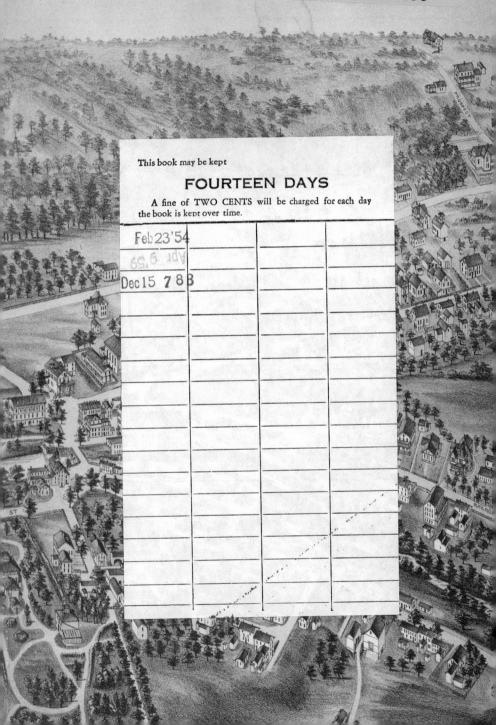

This book may be kept

FOURTEEN DAYS

A fine of TWO CENTS will be charged for each day
the book is kept over time.

Feb 23 '54			
Apr 9 '59			
Dec 15 78			

HARVARD STUDIES IN BUSINESS HISTORY

1. JOHN JACOB ASTOR, BUSINESS MAN
BY KENNETH WIGGINS PORTER

2. JAY COOKE, PRIVATE BANKER
BY HENRIETTA M. LARSON

3. THE JACKSONS AND THE LEES: TWO GENERATIONS OF MASSACHUSETTS MERCHANTS, 1765-1844
BY KENNETH WIGGINS PORTER

4. THE MASSACHUSETTS-FIRST NATIONAL BANK OF BOSTON, 1784-1934
BY N. S. B. GRAS

5. THE HISTORY OF AN ADVERTISING AGENCY: N. W. AYER & SON AT WORK, 1869-1949
BY RALPH M. HOWER

6. MARKETING LIFE INSURANCE: ITS HISTORY IN AMERICA
BY J. OWEN STALSON

7. HISTORY OF MACY'S OF NEW YORK, 1858-1919: CHAPTERS IN THE EVOLUTION OF THE DEPARTMENT STORE
BY RALPH M. HOWER

8. THE WHITESMITHS OF TAUNTON: A HISTORY OF REED & BARTON, 1824-1943
BY GEORGE SWEET GIBB

9. DEVELOPMENT OF TWO BANK GROUPS IN THE CENTRAL NORTHWEST: A STUDY IN BANK POLICY AND ORGANIZATION
BY CHARLES STERLING POPPLE

10. THE HOUSE OF HANCOCK: BUSINESS IN BOSTON, 1724-1775
BY W. T. BAXTER

11. TIMING A CENTURY: HISTORY OF THE WALTHAM WATCH COMPANY
BY C. W. MOORE

12. GUIDE TO BUSINESS HISTORY: MATERIALS FOR THE STUDY OF AMERICAN BUSINESS HISTORY AND SUGGESTIONS FOR THEIR USE
BY HENRIETTA M. LARSON

13. PEPPERELL'S PROGRESS: HISTORY OF A COTTON TEXTILE COMPANY, 1844-1945
BY EVELYN H. KNOWLTON

14. THE HOUSE OF BARING IN AMERICAN TRADE AND FINANCE: ENGLISH MERCHANT BANKERS AT WORK, 1763-1861
BY RALPH W. HIDY

15. THE WHITIN MACHINE WORKS SINCE 1831: A TEXTILE MACHINERY COMPANY IN AN INDUSTRIAL VILLAGE
BY THOMAS R. NAVIN

HARVARD STUDIES
IN BUSINESS HISTORY

HARVARD STUDIES IN BUSINESS HISTORY
XV

EDITED BY N. S. B. GRAS

STRAUS PROFESSOR OF BUSINESS HISTORY

AND HENRIETTA M. LARSON

ASSOCIATE PROFESSOR OF BUSINESS HISTORY

GRADUATE SCHOOL OF BUSINESS ADMINISTRATION

GEORGE F. BAKER FOUNDATION

HARVARD UNIVERSITY

LONDON: GEOFFREY CUMBERLEGE

OXFORD UNIVERSITY PRESS

Aerial View: Main Plant of the Whitin Machine Works, Whitinsville, Massachusetts, 1948

THE WHITIN MACHINE WORKS
SINCE 1831

A TEXTILE MACHINERY COMPANY
IN AN INDUSTRIAL VILLAGE

By

THOMAS R. NAVIN

Assistant Professor of Business History
Graduate School of Business Administration
George F. Baker Foundation
Harvard University

HARVARD UNIVERSITY PRESS

CAMBRIDGE · MASSACHUSETTS

1950

338.45
N 22 W

26923
Jan '51

CONTENTS

PART I

THE PERIOD OF JOHN C. WHITIN

PART III

THE PERIOD OF E. KENT SWIFT

APPENDICES

ILLUSTRATIONS

TABLES

CHARTS AND MAPS

EDITORS' INTRODUCTION

In these days of international turmoil and grave social dissension it is as pleasant as it is instructive to stop to examine one of the cells or units of life and work that have been unostentatiously supporting our material civilization. Much as the world depends upon the management and workers in these units, it knows little about them. The census gives us statistical information which is valuable but completely unreal.

Starting from Providence, Rhode Island, we go up the Blackstone River through many a textile mill town to the little tributary, the Mumford River, and up that river to where there are ponds. There, once driven only by water power, was established a shop or works that has grown during a century, grown in size and service, making the machinery that turns out the yarn for our cotton cloth and more recently for other kinds of cloth. This Whitin Machine Works has operated through five wars in which America has participated. It has employed thousands of workers and produced tens of thousands of machines. One family has managed the Works, stayed on the job, and taken relatively little out of the plant. Just now, at last, is the company broadening out to include the public in its ownership at the very time that the national government is reaching out to control operations through the determination of wages and working conditions, profits, and prices. Recent wars have hastened these determinations from afar, but the closing-in of larger forces has been unmistakable.

In this study we have another example of the creative work of a petty capitalist family that used its ingenuity and capacity for management to build up an industrial capitalist concern that has lasted. Unlike so many industrial capitalist companies, this one has never had to go on its knees to Wall Street or State Street. Indeed, it has built up a financial competence that justifies our putting it into the category of financial industrial capitalism. While it has escaped the financial capitalism of the great metropolitan centers, it has not been free from the domineering shadow of Washington. As this shadow has reached out through the Wagner Act and through the Second World War, the Whitin family and its in-law relatives have felt their control and responsibility lessen. Gradually, in the future, we may expect the substitution of absentee government for an ever-present management that has spent sleepless nights planning for the effective operation of the plant and the welfare of the workers.

We feel that the success of the Whitin Machine Works has been due to a number of factors. The first of these is efficient management: no second-rater, even when a member of the controlling family, has been allowed to occupy a dominant or key position in the company. Earnings have been plowed back into the plant, and not spent on palatial houses, though The Hill is a delightful place of residence. Moreover, the family has been content to live in Whitinsville; like the Du Ponts it has not moved off to New York or some other center of consumptive enjoyment. And, then, there has been a continuous stream of improved machinery available for customers, who have been held close to the company by ties of friendship as well as by bonds of service. Although there has been an evolving and generally assured supply of local workers, the company has not attained its position by means of cheap labor. Perhaps the wage rates have been relatively low, but then the rents and benefits at the expense of the company have been extensive.

The village is a key part of the organization of the company. Whitinsville is a mill village. Many of the cottages are tied to the plant. There is only one other small manufacturing concern in the village. In the pleasant valley there are attractive homes and gardens, a shopping center made up of independent stores, bus service to Providence and Worcester, several churches, and a library; and several ponds nestling between the hills give assurance of abundance of drinking water. A few minutes' walk, and the company executives are at the golf club or the workers are in the hills hunting. There are electricity and gas, street-cleaning service, fire protection, and schools. In the matter of racial origins there is an unusual assortment, from Dutch to Armenians. Although the opportunities are about the same for all, the abilities and inheritances are so different that there is no more social uniformity than in Europe. But there *is* security. The colossal hill, topped by executive homes, and the sturdy plant on the main street stand as guarantees for the present and the future. Long experience has shown that this security is real, even in the most severe depressions. In the village, then, are quiet and orderliness but also a measure of monotony and dullness. There is the over-towering influence of the Works and little effective political life. To many this is ideal; and in other ages than ours it would be regarded as Utopia. Many of the young men, however, drift away to the cities and come back to live only when they fail elsewhere. They know that the company will provide a job and an apartment, care for the streets and sidewalks, cut the lawns, and cart away the ashes. In case of a fire, a family will be put up at The Blue Eagle Inn, owned by the company, until another apartment can be provided. Here we have the welfare state in miniature.

The Whitin Machine Works is one of only a handful of cotton textile machinery companies to survive the ravages of time. The industry has been notable for some striking developments that all scholars should ponder. There has been a combination of copying and borrowing from England and essential improvements at home. In competition with other firms, each company has had to have one or two machines of outstanding distinction, if it is to survive, and a full line of machines, if it is to attain enduring success. While Whitin has purchased other concerns, it has never been merged to save itself from disaster. After the New England market had been satisfied, the South developed new opportunities and offered new hopes. In the South it often proved both necessary and profitable to take the stock of mills buying machinery. In depressions, when new machinery was not in demand, the sale of replacement parts has been sustaining. Indeed, parts for a machine forty or fifty years old may be called for at any time and obtained. The machines are sturdy and parts easily replaced, and new improved parts may be added to old frames. The textile mills, which are the customers, are rather slow in appreciating brand new machines. Indeed, the industry is mature, though not yet quite sick. Opportunities for sales abroad are always a consideration, and the stream-lining and speeding-up of machinery are promising improvements. To the lines of cotton machinery have been added machines for processing rayon, silk, woolens, worsted, and asbestos fibers.

The head of the Whitin Machine Works has long been Mr. E. Kent Swift, as well known in Boston as in southern cities. He is a son-in-law of the Whitin family and has been a strong dynamic factor for a generation. Indeed, when the Whitin family has not produced an outstanding son, a daughter has married an outstanding executive. Such a family can hardly fail to make good. Mr. Swift had a history of the company written just before the Second World War, but it was compiled by a journalist who did not know what is involved in business history: the history was eloquent on the subject of local fires, brought in bits of irrelevant literature, and thinly twined the Plant, the Hill, and the Village. In view of the new developments in business history, Mr. Swift felt that such a treatment was no longer adequate. He wanted a serious, factual, impartial study of the company placed in the midst of the village and managed by the family. There may be a question as to whether he will be satisfied with the present history — a sponsor rarely is satisfied with a self- or family portrait — still the effort has been to produce the results he and we had in mind. We suspect that he wanted to emphasize the village somewhat more than the author has succeeded in doing, but whether that is still his main interest is doubtful in view of the labor troubles that have so recently arisen. He was so proud of the effort of his family on behalf of the workers and of the village which gave them sustenance and security as well as opportunity for growth, that he felt the story of Whitinsville should be widely known. This was precisely our own earliest enthusiasm, and we are not quite sure that this village may not yet prove to be a model for the future in the welfare state that we as a nation are so blindly drifting toward. Whitinsville has been self-supporting and, while it has not reached great heights, it has never been threatened by bankruptcy.

In 1943 one of us started out for Whitinsville in a crowded bus on a wartime schedule. The task was to learn whether there were records adequate for a history and to interview older employees against their passing on before they had a chance to contribute to the story. One official would not at first produce a certain financial record because he regarded it as private, but he swallowed the pill of disclosure. Another could not stretch his imagination far enough to understand what was involved. Others, however, were very sympathetic and helpful. Discussions with the old pensioners at The Blue Eagle Inn proved interesting, though all talk ended abruptly when the meals were announced, for the oldsters were eager for their food, the same as was served to transient guests. One molder, over eighty years old, said that he did not go downtown any longer because the people stared at him as if he were loafing. All in all, the project of a history looked promising. Indeed, we were encouraged to select a whole series of records for deposit in the Baker Library, provided we left the volumes necessary for current business. And what a collection! Is there another like it? Yet, for the day-to-day work in the plant and for inter-departmental relations there proved to be all too little material. We still have no history of an American factory at work during a hundred years.

We were impressed with the readiness with which Mr. Swift accepted our terms. We must have adequate financing. We must have freedom to study and print. And we must wait till we could find a suitable author. He showed amazing patience for a business man. Yes, he would wait till the boys came home.

The boy we were waiting for was Mr. Navin, who had displayed a feeling for scholarship and an understanding of business. In due time the Navy returned him from the South Sea Islands. Unsettled, he debated whether to become a business man or a scholar. The Whitin history as a starting point finally won the decision. During the whole of 1946, 1947, and 1948 he devoted a large part of his energies to research and writing. Part of his time was spent in Whitinsville and part in the Baker Library. His participation in the affairs of the Business Historical Society and in the class work in business history delayed the completion of the manuscript till August, 1949.

Throughout the research and writing of this history the School of Business has given the author and the editors magnificent support, even at a time when the demands for postwar instruction were pressing hard upon us all. The Business Historical Society, to which Mr. Navin gave so much time, will reciprocate by sending copies of his volume to all the members.

N. S. B. Gras
Henrietta M. Larson

August, 1949

AUTHOR'S PREFACE

IN THE classical view of economics there are four factors of production: resources, labor, management, and capital. Recent years have witnessed a rising conviction in many quarters that the productivity of the first two factors is declining. Some of America's key resources are in danger of running out, and America's highly industrialized populace is showing a diminishing interest in working at its drudging job. So far, however, the decline of the first two factors has been more than offset by the advances of the third and fourth. Management is finding increasingly efficient ways of getting work done, and engineers are perfecting constantly better capital goods to do the work with. Hence a study of the management techniques of a capital-goods firm comes close to dealing with the essence of America's modern industrial accomplishments.

This book attempts such a study. It is the story of how one firm helped to build America's productive capacity. It is the story of how four generations of executives were able to achieve consistent success through a policy of conservative management. It is a narrative that is highlighted by no crises, no threats of bankruptcy, no management escapades, no scandals, no struggles for control — none of the trappings of a spanking good yarn. It is simply the story of a group of men who learned how to master themselves, then how to direct others, and finally how to make the best use of their environment. It is not meant as a bedside reader; it is a book of information, not of entertainment. In short, it is the microscopic study of a microcosmic community — the plant and village of Whitinsville, Massachusetts.

The person directly responsible for this book was Mr. E. Kent Swift, Chairman of the Board of the Whitin Machine Works. It was his idea originally and it was his active interest that made the work possible. Having been head of the company for nearly a third of a century, he was able to bring to this study an intimate knowledge of events that could have been obtained from no other source. Yet it should be added that he made no attempt to make this study his.

Though he has read all parts of the manuscript and has pointed out errors of fact, he has let judgments and opinions stand, even where they differed from his own. Consequently the publication of this book in no sense indicates that its conclusions are those of the company. On the contrary, they are in every case mine.

It is inevitable that a certain degree of bias will creep into a work of this kind — though one always hopes that the degree will be slight. Consequently, it is well that the reader know something of my personal background, for it is bound to have had some effect on my work. Born, reared, and educated in the Midwest, I am the son of a manufacturer and the product of an industrial community. Since my father's company is a family-managed concern, I am familiar, not to say sympathetic, with the problems of a company like Whitin. And since I am convinced that men are happiest and achieve most when they strive to do their job well and to give in return for what they receive, I am not so critical of New England's conservatism as others might be, for I find native Yankee self-sufficiency worth admiring, existing as it does in the midst of widely increasing government dependence.

Mr. Swift, when he first discussed the Whitin history with Professor N. S. B. Gras, one of the editors of this book, expressed the hope that substantial attention would be given to the village where the company is located. In large part that hope has not been fulfilled. It soon became apparent that the task of doing research in the community's social structure was something quite different from doing work in the company's records. Here would have been an excellent opportunity for collaboration between the business historian and the sociologist. We can only hope that a collaboration of this nature will some day be undertaken. For the present I have done what little my limited knowledge of sociology would allow. Especially have I been conscious that the most interested readers of this book will be the inhabitants of Whitinsville, and for that reason I have included many facts and data about *their* company and *their* village that I might otherwise have passed over.

When I began research on the Whitin project in 1946, I was greeted in Whitinsville with exclamations of incredulity. No one could believe that I had been given permission to see all the company's records and that I had been granted freedom to publish whatever I found. As a family concern the company had always treated its records as the private property of the Whitins. Executives of the company and their assistants to whom the records were entrusted had come to feel the responsibility of their trust and had learned to shield the records from the prying eyes of outsiders. My work necessarily took me where even the government's agents had not previously inquired and, for the first few months, brought me into one cul-de-sac after another until the company's reticent New Englanders grew accustomed to what seemed to them to be indiscriminate snooping.

My final acceptance by the company's employees would never have been possible without the assistance of Mr. Ralph E. Lincoln, Vice-president of the company. Throughout the project Mr. Lincoln served as liaison between Harvard University and the Whitin Machine Works. No company history should be undertaken without the assistance of such a person within the firm; of that I am sure. Ideally the choice should be a man of high authority, with a record of lengthy service in the company, and with a genuine interest in the project. Mr. Lincoln possessed all three qualifications in high degree. Working with him was one of the most pleasant aspects of a thoroughly enjoyable task.

Doing research in the company's records proved to be both a challenge and a chore. Probably no other American concern of comparable age has kept its records in such complete and organized manner. The very completeness of the records created a problem, for they were so voluminous that I could not have studied them all in a lifetime of work. Moreover, the account books were kept by double-entry only after 1918, so that much reconstruction of accounts was necessary. The information for one chart alone (Appendix 29) — information that the company now compiles regularly — occupied the time of an assistant for seven weeks.

Most of the company's earlier records (those before 1920) were deposited for my use in the Harvard Business School's Baker Library. At the completion of the project the company presented those records to the Library for the use of all accredited scholars. In them may be found some of the finest known source materials on the development of the American textile industry.

Research in the records after 1920 was conducted in Whitinsville in the offices of the company. Working thus within a company's walls puts the historian on his mettle. Soon he begins to identify himself with the institution he is studying, much as though he were a member of it. Many historians feel that a scholar jeopardizes his detachment by coming into such close contact with his subject, and doubtless there is much to be said for such a view. Yet I know of no better way to get the pulse of an organization than to work with it for a time. Perhaps the advantages of a more intimate familiarity offset the disadvantages of lost perspective. Let the reader be the judge.

In writing this book I have had the unparalleled advantage of association with an author already well known for his work in New England business history, Mr. George S. Gibb, whose concurrent efforts were being directed toward a history of Whitin's principal competitor, the Saco-Lowell Shops. The conducting of joint studies on competing companies was not, however, without its trials as well as its compensations. It afforded the unusual opportunity of knowing how several units in the industry reacted to common problems, but it introduced the danger that one author's conclusions might influence the other's. For that reason Mr. Gibb and I worked separately, comparing notes only as we completed chapters. Throughout our studies we scrupulously avoided using each other's materials. I saw none of Saco-Lowell's records, and Mr. Gibb saw none of Whitin's. During the early period of our work, we had little occasion to confer since our companies went their separate ways without much direct competition. But the histories of the two companies since 1900 have inevitably been intertwined, and the reader of one study will probably want to be a reader of the other.

Both the Saco-Lowell and the Whitin studies were made under the direct supervision of Professor N. S. B. Gras. It is always acutely embarrassing to an editor to have his authors pay him public tribute in their books, but often they have no other means of expressing their admiration and gratitude. Professor Gras is one of those rare persons who continue to believe in the dignity of the individual when nearly all others are turning to the worship of the group. To study under him is to have complete freedom of thought and action; small wonder that his associates work for him with enthusiastic devotion and loyalty. He leads not by directing, but by setting the pace, and few are those who can match his energy and scintillating scholarship. For a period of nearly a quarter-century he has plowed the lone furrow of business history and has laid out the work for a generation of business historians to come. Those who have worked with him during that period have been conscious that they were enjoying an intellectual experience accorded very few others in this materialistic and secular world.

In the early part of this study and again at the conclusion, I had the advantage of working with Dr. Henrietta M. Larson, whose knowledge of the business history field is second only to Professor Gras'. For a time I also had the opportunity of working with Mrs. Evelyn H. Knowlton when she was finishing her study on the Pepperell Manufacturing Company.

In Whitinsville no executive has escaped interruption in my search for materials. Wherever possible, I have taken opportunity to acknowledge my individual indebtedness in appropriate footnotes. I am especially grateful to Miss Eve S. Higginbottom, and to Mr. Leroy Rollins for his willingness to give me part of his office as headquarters for my work in Whitinsville during the summer of 1948.

From time to time I was fortunate enough to have the help of several research assistants. Mrs. Martha A. Starr helped me to compile many of the data used in my first five chapters. Miss Alberta Renzaglia read samplings of incoming letters, and Mrs. Mildred Smith helped to accumulate the statistical materials that went into the appendices. Mrs. Marion Farrington assisted me in reading the two hundred thousand outgoing letters included in the pre-1920 portion of the Whitin records. Mr. Richmond F. Bingham drew the graphs, and Miss Helen Ballou did pen and ink sketches for the line cuts. Miss Josepha M. Perry gave me the benefit of her expert advice on matters of style. Miss Helen E. Kosakowski assisted in the final task of getting the manuscript ready for the press. I am especially indebted to Miss Hilma B. Holton for the painstaking editorial job she did and for the index which she compiled. My wife typed the manuscript; only she could have had the patience to bear with me through the book's innumerable drafts.

THOMAS R. NAVIN

Part I

THE PERIOD OF JOHN C. WHITIN

CHAPTER I

FOREBEARS, 1809–1831

IN THIS transient world, Americans spend about three-quarters of their national income on consumers' goods and services; small wonder they know more about the companies that manufacture soap, cigarettes, and soft drinks than about the firms that produce machinery and heavy equipment. Yet, in any highly mechanized civilization, the makers of producers' goods are the real molders of everyday life, for without their labor-saving products modern living standards would never have been attained. All too few people realize the part played by the manufacturers of producers' goods in present-day society. The name of a company like the Whitin Machine Works is almost unknown to the general public. Yet its products are so widely used that every reader of this book will almost certainly be the owner of at least some clothing made of yarn produced on Whitin equipment.

The Whitin Machine Works is a company that employs from three thousand to five thousand men. Its main offices and principal manufacturing plant are located in Whitinsville, Massachusetts, between Worcester, Massachusetts, and Providence, Rhode Island. Its product is textile machinery.

All textile goods, no matter what their composition, are produced on four general types of machines. The first type converts fibers into yarn. The second type transforms yarn into woven cloth. The third changes yarn, by an alternate process, into knit goods. The fourth puts a finish on the woven or knit goods and dyes or prints them.

The first of the four types of textile machinery is called "preparatory equipment" and is produced in America by only a handful of companies, three of the largest of which are the Whitin Machine Works, the Saco-Lowell Shops, and the H & B American Machine Company. All three are located in New England. Until after World

War I, all three specialized in *cotton* preparatory equipment. The
Whitin company and the Saco-Lowell Shops are about equal in size.
For nearly a half-century they have fought a seesaw battle for first
place. The H & B American Machine Company is about a quarter
as large as either of its two great competitors. Inasmuch as the cotton textile industry, which has been dependent on these three companies for preparatory equipment, was, for a century before World
War I, the largest manufacturing industry in the country (and is
even today exceeded in size only by the automobile and the iron and
steel industries) these companies have for years been key members
of America's industrial community.

The first textile machine made for sale by the Whitin company
was a picker based on a design developed by John C. Whitin in
1831. In the years that have elapsed since then, ownership of the
company has been retained by the same family, and operations have
been conducted at the same location, always under the active management of the owners. Around the factory has grown an industrial
village that has been dependent in war and depression, in boom and
peace, upon the company's successful management. The owners,
conscious of a need to preserve a skilled work force and of a responsibility toward the community, have maintained a policy that
no employee with dependents should be laid off because the shop
lacked work. At times, when orders have declined, the owners have
curtailed working hours so that existing work might be equitably
distributed; and in months when order books have been blank, they
have financed maintenance work about the village to provide jobs
for employees; but never have they allowed a worker to hunger or
to want shelter. The stability of the company has transfused security
to the village.

No attempt to explain the company's continued success can ignore
the fact that ownership has been closely held within the family and
that the family has been active in company management. Throughout its century-long history, the Whitin Machine Works has had
only four chief executives, three of whom have been business men
of remarkable cast. The company has always been closely held. In
1917 it had only three stockholders; as late as 1940 it had only 37,
although by that year it had grown to be a fifteen-million-dollar

corporation. Management has been conservative. The owners have paid themselves only moderate salaries and have declared only moderate dividends. Most of the profits have remained in the business or have been invested in the community. No outside capital has ever been solicited. The company has grown entirely from reinvested earnings. Consequently, it has never had recourse to investment bankers and only rarely has sought loans from commercial banks. With the exception of the years 1884 and 1885, dividends have been declared annually since the company's incorporation in 1870.

This record is by no means an indication that the Whitin company has always operated in a stable industry. Like all producers of capital goods, textile-machinery manufacturers have been violently affected by fluctuations in general business activity. In part, Whitin has met these conditions by diversification of product. For many years the company manufactured only cotton-textile machinery. Indeed, in the early period few American textile-machinery manufacturers made anything else; the wool machinery industry was very small and most worsted equipment was imported from abroad. But in recent years the company has broadened its line to include machines especially designed for use with wool, worsted, silk, rayon, and asbestos fibers on the theory that poor years in the woolen and worsted trade often do not coincide with those in cotton or synthetic fibers. In major business depressions, however, when all types of textile firms have suffered, the company has had to rely on the sale of replacement parts and on its strong financial position.

A simplified description of the preparatory processes used in the manufacture of cotton yarn will help to explain what manner of machines the Whitin company turns out. (See Chart I and the accompanying illustrations.) Raw cotton, as it comes from the plantation, is matted in lumps and fouled with seeds and dirt. Before it can be spun into yarn, the lumps must be loosened and the dirt removed. To accomplish this purpose a process known as *picking* is used. The baled cotton is first opened and fluffed up, then beaten and whirled about in a cage, while suction fans remove the foreign particles.

In the next operation the entangled fibers are carded to make them lie parallel. A large cylinder, bristling with fine wires called card

CHART I

Basic Operations through Which Cotton Fibers Must Pass
before Becoming Woven Cloth

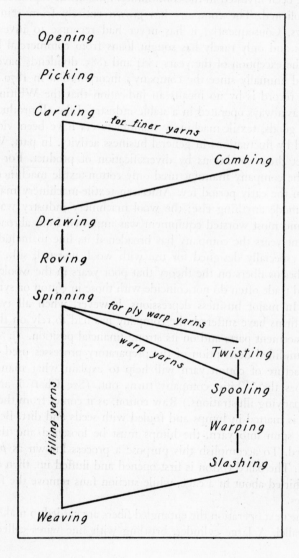

One-process Picker

Model "L" Revolving Top-flat Card

Model "J" Comber

Model "KFS" Drawing Frame

clothing (pronounced CLOTHE-ing), revolves at high speed, carrying the cotton fibers around with it. Other wires, on smaller cylinders or on flats, brush out the fibers as they fly by. The cotton is then peeled off the card cylinder in a sheet, or lap, and is compressed into a sliver (pronounced SLY-ver), giving it the appearance of a long switch of platinum blond hair.

The fibers are then pulled parallel by a process called *drawing* in which several slivers are combined into one and are attenuated, doubled, and re-attenuated until the fibers are thoroughly blended in an even strand. The *roving* operation continues the blending process and reduces the diameter of the sliver to a size suitable for the next process. Finally, *spinning* imparts a uniform twist, binding the fibers together into a yarn of requisite fineness. The yarn is then ready for the beginning steps of either weaving or knitting, depending on the type of cloth to be made.

All kinds of fibers must pass through these five processes (cleaning, paralleling, blending, attenuating, and twisting) before becoming yarn, and nearly every machine produced by the Whitin company is designed to accomplish, by means especially adapted to each type of fiber, one of these five objectives. The illustrations on accompanying pages show recent models of Whitin's basic products.

Like nearly all present-day textile-machinery companies, the Whitin Machine Works originated in the early years of the American Industrial Revolution. Because the company was located nearer Providence than Boston its early history followed the Rhode Island pattern of business more closely than the Massachusetts. Inasmuch as the two patterns were so completely different and since they were to have such marked effects on the future of the two regions, they are worth at least passing comment.

When the Industrial Revolution came to Boston, it found large accumulations of merchant capital standing ready to help finance its way. Providence also had its mercantile fortunes, but they were much smaller than Boston's and fewer in number. Consequently, the Industrial Revolution in the Rhode Island area was principally the work of petty capitalists who were eager to get ahead in the world, while around Boston it was in large part the work of mercantile capitalists who were just then withdrawing from international trade and were looking for a place to invest their funds. Because of Boston's larger resources, its first cotton mills were corporations, large by the standards of that time, started full-blown by groups of wealthy investors. In contrast, early mills of Providence were partnerships, started on a small scale by men with limited means.

The different financial conditions of the two areas profoundly affected the textile-machinery companies that grew up in each. In the Boston area, cotton mills started out on such a sizable scale that they had immediate need for large quantities of machinery. At that time, however, there was no machinery industry of any consequence in America; the only place where machines were being built in quantity was in England. But since British laws forbade the exportation of English-made machinery, Americans had to make provision for building their own equipment. Consequently, one of the first steps taken in organizing new cotton mills in the Boston area was to set up shops for constructing the needed machines. The first great cotton mill in the region was the Boston Manufacturing Company, started in the year 1813, and from its machine shop came products, designed by Francis Cabot Lowell and Paul Moody, that were to be distinctive features of mills in the Boston area for a half-century to come. For, once the Boston mill had been equipped, the machine shop (in which, of course, considerable money had by then been invested) kept itself alive by going out and getting orders from other new mills — mills that not infrequently were promoted by the owners of the original mill or by their friends or relatives. Most other machine shops in the Boston area had similar beginnings, and all three of the shops that were later to become the merged Saco-Lowell Shops, Whitin's largest competitor, began in this fashion.*

So that the reader may begin his acquaintance with Whitin's competitors, it would be well at this point to list the three principal machine shops in the Boston area. They were the Lowell Machine Shop, at Lowell, Massachusetts, successor to the machine shop of the Boston Manufacturing Company, and throughout most of its inde-

* Because the Whitin Machine Works and the Saco-Lowell Shops are now about equal in size and because they make roughly the same line of products, people have come to think of them as being very much alike. Yet anyone who reads both this book and George S. Gibb's history of the Saco-Lowell Shops will be surprised to find how different the two companies have been in the past and how different they still are.

SUPER-DRAFT ROVING FRAME

MODEL "F2" SPINNING FRAME

pendent existence the largest textile-machine shop in the country; the Pettee Machine Works, at Newton Upper Falls, Massachusetts; and the Saco Water Power Machine Shop, at Biddeford, Maine (see Chart II).

By contrast machine shops in the Providence area started on a shoestring, for mills in that area were too small to warrant the establishment of great plants to fabricate their equipment. Most of the early machinery built in the Providence region was consequently

CHART II

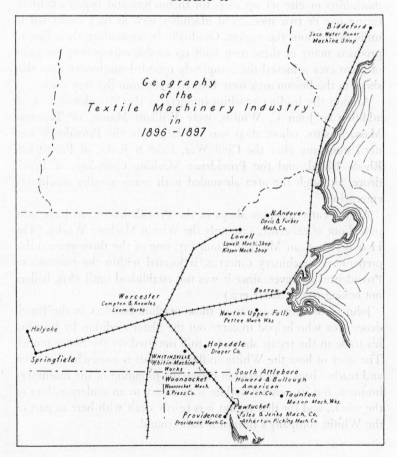

Geography
of the
Textile Machinery Industry
in
1896 - 1897

Biddeford
Saco Water Power
Machine Shop

N. Andover
Davis & Furber
Mach. Co.

Lowell
Lowell Mach. Shop
Kitson Mach. Shop

Worcester
Compton & Knowles
Loom Works

Boston

Holyoke

Newton Upper Falls
Pettee Mach Wks.

Hopedale
Draper Co.

Springfield

WHITINSVILLE
Whitin Machine
Works

South Attleboro
Howard & Bullough
American
Mach. Co.

Woonsocket
Woonsocket Mach.
& Press Co.

Taunton
Mason Mach. Wks.

Pawtucket

Providence
Providence Mach. Co.

Fales & Jenks Mach. Co.
Atherton Picking Mach. Co.

constructed in local blacksmith shops. Moreover, most of it followed the designs, not of Lowell and Moody, but of Samuel Slater and David Wilkinson. Slater was an Englishman who had managed to smuggle British machine designs past government officials by carrying them in his mind. Wilkinson was Slater's American-born brother-in-law and a remarkably clever blacksmith. Under those two men most of southern New England's early machine-builders received their training. Seeing the opportunities that were open to them, Slater's protégés left his employ in large numbers and either went from town to town helping to start new mills as free-lance machinists or else set up shop for themselves and began manufacturing one or two specialized machines such as they could sell to mills throughout the region. Gradually by expanding their line of products many of these men built up sizable enterprises; but none of them ever achieved the completely rounded machinery lines that shops in the Boston area were favored with from the very start.

Among the leading machine-builders in the Providence area, in addition to John C. Whitin, were William Mason, of Taunton, Massachusetts, whose shop was the largest in the Providence area until sometime after the Civil War, Fales & Jenks, of Pawtucket, Rhode Island, and the Providence Machine Company, of Providence, although the area abounded with many smaller machinery enterprises.

All the early machine shops in the Providence region have now passed out of existence, save only the Whitin Machine Works. (The H & B American Machine Company, one of the three present-day preparatory machinery concerns, is located within the environs of Providence; however, since it was not established until 1894, it does not belong to the Slater era.)

John C. Whitin was one of those machine-builders in the Providence area who helped to carry out the Slater tradition by learning his trade in the repair shop of a mill outfitted on the Slater model. The story of how the Whitin mill got its start is somewhat involved and reaches back a generation before the founding of the machinery business. But its general outline is necessary to an understanding of the whole, and for that reason it is briefly dealt with here as part of the Whitin company's historical background.

I. PAUL WHITIN, 1767–1831

One of the promoters of the mill where the Whitin Machine Works originated was Paul Whitin.[1] It was his water privilege that drove the mill's spindles, and it was his blacksmith shop that built the mill's machinery.

Originally, Paul's family name had been Whiting, a name still prominent in the Boston area. Tradition has it that the reason Paul changed his name to Whitin (pronounced WHITE-in)* was that, at the time of his marriage, he wished to avoid confusion with a distant cousin, also named Paul Whiting, who owned a tavern in a neighboring town. Some credence may be given the story, for it is known not only that Paul was a piously strict abstainer but also that a tavern owner of the same name and of very nearly the same age did live in an adjoining town.[2]

Paul Whitin's great-great-grandfather, Nathaniel Whiting, came to America from England about 1636 and settled in Dedham, Massachusetts, ten miles southwest of Boston.[3] There his children and grandchildren were reared, and there his great-grandchild, also named Nathaniel, was born. At the age of twenty-one the younger Nathaniel died, leaving a widow, Sarah, and a son, Paul, an infant of eighteen months. Sarah remarried within a year and moved with her son to Sutton, a town just south of Worcester, where her second husband, James Prentice, owned a farm. There Paul grew up and received what little schooling he ever had. At the age of fourteen he became apprenticed to Jesse White, a blacksmith with a shop in Northbridge Center, not more than five miles from the Prentice farm.[4] How long Paul stayed with White is not known, but apparently either he or his parents quarreled with the blacksmith over the conditions of Paul's indenture, and for the remainder of the lad's seven years' apprenticeship he worked for a man named Chester Williams.[5]

During the years when Paul was living in Northbridge Center

---

* The Whitin name has had its advantages and its disadvantages. It has served the company well as a distinctive trade name, one that has been easy to remember. But it has also plagued the company because it is constantly mispronounced. People who do not refer to the Whiting Machine Works in Whitingsville, go to the other extreme and call it the Whitten Machine Works in Whittensville.

(1781 and after), the district known as Northbridge gained separate status as a "town."[6] In the political geography of New England, a town is a division which, in states farther west, would be called a township. Within a New England town there may be several communities with widely varying names. The town of Northbridge today contains five such communities: Northbridge Center, Rockdale, Riverdale, Linwood, and Whitinsville. The largest of these is Whitinsville, a village which in Paul Whitin's time was known by the anomalous name of South Northbridge.

In the years immediately following the American Revolution, the community life of Northbridge revolved around Northbridge Center. The town hall and the town's only church were located there, as were also the general store and the greater part of the town's sparse population of about five hundred. But the Center possessed few natural advantages. It was situated on a high ridge of land and was accessible to many of the townspeople only after an arduous climb, a fact that made the valley people complain bitterly. Around the Center the rolling hillsides, while attractive to the eye, were rocky and barren, more conducive to the quarrying of granite than to the tilling of fields. The Center's only industry, shoemaking, throve for a while on a putting-out basis, though it later vanished with the advent of machine-made shoes. On the eastern and southern margins of Northbridge, however, ran two rapidly flowing rivers, the Blackstone and the Mumford, on whose waterfalls the gathering Industrial Revolution was to place high premiums. The finest of these power sites was the one around which the small settlement of South Northbridge was developing.

Sometime shortly after the completion of his apprenticeship (it is not known exactly when), Paul Whitin moved to South Northbridge. It is said that he served four years there as a journeyman blacksmith, after which he entered business for himself by renting a smithy from a wealthy farmer named Ezra Wood. Wood was the owner of the South Northbridge water privilege, which, together with 268 acres of land, he had bought on 16 September 1771 for £450. From as early as the year 1727, the South Northbridge water privilege had driven the trip hammers of a small forge that had initially used, as its source of iron, unrefined ore brought down from the Northbridge hills. But the strain of ore must have been thin or of low grade, for by Whitin's time scrap and pig iron were being used at the forge as raw materials.

When Wood bought the forge, it was located several yards south of the river bank and was operated by the power of a stream of water diverted to it through a flume. Probably with the thought of increasing the size of the forge, Wood built a larger dam and, next to it, a building into which the forge was moved (see Chart III). It would appear that Wood's intentions in these undertakings was to provide a dowry for his daughter, Margaret, for on 24 December 1771, three months after he had purchased the forge, Margaret married James Fletcher, who, during the next 42 years, was to be the forge's proprietor.

Sometime during the next score of years, Ezra Wood also erected a blacksmith shop in South Northbridge. The site he chose for the smithy was directly across the river from the forge, and the smithy's power was drawn from the same dam.[7] This was the smithy which, in 1792, Paul Whitin rented as the starting point of his business career. Within a little more than a year, Paul had begun to prosper and had married Betsey Fletcher, the property owner's granddaughter. She was only sixteen years old at the time, but even then was endowed with an indomitable personality, a trait which in later years was to make her active head of the Whitin family and matriarch of the village.

Shortly after Paul and Betsey had married, Ezra Wood agreed to sell to James Fletcher and Paul Whitin the South Northbridge water rights. For £200 he transferred to Whitin not only full ownership in the blacksmith shop, but a one-third interest in "Fletcher's Forge" and in its water rights.[8] For £300 he sold Fletcher the remaining two-thirds ownership in the forge and in the water privilege.[9] From a breakdown of these figures it is evident that the water rights were the really valuable part of the property, for it would seem that Whitin paid only £50 for his smithy, whereas he paid £150 in order to have a share in the power privilege.

Paul's smithy achieved its greatest financial success during the years of the Embargo and Nonintercourse acts (1807-09) when the United States was almost completely cut off from trade with Britain

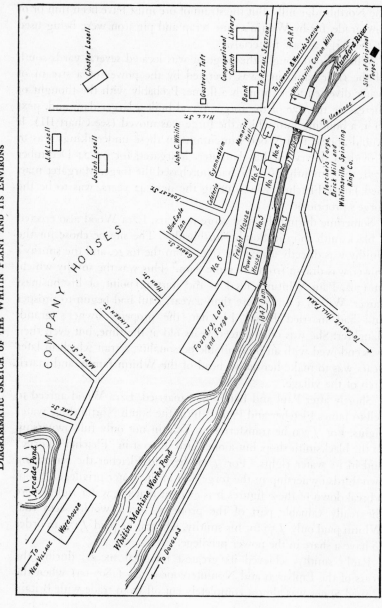

CHART III

DIAGRAMMATIC SKETCH OF THE WHITIN PLANT AND ITS ENVIRONS

NOTE: Shop numbering indicates the chronological order in which buildings were erected; the company's numbering system runs according to location rather than

and France. During those years Paul hammered out large quantities of scythes and heavy hoes and sold them to plantation owners in the South.[10] It would be interesting to know how he went about marketing his products, but no information of that type has survived.

Nor has any likeness of Paul Whitin been handed down by members of his family. But from what is known of him, he seems to have been fitted for his life work as a blacksmith more by temperament than by physique. Although he lived to be sixty-three, his health was never robust. Still physical ailments did not seem to diminish his capacity for work. So conscientious was he that he forced himself to make up in his smithy any time lost because of his numerous excursions into civic affairs. For thirteen years he was town clerk of Northbridge, and for a considerable time he was justice of the peace. His activities in the Militia of Massachusetts won him the rank of Lieutenant Colonel in 1807, and from that time forward he was known as Colonel Paul.

In his way of life Paul followed the ideals now associated with the name of Benjamin Franklin, for he was industrious, virtuous, self-disciplined, and thrifty. Yet he seems to have been a business man of no more than average parts. He contributed small amounts of capital to several enterprises during his lifetime, but he took no active interest in any of them. His smithy was his principal preoccupation. Like Meyer Amschel Rothschild, his chief accomplishment in life was not so much in the business field as in the begetting of five remarkable sons. He was proud of his sons and gave them great responsibilities at early ages. But he did not wish to spoil them and therefore at his death left his entire estate to his wife rather than give the boys too much independence.

2. THE NORTHBRIDGE COTTON MANUFACTURING COMPANY

There is an old tradition, many times repeated, that Paul Whitin was the founder of the Northbridge Cotton Manufacturing Company. That he was one of the founders is indisputable; that he was the driving force behind the project seems very doubtful.

Before 1809, the year when the Northbridge mill was organized, no more than a handful of power-driven cotton mills existed in the United States. For several years after the American Revolution,

England had successfully prevented the development of a textile industry in this country by enforcing its stringent laws against exportation of machines and emigration of mechanics. In 1789, however, Samuel Slater had succeeded in evading the prohibitory statute and had brought to America the first real knowledge of how to make cotton yarn by power-driven machines instead of by hand-operated ones.

Slater produced his first cotton yarn in Pawtucket, Rhode Island, in 1790, but for many years his processes remained unimitated, not only because Slater guarded his secrets as jealously in America as his compatriots had tried to guard theirs in the Old Country, but also because American power-spun yarn was slow to win consumer acceptance. It was not until the embargoes preceding the War of 1812 had eliminated British competition that the cotton textile industry began to take hold in this country.[11]

The manner in which the textile industry of the United States developed from the spadework of Slater is one of the most fascinating stories in the history of business. The first competing power-driven mills were built in 1803 or 1804 and even in 1807 there were only fifteen such mills in operation. But of those mills, nearly all were established by men who had been trained either by Slater or by men who had worked in Slater's mills.[12]

As the mill movement spread, it gained momentum. Imitators increased by geometrical progression. At the end of 1809 there were said to be 62 cotton mills in operation and 25 in the process of being erected.[13] The Northbridge Cotton Manufacturing Company, which was built during the fall of 1809, was thus one of the first hundred water-powered spinning mills started in this country. Like nearly all the others, it had received its heritage from the old Slater mill in Pawtucket.

It is impossible now to piece together with any certainty the exact story of how the company was organized. The only records that remain are entries made in local registries of deeds. In days when no other means of perpetuating legal transactions were available, it was common practice to set down the sale of a partnership share just as though it was a sale of physical property. With these deeds as references, it is possible to make some judicious speculations on how the mill came into existence.

All that is really known about the actual organization of the Northbridge mill is the distribution of its thirty-two partnership shares and the value of the respective holdings. It seems possible, however, that the man who was the real promoter of the mill was Jonathan Adams, a former resident of Northbridge who had moved to Providence and had become a fairly successful merchant.[14] By 1809 he had invested in one of the important mills of the period, the Natick Manufacturing Company, of Warwick, Rhode Island, of which he and his business partner were one-quarter owners.[15] Catching the cotton-mill fever, Adams may have bethought himself of the fine power site on the Mumford River back in Northbridge and he may have approached Fletcher and Whitin with an offer to take them into partnership. Quite possibly he worked out a plan whereby neither Fletcher nor Whitin had to invest a cent in the venture. Perhaps all Fletcher had to do to obtain a 4/32 share of the company that was later formed was to contribute land for the mill together with a share in the Mumford power privilege.[16] Similarly Whitin may have received his 6/32 interest in the venture in exchange for his share in the river's water privilege and for his promise to build the machinery for the mill in his blacksmith shop.

One of the men who became interested in the Northbridge venture was Charles Sabin, the agent of Jonathan Adams' Natick mill.[17] In fact, either at the time the Northbridge mill was started or else shortly thereafter, Sabin moved his place of residence to Northbridge, from which fact we may presume that he became the new mill's agent.[18] He, too, may have contributed no cash, and his 4/32 interest in the firm may have been only an inducement to get him to accept the post.

The only man among the shareholders who is definitely known *not* to have contributed any cash was William Howard, a "machine-maker" by trade.[19] Like Sabin, Howard had formerly worked for the Natick mill. Apparently he was brought to Northbridge to instruct Paul Whitin in the mysteries of textile-machinery construction.* Besides his wages he was given a three-year option to buy two

---

* Through William Howard, the ancestry of the mill at Northbridge may be traced to Samuel Slater. In 1799, Obadiah Brown, one of Slater's partners, placed Slater-type machinery (over Slater's protest) in the Warwick Spinning Mill in which he held part interest. One of the other Warwick owners was William Potter who,

shares at half-price, but for some reason he failed to exercise his right.[20]

The heaviest investors in the new company were the three Earle brothers of Leicester, Massachusetts. Pliny Earle, the eldest brother, was a man widely known in the early years of the textile industry. Using a novel device for pricking holes in leather, he had made a small fortune in the manufacture of card clothing. A Quaker himself, Earle had been called upon by Almy and Brown, Slater's Quaker partners, to solve the difficulties which Slater had encountered when he first tried to reconstruct a carding machine from memory.[21] Possibly the Earles contributed card clothing to the enterprise, but that contribution alone could not have accounted for the size of their investment. It seems likely that they and Jonathan Adams provided the necessary working capital and that with their 43 per cent holdings, they effectively controlled the concern.* (A list of the original shareholders in the Northbridge Cotton Manufacturing Company and the proportion of the partnership owned by each are given in Appendix 1.)

The new mill was a wooden building two and a half stories high, 40 feet long, and 30 feet wide. It was located northwest of Paul Whitin's smithy, about 30 yards back from the bank of the river — approximately where the power plant of the Whitin Machine Works now stands. To provide power for the mill the partners constructed a new dam about 700 feet above the forge-smithy dam (the exact location cannot now be determined), and dug a mill race to conduct water to the new mill's wheel. Near the mill they constructed four dwellings to house the operatives and a mill store to provide for their needs.[22] No one could have predicted that those few structures, so typical of mill groups being built at that time, would one day multiply into New England's leading company village.

---

having thus acquired a familiarity with Slater's machinery, exploited his knowledge by helping to start the Natick Manufacturing Company. William Howard, one of the Natick machinists, then brought the Slater secrets to Northbridge. The relationship may seem humorously devious, but by just such circumvolutions did the textile industry become established in this country.

* The other two investors were Samuel Fletcher, a son of James Fletcher (2/32), and Abram Wilson, a resident of Northbridge (1/32) who was given an option similar to Howard's and who took it up.

Like all mills of the period, the Northbridge firm made wide use of the putting-out system. Baled cotton was delivered by wagon to the homes of Northbridge residents, where it was picked apart and whipped to free it of impurities at a customary remuneration of from four to six cents per pound. Only the carding, drawing, and spinning processes were performed in the mill. The mill is said to have specialized in the production of warp yarn and probably sold its output directly to merchants, though on occasion it may have let yarn out to townspeople to be woven into cloth on hand looms.[23]

The company was capitalized at $32,000 — 32 shares worth $1,000 each. Even if we were to assume that this entire amount was subscribed to either in cash or in kind, the company must have been seriously underfinanced. The Natick mill, with its 568 spindles, was capitalized in exactly the same manner as the Northbridge mill and so had an investment of $56 per spindle,[24] while the Northbridge mill with approximately 1,000 spindles[25] (an average number for early mills in the Providence area)[26] had an investment of only about $32 per spindle. Albert Gallatin, the Secretary of the Treasury, in his 1810 *Report on American Manufactures,* stated:

> The capital required to carry on [cotton] manufacture on the best terms, is estimated at the rate of one hundred dollars for each spindle; including both the fixed capital applied to the purchase of the mill-seats, and to the construction of the mills and machinery, and that employed in wages, repairs, raw materials, goods on hand and contingencies. But it is believed that no more than at the rate of sixty dollars for each spindle is generally actually employed.

By Gallatin's standards, the Northbridge mill started out with only about half the minimum capitalization it needed.[27]

Still, the misfortunes and anxieties which so often follow upon the organization of an undercapitalized company were spared the owners of the Northbridge Cotton Manufacturing Company by the outbreak of the War of 1812. British imports of cotton yarn and cloth ceased abruptly, leaving only the newly established American manufacturers to supply the demand of the home market and the requirements of the Army. Profit margins widened as prices of finished goods soared and costs of raw cotton, affected by the loss of a foreign market, remained low. During the war years the number of mills in this country increased rapidly, but the industry was too young and its ability to increase capacity too limited to enable it to satisfy the heavy demands suddenly made upon it. By 1814, shares in the Northbridge mill were selling at $1,800, a general indication of the profitableness of the enterprise.

Then came the end of the war and a sudden reversal of conditions in the entire industry. British manufacturers and distributors, anxious to regain their lost markets and stocked with goods which they had been unable to dispose of during the war, deluged American auctioneers with cheap cotton cloth consigned on liberal terms. Not even the 35 per cent double duties that were imposed on imports until June, 1816, were sufficient to eliminate the difference in price between American and English goods. American producers suffered a sharp depression. Like nearly every other mill in the Rhode Island area, the Northbridge Cotton Manufacturing Company experienced several years of severe losses and finally suspended operations.

3. THE WHITINS ORGANIZE THEIR OWN MILL

At this gloomy juncture in the history of cotton textiles, Paul Whitin was prevailed upon by his brothers-in-law, the sons of James Fletcher, to enter a partnership with them for the purpose of organizing a second cotton mill. To attempt an explanation of Paul's motives in agreeing to such an undertaking is impossible with the little information available. Sometimes when dealing with friends or relatives, men are induced to make decisions which, if viewed apart from their personal implications, seem illogical and indefensible. It is known that in 1813, James Fletcher, at the age of sixty-seven, had closed his forge and had retired from active work. Why Fletcher's sons were not willing to carry on their father's business we do not know. Perhaps it was because the forge had never been very profitable. Fletcher does not seem to have been the business man Paul Whitin was and there is evidence that he was completely uneducated, for he alone, of all the men he did business with, was forced to sign property deeds with an X. But the more likely explanation is simply that Fletcher's sons had contracted the cotton-mill fever and wanted to try their hands at operating the forge as a mill. It was natural that they should try to interest Paul Whitin in their proposed enterprise, not only because of the financial support he could give but because he was already one-third owner of the forge property.

Whitin agreed to provide half the capital of the new firm; the three Fletcher brothers, Samuel, James, Jr., and Ezra, together with their brother-in-law, Amos Armsby, agreed to supply the other half. James Fletcher made his contribution to the enterprise by selling his interest in the forge property to his sons for the nominal price of $500.[28] The new company, which was to be known as Whitin & Fletchers,[29] was begun in 1816 on an unpretentious scale, for the old forge shop, which was used as a mill building, was so small that its capacity was only 288 spindles (four frames with 72 spindles each). From the beginning, the "forge mill" was operated by the Fletchers; Paul Whitin's interest was merely financial.

How successful the Whitin & Fletchers mill proved to be is not known. Doubtless it experienced difficult times during the postwar depression of 1818–19. A second depression, in 1825, seems to have convinced the Fletcher brothers that a brighter future lay in a return to farming, their former vocation. On 15 January 1826 they sold their half-interest to Paul Whitin for $2,000.[30]

Again it is difficult to understand why Paul was willing to put more money into the forge mill when, as will be related shortly, he had only a few months earlier sold, at a reduced price and in exchange for promissory notes, his interest in the Northbridge mill. The only apparent explanation is that he wanted to provide his sons with a business of their own and lacked the opportunity or the wherewithal to buy out his partners in the much larger Northbridge enterprise.

By 1826 three of Paul Whitin's five sons had reached maturity. The eldest, Paul, Jr., had spent three years in Boston as a clerk in a dry-goods store and four years in New York as part owner of a retail firm.[31] The second son, Nathaniel, had also gone to New York but, unlike his older brother, had not prospered. For a time he sold drugs (an occupation which seems to have won him the title of Dr.

Whitin), but being unsuccessful, he returned to Northbridge and became a farmer. He seems to have possessed some inventive ability but to have lacked the business acumen required for a profitable use of his talents.[32] The executive bent of his four brothers was strangely absent in Nathaniel, and through want of interest or of competence he was precluded from all family enterprises. The third son, John, had spent the greater part of his youth learning the techniques of mill production. As a boy he had worked first in the picker room and then in the machine shop of the Northbridge mill. For the three years preceding 1826, he had been employed as a clerk in Paul's dry-goods store in New York. The other two Whitin sons, Charles and James, were seventeen and twelve respectively, still too young to assume business responsibilities.

As soon as their father had obtained full ownership of the forge mill, Paul, Jr., and John returned to Northbridge to assume active management of the company. They immediately set about tearing down the fifty-year-old forge building and in its place erected a brick structure large enough to house, if conditions ever warranted, several times the thousand spindles with which they equipped it at the outset.[33]

The new firm became known as P. Whitin & Sons but in fact was owned solely by the elder Paul Whitin. Nevertheless, Paul continued to give his full attention to the smithy and therefore delegated the management of the "brick mill" completely to his sons. Paul, Jr., because of his interest in selling, took charge of marketing the mill's products, and John, then only nineteen years of age, became responsible for mill operations.

4. FATE OF THE NORTHBRIDGE MILL

Meanwhile, the original owners of the Northbridge Cotton Manufacturing Company had become so discouraged by depressed postwar conditions that, except for a two-year period when they rented the mill to a firm called Gladding & Cady, they had let the building stand idle. It is not surprising, therefore, that in the spring of 1825 some of the owners were willing to sell their interest to the Buffum brothers, Thomas and William, Jr., a pair of speculators who were just then buying up mills at generous prices. Already the two brothers had become the owners of the Branch Manufacturing Company, of Smithfield, Rhode Island, and within a year they were also to acquire a mill in Holden, Massachusetts.[34] The price they offered the promoters of the Northbridge company was $555 per share. On 25 March 1825, six of the Northbridge shareholders, including Paul Whitin, agreed to sell the Buffums an aggregate of eighteen shares, enough to represent control of the mill.[35]

As has already been stated, a sharp depression occurred during the year 1825. So far did values decline that, by November of that year, Henry Sabin, one of the owners who had already sold a portion of his stock to the Buffums, was willing to sell the rest for $333 per share.[36] Apparently the Buffums felt that this sale constituted an indication of the just and reasonable price of the shares under prevailing conditions; therefore, they called together the former shareholders, for whose stock they had as yet paid nothing, and declared that they were unable to pay the $555 per share first agreed upon, but were willing to renegotiate the sale on the basis of $333 per share. To this proposition the former holders agreed, and on 28 November 1825 each received five notes which were to mature, one annually, over the following five years.[37]

During 1826, 1827, and 1828 the Buffums redeemed their notes promptly, but in 1829, the crash year in which nearly all New England mills lost heavily, they defaulted.[38] To aid them out of bankruptcy their brother-in-law, Samuel Shove, agreed to buy the mill and to assume its debts, of which $3,549.19 was the amount still owed to the noteholders. Unfortunately, however, Samuel Shove was too much embarrassed by difficulties arising out of his own wide mill holdings to be able to do much toward paying off the notes. (In fact, he eventually went bankrupt himself — in 1834.)[39] Such was the situation when, on 8 February 1831, Paul Whitin suddenly died.

It seems possible that the status of the Northbridge mill had been a point of controversy between father and sons for some time before Paul's death. The boys had prospered notably in their five years of mill operations and must have viewed the Northbridge mill as a hopeful means of expansion, especially since the Northbridge company was apparently being poorly, or at best indifferently, managed by outside interests. But Paul seems to have felt the moment unpropitious for such bold expansion.

Scarcely four months had passed after Paul's death when his sons, on 10 June 1831, came to an agreement with Samuel Shove whereby they undertook to pay him $15,753.56 for the twenty-three Northbridge shares he held — $2,246.54 to be paid in cash (so that Shove could pay off the company's remaining noteholders) and the rest in five promissory notes maturing quarterly over a period of the next year and a half.[40] The high price that the Whitins were willing to pay for the mill, approximately $685 a share, may have been in part a reflection of the optimistic spirit of their youth; yet in part it was also an indication of how well they had fared financially during their first five years in business. Even at their young ages the Whitin brothers were beginning to show their keen business acumen. In those few years of prosperity between 1826 and 1829 they had established the foundations of their fortunes. By surviving the depression of 1829 (when even David Wilkinson had gone bankrupt and Slater himself had nearly done so) they had proved those foundations to be secure.

Apparently the Whitins were able to meet the due dates on their notes without trouble, for on 7 August 1833 they received from Shove a receipt formally acknowledging payment in full.[41] Meanwhile Paul, Jr., and John were busy buying up the other outstanding shares in the mill, so that by 1833 they were its sole owners.[42] The smithy had been closed in 1831 after their father's death. Therefore, the two mills comprised the Whitin enterprise, and as owners thereof the Whitin brothers were the town's only large-scale employers. When the villagers met, in 1835, to change the name of their community from South Northbridge to Whitinsville, they were not only honoring the man who had so recently died, but in actual fact they were acknowledging the commanding position achieved since his death by his sons.

Following Paul Whitin's death, the firm of P. Whitin & Sons became for the first time a partnership. On 21 October 1831 Betsey Whitin, Paul's widow and sole heir, sold to three of her five sons (Paul, Jr., John, and Charles) a three-quarters interest in the company for the price of $6,000. The remaining quarter-share she retained for herself. For thirty-two years she was to hold an active and, because of her position in the family, a virtually controlling interest in the company. As the partnership expanded to include still another of her sons, and as the company's interests spread to other mills and to machinery manufacturing and real-estate holding, it was Betsey Whitin whose force of personality dominated the firm and held it unified.

CHAPTER II

FROM PICKERS TO LOOMS, 1831–1859

IN EVERYONE'S lifetime certain dates serve as memory guideposts — the year one finished school, the date of one's marriage, the time one made a certain trip. To the Whitin brothers the year 1831 must have been such a way-mark. It was the year of their father's death, as well as the year they bought the Northbridge Cotton Manufacturing Company. It was also the year that brother John developed and patented his improved picker.

With two mills to manage, John let it be known that he could not continue to act as mill superintendent and still do justice to the experimental work he was conducting in the brick mill's repair shop.[1] Before the end of 1831 he had turned the superintendent's job over to his younger brother, Charles. Previously Charles had been in poor health and had limited his activities to overseeing only one department. But by 1831 his health had improved and he was perfectly willing to take over part of John's work.

Probably no one really begrudged John the hours he chose to spend in the repair shop, for no other single department of the mill was so vital to the success of the whole. In those early days when the textile machinery industry was still in an amorphous stage, mills not infrequently made their own machinery and most of them thought nothing of executing radical changes in their equipment if it suited their fancies. A mill with an alert repair department was bound to enjoy an advantage over its competitors, as the Whitin brothers were doubtless aware.

Furthermore, working apart from the others suited John's temperament, for he was more an independent operator than a teamwork man. Even at an early age he had shown himself to be extremely ambitious — much more so than his brothers — and rather more concerned with watching out for his own interests than his brothers thought he ought to be. It is said that Charles, the brother nearest John's age, was the only one who could get along with him and that Betsey Whitin's firm hand was all that kept the brothers working together in partnership.

In many ways John was the ablest of the Whitin brothers; certainly he was the most dynamic. Paul, Jr., the oldest of the five brothers and the one who became titular head of the family after the elder Paul's death, was a reserved, dignified, and civic-minded young man, very much like his father. John was in many ways the opposite. In manner he was anything but reserved. He took too much pleasure from the things money could buy to live a life of dignified austerity. Later on, after he had become a wealthy man, John picked the best spot in town on which to build the town's largest house and finest estate. Nor was he interested in the community's political life, as his brother Paul was. John was much too busy for politics. His one digression from work was the Congregational Church, and even there one suspects that he attended services more because he believed in setting an example for the townspeople than because he felt a need for divine guidance.*

As a husband, John seems to have been generous and considerate, and, as a father, indulgent. He worshipped his daughter and could never bring himself to find fault with her. He held somewhat the same attitude toward his son, for he gave the lad all the latitude possible to a son of the new-rich; then, having trained the boy for his life work in the worst possible manner, he expected such great things of him that he quickly pushed the young man beyond his depth.

As a business man, John C. Whitin was a product of his times. Like most manufacturers of his day, he was a specialist in production. To him selling was at best a subsidiary function. Occasionally he may have tried to persuade mill owners to buy Whitin products, but for the most part he ran what was essentially an order-taking business. Moreover, like most self-made men, he knew nothing of

---

* Because of his church activities John Whitin was commonly known to the townspeople as "Deacon John." Family tradition has it that, as a staunch Congregationalist, he would hire no one of any other faith, but from the Irish names on the company's payrolls it would appear that at least by 1860 he was employing a number of Catholics.

accounting. All but the most rudimentary forms of bookkeeping escaped his attention. Throughout his lifetime he kept no satisfactory financial records. To familiarize himself with what was going on in his business he relied not on accounting reports but on a direct, personal, and constant association with day-by-day affairs. Under such circumstances elaborate accounts probably seemed to him a wasteful expenditure of time and energy.

Yet despite his apparent shortcomings, Whitin was a man of remarkable accomplishments. With little help from his brothers he built the family machinery business from a one-product beginning into a great, integrated concern. It was men of his kind who made New England the center of the American Industrial Revolution. Indeed without such leaders no society could achieve preëminence. Yet how little the general public appreciates them. Judged as he should be judged, by economic standards, John C. Whitin was a person of rare capacity. With a smattering of mechanical talent he combined such a richness of executive ability that he was able to develop an industrial organization so efficient as to cause men to come to him from all over the country asking him to build machinery for their mills. It is given to few men in this world to be as socially useful to their fellow-creatures as John C. Whitin was.

I. WHITIN'S IMPROVED PICKER

In his machinery experiments John C. Whitin was particularly concerned with finding a way to mechanize the picking process without doing harm to the delicate cotton fibers. For at least a generation, mill owners had been trying to solve the perplexing problem of duplicating hand picking by machine methods. Around 1807 the firm of Hines, Dexter & Company, of Rhode Island, is said to have tried using a water-powered picker, although apparently with little success.[2] In 1809 Seth Bemis of Watertown, Massachusetts, is reported to have devised a mechanical picker, though he too seems to have become discouraged by the harsh treatment his invention gave the cotton fibers.[3] As late as the war period of 1812–15 picking was still being performed by hand in most mills, an expensive process that accounted for about 5 per cent of the cost of finished yarn.[4]

After the war, however, there was great incentive to do away with hand picking, for business in general was depressed and competition from the British was stiff. Gradually American manufacturers learned to concentrate on the production of coarse fabrics, the quality of which did not demand refined picking methods. By the early 1820's machine pickers were in common use, even though no generally accepted picker had yet been put on the market,[5] for each mill customarily designed its own mechanical whipping device. The resulting apparatus was usually a crude affair, called either a whipper or a willow because it was so much like the hand method of whipping cotton fibers with a willow wand. Such machines made no attempt to form the fibers into a lap. Consequently, the whipped cotton still had to be placed on the revolving cylinder of a card, handful by handful, a slow and expensive operation. It was not until the late 1820's that a second type of machine was developed to prepare the cotton in lap form so that it could be fed into card cylinders automatically.[6] By that time the first process had come to be called either scutching, or picking, and the second process was referred to as lapping.

No single idea incorporated by Whitin in his picker seems to have been an innovation; rather he seems to have combined for the first time in marketable form the best features of the many designs that had sprung up separately in mill shops throughout New England. The accompanying illustration reproduces the sketch on which Whitin based his application for a patent, but since no word description of the sketch has survived, it is impossible to be certain in what manner the Whitin picker differed from its predecessors. The *Journal of the Franklin Institute* made the following comments on the new patent:

This spreading and picking machine is constructed *like some others now in use* [italics mine], but the wire cylinders are to have a flanch, or heading, on each end, projecting about two inches, so as to retain the sheet or lap of cotton, with a smooth, compact edge. All the moving cylinders, rollers, &c., excepting the beaters, are to be geared, and these are to be run as usual by straps. The claim is to "the application of gearing to the several movements, instead of belts, and of the flanch or rim to the ends of the several wire cylinders."

Gearing was just coming into common use in the early 1830's.[7] It is easy to imagine that gears greatly improved the way a picker functioned, for they probably prevented the slippage that had bedeviled the picking operation in the days when only belt-driven components had been used.

Whatever its reputed advantages, the Whitin picker was a notable success. The leading mill authority of the period, James Montgomery, reported: "The best lap spreaders, or scutching machines, that I have seen in this country, are made by Mr. Whitings [*sic*], of South North Bridge, Massachusetts, for which he has obtained a patent."[8]

To give John Whitin sole honor for the success of the new picker would be an egregious error, however. George L. Gibbs, who married one of John's nieces, has recorded in his memoirs that credit for the invention was privately claimed by Benjamin Innis, one of P. Whitin & Sons' employees. No doubt there is some truth in what Innis claimed, for he was a man of about Whitin's age, perhaps a little older,[9] and was known throughout his life as an ingenious mechanic, whereas Whitin gave no evidence in later years of native inventiveness.* Innis, however, had spent several years at sea and had acquired a reputation for irresponsibility and heavy drinking; hence he was fitted neither financially nor temperamentally to utilize the picker patent, even had it been granted to him. Consequently, whatever may be said for the unhappy Innis, it is probably fortunate for the people of Whitinsville that the patent was awarded to a man of executive ability, for it is unquestionably true that the village would today number among New England's hard-pressed mill communities, had it not been for the machinery business that John C. Whitin developed from that patent.

There is no positive evidence that Whitin perfected his machine with the idea of putting it on the market. He seems to have had in mind only a method of improving the picking operation in his family's two mills. The patent covering the new picker was dated 20 July 1832, but according to tradition the first sale of machinery was

---

* In Whitinsville's Pine Grove Cemetery, the center plot has traditionally been reserved for members of the Whitin family and for certain key employees — the Tafts, the Trowbridges, etc. One of those buried in the center plot is Benjamin Innis.

JOHN C. WHITIN, FOUNDER

WHITIN'S PATENT PICK & SPREADER.

1831

PATENTED JULY 20, 1832.

The Company's First Product

not made until 1834. In the intervening time only three pickers were made, all of them apparently for use in Whitin mills. By the beginning of 1834, however, a sufficient number of outside mills had learned of, and had placed orders for, the new machine to warrant a steady production of about one picker a month.*

By 1835 Whitin had increased his productive capacity to three pickers a month and, by 1836, to six. It seems impossible that he could have achieved this level of production in the small repair shop where he had made the first picker; in fact, although no history of the town or company contains any record of the erection of a separate machine shop prior to the large one built in 1847, there are several indications that such a shop did exist. In a pamphlet published in 1844 the village of Whitinsville was credited with two mills and a large machine shop.[10] Similarly, in a deed dated the following year, a plot of land was described as lying "between the upper Machine Shop of P. Whitin & Sons and the Whitinsville Post Office, it being the same land upon which recently stood a blacksmith shop." [11] The best available evidence of the location of this early shop is an old, undated map in the possession of the Whitin Machine Works. On the map is shown a machine shop located next to the 1809 dam, between the Northbridge mill and the river. Unfortunately, though, the map gives no evidence of when the shop was constructed.

The Whitin picker soon became established as the best on the market, and for nearly twenty years P. Whitin & Sons held unchallenged leadership in the picker field. As late as 1850 a textile handbook called *The Manager's Assistant* advised that "there are no machines of this, or indeed of any kind, which are more perfectly adapted to their office than those turned out by the Messrs. Whitins, of Mass." [12] Originally Whitin pickers were made with wooden

---

* The earliest available record of Whitin machinery production is a torn and ratgnawed piece of paper which purports to list the number of "spreaders" produced for P. Whitin & Sons by one S. F. Batchelor from 1833 to 1855. Apparently Batchelor was a foreman who had charge of the picker job on a contract basis. He was doubtless the Batchelor (Batchellor?) who married a niece of Betsey Whitin. The authenticity of the figures recorded on this slip of paper may be checked by comparing spreader production with the combined orders for pickers and lappers in the years covered by extant order books. See Chart IV.

frames, but during the 1840's John made available to his customers iron frames on an optional basis and at a price increase of from 15 to 20 per cent, depending on the model. By 1849 he had also acquired a license to manufacture Mumgrill-type pickers and had begun producing what he termed "lappers." Apparently by that time he was advising his customers to perform their picking operation in two steps to ensure more thorough cleaning.

CHART IV

PRODUCTION AND SALE OF WHITIN PICKERS, 1833–1855

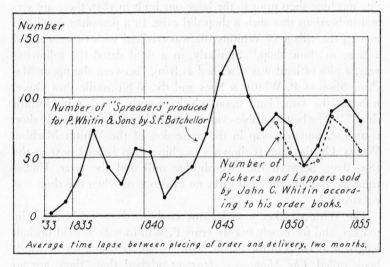

For at least his first five years in the machinery business and perhaps for as long as ten, Whitin seems to have produced nothing but picking equipment. By 1839 he is reported to have been employing eleven men in his machine shop,[13] and his total output for the year is said to have been $25,000.[14] Since we happen to know that P. Whitin & Sons produced 52 pickers in 1839 (see Chart IV), we can be fairly sure that John's shop produced little else besides pickers in that year, for 52 pickers at $500 each (the price for which they were selling a few years later when we happen to have more complete records) would have meant sales of about $26,000 for the year.

After 1849, radical changes occurred in the demand for the company's pickers and lappers. The picker business fell off precipitously and even lapper sales, while holding up, failed to respond to the general boom in the machinery business. Unfortunately our knowledge of competitive conditions in the textile machinery industry before the Civil War is so scant that we cannot be certain why Whitin failed to maintain his lead in the picker market. Two circumstances may have been contributing factors. Shortly after 1853 Richard Kitson of Lowell, Massachusetts, brought out a new type of picker that used, in the place of beaters, a needle-pointed revolving cylinder. Within the next decade he became, and for many years remained, the leading American producer of picking machinery. Meanwhile British manufacturers were beginning, for the first time, to sell textile equipment in the United States. The 1774 Act of Parliament, which had effectively barred the exportation of English machinery for nearly three-quarters of a century, was finally revoked in 1845. In a paper read before the New England Cotton Manufacturers Association in 1884, Alfred Clarke stated that twenty years previously pickers were being sold in America by "such well-known makers as Crighton, Lord, Platt, Walker & Hacking, and others, in England; and Kitson, Lowell Machine Shop, and Whitin, in this country." *

After about 1870, Whitin sold almost no picking equipment. Yet the legend of the original Whitin picker lived on in the memories of the villagers. With increasing pride in his later years, John Whitin took pleasure in showing visitors the old lathes on which he had made the machine that had proved to be the foundation of his fortune. In 1866, when he erected a new and much larger plant, he ordered that there be placed atop the bell tower a weather vane representing the original Whitin machine. Though it was badly damaged in the New England hurricane of 1938 and had to be taken

---

* Evelyn H. Knowlton, in her *Pepperell's Progress*, relates an incident that is an indication of what was happening in the picker market. In 1854 Pepperell decided to erect a new mill in Biddeford, Maine. Bids were solicited from many firms in the United States and, supposedly, in England as well. When the contracts were signed, the order for spinning machinery, dollar-wise the most important item of the mill's equipment, went to P. Whitin & Sons, but the picker order went to Walker & Hacking in England.

down and repaired, the picker weather vane may still be seen prominently displayed high above the plant created by its prototype.

2. A DIVERSIFIED PRODUCT LINE

It is possible that Whitin was producing a diversified line of cotton equipment as early as 1843. But how he was able to put on the market one type of machine after another until he was turning out not just pickers but also cards, railway heads (forerunner of the drawing frame), spinning frames, and looms is something we shall probably never know. Only fragments of the story have survived, and from those fragments we can reconstruct no more than a vague outline of what was taking place.

Many years later, in 1873, Whitin's son-in-law remarked in a letter to a customer that the Whitin company had been in the ring spinning business "for thirty years." [15] Whether he meant exactly thirty years or approximately that length of time one cannot tell from the content of his letter. It is regrettable that he was not more specific, for the early development of the ring spinning system is so cloaked in mystery that a more definite statement by a man who was in a position to know whereof he spoke would have meant much to future historians — and especially to an historian of the Whitin company, for "ring frames" were to become (and remain) the backbone of the Whitin machinery business. As it is, we have only a few scattered facts about how ring spinning got its start.

The ring spinning process was invented in 1828 by a Providence machinist named John Thorp. It was Thorp's hope that his ring frame would eliminate the slow and clumsy throstle-flyer which had remained virtually unchanged for nearly sixty years, that is to say, since Arkwright's time. But though brilliant in theory, Thorp's ring was clumsy in operation, and for many years it was completely ignored by mill men. Apparently the first person to make ring spinning at all practical was William Mason of Taunton, Massachusetts, for Mason is known to have sold a few ring frames as early as 1835. But Mason soon found that, as Van Slyck puts it in his *Representatives of New England: Manufacturers,* "there was at first a limited demand [for the ring frame] owing to the prejudice created by the old [Thorp] machine," [16] and so Mason neglected his lead in the ring-spinning field and devoted his attention instead to the self-acting mule, a competing type of spinning frame.*

It would seem, therefore, that the first commercially successful manufacturers of ring spinning frames were either Fales & Jenks, of Pawtucket, Rhode Island, or P. Whitin & Sons. Van Slyck states that Fales & Jenks began producing ring frames about 1845 and were among the first manufacturers to make this new type of spinning machine.[17] But the Whitin company must have been not far behind, for by 1849 (the first year for which there are any Whitin machinery records worthy of the name), P. Whitin & Sons were making frames at the rate of about fifty a year. To have created that large a market for their product P. Whitin & Sons must have entered the field, at the very least, two or three years earlier.

By 1849, at the latest, P. Whitin & Sons were making a complete line of machinery from pickers to looms, with only two exceptions — mules and roving frames.† The lack of roving frames was a disadvantage that John Whitin tried for many years to overcome, but in vain. The lack of mules, however, was less serious, for ring frames could be substituted for mules in many cases; in fact, the ring frame eventually almost completely replaced the mule as a spinning machine. But the roving frame, or speeder as it was then called, had no

* The beauty of ring spinning lay in its continuous and rapid operation. By comparison mule spinning was slow and awkward, since mules first had to twist the yarn and then wind it on bobbins in alternating operations. At first the reciprocating motion of the mule was activated by hand, but in 1825 an Englishman named Richard Roberts developed what was known as the self-acting mule. In 1840, patterns for the Roberts mule were smuggled to this country by William C. Davol, who thereafter manufactured self-acting mules for the American market. Meanwhile Mason had developed his own idea of how to make mules self-acting. For many years the two men produced between them most of the mules made in America. Typically mules were used in the manufacture of fine goods or in the production of filling yarns. In the Providence area ring frames were used in the production of warp yarn, while in the Boston area the throstle frame lingered on as the means of producing warp.

† Only William Mason, of all the other machine-builders in the Providence area, was ever able to achieve such a well-rounded product line. At least a portion of Whitin's expanded machinery line was achieved by licensing the right to produce patented machines such as the Mumgrill picker. In 1855 he began selling Bacon willows and in 1857 the self-stripping cards that Horatio Gambrill had patented two years earlier. In 1858 he made his first sale of a Bartlett let-off attachment, an important loom invention that had been patented in 1857.

substitute, for it accomplished the indispensable operation of attenuation just before the spinning operation.

The market for speeders was neatly divided between the two New England mill areas. Boston mills preferred the Waltham speeder invented by Paul Moody; Providence mills preferred the Taunton speeder invented by George Danforth. Until about 1850 these two machines dominated the speeder market and unless a shop produced one or the other, which Whitin's shop did not, it had little chance of success in the speeder line. After 1840, British machine-builders began to ship fly frames (as their type of roving frame was called) to America, and in so doing they played havoc with the domestic speeder market.[18] Fly frames were vastly superior to the old speeders, which turned out only the coarsest type of work, and within a very short time the speeder had become completely obsolete. Apparently only one American producer, the Providence Machine Company, owned by Thomas J. Hill, was able to develop a fly frame capable of competing with the British. The Whitin company never did succeed in developing a competing machine, though it tried on at least one occasion. Not until many years later did the Whitin company finally add roving equipment to its machinery line, and then it did so by purchasing the Providence Machine Company outright.

From 1844 to 1847, John Whitin's machinery business expanded so rapidly that he was hard pressed for space to carry on his work. In 1845, his brothers vacated the entire brick mill for his use, and moved all their cotton machinery across the river into a handsome new mill built of native granite on a spot just below where the blacksmith shop had stood.[19] Even then John found himself with inadequate space and decided to build a large machine shop where he could gather all his manufacturing facilities under one roof. Accordingly, in 1847, he erected a shop which from its very dimensions bears evidence that P. Whitin & Sons were no longer making just pickers.[20] The new building, a brick structure measuring 102 feet by 306 feet, consisted of two stories and a basement.* Some idea of its

---

* This building is still being used as an integral part of the Whitin plant. In its century of service its only major repairs have been the substitution of a new roof for the old tin one and the replacement of the original basement posts with steel supports. To provide enough power for the new shop the 10-foot dam opposite the Northbridge mill was replaced by a 20.4-foot dam 300 feet farther up the river. This latter dam is still being used by the company and is capable of providing from 350 to 400 horsepower. On the dam's keystone may be seen the chiseled date, 1847.

THE MACHINE SHOP BUILT IN 1847

View of the Holyoke Machine Shop

relative size in the industry may be gained by comparing it with the shop built by William Mason, in Taunton, two years earlier. Mason's shop was 315 feet long and three stories high. At the time it was built it was regarded as the largest machine shop in the United States.[21]

Remember, though, that in 1847 John's machinery business, fast-growing as it was, still was only a subordinate part of the central interest of P. Whitin & Sons — the production of cotton sheetings.[22] For that reason, even though it may seem a digression from the main narrative, a review of what was happening in the mill end of the family business is necessary to an understanding of the whole.

3. A SHOP AND SIX MILLS

It will be recalled that in 1831 the two Whitin mills had a total combined capacity of 3,100 spindles. By 1844 that capacity had increased to 11,400 spindles simply through the installation of additional machinery.[23] Construction of the stone mill in 1845 added only about 1,750 spindles to the capacity, since most of the new building's equipment was machinery moved over from the brick mill. Till that time the Whitin brothers had confined their cotton-manufacturing activities solely to Whitinsville, but after 1845 hardly another spindle was added to the textile-manufacturing capacity of the village. Instead, the Whitins began to buy mill properties in the contiguous area, principally at bankruptcy sales. It is a comment not only on the business conditions of the times but also on the superior ability of the Whitins that within the next fifteen years nearly every mill in the immediate area, theirs being the only important exception, came on the market as the result of bankruptcy proceedings.

The first outside establishment bought by the Whitins was the Uxbridge Cotton Mills, located on the Mumford River five miles below Whitinsville (see Chart V). The previous history of these mills had been long and kaleidoscopic. Originating in a frame structure built in 1810, the mills had reached the height of their development under Roger Robertson, a Boston merchant, who had replaced the old wooden buildings with a stone mill on either side of the Mumford River, one named the Crown Mill and the other the Eagle Mill, in honor of England, the birthplace, and America, the foster home, of his parents. (During Robertson's time, one of the mills' employees had been George Draper, the man who was later to found America's leading loom-producing company, the Draper Corporation.)[24]

The depression of 1837 forced Robertson into bankruptcy (and incidentally caused him to sell to the Whitins his title to the water privilege at Linwood, where the Whitins later built another mill; see Appendix 10). After Robertson's bankruptcy, the Crown and

CHART V

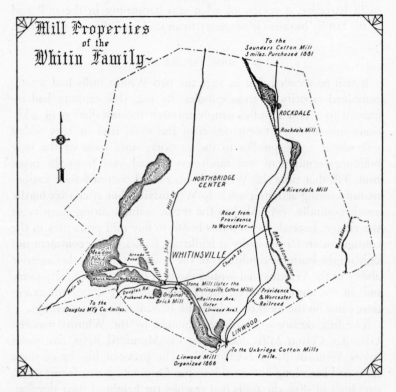

Eagle mills stood idle until 1841, when new owners came in to reorganize them as the Uxbridge Cotton Mills. These owners also had difficulty in making the Uxbridge mills pay, and on 8 May 1849 they sold the mills to the Whitins at a sacrifice price.

Almost at once the Whitins enlarged the mills by spanning the river with a connecting brick structure. The contrast of brick and stone, the symmetry of design, and the verdure of the surrounding meadows in combination with the sparkle of the river must have made the Uxbridge mills among the handsomest in New England, for even now, with the mill buildings in disrepair and the grounds untended, there is a haunting beauty about the place.

In 1856 the Whitins added further to their holdings by purchasing the Riverdale and Rockdale mill properties, both located on the Blackstone River. These mills had at one time been owned by Sylvanus Holbrook,* but in 1855 Holbrook had died, nearly bankrupt, and his mill properties had fallen to the Worcester Bank to which he owed money. From the bank the Whitins bought the Rockdale site on 19 March 1856 [25] and apparently they bought the Riverdale mill on 21 October of the same year.[26] Finally, in 1859, the Whitins bought a sixth mill, located in East Douglas. By that time they owned every mill property of any consequence in the Northbridge area and had become one of the leading mill families in the Blackstone Valley.

Meanwhile, a fourth brother, James, had been admitted to the Whitin partnership. As will be recalled, the 1831 division of ownership in the family firm had been among Betsey Whitin and three of her sons, Paul, Jr., John, and Charles. When James, the youngest son, sought to be included in the firm, his brothers, who might have been expected to offer him an equal interest in the company, evidently refused. It was not until 1847 (by which time James was thirty-three years old and had worked a dozen or more years in the office of the company) that a settlement was finally reached. Even then, the brothers did not give way. Instead, it was Betsey who agreed to sell half of her interest to James — for $10,000.[27]

As the thread of the Whitin story unwinds, Betsey's rôle as matriarch of the family and arbitrator of disputes among the brothers becomes increasingly evident. Within the company there had grown up two distinct enterprises, the shop and the mills. Each operated autonomously, each had its separate set of customers, each had its

---

* Holbrook had bought the Riverdale mill in 1821 and at the same time had obtained the water rights at Rockdale, a few miles farther upstream. Then, in 1832, he had built a mill at Rockdale, but it had soon burned and Holbrook had not been able to finance its reconstruction. Thus when the Whitins bought the Rockdale property, they got not only a piece of land but also the water rights at that spot.

individual manufacturing and marketing problems, each its separate labor force and its contribution of profits or losses to the firm. Yet the books of these two enterprises were kept jointly, profits were jointly shared, and, theoretically at least, control was jointly held. Under such circumstances, Betsey's firm hand was necessary to hold together the factions that must have arisen and to preserve the entity of the family enterprise.

4. ORDER BOOKS, 1849–1859

Since all records were kept jointly, the machinery end of the business lived no separate accounting existence. Consequently, when the family many years later closed all but one of its mills and destroyed all its early mill records, it inadvertently destroyed the machinery records as well. With but two small exceptions the only machinery accounts that have survived are those beginning in 1860, when John C. Whitin launched an enterprise of his own. The exceptions are two small order books which were apparently John's personal notebooks and which therefore escaped the fate of the other records. Within those two small books may be found practically all that is now known about John C. Whitin's machinery business in the ten years before the Civil War.

Glancing at the order books one is surprised to discover how widely Whitin sold his machinery in those early days. At a time when there were only thirty-three states in the Union, Whitin was selling machinery to mills in twenty-one of them. In addition, he was making occasional sales in Canada and Mexico. But, on closer study, it becomes apparent that almost all the machines Whitin was selling outside New England were pickers. The greatest share of his other products went to mills in Rhode Island, southern Massachusetts, and eastern Connecticut — the so-called Providence area. Especially important as a market in the 1850's was the valley region of eastern Connecticut where a group of rivers, the Quinebaug, the Willimantic, the Shetucket, the Yantic, and others, flowed southward into the Thames River estuary. The whole eastern Connecticut region was experiencing a boom in its cotton manufacturing industry at that time, and one is led to believe from a study of the Whitin records that a large, perhaps preponderant, part of the mill equipment installed in the area was being built in the machine shop of

P. Whitin & Sons. In fact, it seems possible that John C. Whitin's rapid advance to the forefront of the textile-machinery business in the 1850's resulted in large part from his fortuitous proximity to such a booming region and to his success in establishing himself as the leading builder of equipment for Connecticut's new mills.

Because of variations from product to product, it is impossible to define the extent of John Whitin's machinery market in any specific way. For instance, the Connecticut area took 40 per cent of his loom output for the decade 1849–59,* but took only 7 per cent of his pickers. The Boston area absorbed little Whitin machinery of any kind, with the exception of drawing equipment; it took only 7 per cent of Whitin's spinning frames and only 8 per cent of his looms,[28] but in the case of drawing equipment it absorbed 24 per cent of his sales. There was a special reason for that exception, however. Drawing sets consisted of a group of cards and railway heads connected in tandem with a group of drawing heads, thus combining in one operation the carding and drawing processes.† The system was first developed in the Providence area and was commonly known as the railway-head system of drawing. Gradually it found acceptance in Boston mills, but many years elapsed before machine shops in the Boston area took up its manufacture. Meanwhile Boston mill owners, if they wanted to buy railway-head equipment, could do so only in the Providence area.

About once each year P. Whitin & Sons received an order to build all the machinery for a new mill. Such an order characteristically required six months to fill, whereas average-sized orders usually required about two months. Customers showed their satisfaction with Whitin machinery by placing frequent reorders. Those who placed three or more orders during the six years covered by the second order book (1854–59) accounted for 45 per cent of Whitin's total dollar sales. Nearly all orders were for complete machines; few

---

* Although the Whitin company no longer makes weaving equipment, in the first years of its history it made a full line — spoolers for winding warp yarn from bobbins to spools, dressers for sizing it, warpers for winding it onto drums, and finally looms for weaving the warp and filling yarn into cloth.

† As laps of cotton came off a battery of card cylinders, they passed immediately through railway-head rollers, which compressed them into bulky slivers and sent them slithering down a series of parallel troughs into a set of drawing heads, which combined a number of slivers into one and drew that one out to the desired fineness.

orders called for parts only. In ordering new equipment, mill owners usually stipulated the spare parts they wanted sent along; it was general practice for mills to do all their repair work in their own repair shops.

The spread of Whitin's reputation as a machinery manufacturer seems to have been accomplished entirely by word of mouth. Mill owners saw or heard of a desirable machine, learned that it was made by Whitin, and wrote for one like it. Order after order requested "spindles like New Bedford" or "two frames like Blackstone" or "looms same as Suffolk has."

Orders were generally placed by the agent of a mill, or as he would now be called, the superintendent. If an intermediary entered the transaction, he did so as the representative of the mill, not of the Whitin company. Except for a short time early in his business career, John Whitin consistently refused to allow outsiders a commission on sales. In negotiating machinery sales, he believed that the only satisfactory relationship was between the shop and the mill itself, and that commission agents tended to disrupt that close connection. However, his policy did not prevent certain other types of purchasers from acting as intermediaries. Many mills allowed their selling agents to buy their machinery. H. J. Libby & Company, of Portland, Maine, bought Whitin machinery for three Maine concerns whose selling agents they were; Parker, Wilder & Company, of Boston, bought machinery for a group of New Hampshire mills; and Hay, McDevitt & Company, of Philadelphia, acted as purchasers for several Pennsylvania firms. Frequently these selling firms held financial control of the mills for which they were buying machinery; and, being located in large business centers, they were in a better position to judge the machinery market than the mill agents themselves. Occasionally Whitin's competitors acted also as middlemen for certain mills, but only when they had orders to furnish complete sets of equipment and could not fill the entire order themselves. Of course, under similar circumstances Whitin himself sometimes became a middleman, since he did not make mules or roving frames. The competitors who most often bought from Whitin were William Mason and Thomas J. Hill.

From notations in the order books we can reconstruct, in part at least, the paths traveled by Whitin machinery from the shop to the customer's mill. On one early order, for instance, the price was quoted "del^d on canal." From 1828 on, there had been a canal between Providence and Worcester parallel to the Blackstone River. It passed within two miles of the P. Whitin & Sons machine shop and must have carried most of Whitin's early machinery shipments. Whitin probably sent machines from his shop to the barge landing by ox-wagon, just as he is known to have done in later years when it was necessary to cart machinery from the shop to the railroad siding. In 1847 the Providence and Worcester Railroad began operations and almost immediately forced the canal to close.[29] No doubt the railroad played an important part in Whitin's early prosperity, for it began operating just as Whitin was building his first big machine shop.

When making shipments northward, Whitin sent his machines as far as Worcester on the Providence and Worcester Railroad and then on lines which connected at that point. When shipping south and west, he sent machinery to Providence and usually thence by sea. Equipment bound for mills along the Mohawk River went to New York and then up the Hudson. Machines for Pittsburgh went first to Philadelphia by sea and then overland. Machines for mills in eastern Tennessee generally went by boat as far as Charleston, South Carolina, while those meant for the western part of the state went via New Orleans. Frequently goods meant for the South had to be sent to New York for transshipment because sailing vessels seldom left Providence bound directly for southern ports.

From the records of Whitin's machinery orders it is also possible to trace something of the cyclical nature of the machinery business in those times (see Chart IV). It is interesting to note that the general prosperity of the years 1844–47 drove Whitin's picker sales to unprecedented heights just as John C. Whitin was deciding to build his ambitious new machine shop. It would appear that Whitin, by expanding into other lines, was able to save himself from a severe setback in the depression that followed. By 1849, his sales amounted to an estimated $85,000 whereas ten years earlier they had been only $25,000.

The depression that most seriously affected Whitin's business in the pre-Civil-War period was the general collapse of 1857–58. The first indication we find of impending trouble was a penciled note placed opposite an order entered in June, 1857. The order was from none other than William Mason, Whitin's principal competitor in the Providence area. The note read simply: "Failed." Actually, however, Mason's failure was owing not to any financial weakness inherent in his machinery business but to the weakness of James K. Mills, the Boston commission agent whose firm owned half-interest in his company. In fact, the strength of Mason's own financial position was such that within a short time he was able to resume his business.

By September, 1857, Whitin's sales were falling off precipitously. In the first eight months of the year, Whitin had received orders for machinery totaling roughly $140,000; in the remaining four months he received only six orders, amounting to not more than $8,750. Throughout the next year orders came in very slowly. Fortunately, though, John was able to provide work for his employees because he and his brothers chose the depression months to build and equip a mill at Rockdale on the property they had bought from the late Sylvanus Holbrook's creditors. It was the first of a series of instances in which the Whitins were to look upon the employment of their workers in time of depression as a matter of family concern.

By late 1858, business was beginning to recover. In 1859 the pent-up demand for machinery burst upon Whitin with unprecedented force. The total value of requests for machinery during that year more than doubled the previous record set in 1855. Whitin took orders for a total of $330,000 worth of machinery, more than he could possibly have delivered in the time promised and with the plant then available. Caught completely off guard by the suddenness of the recovery, he met the situation with a hasty decision. At the time it seemed the logical answer to his problem, though he later came to regret his action and eventually decided to reverse it. Had he been more patient, his new undertaking might have proved a success and might have altered the whole history of the Whitin company. As it was, the venture that he was to undertake at Holyoke merely shows how easily external events can divert a business man from one course to another and then to still another.

CHAPTER III

THE HOLYOKE VENTURE, 1860–1863

By the spring of 1860 John Whitin's backlog of orders had reached a critical limit.[1] If he was to meet his delivery obligations he had to have additional plant capacity; the capacity in Whitinsville was completely inadequate and there was not enough time to erect more buildings.

Whether Whitin would have preferred to build another shop in Whitinsville, given sufficient time, we do not know. Whitinsville, of course, was a very favorable location for a textile-machinery plant. It had ample water power,[2] and there was still plenty of room for additional buildings near the shop built in 1847. There existed a good market near at hand and railroad connections within a mile and a half. Labor was not abundant, but workers could be attracted from Worcester or Providence with little difficulty.

But erecting another machine shop in Whitinsville would have meant using family property and family-controlled water rights. More specifically, it would have meant that P. Whitin & Sons would have owned the new building. Apparently John was not anxious to see his brothers continue to dominate the business he had started. Perhaps he thought it unfair that they, who had done so little for the shop, should continue to enjoy more than half its profits. At least, when it came to buying a shop in another locality, he decided to do it on his own account and not in partnership with his brothers —though he did not relinquish his active interest in the shop at Whitinsville. What alternatives he considered or what other locations he looked into we do not know, but he bought outright, and in his own name, a large and fairly new machine shop at Holyoke, Massachusetts, about sixty miles west of Worcester.

I. PURCHASE OF THE HOLYOKE SHOP

The shop at Holyoke had previously been owned by the Hadley Falls Company, a promotional enterprise launched ten years earlier by James K. Mills' commission company, the selfsame firm that had brought financial failure to William Mason in 1857.[3] James K. Mills and his associates had been impressed by the tremendous success of the mill development at Lowell and were convinced that they could duplicate that success at Holyoke. Like the promoters at Lowell they undertook the entire job of organizing a new mill site: they dammed the river, constructed locks and canals, organized a machine shop, set up cotton mills, and induced their friends to buy property from them and set up additional mills. In other words, they launched their enterprise in typical Boston fashion, establishing among other things a machine-building company that began its existence with a full line of machinery and with orders to outfit several complete new mills.

What had taken more than a decade to achieve on a smaller scale at Lowell, the James K. Mills associates hoped to accomplish in two or three years. But as might have been predicted, the sale of mill sites fell far short of expectations, and in 1854 the company had to reorganize. A separate firm called the Lyman Mills was set up to take over the company's cotton-manufacturing properties, leaving the original Hadley Falls Company in possession only of its machine shop, its water rights, and its undeveloped real estate. The machine shop was managed by Otis Holmes, formerly agent of the Saco Water Power Machine Shop, at Biddeford, Maine. Then, in 1857, the failure of the James K. Mills firm threw the Hadley Falls Company into involuntary bankruptcy.

For over a year the machine shop at Holyoke stood idle. Finally, on 10 February 1859, it was sold at public auction along with the real estate and water rights for $325,000 to a local capitalist named Alfred Smith. Smith immediately organized a new firm, under the name of the Holyoke Water Power Company, and sold part interest to other local investors. But a year later he and his associates had still not succeeded in getting the machine shop back in operation. All that Smith had been able to do was to lease part of one floor (a sixth of the shop's total floor area) to a small job-order firm named Wheeler & Pattee.[4] The Holyoke shop had consequently been idle for about three years by the time John C. Whitin became interested in it. Small wonder that Alfred Smith was a ready seller.

It is also easy to understand why John Whitin looked upon the Holyoke location as a promising site. Even though Holyoke itself had not yet achieved the prosperity anticipated by its promoters, the town of Chicopee Falls, only a few miles to the southeast, had been a thriving mill center for some years past. Four of the large mills there had been organized by Boston investors, many of whom had been concurrently financing the mill development at Lowell,[5] and within a fifteen-mile radius of Chicopee there were nine mills with 10,000 spindles or more each. Many of the mills in the Chicopee area, despite their connection with Boston interests, had been good customers of P. Whitin & Sons. Consequently, John C. Whitin already knew the territory and was himself already well known there. Moreover, the shop at Holyoke was said to have been the largest machine shop in Massachusetts at that time, larger even than Mason's; and, besides being served by what was probably the finest water-power site in New England,[6] it was already equipped for the manufacture of textile machinery.

Records of the negotiations between Whitin and Alfred Smith have not been preserved. All that exists is an undated piece of paper which sets forth a list of the notes which Whitin agreed to pay the Holyoke Water Power Company for the property and equipment of its machine shop. From that list, and from subsequent payments on the notes, we are able to learn the general terms of the sale. The date of the agreement was 18 April 1860.[7] The sales price was $150,-000, to be paid not in cash but in five equal notes maturing over a period of five years and bearing an interest rate of 6 per cent, payable semiannually. (The total price would have amounted to $177,-000 had not Whitin paid off the notes within two and a half years, thus saving himself $5,400.) [8]

For his promissory notes Whitin received a ten-year-old building with a gross floor area nearly 40 per cent greater than the area of his machine shop in Whitinsville.[9] (So excellent was the construction of the building that it is still standing today, scarcely altered in

appearance from the accompanying picture dated 1875.)[10] Behind
the shop were a foundry and a forge of similarly large proportions. Across the canal stood a block of brick company houses (likewise still in existence). Before beginning operations at Holyoke,
Whitin invested an additional $18,000 in the renovation of the shop
and tenement buildings. His major improvement was the installation of a new heating system, probably steam, but at the same time
he had the flooring on the ground level repaired and the plant improved as a fire risk by the addition of new pumps and ladders and
by the erection of a surrounding fence. He also ordered the tenements repainted and, where necessary, repapered.

Title to the real estate included the privilege of using water power
equivalent to eight mill powers (about 480 horsepower) in return
for a nominal semiannual charge of $450.[11] A schedule of the shop's
machinery inventory indicates that its ten-year-old tools had been
depreciated only about 25 per cent from original cost; such a low
depreciation rate seems to have been realistic, however, for Whitin
found that many of the tools which he did not need could be sold
for approximately their book value. Of the 326 pieces of equipment
listed in the inventory, 200 can be classified as some type of lathe;[12]
the remaining items included screw machines, gear cutters, and milling machines, drill presses, boring machines, planers, and saws —
the same general type of machinery found in any metal and wood-
working shop today.

As important as the machine tools were the foundry patterns that
Whitin received with the purchase of the shop. Three types are
worthy of special note even though none of the three proved of great
monetary value to Whitin: patterns for mules, for fly frames, and for
Boyden turbines.

As has already been stated, Whitin had been producing all the
machinery needed to outfit a cotton mill except mules and roving
frames. For a time it seemed to Whitin that his Holyoke purchase
might at last enable him to complete his product line, and he even
went so far as to tell his customers that he was giving thought to
entering the mule and roving frame business.[13] But nothing ever
came of his ambitions in the mule line, and although he toyed with
the idea of building roving frames, he eventually abandoned that

hope too. It seems reasonable to assume that his inability to enter these two fields resulted from the poor design of the Holyoke patterns which had come to his hands.*

The turbine patterns, however, enjoyed a moderate success. The patterns owned by the Holyoke shop were covered by a patent held by Uriah A. Boyden, one of the earliest Americans to build water turbines in imitation of those designed by the Frenchman, Benoit Fourneyron. For many years after his first wheel had been installed in 1845, Boyden's turbines were considered among the best in America and were rapidly adopted, in place of breast wheels, by mills and factories throughout New England. The Hadley Falls Company was only one of several companies that manufactured Boyden turbines on license from the patent-holder;[14] consequently competition was fairly stiff. Moreover, several improved turbines began to appear just as Whitin was beginning to manufacture from the Boyden patterns so that, although Boyden reduced his royalty fee from $2.00 to $1.50 per horsepower, the business was not very profitable.[15] In all, Whitin built only sixteen wheels, two of them for the shop in Whitinsville. Whitin's negligible achievements in the turbine line, however, were not so surprising as his decision to have anything to do with this line. Whereas nearly every other textile-machinery manufacturer in New England was branching out into many diverse fields at about that time, Whitin, with this single exception, concentrated on the one product he knew best: textile machinery.[16]

2. INITIAL DIFFICULTIES

To manage the Holyoke Machine Shop, Whitin counted heavily on the aid of others. He had no desire to give up his home in Whitinsville or to relinquish his direct management of the shop there. Instead he hoped, by spending only a day or two each week

* Following the Civil War, Whitin decided to give up trying to do anything with the outmoded Holyoke Machine Shop's roving patterns and attempted to get permission to build British fly frames instead, arguing that the American tariff would prevent British manufacturers from selling their fly machinery in the United States. Whitin wrote to William Higgins & Sons, of Manchester, England, and asked for a license to build their type of roving machinery in America. Higgins declined. Consequently, it was not until 1909, when the Whitin Machine Works bought the Providence Machine Company, that the Whitin company was able to add roving equipment to its product line.

in Holyoke, to delegate to others most of the management of the new shop. As superintendent he chose Gustavus E. Taft, a young man of thirty whose work in the P. Whitin & Sons shop had disclosed his marked abilities in factory management. For cashier he obtained the services of Josiah Lasell, the young man who had married his daughter, Jane. Until then Josiah had been an instructor in a fashionable school for young ladies, which his brother, Edward Lasell, had established at Auburndale, Massachusetts.[17] The Lasell Seminary for Young Women, it was called — now Lasell Junior College. Jane Whitin had been one of Josiah's pupils there, and shortly after graduation had become his wife. The young couple were still living in Auburndale when John offered his son-in-law a job at Holyoke. For those days Josiah was a highly educated man, having been graduated from Williams College (the Lasells have been going there ever since). His interests were broader than the interests of many business men of his day, for he gave a large share of his time to school, church, and civic activities. Immediately upon arriving in Holyoke he took up his place in the community life of the town, and soon became one of those most active in encouraging the young men of Holyoke to volunteer for service in the war between the states. As office manager of the Holyoke Machine Shop, he was punctilious, earnest, and able. His superior education caused him to be held by his associates in respect, if not in awe; however, his highly trained mind tended to be inflexible and, although he worked in the textile machinery industry for the rest of his life, it cannot be said that he ever developed a commanding knowledge of the field.

As agent, or general manager, of the new shop, John chose his only son, John Maltby Whitin. Young John was twenty-two at the time and had only recently finished college at Dartmouth. When not in school, he had worked in his father's machine shop and had acquired a certain familiarity with cotton machinery. But he was still much too immature for his new responsibilities. His first formal act as agent of the Holyoke company was to order a batch of official calling cards so that he could distribute them among his acquaintances in Whitinsville.[18]

Members of John M.'s home community received the news of the young man's appointment as agent of the Holyoke shop without enthusiasm. They had seen him grow up, a spirited, willful son of an indulgent father who was too busy to pay much attention to his upbringing. His mother, never in good health, had spared him the discipline he might have received at home, and his acquaintances, always in awe of him because he was John C. Whitin's son, had never given him the benefit of the normally competitive life that children lead. That Whitin completely ignored his son's limitations was not so much an evidence of the blindness of paternal pride, as it was an indication that the father felt he was giving his son exactly the kind of exciting challenge that he himself would have gloried in as a boy.

The unfortunate effect of the decision to make young John agent of the new shop was almost immediately apparent; from the beginning, matters at Holyoke went badly. Although the shop had been bought in April, 1860, it did not begin to turn out textile machinery until late in the year; meanwhile, only the foundry was in operation producing pipe for soil, gas, and steam installations.[19] The illness of one of the key production heads at Whitinsville, a man named Cleveland, kept Whitin from spending as much time in Holyoke as he had planned,* so that nearly the entire burden of organizing the new company fell on his son.[20] The boy's lack of training and the father's failure to provide suitable instructions for carrying on the business when he was not present are clearly shown by a few sentences contained in a letter written by young John to his father on 13 July 1860:

Twould be quite an accommodation to me if you would make out a list of different kinds of mac[hinery] you build & affix a price as I am often called upon to know prices and don't like to *display* my ignorance. Will you please write by return mail what I shall pay the men whose names are on list encl. I will not pay them until I hear from you. I encl.

---

* At first the people of Holyoke were overjoyed when they learned that Whitin was reopening the old Hadley Falls Machine shop, for the shop had been the town's largest employer of male workers. (The town's other large employers, the Lyman and the Hampden mills, hired principally women.) But when it was learned that Whitin planned to be an absentee owner, the press was bitter in its condemnation. See Holyoke *Transcript*, 11 July 1863.

a letter fr. Mr. Adams of Dwight [Mfg.] Co. I did not know their Pulley was contracted to be done in 8 days.

The significance of this letter lies not only in Whitin's failure to instruct his son in the simple details of management but also in his neglect to establish a policy covering product and price. Perhaps one of the reasons that there was some confusion over what machines would be made at Holyoke was because of the difficulty of securing the necessary patterns. Apparently Whitin had decided to make use of only a portion of the patterns he had obtained from the Holyoke Water Power Company, for many of them were either obsolete or inferior in design. Yet if he was to use P. Whitin & Sons' patterns, he would have to make some arrangement with the firm's other partners. Just what the disposition was we do not know, but the general result is clear. P. Whitin & Sons at that time were producing two types of cards, one on license from George H. Wellman of Lowell, and the other on license from Horatio N. Gambrill of Baltimore. The production of these two cards was to be split between the two shops, Wellman cards being made at Whitinsville and Gambrill cards at Holyoke. All other machines requiring large and expensive patterns were to be made only at Whitinsville (although a few spinning frames were made at Holyoke at first). All machines requiring small patterns which could easily be reproduced (railway heads, drawing frames, spoolers, warpers, looms, and so on) were to be made at both shops.[21]

To finance the early stage of developing the new company, Whitin was forced to arrange for a considerable amount of working capital in the form of cash or credit. While plant alterations were being made, machines renovated, and patterns shipped, payrolls had to be met and stockpiles of raw materials built up. Furthermore, even after machinery construction had commenced, several months were bound to elapse before machines could be completed and payments received. To finance the first nine months of operations, Whitin contributed $111,201.29 of his personal funds, after which he turned to his brothers and, between February and May of 1861, borrowed from them $36,000 on four-months' notes, secured probably by the machinery that was in the process of being built.[22]

Apparently the difficulties of getting into production proved far greater than Whitin had expected. His early optimism is clearly reflected in his letters to W. C. Chapin, agent of the Pacific Mills, a large new cotton-manufacturing company at Lawrence. Whitin had persuaded Chapin to place a heavy order for machinery with him on the assurance that the opening of the Holyoke shop would permit delivery beginning in October and running through December of 1860. Chapin had just received from Whitinsville nine Gambrill cards that he had ordered more than seven months earlier. Therefore, he was skeptical of Whitin's ability to meet his delivery schedules in the future, but the prospect of new facilities at Holyoke made him decide to go along with Whitin on another order. To Chapin's dismay, however, the Holyoke shop did not succeed in beginning deliveries before the end of January, 1861, and did not complete the order until June, six months after the promised date.

Aside from the inexperience of Whitin's son, the problems which delayed production at Holyoke were merely the normal difficulties of moving to a new location. There existed virtually no problem of obtaining a suitable labor force. Many of the skilled workmen who had formerly been employed by the Hadley Falls Company were still in Holyoke and were anxious to resume the practice of their trades. Others from as far away as Ballston Springs, New York, and Moodus, Connecticut, learned of the new enterprise at Holyoke, perhaps through articles in local newspapers, and wrote asking for employment. However, the payroll books indicate that Whitin hired only those who came from locations not more than a few miles from Holyoke. Establishing new connections for the purchase of supplies and raw materials was a difficulty which Whitin sidestepped insofar as he could by continuing to rely on his established sources of supply in Providence and Worcester.[23]

By January, 1861, the Holyoke Machine Shop was in full production. How it compared in output with the shop at Whitinsville cannot be stated with certainty, since the records for the Whitinsville unit are not complete. But it would appear, from a comparison of orders at the two shops, that by the early months of 1861, the Holyoke shop was producing about as much machinery as the shop in Whitinsville. The payroll records indicate that Holyoke reached its production peak in March, 1861, when 572 men appeared on the pay lists. In the following month war broke out between the states, and employment immediately began to fall off.

3. WARTIME OPERATIONS

As soon as war was declared the younger employees of the Holyoke Machine Shop rushed to volunteer for armed service. Even the older ones began to evince noticeable unrest. On 4 May 1861, John C. Whitin wrote to a customer: "We should have had your grinder [ready] sooner, but the war has played the mischief with our men and troubled us a good deal — but we must stand by our country anyway." On 8 June the weekly issue of the Holyoke *Mirror* gave the names of thirty-eight men who had formed the first volunteer group from Holyoke. Thirteen of them, more than a third, were former Whitin employees.

Greater even than the loss of men to the Army was the transfer of many of the shop's most skilled men to the near-by gun factories. Both the Ames Manufacturing Company, makers of side arms, cannons, and gun-stocking machinery, and the Massachusetts Arms Company, producers of the Maynard rifle, were located in Chicopee. Within a short time after the declaration of war these shops are known to have doubled the number of men they employed.[24] It is not unlikely that some of their war workers were former Whitin employees. The important magnet attracting workmen away from the Holyoke shop was, however, the vital United States Armory at Springfield where liberal wages were drawing skilled workers from a wide radius.

During the first five months of the war the loss of workers from the Holyoke shop was especially rapid. At first this loss was caused by the war's disturbing influence on the labor market, but before long Whitin was finding difficulty in getting enough business to keep his workers busy. In the face of a threatened interruption in the delivery of raw cotton from plantations in the South, mill after mill began to reduce operations and curtail machinery purchases. By July, Whitin was forced to cut his machinery prices in an effort to secure enough work to keep together his dwindling labor force. Other textile-machinery builders, faced with similar problems, shifted to war work. Fales, Jenks & Sons made milling machines for the government. William Mason produced rifles. George Crompton turned to the manufacture of gun machinery.[25] But Whitin, either because of his natural reluctance to abandon the field in which he had become a specialist or because of an optimistic belief that the war would soon be over, delayed taking war orders until October, 1861, and even then converted his shop to war work only partially.[26] The one large government order that he undertook was a sub-contract for fifty-one milling machines for the Ames Manufacturing Company.[27] For a while he also made a few machines for various other war plants, notably hammers and drill presses for E. Remington & Sons, using patterns furnished him by the Springfield Armory. Soon, however, the Armory, in an effort to centralize its production, ordered the patterns returned, so that Whitin was thenceforth forced to refer inquiring customers to Springfield.[28]

If Whitin's reluctance to assume the risks and problems of war work was the result of a conscious policy of waiting out the storm, he must soon have felt that his position had been justified. The severity of the textile depression, which had caught Whitin just as he was beginning to operate his Holyoke shop at a profit, proved to be only temporary. Many textile mills received from the government orders for military clothing together with allocations of raw cotton.[29] Many others, while closed, took the opportunity to modernize their equipment or to expand their facilities. From these two sources Whitin received a few large orders for new machines and for repair parts. Operations during 1862 were kept at a profitable level as a result principally of a $56,000 order from the Dwight Manufacturing Company and one for $65,000 from the Chicopee Manufacturing Company.[30] Under the existing conditions, however, mills were able to dictate stiff price terms, putting pressure on Whitin's margin of profit at a time when the costs of raw materials and labor, reacting to shortages and to the beginnings of greenback inflation, had commenced to rise.

As late as the summer of 1862 Whitin thought that the war would soon be over. But when Union troops experienced reverses in the fall of that year, he seems to have become convinced that the struggle might after all be a long one. Business prospects under a continuing war seemed none too bright. The large orders from the Dwight and Chicopee companies had been completed. Further orders of comparable size would be difficult to obtain. Operations had already declined to an unprofitable level. Only the receipt of payments for machinery already delivered kept the company's cash account from dwindling.

TABLE 1

HOLYOKE MACHINE SHOP
CASH PROFITS AND LOSSES, 1860–1863, COMPILED QUARTERLY

Quarter		Profits	Losses
1860	1st	....	....
	2d	....	$16,480.21
	3d	....	45,851.08
	4th	....	32,817.47
1861	1st	....	28,546.29
	2d	$2,215.54	....
	3d	32,014.58	....
	4th	6,372.72	....
1862	1st	11,791.59	....
	2d	2,130.78	....
	3d	19,826.45	....
	4th	67,042.29	....
1863	1st	....	12,184.88
	2d	....	5,775.72
	3d	....	10,027.22
	4th	133,938.06	....
Totals		$275,332.01	$151,682.87
Net cash profit		....	123,649.14
		$275,332.01	$275,332.01

Table 1 indicates something of the downward course of business at Holyoke as the year 1862 neared an end. The figures are taken from the company's cashbooks and represent the difference between cash income and outgo. Note that the figures tend to lag behind production activity because of the lapse of time between the production of goods and the receipt of payments.

Meanwhile, the task of managing both the Whitinsville and

Holyoke shops had grown still more difficult under the pressure of war conditions. Whereas Whitin had planned to spend little of his time in Holyoke, he had found it necessary to be there on at least Tuesday, Wednesday, and Thursday of every week, leaving the shop at Whitinsville temporarily under the supervision of his younger brother, Charles.[31] Traveling between the two shops required an arduous, five-hour trip over seventy miles of railroad with transfers at Worcester and Springfield.[32] At the same time rheumatism had begun to trouble John, forcing him to admit what was undoubtedly for a man of such vitality the disagreeable necessity of taking a vacation for his health.[33]

The combination of physical ailment and of anticipated financial losses caused Whitin to consider either closing the Holyoke shop until after the war or disposing of it entirely and returning to Whitinsville as partner-manager of the family shop. Had young John M. Whitin measured up to his father's expectations, the first alternative might have been a feasible choice; but after a few months as agent, the son had displayed so little interest in his job that he had neglected all but the most routine work about the shop. Josiah Lasell's handling of the Holyoke company's correspondence and books of account had been creditable enough, but his temperament and training were such that he could not have taken over management of the shop.

It seems doubtful whether Whitin ever seriously considered selling his interest in P. Whitin & Sons and moving to Holyoke, for at his age it would have been difficult for him to forsake a lifetime acquaintance with friends and locality. Moreover, the shop with the better location was the one at Whitinsville, for the Rhode Island mill area was already an accomplished fact, whereas the mill area of western Massachusetts was still little more than a potentiality — and one that in the course of events was to prove unpromising in textiles.* With all those considerations in mind, Whitin might well have decided to sell the Holyoke shop even had family affairs in Whitinsville not taken a sudden new turn.

---

* After the Civil War, Holyoke turned from cotton to paper manufacture. The promising area for textile-mill development proved to be not western Massachusetts but Fall River and New Bedford.

No reference to what took place in family council has come down to us, but from subsequent events we can reconstruct some of the story with what should be fair accuracy. During the war the mills belonging to the four brothers were hard pressed by the shortage of raw cotton, while the machine shop continued to operate at very nearly full capacity. By a combination of good fortune and hard-headedness, John C. Whitin was able to keep the Whitinsville shop busy during the depressed months at the beginning of the war by working on a very large order to equip a new unit for the Wamsutta Mills, of New Bedford. When the owners of the Wamsutta Mills realized that war was going to interfere with their operations, they tried to cancel the order for machinery.[34] But Whitin chose to protect himself and his workers even at the risk of creating bad customer relations and so forced the Wamsutta owners to honor their contract. (Wamsutta remained a good Whitin customer, nevertheless.) By the time the Wamsutta order had been completed, many mills were again seeking to place orders, so that the Whitinsville shop (thanks also to the fact that there were no war plants near Whitinsville to entice away its skilled labor) was able to maintain a level of operations seldom equaled even during previous years of peace.

The sources of irritation existing within the family under such conditions were too important to ignore. While his brothers had been left with little to do as their mills stood idle, John, though in poor health, had worked harder than ever before even though his quarter-share in the firm's earnings was a constant reminder that much of the machine shop's profit was being divided among his brothers. The only means by which John could have prevented the flow of profits from the machine shop into the pockets of his three brothers would have been to divert the more profitable portion of large orders to his wholly owned company at Holyoke. Although he may never have consciously discriminated against the Whitinsville shop, he had of necessity divided many orders between the two companies, a practice which may well have aroused the resentment of his brothers.

How much bitterness was engendered by conflicting family interests we do not know, but apparently the time had arrived when the matriarchal Betsey Whitin, now in her eighty-sixth year, could no longer hold the family enterprise together. It was agreed that the manufacturing properties of P. Whitin & Sons should be distributed among the owners of the company, each shareholder receiving a just portion of the firm's assets. The shop was to go to John.

The distribution of the firm's assets became officially effective on 1 January 1864, although final dissolution was not accomplished for many years. After that date the brothers of John C. Whitin took no further part in the manufacture of cotton machinery, and John took no further interest in cotton manufacturing. Each brother went his separate way. Each established his own business and founded a separate family dynasty. All continued to have a considerable influence on the village of Whitinsville, but thereafter they had only limited dealings with each other.*

4. SALE OF THE HOLYOKE SHOP

John Whitin, meanwhile, was growing eager to dispose of the plant at Holyoke. As early as 11 September 1862 he had written George M. Bartholomew, president of the Holyoke Water Power Company, that he would sell the Holyoke Machine Shop property, exclusive of the tools and patterns, for $135,000. But not until 20 January 1863 did he mention the matter again in his correspondence. Then, in a letter to Henry Saltonstall, treasurer of the Chicopee Manufacturing Company, he offered the property for $125,000. Saltonstall countered with an offer to buy the shop, provided that Whitin would agree to contribute capital (in the form of newly built machinery) toward establishing a cotton-manufacturing company to occupy the shop building. But Whitin replied that he definitely did not wish to invest in a cotton mill and that he was unwilling to continue his interest in the Holyoke shop long enough to complete an order of machinery for a new mill, so anxious was he to be rid of his Holyoke responsibilities.

In the end, however, Whitin found that he would have to agree to outfit the shop as a cotton mill if he expected to find anyone in-

---

* A brief account of the division of the company's assets and the subsequent history of the various mills during the general decline of the cotton textile industry in New England is presented in Appendix 10.

terested in buying the property.[35] Therefore, on 15 April 1863 he finally consented to a sale agreement proposed by the owners of the Lyman Mills in Holyoke. The Lyman owners were to buy the shop for $110,000 and were to organize it as a thread mill under the name of the Hadley Company. Whitin was to build the mill's machinery — $90,000 worth — partly at Holyoke, partly at Whitinsville.[36] To make matters even more difficult for Whitin, the Hadley Company

TABLE 2

HOLYOKE MACHINE SHOP
SOURCE AND APPLICATION OF FUNDS, 1860–1863

Source of funds	
Working capital furnished by Whitin[a]	$156,568.11
Sale of property and tools	164,811.25
Net profit including return from rentals[b]	123,649.14
Total	$445,028.50
Application of funds	
Payment for Holyoke property[a]	$171,600.00
Transferred to Whitin's account at Whitinsville[c]	158,857.80
Cash on hand at time of liquidation	114,570.70
Total	$445,028.50

[a] Includes $8,100 paid by Whitin on notes due the Holyoke Water Power Co. but not recorded in the Holyoke Machine Shop books of account.

[b] Figure derived by subtracting known sources from known applications of funds.

[c] Includes $16,258.04 worth of raw materials shipped to Whitinsville.

wished to begin immediate remodeling of the shop building, for they wanted dormer windows cut in the roof to permit the use of an additional floor, and a coal cellar dug under one wing.[37] Working in the midst of these alterations, Whitin's men were finally successful in finishing up all foundry work by 10 October 1863, and by the end of December they had finished the Hadley Company order and closed the shop.[38]

Whitin had hoped that he could sell the manufacturing equipment of the Holyoke shop for at least $70,000 (except for the patterns which he intended to ship to Whitinsville),[39] but many of the tools would not bring the price he thought them worth. Fortunately, he was able to sell the shop's turbine patterns and foundry equipment to the Ames Manufacturing Company for approximately $30,000,[40] and he disposed of nearly $25,000 worth of tools to various individuals. But the remaining equipment he finally decided to ship to Whitinsville, along with the patterns.

The Holyoke venture, though it was fraught with cares and disappointments, proved on balance to have been a financial success. The sales price of the real estate and machinery very nearly equaled the property's original cost, while the operation of the shop had yielded a respectable return on Whitin's investment. For the three years and nine months during which the Holyoke Machine Shop existed, its source of cash funds and the use to which those funds were put are shown in Table 2.

The figures indicate that, in addition to his investment of $150,000 in the property at Holyoke, Whitin contributed working capital in the amount of $156,568.11. His total investment at Holyoke, therefore, must have been something more than $300,000, perhaps $325,-000.* On this investment he obtained a total net profit of $123,649.14, giving him an average annual yield on investment of about 10 per cent.

These Holyoke figures are especially important because they are all we know about Whitin's capital investment during the early period of his operations. At Whitinsville, where the shop had been built and equipped chiefly by local labor and partially from local materials, the cost of Whitin's fixed assets is not only unknown but unknowable. If the Holyoke shop had been able to realize 10 per cent on its investment despite its having operated at a loss during half its existence, the shop at Whitinsville must have realized even greater returns. These inferred profits will go far to explain how John C. Whitin, without aid from his brothers, was able to embark on such an ambitious expansion program immediately upon returning to Whitinsville.

---

* The figures take no account of the value of the P. Whitin & Sons patterns that Whitin used at Holyoke.

CHAPTER IV

COMPANY VILLAGE, 1864-1870

In choosing Whitinsville rather than Holyoke, John C. Whitin had to face the fact that the labor supply in Whitinsville was less plentiful than the supply at Holyoke was certain to be once the war was over. Whitinsville's labor market had always been tight. Even in 1847, John C. had been forced to bring in Irish workers to man his newly constructed machine shop.[1] Now, in 1864, he was faced with the necessity of building additional houses to attract the workmen he needed.

Labor scarcity was to be a theme that would recur again and again in the company's subsequent history. A shortage of labor was to force the company to develop and maintain its own village. It was to create the need for a blending of several European national groups in an otherwise typically Yankee community. Its saving grace was that it kept Whitinsville from becoming one of the festering industrial centers of New England's maturing economy.

The houses which John C. Whitin built during the years immediately following the Civil War were not the first company-financed dwellings in Whitinsville; even in 1809 the Northbridge Cotton Manufacturing Company had erected houses for its operatives. But John's were the first to be built on a large scale and were the origins of the notable company village that was to grow up around the Whitin plant. A history of the Whitin firm would be without meaning if it were to neglect the story of the village the firm created. In Whitinsville, village, firm, and family have always been almost indistinguishable.

I. WHITINSVILLE AT THE END OF THE CIVIL WAR

Despite its manufacturing activities, the Whitinsville of 1864 was little more than a rural village. Its inhabitants could still devote their most heated discussions in their annual town meetings to the means of preventing cattle from roaming untended through their village streets. The community had acquired none of the drab monotony or the crowded populousness of those other textile centers where massive mill structures of unrelieved brick had grown up amidst row on row of multiple dwellings; it was as yet too small to require any such concentration of living conditions. Even today, after nearly a century of growth, when the number of its inhabitants has increased tenfold and the value of its factory production has multiplied more than a hundred times, the community still maintains its Arcadian atmosphere, partly through conscious endeavor and partly through the necessities imposed on it by the physiography of its location.

The Mumford River, which passes through Whitinsville on its short but steep descent to the broad valley of the Blackstone, has worn from the countryside a deep and narrow valley, laying bare rocky hillsides that have proved discouraging both to settlement and to farming. Over those hillsides has spread a second-growth woodland which conceals, with its summer verdure, the unreceptiveness of the land. Among the hills lie a series of man-made ponds and reservoirs, the lower of which have reduced still further the scanty width of the valley's habitable basin. As a result, Whitinsville has grown only by extending itself either upstream or down and has remained, with the exception of that small portion of the village that lies south of the river, only two streets in width.

By the end of the Civil War, Whitinsville's elongated development had already deprived it of that most typical feature of early New England towns, the village common.[2] Instead, the focal point of the community, both physically and figuratively, was the homestead of Betsey Whitin (later to become the site of the town hall). At the age of eighty-seven, Betsey was living out the last four years of her remarkable life. Her house was the geographical center of the village; her sons were its leading citizens, and her direct descendants numbered, out of a population of a little more than one thousand, no less than twenty-eight.

The village might have developed more rapidly had the Whitin brothers not adopted the policy of expanding their family enterprise by the purchase of mills in other centers. In 1864 fully half the physical assets of P. Whitin & Sons consisted of properties in Rockdale, Riverdale, North Uxbridge, and East Douglas. Such a policy naturally tended to build up rival communities at Whitinsville's expense.

No accurate information concerning the population of the village has ever existed. Never having had a separate legal status, the community has always been considered for census purposes a part of the town of Northbridge. However, there exist two old maps, one dating from 1849 and the other from about 1871, showing in detail an arrangement of the dwellings in the village. From those two maps and from other references to early life in Whitinsville we may draw a few circumspect generalizations about the village as it was when John C. Whitin obtained sole ownership of the family machine shop.[3]

Of the hundred houses in the community, about half were owned by P. Whitin & Sons and were rented to its employees. Inasmuch as all company-owned houses contained at least two family units, and in some cases four, a total of more than two-thirds of the village families were probably company-housed.* According to the Massachusetts census for 1865 the average family in Northbridge consisted of five members; hence, the number of individuals living in each multiple dwelling must have been large.

The male population of Whitinsville found occupation in one of several ways. About two hundred men were employed in the shop and foundry of the machinery branch of P. Whitin & Sons. (In the cotton-mill branch there were probably not more than twenty-five men, the rest being women and boys.) The remaining townsmen, perhaps two or three dozen in number, were either professional men, tradesmen, or farmers. They included three clerks who worked in the company-owned store,† a tailor, a cobbler, a blacksmith, a

---

* Strictly speaking, these company-owned houses are "tenements" and that is what they are commonly called in Whitinsville. But the word *tenement* has such a derogatory meaning that I have avoided its use throughout this volume. The clean, airy, well-maintained company houses in Whitinsville bear no resemblance to the squalid and ramshackle buildings that tenements are usually thought to be.

† The company-owned store had been a part of P. Whitin & Sons since 1810. As part of the dissolution of the family concern, the store was sold to P. Whitin Dudley, a cousin of the Whitin brothers.

stagecoach operator, a quarry owner, and a station master hired by the Providence and Worcester Railroad to tend the Whitins station, a small freight and passenger stop about a mile and a half southeast of the village. The professions were represented by a doctor, who claimed the qualifications of both surgeon and physician, and two full-time ministers, one for the Congregational and one for the Methodist church. As yet there was no resident priest, and the Irish Catholics (at the end of the war about 20 per cent of the workers in the shop had Irish names) had to make the four-mile trip to Uxbridge, usually on foot, to attend Sunday Mass.

The educational facilities of the town included only the primary, intermediate, and grammar schools. Plans were already under way to build a high school, however, for the state required that one be supported by all towns having more than five hundred families, and Northbridge had just passed that mark. Since nearly half the population of the town resided in Whitinsville, it was only natural for the school to be built there.

To the boys of the village a form of education more popular than schooling was an apprenticeship in the machine shop. Apprentices were placed directly under the supervision of Gustavus E. Taft, a stern, impartial disciplinarian who put fear and a respect for hard work into their hearts.[4] In accord with John C. Whitin's general philosophy, the apprentices were paid a little something for their work to give them a sense of importance and to serve as a measure of their progress. The period of training customarily covered three years. During the first year the boys received 63 cents a day, during the second 82 cents, and during the third $1.00. Not uncommonly customers sent their sons to Whitin to obtain a basic training in the construction of cotton machinery before entering upon the management of the family mill. Apprentices from out of town sometimes lived in the company boarding house, but when possible they stayed with private families. Invariably they were required to attend church on Sundays, unless poor health prevented.[5]

The apprentice-training program formed an important part of the factory system in those days. Work in the foundry and machine shop had not yet been divided into a series of separate and distinct operations. Each worker had to develop a number of skills, and every man eventually had to be the equivalent of a bench molder or a tool-maker. Probably for the greater part of his training period an apprentice was worth no more than he was paid. The magnitude of the training program in the Whitin shop is best illustrated by the fact that in March, 1868, 21 per cent of the company's employees were in the apprenticeship pay scale.[6]

In a village of a thousand inhabitants, personal relations were bound to be closely knit. Friendships were based on long association and very often on blood ties. Joys and misfortunes were widely aired and broadly borne by everyone in the community. This close identification of self with neighbor in the social intercourse of Whitinsville is clearly shown in the closing remarks of a letter written by John C. Whitin after a fatal accident to one of his employees. The paragraph is the more remarkable because of Whitin's customary stolidness and because it reflects an obvious desire to unburden himself of a real disaster. The letter was written, on a matter of business, to a customer in Taftville, Connecticut, a man who could not have been personally acquainted with the victim of the accident.[7]

I feel a little sad this evening having just ret^d from the house of one of our most worthy citizens, a man who has been in our employ 33 years. While using a circular saw yesterday a piece of board was thrown against his bowels &, without breaking the skin, injured him internally so much that his physician says he cannot live until morning. We shall feel his loss.

In such a community, where three-quarters of the inhabitants earned their livelihood in one shop, the terms employee, fellow-citizen, and friend were almost synonymous.

2. CONDITIONS OF WORK IN THE MACHINE SHOP

Before the Civil War, the usual length of the working day was eleven hours. During the war, however, the workers in Whitinsville, as elsewhere, began agitating for a ten-hour day. Realizing that he must either reduce his hours or lose his men to war industries, Whitin met his employees' demands on 1 April 1864. Whitin was not alone in adopting the ten-hour day at that time; many of New England's more prosperous and progressive manufacturers were doing the same thing. But the state law establishing ten hours as a maximum day's work was not passed until 1874 and was not made really enforceable until 1879.[8]

Along with the reduction in hours, Whitin gave nearly all his workers an additional wage increase of from 3 pence to 1 shilling 6 pence per day. Translated into dollars and cents these rates meant an increase of anywhere from four to twenty-five cents per day. It did not mean that they were to be paid in shillings and pence. The custom of quoting labor rates in terms of British colonial currency dated from pre-Revolutionary days when the Massachusetts shilling was equivalent to one-sixth of a Spanish dollar.

Many New England manufacturing companies have carried the practice of quoting wage rates in shillings down into the present century. Why the custom was continued for so many years after the shilling had become obsolete is difficult to explain. One reason for the continuation may have been the convenience with which daily rates quoted in shillings could be translated into weekly wages payable in dollars. Since there were six full working days in a week, and six shillings in a dollar, a daily rate in shillings was always the same as a week's pay in dollars. Ten shillings a day amounted to ten dollars a week.

Few companies, if any, adhered to the practice as long as Whitin did. In its machine shop the company did not adopt dollar wage rates until 1907 (perhaps the shift to a 5½-day week in that year accounts for the change), and in the foundry it did not convert from the shilling until 1915. Then, at last, more than a century and a quarter after the defeat of the British at Yorktown, Whitinsville abandoned the final vestige of America's colonial period.

Discipline in the Whitin shop appears to have been maintained on an easy-going basis and workmen seem to have been given considerable freedom on the job. One account said: "The working hours [were] nominally eleven; if a workman was five or ten minutes late, it was not noticed, and if a hand wanted a piece of pie in the forenoon, he simply walked out of the shop to his home after it."[9] In the pattern loft of the foundry one may still find patterns of andirons, mud scrapers, even G. A. R. flag holders—mute evidence that foundrymen were allowed to devote at least a portion of their worktime to their own personal ends. In the summertime employees frequently took time off to work either in their gardens or on their farms, or perhaps even to enjoy a vacation without pay (a practice which continued until very recent times). This loss of man hours during a busy season seems to have caused Whitin occasional embarrassment, especially when he did not count on the attendant delay in quoting delivery dates.

There is no evidence that occasional absences from work were considered cause for disciplinary action. On the contrary a day or two off each month seems to have been an accepted practice. Take October, 1864, as a random example. Ordinarily one would expect October to be a month of low absenteeism. Men are not likely to be off working on their farms, and winter illnesses are not likely to have begun taking their toll; yet, even excluding the 11 who were hired during the month (and hence did not work full time) and the 12 who left the company's employ during the same period, the absentee rate was surprisingly high. That particular October had five Sundays, leaving 26 workdays in the month. Only 36 per cent of the workers were on hand every day; that is to say, 64 per cent took at least one day off during the month. Forty-four per cent took off two days or more, 32 per cent three or more, and 23 per cent four or more. In other words, to nearly a quarter of the shop's employees the average workweek in that particular month was really only five days long. A spot check of other months yields similar results. It would seem that the common belief that men worked long, hard hours in the "old days" does not hold true for Whitinsville.

Night work was virtually unknown. Occasionally heavy orders caused a bottleneck in the planning department and forced overtime work until 11:00 P.M. (the standard workday ran from 7:00 A.M. to 6:00 P.M. with an hour off for lunch). But the fire insurance companies with which Whitin dealt were loath to permit work after dark and were willing to grant exceptions only in case of a short-term emergency.[10]

The machine shop employed as many as three hundred full-time workers, about two hundred of whom, as has already been stated, were drawn from within the limits of the village. Although a few of the resident employees, chiefly those of the foreman class, owned private homes, at least 90 per cent either occupied company houses or else roomed with families who were company tenants. Of this 90 per cent, only about half paid any rent to the company, indicating that the other half consisted of workers who were either dependents of, or roomers with, men who were renters. The tight state of the labor market in Whitinsville is further revealed by the fact that about a third of the shop's employees came to their work from points outside the immediate vicinity. About half of these nonresidents ate their noon meals at the company's boarding house, while the remainder must have eaten with private families or brought lunches to work.*

Such were the conditions of life in the village and in the machine shop when, upon the agreement to dissolve P. Whitin & Sons, John C. Whitin decided to concentrate all his manufacturing facilities in Whitinsville. The village was removed at some distance and in spirit from the growing industrial centers of Worcester and Providence. Life was unhurried and times were prosperous. The machinery business had grown so large that it had drained the countryside of available man power; if it was to expand further it would have to look elsewhere for laborers.

3. A FACTORY VILLAGE EMERGES

During the years between 1864 and 1869 both the physical appearance and the social organization of the Whitinsville community underwent remarkable change. The machine shop more than doubled in size and the number of company-owned houses multiplied two and one-half times. The working force in the shop grew from around three hundred to nearly five hundred men, bringing in

---

* From time immemorial to the present, the Whitin shop has allowed an hour off for lunch so that workmen could go home for a full noon meal.

The dissolution of P. Whitin & Sons gave the company boarding house to Charles P. Whitin. Consequently, John was forced to build another boarding house for his own men. To run the new house he hired Mr. and Mrs. William DeWitt for $14 a week plus room and board. Boarders were charged $3.50 per week, which was deducted from their pay. Provisions were purchased and charged by the DeWitts against Whitin. At the end of the year, Whitin balanced the income from boarders against the expense for provisions. Any favorable balance was given to the DeWitts as a bonus for good management. Nothing was said about the eventuality of an unfavorable balance; the implication is that there never was one. (See letter of John C. Whitin to William DeWitt, 21 March 1870.)

a whole new group of families whose ties with the locality were not indigenous. In those few years the rural past merged into the industrial future.

Division of the physical assets of P. Whitin & Sons seems to have been determined, in part at least, by rule of thumb. All the property that lay near, or was served by, the water power from the upper dam was apportioned to John; all that lay in the area contiguous to the lower dam was given to Charles.[11] By this division John obtained, in addition to the machine shop, the old mill built by the Northbridge Cotton Manufacturing Company and the thirty-eight company houses nearby. Charles received the brick mill built in 1826 and the stone mill built on the other side of the river in 1845. He also acquired those company houses which were located on the river's south bank. In later years this chance division of property came to exert an unexpected force on the development of the village. Whereas the machine shop prospered and extended its area of influence up and down the north bank of the river, the cotton mill advanced but slowly, then paused and gradually fell behind. As a result, the southern bank has remained largely open country, with but a few dwellings more than it had when its fate was sealed in 1864.

The new machine shop which Whitin proposed to build was to be erected beside, and connected to, the old one and was meant both to replace the productive capacity lost by the sale of the Holyoke shop and to house those tools which John C. Whitin had brought with him from Holyoke to Whitinsville.* It was to be built of brick and was to be constructed on a scale that would make it larger by 15 per cent than the shop at Holyoke. Most of the new capacity, however, although it was to multiply the manufacturing floor space at Whitinsville by two and one-half times, was in effect a belated recognition of that growth of demand which had occurred before 1860 and which had been met temporarily by the purchase of the Holyoke Machine Shop.

In former years the new shop would have been conceived, designed, and erected by men from within the firm; now, for the first

---

* Before making other plant changes Whitin dismantled the old Northbridge cotton mill and moved it alongside the upper dam, where he converted it to a carpentry shop. Then, on the spot where the old mill had stood, he erected a foundry and smithy large enough to meet the requirements of an additional machine shop.

time in the company's recorded history, construction work was placed under the supervision of an outsider. The person hired for the job was a man from Worcester named Captain Edward Lamb. Apparently Lamb's first connection with Whitinsville was as architect for the house that John C. Whitin built for his daughter and her husband, Josiah Lasell, when they moved from Holyoke to Whitinsville. Being pleased with Lamb's work, John retained him for several years to do further work in the village.

Besides designing the company's new shop and foundry, Lamb was expected to supervise their construction. He was permitted to hire such men as he needed for his work but he was also obliged to take any men hired for him by Whitin. (All men, once hired, were immediately put on Whitin's payroll.) Lamb was expected to suggest the quality and quantity of materials he would like to see used in the buildings constructed, but responsibility for obtaining the materials remained with the company. His remuneration derived not from a contractor's profit but from the fee he received for his services. In this manner Whitin could keep strict account of the costs of his buildings and could benefit from whatever bargaining powers his position as a large purchaser gave him. For many years thereafter when buildings were erected, the policy of hiring an architect-superintendent was followed at Whitinsville, and even in recent times the company has signed construction contracts permitting it to furnish the building materials required.

Work on the new shop began in the spring of 1864 as soon as the weather permitted. For three years construction pushed steadily ahead, although, in wintertime, days suitable for outdoor work were sometimes infrequent. As the buildings progressed, portions of the shop became available for manufacturing purposes. Finally, in the spring of 1867, Whitin could write, "I have started up new machines and have doubled my producing power for building spinning and can now get out about two frames per day when I get fairly under way." [12]

The "new machines" referred to must have been, in part at least, the machinery Whitin had brought with him from Holyoke. The "Tools" account in the ledger reveals that, during the years 1864–67, Whitin bought only $4,533.80 worth of machinery, of which amount $3,137.80 was spent for eight secondhand milling machines made by the Providence Machine Company and put on the market by the Burnside Rifle Works as war surplus. If Whitin installed any "new" machinery, it must have been equipment built in his own shop.*

Concentrating his entire manufacturing investment in Whitinsville required of John C. Whitin not only a doubling of his plant capacity but also an enormous expansion of his interest in employee housing. Therefore, as rapidly as he could realize enough cash beyond what he required either for working capital or for plant construction, he pushed the erection of new houses. Each summer he constructed a separate group, first on Forest Street, then on High, Central, and Water streets.† Even as late as the spring of 1868 he could write that only the lack of housing prevented him from securing an additional fifty workmen. By the end of 1869 he had spent $219,000 on the erection of two hundred family units.

Rentals for the new houses varied according to the size of the units. Two sizes seem to have been standard, one renting for $3.00 a month and the other for $5.00. A few scattered units for foremen and executives were built to rent for as high as $10. The average price charged for these new houses was somewhat higher than the average for the older houses had been, for despite rapidly rising wartime prices, Whitin had maintained the old rentals at their former level. The

---

* The power unit installed in the new shop deserves passing comment. While still at Holyoke, Whitin ordered two Boyden turbines built there for his proposed shop expansion at Whitinsville. These wheels measured 84 inches and 26 inches respectively and cost a total of $4,000 (Holyoke Machine Shop blotter, no. 3, p. 96). The smaller of these wheels was used for pumping water to the village reservoir; the larger was said to have had a capacity of 200 horsepower. In the late fall of 1870 the shop was forced to close for three weeks because of water shortage. To prevent a similar occurrence Lasell ordered a Corliss-type steam engine from William A. Harris of Providence. During the severe drought of 1880 this engine served to keep the shop running for more than three months, though doubtless on a reduced basis. (See letters dated 3 December 1870, 8 September 1880, and 30 November 1880.)

† The houses on Forest Street were first occupied by men whom Whitin had brought back with him from Holyoke. It is said that these men wanted to call their thoroughfare Holyoke Street, but Whitin would tolerate no such display of cliquishness and ordered that they give their street a more general name. The Forest and High Street buildings are still standing. Most of those on Central and Water streets were torn down or moved, in 1906, preparatory to building a new foundry where they had stood.

new houses brought the average rent up 6 per cent, but in the same period labor rates in Whitinsville had advanced 24 per cent.

The immediate result of this expansion of plant and housing was an unprecedented influx of Irish workers. By 1870 the size of the village had nearly doubled, and whereas formerly one-third of all the families in town had lived in their own homes, now only about one-seventh did. The independent portion of the citizenry was being pushed to one side and a company village was beginning to develop. In those five years following the Civil War, John C. Whitin cast the die of Whitinsville's industrial future.

4. DESTINY OF THE FACTORY VILLAGE

At about this same time, the Stafford Mills in Fall River were solving their comparable housing problem by inducing a group of the community's leading citizens to sponsor a housing project with money loaned them by the company. The undertaking proved so successful that the loan was shortly repaid, and thereafter the company was freed of all connection with its employees' homes.[13] But Fall River was a busy industrial city where individual capitalists felt safe in assuming responsibility for funds invested in employee housing; Fall River houses could always be rented to others even if the sponsoring company should fail. In Whitinsville no outsider would have been willing to underwrite an investment in housing, inasmuch as the value of the property depended almost wholly on the success or failure of a single company.

Some firms, fortunate enough to be located near a large city, found that, with the normal growth of population, a favorable market for their houses soon developed, enabling them to sell to others their interest in residential real estate. For instance, the costly housing experiment of the Pullman Palace Car Company, at Pullman, Illinois, found redemption in the rapid growth of the city of Chicago.[14] But in New England, at a time when water was the cheapest source of power, the location of a plant near a growing city was not always possible. In most cases mills and plants had to be located in remote regions, near river rapids, where there was seldom a ready labor market. Under such conditions manufacturers had little choice but to build houses for their employees.

Had he wanted to, Whitin might conceivably have built his houses with the idea of selling them to his employees. Other companies have carried out such plans, although in so doing they have had to accept long-term mortgages in part payment.[15] But in a village like Whitinsville, where there was little other chance of employment, an employer who was a landlord was probably more to be desired than one who was a mortgagor for there would have been endless trouble over the resignation or discharge of an employee whose mortgage was held by the company. Furthermore, had Whitin's houses been built for sale they should really have been single dwellings rather than the less expensive multiple dwellings that Whitin erected. At that particular point in his career, however, Whitin was in no position to tie up more funds in employee housing than he absolutely had to.

In England, companies faced with a housing dilemma found aid in public-utility building societies. These societies — government-financed and government-supervised — were designed to exempt companies from the responsibilities, dangers, and criticisms of owning their employees' homes. The town of Bournville, built for the Cadbury cocoa firm, and Port Sunlight, built for Lever Brothers, were sponsored under such a plan and were looked upon as models of their type.[16] But in America, where public policy was determinedly *laissez-faire,* the government left employers to solve their problems in whatever commendable or undesirable manner they saw fit.

The company housing problem was by no means new in 1865. The first small-house industrial colony known to modern man was the so-called Fuggerei, built by Jacob Fugger in fifteenth century Augsburg.[17] Company-owned housing developments have often been the boon companion of pioneer or remote industrial enterprises; they are still numerous in American mining regions and in the recently industrialized South. In other parts of the world, in Brazil, in India, in Italy and in Israel, they are still springing up. In New England, however, most of them have disappeared. Of those that have catered to both salaried and hourly workers, Whitinsville is the only sizable one left. Nearly all the others have been torn down or sold off, piecemeal or in blocks. New England towns that were once pioneer industrial communities have become mature manufacturing centers. In addition, the automobile has done much to make company housing in New England no longer necessary. Commuting to work over many miles of highway has become a commonplace. And, more recently, other groups have stepped forward to take over the function of providing mass housing, notably the government and the larger insurance companies.

Meanwhile, the Whitinsville project lives on, partly because the company found that once it had started it could not easily withdraw or change its course. Had it abandoned its low-rent policy, it would have discouraged workers from moving to Whitinsville and would have negated its own purpose. Yet by continuing to charge only nominal rents, it discouraged its employees from building their own homes, since they could get their housing at a lower cost as tenants than they could as home owners. At the same time, the comparative isolation of Whitinsville removed the possibility that it might some day become a part of an expanding metropolis, and because of that isolation, its housing needs had little chance of attracting outside investors. Large investors would have felt that Whitinsville did not offer enough security for their funds, and small ones would have hesitated to compete against the company's subsidized low rentals.

Whether John Whitin based his housing policy on economically sound considerations is difficult to say even in retrospect. Some observers have argued that one of the chief economic reasons why employers build homes for their workers is simply to reduce the cost of their labor turnover by giving workers such comfortable and inexpensive places to live that they would find moving undesirable.[18] The argument is most applicable to those companies, such as the American Woolen Company at Shawsheen, Massachusetts,[19] and the Draper Corporation at Hopedale, Massachusetts, which have built houses only for their executive and clerical forces, where turnover is the most costly. John Whitin's effort was more immediately connected with the initial recruiting of factory workers than with the problem of labor turnover. Reduction of labor turnover may have been a result of the company village Whitin founded, but it certainly was not an originating force.

Others have argued that manufacturers more than compensate themselves for the low return they get on industrial housing by paying low wages. Whether Whitin was able to achieve a low labor cost as a result of his housing venture, no one knows.[20] The Whitin pay-roll records give no indication of the jobs individual employees per-formed; consequently, there is no possibility of comparing wage rate with wage rate among competitors in the industry. In letters of that period, however, Whitin conveyed the impression that his labor costs were actually higher than his competitors'. "I cannot build machinery as low as the Lowell Shops can," he wrote, "as I pay more for doing the work and think I do it better." [21] Or, "I cannot make machinery as low as some can who job out their work to the lowest bidder. A good manufacturer a short time ago wrote me that . . . [the Lowell Machine Shop] offered to build frames for 20 cts. less than I did. I wrote him I thought I paid in labor 25 cts. per spindle more than they did and that my frames were worth 50 cts. more." [22] Or again, "I know some loom builders get their labour done on looms for 6 or 8 dollars each less than I do." [23]

Of course higher labor costs do not necessarily mean higher wage rates; they may simply mean better and more painstaking workman-ship. Being unable to compare quality of products, we cannot know whether Whitin's machinery was well but expensively built or whether it was merely inefficiently built. Judging from Whitin's suc-cess as a manufacturer, however, we must assume that his customers thought that his products were well constructed and were worth whatever premiums he may have asked for them.

In a later period, after accounting practices had improved, a more specific judgment is possible. But for the years before 1918, it would appear that Whitin enjoyed no appreciable competitive advantage because of his company village. The original cost of the village was about a quarter-million dollars. Income from rentals provided enough to cover maintenance expense and to yield a very small re-turn on investment, far less than Whitin could have obtained had he invested his money elsewhere. If any reduction in wage levels resulted from his housing venture, the savings were not enough to offset the high labor costs he built into his products.

5. TROUBLED FINANCE

Whitin could have picked no more critical period to establish a factory village. So troubled were business conditions toward the end of the war that only with the aid of a graph such as the one in Chart VI can the course of events be fairly traced.*

In the spring of 1864, when housing and shop construction was just getting under way in Whitinsville, a wave of unrestrained optimism swept the textile-manufacturing centers of the North. The victory at Vicksburg and the reopening of the Mississippi River gave

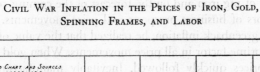

CHART VI

CIVIL WAR INFLATION IN THE PRICES OF IRON, GOLD, SPINNING FRAMES, AND LABOR

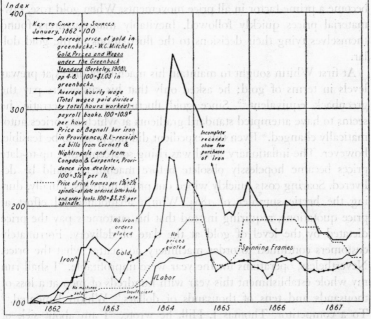

* The line showing average hourly wages represents only shop and foundry workers, not construction men. It does not include job-work payments which were essentially efficiency bonuses; consequently the average wage tends to be a little lower than the average take-home pay would have figured out to be — it also tends to be freer of random variations. Labor has always constituted the most important single item in the manufacture of textile machinery; however, because of the more rapid rise of other costs during the war, labor declined in relative importance from more than half to less than a quarter of total costs.

promise that cotton would soon be arriving from the plantations of the Southwest. Textile men immediately began a race to reëquip their mills in anticipation of a busy season.

Simultaneously a final, powerful spurt of inflation was sending prices two and one-half times above their prewar level. Like everyone else, Whitin was finding it necessary to look to his local newspaper for current quotations in the gold market as a barometer of business conditions.[24] In former years he had depended on the trend in the cost of pig iron and on the forecast of the coming cotton crop as indicators of business prospects and price movements. But with continued greenback inflation, he realized that the value of gold had become a prime factor in all price movements. When gold rose, raw-material prices quickly followed. Inevitably manufacturers found themselves tying their decisions to the fluctuations of the gold dollar.

At first Whitin sought to maintain his machinery prices at prewar levels in terms of gold; he asked only that his customers pay the greenback equivalent.[25] Since gold fluctuations were erratic, he seems to have attempted standard gradients at which his prices automatically changed.* Even this expedient did not prove to be feasible, however. The inflationary spiral was rising so steeply that up-to-date prices became hopelessly obsolete before machinery could be delivered. Soaring costs quickly wiped out profit margins. Finally, during the hectic summer of 1864, Whitin abandoned all effort at price quotations, requiring instead that his customers pay the price dictated by the level of gold at the date of delivery. Fortunately customers continued to order machinery no matter what the price. Nevertheless, operations for the year were unprofitable. "I shall run my whole establishment this year with hundreds of men at a loss of thousands and tens of thousands of dollars," Whitin lamented.[26] To a competitor, Thomas J. Hill, he wrote, "I am about sick of machine building," and to a customer, "If McClelan [sic] is elected [President] I shall stop business as soon as I can." [27]

---

* "If there is an advance in gold beyond 80," he wrote, "I think I should be obliged to advance the price" (letter of John C. Whitin to Arbucle, 17 May 1865). Whitin apparently meant to write "beyond 180." The average gold quotation for the month of May, 1864, was $176.30 in greenbacks. The average for the following month was $210.70 (see Wesley C. Mitchell, *Gold, Prices and Wages under the Greenback Standard*, Berkeley, 1908, p. 6).

An immediate result of the sharp rise in the cost of materials was the rapid disbursement of Whitin's available cash. By the end of the year the company's inflated working-capital demands had forced him to reinvest in his firm $144,000 of the funds he had realized from his liquidation of the Holyoke venture. The erection of merely the first third of the new shop soon required an additional $78,000. Weakened in his cash position and committed to an expensive building program, Whitin was in a poor condition to face the tribulations which 1865 and the end of the war were to bring.

The first sign of trouble came with the slackening of demand for machinery in the early months of the year 1865. Shipments of cotton from the liberated South did not measure up to expectations. Mills had to curtail their expansion plans. The level of prices fell rapidly. Manufacturers everywhere postponed their purchases as long as possible, hoping to obtain goods at lower figures. Driven partly by competition, partly by a sanguine belief that his costs were declining, Whitin slashed his prices a generous 25 per cent.

This price-cut in the spring of 1865 proved to be a shortsighted expedient and had to be revoked at the end of the year. Although the decline in the price of gold early in the year seemed to warrant Whitin's price reduction, his own manufacturing costs certainly did not. Iron, because of its scarcity, was still expensive, and labor rates, largely as a result of a reduction of the workday from 11 to 10 hours, were higher than ever before. The situation was not unlike that which obtained at the end of World War II, when many companies cut their prices prematurely in anticipation of a business decline.

By August, at prices that were yielding little if any profit, Whitin had taken so many orders that he was forced to extend his promises of delivery. Meanwhile a sharp business revival had occurred and general prices had quite unexpectedly reversed their trend in an upward leap. By October, Whitin was paying ruinously high prices for materials to build the machinery he had contracted to build at bargain rates. Thus, in the midst of a period looked upon as one of general prosperity, Whitin was experiencing the heaviest losses in his career.

By November, a crisis threatened. At the close of business on the second Saturday of the month, Whitin had on hand only $10,000

in cash. To meet his payroll on the following Wednesday he needed
$17,000. Happily, the emergency was forestalled by the timely arrival
of a draft for $19,000 from the Chicopee Manufacturing Company
in payment for machinery purchased. But to meet his other obligations Whitin had to cash $32,000 of his personal holdings of govern-
ment bonds.[28] By the end of the year his operating expenses had so
far exceeded his operating income that he was left with an out-of-
pocket deficit of $133,000. Nor did his hasty return to the peak
machinery prices of wartime inflation save him from having to borrow $8,000 from his brothers and an additional $10,000 from the local
bank. Because operations had been unprofitable throughout the
greater part of 1864 and 1865, Whitin had to pay income taxes for
only the second and third quarters of 1864.*

---

* He did not, however, escape paying excise taxes both on his production of castings and on his sale of completed machines. In 1864 these taxes amounted to
$14,912.03, in 1865 to $25,095.69. Insofar as possible he passed his taxes on to his
customers in the form of higher prices, but sometimes the ambiguity of rulings by
the Commissioner of Internal Revenue forced him, in the interest of preserving customer relations, to assume the tax burden himself.

The most controversial of the tax decisions centered in the government's definition
of what constituted a proper tax base. The local collector of internal revenue ruled,
in what seemed to Whitin a highly arbitrary and unreasonable manner, that the
value of a product was the price the consumer paid for it and that the product
should be taxed accordingly. If, therefore, a manufacturer chose to include the internal revenue tax in pricing an article, his tax should be computed on the basis of
that inclusion. Take, for example, an item which would ordinarily sell for $100. If
a manufacturer found himself forced to pay a 5 per cent tax on that article, he would
in all probability raise the article's price to $105, passing the tax on to the customer.
The value of the article would thereby become, so the tax collector argued, $105 and
should be taxed at that figure. The tax would therefore be not $5 but $5.25 (5
per cent of $105). In that case the manufacturer might justifiably charge $105.25
for his product — and so on. If carried to its logical conclusion, the process would
go on indefinitely, but the tax collector was willing to stop, having proceeded only
one step into absurdity. By his interpretation of the tax law he was able to collect
what was actually a 5¼ per cent tax on machinery sales.

At first Whitin refused to pay the extra amount, thinking he was the victim of an
irresponsible decision by the local tax agent. But after corresponding with his competitors he learned that they, too, were experiencing the same difficulties with their
local collectors. Finally, when a trip to Washington had convinced him that he
could not prevail against the policies of government officials, he acquiesced and paid
some two thousand dollars in tax arrears. He had so much difficulty in explaining
the tax collector's ruling to his customers that he sometimes simply resigned himself
to paying the extra amount personally. At length, in April, 1868, the tax was
abolished.

Fortunately, however, the demand for machinery continued heavy after this jump to record prices. In February, 1866, Whitin was able to write, "I have more than I can possibly do for 12 months . . . and prefer to take no more orders at present, and I do not know of any builder in the country who can take . . . an order to execute in less than 12 months, certainly no one that I can recommend. [Three] months ago I could have doubled the machinery in this country if I could have furnished it in 6 months." [29] The margin on these orders was the largest Whitin had ever enjoyed. In contrast to 1865, a year of heavy losses, 1866 was to prove the most prosperous in Whitin's experience.

The last half of 1866 was marred by a slight recession in the textile machinery business, but the year 1867 and the greater part of 1868 were periods of high prosperity and handsome profits. During those years Whitin was able to recover his earlier losses and soon had excess cash funds on hand despite the large sums that he was still spending on construction expenses. At last he felt able to repay himself for the Holyoke profits he had contributed three years earlier. Rather than leave these funds idle, however, he elected to invest them in $141,000 worth of stock in the Providence and Worcester Railroad and in $54,000 worth of stock in the Rome, Watertown and Ogdensburgh Railroad.[30] In both purchases he seems to have been seeking a safe investment rather than a speculative profit.[31] By the end of 1869 he had expended a total of $454,000 on his completed shop and houses. For this sum he received little more than a replacement of the Holyoke properties he had parted with for $110,000. The gap between these figures resulted in part from the sacrifice price for which the Holyoke assets had been sold and in part it represented the comparative age of the Holyoke shop and tenements. But the principal cause of the discrepancy was the inflated cost of the labor and materials that had gone into the new structures at Whitinsville. Nearly all the generous profits that had come to Whitin in the five years following the war had been poured into brick and mortar. Even though by 1870 John C. Whitin was generally regarded as being a millionaire, he was in actual fact very little richer in material goods than he had been at Holyoke. Neither his personal property nor his productive capacity had greatly increased. From an immediate point of view, the disposal of the Holyoke shop had been a costly decision.

If Whitin had remained in Holyoke, he would have found himself in the midst of the most prosperous Massachusetts community of the decade. (The population of the town tripled in the ten years following the war.) [32] However, since Holyoke's subsequent prosperity was to come not in textiles but in paper-making, it is questionable whether Whitin would really have benefited by staying. Again, if Whitin had remained in Holyoke, where water power and a large population were coexistent, he would have avoided the responsibility of the industrial village which became so intrinsic a part of the company. The cost of the village was the price John C. Whitin paid to do business in his home town.

CHAPTER V

POSTWAR PROSPERITY, 1870–1874

The founding of a company village was John C. Whitin's crowning achievement. Ill health was to force his retirement in 1870, just after factory and housing construction work had been completed and just as his company was in the midst of one of the greatest booms in its history — a boom that was to last off and on until eight years after the close of the Civil War. It was during those eight years that Whitin became a rich man — a "millionaire" if you like, though we know too little of his financial situation to be able to say in any exact way what he was worth.

The most profitable part of the postwar boom occurred between 1870 and 1873, after Whitin had withdrawn from business. Like so many of America's wealthy men, Whitin added more to his fortune in retirement than he accumulated in his active career. In a capitalistic system wealth grows by compounding itself, and often the wealthiest men are those who make their fortunes early and then live longest to see their incomes mount.

Throughout his active business career Whitin lived well but without ostentation. Most of his profits went into the expansion of his business. By 1870 he had built up a productive unit of sizable capacity. With that capacity his firm was able to go on despite his retirement, to reap a bountiful harvest in the first booming years of the 1870's.

I. JOHN C. WHITIN RETIRES

Provoked by worry and overwork, John C. Whitin's rheumatic affliction grew steadily worse in the period immediately following the Civil War. By 1868 he was able to get about only with the aid of crutches. For several years he and his wife spent their summers at the famous Canadian watering place at St. Catharines, where they hoped that the mineral waters would have a salutary effect on John's rheumatic condition. But nothing seemed to alleviate his distress. More and more John found himself relying on Josiah Lasell and Gustavus Taft to run the shop.

These two men carried on in Whitinsville much as they had at Holyoke. Lasell became, in effect, the company's office manager. Besides writing most of the firm's letters, he acted as accountant, purchasing agent, traffic manager, and to some extent sales manager. Taft took charge of the plant. From 1847 to 1864, the superintendent of the Whitinsville shop had been William Kendall, but Kendall was getting along in years, and Whitin felt that the job should be given to a younger man. Being particularly pleased with Taft's performance at Holyoke, Whitin decided to give him Kendall's job. Apparently the promotion stirred up considerable ill feeling in the village, where many people thought that Kendall had been unfairly treated.[1]

Lasell and Taft were complete opposites in temperament and appearance. Lasell had the slight build, the delicate features, and the quiet temperament of a scholar; Taft had the large frame, the stern bearing, and the positive manner of a man whose education had been acquired at the bench rather than at the blackboard. For sixteen years the two men were to manage the company almost as a partnership. Each remained boss in his own precinct — Lasell in the office and Taft in the shop. Lasell gradually acquired a working knowledge of the company's products and became competent to advise customers on technical problems, but he made no attempt to dictate product policies or manufacturing procedures. When Lasell was absent because of illness or away visiting customers or perhaps just on vacation, Taft attended to the necessary office matters, but it is obvious from the turbid and opaque letters he wrote, that he found such responsibilities distressingly difficult. For many years both men drew approximately the same salaries. From 1864 until 1873 their incomes ran about $5,000 apiece and then for several years varied between $10,000 and $20,000 a year depending on the company's prosperity.[2] In those years and for many decades thereafter Whitin executives received no specific salaries, they merely drew against their accounts; then at the end of the year their accounts were credited with a round sum, the size of which generally

JOSIAH LASELL, TREASURER, 1870–1886

GUSTAVUS E. TAFT, SUPERINTENDENT AND AGENT, 1864–1888

reflected the company's profits for the year. Any balances, whether debit or credit, simply carried forward to the next year's accounts.

Whitin seems to have become very fond of both Lasell and Taft, perhaps because they compensated for his disappointment in his son. While still at Holyoke young John Maltby Whitin had married a Springfield girl named Jennie Thomas, of whom John C. is said to have disapproved. In the spring of 1864, John M. and his wife had returned to Whitinsville and had moved into a house on Hill Street which the older John had bought for them. But, although John M. continued on the company's payroll, there is no indication that he ever did any work. Finally in 1867, after a short and stormy marital life, he sued for a divorce charging adultery.[3] A year later he married again, this time a widow named Achsah Crane Haggerty, who had been left by her husband with little else save his son and daughter by a former wife.* If this marriage seemed to John C. more suitable than the first — as apparently it did — it seemed even less so to John M. In 1870 he separated from his wife and left Whitinsville for western Massachusetts. The rest of the story, although anticipating events somewhat, is quickly told. For a time no one heard from the prodigal until, one day in the fall of 1872, his father received word that the young man had been taken seriously ill in the small town of Cheshire, Massachusetts. Hurrying to his son's bedside John arrived just in time to see him still alive.[4] A few days later death came, closing the young man's life at the unripe age of thirty-four.†

* The boy died shortly after his stepmother's marriage to John M. Whitin. The girl was eventually taken by the good-hearted Josiah Lasell, who became her legal guardian. (See Registry of Probate, series A, nos. 64587 and 64588, Worcester County Court House, Worcester, Mass.) Achsah seems to have remained on good terms with the Whitin family even after the death of John M. Whitin. She died in Whitinsville in 1895 and was buried in the Whitin family plot.

† In 1873, just a few months after the death of his only son, John C. Whitin also lost his wife. Mrs. Whitin was returning in her carriage from a visit to her ailing brother in Sutton when she was seized with a fatal heart attack. Two years later, with the approval of his family, John C. Whitin remarried. His second wife was a woman of forty, the cultivated and charming Sarah Elizabeth Pratt, of Hopkinton, Massachusetts. For years Sarah had been a friend of Whitin's only daughter, Jane Lasell. The two women had first met at the Lasell Seminary in Auburndale. A year following the marriage, Sarah gave birth to a son, John Crane Whitin, Jr. Unhappily, the baby lived only a few weeks. His loss was a great grief to his sixty-eight-year-old father, who had seen in the infant a possible fulfillment of the blighted hopes he had had for his other son.

The combination of his son's waywardness and of his own chronic illness made Whitin conscious that he should be looking for a suitable means of perpetuating his company in the event of his death. He had been conducting his machinery business since 1864 as a personal proprietorship under the straightforward title of J. C. Whitin, Whitinsville.[5] Now he felt that the time had come to incorporate his firm. On 22 April 1868 he obtained from the legislature of the Commonwealth of Massachusetts a special charter to incorporate his business as the Whitin Machine Works.[6] The charter read as follows:

An Act to Incorporate the Whitin Machine Works
Be it enacted &c. as follows:
Section 1. John C. Whitin, Josiah Lasell, John M. Whitin, their associates and successors, are hereby made a corporation by the name of Whitin Machine Works, for the manufacture of castings, and various kinds of machinery; also, for the manufacture of fabrics from cotton and other fibrous materials, in the town of Northbridge, in the county of Worcester; with all the powers and privileges, and subject to all the duties, restrictions and liabilities set forth in all general laws, which are now or may hereafter be in force relating to manufacturing corporations.
Section 2. The capital stock of said corporation shall not exceed one million dollars, and shall be divided into shares of one hundred dollars each; and said corporation may hold such real and personal estate, as may be necessary or convenient for the purposes set forth in this act, and shall not commence business until five hundred thousand dollars of its capital stock shall have been paid in.
Section 3. This act shall take effect upon its passage.

The new corporation officially got under way at a meeting of the stockholders and of the new board of directors on 4 January 1870. What occasioned the delay of nearly two years between the chartering of the company and the first stockholders' meeting, I have been unable to discover. All five of the company's stockholders were also members of its board (see also Appendices 2, 3, and 4).

Each of the minority stockholders paid for his five $100-shares in cash. John C. Whitin "sold" his plant and equipment[7] to the new company in return for $550,000 in Whitin Machine Works

John C. Whitin	5,980 shares
John M. Whitin	5 shares
Josiah Lasell	5 shares
Gustavus Taft	5 shares
Charles P. Whitin	5 shares
Total	6,000 shares

stock. In addition he bought $48,000 worth of stock for cash. Consequently the company began its existence with a $600,000 capitalization, $50,000 of which was working capital.[8]

It is a point of some significance that John C. Whitin, the company's principal stockholder, designated Josiah Lasell as treasurer of the new corporation. By law the treasurer of a Massachusetts company, not the president, was the man elected directly by vote of the stockholders.[9] By custom the treasurer was also the man who was specified in the bylaws of most New England firms as the officer charged with the top administrative duties in the corporation. Obviously therefore it was Whitin's intention, when he elected Lasell to the treasurership, to relieve himself of some of the burden of management and to shift to Lasell the direct responsibility for conducting the company's affairs.

Shortly after the incorporation had been effected — perhaps as soon as all legal details had been settled — Mr. and Mrs. John C. Whitin left for Florida. With business affairs in good order, Whitin hoped that a winter in the warm climate would afford him relief from rheumatic pains. He intended to be gone not more than three months, but unhappily his plans were soon shattered. Instead of relief he found only added misery. In Florida he became so crippled that he was unable to walk even with crutches. Moreover, his eyes began to trouble him, giving him such pain that he could neither read nor write. His condition continued to be so bad that even after summer had arrived, he could not make the return trip north. Finally, in the following December, too impatient to wait out another winter, he declared himself well enough to travel and set out for Whitinsville, having been away from home for nearly a year.

Back in Whitinsville, John's health began to mend and his energies revived. With characteristic restiveness he threw himself into planning a new home. He had been living directly across the street from the factory, an undesirable spot. He now conceived the idea of crowning the hill in front of the plant with a mansion set in a handsomely landscaped estate. The house was to be designed in the best mid-Victorian manner and was to be elaborately ornamented with hand-wrought decorations.* The grounds of the house were to be laid out with formal gardens and were to include a magnificent greenhouse.

Before beginning this project, however, it was necessary for John to buy the houses on the desired land and move them to other locations. In this negotiation he was completely successful except for the house on one corner which belonged to Gustavus Taft's father, Cyrus. Out of pride or obstinacy, Cyrus refused to sell, and so the little house remained on the corner, marring the symmetry of the estate. Not until after the death of both Cyrus and John did the Whitin and Taft families finally agree to have the house torn down.

Meanwhile, John was continuing to formulate the company's major policies and to act as adviser to Lasell and Taft. Sometimes, in fact, when his health permitted, he even called occasionally on customers. He was not a man to give up his work easily and he did everything he could to keep up with what was going on in the shop even though it meant being pushed about in a wheelchair by Robert K. Brown, the company's bookkeeper.[10] Nevertheless control of the day-to-day details of the business inevitably slipped into the hands of the younger generation.†

---

* William B. Stall was the architect. Just at that time he was building a similar house for Frank Sayles in Pawtucket, R. I. The Whitin mansion remained standing until 1943 when, for reasons of taxation, it was torn down. The estate is now a recreational park owned by the Whitinsville Community Association.

† John C. Whitin lived for a dozen years after his retirement, but his hand reached out to business affairs less and less frequently during that period. In winter, whenever he felt well enough, he made the trip to Florida. He occupied the rest of his time with such incidental activities as supervising the work in his greenhouses and on Castle Hill Farm. Occasionally he engaged in civic affairs but only when they required little energy and promised to enhance his reputation and prestige. In the closely contested Hayes-Tilden election, he served as a member of the electoral college, and for ten years he acted as a director of the Providence & Worcester Railroad and of the Ponemah Mills, in both of which he was a large stockholder.

2. BOOM OF THE EARLY 'SEVENTIES

Fortunately Whitin could afford to leave matters to the younger men, for between 1870 and 1874 the textile machinery industry was coasting through a period of effortless prosperity. Quotations of twelve-month deliveries were standard, and impatient customers who insisted on better service were advised to place their orders with the British. Their chances of getting better attention abroad, however, were problematical, for the British shops were likewise heavily booked.[11] Some idea of the prosperity of the Whitin company may be derived from the ledger accounts which show that for three consecutive years (1871–73) gross sales exceeded a million dollars; in only one previous year (1867) had the company's sales been so large.*

Most of the firm's customers during those busy years were located in the Rhode Island area. Ninety per cent of all deliveries went to mills within fifty miles of Whitinsville. Even before the war, sales to other parts of the country had fallen off because of the decline of Whitin's picker business. In the South, war's devastation had left few mill owners who were financially able to buy new textile equipment. In the entire period from 1870 to 1874, only three Southern mills, all of which had been Whitin customers before the war, placed orders totaling as much as $10,000, a comparatively negligible figure.[12]

Even in and around Rhode Island, the number of Whitin customers did not exceed two hundred, a narrow base on which to build sales of a million dollars. Some of these customers placed exceedingly large orders. Four of them — the Ponemah, Chicopee, Grosvenor Dale, and Wamsutta mills — bought over a quarter-million dollars' worth of machinery each, the total being nearly 30 per cent of the company's sales for the period. Twenty mills — those buying more than $50,000 worth of machinery — accounted for more than 60 per cent of the company's sales.[13]

This obelisk of sales, with its narrow base and its astonishing height, was the more unstable because of the lack of vitality in the

---

* At the height of its boom, the company was building 150 cards a month — more than at any other time in its history.

company's market pattern. Not one new customer of any significance was won over from a competitor during the period. In fact, sixteen of the company's twenty principal customers had been buying machinery from Whitin for ten or more years; the other four were newly established firms.

The company's failure to reach out for new customers may in part be explained, if not justified, by pressure of business during those years. Being unable to satisfy the demands of its old-time customers, the company could hardly be censured for failing to develop new ones. Moreover, the number of textile mills in the country was actually declining. In every decade after the 1840's there was a decrease in the number of the nation's cotton mills until the emergence of the South as a textile-manufacturing region in the 1880's. Throughout the decline in the number of mills, the nation's spindle capacity continued to increase — not in newly founded mills but in the expansion of already established ones. Consequently, the important market for machinery lay not with new customers, but with old.

Of course, there were exceptions to the general trend. As has been mentioned, four newly incorporated mills were among the company's largest customers. Surprisingly enough, however, the company failed almost completely to participate in the greatest textile-mill development of the decade, the spectacular growth at Fall River. In all the years before the Civil War, only eight cotton mills were built in Fall River and of those eight only one had a capacity of as much as 40,000 spindles. In the five years following the war seven mills were built, most of them with capacities greater than 40,000 spindles. Then, in the single year 1871, eleven more mills were incorporated, and in 1872 an additional four. The city's spindle capacity doubled in the latter two years alone. If one includes the years 1865 through 1872, the increase in Fall River's spindle capacity was fivefold.[14]

Subsequently, many of the companies established in Fall River became important customers of the Whitin Machine Works, but during the period when they were getting under way they bought very little Whitin equipment. Aside from some Wellman-type cards ordered by the Chace Mills and the Richard Borden Manufacturing Company in 1870–71, the only Whitin machines purchased by Fall

River mills in significant quantities were drawing heads. According to a contemporary account of the mill development in that area,[15] a large number of the mills ordered their cards from William Mason of nearby Taunton, Massachusetts. They seem to have obtained their looms quite generally from Kilburn, Lincoln & Company, a local firm, while they bought their spinning frames from Fales, Jenks & Sons, of Pawtucket, Rhode Island, and from the Saco Water Power Machine Shop, of Biddeford, Maine. Frequently they obtained their pickers, roving frames, and mules from English machine-builders.[16]

Without knowing either the economic or the personal reasons why Fall River mill owners placed their orders as they did, we can well guess some of the considerations that must have motivated them. Since William Mason was both a stockholder and a director of several of the new mills, he naturally may have been accorded first consideration as a manufacturer of cards; however, it is not certain which came first, the investor who influenced the choice of machinery or the manufacturer who took stock in payment for his goods.[17] The preferential treatment given Kilburn, Lincoln & Sons is easily explained in view of the firm's local character, and here again the owners were directors of many of the new mills.[18] The admitted quality, if not indeed the superiority, of most of the pickers, roving frames, and mules made in England is reason enough why so many mills bought those particular machines abroad, especially if better delivery was to be expected.

The failure of the Whitin Machine Works to sell in Fall River any machinery except drawing frames is, however, a puzzle. The drawing-frame sales were natural enough, for John C. Whitin's railway-head type of drawing equipment had long been the most popular in the Rhode Island area and had attracted attention even in the Boston region. By Whitin's own estimate he produced twice as much of this type of equipment as anyone else in the Rhode Island area and five times as much as the Lowell Machine Shop, the premier manufacturer of machinery in the Boston area.[19] Yet from the standpoint of dollar volume, Whitin's drawing-frame sales were not of great importance, for equipment of that type represented only about 5 per cent of the total cost of outfitting a mill with machinery.[20] Ring spinning, on the other hand, accounted for at least a quarter of the final cost of machinery for a new mill; hence it was ordinarily a heavy-selling line, and it is difficult to see why Whitin placed none in Fall River. The reputation of Whitin's spinning frames was even more notable than the reputation of his drawing heads and should have attracted as much favor among the new mill owners.[21] True enough, Fales, Jenks & Sons, the firm which supplied the Fall River mills with so much of their ring spinning equipment, was at that time as well-known a machinery builder as Whitin. But the Whitin company, by the 1870's, had so far outstripped everyone in the spinning field, that Lasell could lay claim to having built more ring frames than all the other manufacturers combined.[22] How, then, could he have failed to sell at least one order of spinning frames to the new mills at Fall River? To some extent at least the explanation may lie in the selling methods of the time.

3. BUSINESS PRACTICES IN A SELLERS' MARKET

It must be remembered that the textile machinery industry had been enjoying an almost continuous sellers' market since its inception. Of course, a sellers' market does not preclude unprofitable operations, and many machinery companies experienced grave difficulties in their early years. But a sellers' market does create a certain pervasive attitude of mind, an attitude so strong that it is not dampened by such temporary setbacks as the unprofitable period that occurred in 1857–58 or again in 1864–65. It means that manufacturers begin to have a feeling of being able to sell all they can produce. It means that they feel there is little need to solicit business actively since there is plenty to do just taking care of business as it comes in. It means an emphasis on production, on labor, and on delivery dates. It means that selling and competition are considered of secondary importance. The entire period from 1843 to 1873 saw great prosperity among America's new manufacturing concerns. During those three decades there were no major depressions, only occasional sharp readjustments which, though they eliminated the weak, did little more than castigate the strong for their over-optimism.

When John C. Whitin began his machinery business in the 1830's, competition in the textile equipment industry was localized according to region and vicinity. The schism that separated the machinery designs of Boston from those of Providence effectively discouraged manufacturers in one area from trying to sell their goods in the other. Even within each region, competition tended to be compartmented by the expense and difficulty of transporting anything so bulky as textile machinery over very great distances. Machinery that was expected to travel very far had to be boxed at an expense of about 5 per cent of the cost of the finished product. Shipping rates added another 5 per cent or more, depending on the distance the machinery had to travel.[23] Under such conditions, local manufacturers usually found no difficulty in excluding competitors on a price basis.

Even without a price advantage most producers managed to exclude their competitors simply by keeping on such close personal terms with the mill owners in their region that outsiders had no chance of breaking in. For instance, it is doubtful whether any competitor could have sold machinery to John C. Whitin's brothers. In addition to the advantage of propinquity, John's brothers customarily received a 3 per cent price concession, and family loyalties must have counted for something, even though among Yankee families blood was not always more puissant than gold. A similar situation existed at Lowell. Many of the mills there were owned by the same people who owned the Lowell Machine Shop. Only under the most unusual conditions would Lowell mills have bought their equipment from any other shop. So also at Fall River, where sales frequently were dictated by financial consanguinity. In a sense the textile machinery industry had still not outlived the time when it was the handmaiden of New England's cotton mills. Many years were to elapse before the industry was to achieve complete independence, and even today it retains certain remnants of its old servitude.

As late as 1863 Whitin was still making no sustained effort to expand his machinery market into the territories of his competitors, although it happened that in that year he and Thomas J. Hill, of the Providence Machine Company, did agree to furnish machinery to Amos D. Lockwood, a Rhode Island and Connecticut mill owner, who was about to build a new mill in Lewiston, Maine. Quite logically Lockwood wanted his machinery built on Providence designs even though his mill was to operate in what was really Boston territory. News of the arrangement soon reached the ears of William H. Thompson, superintendent of the Saco Water Power Company whose machine shop at Biddeford, Maine, was located nearest the proposed mill. Thompson looked upon Whitin and Hill as interlopers in an area that he had long thought of as belonging exclusively to his company and he did not hesitate to let it be known that he considered Whitin and Hill to be venturing outside their territories. Upon learning that Thompson was charging him with unfair interference, Whitin sent his critic a chilly letter, part of which read as follows:[24]

Friend Thompson, I heard a rumor of yours a few days ago which led me to think you had a wrong impression of my work. I heard you said, Hill and Whitin have no business to come down your way to get machinery to build, as you did not come this way. I can assure you I have not been after work your way or anywhere else for a long time as I have had all I wish to do without, and I do not need to go after work. I do not know when I have come into competition with you, but once, for years. . . .

There Whitin seems to have let the matter stand, not with an agreement to restrict competition but with a frank statement that he could see no present advantage in trying to expand his market area.

For more than a decade thereafter, the competitive situation seems to have hung in the balance. Machine-builders frequently interchanged price information, indicating that they were beginning to recognize the importance of pricing policies. Yet the freedom with which they dealt with one another is an evidence that the period of bitter competition had not yet arrived. Whitin met all requests for price lists fully and in good faith — but with obvious ill humor. He apparently preferred to travel his own way, neither expecting nor desiring assistance from others.

In many ways Whitin conducted his business in what we call today a professional manner. We think of the professional business man as a newly enlightened individual who has developed an ethical code much like the code of a doctor or a lawyer. Actually the "professional" attitude in business is very old. At one time, when the gilds were flourishing in Europe, it was the only accepted mode. Customers were regarded as rational beings, capable of making their own choice of wares, and any business man who attempted to coerce them or to influence their decision by so much as an attractive display of goods was considered guilty of an unfair practice.[25]

Both John C. Whitin and, to a lesser extent, Josiah Lasell belonged to this honored tradition, for it was not until late in the nineteenth century that the professional philosophy of selling — the "build a better mouse-trap" philosophy, it might be called — finally passed from the American scene. Both these men preserved the credit standing of their company not simply because they thought it was good business policy to do so, but because it was the only virtuous thing to do. They were surprised when anyone considered their manner of business unjust. "You do not of course intend to impute intentional unfairness," wrote Lasell to a customer with indignation. "If you knew our house better, you would not even seemingly do us this wrong." Both thoroughly believed that sales promotion was unessential and almost unethical and that the best way to sell a product was to improve it. "We do not build cheap machinery but use the very best stock and have the stock as thoroughly worked up as we possibly can." They were further of the opinion that they could not be impartial judges of their own products. "It is not for [us] to say that [our] Lapper is the best there is made. [We] can only say that very many people think it is." And again, "We are sure we put much more labor into our looms than other builders, though whether our looms are any better, others must judge."[26] This attitude was to be tempered with the passing years as competition became more severe, but in diluted form it is with the company yet, for the company still does not believe in touting its products to the sky or in running the risk of overselling its products to its customers. With such an attitude toward selling, it is not surprising that the Whitin company, of the 1870's, did not enter the newly developing market at Fall River in an aggressively competitive spirit.

4. SELLING METHODS AND CREDIT POLICIES

For the first half-century of its existence, the Whitin machinery business maintained no salesforce. Except for occasional personal visits made by John C. Whitin to his customers, sales promotion was limited to correspondence. For a few years, when he was first reaching out for a wider market, Whitin allowed commission agents to represent him in what were then such distant textile centers as Philadelphia and Baltimore. But after 1860 he withdrew this privilege from all except Hay, McDevitt & Company, of Philadelphia, one of the first and most loyal of the commission firms which had served as his agents.[27] Thereafter Whitin informed all who wrote offering to sell machinery for him that he maintained a strict one-price policy with every customer, leaving no commission margin for the work of an agent. Inevitably such a policy eliminated all middlemen, precisely as Whitin expected it to do, for he continued to believe that the only satisfactory way to conduct a machinery business was by direct dealings between the manufacturer and his customers.

Both Whitin and Lasell urged mill owners never to buy equipment without first having seen it in operation. If customers wrote the Whitin Machine Works for catalogues or descriptive material, as they often did, they were informed that the company printed no catalogues because printed matter was a wholly inadequate substitute for a firsthand view of the machinery at work. Whenever feasible, customers were urged to visit Whitinsville to see equipment being erected in the shop and to watch it being operated in one of the Whitin brothers' mills. Sometimes they were induced to accept an invitation to stay overnight at John C. Whitin's new mansion on the hill; otherwise they could return by the evening train to their hotel room in Worcester or Providence.

If mill men were unable to visit the plant to settle the specifications of the machinery they wanted, they were directed to a textile company near their home where they could see Whitin machinery in operation. Sometimes, if requested, either Lasell or Taft arranged to pay visits to prospective customers, traveling on occasion as far as Georgia or Wisconsin. The first such visit by a Whitin executive to a distant mill seems to have been made by John C. Whitin, while he was on his way to Florida, in 1870.

Most Whitin machinery sold during the company's first half-century of existence was used by its customers in expanding their mill capacity rather than in replacing worn-out or outmoded machinery. So little technological improvement took place between the 1840's and the 1870's that the rate of obsolescence was negligible. On a few occasions Whitin agreed to accept partially worn equipment in trade if a mill wanted to replace its old machines with new model equipment. But Whitin's letters indicate that his experience in trying to renovate and resell this secondhand equipment was never very happy. Therefore he usually urged customers to dispose of their old machines by advertising in their local newspapers. Fortunately, toward the end of the 1870's, when the introduction of new models was beginning to force machinery into obsolescence in large quantities, specialists, such as Jeremiah Clark of Lowell, were setting themselves up as dealers in used machinery.[28] Thereafter, the Whitin company conscientiously avoided the secondhand market.

In the early years of the company's machine-building, the sale of repair parts constituted a very small portion of its total business. Although there was never a time when Whitin did not feel responsible for keeping in operating order the machinery he had made, still, for many years, he apparently did not find this responsibility heavy. The company sought consciously to reduce its repair sales, and to obviate the need for carrying an inventory of extra parts, by the custom of sending out with each new machine a spare set of those parts most likely to break or wear out. When it did receive requests for repair parts, however, the necessity of running small orders through in special lots must have resulted in heavy unit costs. Parts produced in this manner were billed at a price (out-of-pocket costs plus 20 per cent for indirect costs and overhead)[29] that could not have brought the company a profit,[30] although to customers it probably seemed high. Many mill owners found it cheaper to attempt all but major repairs in the machine shops of their own mills. In the days when parts were simply designed and tolerances were loose, such an expediency was easily feasible. Gradually, however, parts became too difficult for mills to reproduce. By World War I spare parts sales had come to be an important factor in every textile-machinery company's business.

Like any manufacturer whose products have a high unit value and whose customers are limited in number, the Whitin company was

forced to accept heavy credit risks. Work on an unusually large order might require an inventory outlay of as much as $100,000, over
a period of several months. Sometimes an order from an individual
mill was large enough to represent a quarter of the company's total
sales for the year.[31] Obviously if such a mill were to fail any time
between the day it placed its order and the day a year or more later
when it made final payment, the Whitin company might suffer a
heavy financial loss.*

Whitin required all mills to make their payments in cash.[32] His
definition of "cash," however, varied with the prosperity of the times.
When orders were running heavy and he was in need of liquid
funds for working capital purposes, he usually took advantage of his
ability to dictate terms by requiring prompt payment. Under such
conditions "cash" meant settlement in full within fifteen days of delivery. If inventory demands were light and collections were slow,
he might allow thirty days. If business conditions were depressed
and collections were at best difficult, he sometimes allowed an order
to be paid half in cash and half in notes running up to six, nine, or
twelve months; such an arrangement he also referred to as "cash,"
probably to distinguish it from a long-term mortgage with machinery as collateral, an arrangement that he almost never agreed to.

With limited credit information available, Whitin kept check on
his customers as best he could through personal inquiries. Too often,
one suspects, the reputation of a mill's owner was the only basis on
which he could pass judgment, and not always did a good reputation

* Probably the most serious credit loss sustained by the company during the 1870's
was the failure of George Ballou & Son, of Woonsocket, Rhode Island. In November,
1873, the Ballous received delivery of $155,000 worth of Whitin machinery. Because
of the sudden depression that occurred in the final month of 1873, the Ballous were
able to pay the Whitin Machine Works only $15,000 of the amount they owed. A
reorganization of their company under the title of the Ballou Manufacturing Company, with David Ballou, the son, as treasurer, proved no solution to their problem.
Lasell tried to help them get back on their feet by selling them $12,000 worth of
additional machinery so that they could get into a new line of fabric production, but
he received only $5,000 in payment. In 1877 the company was again reorganized,
this time with P. H. Brown as trustee and David Ballou as superintendent. Apparently by liquidating some of the mill's capacity, Brown was able to arrange a payment of $56,000 to the Whitin company. No further payments were ever made. If
interest charges are included, the total loss to the Whitin company was approximately
$100,000.

mean business success. In the case of S. Angier Chace, one of the leading manufacturers of Fall River, confidence in the man seems to have been misplaced. When Chace's Union Mill Company went bankrupt in 1878, the Whitin company had not yet received payment for the $50,000 worth of ring frames it had recently shipped the mill. Since the frames were made to non-standard specifications, they were difficult to sell to anyone else. Even after their price had been reduced from $3.25 to $2.90 per spindle, they sold very slowly, causing Whitin what was probably a substantial loss.[33]

Customarily, if an order for machinery was received from an unknown firm, either Whitin or Lasell made inquiries about the prospective customer's credit from mutual friends or from firms that had had business dealings with the company. If no information was available, the stranger was required to pay for his machinery before the Whitin company would agree to ship it. If the sale appeared to be particularly risky, the unknown customer might even be required to deposit a portion or all of the price with the company before the company would begin work on the order; in such a case 6 per cent interest was always allowed on the deposit until the completed machinery had been delivered.[34] Foreign sales are still handled in this manner.

Sales were usually made on a contractual basis, though sometimes the contract seems to have been no more formal than a gentleman's agreement. If a contract was canceled before work on the machinery had begun, no penalty was exacted. But if construction was already under way, the customer was required either to accept his obligation or to pay a forfeit amounting generally to 10 per cent of the contract price. The amount of the forfeit was designed to protect the Whitin company from whatever loss it might sustain by having to complete the machinery and sell it to someone else at a reduction. Sometimes a customer was given the privilege of applying the amount of his forfeit against future orders.

An indication of the general prosperity of the times and the sellers' supremacy in the market was Lasell's attempt to adhere to a one-price policy. Overtly such a policy was an effort to treat small and large purchasers on a fair and equitable basis. Actually it was nothing more than a suspension of quantity discounts. As a sales policy it was economically unjustifiable. Since the Whitin company manufactured machines for order and not for stock, small orders were almost certain to be more costly than large ones unless several small orders could be grouped and run in a lot. Furthermore, small orders were likely to disturb the production balance or "mix" of the shop and foundry, whereas a large order preserved the balance almost automatically. For instance, all new mills ordering complete equipment required something like a standard ratio of machinery — e.g., forty spindles of ring spinning for every loom. On the other hand, miscellaneous orders might call for a large number of looms and no ring frames whatsoever. Not infrequently production was thrown so out of balance that Lasell had to turn down orders for, let us say, drawing heads at the very time when he had spare capacity in his picker department. Sometimes he even found it expedient to hold a reserve capacity in one or more departments rather than find himself embarrassed by an overload in those departments in case he had an opportunity to sell a full-mill order of machinery. In the case of looms, where margins were particularly low, he sometimes refused to accept an order unless it was accompanied by a request for other machines on which he could make a better profit.

Lasell's one-price policy was characteristic of his professional attitude toward business — his desire to deal with all customers on an equal basis. It was tolerated by the Whitin company's larger customers — against whom it was really a subtle form of discrimination — only as long as the sellers' market in textile machinery continued. The country's large mills were finding the boom of 1870–73 extremely profitable and were more concerned with getting delivery of new equipment than with getting the lowest possible prices. Once the boom had rounded the corner, however, mill profits became more difficult to achieve and customers began to watch their costs more closely. It is not surprising, therefore, that, when at last the sellers' market began to show signs of crumbling in the fall of 1872, one of the first cracks in its structure was Lasell's forced abandonment of his idealistic one-price policy.

CHAPTER VI

WHITINSVILLE'S FIRST GREAT DEPRESSION, 1874–1879

THE first evidence of prosperity's turning tide came in the latter part of 1872, when Lasell was forced to bow to those among his larger customers who were importuning him for price advantages. By April he was receiving so few orders for machinery that his company's backlog of work was beginning to shrink. By July, he was conceding to all his customers a 5 per cent reduction in the price on all ring frames. The peak of the boom had clearly passed.

Nevertheless, when the nationwide storm finally broke in September, with the failure of Jay Cooke & Company, of New York and Philadelphia, the Whitin firm still had on its books sufficient orders to keep it operating at full capacity for at least a year. While business generally was suffering deficits and bankruptcies, the Whitin company went its way as though unaffected by the depression. Indeed, if collections rather than orders are used as a measuring stick of activity, 1874 was a better year than either 1872 or 1873 had been.

However, throughout those months of false prosperity there ran recurrent warnings of a troubled future. Three times ring frame prices had to be cut. By the fall of 1874 they were lower than they had been at any time since before the Civil War. Still, customers hesitated to order, expecting that prices would drop further. In April, 1874, as an added sales inducement, Lasell began promising that prices would be adjusted to meet whatever conditions prevailed at the time of delivery. By November he was complaining that new orders could be obtained only at a loss, since the drop in raw-material prices had failed to keep pace with the rapid fall in machinery prices. A buyers' market was under way.

I. ADJUSTMENT TO NEW CONDITIONS

One of the first results of the depression was a tightening of La-sell's purchasing practices. The company's procurement policy which had developed over a long period of prosperous operations was hardly suited to withstand the high pressures of a shrinking profit margin. Both Whitin and Lasell had commonly done business with only one dealer in any commodity. They had made no effort to spread their purchases over several firms or to play one supplier against another in an attempt to gain price advantages. Their only control device had been their familiarity with prices as quoted in newspapers and their occasional comparison of costs with their friends and business acquaintances. For most small items they had preferred to rely on the integrity of their suppliers rather than to haggle over prices. "We have always acted upon the presumption that our orders by letter would be filled at the lowest cash prices," Lasell explained, "and therefore it was unnecessary to solicit per-sonally propositions from your house." [1] After November, 1874, how-ever, the dangerous drop in profit margins quickly converted Lasell to a more aggressive attitude toward his suppliers and drove him to threaten them with the loss of his business if they did not reduce their prices to him.

The company's backlog of orders was liquidated by October, 1874, and thereafter activity in the shop went into a rapid decline. Men had to be laid off and hours of work had to be curtailed. At peak employment in October, 1873, there had been 680 workers on the company's payroll; by July, 1876, there were only 250. In September, 1875, there occurred the first recorded pay cut in Whitin's history. The worst months of the depression came in the summer of 1876 when cash receipts barely met payroll expenses. In 1877 business im-proved a little when several large and well-financed mills decided to take advantage of low prices to reëquip or expand their facilities. But after returning for a short time to a six-day basis, activity in the shop soon fell off again, until, by the summer of 1878, work was back on a spotty three- and four-day schedule.

As fewer and fewer new orders came in and as the company finished up the old orders on its books and received payment for them, it found that its investment in inventories and receivables was being converted into cash. Ordinarily a third to a half of the total assets of a textile machinery company are tied up in unfinished products and in products sold but not yet paid for; thus when depression comes and there is no further reason for large inventories and receivables, such companies find themselves surfeited with cash. Many companies with widely fluctuating demands for working capital make it their stated policy to borrow from commercial banks in order to tide themselves over periods of peak activity and in order to avoid having a superfluity of idle funds in dull times. But John C. Whitin preferred to have as few dealings with banks as possible. It was his ambition to have a company that was capable of acting as its own "bank" (the Whitin company still holds to that ideal). During the early 1870's, as controlling director of the company, John let his profits accumulate in the business. He declared dividends which entitled him to withdraw about $60,000 a year between 1870 and 1873 (see Appendix 5), but actually he withdrew only about $40,000 a year — much of which probably went into building his mansion and developing his estate. By 1874, however, he found that because of the depression his company had no immediate need for about a quarter-million dollars of current assets. Therefore, he declared a 50 per cent dividend permitting himself to withdraw $260,000 from the firm.* For the first time he could consider himself a wealthy man quite apart from his interests in the machinery business.

---

* There exist a few scattered bits of information from which we can piece together the way in which Whitin invested a part of this sum. In general he bought common stock in New England railroads, as he had with the funds he invested in 1868. His portfolio was, thus, almost without diversification of type or region and, although selected for purposes of security, was in reality highly speculative. Furthermore, most of his stocks were bought just as they were beginning their depression slide. Not until the time of his death, eight years later, had they recovered to a point where they were worth what he had originally paid for them. Following is a list of the investments Whitin made in the year 1874:

Connecticut River Railroad	340 shares	@ 136½	$46,410
Boston Light Gas Company	50 shares	@ 730	36,500
Boston & Providence Railroad	200 shares	@ 148	29,600
Fitchburg Railroad	150 shares	@ 125	18,750
Norwich & Worcester Railroad	120 shares	@ 122	14,640
Boston & Maine Railroad	100 shares	@ 108	10,800
Chicago & Alton Railroad	100 shares	@ 106¼	10,625
Worcester & Nashua Railroad	58 shares	@ 122	7,076
Massachusetts State Bonds (gold) 6s.	100 shares	@ 106¾	10,675
Total investment			$185,076

The liquidity of the Whitin company helped in turn to finance its workmen through the depression. During 1875, large numbers of workers were laid off, supposedly to return to their farms to eke out a living for the duration of the emergency. But in the village every married man was tacitly guaranteed a job. Insofar as possible the older employees were kept in the shop where what little work was to be had was spread among them all. For the younger men, outside jobs were "made." In the wintertime there was ice to be cut from the pond and stored; in the summertime there was work to be done on Castle Hill Farm.

The "farm" was a 70-acre tract of barren land belonging to John C. Whitin. It was handsomely situated on the crest of a hill across the river from the machine shop, where it commanded an imposing view of the whole lower Mumford valley. As farmland, however, its value was seriously reduced by the rocks and boulders which bestrewed the greater part of its surface. To give employment to his idle men, John C. Whitin set them to work removing the stones and building a wall around the farm. Apparently such work was made available to anyone who chose to accept it, for the names on the pay list appear and disappear with irregularity.

Clearing the field must have been an arduous task; the great stone wall still stands to testify to the size of the undertaking. It is approximately six feet high and very nearly as wide. The stones which form its facing are exceptionally large and, although not cemented, are smooth-hewn and fitted into place, while the interior of the wall is filled, as if it were a huge trough, with stones sufficiently small to have permitted easy handling. One can imagine that John C. Whitin countenanced no boondoggling on the job, but, for the men who were willing to work, the job was comparatively remunerative. Previously, while working in the shop, the wall builders had received a median wage of $1.50 a day (9s.). Had these men continued working in the factory, with its reduced four-day schedule, their median wage would have been $6.00 a week (four days at $1.50). On the farm, although their pay was only $1.10 a day, they were allowed to work a six-day schedule and could earn as much as $6.60 a week. Thus, although they had to work longer and harder hours for their money, it was possible for them to earn more on the farm during this period than in the factory.

The Great Stone Wall Still Stands as a Memorial to a Depression Emergency

PLANT OF THE WHITIN MACHINE WORKS, AROUND 1879

For the three darkest years of the depression (1876–78), work on the wall continued. Actually, the number of men engaged on the task at any one time was not large — seldom more than forty — yet the wall in all its indestructibility became a monument to the fact that John C. Whitin, in his concern for his workers, had guaranteed all those who resided in Whitinsville a basic living wage through the worst depression they had ever known. As years passed by, the wall became a legend in the village, illustrating how John C. Whitin had taken care of his workers in bad times. The total cost of the wall to John was in excess of $13,000. Certainly if other New England stone walls had cost as much, there would not be so many in existence today. But the value of the wall as an immutable reminder cannot be calculated in dollars, for it afforded the villagers a visible proof of their protection against depressions. Probably no other company has ever purchased greater employee good will for so few dollars.

2. EFFECT OF THE DEPRESSION ON SALES POLICIES

Depressed conditions within the textile machinery industry made Lasell's conservative business policies seem obsolete, or at least inadequate. No longer could the Whitin firm afford to rely wholly on its customers to carry the burden of its sales promotion by their word-of-mouth recommendations. An improved line of products, better manufacturing methods, and more aggressive selling techniques were necessary if the company was to meet the new competitive challenges.

Gradually during the depression years, Lasell instituted major revisions in nearly all the company's time-honored selling policies. The task was not an easy one for him. Being a professional man by training, he abandoned with great reluctance the gentleman's way of doing business. Only the pressure of circumstances could have brought about his conversion to a hard-fisted, tough-minded business policy. In actual fact, of course, he never did complete the transition. He did what his position required him to do. But after 1874 his letters indicate that his job grew less and less congenial to him. Under the circumstances, he deserves all the more credit for what he accomplished.

The decisive action in Lasell's quiet management revolution took place in the company's pricing policy. As has already been stated, Lasell made broad slashes in the prices of his machines on several occasions during 1873–76 amounting in total to a reduction of about 33 per cent. In line with stated company policy, he made these cuts available to all customers. But in the pragmatism of the business world, stated policy and temporary expediency come often into conflict. Customers soon began to demand even further price reductions, and Lasell, being unwilling to agree to yet another general cut, began to make concessions in individual cases. To prevent these shadings of price from becoming common knowledge in the industry, he frequently made them in covert form. The methods he resorted to were not wholly new, but he used them more generally than before. For instance, in many cases he allowed quantity discounts. Sometimes he provided boxing free of charge (the equivalent of about a 5 per cent reduction in price); and at times he even prepaid freight expenses which ordinarily the customer would have paid. But the price-shading method which was to have the greatest significance for the future was one that the company had seldom used before. Lasell would round off the price of a large order of machinery to some lower figure, basing his price on no apparent percentage reduction and relying on what seems to have been a substantial degree of guesswork. An order placed by the Warren Cotton Mills on 2 July 1874 gives an example of how this type of discount operated.

The Warren company wanted 28 ring spinning frames, 4 spoolers, and 160 looms. At going prices the types of machines desired would have cost Warren $34,584. Lasell, however, after some negotiations, agreed to round off the total price to $33,400. Although in a strict sense this latter figure was the result of nothing more than a quantity discount, still it was not arrived at, as most discounts are, by a straight percentage reduction. Instead, it was merely the result of some process of mental arithmetic known only to Lasell. (Since Lasell frequently complained of the low margins at which looms were sold, one is tempted to conclude that most of the discount was squeezed out of the ring frame price.) The result of these calculations actually figured out to be a discount of 5.829 per cent.

The "rounded-off" discount was first adopted as a matter of temporary expediency. Later it came to be used regularly since it helped to disguise the company's selling prices. In subsequent years, during a period of cutthroat competition, the company often had to give price concessions in individual cases. To prevent these concessions from becoming general knowledge, the Whitin company simply quoted a round figure for an order involving many different types of machinery. No customer could say, under such circumstances, what price it had paid for looms or for cards. Even the company itself made no attempt at a breakdown of such orders. Instead it merely used an unimaginative system of straight proration of the discount, without making any effort to determine which machines could most easily absorb the price reduction.

Concurrently with his efforts to stimulate business through price-cutting, Lasell engaged in what was, by comparison with former years, an aggressive promotional campaign. In place of his usual modest reticence, he began to inform customers that both the company's railway heads and its ring frames were unquestionably the best on the market. Furthermore, he now placed frequent advertisements in trade media.* By 1875 both *Dockham's Directory* and the *Textile Manufacturers' Directory of the United States* were carrying Whitin announcements. Gradually Whitin's advertisements appeared in other media until by 1884 they were to be found in the *Boston Journal of Commerce, Niles' National Register, Cotton, Wool & Iron,* the *Manufacturers' Review and Industrial Record,* and the *Georgia State Gazetteer.*

During the depression years Lasell also gave way before the demands of his customers for circulars and catalogues of Whitin machinery. In 1876 the company began sending prospective buyers small cards, on one side of which was a heliotype cut of a loom or a frame, while on the other side was printed information on such subjects as the floor space occupied by the machine or the productivity of the machine at various levels of operation. The company did not put out its first catalogue, however, until 1883. (It issued a second and slightly revised edition in 1890.)

---

* The only earlier company advertisements that I have been able to find were two perfunctory announcement-type, small spreads in the 1867 and 1872 *Massachusetts Register*. In contrast, the advertisements after 1875 were full-page spreads, occasionally illustrated with pictures of the plant, and frequently repeated in successive issues.

Something of Lasell's new solicitude for his customers is shown by his increasing willingness to act as their agent in buying numerous devices such as spools, bobbins, shuttles, and grinders — appliances that form an important though ancillary part of textile machinery. One of the most costly items in this group was card clothing (that strip of bristling wires that is wound on a card cylinder to form its brushing surface). John C. Whitin had always maintained that the mill owner gained no advantage from having his card clothing ordered for him by the manufacturer of the card. A card cylinder in those days had to be machined after being set in place in order to make it revolve with perfect concentricity; thus in any event the clothing could not be wound on the cylinder until after the machine was in the mill. Whitin argued that it was only logical for the mill owner to order his own card clothing. Furthermore, since the clothing was subject to wear and would have to be replaced, the mill owner was better served if he was encouraged to form an early acquaintance with the man who would act as his clothing supplier. Of course, it might be added that it was to Whitin's advantage to omit the price of the clothing when quoting his card prices, for in those days the cost of clothing was so great that it would have added 30 per cent to the basic price of his card.[2] During the depression Lasell found himself forced to reverse this long-standing Whitin policy by offering, if customers so desired, to have J. S. Kimball of Pawtucket, Rhode Island, equip their cards with clothing. By recommending Kimball to his customers he, of course, virtually guaranteed Kimball's work. But whether he ever encountered any difficulty with his customers because of their dissatisfaction over Kimball's work has not been recorded.

In connection with Lasell's willingness to act as agent for his customers, there occurred, at about this time, an incident that is indicative of a growing competitive tenor. Upon taking an order for machinery from a representative of the Tuckaseege Manufacturing Company, of Mount Holly, North Carolina, Lasell agreed to buy the spools and bobbins that the mill needed. After leaving Whitinsville, the Tuckaseege spokesman apparently traveled to Lowell, where he met A. T. Atherton, the venturesome spirit behind both the Whitehead & Atherton Machine Company and the Lowell

Spool & Bobbin Company. Within a few hours, Atherton had not only acquired the spool and bobbin order for himself but had written Lasell informing him that Tuckaseege wished to cancel the order that it had recently asked him to fill. In the face of such forthright competitiveness, it is easy to understand why Lasell's gentler and more professional business policies had such difficulty surviving.

3. A BACKGROUND OF TECHNOLOGICAL STAGNATION, 1840–1870

Depressions seem to have the same toughening effect on business that obstacle courses have on Army inductees. Depressions convert a corporation that has been softened by easy prosperity into a tough-fibered organization capable of fending for itself against economic adversity. The cotton-textile machinery industry of the 1870's had been softened by three or more decades of heavy demand. In those decades the advance in machine technology had been very slow. On every hand there were complaints from mill men that machinery companies had not changed their models in thirty years.

After the first burst of American inventiveness had died away (around 1840), there had been few radical innovations in textile equipment.[3] Machine-builders continued exploiting their old patterns, and mill owners kept on buying machinery so nearly like their existing equipment that it caused them no new operating problems. In England, mechanical creativeness was likewise at neap tide. A Frenchman named Josué Heilmann contributed the only invention of revolutionary importance during the whole period: an intricate machine known as a comber, developed in 1845 and designed to separate the short cotton fibers from the long so that finer goods could be produced.

During those three decades the only patent for which John C. Whitin applied pertained to the device called a Union Card. It was so named not for political reasons, although a psychological advantage must have attended his decision to place it on the market in 1863, but because it combined features common to both roller and top-flat cards. Its only notable feature was its size, for it was larger than most cards and had a greater capacity, but its proper adjustment required such careful attention that it achieved only limited popularity.[4] Clearly Whitinsville was not a font of machinery invention. Only ten patentable machines came out of the Whitin shop in its first forty years of existence (see Appendix 9).

So little technological progress had there been in the decades before the 'seventies that the company's bolsters, for example, had remained exactly the same for seventeen years. Similarly, no special improvement in the firm's Wellman-type cards had been made since they were first put on the market in 1861.[5] A report read before the 1872 meeting of the New England Cotton Manufacturers' Association made a sweeping indictment of the industry's antiquated carding techniques; it charged that, except for the Wellman-type stripper, no advances had been made in carding practices since the improvements instituted by Slater and Wilkinson in the preceding century.[6] Drawing frames and railway heads, it is true, had undergone considerable improvement, but the mere fact that Whitin was obliged to point out to customers that they could not expect to buy the same frames in 1869 that they had bought in 1850 is an indication that changes in design over a period of two decades were neither looked for by customers nor considered especially desirable.[7]

Over a period of years the general inattention of the Whitin firm to product development resulted in a gradual shrinkage in the company's line of products. About the time of the Civil War, Charles Hardy of Biddeford, Maine, brought out a new card grinder so superior to the one that Whitin was making that it very soon came to dominate the market. (A card grinder is a machine used to dress clothing wires so that their points will all be of proper level.) Although more than half again as expensive as Whitin's grinder, Hardy's was capable of working from four to six top flats simultaneously while Whitin's could handle only one at a time.[8] Likewise, about 1870 J. E. Van Winkle, of Paterson, New Jersey, began marketing a small opener which almost immediately displaced the Bacon-type opener which the Whitin company had been manufacturing for twenty years or more.

Of greater importance than the loss of either the grinder or the opener market, however, was the Whitin company's failure to keep pace with the changing methods of sizing yarn. Warp yarn, which has to be made strong enough to withstand the strain of the weaving process, is commonly passed through a machine which starches or "sizes" it. From around 1815 until after the Civil War, a machine known as a dresser had been used to perform this operation. In 1867, however, a new type of sizing machine, called a slasher, was brought to the United States from England.[9] The new machine's output, as to both quality and quantity, was so superior that it almost immediately made the dresser obsolete.[10] Some of the larger mills, in fact, went so far as to sell all their dressers, no matter how recently bought, and replace them with slashers.[11] Inasmuch as Whitin had been, by his own claim, the largest producer of dressers in the country, he stood to be the hardest hit by the slasher's fast-growing popularity. Moreover, the particular type of warper that he made was not suitable for use with the new slashers. Consequently, he lost sales in the warper field as well.

One should not imagine, however, that the rest of the textile machinery industry was passing the Whitin company by; indeed, the company's principal competitors seem to have behaved just as Whitin did. Machine-builders strove constantly to improve their manufacturing methods with the idea of producing better-quality machines at less expense, but they did almost nothing to improve their product designs, merely accepting whatever changes were forced upon them from the outside.

New ideas in product development typically came from two sources — from competing English machine-builders and from American textile men. In the 1870's the British were building equipment that was far superior to American equipment for the production of fine yarns. A protective tariff, plus the fact that American mill men were more interested in mass production than in the manufacture of fine cotton goods, kept British machinery from being a threat to American machinery builders. But British machinery designs continued to lead American designs at least until World War I.

In addition to learning from their friends and competitors across the ocean, American builders leaned on their own customers for new ideas. Textile men were constantly working out methods of cutting costs and improving output, and since some mills had extensive repair shops, their experimentation on machinery design sometimes proceeded on a large scale. Machine-builders watched the work of mechanics and overseers in their customers' mills,[12] checking on

TABLE 3

Use-license Royalties Collected from Customers and Paid by the Whitin Machine Works to Patent Holders during the Year 1870

Patent Holder	Residence	Licensed Invention	Used on	Rate	Total Royalties
Horatio N. Gambrill	Baltimore, Md.	Card with cylinder stripper	Card troughs	$20.00	$ 120.00
George H. Wellman	Lowell, Mass.	Card with top flat stripper	Railway heads	$18.00	11,934.00
Geo. Draper & Sons	Hopedale, Mass.	Revolving trumpet	Railway heads	.50	$ 120.00
		Evener	Railway heads	[a]	896.10
		Weighting motion	Drawing heads	2.00	134.00
		Weighting motion	Ring frames	1.25	61.25
		Spinning bolster	Looms	.05	1,523.20
		Thin place preventer	Looms	.75	6.00
		Let-off motion	Looms	1.00	1,737.00
		Picker[b]	Looms	.50	504.50
Total royalties					4,982.05
					$17,036.05

[a] Charge based either on the number of spindles which the railway head was to supply (at 2½¢ per spindle) or on the number of looms supplied (at 50¢ per loom).
[b] Either the Wright or the Stearns model.

Source: Statements rendered either quarterly or semiannually to the above patent holders by the Whitin Machine Works.

their progress and negotiating for the right to manufacture on a license basis the new devices being developed there.*

Developmental work at the mill level was a slow, gradual, adaptive process. It was never revolutionary, but cumulatively it produced far-reaching results. Moreover, in a depressed period, like the 1870's, it promoted a marked change in textile-machinery design, for in times of depression a strong pressure to reduce costs always made itself felt on the mill floor where developmental ideas typically originated.

* When the Whitin company negotiated with a mill overseer to build a new invention, it usually effected one of two types of licensing agreements. The company either obtained a license to *manufacture* the new device, or else it arranged to have its customers obtain the right to *use* it. In cases involving licenses to manufacture, Whitin and Lasell preferred to pay the patent holder a lump sum for permission to produce the patented item in unlimited quantities. In case of licenses to use the device, the Whitin company acted merely as an intermediary between the patent holder and the customer who was to buy and use the Whitin product. Under the use-license arrangement, the company was theoretically obliged to report to the patent holder only the number of sales it made, but in actual practice it often acted as the patent holder's agent in collecting the royalty. Usually the company settled its debt with the patent holder either quarterly or semiannually. Patent holders obtained the coöperation of manufacturers by allowing them to grant a discount to those customers who paid their royalties at the time of purchase. Thus, George Draper & Son charged only $1.25 to any mill owner who paid Whitin for the Draper loom royalties when they bought their machines; if, on the other hand, the Drapers had to go to the trouble of collecting the loom royalties themselves, their charge was $1.75.

Table 3 shows the use-license royalties collected by the Whitin company and paid over to patent holders during 1870. The first item in the table, the Gambrill device for stripping card cylinders, had once been in popular use, but by 1870 had been largely abandoned in favor of the older and more thorough hand-stripping method; hence its poor showing in the table. The second item, the Wellman patent for cleaning card-top flats automatically, was one of the few significant improvements in cotton-machinery design made in America during the 1840–70 era. This stripping device had been patented in 1853 by George Wellman, an employee of the Merrimack Manufacturing Company in Lowell, and within a short time it had achieved wide popularity in both America and England. In 1866, as a result of a suit initiated by Horace Woodman of Biddeford, Maine, Wellman had been forced to raise his stripper royalty from $13 to $18 per card, paying to Woodman the added $5.00 in a compromise settlement of the latter's claim. Nevertheless, so much did the Wellman-Woodman stripper enhance the efficiency of the carding operation that mill owners were willing to pay the high royalty fee even though it added 15 per cent to the cost of their carding equipment. Nearly all the other large manufacturers of textile machinery were also licensed to make Wellman-type cards, but the Whitin design, so the company claimed, was sturdier than the rest, weighing approximately a hundred pounds more than the cards made by competitors. The company also maintained that its Wellman cards were capable of finer work than were the cards of other manufacturers.

4. IMPROVEMENTS IN PRODUCTS, MATERIALS, AND TECHNIQUES

The depression years of the 1870's created a demand for better products and a need for better production methods. With business in a demoralized state, the Whitin company could not hope to interest its customers in buying new machinery unless that machinery was considerably more productive and less expensive to operate than the machinery which customers already had on their floors. Mills were not expanding their capacity and so were not in the market for additional equipment of the types they already owned. Nor was much machinery wearing out. The only market was for new-type machinery, a market that the industry had to create by first creating obsolescence. In a buyers' market, it was the customer who was bringing pressure on the manufacturer to improve his methods and products.

Here is a point of first-rate significance, for it has been generally assumed that competition is necessary in business, if stagnation is to be prevented. Yet competition in the textile machinery industry of the 1870's, while stronger than before, was not a factor governing management decisions. Lasell's letters give no indication that he was thinking about or was even aware of what his competitors were doing. Competition in the industry did not cause distress until the 1890's and, when it did, it vented its force not by compelling manufacturers to improve their product designs but by making them sell their products more aggressively. Though it may not be true of business as a whole, in the textile machinery industry at any rate, product innovation has typically been spurred on by periods of slow sales, not by periods of out-and-out competition. The two forces sometimes coincided, but it was the former, not the latter, which predominated.

Fortunately for the Whitin Machine Works, Gustavus Taft was gifted with considerable mechanical ingenuity and insight. Unfortunately, however, he lacked the inventor's original touch. He did much to revamp the company's product line and to improve its methods of production, but his changes were adaptive rather than creative. It has been said of John C. Whitin — and it might equally well have been said of Taft — that "his conservatism kept him from costly and fruitless experiment." Similarly it was said of Taft's eldest son that "a new application of a principle commended itself to him only after thorough and careful investigation." [13] Those two statements might well be combined into something like a motto for the Whitin company, for beginning with John C. Whitin and continuing to the present, the company has adhered to the policy of avoiding radical departures in machinery design as long as they remain radical.

Under Taft's administration virtually every machine in the Whitin product line underwent some sort of change. The lapper became equipped with an evener device which made possible an elimination of the opening process — and which seems to have involved the Whitin company in the threat of litigation by the Lord Brothers firm, of Todmorden, England.[14] Cards were redesigned to increase their capacity. Three new card models, the Full Roller Card, the Combination Card, and the Arlington Card, were brought out between 1876 and 1879 (see Table 4).[15] Applied to these new models were two patented attachments developed by Gustavus Taft himself, one of them a self-stripping device (1872)[16] and the other a mote separator (1880).

The Whitin company's ring spinning frames were completely revolutionized in the 1870's by two important developments, the high-speed spindle and the evener. But both these developments came from outside the company. By making possible a considerable reduction in power consumption and a tremendous increase in the output of the ring spinning frame, the high-speed spindle caused throstle-frame spinning to become immediately obsolete.[17] The evener improved the quality of the ring frame's output so much that it made ring spinning suitable for fine-count production and for the first time put ring spinning into effective competition with mule spinning for the production of filling yarns. Both these improvements were chiefly the work of George Draper & Son, of Hopedale, Massachusetts, a firm which had originally specialized in loom attachments but which, beginning in the 1860's, had seen profitable opportunities in buying up and consolidating the patent rights of

TABLE 4

CHANGES MADE IN WHITIN CARDING MACHINERY DURING THE 1874-1879 DEPRESSION

Purpose of Card	Name of Card	Year First Made by Whitin	Description	Price in 1879	Replaced by	Year First Made by Whitin	Nature of Change	Price in 1879
Coarse work	Gambrill Card	1857	10 rollers	[a]	Full Roller Card	1879	5 rollers added	$300
Fine work	Wellman Card	1861	19 top flats	$120	Arlington Card	1878	2 rollers added beneath lickerin tops placed next to feed rolls	$175
Heavy-duty work	Union Card	1863	7 rollers, 16 top flats	[a]	Combination Card	1876	3 rollers added 4 top flats removed	$225

[a] Not being sold in 1879.

many inventors.* The Draper firm was *sui generis* and followed none of the set patterns in the textile machinery industry's development. During its formative years it possessed what was unquestionably the most dynamic developmental organization in the industry, an organization quite unmatched in any other textile-machinery firm in any other period in American history.

In the drama of the high-speed spindle, Gustavus Taft played only a supporting part to the Drapers' starring rôle. His part was nevertheless a vital factor in the Whitin company's success in the spinning field and was important enough to have precipitated one of the notable legal cases in textile-machinery history. Because of its importance, the lawsuit, and with it the entire development of the high-speed spindle, has been left to a later chapter.

Besides doing experimental work personally, Taft drew upon others for new ideas. Table 5 lists the licensing arrangements that the Whitin Machine Works entered into with several outside patent holders between 1870 and 1883, and Appendix 9 lists the patents developed or purchased by the Whitin Machine Works between 1832 and 1910. When Taft saw a need for product improvement, he either referred the problem to someone in the plant or else brought in outsiders to work on the assignment. On one occasion, having canvassed several different sources of supply for a satisfactory material out of which to make a bobbin lighter than the standard wooden bobbins and at the same time capable of holding more yarn, he turned the problem over to Charles E. and Charles H. Pollock, two Whitin employees.[18] Cotton textile men had toyed with the idea of a lightweight bobbin for several years but without achieving results. After some time the Pollocks devised what at first seemed to be a satisfactory bobbin made of cardboard, and on 20 January 1877 they assigned their rights in the invention to the Whitin Machine Works.[19] However, the cardboard bobbin was never a success, although the ideal of a lightweight bobbin still titillates the fancy of cotton-machinery inventors.

* Realizing the tremendous potential market opened up by their evener, the Drapers wisely refrained from charging a royalty for it. They were not the losers thereby. As the evener made headway against the stubborn competition of the mule, it brought the Drapers an income in the form of royalties on every high-speed spindle sold with evener-equipped frames.

TABLE 5

Patent-licensing Arrangements Entered Into by the Whitin Machine Works between 1870 and 1883

Date	Patent Holder	Residence	Invention Licensed	Used on	Rate
1871	Geo. Draper & Sons	Hopedale, Mass.	Sawyer Spindle	Ring frames	$ .38
1872	John N. Pierce	Lowell, Mass.	Self-stripper	Cards	1.25
1872	D. W. Hayden	Providence, R. I.	Front stop motion	Drawing heads	5.00[a]
1874	Geo. Draper & Sons	Hopedale, Mass.	Bobbin holder	Spoolers	.40[b]
1877	S. H. Seward	Putnam, Conn.	Arm	Pickers	550.00[c]
1877	Geo. Draper & Sons	Hopedale, Mass.	Evener	Ring frames	[d]
1877	John Lord	Todmorden, England	Evener	Lappers	25.00
1879	Edw. Wright & Co.	Worcester, Mass.	Comb	Cards	2.00
1879	P. Dawson	Providence, R. I.	Front stop motion	Railway heads	6.00
1880	Geo. Draper & Sons	Hopedale, Mass.	Separator	Ring frames	.04
1880	Taylor & Curtis	Springfield, Mass.	Guide	Spoolers	.10[e]
1883	George H. Clark	Newburyport, Mass.	Saddle	Ring frames	[f]

[a] The Whitin Machine Works bought these motions already fabricated from the patent holder.

[b] This is the cost of the bobbin holder itself, with royalty included.

[c] Lasell made a lump-sum payment to avoid a possible lawsuit. See ltr. JL to S. H. Seward, 16 June 1877.

[d] The Drapers charged no royalty for their eveners, since the sale of eveners increased the sale of spindles.

[e] This was the Partridge guide, half of the rights to which the inventor had given to Curtis for help in securing the patent. The other half he had sold to a man named Smith who had in turn sold to Taylor. See ltr. A. Partridge to GET, 29 Sept. 1880.

[f] The Whitin Machine Works manufactured these saddles for Clark at a mutually agreeable price and divided evenly the profits which arose from their sale. See ltr. GET to Geo. H. Clark, 9 Oct. 1883.

Source: Letterbooks, *passim*. For some inexplicable reason license payments were not recorded in the Whitin ledgers; hence the only source of information concerning them is the letterbooks. Dates are therefore subject to slight errors, since licensing arrangements were no doubt sometimes made orally and quite possibly had been in existence several months before the first mention of them was made in a letter.

On another occasion Taft was instrumental in getting the shop's master-mechanic to develop a multiple drill head designed to drill more accurately-aligned holes in ring-frame rails. The shop had been troubled by its inability to control the spacing of the drilled holes in the two rails of a spinning frame. So long as the hole in the spindle rail and the one in the ring rail were drilled separately, concentricity of the two was difficult to achieve. Taft's idea was to drill both holes simultaneously. The new machine attracted considerable attention throughout the industry and brought inquiries from several competitors. Particularly illuminating is a letter written by Lasell in answer to William Mason's request for information concerning the machine:[20]

Our drilling machine was built at our works. The bed of the machine was an old one we had on hand, bought of the Essex Co. The other parts — bed plate, gears, etc. were from patterns modified temporarily to meet the case. We made drawings at first, but they were so much modified in the progress of building the Drill as to be of very little practical use to anyone but the machinists who were engaged in the work. You will at once perceive, we are not in a situation to aid you very much in building one for yourself, though we will be happy to render such assistance as we can.

On several occasions during the depression years Taft went so far as to induce individuals with inventive ability to use the Whitin shop as a developmental laboratory. In 1875 a man named J. P. Richards was brought to Whitinsville to perfect a punch for perforating the tin sheets that form the friction surface on loom take-up rolls. After completing his work, Richards gave the Whitin Machine Works unlimited rights to the use of his machine for the nominal price of $75.

At about the same time, John F. Foss was in Whitinsville conducting experiments of an undisclosed nature. It is known, however, that while he was there he and a man named John M. Pevey took out a patent (27 July 1875) on a card that made use of under flats as well as top flats. Since the witnesses for this patent were R. K. Brown and H. B. Osgood, both Whitin employees, it seems probable that Foss had either been developing or else testing his new card while he was working in the Whitin shop. The Foss and Pevey card, which in subsequent years was to achieve great popularity among cotton-mill owners, was, for reasons not now known, never added to the Whitin Machine Works' product line.

The depression years also witnessed the acceleration of a trend that had begun many years earlier. In the days of the Holyoke Machine Shop the framework of many Whitin machines had been made of wood, but in the period following the war, cast-iron frames came gradually into use, until by 1879 the entire Whitin line was being constructed of metal parts.

At first all the pig iron that the shop used for frame castings came from Scotland, preference being given to a brand known as Eglinton iron.* Bar iron for machining purposes (Bagnall brand) usually came from England. What little steel the company used also came from British sources. Being intensely patriotic, Lasell resented his company's dependence on Old World suppliers and strove to use American products whenever American iron or steel met his standards.

By 1873 Lasell had found, as many other manufacturers were finding at about that time, that the quality of American steel had improved sufficiently to be on a par with British steel. By 1875 he had also found a combination of domestic pig irons that were up to his specifications.[21] But the bar iron he obtained from American producers continued to give him trouble. In a letter written 3 March 1873 to Jones & Laughlin, of Pittsburgh, he criticized American iron men and called upon them to improve their products:

We use some 300 tons bar iron [a year] — turning most of it. On account of the imperfection of American in its mechanical execution, being untrue to size, & out of round, we have been obliged to use Bagnall's English against our wishes, as we fully believe in patronizing our home industries, if possible. Other machinists are driven to use English iron for the same reason.

* Although he bought iron from many dealers, Lasell placed most of his orders through two Providence firms, Congdon, Carpenter & Company and Cornett, Nightingale & Company. Both firms are still in existence (as the Congdon & Carpenter Company and the Nightingale, Baker & Salisbury firm) and both still do business with the Whitin Machine Works.

I am satisfied that if some manufacturer would make a good turning iron & have it well rolled — true to size & round — he would secure a very large trade & drive the English out of the market & that too at an advantage of ½ or ¾ ¢ per #.

The steel manufacturers have come up to the standard & today we are using American steel in preference to the English.

Unfortunately the sample of bar iron sent by Jones & Laughlin in response to Lasell's challenge proved to be as defective as previous lots. Especially for the machining of drawing rolls (which had to be fluted) it was important that the company's iron be free from imperfections. Throughout the 'seventies Lasell relied wholly on Yates Booth of Lancashire, England, to furnish bar iron of the quality he required. Finally, in 1881, the Burgess Steel & Iron works, of Portsmouth, Ohio, and the Cleveland Rolling Mill Company, of Cleveland, convinced Lasell that he could use their bar steel instead of iron and that he need no longer depend on the British for his fluted roll stock.*

Another source of new ideas for machinery design was appearing with the advent of the mill engineer — for it was during the 1870's that mill engineering became a recognized profession. At an early period, a few men had instituted the practice of offering their services to mill owners as engineering consultants,[22] but they had seldom devoted full time to their consulting work. Beginning in the 1870's, more and more individuals took up this new profession. In general the machinery companies welcomed their coming, for mill engineers relieved the machine-builders of the troublesome necessity of giving prospective customers advice on problems of mill construction, power equipment, plant layout, and the numerous other vexatious incidentals that are tangential to the job of providing a new mill with machinery.

It is not easy to assign a reason for the development of mill engineering in this period. The greatest need for such a service did not

---

* Even as late as 1895, however, the company was still having difficulty with American metals. "We have had some trouble with American steel," wrote the treasurer on 28 December 1895, "and are now using English steel. We now have quite a large stock on hand and are so busy in that department that we dislike to make any change."

arise until the next decade, when the South began developing as an important textile-manufacturing region. In the 1870's there was very little construction in the South. However, what little there was seems to have attracted the services of engineering specialists, inasmuch as three out of the eight mill consultants recommended by Lasell to his customers during the decade were Southerners.[23]

Perhaps mill engineering was the result of a general trend in the industry and was only incidentally aided by the growth of cotton mills in the South. Certainly, new mill owners everywhere must have found that the intelligent selection of machinery was a difficult undertaking. Not only could they choose from a vastly larger number of suppliers (including the British) as the market area of machine-builders expanded and overlapped, but they could no longer fill all, or even most of their requirements from one shop as formerly they had been able to do. With other manufacturers as well as with Whitin, the expansion of market areas seems to have resulted in a reduction in the variety of machines each produced. As builders came more and more into competition with one another, they found that the weaker items in each product line lost out to a competitor's superior machine.

Fortunately we have for the year 1874 a fairly complete picture of who in the industry was making what. From Appendix 7, it is clear that only five American manufacturers — the Amoskeag Manufacturing Company, the Lowell Machine Shop, the Mason Machine Works, the Saco Water Power Machine Shop, and the Whitin Machine Works — could offer a substantial variety of machinery, and all of them lacked one or more items necessary to make up a full line. Moreover, this appendix indicates that mill owners could select most types of machinery, if they wished, from among as many as eight or nine American manufacturers and from perhaps three or four British.

Into this welter of products stepped the mill engineer. From the initial selection of a mill site to the final purchase of bobbins, he guided the course of new mill construction. Familiar with all makes, he could see the advantages of one machine over another; conversant with prices, he knew where to secure the best bargain; trained in engineering, he could spot defects and recommend improvements in machine design. In a sense he was a harbinger of the cutthroat competitive era. His continual pressure on the machine-builder to produce a cheaper and better machine must have resulted in many innovations which would otherwise have been slow in coming. But striking a balance, one is tempted to question whether the good he did the industry was enough to offset the harm. His continual insistence on special devices, sizes, and specifications — often perhaps only in a subconscious effort to justify his existence as a specialist — introduced to the industry a lack of conformity to standards from which it has not even now managed to divorce itself completely. By 1876 Whitin was offering ring frames in a half-dozen different gauges.[24] In addition, the customer could order his frames in two widths, either the narrow type (27 inches wide) or the standard (39 inches).[25] His spindles could be either common or high-speed and could be set in their frames in multiples of either 12 or 16. His rings could be any of a number of sizes and could be either plain or double-adjustable. His front rolls could be either plain or shell-type. His frames might have separators or not, just as he desired. Conceivably a certain amount of what appeared to be progress in the 1870's might better be termed change and might be traced to the insistent, sometimes whimsical, demands of the mill engineers for special concessions.

CHAPTER VII

THE PASSING GENERATION, 1880–1888

In 1882, at the death of John C. Whitin, Josiah Lasell took over the presidency of the company, although continuing at the same time to serve as treasurer. Far from increasing his administrative duties, however, Lasell's added title of president merely brought him a step nearer retirement. In Whitinsville, as in so many other New England communities, the presidency of a company was an honorary position only, not unlike the board chairmanship of many present-day corporations. By taking the presidency, Lasell was in effect letting it be known that he intended to begin turning over his responsibilities to younger men. It would, in fact, seem almost as if his father-in-law's death had at last released Lasell from the moral obligation of having to live up to what John C. Whitin had expected of him.

Furthermore, Lasell was beginning to feel concern about his health. News of the sudden and unforeseen death of one of his brothers appears to have convinced him that his family suffered from an hereditary tendency toward angina pectoris and that he would have to take strict precautions if he was to guard against his own untimely death from that source. Therefore, after 1882, Lasell more than ever left the management of the shop to Gustavus E. Taft, whom he had elevated a year previously to the newly created post of (factory) agent in recognition of the indispensable part Taft was playing in shop affairs.

Meanwhile, younger men were being groomed for top-management positions in the firm. In every case they were either sons or sons-in-law of the company's two operating families, the Tafts and the Lasells. By what process a treasurer of the company was selected as successor to Josiah Lasell, no one now knows, but the circumstances surrounding the selection are sufficiently pertinent to the company's history to warrant speculation as to how the choice was made. The reader is cautioned, however, that the following account, while based on substantiated and clearly recognizable facts, is put together in a way that is wholly hypothetical.

1. "THE LAYING ON OF HANDS"

It seems possible that the aged John C. Whitin, contemplating his own approaching demise and pondering what the future of his company might be in the hands of the next generation, saw certain difficulties that he wished, if possible, to forestall. Whitin was well aware, for instance, that, for another two generations at least, the company he had founded would continue to be a closely held family concern, for although he was to die technically intestate, he in fact arranged for the disposition of his property well in advance of death and so knew exactly how his stock in the company would be distributed. All his company holdings were to go to his daughter and son-in-law, except for a 10 per cent interest which he had already given (in 1876) to Gustavus E. Taft. It must have been evident to him, therefore, that control of the company would some day pass into the hands of Josiah and Jane Lasell's four children, Catharine, Jeannie, Chester, and Josiah M. Lasell.

In 1881, the year in which Lasell's successor appears to have been selected, Chester Lasell was only twenty years of age and J.M. was only eighteen. Catharine was married to her twenty-five-year-old second cousin, George Marston Whitin (known to his friends as Marston and to his intimates as "Mart"), who was a son of Charles Edward Whitin and a grandson of Paul Whitin, Jr. Jeannie was not yet married.

Now, under ordinary circumstances, it would have been natural for the elder members of the Whitin-Lasell families to let the three young men mature for a few years before singling out any one of them as the person to be trained as the next company treasurer. Instead, however, the selection seems to have been precipitated at a very early date and through pressure brought to bear by John C. Whitin.

It may have been that John C. did not wish to leave the question of management succession in the hands of Josiah Lasell for fear that Lasell would show favoritism toward his two sons. It may have been, also, that John C. had already sized up the capabilities of the three young men in the family and had concluded that one of them possessed incomparably greater business acumen than either of the others. At any rate, in the fall of 1881, someone, perhaps John C. himself, induced young George Marston Whitin to take a job at the Whitin Machine Works with a beginning salary of $3,750.* At about the same time, John C. made Marston a gift of five shares of company stock, without at the same time giving his two grandsons any.

There is no certainty that the offer extended to Marston Whitin in 1881 was any more than the tender of a job, but it seems unlikely that Marston would have given up the work he was doing, merely upon receiving a block of five shares of stock together with an opportunity to work for $3,750 a year, without at the same time receiving some assurance that the way was being opened for him to ascend to the top. Marston was already serving as superintendent of his father's Riverdale Mill and must have expected that in due time he would inherit that mill outright. Furthermore, it is reported that Marston's father was actively opposed to his accepting the Whitinsville offer. One must assume, therefore, that, whatever the inducements which led Marston to abandon his job in Riverdale simply to take up a place alongside his brothers-in-law in the Whitinsville plant, and especially in the face of parental opposition, they must have been much stronger than there is any record of. There is just one substantial piece of evidence to indicate that Marston was at an early date given to understand his preferred position in the company: a few months after beginning work in Whitinsville (on 16 January 1882, to be exact) and while still serving an apprenticeship stretch in the shop,† Marston was elected a member of the com-

---

* Marston was not wholly unfamiliar with operations in the plant. After spending three years at Williston Academy, in Northampton, Massachusetts, (1872–75), he had worked for a while in the Whitinsville shop. Later he worked in a New Bedford mill, perhaps Wamsutta, and then, following his marriage to Catharine Lasell, he became superintendent of his father's mill at Riverdale, his older brother "Harry" having already been put in charge of the family mill at Rockdale.

† For fourteen strenuous months, Marston underwent an intensive training course in all departments of the factory. By March, 1883, he was working as an assistant in the accounting office, and by September he was handling most of the correspondence and was working his way toward a mastery of the company's sales problems.

pany's board of directors. His two brothers-in-law were not similarly honored with directorships until five years later.*

By 1883 Marston Whitin was serving as second-in-command in the company, with Gustavus Taft continuing responsible for operations in the shop. In due time both Chester and J. M. Lasell entered the shop as apprentices and took positions in the company's office. Cyrus Taft, the eldest of Gustavus Taft's three sons, did likewise and eventually became plant assistant to his father.

However, the four young men, not one of whom was over thirty, had only begun working together as a team when, one Sunday evening in mid-March, 1886, Josiah Lasell experienced the heart attack he had been predicting.[1] He had attended both the morning and evening church services, as was his wont, and had thought that a walk home in the fresh air might be good for his health. At first his illness did not seem serious, but after a restless night, he suffered another, and this time a fatal, attack at four o'clock in the morning.

As successor to his father-in-law, George Marston Whitin became the company's treasurer,[2] but one suspects that the experienced Gustavus Taft must have continued to have a great deal to say in the firm's management.

Taft, himself, was not at all well, however.[3] For years he had had recurrent trouble with a painful leg injury received in a factory accident shortly after his return to Whitinsville from Holyoke,† and in January, 1884, while on a trip to Palmer, Massachusetts, he had suffered what he referred to as a "shock." But of greater importance in his later years was the fact that his once robust body had become emaciated because of diabetes. Indeed, it was only a little more than two years after Lasell's death that Taft succumbed to his diabetic ailment, leaving the company entirely in the hands of the younger generation.‡

Ordinarily a company left in the hands of such young men would

---

* N.B. John C. Whitin personally presided over the meeting at which Marston was elected and personally voted his 65 per cent block of stock.

† One day when riding in an open shop elevator, he had been preoccupied with other thoughts and had moved his foot forward before the elevator reached its landing. His foot had been badly crushed, and although he did not lose its use, he suffered increasingly from the effects of the injury in the later years of his life.

‡ Taft's successor as factory agent was his son, Cyrus.

have had difficulty surviving the experience. Few men of thirty could have carried on such a large enterprise without the sage advice of at least a counseling board of directors. But the Whitin board in 1888 consisted only of the four young men already mentioned, plus Cyrus Taft's younger brother, William. There was consequently no one they could turn to for advice.

Fortunately, however, Marston Whitin, at the age of thirty-two, was already a fully mature business man, as the events related in succeeding chapters will reveal. With complete self-assurance, he proceeded to make himself personally acceptable in the shop where once Gustavus Taft had held sway. Then he went forth to do business with customers and to do battle with competitors. Within ten years his company, which, when he took command, had been the largest textile-machinery producer in the Providence region, had become the largest in the entire country. By the age of forty, when most business men think they have done well to reach the top ranks of their companies, Whitin had come to be regarded as the leading figure in the entire textile machinery industry. What John C. Whitin had accomplished as founder and developer of a high-quality machinery firm, George Marston Whitin was to inherit and enhance by the force of his competitive skill.

2. THE WHITIN–LASELL PERIOD IN REVIEW

By 1888 — sixty years ago and more — the Whitin Machine Works already could boast a corporate history that extended back over a half-century, a record that many concerns even today would consider worthy of an anniversary publication. A mature business unit, the company had already developed something of the corporate "individuality" that it has today.

The person responsible for making the company what it was then, and what it has continued to be, was its founder, John C. Whitin. The company's individuality began to be recognizable as soon as John C.'s machine shop emerged from its cotton-textile mill past.

For the first ten or fifteen years of his career as a machine manufacturer, John C. Whitin conducted his shop as a small, one-product enterprise, operating it on a petty capitalist's scale and using petty capitalist management techniques. He was not just owner-manager of the concern; he was supervisor-laborer as well. He ran the business personally, not through intermediaries. And he focused his principal attention on production. His capital funds were limited: his inheritance was modest and his expanding enterprise was financed out of earnings, not from the investment of any outside capital. His unit profits must have been very large to have permitted such rapid growth, yet for many years his profits did not appreciably enhance his living standards, for most of them went directly back into his business. That his risks were very large is suggested by the fact that his picker sales fell off abruptly after 1849; had he not diversified a few years earlier, he very likely would have been faced with financial ruin in the 1850's, making his story just one of a thousand others of a similar kind.

In short, John C. Whitin began as a typical petty capitalist. What made him soon cease to be typical, however, was his remarkable management ability. By the 1850's he had expanded his enterprise into what may best be called an industrial capitalist concern. Unfortunately, we do not know by what means he succeeded in making the transition from being the producer of one product only to being the producer of many products, for the records of the critical period, the 1840's, do not exist. All we know is that, judging from what was accomplished, the story must have been a remarkable one. We can, however, distinguish some of the strengths and weaknesses that came out of Whitin's past and ran on into the future.

It is interesting to observe how John C. Whitin, the newly arrived man of big business, continued to show evidence of his petty capitalist background. Like so many others in his position he tried to solve the large-scale problems of industrial capitalism with petty capitalist measures. For instance, even after his shop had multiplied many times in size and in fact had split off into two divisions, John C. continued managing it in person. It seems fair to say that the two-shop experiment of the Civil War period failed not so much because of the war itself, although admittedly the war was a contributing factor, as because Whitin still had not learned to run his business through the agency of others and was unable to continue running both shops himself.

Then, too, in matters of accounting Whitin never progressed beyond the petty capitalist stage. As will be shown in some detail in the next chapter, the Whitin company continued to follow a single-entry system of household-like accounts, taking no advantage of the superior accounting methods being used by other industrial firms either in that period or later.

Similarly, Whitin's emphasis on production continued even after he had become a large-scale manufacturer, primarily because production was the field he knew best, but also because most of the business problems of a manufacturing concern in that era were production problems; in a sellers' market, selling was a secondary worry, and finance tended to take care of itself.*

Another policy brought over by John C. Whitin from his earlier days was his product specialization. Although he managed to change from his single-product line of the 1830's to a multiple line in the 1850's, he never succeeded in rounding out his line completely. At the time, his narrow specialization was probably an advantage, since it made him competitively strong in a limited field, but in later years it had serious drawbacks. For about twenty years after 1890, the company suffered because Whitin had not succeeded in adding roving equipment to his line, and not until the 1920's did the company regain the strength it had lost in the 1850's when Richard Kitson drove Whitin practically out of the picker business.

Finally, it should be noted that, for better or for worse, John C. Whitin's petty capitalist vision prevented him from breaking away from his place of origin and forced him to build around the shop a company-owned and company-dominated community. Like his other policies, this one had its roots in the nurturing soil of ex-

* In financial matters, however, it should be noted that Whitin was an exception to the rule. Most industrialists, once they had discovered that a well-run production unit tended to solve its own financial problems by returning ample profits, gave no further attention to financial matters. Too often, however, they ran along, making money and investing it in expanded plant, only to encounter a period of financial stringency when their liquid resources were too low to carry them through. Not so Whitin. Partly because the very nature of his type of business required him to keep an unusually large portion of his capital in working funds and partly because of the extreme financial conservatism drubbed into him by his father, John C. set a financial policy that was to be followed by his successors consistently thereafter, a policy that was to make the company so financially strong that it managed to escape completely any reliance on the financial capitalist bankers on State Street in Boston or on Wall Street in New York.

pediency; but by reason of its early growth and continued cultivation, the policy eventually became so firmly established that any attempt to discontinue it would have caused a major upheaval in the company's affairs.

Under Josiah Lasell, John C. Whitin's basic policies were continued in force with few exceptions. Indeed, from an administrative standpoint, Lasell's career in office was merely an extension of John C. Whitin's. During all but four years of Lasell's comparatively short sixteen-year span as treasurer, his administration was overshadowed by the pervasive influence of his dynamic father-in-law. In addition, Lasell's star was somewhat dimmed by the planetary brilliance of his shop superintendent, Gustavus Taft. Nevertheless, Lasell succeeded in making his own individual contribution to the growing tradition that was to form a basic part of the company's distinctiveness.

To begin with, Lasell helped make certain, by forsaking his scholarly calling and taking up the responsibilities that had come to him as a part of his wife's dowry, that the company would continue in family hands and under family management. Simply by establishing that precedent he went far toward ensuring its continuance, for, where a sense of family pride exists, such precedents are not easily broken. The very fact that he, Lasell, was a son-in-law and not a son was also in its way a precedent, for the line of management succession in the next two generations was to follow the same pattern. Apparently the strong character traits of the Whitin family were to be dominant in the daughters, but recessive in the sons. It will be recalled, for instance, that John Maltby Whitin, the errant son of John C., in all likelihood would have succeeded his father had he measured up to his opportunities. Instead, in that generation as in succeeding ones, it was the distaff side of the family that was to show strength of character and that, probably by being attracted to persons of similar strength, was to marry men who would bring to the company's management the drive and enthusiasm that was lacking in the family's sons.

Compared with the accomplishments of his father-in-law before him and of his son-in-law in the next generation, Josiah Lasell's career seems lacking in luster and tone. But it must be remembered that Lasell guided the company through one of the most difficult periods in its history.* By the time Lasell became treasurer, the textile machinery industry had become mature enough to begin reacting to those economic fluctuations that have come to be known among historians as the secular trends in business behavior. The concept of the secular trend in business, briefly stated, is that business profits vary in much the same way, and in response to much the same pressures, as do commodity prices. It has been observed, for instance, that during long periods of falling prices, profits become more difficult to earn and depressions become longer lasting. Young industries may, and often do, run counter to the trends, but older ones are likely to follow the trends closely. As yet the field of business history is too new to have produced enough examples substantiating the trend theory to make it unassailable, but the experience of the Whitin company tends to bear the theory out.

The Whitin company started operations in the downtrend of prices following the War of 1812. Being a new company in a new industry, it was able to go through the depression of 1837–43 with only a temporary setback in sales. Then, from 1843 until after the Civil War, prices rose steadily and John C. Whitin's business flourished. It continued to flourish for several years after the war despite falling prices. (In fact, as in every postwar period in its history, the company enjoyed its best profits during the period when commodity prices were falling rapidly while machinery prices, because of their contractual nature, were staying at relatively high levels.)

Beginning in 1874, however, the company felt the strong tug of falling prices on its profit margins. Appendix 25 shows how spinning machinery prices sagged lower and lower from 1866 onward,

---

* The depressed state of business during Lasell's career was reflected in the town's population growth. Figures from the U. S. Census show that for several decades before 1870 the rate of population increase in the town of Northbridge deviated little from an average of 14 per cent. In each of the two following decades (1880 and 1890 census reports) the rate of increase fell to 11 per cent. The Massachusetts census (which was also taken decennially but which alternated with the U. S. Census at five-year intervals) gives a somewhat clearer picture of how the years of business hardship affected the population of the town. Between 1875 and 1885, both depression years, the population of Northbridge actually fell off by 6 per cent. If what was true for the town as a whole was also true of that portion of Northbridge known as Whitinsville, it is clear that depressed conditions must have driven the more mobile portion of the company's labor pool to look for work elsewhere.

and Appendix 5 shows how the company's dividend payments, which from 1872 to 1875 had never fallen below $60,000, managed to rise above that figure in only four years out of the next twenty. Blame for the poor showing of those years could hardly be laid at Josiah Lasell's feet. All his piety and wit could not have canceled out the national trend that was causing recurrent depressions in the cotton textile industry and, by reflection, in the textile machinery industry as well. No less than eight of Lasell's sixteen years in office were marred by the stunting effects of two severe national depressions (1874–78 and 1883–85), depressions from which the company could no longer recover with its one-time youthful buoyance.

Throughout the 1870's, the 1880's, and the 1890's, the Whitin Machine Works found business conditions very difficult. The period was to be as difficult for Marston Whitin as it had been for his father-in-law. Indeed, had Marston's career ended in 1898, it is possible that he would not today be remembered as one of the company's outstanding figures. But instead his career went on into a period of upward secular trend when the company was to enjoy some of the greatest prosperity in its history. The period of the company's experience under Marston was thus to be compounded, in about equal parts, of depression and prosperity. Perhaps the greatest tribute that can be paid to the young man who was about to take over the company's management is that he was to prove himself capable of handling the problems peculiar to both bad times and good.

Part II

THE PERIOD OF GEORGE MARSTON WHITIN

CHAPTER VIII

MANAGEMENT AND CONTROL, 1888–1900

LIKE most of the members of his family, George Marston Whitin
was short in stature but wiry in build. Although he had a youthful
predisposition to rheumatism, it happily abated in later years, and he
was able to lead an active outdoor life. His only diversion from work
was hunting and the attendant hobby of raising pheasants. Occasionally he golfed for business reasons, but he held no real love for the
game. His work was his life; vacations were likely to make him
restless and anxious to get back to the job. Only by taking him on
occasional trips to Europe — sometimes he came back by return
boat! — could his family combat his constant tendency to overwork.

Like the business men of his era, Marston ran his company with
the stern and uncompromising independence of an absolute, if be-
nevolent, despot. As the company expanded in the final years of the
century, his management burdens mounted until they exacted an
inhuman share of his time and energy. Still he loathed to delegate
responsibilities. Functions of staff were all but unknown to his organization, while the niceties of chain-of-command were often ignored when expediency dictated. If, upon occasion, he felt that a
problem required immediate solution at the bench level, he did not
hesitate to by-pass his foremen in seeing that the matter was carried
through. Under ordinary conditions such disregard for the rank and
position of his subordinates might have proved demoralizing. But
Marston Whitin had a gift for inspiring loyalty in his workers, many
of whom had known him as a classmate in the village schools and
had come to look upon him as a personal friend.

Unlike his predecessor, Josiah Lasell, Marston considered the
shop and foundry as much his province as the office;* he left no

---

* He also thought of each as being reserved for men only. During his lifetime
women visitors were allowed in the plant only when it was not operating and women
stockholders, his wife included, were not encouraged to attend stockholders' meetings.

thought that Cyrus Taft, as agent, would succeed to his father's place as co-equal in the business. Nor did he hesitate, when sales declined, to take to the road, making arduous trips to see customers in North Carolina, South Carolina, and Georgia. Seldom did he return without a notebook penciled with orders. Still he disliked the traveling life of a salesman. "I had a very pleasant trip down to Anderson [South Carolina]," he once wrote to his agent in the South, "but was glad when I was homeward bound as really the living is too high for me in that country." Serious-minded, intense, shrewd, uncompromising, he was the very antithesis of the traditionally expansive salesman. Yet his thorough knowledge of the company's products, his unquestioned reliability, and his vigorous prosecution of business secured for him orders where the hail-fellow would have failed. Thanks to his early training in his father's mills, he knew the cotton business from the mill man's point of view and could readily visualize the problems with which mill owners were faced in their operation of cotton machinery.

In his quiet, self-assured, yet forceful way, Marston became a recognized leader in the cotton-textile machinery industry. His uncanny ability to judge men and to gauge economic trends made him respected by customers and competitors alike. Being in a key spot, with a wide acquaintance among mill owners, he was often called upon to recommend men for responsible mill positions. For similar reasons he was widely sought as a mill director. He conscientiously refrained from serving on the board of any mill so far from Whitinsville that he could not attend its directors' meetings regularly. Therefore he accepted few invitations to serve on Southern boards, limiting his directorships in the South to mills in which his company had heavy financial interests. At the time of his death he was serving as a director of 14 mills, 7 of which were located in New Bedford, where the Whitin comber was a potent influence among the mills that were producing fine, combed yarns.*

* Marston's New Bedford directorships were held in the Kilburn Mill, Manomet Mills, Nashawena Mills, Nonquitt Spinning Company, Quisset Mill, Whitman Mills, and Sharp Manufacturing Company. In Lawrence, Massachusetts, he was a director in the Arlington Mills. In Rhode Island he was a director in the Crown Manufacturing Company and the Nyanza Mills, and in Connecticut in the Lawton Mills. In South Carolina he held directorships in the Brogon Mills, the Calhoun Mills, and the

GEORGE MARSTON WHITIN, TREASURER,
1886–1920

Under Marston Whitin's leadership the Whitin Machine Works became for the first time an integrated productive unit. In the days of John C. Whitin and Josiah Lasell its growth had been so hasty that its organizational pattern had failed to keep pace with changing times. In 1886 the shop was still as loosely decentralized as in 1860. Theoretically, full control over operations reposed in the superintendency, but in actual practice the superintendent was more a coördinator than an administrator, for his principal duty was to keep individual departments working together smoothly and in harmony. Real authority in the shop rested in the hands of department heads who brooked no interference in the conduct of their departments' affairs.* The chief executives of the company — both John C. Whitin and Josiah Lasell, but especially Lasell — dealt with the shop almost exclusively through their superintendent, Gustavus Taft; although on occasion they doubtless enforced their will on the middle and lower management echelons, in general they appear to have avoided interfering with day-to-day shop management.

At a time when the shop was small and when individual department heads had not yet become set in their ways, the company's decentralized organization probably functioned well. But by the time when Marston Whitin assumed the treasurership, the Whitin Machine Works was not just one unit but a dozen or more small enterprises housed under one roof and headed by men who were accustomed to acting with independent disregard for the welfare of the whole. These enterprises constituted the departments of the shop, set up on the basis of product rather than of function. All card

---

Williamston Mills. When William F. Draper asked Whitin if he would be willing to serve as a director of the First National Bank of Boston, Whitin replied that he could not accept the position because (a) he was too busy to do the position justice, (b) he could not easily attend meetings, and (c) he kept his cash funds in Whitinsville and Providence, not in Boston.

* Before the Civil War there seems to have been no specific appellation by which such department heads were known. The Whitin shop had only one "foreman" and he was the man in charge of all shop operations. The title "superintendent," as applied to this position, did not come into use in Whitinsville until about 1860. The title "agent," which the company presumably borrowed from the cotton textile industry, was always a misnomer as used in Whitinsville and was eventually dropped. The first persons to be called agents, Gustavus Taft and his son Cyrus, were something akin to works managers. The third and last agent, L. M. Keeler, was practically a sales manager, although he was never given authority over sales in the South.

parts, for example, were made and assembled in one area instead of being turned in one department, milled in another, and ground in a third. Under a single supervisor's direction, a complete machine might be manufactured from castings to the assembly of finished parts — in the case of the more complex machines a separate department might take over the final erection. The department heads (whom I shall call supervisors for the sake of simplicity) therefore had a multiplicity of operations under their charge.

How Marston Whitin set about breaking down the independence of his department supervisors is the theme of this chapter. To accomplish his purpose he deprived them of their erstwhile prerogatives and transferred to the superintendent's office many of their former responsibilities. In so doing he had to convert the superintendency from a one-man job to an office organization, for Marston's superintendent, Harvey Ellis, was not the rounded executive that Gustavus Taft had been.

Marston might have carried his centralization program to even greater lengths had Cyrus Taft, who was then the company's agent, been an abler administrator. As it was, Marston had to assume, personally, a disproportionate share of the shop's responsibilities. Also, his task would have been easier had his accounting controls been more effective. But like so many manufacturing concerns with petty capitalist backgrounds, the Whitin company's accounting system was rudimentary in form and almost valueless except as an historical record of what had taken place in the past. However, Marston Whitin more than made up for the deficiencies of his organization by his close, personal control over operations and by his keen executive incisiveness. Many competing firms had better accounting systems and some had abler administrative assistants, but none had a chief executive as competent in plant management as Whitin was.

1. THE RÔLE OF WHITIN SUPERVISORS

At the time when Marston Whitin entered the company, department supervisors in the Whitin Machine Works held positions of considerable authority and prestige.[1] They hired their own men, trained them, determined their rate of pay, set their jobs, and had the power to fire them or transfer them to another department.* In addition, each supervisor acted as his own production manager. Theoretically, he was required by the shop's building orders to comply with a number of restricting regulations (see accompanying illustration), but in actual fact he ran his department with independent autonomy. Although he was required by the building orders to requisition forgings and castings "in such quantities as shall be determined by the Superintendent" and was expected to include a report of "all spare pieces of Castings or Finished Work on hand," in actual practice he seldom did either. So well was he acquainted with the parts needed for the machines made in his department that he could place his foundry and forge orders from memory without any reliance on the superintendent. Similarly the report of parts on hand was a formality that he seldom observed. Most department heads took pride in their ability to have hidden away in some obscure bin a store of spare parts on which to rely in a pinch. To accumulate such a store they often took it upon themselves to turn out a larger number of pieces than an order called for. Then, if a small request for repair parts came in, they could fill the order out of stock without the expense of a special run. In effect they were performing a stock-control function on an informal, decentralized basis.

From experience, department heads knew how far in advance to order their castings and how much faith to put in the foundry's

* Since a supervisor's workers were literally "his" employees, the supervisor also kept track of his workers' time. Every morning a young lad, known as a timekeeper, made the rounds of the shop to collect from each department head the names of any men who had been late or absent the day before. An additional check was provided by a gatekeeper who stood at the only gate left open after work began, noting all men who came in late. This method of checking workers' time was continued after the supervisors had lost much of their authority. Commenting on the Whitin timekeeping system, Marston wrote E. D. Bancroft of the Draper company on 25 September 1899, "We take the time of our men through the various foremen about the shop. Our time-keeper goes about every morning and takes the time from foremen. We have used this system for a number of years, but we do not think it is quite up to date. We expect to put in a system of time registers, but our idea is, in using this system to employ it in connection with our present method, each to check errors that creep into the other system." However, time clocks were not finally installed in the shop until November, 1917. Ernest Booth, foreman of the carpenter shop, has shown me his time book in which he continued to keep the time of his men through August, 1918.

promises of delivery. If castings were not forthcoming, they acted as their own expediters, perhaps taking along a young apprentice to help truck back such castings as were ready. From experience they also knew what machining operations each piece required. Indeed, part of the supervisors' strength (and part of the system's weakness) was their ability to carry in their heads what would otherwise have had to be committed to paper. So long as each one knew his job thoroughly, production flowed with almost autokinetic ease. Administrative red tape was kept at a minimum, and so-called indirect labor was all but unknown.

In short, the system was as good as the men who ran it. To make the system work, each supervisor had to be an administrator of superior ability. Even to qualify for the job he had to have years of training and experience. In addition, he had to have a knack of fitting his department's work into the flow of shop production. His rôle in the company's organization required him to be farsighted and coöperative, but unfortunately his position of authority, more often than not, encouraged him to be arrogant and autocratic.

2. JOB WORKERS

It seems possible that sometime early in the pre-recorded past, all Whitin department heads worked for the company on a contract basis. How the contract form of plant organization originated is not known, but in all likelihood it came to this country from England where industrial development in the late eighteenth and early nineteenth centuries was considerably more advanced than in the New World. Certainly by the 1830's contracts covering departmental work were in common use by many New England manufacturing firms.[2] The owner of a shop made agreements with skilled men whereby they were to furnish him a certain number of finished products at a specified price. In their turn, the skilled men selected such workers as they needed to fulfill their individual contracts, paying whatever wages they considered suitable, or allowing the wages to be paid by the shop owner and deducted from their contract account. Usually the shop owner furnished not only plant and tools but also all necessary materials and supplies.

Whitinsville supervisors who were employed on a contract basis

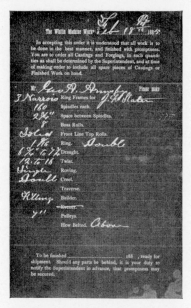

An Example of a Superintendent's Building Order

A Whitin Machine Works Electric Freight Locomotive,
Believed To Be the First Built in America

WHITIN OBSERVATORY, WELLESLEY COLLEGE

LASELL GYMNASIUM, WILLIAMS COLLEGE

were said to be "on job work." The first Whitin job records begin
in 1864, at which time the system must have been in full effect, since
fifty-six of the company's employees, or about one in ten, were being
paid on a job-work basis. This meant that they were receiving a
daily base rate, in addition to which they were being paid the differential between the job price and the labor costs on the work for
which they had contracted.

The jobbing system can best be understood by observing how it
worked in a particular instance. The Whitin records show that
Henry F. Woodmancy, head of the spindle department, worked on
a jobbing basis from 1864 until his death in 1898. He began with only
two assistants and ended with a department comprising fifty or
more. Like all other job workers, he was allowed a base wage in
addition to his jobbing pay. For the last twenty-three years of his
life, his base pay remained unchanged at 12 shillings ($2) per day —
a maximum of about $600 per year. Yet his total income during that
period fluctuated widely. In general his income followed the business cycle, growing rapidly in prosperous times and falling off in
periods of inactivity. In 1888, a fairly good year, job work paid him
$5,216.51. In the following year jobbing paid him $7,931.78; a year
later it fell to $6,277.35 and in the year after that to $3,254.21.

Woodmancy was an inventor of some ability, but as a company
employee he reaped little financial benefit from his inventions since
he customarily assigned his patents to the Whitin Machine Works.
Therefore, a grateful management seems to have permitted him
extra compensation through the liberality of his job-work rates. During the last ten years of his life, he ranked as the most highly paid
department head in the shop. Yet he was but first among peers, for
the company had four other department heads who always earned
more than $2,000 annually from their job-work pay.[3] The relative
size of the income enjoyed by these men is best indicated by the fact
that the company's most skilled day laborers never received more
than 24 shillings a day, or about $1,200 a year.

Since Woodmancy's department produced not only spindles but
also collars, skewers, and caps, he was required to submit to the
paymaster an itemized report of his department's output. The paymaster then computed the amount of his job-work earnings on a

so-much-per-piece basis and credited the amount to his account. Each item of production carried a different jobbing price. The old taper-top spindles grossed him 15 cents apiece. The new high-speed spindles brought him 16 cents in 1874, but during the ensuing depression the rate gradually fell until by 1879 it was only 13 cents per spindle. Records beyond that date are fragmentary, but in 1882 the rate was still 13 cents while by 1904 it had fallen to 10¾ cents per spindle.

Since the paymaster also entered on the debit side of Woodmancy's account all the wages of the men in the spindle department, Woodmancy's net income per spindle was very small compared with his gross income — at no time more than a cent or two. Theoretically, the paymaster settled with Woodmancy only four times a year, at which times he balanced Woodmancy's account. In actual practice, however, Woodmancy did not wait for his job-work earnings to be paid him in quarterly sums but instead drew against his account at irregular intervals.

Since job work froze the company's direct labor costs at a certain level per unit, the company benefited from efficient department supervision only through increased output. All the monetary benefits of the system accrued to the job workers. Yet the system's effectiveness in getting job workers to improve efficiency in their departments must have had certain natural limitations. Although job workers no doubt realized the theoretical advantages to be gained through their constant efforts to maintain a smooth and effective flow of work, they must have had difficulty in reconciling theory with reality. The infrequency with which job-work accounts were settled made it impossible for them to follow closely the dollar effects of any specific efforts to improve their department's output. Then, too, since their own prosperity was necessarily dependent on the busyness of their department, a factor over which they had no control, job workers must have felt that their ability to increase their jobbing income was not very great.

No doubt most job workers directed their attention chiefly toward the level of wages they paid their men, for there at least they could watch figures which they knew had a close connection with their dollar income. One jobbing man, Oscar Taft, is said to have judged the performance of his workers by whether or not they produced each day a 15-cent differential between what they earned for him by their output and what they drew in wages. B. L. M. Smith, head of the roll department, where the machining operations were comparatively simple, is said to have hired only boys who could be trained quickly, paid little, and transferred to another department when they grew old enough to expect higher wages.[4] As long as a job supervisor could dictate how much he was willing to pay a man, he was probably slow to grant a raise, for by the very nature of the system, individual raises were virtually taken from the job-worker's pocket. Of course, the farsighted job worker might feel that his employees were likely to produce more if they were given more incentive to work, but on the whole the system probably invited petty tyrannies rather than an attitude of intelligent self-interest.

In many departments the employees who were supervised by job workers were paid on a piece-rate basis. This method of payment followed logically from the fact that the department head was paid according to the number of pieces produced on his job-work contract with the shop. Piece rates were used in the Whitin company at least as early as 1860, but how the rates were set or administered is not known. Apparently they were paid in connection with a guaranteed daily wage. When the worker's production exceeded the amount covered by his "day rate," straight-line piece wages, or "extras" as they were called, were computed for him. The base wages were paid weekly, beginning in 1886 when a state law required weekly payment of wages, but the piece-rate earnings were accumulated and paid in the last week of each month.

At first the amount of the piece rates must have been determined by each department supervisor for the men under him, but by 1896 the shop superintendent was determining at least under what circumstances piece rates were to be paid. The piece rate was evidently recognized as an incentive device and was put into effect when increased production was desired. A magazine article published in 1896 cited the Whitin Machine Works as an example of successful shop management and reported as follows:[5]

A large part of the work [at the Whitin shop] is always at piece rates, but under varying conditions the piece rate on a certain job may be discontinued and day prices be substituted. The spindle-forgers, for instance, are now on day-pay, though if the demand for extreme production was urgent, these hammer-men would be put on piece rates, which would increase their day-pay and the output together. "When I want more work," said Mr. [William] Taft, "I put the spindle-forgers on piece prices; then they fix their fires on their own time, and run their pay up, and get out more work for me; when we are not driven, we put the spindle jobs back on day-pay, and get less work and maybe pay a little less per spindle. I don't know exactly." *

From the company's standpoint, the job-work system's chief merit was its standardization of direct labor costs. As long as the shop operated on a jobbing basis, management always knew in advance how much it would have to pay its employees to have a machine built, since the company's job workers bore the full effect of all fluctuations in labor costs, whether favorable or unfavorable. With the cost of labor pre-determined, the owners found that they had to watch only material costs, especially the cost of pig iron, to know at what level to quote machinery prices.

Job work was a handy and simple management device. To some extent it took the place of a cost-accounting system. It gave the company's department heads, virtually, a base income plus a share in management's profits. And it went at least part way toward encouraging efficiency. But it was less automatic in its effect than was generally assumed by those who used it. In practice there was no discernible correlation between efficiency and jobbing profits. Moreover, rates had to be continually reset to be kept realistic. To a fair extent the increase in a department's productivity was due to nothing the supervisor had done but rather to the installation of new machine tools or improved jigs and fixtures. Changing job rates

---

* Since the spindle-forging department was not operating on a jobbing basis in 1896, it is possible that Taft, who was then superintendent, was accurately quoted. If the department had still been on job work, it would have made no difference to the company whether the men were on day pay or on piece rates because any saving in labor cost per unit would have accrued to the job worker. The company gained from high productivity only through savings on burden costs per unit. In this connection it is instructive to note that Taft failed to include overhead charges in estimating the difference in costs between forging spindles with piece rates and forging them without.

to meet changing conditions was not an easy thing to do, however. Job workers naturally resented having their rates modified, and, furthermore, top management had no accurate way of knowing what the new jobbing rates should be.

Since job work seemed to create more problems than it settled, Marston Whitin decided to abolish it altogether. Such action, however, could not be accomplished in one step. Eight years were to elapse before the shop's department heads could be converted to a strictly foremanship basis, and another sixteen years were to go by before all vestiges of job work disappeared.

3. THE DECLINE OF JOB WORK

A decline in the number of men who worked on a job-contract basis shows up almost immediately after the earliest records start. From 56 in 1864, the list of names dropped to 49 in 1870, and by 1886 it stood at only 25. Yet there is no evidence that the company was following a clear-cut policy of doing away with the system at that time, since between 1870 and 1886 eight new names were added to the list.

There seem to have been three general circumstances under which job work was dropped during those years. Sometimes the company replaced a job worker, when he retired or died, with a department head who was called a foreman and who was paid a straight salary plus an annual bonus. Secondly, a man was sometimes taken off job work, perhaps at his own request, because his department was running a recurrent jobbing deficit. Thirdly, a man whose average income from job work amounted to only a few hundred dollars a year was sometimes permitted to change to a foremanship with the privilege of an annual bonus.*

Whitin's most drastic, and probably his most effective maneuver to put an end to job work was his transfer of the hiring function from the departmental level to the superintendent's office. The exact year of the transfer is not a matter of record, but Ernest Booth, one of the company's oldest foremen, recalls that the date was about 1888. If Booth's memory serves him correctly, the explanation of the

---

* In 1890 the median annual bonus paid Whitin foremen was $200. The largest bonus, $1,000, went to George Armsby, head of the carpenters' shop.

change seems easy enough. It was about 1888 that Marston Whitin became aware of the necessity of recruiting additional laborers from outside Whitinsville. With the local labor pool fast drying up, individual department heads had little opportunity to secure the workers they needed. A centralized hiring agency became imperative if the company was to secure sufficient imported labor. Probably nothing that Whitin could have done would have gone further toward weakening the position of his job workers. Hiring constituted a very small part of their prerogatives, but it was the keystone of their authority. With the loss of the ability to hire went the loss of the ability to set beginning wages, and with that loss went the foundation of the job-work system.

Further emasculating what remained of the jobbing system, Whitin gradually reduced the level of jobbing rates until they yielded low net returns. A memorandum book kept during the closing months of 1890 shows clearly how he went about making his reductions. First he estimated what income he thought a certain "job worker x" should receive commensurate with his ability. Then he compared that "fair" income with the income "worker x" was likely to receive during the year at going job rates and under existing business conditions. If it looked as though the "fair" income of "worker x" ought to be 25 per cent less than his "likely" income was going to be, Whitin reduced all the jobbing rates in "worker x's" department by an appropriate amount. As a result of Whitin's calculations in 1890, Oscar Taft was cut a flat 5 per cent on all bolster prices; David Smith's rate per railway head was reduced from $40 to $35; John Harrington was cut from $5.50 to $5.25 on card parts; and both J. F. Scofield and J. H. Burbank were permanently dropped from the job-work list.

It is to Marston Whitin's credit, however, that he allowed the older department heads the satisfaction of keeping their job-work status even though he took away most of their economic privileges. By 1895 job work as a system was a dead letter, but twelve of the company's veteran supervisors were still permitted to retain their jobbing category. No doubt Whitin, being keenly aware of the debt he owed his senior department heads, was anxious not to offend their sensibilities. It must be remembered that Marston had been a lad of only twenty-five years when he came to work for the Whitin company and that, because of Gustavus Taft's death, he was left virtually on his own by the time he was thirty-two. Of the company's new officials, all but Cyrus Taft were his junior, and Cyrus was only five days older. Under such circumstances the decentralization of the Whitin organization had been a blessing, and the company's veteran job workers had been a rock of strength to the young treasurer. Of the 25 men who were job workers in 1886 when Whitin took over as chief executive, 13 (or more than half) had been in supervisory capacities since the company's incorporation in 1870.[6] Moreover, eight of them (or about one-third) remained at their posts for ten years or more after Marston's accession to the treasurership. To those men must go much of the credit for carrying the Whitin Machine Works over the critical period when the new management was still young in years and experience.

After 1895, deaths and resignations rapidly took their toll of the men who retained the right to serve as job workers, until by 1907 only four of the final twelve were left — Oscar Taft, B. L. M. Smith, John Fisher, and George Parker. The last to depart was John Fisher; with his retirement in 1911 went the last trace of the Whitin job-work system.

4. ACCOUNTING METHODS AND CONTROLS

Part of Marston Whitin's effort to centralize management controls took the form of an earnest attempt to improve the company's accounting methods. Marston was not an accountant himself and fundamentally he had very little patience with what he considered accounting falderal. But he recognized the need for central administrative controls, and he did what he could to develop a workable set of accounts for his own personal use. Compared with modern techniques his system was primitive and crude, but one must remember that neither he nor his company had any background in accounting experience.

Like so many American companies that sprang from inconspicuous beginnings, the Whitin Machine Works possessed few of the sophisticated management techniques known to companies that could trace their ancestry to the merchant-era past. In a very general way, American manufacturing firms of the nineteenth century followed two management patterns. There were those which, founded by wealthy investing capitalists, were fair-sized institutions from the start, and there were those which, started by petty tradesmen or shop owners, were small in their beginnings but large in potentiality. Companies of the first group, having been promoted by experienced capitalists, were the beneficiaries of the business experience handed down to them through the ages of mercantile capitalism. Typically companies in that group had well-developed double-entry bookkeeping systems with such refinements as unit cost data and special manufacturing accounts. Companies in the second group, having been promoted by petty capitalists whose knowledge of business was limited to what they had learned from practical experience, usually kept their financial records on the same informal basis as their owners kept their personal accounts. Indeed, in such companies corporate and personal accounts were often indistinguishable.

As we have seen, the textile machinery industry of New England was split geographically into two sections, each with a different heritage. In the Boston area most shops possessed the superior accounting practices of their mercantile ancestors, while in the Providence region most shops revealed through their records the humbleness of their business origins.* The Whitin company's records were kept on a single-entry, cash basis until as late as 1918, whereas the Lowell Machine Shop's records were double-entry from the very beginning of its history.

There are a few shreds of evidence indicating that at one time Whitin's accounting practices may have been better than they were in the 1880's, but what the evidence may mean is uncertain. Among the records for the years 1860–63 are definite indications of a double-entry concept of bookkeeping. For example, an 1861 sale of machinery to the Pacific Mills was recorded in this manner: "Pacific Mills, Dr. to Merchandise [the old term for Sales]." Both sides of

---

* That the Whitin shop was not alone in its undeveloped accounting methods is shown in a 1916 report by the United States Bureau of Foreign and Domestic Commerce (Misc. Series, No. 37, p. 11). According to the report, one firm in the textile machinery industry (the firm is not named but quite obviously it is not the Whitin Machine Works) "made no effort to keep books except in the most old-fashioned way, and until [1912] . . . had not taken an inventory of stock on hand for 25 or 30 years."

such transactions were posted to the ledger in true double-entry fashion, but there the bookkeeping procession halted. No attempt was made to strike a trial balance; hence no profit and loss account was developed. Most entries were not even totaled at the end of the year. Some accounts, such as receivables, were balanced only at the bottom of each page when it became necessary to know what figures to carry to the next folio. Obviously the little double-accounting that was practiced was of slight value and was, in fact, more an obstacle than an aid in expediting the bookkeeping task.

Why then was this touch of double-entry bothered with? And whence had it come? Could it be that John C. Whitin had learned the rudiments of double-entry bookkeeping during his youthful employment in the mercantile firm owned by his brother in New York only to forget it? It seems certain that Paul Whitin, Jr., had known how to keep books, for in 1824 J. Gordon Bennett, in an advertisement for his classes in "bookkeeping and merchants' accounts," gave the name of "Mr. P. Whitin, Jr., Maiden Lane," as a reference.[7] Possibly, having learned the form but not the essence of bookkeeping, John C. Whitin had used the double-entry concept for a while, only to drop it when it seemed to be accomplishing no purpose.

By Marston Whitin's time, the company's accounts were being kept in a manner that can only be described as casual. Since, in a company like the Whitin Machine Works, the number of individual business transactions per day was usually small, the bookkeeping task was not a full-time job. Consequently, it was a job that was often neglected. In the entire year 1886 the cash book, which was really the controlling record since the company was on a cash basis, contained only 1,556 credit postings. Figuring the year on the basis of 300 working days, it is apparent that the expenditures recorded per day averaged only about five. When at the end of the month the cashbook was out of balance by $20 or $30, as it not infrequently was, the difference was simply debited or credited to miscellaneous expense. If the bookkeeper was busy with other duties, he sometimes did not even bother to strike a month-end balance; after all, the checkbook always revealed the amount of cash in the bank, and the amount in the safe could easily be counted if anyone wanted to know how much cash the company actually had.

Frequently the clerk let his postings fall many days behind. On one occasion, in 1889, the postings were so delayed that a letter of explanation had to be sent to a customer. "In reply to yours of [Aug.] the 26th," it read, "would say that we received your remittance of $1314.50 as stated. Our cash book has not been posted since Aug. 1st, & I think this must account for our sending you a second statement." [8] Apparently the company's accounting gradually became an historical record of past activities, to be referred to only in case of doubt or controversy. As a live aid to management, it could have performed almost no service.

Knowing virtually nothing of accounting, Marston Whitin was powerless to remedy the situation. Yet, since he made a real effort to put into practical use the little data he had, he must have sensed the need for improvement. One of his first changes in company policy, for instance, was to inaugurate an annual report to stockholders. Previously such reports had hardly been necessary. As late as 1885 there were only five individuals holding company stock, of which the treasurer, Josiah Lasell, and his wife, Jane, owned 89 per cent. By 1889, however, the company's stock had been divided into 12 blocks and had passed into hands other than the treasurer's. The stock held by Marston Whitin and his wife in 1886 accounted for less than a 9 per cent interest in the company. Marston's own share in the company was less than one-tenth of one per cent when he became treasurer (increased to 8 per cent in 1897 and to 10 per cent in 1910). For the first time in the Whitin company's history, ownership and management were not completely identical.

Marston seems to have been quick to sense his new responsibilities to the other members of the ownership group, for they held far larger stakes than he in the concern's financial success and had a right to know how he was managing their affairs. It might be remarked that he did not tell them much, but he did summarize for them, in convenient form, a record of the shop's yearly operations.

As a basis for his reports Marston used the same information that the company submitted to the Commonwealth of Massachusetts in its annual "statements of condition." [9] Contained in these compulsory statements were short, formal balance sheets. Typically, these balance sheets included the following eight items, of which only those in italics were representative of what might be considered reasonably accurate values:

Assets	Liabilities
Cash	*Payables*
Receivables	Reserves
Inventories	Capital
Plant	Surplus

The items not italicized require a sentence or two of explanation. Inventories in the 1880's were valued by a process no longer remembered. Perhaps the procedure was not dissimilar to that in effect at least as early as 1900 (and not abandoned until 1938). If so, the physical volume of inventory was determined as much by weight as by count. Poundage figures were computed by whatever method seemed simplest. The company always kept in mind that it was making only an approximation and so it wasted no time on elaborate refinements. At the end of each year all foremen submitted to the front office an estimate of the pounds of castings on hand in their departments. The weight of finished castings was lumped with the weight of castings not yet machined. Loss of weight resulting from machining was approximated. The front office then multiplied the foremen's weight figures by the dollar costs of the raw materials involved. The value added by labor was also guessed at. Since the shop was so organized that a machine part was generally converted from the raw material (or casting) stage into a finished piece within one and the same department, the foreman of that department had a fairly clear idea of the value of the labor involved in the process. The front office then added raw material and labor values together to get a figure for in-process inventory. No overhead was included.

The completed inventory report was then handed to Marston Whitin, who proceeded to adjust the final sum by whatever amount he thought current business conditions justified — and perhaps to whatever extent he wished to influence his final profit calculations. Not infrequently his write-downs amounted to 20 or 30 per cent. In fact, everything in Whitin's annual statements reflected his constant effort to view profits as conservatively as possible.[10]

Except for the profits continually hidden by persistent undervaluations, it mattered very little in the long run what the company thought its inventories were worth. If inventories were valued at too low a figure in one year, the undervaluation merely tended to increase the profit figure in a subsequent year.* Since there was no income tax, and since there was no trading in Whitin Machine Works stock, neither the government nor the company's stockholders objected to having a portion of the profits concealed during any one period.

The plant account, which included not only land and buildings but machinery and water rights as well, was kept at an unvarying figure of $500,000 from 1878 to 1883.[11] In 1884 it was increased to $525,000 for the apparent purpose of capitalizing a portion of the cost of erecting Shop No. 3.[12] Then for 27 years (until 1910) it remained unchanged, even though during that period the company's productive facilities more than doubled.[13]

On the liability side, the depreciation reserve seems to have been adjusted with similar infrequency. Before 1883 the reserve was allowed to build up gradually until by that year it amounted to $150,000. Then, in 1884, it was summarily reduced to $50,000, apparently to compensate for that part of the cost of Shop No. 3 not added to the plant account. Thereafter, until the introduction of the new accounting system in 1918, a span of 34 years, the depreciation reserve stayed at a figure of $50,000 without a single change.[14]

The capital account was even more static. Established at $600,000 when the company was incorporated, it remained unaltered for fifty-two years, all capital needs being provided for out of earnings. Surplus, the final item, was in effect the balancing account and hence was the repository for all the errors in the other items.

With such figures as these at hand, Marston Whitin, at the end of his first year as treasurer, set about determining the company's first recorded profit figures. Taking the surplus figure (which he had discovered by the derivative method described above) he subtracted the comparable figure for the preceding year. Then, after adding the $36,000 which the company had paid in dividends in the interim, he arrived at a dollar figure — $97,379.85 — which he termed his

---

* In 1918 the accounting firm of Scovell, Wellington & Company, in the process of setting up a modern accounting system for the Whitin Machine Works, re-computed the company's earnings back to 1909. It discovered that the Whitin company's profit figures for the boom years 1909–12 were understated but that for the depressed years 1913–16 they were overstated. Minutes of the Board of Directors' Meeting, 29 May 1918.

"net" profit. However, since a large portion of the company's income during the year had been derived from non-manufacturing sources, Whitin seems to have felt that the "net" figure was deceptively *over*stated. Interest on notes receivable, for instance, amounted to $11,604.71. Gravity spindle royalties (see Chapter X), amounted to another $28,399.02. Consequently Whitin felt that he should deduct those two figures from his "net" profit to arrive at a true "manufacturing" profit — $57,376.12. (A few years later he began deducting also as a non-manufacturing profit the net income received from housing rentals, a figure which during the 1890's amounted to about $10,000 a year.)[15]

Looking at the matter from another angle, Whitin then appears to have considered that for certain purposes his "net" profit was *under*stated rather than *over*stated. Because of the company's policy of keeping its plant and depreciation values at static levels, capital expenditures were in effect treated like current expenses. Consequently, Whitin felt that he should compute still a third figure that would show the amount of his "profit before capital expenditures." This he did by *adding* to his "net" profit all capital expenditures made during the year.

Faulty as it may have been, Whitin's "profit before capital expenditures" is the only source of information on which it is possible to base an estimate of how the company distributed its income. Between 1886 and 1912, Marston Whitin's figures indicate that 46.9 per cent of all profits was plowed back into the company — 18.9 per cent in the form of expanded working capital, 10.1 per cent in new tools, 9.0 per cent in new plant, 6.7 per cent in new employee houses, 1.4 per cent in a reservoir for the village water supply, and 0.8 per cent in the railway connection between the shop and Whitins station. The remaining 53.1 per cent was paid out in dividends.

Of other existing records, Marston Whitin made further ingenious use. Demanding few new statistics, he built upon the old a superstructure of resourceful ratios by which to gauge the company's progress. Some of his ratios were compiled weekly, some monthly. Usually they were submitted to him by the company's paymaster as informal reports. It is unfortunate that, with but few fragmentary exceptions, these reports were destroyed soon after they had served their purpose. But judging from the fragments that have survived, Whitin's control ratios fulfilled, or attempted to fulfill, three primary needs: (a) they gave him information on which to base his machinery prices, (b) they served as a means of checking the effectiveness of the company's quality controls, and (c) they provided a method of detecting weaknesses in cost controls.

Whitin's method of determining his selling prices, one suspects, was not so much absolute as comparative. There is no evidence that the Whitin company had any system of unit costs such as the Pettee shop had.[16] Instead Whitin seems to have determined his prices partly on a basis of what the company's prices had been when he became treasurer, and partly on a basis of average annual costs. Probably he arrived at his estimate of direct costs in much the same manner as he arrived at inventory valuations. But how he figured his burden rate is not clear, although it seems evident that he applied the same rate to all types of machines built. How much he allowed for profit margin is also not evident, but the rate was doubtless sufficient to give him at least a 30 per cent net return on sales, before capital expenditures.[17]

Once having satisfied himself as to the proper price relationship among his various products, Whitin seems to have moved his prices in a fairly set pattern. For instance, the list price of cards for many years after 1896 was always 200 times the price of a standard spinning frame per spindle. Thus, when a frame was selling for $3.25 per spindle, a card sold for $650.[18]

The prices of various sizes of frames likewise moved in constant ratio. Once a base price had been set for a standard machine, all prices for larger or smaller machines of that type were computed by multiplying the standard price by constant ratio figures.* At least some of the ratio figures seem to have been carefully computed. The

* For instance, a spinning frame with a certain size of ring and a certain number of spindles might be picked as a "standard" frame, in which case it was given a constant ratio number of 100. A slightly larger frame might be given a ratio of 110, and a still larger one a ratio of 125, and so on. When standard frames were selling at $3.00 a spindle, frames that carried a ratio of 110 automatically sold for $3.30. It is not unlikely that the ratio figures used by the Whitin Machine Works were computed by someone in a competitor's employ, since the same ratios seem to have been commonly used by the industry at large.

company's present roving-frame ratios have remained unaltered for at least 35 years and perhaps longer,[19] yet they are still considered fairly accurate even by the best modern accounting methods.

Apparently in an effort to determine if and when the whole price structure needed adjustment, Whitin watched a few indices that were computed for him by the paymaster, Arba S. Noyes. One of these indices was the per-pound cost of pig iron. So important was this item in the manufacture of textile machinery that Marston Whitin made all the company's pig-iron purchases personally.[20] He also kept a careful, weekly check on the cost (including raw materials, labor, and supplies) of rough castings per pound, knowing that a steady rise in castings costs would necessitate a boost in the price of all machinery. Total labor costs, the shop's biggest single manufacturing expense, were computed only once a month, as a percentage of dollar sales. Whenever labor costs exceeded 40 per cent of sales, Whitin considered an increase in prices. (It is said that whenever they reached as high as 45 per cent of sales, the company's employees knew from experience that it was useless to ask for a raise.)

The ratio of coke consumption per pound of iron cast in the foundry seems to have been computed solely for purposes of quality control. How valuable a device it was is open to doubt. On one occasion Whitin wrote, "We think the Davis coke is not giving us as good results as when we first commenced its use, as it seems to take more coke per pound of iron." [21] But since poor iron would have produced the same result, the ratio was presumably valuable simply as an indication that something was amiss in the foundry cupolas.

The calculation of foundry labor costs per pound of castings produced seems to have fallen into a third category of ratios, the category of cost controls. C. T. Moffett, assistant foundry foreman from 1894 to 1899 and foreman from 1899 to 1937, remembers that a report showing a rise in the ratio of labor cost to pounds of castings produced was almost always followed by a visit to the foundry by both Marston Whitin and Cyrus Taft. Usually Moffett was able to explain the ratio's rise by showing that there had been an exceptionally large run of light castings during the month. Since light castings required a proportionately greater amount of work per pound than heavy ones did, the cost per pound was almost certain to increase whenever the number of light castings poured was larger than usual. It seems that Whitin and Taft were generally satisfied by whatever explanation Moffett had to offer, for the last-mentioned can remember no occasion on which a high labor cost ratio resulted in remedial action. However, the fact that such cost ratios kept him constantly alert to cost variances was in itself probably beneficial.

On balance, one cannot feel confident that Marston Whitin's control schemes would have worked had it not been for the man himself. After all, accounting figures can only indicate the existence of a problem — they cannot effect its solution. It takes an executive of considerable competence to do that. To some extent, of course, accounting does perform the scalpel service of cutting through masses of detail into the heart of production problems, but Marston Whitin seems to have been gifted with an almost intuitive sense of what was important and what was not. Among those who worked with him, he is remembered as having had an astonishingly quick grasp of figures and an undeviating sureness of the correct way to get manufacturing results. Finally, and in the last analysis, accounting controls are useful chiefly as substitutes for on-the-spot observation. But Whitin, it seems, was so familiar with the shop that he really had no need for such substitutes. Weeks before a situation began to show up in his somewhat haphazard accounts he doubtless already had become aware of its existence. Not for another generation — by which time the plant had doubled in size — did shop operations become so complex that one man could not comprehend the whole without the assistance of a refined reporting mechanism. By that time, Marston Whitin was in retirement and another family member had taken his place.

CHAPTER IX

THE VILLAGE SOCIETY, 1888–1900

WHEN George Marston Whitin assumed the treasurership of the Whitin Machine Works, the bracing atmosphere of a new régime was at once distinguishable. The younger members of the Whitin and Lasell familes, having less of the austerity that characterized their elders and more of the zest and enthusiasm for good living that is so often typical of the third and fourth generations in well-to-do families, felt that life held more for them than the constant, fifty-week-a-year attention to business that their forefathers had given. For the first time, the family tasted the pleasures of a social life made possible by the continuing productivity of the factory in the valley.

At the same time, but at the other extreme, the new management under Marston Whitin was following a course of action that was further extending the social spread in the village. To provide the shop with the additional workers it needed, Marston initiated the hiring of large numbers of European workmen, giving them their first jobs in America. Within a few years the very nearly classless structure that Whitinsville had known under John C. Whitin and Josiah Lasell had given way to a clearly defined stratification. The heterogeneity of Whitinsville's present-day social structure may be traced directly to the period between 1888 and 1900 when the Whitin family was deciding to take advantage of its wealth in consumptive living and when the Whitin company was choosing to increase its labor force by hiring workers who had only recently come from the overcrowded and underprivileged sections of Europe.

1. WORKER GROUPS

Before the 1880's the population of Whitinsville was not unlike that of most New England villages of the period. The inhabitants were predominantly of Yankee stock, descendants of early New England settlers. Those who were not Yankee were either English, Irish, or French Canadian.

The English constituted the foreman group. They were hired because of the skills they had learned in the Old Country and because they were able to teach Whitin workers the superior methods they had seen used in English machine shops. They were never numerous, but they held key positions in the community's economic life. The small Episcopal church in Whitinsville still stands as a tribute to that band of skilled employees who brought to the village their knowledge and their religion.

It is said that the first "foreigners" to move into Whitinsville were the Irish, who came as day laborers in the 1840's. By the Civil War period perhaps as much as a quarter of Whitinsville's population stemmed from either the northern or the southern part of the Emerald Isle. In general the Irish were assigned those jobs where work was the heaviest, particularly jobs in the foundry. Among the second-generation Irish, however, there were many who refused to endure the hardships of foundry work and who preferred to work in the shop's machining departments even at lower pay. Thus, when business began to pick up in 1886, the foundry was the first to feel the pinch for manpower.

After the depression reached its nadir in the summer of 1885, employment began a steady rise. By 1888 the payroll was carrying more names than at any time in previous history.* So inadequate was the local labor market, in view of the growing demand, that some means had to be found to swell the population in the surrounding area. At first French Canadians were hired to work in the shop. For years there had been families of French descent in Whitinsville, but they had lived on the south side of the river (in the houses owned by the Charles P. Whitin branch of the family) and had worked only in the Whitinsville Cotton Mills. After 1886, however, the Whitin Machine Works employed French Canadians in large numbers, a dozen or more new names being added to the pay lists every month. Whether the company depended wholly on recruits from the Black-

---

* To house the expanded work force, the company built (in 1888) 16 two-family houses on Maple Street at a cost of about $40,000.

stone Valley's large French Canadian population or whether it attempted to obtain workers from Quebec is not known. (One old-time foreman recalls that Worcester employment agents frequently visited Whitinsville with offers to procure men for the shop.)[1] But for every three French Canadians hired, only one became a perma-nent employee, so rapid was the turnover. Nevertheless, by 1893 there were listed on the Whitin payrolls more than sixty employees with French names. Docile workers, loyal and industrious, the French Canadians came to be one of the important national elements in the Whitin shop.[2]

Many of the French accepted jobs in the foundry, but still there remained a labor shortage in that department. In his concern over the scarcity of foundrymen, George Marston Whitin is said to have counseled with William Draper, who was experiencing similar diffi-culties.[3] The Drapers' textile machinery company in Hopedale was only about ten miles east of Whitinsville. In many respects the vil-lage of Hopedale was similar to Whitinsville, being company-dominated and largely family-owned. But it was separated from Whitinsville by a ridge of hills that discouraged east-west travel. Even today there are few cross-country roads in that locality and there is little travel in an east-west direction. The two companies were thus separated enough to be free of competition for their labor supply, yet were near enough to be similarly affected by the general labor conditions of the region. Not infrequently William Draper and Marston Whitin met to exchange information concerning their labor problems.[4] In hiring men for his foundry, Draper is said to have had trouble with some Italians and is believed to have recom-mended that Whitin try to obtain Armenians.

At about that time many Armenians were taking flight from Turkish oppression and were making their way to this country. Per-haps the company's first Armenian workmen were obtained through the listings of employment agencies in New York; at least, it is known that at times the firm did make use of that method of pro-curing laborers.[5] By 1888 the distinctive -ian endings of Armenian surnames were beginning to appear frequently on company pay lists. Once settled in Whitinsville, the new immigrants immediately strove to accumulate enough cash to finance the escape of their relatives and friends.[6] Within five years the number of Armenian names appearing on Whitin pay lists swelled to more than forty-five.

In 1894 and 1895, when Armenians in the homeland were being massacred by the Turks, the number of Armenians newly hired by the Whitin company was more than offset by the number who quit in protest over the company's refusal to discharge a handful of Turkish employees. To win their point, a few radical Armenians attempted to lead their compatriots out on strike, but failing ignominiously, they departed, half in indignation, half in disrepute.[7] In the midst of this carryover of Old World animosities, the company seems to have maintained an attitude of aloof neutrality.* Like the French Canadians, the Armenians often worked for a short while and then moved on to other localities. Yet gradually there was built up in Whitinsville one of the largest per capita concentrations of Armenians in the United States.[8]

Being able business men, many second-generation Armenians rose to a middle-class status in the village. Exercising their seemingly innate urge to own property they came to possess a large portion of the privately owned (as against company-owned) real estate in Whitinsville. As small shopkeepers they also gained prominence beyond the proportion of their numbers. By World War II, Armenians were the owners of two clothing stores, a private money-lending agency, two small grocery stores, two cobbler shops, and a tailoring establishment. One might add that the presidency of the machineshop union, a salaried office, is held by a man of Armenian descent.

A third national group, the Dutch, came to Whitinsville almost by chance. According to the recollection of some of the older Dutch residents in the village, the first Dutch settlers came as the result of a purchase of Holstein-Friesian cattle for the farm on Castle Hill in 1886.[9] After John C. Whitin's death, the farm which for so many years had been his hobby was maintained by his widow. Within a

---

* In a letter written 17 December 1895 to the Turkish consulate, Boston, J. M. Lasell reported, " . . . the trouble with our Armenians was very slight and lasted but a few days. The Armenians requested us to dismiss three or four Turks in our employ, stating that unless we did so they should stop work. We declined to dismiss the Turks and the Armenians went out. They remained out about two days when the larger part of them returned to work. We think the Armenians acted on the bad advice of one or two men who did not understand the situation."

few years, however, a scourge of tuberculosis had nearly wiped out the farm's herd of registered Jersey cattle. An old notebook has survived to disclose that, by the early part of 1886, fifteen of the twenty-six registered cows were dead. To restock her herd, Mrs. Whitin ordered an unrecorded number of Holsteins sent over from the Netherlands.

Accompanying the cows on their ocean voyage was a Frisian lad named John Bosma. Upon arrival in Whitinsville, in the spring of 1886, Bosma asked to be allowed to stay and work on the farm. Soon he was sending home for his relatives. In May, 1887,[10] a sister and her husband, William B. Feddema, arrived, followed by Feddema's brother, Peter, and, in September, 1888, by Peter's wife and five children. The group expanded rapidly, drawing always on the Frisian Dutch. Around 1895 the arrival of a Dutch Reformed lay leader, F. J. Drost,[11] attracted to Whitinsville many of the church-loving Frisians who had already settled in other parts of the United States but who were eager to live where regular Sunday worship was possible.[12] By the middle of 1893 the company was employing at least sixty men with names that were unmistakably Dutch.

With typical thrift and industry the Frisians quickly distinguished themselves from the ranks of the laborers. Of those who worked in the shop many became foremen. Of those who established an enterprise of their own, most went into dairy farming, the only agricultural industry which the rocky slopes of the Northbridge countryside would profitably support. By World War II, nearly 65 per cent of the privately owned (again as distinguished from company-owned) cattle in Northbridge were in the hands of Dutch farmers.[13]

The heavy influx of foreign nationals, which had begun about 1888, had spent its force by 1900, although immigration to Whitinsville did not die out completely until the beginning of World War I. After 1900 most of the new labor recruits came not from abroad but from the Penobscot Bay region of Maine.* Occasionally in the years before 1900, natives of Maine had found their way to Whitinsville, but their number had not been large. One of the early Maine men was Benjamin R. Graves, foreman of the comber department,

---

* Most of the Maine men came from within a radius of ten miles of the town of Rockland.

which was newly established in 1899. Starting with an initial crew of ten men, Graves rapidly developed his department until by the end of 1902 he had nearly a hundred men under his supervision. Most of those whom Graves induced to work for him were friends and acquaintances of his from "down home." Proving themselves intelligent and industrious, these men soon convinced the management of the company that more of their like would be an asset to the plant's work force. Consequently Graves was encouraged to use his summer vacations in Maine as recruiting trips for the shop. Through his wide range of acquaintances and through advertisements in local newspapers he encouraged as many as thirty or forty young men at a time to take jobs at the Whitin Machine Works.

The "down-homers" or "Mainiacs," as they were jocularly called, made excellent machinists, for they had great mechanical talent. But most of them looked upon their factory jobs solely as a wintertime occupation. In the summer they returned to their homes to fish, to work in the quarries, to farm, or to sail the yachts of wealthy Boston and New York vacationers. In the shop the summertime absence of the down-homers was looked upon as a matter of course. What better indication of the leisurely manner in which the company was run in those days!

The various national groups, although they mixed freely in the shop, held rather closely to themselves in after-work hours. For the Irish and the French Canadians, life centered around the Catholic Church and its numerous affiliated organizations. For the Dutch, too, the nucleus of social existence was their Church in which services were conducted in their homeland language. For their children, there was the Church-sponsored Dutch grammar school established to combat the heretical theories of evolution that were being taught in the public schools. It was not until the period of World War II that the Dutch finally abandoned their esoteric custom of conducting religious services in their native tongue. Even then they continued to maintain their own redundant elementary school.

The Armenians, having no local church, formed New World counterparts to the political societies they had known in the Old Country. The Armenian Revolutionary Federation, established initially to help promote the overthrow of the Turkish government, became by far the strongest of the Armenian organizations in the village. Belying its name, it came to represent the moderates who wished to see Armenia made an independent republic. The Social Democrat Hunchagist group, on the other hand, voiced its radicalism by approving the 1920 absorption of Armenia into the Soviet sisterhood of states. As the burning question of Armenian independence lost some of its fire, the political activities of the two groups gradually faded until they became little more than social clubs. Still they continued to stand apart from each other. The "Dashnags," or liberal republicans of the Armenian Revolutionary Federation, came to follow the social and intellectual leadership of the *Hairenik* (Fatherland), a newspaper published at the Federation's headquarters in Boston. The pro-Soviet (but not pro-Communist) group, the "Hunchaks," came to look to the New York newspaper, *Yeridasard Hayastan* (Young Armenia),[14] for political guidance. Each group established its own clubhouse and led its independent social existence.*

Before the 1880's the village churches (among which the Congregational and Catholic were by far the strongest) served as the principal social centers of the community. Choir rehearsals, church suppers, prayer meetings, and missionary gatherings helped to enliven the workaday drudgery of a small-town existence. But as the population of the town increased and as the age of skepticism reached out to shake man's religious faith, the churches began to lose their prominence as the focal points of society.

Supplementing the ritual and camaraderie of the religious service there sprang up in Whitinsville, especially during the 1880's and 1890's, a host of secret fraternal orders. An enumeration of but a few of the larger societies will indicate the nature of the movement. Among the earliest were the Irish-sponsored Ancient Order of Hibernians (1873) and the Knights of Pythias (1874). The Ancient Free and Accepted Masons lodge was established there in 1880, the Independent Order of Odd Fellows in 1882, both the Order of the

---

* There is a third Armenian group in Whitinsville, but its number is very small and its social affiliations are with the Hunchaks. Designated "Ramgavars," the members of this group read the *Baikar* (the Fight) newspaper published in Boston. Like the Hunchaks they are content to see Armenia's status quo — that is, its inclusion in the Soviet Union — maintained.

Eastern Star and the Social Rebekah Lodge in 1887, the Ancient Order of Foresters of America in 1891, and the Eureka Temple Pythian Sisters in 1895.[15]

These organizations, in addition to performing a social function, served as mutual-assistance societies in a period when health and accident insurance was all but unknown. Beginning in 1889, the company insured itself with the American Mutual Liability Insurance Company, but in order to secure the lowest rates possible it sought coverage only for accidents in the shop that resulted in suits for damages. All other claims it settled privately, if the injured person was not otherwise provided for by one of the secret societies.

When the Massachusetts legislature, in 1904, took up the consideration of compulsory accident insurance, the Whitin company's methods were looked to as a model by several of the other manufacturing concerns in the area. Answering a letter of inquiry from Henry D. Sharpe of the Brown & Sharpe Manufacturing Company, of Providence, Marston described the personal basis on which his company dealt with accidental injuries:

When a man is injured while doing his work we invariably pay him all or a portion of his time, during the period of disablement, and also the expenses of medical attendance and care, where the resources of the man in question are limited. With this method, the insurance policy we have is not in sympathy as we secure a low rate in consideration of the fact that we waive the right to apply to the insurance company for aid in such cases. We have been very fortunate both in regard to the number of accidents we have had here for the last few years with the exception of one recent case, where, through the bursting of a steam pipe, one man was killed and another badly scalded.* These 2 cases the Insurance people have in hand for adjustment and are practically the only instances where the Insurance Company has taken hold of any of our cases for the last 7 or 8 years. . . . The only practical benefit we receive is the immunity from damage by law suit and as we try in every case to avoid such contingency, the actual benefit from our insurance is very slight.

---

* It is said that two doctors were called to administer to the scalds of the man who survived. One of the doctors believed in using ointments for scalds, one in using saline solutions. To hasten their work, each treated one half of the scalded man's back, each using his favorite technique. The sides are said to have healed equally well.

At about the same time Marston wrote a similar letter to George A. Draper:

It must be borne in mind that we have in our village some twenty odd secret societies and there are very few of our employees who do not belong to one or more of these and, when hurt, receive weekly benefits and other assistance. It is not our policy to indemnify men for their time lost when they receive this aid from other sources and this being understood accounts for some of the cases where no request for help has been made — probably, in fact, the majority of them.

We frequently, where the circumstances of men do not warrant their receiving too much consideration, only partially assist; but where men have families and are dependent on their wages from week to week, our policy is to see that they lose nothing pecuniarily.

Marston made it clear in his letters that he believed the company had a responsibility to employees who were injured. But he also made it clear that he thought government intervention in employee welfare should be resisted, since it deprived management of all possible exercise of discretion by requiring that standardized benefits be given to the deserving and the undeserving alike. In a later part of the letter quoted immediately above, Whitin wrote:

We are not very familiar with the proposed legislative scheme compelling corporations to insure their help against accidents. It seems to us that any statute obliging us to do what is and has been our custom would work greatly to our injury in that it would mean much additional expense, make it possible for employees who so desired to put in fraudulent claims, or unnecessarily prolong their period of idleness (which would require constant attention on our part to properly follow up), and be the cause of many disputes with, and more or less hard feelings from, numbers of our men; whereas, under present conditions we have the satisfaction of knowing that our mutual relations are most amicable and that our employees feel that our position towards them is liberal and just.

The 1880's also saw the beginning of Whitinsville's prohibition era. For many years a strong anti-saloon feeling had existed in Whitinsville, early evidence of which may be found in property deeds drawn up for Grandmother Betsey Whitin. By such deeds Betsey tried to make sure not only that no buildings would be erected closer to the road than 25 feet but that no intoxicating beverages would be sold in any buildings erected.[16] Apparently the early opposition to drinking was very strong, for in 1831, only two years after the country's first known ban on liquor sales, the town of Northbridge voted not to grant any liquor licenses during the year.[17] The following year, however, the ban was revoked, to be clamped on again only once (in 1835) in the ensuing twenty years. Beginning in 1852 the Commonwealth of Massachusetts made various attempts to enforce either moderation or outright prohibition but with indifferent success.[18] Finally in 1875 the state adopted local option under which, in 1881, Northbridge again chose to forbid the sale of intoxicants. For 37 years thereafter the voters of the community consistently refused to allow the granting of liquor licenses, although in the years 1881, 1890, 1891, and 1892, the heavy voting and near upsets indicate that from time to time there must have been spirited opposition to the measure.[19] Finally in 1919, when ratification of the Eighteenth Amendment was certain, the people of Northbridge, in a display of Yankee independence, voted to allow the sale of liquor in their town.*

2. THE SUPERVISORY GROUP

No doubt in the 1880's one could easily have named all the people in the village who were neither day laborers nor members of the Whitin family. There were, for instance, the Tafts and the Trowbridges. The Tafts were descendants of Gustavus E. Taft, the shop's able superintendent and agent. The Trowbridges were associates of one of the cotton-mill branches of the Whitin family and were key men in the management of the village's only other metal-working concern, a spinning ring shop.

The Taft fortune consisted, in part, of the savings put aside by

---

* The Worcester *Evening Gazette* of 15 April 1919 explained the upset in the Northbridge liquor vote as follows: "The people consider the bone dry prohibitory amendment an encroachment on their liberties, and, as a rebuke, voted in favor of licenses in many towns and cities that have been in the dry column for years. Here in Northbridge another reason is advanced. . . . What the voters really wanted, and the thing that made them sore, was stopping the pony license that brought the goods [from outside of town] right to their doors."

Gustavus out of his salary of about $15,000 a year and, in part, of the block of Whitin Machine Works stock that John C. Whitin had given him in 1875 in recognition of his services to the firm. By 1888 Taft had received $168,300 in dividends from the company.

Taft had three sons, Cyrus, William, and Edmund, all of whom worked for the Whitin company at one time or another. Cyrus followed his father as company agent, remaining in that position from 1888 until his retirement about 1902. William served for seven years (1891-97) as superintendent of the machine shop. Edmund spent several years on the road working as an erector. But inasmuch as Gustavus had left his sons financially independent, all three were able to retire at fairly early ages.

Since the Tafts did not figure in the management of the company after 1902, the story of their retirement from company ownership might well be included here. In 1908 Cyrus Taft died, leaving his property in trust. William died in the following year, leaving his possessions to his two daughters. The death of the two Taft brothers made the members of the Whitin family realize that the Taft stock was in danger of becoming widely scattered; therefore, early in 1910 the Whitins offered to buy all the outstanding Taft-held shares, including those owned by Edmund, the still-surviving brother. Whatever agreement was reached among the various parties was a personal and not a company transaction; hence the terms are not a matter of corporate record, but it is understood that the daughters of William took cash for their stock while Edmund chose to take New England cotton-mill securities for his.[20] On the pages of most business histories the next sentence would read: "Had William's children agreed to take stock instead of cash they would now be millionaires." But in this case tradition did not hold to form. As mill after mill in the North went through bankruptcy during the 1920's, Edmund's fortune in stocks virtually vanished. In contrast, William's two daughters went through the depression without heavy losses and are still comfortably well off.[21]

The Charles E. Trowbridge family, like the Tafts, rose to prominence in the village through business associations with one of the Whitin family members. During 1871 and 1872 Charles Trowbridge, the master mechanic of the Whitinsville Cotton Mills, and Arthur F.

Whitin, a nephew of John C. and a son of the owner of the Whitinsville mills, obtained several patents on spinning rings and on the
ring-making process by which they were able to produce superior
rings faster and at less cost than had formerly been possible.[22]
With money borrowed from his father, Arthur formed a partnership with Charles on 1 January 1873, and, under the firm name of
the Whitinsville Spinning Ring Company, set up shop to manufacture spinning rings in the old brick mill built by P. Whitin & Sons
in 1826. Although they employed at most only fifty or sixty men,
the partners did very well, partly because until 1912 they sold the
Whitin Machine Works all the rings it installed in its spinning
frames[23] and partly because they turned out a product of superlative quality.*

On a social plane just below the Tafts and the Trowbridges were
the foremen of the Whitin Machine Works. At a time when shop
management was strictly departmentalized, the foremen held positions of key importance. They were all well paid, often earning
enough to own their own homes, to send their children to college,
and eventually to retire in modest comfort. Because of their level
of income and their importance in the shop, they occupied a high
position in the village social scale. Without important exceptions
all were of English or Yankee descent. In fact, other than Anglo-
Saxon names did not begin to appear on the list of department heads
until after 1904. Having a remarkable social cohesiveness, they
formed a distinct group within the village, attending their own
dancing parties and holding their own annual picnics. But for reasons which have, in part, already been set forth, their class gradually

---

* Trowbridge had only two children, a son, George, who succeeded him in the
ring shop, and a daughter, Elizabeth, who never married. During his father's life-
time, George served as superintendent of the shop and was a partner in the concern.
He in turn had two daughters, one of whom, Clara, did not marry, while the other,
Ruth, became the wife of Stuart F. Brown, production manager of the Whitin
Machine Works. When George died in 1920, he left his share in the firm to Arthur
Whitin, who thereupon admitted young Brown as a junior partner. Upon the death of
Arthur Whitin in 1928 the Trowbridge interests bought Whitin's stock in the company (the ring shop had meanwhile been incorporated in 1923) and continued the
company's operation under Stuart Brown's management. After the Whitinsville Cotton Mills closed in 1923, the Whitinsville Spinning Ring Company was left the only
manufacturing concern in Whitinsville other than the Whitin Machine Works.

disintegrated. In a few instances the sons of foremen followed in their father's footsteps, but more commonly they took advantage of their college training to become professional men. As a result, the old English and Yankee foreman class gradually disappeared, and in its place there arose a heterogeneous and socially disunited foreman group composed of men from all the nationalities in the village.

It was probably inevitable that the merchant and professional groups in Whitinsville should fail to keep pace with the growing worker group. Since Whitinsville was a small and almost exclusively manufacturing community, there was insufficient purchasing power among its wage-earner inhabitants to attract business men of the petty capitalist type. Moreover, the gradual absorption of Whitinsville into the economy of the Worcester area, already well under way by the late 1880's, was hastened during the 1890's by the construction of an electric street-railway line between Northbridge and Worcester. As villagers found travel to the larger shopping center increasingly easy, they began to rely on Worcester department stores for clothing and durable consumers' goods and on city doctors and lawyers for specialized medical care and legal advice. (It is significant that even now Whitinsville has only a small hospital, which it uses principally for emergencies and lying-in cases. For other hospital purposes nearly everyone in the village looks to Worcester.) [24]

The streetcar line that brought Worcester within easy commuting distance of Northbridge consisted of a series of extended links, the last of which reached Rockdale in 1894.[25] For the following six depression years further construction was abandoned, so that whoever would make the trip from Whitinsville to Worcester had first to drive to Rockdale by carriage, there to catch the interurban car. Of course railroad travel was still available, but its schedules were neither so complete nor so convenient as the electric trolley's. Finally, in 1900, the construction of two spur lines into the village brought Whitinsville within the Worcester interurban system. The first spur, coming down Church Street from the northeast, was built by the Worcester & Blackstone Valley Street Railway Company.[26] The second, coming down Linwood Avenue from the southeast, is of special significance to Whitin history, not only because the line was constructed and operated by the Whitin Machine Works, but also because it carried passengers from Whitinsville to Linwood and hauled freight between the shop and the Whitins railroad station; then, too, over it was run what is believed to have been the first electric freight locomotive built in America. A picture of the locomotive is shown on a preceding page and a discussion of its history may be found in Appendix 12.

3. THE FAMILY

As Whitinsville began looking toward Worcester economically, so also did the Whitin family turn toward the nearby city socially. Many of the Whitin children began attending dancing classes in town and eventually married scions of Worcester's leading business families. Among the Worcesterites with whom the Whitins formed alliances were Sydney R. Mason, whose family manufactured brushes, Matthew and Edgeworth Whittall of the Whittall carpet family, Frances Sumner of the department store Sumners, and John E. Sawyer, whose father was a leading dealer in building supplies.

Yet the social influence of Worcester on Northbridge can easily be overstressed. Worcester was simply the farthest afield the Whitins cared to venture. Their social life centered predominantly in the Blackstone Valley, where many other similar families had built communities around their closely held mills and shops. Among the leading families of the valley existed an extensive social intercourse, which lessened their dependence on Boston, Newport, or New York for social outlet. Virtually the only function which attracted the Whitins to Boston was the weekly symphony concert to which the women of the family were loyal subscribers.

The self-sufficiency of life in Whitinsville is best illustrated by the manner in which the Whitin children selected their husbands and wives. In John C. Whitin's generation, all the boys married girls born no farther than 15 miles from Whitinsville. In succeeding generations the Whitins chose marriage partners from a wider area, but still they characteristically met those partners in Whitinsville or through their Whitinsville relatives. Partly as a result of that compactness of the family inner circle, intermarriages within the family were frequent. Often such matches were not blood ties but were alliances between two Whitins and two members of some other family. For instance, two Whittalls, brother and sister, married two Whitins, sister and brother (see Chart VII). Likewise, two Keelers, a sister and a brother, married an uncle and a niece in the Whitin clan. Then, too, a grandaunt and a grandniece in the Pratt-Krum family married a grandfather and a grandson of Whitin-Lasell kin. As one of the direct results of these involved family ties, the family-owned business ventures in Whitinsville were for generations very closely held.

Family solidarity also influenced and flavored the lives of the villagers. Family parties highlighted the social season, and the family's participation in village festivities was a necessary part of their success. But one should not mistake the close identification of the family and the village for social homogeneity. For a villager an invitation to attend a social function on the "hill" was a rare and coveted privilege. The best indication of the gap that existed between those who lived in the valley and those who lived on the hill is the fact that, after John C. Whitin's generation, marriages between the two groups were rare. On the other hand, the Whitins were careful to avoid all appearances of being superior to their neighbors in the valley. In a New England community as democratic as Whitinsville, the owner class would quickly have alienated the loyalty of its employees had it seemed unduly influenced by considerations of social status. Furthermore, the Whitins were New Englanders themselves and so found it easy to be democratic and even self-effacing.

With unassuming diligence the women of the family served on village committees, entertained local clubs, and lent moral as well as financial support to drives for charitable purposes. In no respect was their reticence more marked than in their manner of handling charities. Eschewing any attitude of *noblesse oblige,* they followed the dictum that he is best helped who is encouraged to help himself. For that reason their charities were individually small and generally unobtrusive. Yet in the aggregate they totaled far more than anyone in the village realized. The administration of the Arthur Whitin estate is a case in point. When Arthur Whitin died without direct heirs, he made the village of Whitinsville his residual legatee. The income from his estate was to be spent for civic purposes by a group of town officials who, as it has turned out, were also in some cases members of the family.* Over the years the administrators helped a multitude of worthy causes, quietly, inconspicuously, and without thought of earning personal recognition. Yet so anonymously did they handle their trust that, if you were to ask a chance passer-by in Whitinsville what had become of Arthur Whitin's fortune, you would probably be told either that the old man had died bankrupt or that the settling of his estate had consumed whatever money he had left in his will.

To speak of the Whitins as though they were all alike is of course to over-generalize. By the 1880's the family had split into four distinct groups, each group descended from one of the four sons of Paul Whitin. Even within each group there were naturally many dissimilarities of personality. Josiah Lasell seems to have introduced to the inherited characteristics of the machine-shop branch of the family a completely different set of traits. The Lasells were warm-hearted, sensitive, artistic people, socially gracious and fond of good living. The Whitins were tense-lipped, stern-countenanced drivers, men and women alike. They had no social ambitions; they lived without ostentation; and they believed in spending their time constructively.

In the machine-shop branch, the fourth generation's only members were the two daughters and two sons of Jane Whitin and Josiah Lasell (see genealogy, Chart VII). One of the daughters, Jeannie, died without issue soon after her marriage to Dr. Ogden Backus, a physician from Rochester, New York. The other daughter, Catharine, became the wife of George Marston Whitin. Catharine participated in social life somewhat less than her two sisters-in-law did, for her existence was much more strictly governed by the demands of the business than theirs was. Because Catharine's husband was active head of the company and was expected to greet and entertain all visiting customers, Catharine was frequently called upon to perform as official company hostess. During her husband's early

---

* The trust still exists. Its administrators are the president of the Whitinsville National Bank, the parson of the Congregational Church, and a townsperson appointed by the Judge of Probate.

years as treasurer, the South was becoming an important market for Whitin machinery, and Southern mill owners were beginning to arrive at Northern shops with sizable orders in their pockets. Often the hospitality of a host was one of the important criteria on which a Southerner based his decision to do business with a particular Yankee firm. Fortunately, Catharine Whitin was a cordial hostess and hence an invaluable business asset to her husband.

There are some women who, one suspects, would have made excellent business executives had they decided on a career. Catharine Whitin was such a person. Strong-willed, energetic, sharp-witted, she was the firm mistress of her household. It has been said in jest that one of the reasons for the business success of the men in the Whitin family was that the women of the family gave them little opportunity for outlet at home. Because her husband was bound and tied to his work, Catharine had ample opportunities to develop her independence of spirit. At home she was the disciplinarian of her four daughters, Marston being too indulgent a father to reprimand or punish them. In town she was active in many a religious and charitable organization. Beyond the village she traveled frequently, taking along her children or a traveling companion or, whenever she could entice him away, her husband.

It was on a trip to Boston that she met and formed one of the closest associations of her life — her friendship with the glittering and unconventional actress, Ada Rehan. Catharine had seen the famous Irish comedienne perform and, after the play, had sent flowers backstage. Something in the note accompanying Catharine's bouquet had attracted Miss Rehan's fancy and had led her to arrange an interview. From that meeting there developed an intimate friendship between the two women — the one a toast of the Old and New Worlds, the other a wealthy matron. In 1893 or 1894, after a serious fall from her horse, Catharine was urged by her family to travel abroad for her health. While she was in London, where Ada Rehan was playing, she commissioned John Singer Sargent to do a portrait of the actress, now one of the prize Sargent pieces owned by the Metropolitan Museum of Art in New York.*

* The painting was left to the Metropolitan Museum by the terms of Mrs. Whitin's will.

Catharine's brother, Chester, the older of the two Lasell brothers, was every inch a Lasell, just as Catharine was every inch a Whitin. Chester attended Phillips Andover Academy, following which he toured for a time in Europe. Like all the other young men in the family, he then entered the company to serve an apprenticeship in the foundry and machinery departments.[27] In 1885, at the age of twenty-four, he met and became engaged to the daughter of a Lincoln-appointed provost-marshall of the Oregon Territory, Jessie Maud Keeler. Jessie was born in Salem, Oregon, but had spent most of her youth in booming San Francisco where her father had become interested in mining ventures. Upon completion of her education at the well-known Mills school for girls in Oakland, California (the year was 1884), she had embarked on an extended tour of the East accompanied by an older friend of her family. In the course of the trip the two women visited the Josiah Lasells, distant relatives of Jessie's traveling companion. Chester was immediately fascinated by the verve of his family's lovely young visitor and before long was married to her at the home of relatives in Wallingford, Pennsylvania. It was while the two were on their wedding trip to visit the bride's parents in California that they received news of the death of Chester's father, Josiah Lasell.

Returning to Whitinsville as soon as they could, the young Lasells settled temporarily in a small cottage on Church Street where they lived while a home was being built for them amidst the oaks and virgin pine across the road and up the hill from the John C. Whitin residence. An attack of typhoid fever prevented Chester from beginning work at once, but as soon as he was on his feet, he took up duties in the company's front office. At the first board of directors' meeting after his father's death (held 17 January 1887), he was elected president of the company, a position of honor that he was to hold throughout his life.

For about seven years (1890-96) Chester handled much of the company's correspondence, especially that portion of it dealing with customer relations. But the confining life of a business man held little appeal for him. He was a lover of the out-of-doors, a great sportsman, and an enthusiastic horse-fancier. After 1896 he gradually retired from business and, with the same unstinting energy that an earnest business man expends on his job, devoted his time to the breeding and racing of horses.* His Oakhurst Farm came to boast one of New England's finest stables, and his trotters, which he always raced in person, soon were recognized as among the best in the New England circuit.[28]

Chester's enthusiasm for horses was shared and abetted by his witty and vivacious wife.[29] In those days the social life in Whitinsville centered in horses, and anyone who would cut a social swathe had to be adept at riding. Each man, woman, and child in the Whitin family owned a horse. The Grafton Hunt and the Blackstone Valley Hunt were favorite convivial foci. For about a generation (roughly 1885–1910), society in the Blackstone Valley paralleled closely the life of the gentry in rural England. The environment was countrified, the pace of life was leisurely, the place of entertainment was the out-of-doors, and the nexus of society was the established family group. Jessie's spirited participation in riding events made her one of the most popular hostesses in the valley. Her hunt breakfasts were traditionally bountiful affairs, attracting at least on one occasion over a hundred guests.

Chester's younger brother, Josiah M. Lasell, married a girl whom he had met through his step-grandmother, Sarah Elizabeth Whitin.[30] It will be recalled that Josiah M.'s grandfather, John C. Whitin, after the death of his first wife, had married a former school companion of his daughter, a woman many years his junior. The second Mrs. John C. Whitin was a person of wide acquaintance and considerable charm. After her graduation from the Lasell Seminary for Young Women, she had spent much of her time in Washington, D. C., at the home of her sister, Mrs. Samuel Clarke Pomeroy,† the wife of a prominent Republican who, from 1861 to 1873, served in Washington as one of Kansas' first two senators.[31] At the Pomeroys', the future Mrs. Whitin developed the art and charm of an accomplished hostess and came to know well the social and political élite of Capital circles. Even following her marriage to John

---

* After 1896 few letters in the company's letterbooks are signed by Chester. It is said that he grew so impatient with business affairs that he even objected to the check-signing duty imposed on him by his position as company president.

† Wellesley's Pomeroy Hall and Whitin Observatory stand as lasting evidences of the financial support given the college by the two sisters.

C. Whitin, she often visited Washington and frequently she opened her Whitinsville home to week-end parties honoring prominent Republicans.

Following her husband's death, Mrs. Whitin found life lonely in her high-ceilinged mansion and on occasion she invited her attractive young grandniece, Mary Frances Krum, to pay her a visit. Mary was the daughter of Chester Harding Krum, a prominent St. Louis circuit court judge and United States district attorney. It was as a result of those visits to Whitinsville that Mary Krum met and eventually married Josiah M. Lasell.

Like his father and his uncle before him, J. M. was graduated from Williams College.* Like his brother, he served his apprenticeship in the shop before taking up duties in the office. Then, for a dozen years or more (beginning 19 January 1891), he served as assistant treasurer under Marston Whitin, assuming responsibility for company management whenever Marston was out of town. In the spring of 1904, however, J. M. suffered an inexplicable inflammation that totally impaired the sight of one eye. As a result he retired from business to take up the life of a country squire. (His resignation as assistant treasurer took place 16 January 1905.) He continued to maintain a desk at the office and kept himself posted on company affairs so that he might intelligently discuss the problems arising at directors' meetings. But most of his energies after 1904 went into village affairs.

Again like his father, whom he is said to have resembled, J. M. Lasell took a keen interest in community welfare. For years he served as town selectman, as member of the school board, as president of the national bank, as trustee of the savings bank, and as head of the sewer commission. When the need for a larger high school became apparent, J. M. and his cousin, Arthur Whitin, donated the necessary money to erect a new building. When a home for the high school principal was suggested, J. M. stepped forward to provide one.

After 1905 neither J. M. nor Chester concerned himself any longer

* The Lasell Gymnasium at Williams College was given by J. M. Lasell in honor of his father, Josiah, and his uncle, Edward, co-founders of the Lasell Seminary for Young Women and both Williams men.

with the company's immediate management; yet between them they continued to hold a controlling block of the company's stock. Each had inherited a 27 per cent interest in the concern from his parents, and each had brought his individual holdings up to 30 per cent at the time the family bought out the Tafts. Thus, between them they held a 60 per cent interest in the company.*

There is no evidence that the Lasells ever took occasion to exercise the control that was legally theirs. Apparently they had complete faith in Marston Whitin's business ability and relied on whatever bounties his good management produced. It is fortunate that they did so, for Whitin would almost certainly have brooked no interference from them. In Marston's mind the company came first; he would never have tolerated any action favoring the personal interests of the stockholders if he thought it might jeopardize the company's security. He constantly laid stress on the need for liquidity to weather the kind of storms a producers'-goods firm is subject to, even if that meant reducing the stockholders' dividends. Or if the company needed cash for expansion purposes, he also kept dividends low, no matter what the current rate of earnings. Always, the company came first. Family members were expected to adjust their personal finances accordingly. Had members of the family attempted to thwart his actions, precipitating an internecine struggle for power, they would have rendered the company competitively impotent at the very point in its history when dynamic and aggressive leadership was needed for survival. In the first decade of his treasurership, Marston Whitin was faced with (1) a struggle with the Drapers over control of the spindle business, (2) a tooth-and-nail fight for business in the South, and (3) an opportunity, heaven-sent, to seize first place in the industry from the ponderous and venerable Lowell Machine Shop. Probably the greatest single contribution made by the Lasell brothers to the company, which between them they owned, was their willingness to give their talented brother-in-law a free hand in running the firm as he saw fit.

* Their sister, Mrs. George Marston Whitin, held a 30 per cent interest, while her husband held the remaining 10 per cent; the latter bought out the stock inherited by the other Lasell daughter, Jeannie Lasell Backus. From 1910 to 1917, Chester and J. M. Lasell and Mr. and Mrs. George Marston Whitin were the company's only stockholders.

CHAPTER X

THE SPINDLE CONTROVERSY, 1871–1893

IN THE second half of the nineteenth century the American textile machinery industry produced two new and revolutionary devices, the high-speed spindle and the automatic loom. Both were the products of native inventiveness and owed little to European technology. Indeed, for many years neither gained acceptance abroad. Even to-day the automatic loom is something of a novelty outside America. But in the United States both the spindle and the loom have won universal acclaim. Taken together they were to make the man-hour output of American cotton mills the highest in the world.

Historically the spindle and loom inventions are affiliated with the name of George Draper & Sons, for it was the Draper firm that promoted the one and originated the other. Even though they lie on the periphery of the Whitin story, the two inventions are dealt with in this book because both seriously disrupted Whitin's product line.

Chronologically the first of the two inventions was the high-speed spindle. Between 1871 and 1893 the American textile machinery industry gave birth to the modern spindle[1] amidst the pains of recurrent and bitter lawsuits over conflicting patent claims. For nearly a generation the thinking of American textile-machinery men was dominated by the radical changes being made in spindle technology.

In size a spindle is a mechanism of comparative insignificance, for its shaft is not much larger than an unsharpened lead pencil. But though small in proportions, it is the key to the whole yarn-making process. It holds the revolving bobbin onto which the yarn is spun. Though other machinery parts are as indispensable, the spindle is of especial importance because it governs the whole preparatory operation, much as a nozzle governs the flow of water from well to tank to pipe to hose. Because the spindle is the controlling factor in yarn output, it is customarily selected as the unit by which the productive capacity of a mill is measured. The whole cotton preparatory-machinery industry looks upon spindles as being symbolic of the industry's special rôle in the economic world. The Whitin company appropriately calls its employee magazine the *Whitin Spindle* and uses a sketch of a spindle as its official trademark.

Around the principle of the high-speed spindle, the firm of George Draper & Sons organized one of the earliest patent pools in America.* Spindle patents, the Drapers found, often overlapped, and since frequently one patent could not be used without infringing on patents held by others, some means of reconciling conflicting interests became necessary. The alternative to pooling would have been cross-licensing, but the Drapers preferred to keep control in their own hands. Sometimes they bought patents outright. Sometimes they let owners of key patents share in their pool through stock participation in the company they had formed to operate the pool. On not a few occasions they resorted to law courts when competing patent holders threatened their position. At the height of their power the Drapers owned or controlled every important spindle patent in America and Europe — some two hundred in number.[2]

Although the spindle controversy centered in the Drapers, it reached its climax in a lawsuit which involved the Whitin Machine Works. To understand the issues of that suit one must see at least part of its background. At the same time, however, one must bear in mind that not all the background is known, for the Draper version of the story has never been told. The following version is consequently limited by circumstances to a heavy reliance on a few limited sources—letterbooks in the Whitin collection and printed court testimony.

---

* Though the Draper pool was early in time, it was not unique in type. Business men, both in this country and abroad, learned that they had to resort to pools or cross-licensing if they were to prevent industrial progress from being strangled by the outmoded complexities of patent law. In accomplishing this purpose, however, they raised the fear in many quarters that such pools might prove a dangerous cudgel of concentrated economic power. Arguments for and against the pooling of patents are still being voiced before this country's federal courts, but to date no governing decision has been handed down and no substitute for pooling has been found practical.

I. "WHAT'S PAST IS PROLOGUE"

Before the Civil War the standard spindle in America was the so-called taper-top, or common, spindle. It is said that John C. Whitin was the one who, in 1854, conceived the idea of having a tapered spindle which would convey its rotative motion to a bobbin simply by friction.[3] But the idea could not have been wholly new or original with Whitin, for he applied for no patent to cover it. Between 1854 and 1870, practically all ring spinning frame builders in America equipped their machines with taper-top spindles, the only important exception being the Bridesburg Manufacturing Company, of Philadelphia, which used a straight-top spindle that drove its bobbin by a key-and-slot arrangement.

The common spindle, so far as we need be concerned with it here, contained only four essential parts: a shaft, a step, a bolster, and a whorl (see Chart VIII) — the same basic components that are to be found in modern spindles. The shaft carried the bobbin. The step supported the shaft as it revolved. The bolster encircled the shaft about halfway up its elevation and helped to hold it upright. The whorl formed a collar around which passed the driving band.

In the old common spindle design, the bobbin rode on the shaft far above the shaft's bolster support. Consequently, whenever the spindle's speed was increased above 6,000 revolutions per minute, the top-heavy shaft developed a whipping or gyrating motion.

The total weight of the assembled common spindle was about twelve or thirteen ounces. There had been several attempts to produce a lighter spindle but always with unsatisfactory results. John C. Whitin made a 9½-ounce spindle in 1860 for the Attawaugan Mills and an 8-ounce spindle in 1863 for the Hadley Company (the firm to which he sold the Holyoke Machine Shop) but on neither occasion did he get repeat orders.[4]

Meanwhile mill men were becoming interested in the general problem of improving the spindle. In 1867 both John E. Atwood of Willimantic, Connecticut, and Francis J. Rabbeth of Ilion, New York, brought out spindle improvements,[5] and in 1870 Oliver Pearl, an overseer of the Atlantic Mills, Lawrence, Massachusetts, patented a bobbin that made possible the use of a shorter and lighter spindle.

But all such developments seem to have occurred independently and without arousing very wide recognition in the industry at the time. Interest in the potentialities of a lighter and faster spindle did not really awaken until 19 April 1871, the day on which Jacob H. Sawyer went before a semiannual meeting of the New England Cotton

CHART VIII

DIAGRAMS OF THE PRINCIPAL SPINDLES FIGURING IN THE
WHITIN-SAWYER SPINDLE PATENT CONTROVERSY

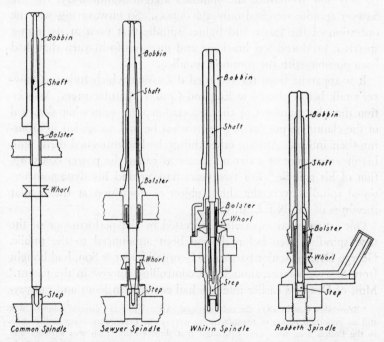

Manufacturers' Association to describe the successful results of a series of experiments he had been conducting in the Appleton Mills, at Lowell, where he was the mill agent. The spindle controversy dates from that memorable occasion.[6]

As a mill man, Sawyer had been observant enough to note the effectiveness of the high bolster perfected by William Higgins & Sons, of England, and by William Mason, of this country, for use

on throstle spinning machinery.* As a mechanic he had been ingenious enough to adapt that principle to use on ring spinning machinery. Basically his adaptation consisted of raising the bolster
to the spindle's center of gravity and chambering out the bobbin
to fit down over it. His original ambition had been merely to
steady the spindle at high speeds, and indeed with a steadier spindle
he was able to achieve as many as 7,500 revolutions per minute — an
increase of roughly 25 per cent over former speeds. But in addition
he was able to reduce the spindle's weight significantly, for the
Sawyer spindle weighed only 3¼ ounces.[7] So unwavering was the
operation of the faster and lighter spindle that even at its higher
speeds it produced less breakage and more uniform yarn than had
been possible with the common spindle.

It is apparent from the recorded discussion which followed Sawyer's talk before the New England Cotton Manufacturers' Association that the members of the Association were somewhat skeptical
of the claims he put forth. Nevertheless he had succeeded in arousing their interest. Among other things, he had intrigued them with
his ingenious use of a dynamometer to gauge the power consumption of his spindle.[8] For two years Sawyer and his dynamometer-
tested spindles were the chief subject of discussion at the regular
meetings of the N.E.C.M.A.

One person was especially impressed by the performance of the
new spindle. Even before it had been announced to the public,
George Draper, senior partner of George Draper & Son, had bought
from Sawyer a large, though not controlling interest in the patent.[9]
Most of Draper's earlier interests had centered in loom and railway-

* Remember that in 1871 the old-fashioned, Arkwright-type, throstle spinning was
still an important means of manufacturing warp yarn. There were many mill owners
in the Boston area who were convinced that throstle-made yarn was stronger and
sturdier than yarn spun by the ring frame method. An 1866 survey of 47 mills in
the Boston area showed that throstle frames were twice as widely used as ring frames
(see N.E.C.M.A. *Transactions,* no. 1, pp. 16–17).

There exists no reliable breakdown of spindle figures for 1871. The Ninth U. S.
Census segregates mule spindles from frame spindles, but it does not differentiate
between throstle and ring frame spindles. William F. Draper, in N.E.C.M.A. *Transactions,* no. 50, 1891, p. 21, stated that ring frames had gained the ascendancy by
1860, throstles being used only for coarse work. Perhaps it would be safe to estimate
that, by 1870, two out of every ten spinning frames being sold were throstle frames,
three were ring frames, and five were mules.

head patents, but in 1871 he was already in possession of at least one patented ring frame appliance, the Richards bolster. The speed and incisiveness with which Draper acted after learning of the Sawyer spindle's potentialities were but a foreshadowing of the daring manner in which his company was to seize and maintain a position in the vanguard of new developments in the textile machinery industry.

On 8 June 1872 the Sawyer Spindle Company was formed to hold the valuable Sawyer patent and to carry on the business of marketing the new invention. Ownership in the company, as of the end of its first year in operation, is shown in Table 6. Despite the predominance of Sawyer interests, the company was a Draper tool, for its entire business was handled through the firm of George Draper & Son, which served as its business agent.

From its inception, the Sawyer spindle was blessed not only with certain innate mechanical virtues but also by the vigorous and famed promotional skill of the elder George Draper. Draper's forceful personality made him one of the most colorful figures in the cotton textile industry. Everyone knew him and nearly everyone paid him some kind of tribute in patent royalties. His candid self-description before a meeting of the N.E.C.M.A. (recorded in paraphrased version by the clerk of the session) neatly summarizes the conflicting rational and emotional reactions he aroused among his associates, in both the mill and the machinery branches of the textile business:[10]

George Draper, Esq., of Hopedale, Mass., said that . . . he had spent twenty years of his life in making and introducing improvements among cotton manufacturers, and had dealings with nearly every member of the Association during that period of time. No doubt some individuals had at some time considered him a bore, [individuals] who a few years afterward had changed their minds and come to the conclusion that he was a necessary evil, if an evil at all, when he had given them some improvement which was better than anything they had ever had before.

Draper pointed his promotion of the Sawyer spindle toward two markets — the primary, or new, machinery market and the secondary, or replacement, market. Since Sawyer spindles could be installed in old frames with little difficulty, the Drapers decided to reserve the secondary market for themselves.[11] At first they also attempted to control the primary market through their manufacturing subsidiary, the Hopedale Machine Company, which was to produce the spindles ordered by machinery manufacturers for installation in new frames. They soon found, however, that the demand was too heavy for the capacity of their small subsidiary. The Hopedale company had always been a diminutive organization, for the Drapers had never had much need to do any manufacturing. Before the 1870's their principal business had been granting licenses and collecting royalties.

TABLE 6

Stock Ownership in the Sawyer Spindle Company in Selected Years

Name of Stockholder	Number of Shares Held (par value $100)		
	1873	1875	1880
SAWYER GROUP	650	250	250
Jacob H. Sawyer	400	150	150
Edward Sawyer	250	100	100
DRAPER GROUP[a]	300	1,000	1,150
George Draper	290	702	855
William F. Draper	10	225	225
George A. Draper	....	2	4
Eben S. Draper	....	1	1
J. B. Bancroft	....	50	50
E. D. Bancroft	....	5	5
George W. Knight	....	10	10
John E. Prest	....	5	....
OUTSIDE GROUP[b]	50	....	....
Edward Kilburn	25	....	....
J. H. and J. Chace	12	....	....
Henry Howard	13	....	....
FALES & JENKS GROUP	....	....	600
John R. Fales	....	....	200
Stephen A. Fales	....	....	200
Jane M. Jenks	....	....	200
Totals	1,000	1,250	2,000

[a] George A. Draper and Eben S. Draper were younger brothers of William F. Draper. J. B. Bancroft was a brother-in-law of George Draper and the managing head of the Hopedale Machine Company. E. D. Bancroft was his son. George W. Knight was a nephew of George Draper. John E. Prest was a Draper employee who had formerly worked for John C. Whitin and who later returned to the Whitin Machine Works.

[b] These men seem to have been friends of Draper and probably assisted him in getting the Sawyer spindle accepted by the trade. Edward Kilburn was a prominent Rhode Island mill engineer and manager. The Chaces acted jointly as treasurer of the Albion Mills. Henry Howard was probably the Henry Howard who was treasurer of the Arkwright Manufacturing Company, Coventry, Rhode Island.

Source: Statements of Condition, filed in the Secretary's Office, Massachusetts State House

According to one report, the Hopedale company had employed only about thirty men as late as 1865. Even in 1873 the firm had only about one hundred forty men on its payroll.[12]

As a temporary expedient, the Drapers decided to contract for the manufacture of spindles with several small specialty manufacturers in their vicinity, such as A. Hopkins & Company, of Pascoag, Rhode Island, Asa Ross, of Worcester, Massachusetts, and A. A. Westcott, of North Scituate, Rhode Island. These suppliers seem to have been the source of continual trouble and irritation, for they were periodically behind in their deliveries and their products were seldom of dependable quality. But the Drapers tolerated them for some time rather than risk licensing the large machinery manufacturers to produce Sawyer spindles.

Meanwhile, George Draper & Son had approached several large machinery firms to interest them in building frames ready to receive spindles of the Sawyer type. Apparently the first concern so approached was the Whitin Machine Works, and rather naturally so, since Whitin was the country's leading ring frame builder and was located only a short distance from Hopedale. In March, 1871, the Whitin company accepted an order from the Drapers for a pilot set of frames to be installed in the Ashton Mills, a subsidiary of the Lonsdale Company, of Lonsdale, Rhode Island. Whitin was to build the frames complete except for the spindles, which were to be supplied by George Draper & Son.*

By the beginning of 1872 the success of the Lonsdale experiment had stimulated the Boston Manufacturing Company, the Saratoga Victory Manufacturing Company, and the Ponemah Mills, as well as many smaller companies, to place orders with the Whitin Machine Works for frames equipped with Sawyer spindles. In each case George Draper & Son provided the spindles. On the seemingly insubstantial ground that his one-year guarantee required him to maintain direct control over quality, George Draper refused to grant

---

* Lonsdale thus apparently became the leader in adopting the new spindle on a large scale (4,000 spindles). Perhaps Lonsdale's progressiveness may be attributed to its mill engineer, Edward Kilburn, a man who is also generally credited as being the first to introduce the French-designed, but British-perfected, cotton comber to this country — and at about the same time. It may be significant that Kilburn was made one of the original stockholders of the Sawyer Spindle Company.

the Whitin company a license to make Sawyer spindles. However, it was not long before incidents arose to test the merit of so restrictive a policy.

After the installation of the Sawyer-equipped Whitin machinery in the Ponemah Mills, serious operating difficulties developed. The Whitin company attributed the difficulties to the defectiveness of the spindles furnished by the Draper firm; Draper countered that Whitin's frames had been poorly made. Eventually, they came to an agreement to share the cost of remedying the imperfect machinery, but Whitin officials did not miss the opportunity to point out that many such mutual recriminations would hardly be conducive to customer confidence.

Still other irritations arose. In the interest of standardization, the Whitin company went to the expense of redesigning its frames so that they could be used with either common or Sawyer spindles. Draper complained that the sale of such frames insinuated that the Whitin company was not confident of the Sawyer spindle's ultimate success and so was selling frames that could be converted if necessary. In the end, rather than risk antagonizing the Drapers, the Whitin firm agreed to revert to its former policy of making special frames for the two types of spindles.

Finally, on 9 December 1873, exasperated with the unreliability of his several small suppliers, Draper consented to allow the Whitin Machine Works the right to equip its frames with Sawyer spindles of its own make.[13] Besides the Whitin Machine Works, he also licensed the Lowell Machine Shop, the Saco Water Power Machine Shop, the Mason Machine Works, Marvel, Davol & Company, the Bridesburg Manufacturing Company, and the Franklin Foundry & Machine Company — in short, virtually every sizable textile machine shop in the country. Everyone wanted a cut of the juicy high-speed spindle pie.

For permission to use Sawyer spindles, Draper charged a royalty of 38 cents per spindle. Until 1886, through boom and depression, the charge remained the same. When the Whitin Machine Works felt compelled to make reduction after reduction in its machinery prices during the depression of the 'seventies, it besought the Drapers to help stimulate business by reducing their royalty fees.

But in vain. Draper royalties were like the laws of the Medes and the Persians — so said Whitin's treasurer — for they altered not.[14]

After the first blush of enthusiasm for the Sawyer spindle had paled, mill owners discovered that, remarkable as it was, the device stood in need of much improvement. Four years of experience was enough to teach the Whitin company that the spindle's only real advantage lay in its saving of from 15 to 20 per cent in power consumption.* Under standard operating conditions, its great potential speed, which seemed to promise such an enormous increase in productivity, could seldom be achieved, for as soon as wear set in, the Sawyer spindle chattered as badly as did the old taper-top spindle.[15] Furthermore, its high royalty made Sawyer frames much more expensive than common frames (as much as 14 per cent more during years when frame prices were depressed). Consequently many mill owners, when working on yarns coarser than no. 28, preferred to use the older and cheaper common spindle.[16]

In an attempt to remedy the Sawyer spindle's defects, investors soon began bringing forth all manner of variant designs. Whenever possible, the Drapers purchased the rights to these inventions and consolidated them into their patent pool.[17] If purchase proved infeasible, court action generally followed. Two lawsuits — one over Oliver Pearl's patent and one over the inventions of Francis J. Rabbeth — turned out to be especially significant both to the future of the textile machinery industry in general and to Whitin's future in particular.

2. LITIGATION

Oliver Pearl has already been mentioned as being among the early experimenters with lightweight spindles.[18] Like Sawyer he was a mill man, being overseer of spinning in the Atlantic Mills, in Lawrence. His interest in the spindle was really overshadowed by his interest in bobbins. Indeed, it was merely as a corollary to the perfecting of a high-capacity bobbin that he designed a lightweight

---

* The ability of the Sawyer spindle to cut down on power consumption was a real advantage, however, for half of all the power consumed by machinery in a cotton mill was consumed by spinning frames, and half the power consumed by spinning frames was consumed by spindles. (N.E.C.M.A. *Transactions,* no. 10, 1871, p. 47.)

spindle in 1870. Consequently, when he drew the specifications for his bobbin patent, he gave only scant attention to the completely new type of spindle that his bobbin required. His patent clearly pre-dated Sawyer's, but the vague manner in which he phrased his spindle specifications made the validity of his claim to priority over Sawyer open to question. Nevertheless, on 12 July 1877, he and a colleague, Joseph Battles, brought suit against two mills in Lowell — the Appleton Company, of which Jacob Sawyer was agent, and the Hamilton Manufacturing Company, a cotton mill closely affiliated with Appleton in both ownership and management. Both mills had been using spindles of the Sawyer design. Pearl and Battles de-manded that the two mills pay them royalties for using spindles that infringed on their patent.

On its surface, the case was no more than a dispute between an inventor and two alleged patent violators. But in actual fact it in-volved practically the entire cotton textile industry. If Pearl could prove that his patent held priority over Sawyer's he could force royalty payments from every mill using Sawyer spindles. By 1877 more than a million Sawyer spindles were in use; consequently the royalties at stake amounted to a small fortune. As the country's largest builders of Sawyer frames, the Whitin Machine Works was among those interested in seeing the Pearl cause defeated.[19] But, of course, the real defendants in the case were the Drapers. If Pearl was to win his suit, the Sawyer patent, around which the main business of George Draper & Son had come to revolve, would be virtually worthless.

For three years the case remained before the federal bench. Testi-mony covering 3,360 printed pages was taken, and the merits of nearly every type of lightweight spindle ever patented were re-viewed. Finally on 17 July 1880, Circuit Court Judge John Lowell announced the result of his deliberations.[20] In jubilation, George Draper's son, William, telegraphed the Whitin company, "Deci-sion that common Sawyer spindle does not infringe Pearl."

Well might young Draper feel jubilant, for his company had meanwhile met and defeated yet another rival, Francis J. Rabbeth. (The Drapers had also meanwhile increased the capitalization in the Sawyer Spindle Company and had bought control from the Saw-yers.) Early in the 1870's reports of Rabbeth's experiments on high-speed spindles had come to the attention of the partners of Fales, Jenks & Sons. On the basis of those reports the partners had decided to invite Rabbeth to their plant in Pawtucket, where he could carry on his experiments with all necessary facilities at his disposal. Apparently the Fales and Jenks partners felt that they stood to gain more by developing their own style of spindle than by paying tribute to the Sawyer-Draper interests. There seems no reason to believe that they were forced to develop a spindle of their own because of any effort on the part of Draper to exclude them from use of the Sawyer rights.[21]

By 1872, Rabbeth had arrived at a new spindle model, described as follows in a letter written by an executive of the Whitin Machine Works:[22]

We have no definite information in regard to the "new" Rabbeth spindle except as it has been incidentally mentioned by some parties calling at our office. The "old" Rabbeth spindle was quite generally regarded as a failure. The new is substantially the old except it is made lighter & the bolster is gun metal instead of iron. I think upon examination you will find that the "whirl" in reality is placed above the bolster though apparently below & thus the wear of bolsters must be very great & as a consequence, the bobbin [must] become unsteady very soon. . . .

After seeing the new Rabbeth invention in operation, Draper wrote to the Whitin company that he found nothing but "wear, unsteadiness of top of spindle, heated bearings, & trouble with bobbins." [23] But apparently Draper thought the new spindle a greater threat than he was willing to admit, for on 7 September 1874 he wrote to Fales, Jenks & Sons charging them with infringing patents held by the Sawyer Spindle Company and forbidding them either to make or to sell additional Rabbeth spindles without paying him royalties thereon.[24]

Apparently the owners of the Fales & Jenks Machine Company (under which name the firm had been incorporated in 1876) eventually capitulated to Draper's demands — and with good reason.*

* How this particular dispute was settled I do not know. In later years George Draper's oldest son, William, stated on the witness stand that his firm had won a "court" decision against the Fales & Jenks Machine Company in February, 1878 (Whitin Machine Works v. Sawyer Spindle Company, p. 391), but I have found no record of the suit coming to trial. A little later in the same testimony (p. 394), Wil-

Their spindle expert, Francis Rabbeth, had hit upon still another, and this time a radically different spindle model, the unchallengeable originality of which the Fales & Jenks owners had great confidence in. So sure were they that their new spindle would make the Sawyer spindle obsolete that they announced its existence to the Drapers immediately following the conference at which the two parties settled their differences over Rabbeth's earlier invention.[25]

Rabbeth's new spindle had many distinguishing features, but the most important was the freedom of action it allowed the spindle shaft. In Sawyer's design, the shaft had been held rigidly in place at both points of support — at the step and at the bolster. In contrast, Rabbeth's design allowed the shaft considerable play by leaving space between the bolster bearing and the bolster case and by filling that space with a soft and pliable packing, such as felt or cotton wicking. In making such a radical departure from traditional spindle design, Rabbeth advanced a completely new theory on how spindles behaved in operation. It is impossible, he claimed, for a spindle to carry a constantly balanced load. Bobbins are bound to vary in dimensions, some being warped and others having holes that are inaccurately bored. Inevitably, unbalanced bobbins throw the spindle off center as it rotates. Furthermore, the balance of a bobbin changes somewhat even in the spinning process. Yarn, as it is being spun, exerts a constant pull on the bobbin. As the winding operation moves up and down the bobbin's length, the pull of the yarn causes a constant shift in the spindle's rotational axis. Rabbeth purposely designed his spindle shaft with room for play to compensate for such variations.

Because of its flexibility, the Rabbeth spindle was capable of speeds up to 10,000 revolutions per minute, a third greater than the maximum speeds achieved by the Sawyer spindle. In speaking of his new spindle, Rabbeth sometimes referred to it as being "self-centering," and on other occasions as being a "top" spindle, because the movement of the shaft in the step resembled the meandering motion of a child's top when it begins to run down.

Draper was quick to realize that the Rabbeth spindle was founded

---

liam Draper stated that a settlement with Fales & Jenks had been reached in September, 1878, in the office of Benjamin Thurston, the Drapers' patent consultant in Providence.

on a completely new principle and that its existence was a threat to the lucrative business he had built around the Sawyer patent. For the three years 1875–78, virtually every spindle sold in the United States had been a Sawyer spindle.[26] If Draper hoped to continue in command of the spindle business, he had little choice but to invite the Fales & Jenks group to join him. His proposition to them ran somewhat as follows (again see Table 6):

(1) Francis J. Rabbeth to sell his interest in the new patent to the Sawyer Spindle Company for cash.

(2) Fales & Jenks Machine Company to sell its interest in the new patent in exchange for 600 shares of newly issued Sawyer Spindle Company stock.

(3) George Draper to be given an opportunity to buy enough shares of the newly issued stock to ensure his unquestioned control of the company.

(4) Fales & Jenks Machine Company to be made a licensed manufacturer of the self-centering spindle; others to be licensed only by mutual consent.

(5) George Draper & Sons (in 1877 a second son had been admitted to the partnership, thus changing the name slightly) to continue serving as sole selling agents of the Sawyer Spindle Company and to bear full responsibility for promoting the interests of the Rabbeth self-centering spindle.

By the terms of this agreement, reached in July, 1879,[27] the balance of power in the ring spinning field was suddenly upset. Before 1879, all manufacturers in the industry had had an equal chance to produce Sawyer spindles on license from the Sawyer Spindle Company. If any machine-builder had an advantage over the others it was the Whitin Machine Works, which, by reason of its early lead in ring spinning production, was selling as many frames in the 1870's as its three next largest competitors combined.[28] Draper's sudden realignment with the Fales & Jenks company now shifted leadership in the ring frame business to one of the Whitin company's strongest competitors. Exercising the right granted it by agreement with the Drapers, the Fales & Jenks firm refused to allow the Sawyer Spindle Company to license the Rabbeth patent to any other producer. Immediately the Whitin Machine Works (and, in fact, practically every other large builder of ring frames) set about trying to find a way to get around the Rabbeth patent.

3. THE WHITIN GRAVITY SPINDLE

As the result of a series of legal decisions, it became fairly well established that any spindle showing freedom at its bolster bearing infringed the Rabbeth self-centering principle. Consequently, when Henry F. Woodmancy, the head of Whitin's spindle department,[29] and Gustavus E. Taft, the shop's experiment-minded superintendent, began to look for a means of achieving a spindle that would duplicate the Rabbeth's high speeds without infringing on it in principle, they kept one fact in mind: the bolster bearing had to be designed with a tight fit.

By 1883 they had hit upon what they thought was a superior spindle yet one that would not infringe on the Rabbeth patent.[30] In certain respects it resembled another recently patented spindle, known as the Sherman spindle, the patent for which was held by the Drapers. But in one respect it was unique: the bolster bearing was fitted into the bolster case with a "close sliding fit." Only the step was allowed freedom of play. The new spindle had the same self-centering tendency as the Rabbeth and Sherman spindles, but it obviated the annoying necessity of constantly replacing the worn-out packing around the bolster bearing. Because the spindle tended to adjust its rotational center to "any change in the center of gravity caused by an inequality of bobbin or yarn load," [31] Taft and Woodmancy dubbed it the Whitin Gravity Spindle. A few years later they might have called it a gyroscopic spindle, but the word *gyroscope* had not yet come into common use in the early 1880's.

After 1883 virtually all spinning frames made by the Whitin company were equipped with Gravity spindles. Prices for frames with Gravity spindles remained the same as the prices for frames with Sawyer spindles, the only difference being that the Whitin company pocketed the 38-cent royalty that it had previously forwarded to the Sawyer Spindle Company. To clear the matter with the Drapers, Taft sent a model of the new spindle to Hopedale for examination. The Drapers submitted this model to their patent expert, George L. Roberts, who pronounced the Gravity spindle an infringement of no less than four patents held by the Sawyer Spindle Company. Not content with Roberts' opinion, however, Taft submitted the question to two independent experts in Providence, Joseph A. Miller and Causten Browne, who in their turn pronounced the Gravity patent unquestionably free and clear of all infringements. The Drapers nevertheless claimed that Whitin owed the Sawyer Spindle Company royalties on all Gravity spindles sold; Taft denied any such debt. At this impasse the two parties agreed to compromise.

The contract signed 21 November 1885 by representatives of the Sawyer Spindle Company and the Whitin Machine Works is reproduced in Appendix 11. In essence it contained five provisions:

(1) All existing Whitin spindle patents were to be assigned to the Sawyer Spindle Company.

(2) George Draper & Sons were to be allowed exclusive right to equip all old frames with any spindle covered by any Whitin Machine Works patent either issued or pending.*

(3) The Whitin Machine Works was to be allowed exclusive right to equip new frames with Gravity spindles.

(4) Whitin was to pay the Sawyer Spindle Company a royalty on all Gravity spindles sold, both past and present.

(5) The amount of the royalty was to be determined by arbitration.

By this agreement the Whitin company tacitly admitted its infringement of the Sawyer Spindle Company's patents. At the same time the Drapers also admitted that the Gravity patent contained elements of independent value. So ruled Judge Morton when the controversy later came before him for decision.[32] In other words, the agreement was tantamount to an admission by the Drapers that the Gravity patent contained new and original ideas. The agreement also made it clear that those ideas could not be put into use without infringing rights controlled by the Sawyer Spindle Company. By

---

* This clause effectively prevented the Whitin company from furnishing any spindles as replacements. Hence, Whitin customers, when their spindles wore out, had to go to the Drapers for additional ones. To meet such requests, the Drapers bought Gravity spindles from Whitin rather than making them in their own shop. Quite naturally the price of replacement spindles became a further subject for dispute. After the Draper monopoly had been broken by virtue of the expiration of patents (after 1911) the Whitin company vigorously took up the sale of replacement spindles. At the same time, several smaller firms stepped in to try to capture the market that the Drapers had held so long. Notable among these specialty manufacturers was the Easton & Burnham Machine Company, of Pawtucket, Rhode Island.

the 1880's spindle patents had become so complicated and interinvolved that to produce a spindle, some feature of which did not infringe upon one or several existing patents, had come to be a virtual impossibility.

In compliance with the terms of the agreement, the disputants appointed two arbitrators to determine what royalty the Whitin company should pay the Sawyer Spindle Company.[33] The Draper interests delegated Benjamin F. Thurston, of Providence, to serve for them; the Whitin interests chose Edward N. Dickerson, of New York. On 13 January 1886 the two men submitted their report. How they arrived at their decision they did not say, but they agreed that the rights held by the Sawyer Spindle Company were worth a royalty of 38 cents per spindle as established by practice and that the Gravity patent was worth a royalty of 19½ cents per spindle. The balance, or 18½ cents per spindle, thus became the amount owed the Sawyer Spindle Company by the Whitin Machine Works for all Gravity spindles sold in the past and all to be sold in the future. The Whitin company, therefore, remitted to the Drapers a check for $29,398.72 covering the 158,912 Gravity spindles that it had sold between 1883 and the date of the agreement.

The settlement should have been mutually satisfactory, for both parties achieved their main objectives. The Drapers withstood yet another attempt to storm their patent citadel, and the Whitins gained a preferential royalty rate that gave them a considerable edge on all their competitors. But in actual fact neither party was satisfied and both sought to negate the agreement without actually violating it. The Drapers, who were supposed to use the Gravity principle only for spindles installed in old frames, saw the advantage in the tight bolster feature and immediately adopted it in modified form in a new model of the Rabbeth spindle which they named the Rabbeth 49D. Meanwhile Taft and Woodmancy had already applied for another spindle patent in which they made claims that were designed to meet the Drapers' objections to their previous patent.*

* Since the Drapers assumed that, once it had been issued, the new Gravity patent would be assigned to their pool in accordance with the terms of their contract with the Whitins, they directed their lawyers to defend it when it ran into an interference while going through the Patent Office.

Before this second Gravity patent had been issued, both Gustavus Taft and George Draper died, leaving to the heads of their respective businesses, George Marston Whitin and William F. Draper, a legacy of tension and hostility.

4. *Whitin Machine Works* v. *Sawyer Spindle Company*

It was Marston Whitin who led off the second round of the Whitin-Draper dispute by writing a curt letter to William F. Draper on 15 January 1890, shortly after receiving word that the second Gravity patent had been granted.[34] In his letter Marston said simply that in his opinion the new Gravity patent was the patent necessary to "hold the spindle business for the next 17 years." He added, "In view of [this fact], we are anxious to ascertain the exact position we occupy under our contract." In brief, Marston felt that the Drapers' practice of making their Rabbeth 49D with close-fitting bolsters was an infringement of the principle of the Gravity spindle.

William Draper's reply was one of surprise. He felt not only that the new Gravity patent was far less significant than Whitin claimed it to be, but that the Whitin-Draper agreement of 1885 explicitly stated that the pending patent, when issued, would be administered by the Sawyer Spindle Company just as its predecessor had been.[35] Actually the agreement contained no reference to the manner in which the patent was to be treated, once issued. Thus, neither the Whitin nor the Draper position was entirely clear.

In substance Marston Whitin's letter to William Draper charged that *all* spindles being made under Draper licenses infringed the Gravity principle. In its way the charge was as sweeping as Pearl's charge had been a few years earlier, for it embraced all the country's leading ring frame producers. (In 1882 the Fales & Jenks Machine Company had allowed the Sawyer Spindle Company to license the Hopedale Machine Company, the Lowell Machine Shop, and the Saco Water Power Machine Shop to build the Rabbeth spindle.) Yet it is evident that Whitin had no real thought of challenging Draper's control of the spindle market. His sole motive was to achieve a reduction in the 18½-cent royalty being paid by his company to the Sawyer Spindle Company on all the spindles which it manufactured.

Only the foolhardy or the ill-advised would have had the daring to back the litigious Drapers into a corner as Whitin was doing. Court actions were part of the Draper stock-in-trade. The very foundation of their firm was cemented with lawsuits and reinforced with injunctions. George Draper & Sons were famed for invincibility before the bar. Furthermore, by 1890, the Sawyer Spindle Company was charging all its other licensees a royalty of 45 cents per spindle, whereas the Whitin company was still paying only 18½ cents. The Whitin Machine Works was already the most strategically situated company in the industry.

Under other circumstances Marston Whitin might have been able to look to his competitors for at least moral support in trying to break the Draper monopoly. As it was, his competitors really hoped that he would lose, for they were anxious to see the Whitin company's preferential contract abrogated. One wonders if Marston Whitin would have proceeded differently had he been an older and less impulsive man.

Whitin's first attempts to get William Draper to admit the independent merits of the new Gravity patent were interrupted by Draper's departure for Europe.[36] As soon as Draper had returned, however, he resumed negotiations and offered to settle the matter amicably by granting the Whitin Machine Works a mutually agreeable share in the ownership of the Sawyer Spindle Company. But Edward Wetmore, Whitin's New York attorney, advised against accepting the offer — a bit of advice Whitin later wished he had not taken. Wetmore recommended that the dispute be submitted either to arbitration or to the Massachusetts Superior Court.[37] Therefore, on 29 December 1890, Whitin informed Draper that he had decided to bring suit in the state court. Inherent in Whitin's charges were two main points: first, that all spindles manufactured under Draper licenses infringed upon the new Gravity patent; and, secondly, that Draper had violated the terms of the 1885 agreement by not observing the Whitin Machine Works' exclusive right to the manufacture of spindles with tight-fitting bolsters. If Marston Whitin had originally intended merely to free his company from the necessity of paying tribute to the Drapers, he should never have followed Wetmore's advice. The point Wetmore wished him to establish through a lawsuit was so broad that, had Whitin won, he would have been in a position to force the Drapers completely out of the spindle business.

For some unexplained reason Whitin did not get around to filing his bill of complaint until 29 June 1892. Once his challenge was on record, however, the Draper firm quickly retaliated with a bold counter-offensive. The Whitin company, William Draper charged, was no longer making the spindle described in the 1885 agreement but was making an altered spindle with a loose bolster in violation of the Sherman patent purchased by the Sawyer Spindle Company in 1883.[38] Because of this violation, Draper argued, the royalty paid by the Whitin Machine Works should be 45 cents instead of only 18½ cents. In addition to launching this counter-charge, Draper peremptorily refused to accept the recently delivered Whitin check for royalties due 31 December 1891. In view of the failure of the Whitin company to pay the full 45-cent royalty, he explained, the statement that their remittance was a payment "in full" was clearly in error. Such was the angry state of affairs when, in the spring of 1893, the case — which Marston Whitin now referred to as "an unfortunate dispute" — came before Judge James Madison Morton for decision.[39]

Most of the testimony given before Judge Morton was technical and centered in the question of how the bolster bearing actually behaved under operating conditions.* At times the discussion seemed to be mere tail-chasing, for the fact of the matter was that both parties, proceeding from opposite theoretical extremes had met, in their manufacturing practice, at a point close to the center. Originally the Whitin Machine Works had defined a "close sliding fit" as having two-thousandths of an inch clearance.[40] But in actual production the company had found it could not keep to such close dimensions. One reason was that Whitin gauges were made of cast iron ("hardened and afterwards ground on the plan of Whitworth's gauges")[41] and consequently wore so rapidly that they sometimes lost two-thousandths of an inch in diameter within three days' time.[42] Under production conditions the company found that a

---

* The counsel for Whitin was William A. Jenner of Wetmore & Jenner, a New York patent law firm. The counsel for Draper was Frederick P. Fish, of Boston's famed general law firm, Fish, Richardson & Storrow. Fish later became president of the American Telephone & Telegraph Company.

clearance of four- or five-thousandths of an inch was the best it could hope to achieve. To Marston Whitin's embarrassment, Draper's experts were able to show in court, by testing a random selection of Whitin spindles, that some had clearances of as much as eleven-thousandths of an inch. Meanwhile the Drapers, having begun manufacturing Rabbeth spindles with wide bolster clearances, had gradually reduced those clearances until the so-called model 49 D had clearances of from five- to ten-thousandths of an inch. Hence there was really little practical difference between the bolster bearings made by the two companies.

Whitin's attorney tried to argue that, since the pull of the driving band held the bolster tight against the case and allowed no play anyway, a variation of a few thousandths of an inch made very little difference in operation. In his autobiography William Draper describes how his lawyers set about refuting that point:[43]

The vital question between us was whether the loose bearing of a spindle revolving at high speed, vibrated — or moved back and forth — against the pull of the driving band. Our contention was that it did, and our case rested largely on that contention, while our opponents took the position that it could not, and did not, move. The loose bearing was held in a case whose socket was only a few thousandths of an inch larger than the exterior of the bearing, and it was surrounded by a sleeve pulley which prevented any ocular observation of the point at issue. Each party prepared ingenious mechanical instruments, and experts on both sides made tests lasting weeks or months, with the result that each was satisfied that the use of his instrument justified his previous view. The idea of an electrical test came to each of us, the idea being to arrange the points of contact so that a touch on the side of the case away from the one where the bearing was held by the band, would ring a bell. We ordered a machine made, but before it was done theirs was brought into court and tests made with it before us and Judge Morton, — showing conclusively that the bell did not ring. The Court adjourned, and we were permitted to examine their machine, but could find nothing wrong with it. That night our machine was completed and brought to us at Young's Hotel, Boston, where were assembled several of our company officers, with our counsel and experts, in a private dining room. The Machine was placed on the table, connection made with the electric wires, and the spindle commenced its revolution. Listen as best we could there was no bell ringing, and the performance of our opponents' machine was corroborated. At this juncture Professor Cross of the [Massachusetts] Institute of Technology, one of our experts, said that the revolution of the spindle was so rapid and the contact so brief that perhaps there was not time to ring a bell, and he suggested making an attachment to a telephone receiver. This was done, and when he placed it to his ear, the smile on his face showed that the problem was solved. Like Galileo, he said, "It does move." I tried it next and could hear the clicks with perfect clearness; and then the receiver went the round of the room, so that each might be sure that the others' ears were not deceived. There was no doubt about it, and we went to bed secure in our position. A day or two later, in court, after a suitable statement from Professor Cross, our machine was started before the judge and the representatives of the other side, and the clicks were as evident to them as to us. For want of something better to say, the counsel for our opponents suggested that there might be something peculiar about our machine, and challenged us to attach the receiver to their apparatus and note the result. They had nothing to lose by this, after our demonstration, but we had to take the chance that something might happen which would interfere with the registration. However, we took the chance; applied the receiver to their machine; and the clicks were as evident as before. We all heard them, — judge, counsel, experts, and clients, — and the decision in our favor after this test seemed as certain as when it came a few months later.

The telephone-receiver test was the dramatic climax of the case. (Incidentally, the receivers are still in existence and are part of the Whitin collection in Baker Library.) But in making his decision, Judge Morton stated that he was not swayed by the technical demonstration staged for his benefit. Instead, although he had spent several weary months listening to the technical evidence presented in the case, he ignored what he had learned concerning spindle technology and reverted to a strictly legal approach by basing his decision on the apparent "intent" of the agreement signed in 1885. The agreement was quite obviously meant to give the Drapers control of the Gravity patent; therefore, Judge Morton ruled this intent should be construed to extend to all and sundry modifications of that patent. Such being the case, he concluded that the Whitin company had no grievance and that, having brought trial for insufficient reasons, it should pay all court charges — the total of which was $14,-755.86.

When Marston Whitin learned of the decision he irately threatened to appeal the case. William Draper immediately threatened a countersuit charging the Whitin company with infringement of the Sherman loose-bolster patent. Draper seems to have known when not to overpress his advantage, however — especially against a firm that was his best customer — for he tempered his counter-charge by renewing his proposition to let the Whitin Machine Works become a stockholder in the Sawyer Spindle Company. Nevertheless, he insisted that thenceforth Whitin pay a 45-cent royalty like all other manufacturers. By then, aware of his weak position, Marston Whitin assented to the plan.*

The terms of the Whitin company's new servitude show what a stinging defeat it had suffered. Before 1893, all Whitin's principal competitors had been charging their customers 45 cents per spindle in addition to their base ring frame prices and had been turning the entire 45 cents over to the Drapers as a royalty payment. Whitin, on the other hand, had been charging its customers only 38 cents extra

---

* In 1894 the Sawyer company increased its stock from 2,000 to 3,000 shares and sold the Whitin Machine Works 850 shares (par value $85,000) for $100,000 (Whitin cashbooks, 27 July 1894). The return on this investment seems to have been only fair, considering the self-liquidating nature of the Sawyer firm. Sample years show that Whitin received dividends amounting to $6,800 in 1894, $7,365 in 1896, $10,311 in 1897, $1,479 in 1898, and $32,406 in 1904 (G. M. Whitin's personal notebook). On 20 May 1895 the Sawyer Spindle Company shifted its corporate charter to Maine and split its stock four to one. At that time the Whitin company's shares were registered as follows:

    1 share — G. M. Whitin
    1 share — J. M. Lasell
    2,831 shares — G. M. Whitin and J. M. Lasell, trustees
    567 shares — held in trust for the Whitin company by the Sawyer Spindle Company.

To whom dividends on these respective shares were paid is not clear. On 21 February 1897 the Sawyer Spindle Company delivered to the Whitin Machine Works 113 shares of the 567 shares of trustee stock that it held, repaying Whitin in cash for the remaining 454 shares. On 13 May 1904, G. M. Whitin and J. M. Lasell sold 83 shares of the trustee stock to George A. Draper at $50 a share. On 23 June 1910 the stock's par value was reduced from $100 to $5 a share. On 8 December 1911 the Whitin company sold its remaining 2,863 shares to the Drapers at the new par value — $14,315. On 3 September 1912 the Sawyer Spindle Company (Maine) was dissolved.

and had been turning over only 18½ cents to the Drapers. Between 1885 and 1894, Whitin had netted approximately $140,000 on its Gravity spindle royalties, and at the same time had enjoyed the luxury of a selling price that was potentially at least 7 cents lower than its competitors' prices. In the ten years following 1893 — years when spinning frame sales climbed to a record level — the Whitin company not only had to charge its customers the same royalty rate that its competitors were charging, but also had to forego its own separate royalty income, which in those ten years would have amounted to approximately a half-million dollars.

Glancing back over the entire period when the Drapers were in control of the spindle business, one might add that the $2,079,738 in royalties paid by the Whitin Machine Works to the Sawyer Spindle Company between 1875 and 1904 was a heavy fine indeed for the Whitin company's supineness in letting control over the key part of its machinery business slip into the hands of a company that previously had scarcely even been in the ring frame business. One wonders how much the Whitin Machine Works might have accomplished had it been spending a like amount on applied research over those same years.

The Whitin-Sawyer suit was the last battle fought in the spindle war. After 1893 all manufacturers paid the Sawyer Spindle Company a uniform 45-cent royalty on every spindle sold in new frames, until at last the final governing patent had expired.

Meanwhile the Drapers had already turned their attention elsewhere — toward the development of an automatic loom. The automatic loom was to be even more profitable to the Drapers than the high-speed spindle had been — and far more devastating in its effects on the textile machinery industry. But because several years were to elapse before it came fully into its own, the story of its effect on the Whitin Machine Works is deferred till Chapter XIII.

CHAPTER XI

RISE OF THE SOUTHERN MARKET, 1880–1900

No DEVELOPMENT during George Marston Whitin's management of the Whitin Machine Works (1886–1915) was to equal in significance the spectacular rise of the South as a cotton-manufacturing region. At the time when Whitin became company treasurer, the production of cotton goods in the South was unimportant; of the country's spindles barely 5 per cent were then located below Mason and Dixon's line. Yet by the time of Whitin's retirement from active business affairs, the South had come to be nearly the equal of New England as a producer of cotton yarns and fabrics; in four Southern states alone (North and South Carolina, Georgia, and Alabama) was located nearly 40 per cent of the nation's total cotton-spindle capacity.

To the machinery industry this development meant the opening of a virtually new and untried market. To the South it meant the first long step away from the blight of war and reconstruction toward industrialization and prosperity. Throughout the country the South came to be regarded as the source of inexpensive cotton goods. Even in the world market its competition was soon felt, for beginning with the organization of the Piedmont Manufacturing Company (1875) and extending down to the Boxer Rebellion in China (1900) — and even, although to a lesser extent, down to the First World War — many of the mills in the South sold their products abroad, particularly to the Orient. By the turn of the century the lower Piedmont Belt of the Appalachian Mountains had become one of the world's three great cotton-manufacturing centers, ranking after Lancashire in old England and after New England in the United States.

If one is to appreciate fully the rapid rise of this new market for cotton-mill equipment, one must first know something of the Southern machinery market as it existed before the 1880's. It is known, for instance, that the Whitin company was selling some machinery in the South at least as early as 1849, the first year for which there are any company records. But until the Civil War, Whitin's sales were generally limited to pickers, its one product which had a national reputation and which could be sold with little or no promotional effort. Only rarely did the company sell any railway drawing systems or any ring spinning frames. Whence, then, came the other machinery that went into early Southern mills?

1. THE SOUTH AS A MACHINERY MARKET BEFORE 1880

It is said that some of the first Southern mills, built during the War of 1812, were equipped, just as were Northern mills of that period, with machinery constructed on the mills' premises under the supervision of skilled machinists who had acquired somewhere a familiarity with cotton-textile equipment.[1] But where Southern mill owners obtained their machinery during the ensuing thirty-five years remains something of a mystery. Perhaps they bought from British manufacturers just as they did in the case of so many other fabricated items in the ante-bellum days, although English export regulations must have prevented such trade from becoming widespread. More likely, they began buying from Northern machine shops at a date much earlier than we have any record of. Not until 1848, when William Gregg purchased from Northern manufacturers the machinery for his Graniteville Manufacturing Company of Graniteville, South Carolina (one of the largest and best-known of the ante-bellum enterprises), do we begin to have specific information concerning the source of Southern mill equipment. Graniteville's first machinery seems to have come from P. Whitin & Sons, Fales & Jenks, or William Mason, for Gregg mentioned in his correspondence that his spinning frames were of the ring spinning type and were shipped to him from Providence.[2] Yet it is worth noting that Gregg himself, upon discovering that Northern manufacturers were too busy in 1859 to give him reasonable delivery dates, went to England to place an order for additional equipment.[3]

Of the several Northern companies which sold cotton machinery to the South before the Civil War, the most important was probably the Lowell Machine Shop, although this fact can be established only by inference. Lowell enjoyed the distinction of being not only the largest shop in the country at that time but also the best-known, for it was fortunate enough to be located in what was then as much the industrial showplace of the country as Detroit is now. Lowell's location and reputation were of inestimable value in an era when advertising was uncommon and when sales initiative came not from the manufacturer, who seldom played an aggressive rôle, but from the customer, who was likely to place his order with the manufacturer he had heard most about.

The extent to which the Lowell shop was a leader in the Southern market is difficult to establish, however, because of the unknown competitive puissance of the Bridesburg Manufacturing Company, of Philadelphia. This company, founded about 1810 by Alfred Jenks, a former pupil of Samuel Slater and David Wilkinson, and known until about 1866 under the name of Alfred Jenks & Sons, had begun its existence in a fashion typical of shops in the Boston area, by providing full complements of machinery for mills as they were being built. By 1858 the company's plant facilities were said to cover about 50,000 square feet of floor space,[4] or about the area covered by the contemporary machine shop of P. Whitin & Sons. That Bridesburg was an important builder of machinery for Southern mills seems to be implied by the publication, in 1845, of a Bridesburg price list in William Gregg's celebrated *Essays on Domestic Industry*. As late as 1880 a manufacturers' agent, writing to the Whitin Machine Works from North Carolina, reported that the Bridesburg Manufacturing Company was a strong contender for the growing Southern machinery market.[5]

But whereas the shops of New England expanded rapidly in the post-Civil War years, the Bridesburg company appears to have stagnated. Bridesburg advertisements, published in 1867 and again in 1888, contain pictures which reveal little or no change in plant facilities over a period of more than twenty years.[6] (Indeed, the only noticeable difference in the two illustrations is the altered location of a steamboat floating on the river in front of the shop.) By the 1890's Bridesburg had ceased to be a competitive factor in the South.

Although Whitin is known to have been among the early companies selling to the South, it seems to have been by no means a challenger of Lowell's supremacy. For fifteen years following the Civil War, the company's total annual Southern sales seldom exceeded $20,000 — the equivalent of about a single order to outfit a small Northern mill. Moreover, its sales were scattered widely among all the eleven states that had once been a part of the Confederacy. If any one market area could be said to have ranked above the others, it was the territory around Richmond and Petersburg, Virginia. Yet even there the mills were small, and individual orders were all but insignificant. Table 7 lists the only Southern mills that

TABLE 7

SOUTHERN MILLS WHICH PURCHASED A TOTAL OF MORE THAN $10,000 OF WHITIN MACHINERY DURING THE PERIOD 1865–1879

Name of Mill	Location	Total Purchases	Year in Which Orders Larger Than $5,000 Were Placed
Ettrick Mfg. Co.........	Petersburg, Va.	$15,708.01	1872
Marshall Mfg. Co........	Manchester, Va.	24,731.83	1871, 1875
Beaver Creek & Bluff Mfg. Co...................	Fayetteville, N. C.	19,432.69	1872
Piedmont Mfg. Co.......	Piedmont, S. C.	81,322.48	1875, 1877
Tallassee Mfg. Co........	Mobile, Ala.	42,616.56	1869

Source: J. C. Whitin Ledger and Whitin Machine Works Ledger No. 1.

bought a total of $10,000 of Whitin machinery in the entire period 1865–79. In most cases orders were limited to railway drawing systems or to ring spinning frames, the two styles of machinery developed in the shops of the Rhode Island area that had spread in popularity to the rest of the country. Whitin pickers and lappers no longer commanded their once important share of the Southern market (probably because of the competition of Kitson's superior picking equipment).

The largest and by far the most notable Whitin sale made during the postwar reconstruction period was the nearly full complement of machinery which the shop built in 1875 for Henry P. Hammett's new Piedmont Manufacturing Company, of Piedmont, South Carolina. In the history of America's cotton manufacturing industry, three mills may be singled out as leaders in their areas. The Slater mill, which began producing yarns in 1790, was the first successful power-driven mill in the New World and was the predecessor of the mill development in the Providence region. Francis Cabot Lowell's Boston Manufacturing Company, which was organized in 1813, was the progenitor of cotton manufacturing in the Boston area. Henry P. Hammett's Piedmont Manufacturing Company was to the South what the other two mills had been to the North.

Why Hammett chose to use Whitin machinery is not known, although he may have been influenced in his decision by the experience of his father-in-law, William Bates. Bates, before moving to the South, had worked in the mills at Pawtucket, Rhode Island, where he may well have developed a partiality for Whitin equipment. It is known, at least, that, after establishing a mill of his own in South Carolina, he had become one of Whitin's most important prewar Southern customers. For many years before the war, Hammett had worked in his father-in-law's mill in the midst of Whitin machinery. His familiarity with the Whitin product is probably explanation enough for his decision to place Piedmont's order with the Whitin Machine Works.

With characteristic caution, Josiah Lasell, in quoting terms to Hammett, stipulated that payments would have to be made in cash, as bills were rendered. When it became apparent, however, that because of the great depression of the 1870's Piedmont would not be able to meet its payments, John C. Whitin stepped in, gave Hammett nearly two years to meet his obligations, and agreed personally to accept stock in the Piedmont enterprise as part settlement of the mill's obligation to the Whitin Machine Works (possibly the first instance of a practice which was later to become widespread and exceedingly troublesome).[7] Whitin's gesture seems to indicate that he had considerable confidence in the South as an industrial area. In fact, on an earlier occasion (in 1869) he had written, "as to the future of the South, I honestly think if our friends there will work half as hard as we poor Yankees do, they will come out altogether ahead of us — and I hope I may live to see it." [8]

To some extent Whitin did live to see a change, for within a few years the Piedmont mill was being heralded as the rejuvenated

South's first successful venture into cotton manufacturing on a large scale.[9] Its owner was looked to as the leading exponent of Southern industrialization, its sale of plain goods to China was considered the answer to the South's marketing problems, and its labor force was regarded by other new mills of the Piedmont region as an incomparable pool of promising superintendents and overseers.[10]

Whitin's liberal treatment of the Piedmont mill's indebtedness and his farsighted confidence in the mill's ultimate success were in marked contrast to the conservative policy followed by the Lowell Machine Shop when at about that same time one of its early Southern customers, the Atlanta Cotton Factory, failed to meet its payments for machinery. Unwilling to extend sufficient financial assistance to get the company on its feet, the Lowell company eventually dismantled the mill, sold part of the machinery, and shipped the rest back North.[11] How much damage the Atlanta incident did to Lowell's prestige cannot, of course, be estimated. Yet it seems possible that Whitin's generous attitude toward Piedmont may have caught the attention of other mill promoters in the South and may have accounted in part for the company's remarkable sales record during the years immediately following. Certainly the existence of Whitin machinery in the Piedmont mills must have proved of inestimable value as an advertisement of the Whitin name.

2. THE COTTON MILL FEVER, 1880–1883

The early success of a few such mills as Piedmont, which in January, 1881, paid its shareholders a 50 per cent dividend in stock,[12] attracted Southern capitalists from a variety of backgrounds — cotton factors, plantation owners, lumber men, grain merchants, and bankers, to name only a few — men who, with occasional exceptions, knew almost nothing about managing cotton mills.[13]

For advice on how to establish and operate their new mills, these men turned to experienced Northerners. If their undertaking was large enough to warrant the additional expense, they hired an engineer to design, erect, and start their mills.* For advice on mill ma-

---

* Most of the South's early mill engineers were Northerners; the few who were originally from the South were usually men who had received their technical training in Northern schools. The contribution made by these men to the industrialization of the South is a subject that has never attracted the attention it deserves.

chinery and on how it should be operated, they relied on the machine-builders from whom they planned to buy their equipment. To
develop a corps of skilled operators — a class of workers that was at
first very scarce in the South — they sometimes sent their own men
North for training or, if possible, hired men from Northern mills to
serve as their overseers and superintendents. If these mill men had
no prearranged outlet for their finished products, they usually approached a commission house in Baltimore, Philadelphia, or New
York and arranged to have it handle their entire line of goods.

If the promoters of a mill felt that their enterprise was too small
to justify paying a mill engineer for the design of a special building, they sometimes accepted the standardized plans offered them by
machinery builders as buying inducements. These plans contained a
set of architect's drawings showing a standard brick mill, a complete
list of all the materials required to construct the mill, and an enumeration of the machines best suited to produce any of several types
of yarns or fabrics. In general such plans were designed for mills
with a 10,000-spindle capacity or less. Most machinery builders encouraged customers who were planning to build mills with a capacity of more than 10,000 spindles to secure the assistance of an
engineering specialist, but some manufacturers were willing to supply drawings for mills having as many as 20,000 spindles.[14] The
Whitin Machine Works, at least by 1885, was offering for sale at
prices from $50 to $100 four standard sets of plans, one for a mill of
864-spindle capacity and another for a mill of 1,728-spindle capacity,
a third for a mill of 3,456-spindle capacity, and a fourth for a mill of
10,000-spindle capacity.[15] If the purchaser of one of these sets of plans
thereafter bought Whitin machinery, he was permitted to deduct the
purchase price of the plans from his machinery bill. As a result,
most of these standard plans were, in effect, given free to the promoters of new mills.

In theory at least, Marston Whitin was opposed to the company's
participation in mill planning, first because he felt that it took the
company into a field in which it had little specialized knowledge
and, secondly, because it caused the company to encroach upon the
activities of engineering consultants. Whitin was anxious not to offend these mill engineers. One of them especially, Charles R. Make-

peace of Providence, who was among the most successful of the engineers operating in the South, was a loyal supporter of Whitin products. Whitin realized that mill engineers could often dictate the type of machinery to be placed in new mills. But since the promoters of small mills sometimes refused to pay a mill engineer's fee when they could go to a machine-builder and get standardized plans without charge, Marston felt compelled to have plans available to keep small customers from transferring to other machinery manufacturers.

Except for its rather desultory use of mill plans as a promotional weapon, the Whitin company seems to have expended little effort to develop its Southern market. On one occasion (in 1880) the company had an opportunity to obtain the services of a manufacturers' agent operating in the South,[16] but it turned the offer down because of its long-standing policy (in effect since the Civil War) not to sell through middlemen.*

At the International Cotton Exposition held in Atlanta, Georgia, from 5 August to 31 December, 1881, the Whitin company apparently did not even exhibit its machinery, although it did carry an advertisement in the exposition's official catalogue.[17] Again in extenuation of the company's passive attitude toward its Southern market, one should add that its competitors seem to have shown a similar tendency. Those were the days when manufacturers believed that a reputation for superior products was the best advertisement possible and the only one they needed. And in many respects customer reaction bore out their theory.

Southern mill men customarily bought their machinery in one of two ways. Those who were price-conscious traveled North, established themselves in a suite of rooms at Boston's Parker House or

---

* In fairness to the company it should be pointed out that in this particular case the agent, one C. T. Harden, was also the exclusive Southern representative of the "New Process" Clement Attachment, a crude forerunner of the modern long-draft system. The Clement Attachment was reputedly able to eliminate many of the traditional steps in the drawing and roving processes and was fashioned to catch the fancy of the South's ingenuous new mill owners. As a result of his connection with the unaccredited Clement process, Harden would no doubt have been rejected as Whitin agent no matter what the company's general policy had been. Still, it is significant that the company did not get around to secure representation in the South until 1894, fourteen years later.

Hotel Touraine, and proceeded to "entertain" bids from machinery manufacturers. Marston Whitin detested that method of doing business and seldom dealt with such customers. On the other hand, those mill men who placed high value on quality, delivery, and service typically singled out one manufacturer, dealt with him exclusively, and counted on getting the best going prices simply by letting it be known that otherwise they would withdraw their patronage and take it elsewhere. Marston liked that type of customer and preferred to work on those terms. With customers of that kind, reputation and reliability were far more important than high-pressure salesmanship.

So it was that the Whitin company, without pushing its products, was able to build its Southern sales to an annual average of nearly $200,000 during the years 1881, 1882, and 1883 — more than ten times the level at which Southern sales had been running in the years preceding the Piedmont order. It is apparent that one of the reasons that the Whitin Machine Works fared so prosperously was because several of its established Southern customers enlarged their mills during the early 1880's. Of the nine Southern mills that bought more than $10,000 of Whitin machinery each during those three years, three were already regular Whitin customers and were alone responsible for nearly a quarter of the company's total sales to the South for the 1881–83 period.*

Shipment of machinery to the growing Southern market involved a development in methods of handling and of transportation. Before 1880 most Whitin machinery had been erected on the floor of the shop and then had been boxed in carefully dried lumber at an added cost to the customer of a blanket 5 per cent of his machinery bill. The only machines not boxed had been cards which were too large to fit into the small railroad cars of that era and which were therefore bolted to flat cars and covered with tarpaulins as protection from the unpredictable New England weather. Machinery shipped to the South had traveled by rail to Boston or Providence and

---

* Two of the best Whitin customers were located in New Orleans where, in the winter of 1884–85, a second exposition was held; this time the company contributed an exhibit of twelve looms shown in actual operation. Gustavus Taft attended this exposition personally. The company also exhibited at the Raleigh exposition the following year.

thence by steamer to Norfolk or Charleston. As protection against the corrosive effects of the salt air, machined surfaces had been slushed with white lead or grease.

Unfortunately, shipment by water involved numerous transfers, thus increasing the likelihood of damage en route. Delivery of machinery to South Carolina, for instance, required as many as eight transshipments along the way. At Whitinsville, machinery was first loaded aboard a horse-drawn wagon and then hauled, on one of four daily trips, to the Whitins railroad station a mile and a half away.[18] There it was transferred to a railroad car and sent either to Boston or, more generally, to Providence, depending on which port had a steamer leaving for the desired Southern destination. Since there was then no provision for switching railroad cars directly to the wharves, machinery boxes had to be unloaded at a siding and carted to the dock by wagon. In Boston the Whitin company relied on the firm of Frost & Company to haul its shipments from siding to wharf, since Frost's draymen were accustomed to handling the bulky but fragile boxes of textile machinery; in Providence a Whitin employee usually went along to supervise the transfer and loading. If possible, the machinery was put aboard a steamer bound directly for the South, although sometimes transshipment at New York was unavoidable. In the Southern port the machinery was again transferred to a railroad car and then was finally hauled to its destination.

As through rail shipments to the South became possible in the late 1870's, Whitin executives advised customers to take advantage of railroad transportation because of the added protection made possible by the reduction in handling. However, in most cases the cost of rail shipments proved much higher than the cost of shipments by water. Moreover, machinery sent long distances by rail still had to be boxed securely. Since the boxes were bulky and of awkward size, efficient loading was difficult to achieve. Many boxes, in fact, were too large to fit into cars with side doors and hence could be shipped only in cars equipped with doors at the end, which unfortunately were difficult to obtain. There was a time during 1879 when Lasell complained that he had fifty carloads of machinery waiting for shipment because of the shortage of that type of rolling equipment.[19] Once, upon being sent a side-door car instead of one with end doors,

Lasell in exasperation ordered the shop's carpenters to rip out one end of the car. Then, after loading and sealing it, he reported the incident to the railroad company and at the same time wrote to his customer explaining that only by similarly breaking into the car could he unload his machinery.[20]

Credit for devising a method of making railroad shipments economically feasible seems to belong to the Lowell Machine Shop, although the evidence is incomplete. The solution lay in loading machinery unboxed, with shoring as its only protection. To make economical use of all available space, some machines were partially disassembled before loading. This method of shipment came to be known as "partial boxing." The first, somewhat oblique, reference to partial boxing in the Whitin correspondence was made in a letter written by Josiah Lasell on 1 September 1881 to the Pendleton Manufacturing Company, of Pendleton, South Carolina. "It was . . . proposed," the letter reads, "to 'knock down' and partially box [your machinery], but as we had never in all our business experience done the proposed thing, nor ever had heard of it being done, we concluded the only proper thing to be done was to box complete."

Just one month later, in a letter to a prospective customer, Thomas M. Holt, of Haw River, North Carolina, Josiah Lasell wrote, "It has been our theory, that the extra cost [of shipping machinery by rail, erected and fully boxed] was more than made up by the better condition in which the frames would reach the mill. But I am confident we can put as many frames (knocked down and unboxed) into a car, and as securely, as any other builder." Since Lasell's letter then goes on to discuss the freight differential between shipments from Whitinsville and those from Lowell,* one is led to surmise that the whole matter of partial boxing had been brought to Holt's attention by a competitive bid made by the Lowell Machine Shop. Unfortunately the letter from Holt which provoked Lasell's determined reply and which probably explained where Holt had learned about partial boxing, is missing from the Whitin collection.[21] It is significant, however, that shortly thereafter Lasell began quoting standard

---

* Until about 1890, Lowell seems to have enjoyed a freight-rate advantage over Whitin. After 1890, however, all New England points were assigned the same rates in shipping cotton machinery to the South.

2 per cent rates for partial boxing instead of the old 5 per cent rate for full boxing.* Thus, although the freight charges on shipments by rail continued to be higher than on shipments by water, the saving in boxing charges was nearly sufficient to offset the difference.†

In the earlier years, when machines were shipped completely erected, it was usually not necessary to send anyone from the Whitin plant to supervise putting them in operation in the mill. During the

* Perhaps it is also significant that within a year Lasell and Taft were laying plans to build a new carpenter shop to handle the increased amount of carpentry work required by partial boxing. The new shop, designated Shop No. 3 in Chart III, was located across the Mumford River where formerly the lumber yard had been. A construction superintendent named William A. Chapman was paid a $10,000 fee to design the building and supervise its erection.

One of the notable features of the new shop was its lack of a power unit. Rather than provide for a separate water turbine, Chapman stretched a rope drive across the river, protecting it from the elements by an enclosed bridge. In an article that appeared in the company's employee magazine in March, 1920, the rope-drive arrangement was described as follows: "Cotton rope for belting was introduced in our shop by Mr. Taft just after his return from [a trip to] England. The rope was purchased over there. Mr. Whipple had charge of these belts and tells us that there were nineteen separate ropes used. They were spliced together in splices of 12 feet in length, each splice of the same thickness as the rope. In repairing these ropes, Mr. Whipple says, they had great difficulty in doing the splicing. Sailors who were set at the task would make the splices too thick and it was necessary to send to England for instructions. Short splices were received from abroad, showing the different processes, which were then easily copied. Manila rope was found to be more enduring than cotton and was used to replace the ropes as they wore out. The difficulties of a rope drive were that the ropes rolled and soon wore themselves out in doing so; also the spliced parts were continually breaking away which meant that the power would have to be shut off or the ragged end would become twisted up in the other ropes."

† For instance, an order of machinery shipped in 1886 to the Mount Holly mill in Mount Holly, North Carolina, cost $210 when shipped by rail "released." By water it would have cost only $160, but the added boxing costs would have brought the amount up to $195 and insurance would have added $6.00 or $7.00. (The company insisted that its customers carry enough insurance on machinery being shipped them by water to cover the billed price plus 10 per cent for shipping charges. The insurance rate on a water shipment to South Carolina varied between .5 and 1 per cent. Although the cost of insurance was borne by the customer, the insurance itself was made payable, in case of loss, to the Whitin Machine Works.) Thus, the Mount Holly shipment, if sent by water with all the attendant risk that the machinery might be damaged en route, would have cost $202, whereas shipping by rail cost $210. The company usually recommended that its customers have their machinery sent by rail "released." "Released" meant that the railroad was released from all liability for breakage except in case of train wreck, in which case it was still liable. Shipments sent "not released" were prohibitively expensive.

1880's, however, as the practice of shipping machinery disassembled became common, it was essential to have skilled men available to erect the machines at their destination. These erectors traveled from mill to mill, setting up Whitin machinery and making sure that it was in proper operating order. The Whitin company charged the mills a flat daily rate ($2.00 in the 1880's) for the services of each erector, plus the cost of their transportation and of their room and board while on the job.

In order to make sure that all parts fitted properly, machines were always erected on the floor of the shop before shipment, even when they had to be dismantled for packing and reërected at the mill.* However, some adjustment of parts was frequently necessary after machines had been reassembled in the mill. In the earlier years when parts were not well standardized, some filing and fitting may have been required to obtain proper results, and for that reason the erectors were at first called "fitters." As the company became sensitive to the implications of the term, that name was abandoned and the euphemistic title of erector was adopted.

As the Southern market continued to expand and as the shipment of disassembled machinery became more common, the demand for erectors grew rapidly. At first three or four were enough to handle the entire Southern area, but by 1900 it was necessary to have fifteen or twenty in the South at all times. By 1917 the number had to be increased to a hundred.[22]

Occasionally the home shop asked these erectors to interview Southern mill owners who had written to Whitinsville for information or price quotations. Such requests, however, were surprisingly few. Probably the home management looked upon erectors as technicians, unequipped to handle the niceties of price negotiations, especially since those negotiations not infrequently involved tens of thousands of dollars' worth of machinery.

---

* The practice of making trial erections is still adhered to today, although many in the industry condemn it as a needless duplication of effort. No one denies that machines such as spinning frames must be shipped disassembled (some Whitin frames are so long that surveyors' intruments must be used to line them up); nor does anyone believe that it would be possible under existing conditions to erect a spinning frame for the first time on the floor of a customer's mill. As yet the flow of parts is not reliable enough, nor are the dimensions of parts true enough, to enable field erectors to do their work expeditiously without the advantage of a preliminary erection at the shop.

3. A REPRESENTATIVE IN THE SOUTH

The first boom in Southern mill building was cut short by the nationwide depression that began in 1883. For the four ensuing years, orders from the South were small and spotty.* Then, in 1888, revival came with a surge. In that year alone Whitin's Southern sales exceeded a half-million dollars. For the first time in history the Rhode Island area lost its position as the leading market for Whitin products.

Between 1889 and 1893 the company enjoyed moderate prosperity, with about a third of its orders coming from the South (see Appendices 29 and 30). Finally, in the fall of 1893, the era of prosperity came to an abrupt end as the entire nation's economy contracted sharply in another general depression. Between August and November the company's weekly payroll fell off from $11,700 to $4,700, a drop of 60 per cent. Throughout the following year business continued in a depressed state. Northern mills were especially hard hit, and many of them experienced heavy losses. But the new mills in the South showed that already they had developed competitive strength, for even in depression they continued to enjoy respectable, if slightly diminished, earnings.[23]

Desperately in need of sales, Marston Whitin now realized that the South was his only promising market. In July, 1894, he abandoned his company's resolute policy against selling through agents and, as if feeling his way forward, promised Godfrey's Textile Machinery Agency, of Providence, a 5 per cent commission on the first six Whitin cards it sold in the South. Later in the year he granted a similar commission to the D. A. Tompkins Company, of Charlotte, North Carolina; this time, however, the commission was to

* During the boom years, 1881, 1882, and 1883, Lasell paid out dividends at the rate of 50 per cent (of capital) a year. Then in the following two depression years he paid no dividends whatsoever. It was to be the only occasion in the company's entire incorporated history when dividends would be passed. Probably, had Lasell realized what a break he was causing in the company's record, he would never have allowed the gap to occur. From the standpoint of cash resources there was no occasion for not paying dividends. But with business conditions uncertain, and with the more-than-generous dividends of preceding years, he probably felt that the way of caution was to remain liquid. And since 89 per cent of the company's stock was held either in his name or in the name of his wife, it really mattered little whether or not the company maintained a regular dividend policy.

cover the entire machinery order for a 5,376-spindle venture to be known as the Statesville Manufacturing Company. Whitin's initial agreement with D. A. Tompkins was followed shortly by a second in which Tompkins was granted, for a trial period of one year, a 5 per cent commission on whatever orders he directed to the Whitin shop.

This man Tompkins was by all standards the leading mill engineer of his era and probably one of the best-known men in the South. Unlike many of the early mill engineers, he was a Southerner by birth. Following two years at the University of South Carolina he had studied engineering at Rensselaer Polytechnic Institute, in Troy, New York. Then, after holding various jobs in the North and abroad, he had returned to Charlotte in 1882[24] where, to take advantage of the current boom in mill construction, he had set up offices as a mill engineer and contractor. By 1894, he was also sole owner of a small machine and repair shop* and was principal owner of the Charlotte *Daily Observer*. Possessed of remarkable vitality, he was recognized widely as a gifted speaker, an ardent sponsor of textile schools, and a leading proponent of Southern industrialism.

One might expect that Whitin would have found reason to congratulate himself on having secured so able a man as his Southern representative. Yet this was not the case. The temperament of Tompkins the promoter was too dissimilar from that of Whitin the business man for the two men to work in harmonious collaboration. Whitin viewed with disfavor Tompkins' enthusiasm for every mill venture no matter how unsoundly financed. He disliked Tompkins' energetic pursuit of a dozen interests apart from his machinery selling. Especially did he fulminate when he learned that Tompkins was planning to take on, in addition to his Whitin line, the agency of a British firm.

Even had the two men not clashed in personality, it is apparent that contention over Tompkins' rate of commission would eventually have disrupted their relationship. It happened that the year 1895,

* By 1894, Charlotte, which was located at the center of Southern mill activity and which was a main station on the Southern Railroad (the line which served four-fifths of the mills in the South), was the leading cotton-textile machinery center in the South.

even though it came in the midst of a general depression, was unusually busy for the textile machinery industry, especially in the South. Whitin felt, therefore, that many of the orders sent in by Tompkins would have been forthcoming anyway. At least he was not convinced that his agent's services were worth the rate of about $15,000 a year at which Tompkins was earning commissions. In the future, Whitin felt, the commission should be 3 per cent instead of 5 per cent. Tompkins disagreed. Before the trial year had expired, Whitin informed his agent that the year's experience had proved less than satisfactory and that continuation on a permanent basis would not be possible.*

As a side-lines observer, Stuart W. Cramer, the manager of the D. A. Tompkins Company, had witnessed with interest the gradual breakdown of the trial arrangement. In his position as administrator of Tompkins' business affairs, Cramer had become well acquainted with the Whitin company and its officials. Indeed, he had on two occasions during the year paid a visit to the plant in Whitinsville. Apparently a tie-up with the Whitin company seemed desirable to him. Perhaps he saw little future in his job with Tompkins or perhaps he found Tompkins' erratic nature difficult to work with (he gave as his official reason his disapproval of Tompkins' connection with British manufacturers). At any rate, Cramer took it upon himself, after Whitin had made clear his intention not to renew the agreement with Tompkins, to ask for the job as Whitin representative for the Southern territory.[25]

Benefiting from his knowledge of Whitin's views on the matter, Cramer proposed either that he be paid a 3 per cent commission or, as an alternative, that he be retained on a straight salary basis. The reason for suggesting a salary, he said, was because so many mill men preferred to deal directly with the machinery manufacturer himself rather than through a commission agent whose income depended on the prices he charged. Moreover, much of the work in the South, at least initially, would have to be of the missionary type, work for which a commission arrangement did not provide adequate incentive.

* Shortly after he had severed his connections with Whitin, Tompkins became agent for the Mason Machine Works.

In specific terms, Cramer proposed that he be allowed a salary of $10,800 a year, out of which he would be expected to pay all expenses incidental to (a) maintaining an office, (b) employing an assistant, a draftsman, and a secretary, and (c) traveling in the states of Virginia, North Carolina, South Carolina, and Georgia. (Traveling in other states would be at the Whitin company's expense.) In practical terms, Cramer's recommendation meant that he would receive a net salary, after expenses, of about $5,000 a year, since out of his $10,800 allowance he would have to spend at least $1,500 for an assistant and $1,000 each for a draftsman and a stenographer.[26] His office rent would probably be nominal,[27] but his traveling expenses would necessarily be heavy. (In at least one month, later on, he reported having covered 5,000 miles.)[28] Yet he seems to have considered that he would be well rewarded by such a contract, and it is evident that Marston Whitin, in accepting the proposal, wanted him to feel that way.[29] In relation to the men with whom he would have to do business, it seems apparent that Cramer's emolument was handsome, for according to one estimate,[30] Southern mill presidents at that time characteristically earned at most from $5,000 to $10,000 a year, while superintendents seldom received a salary of more than $3,000.

There can be no doubt that, in Cramer, Whitin found an ideal Southern representative. Cramer was a younger man than Tompkins by sixteen years and was junior to Whitin by eleven. Born in Thomasville, North Carolina (31 March 1868), he had received his schooling at the United States Naval Academy at Annapolis (1884–88).[31] He had then returned to civilian life and had gone to New York to study for a year at the School of Mines, Columbia College. Upon graduation he had been appointed assayer-in-charge of the assay office at Charlotte where he had become acquainted with and finally (in 1893) had gone to work for D. A. Tompkins, serving as general manager of the Tompkins engineering and construction company.

Unlike Tompkins, Cramer was conservative in his business methods, friendly with the banking group and the well-to-do, and scornful of the popular favor that his former employer sought so sedulously to cultivate. Yet he was a jovial man, big in build and

Stuart W. Cramer, Southern Agent, 1895–1919

hearty in laughter. He had the magnificent self-confidence and buoyant optimism of the natural salesman and on occasion gave Whitin wry amusement by his ability to sell a customer machinery that the customer did not really need. Most of the few storms in their otherwise tranquil relationship arose, in fact, when Whitin, in an effort to maintain the standard of industry ethics, was obliged to restrain Cramer from his occasionally ruthless selling tactics.

One of Cramer's chief assets was his happy facility for working closely with home management, often making several lengthy reports in a single day. His letters were detailed, comprehensive, and yet straight to the point. On matters of competitive gossip he was particularly careful to keep Whitin posted. His criticisms of company policy were always judiciously worded and were often too cogent to be ignored. One gains the impression from reading his daily reports that he sincerely regarded Marston Whitin as the most able man in the business.

His attempts to influence home-office management proved particularly successful in matters concerning advertising. One example is notable because of the subtle illumination it cast on the men involved. When Cramer first became Whitin agent in the South, he asked permission to advertise in the Charlotte *Daily Observer,* the newspaper owned by D. A. Tompkins. The rate was to be only $235 a year, but J. M. Lasell, who was responsible for all company advertising, felt that the company's display in the *Textile Excelsior* was all the promotion that circumstances justified.* By replying that the two media reached completely different reader groups, Cramer succeeded in winning support for his proposal. Upon submitting his first fly sheet for approval, however, he received a scorching reply and a peremptory order to cancel the contract. Heading the offending page was the newspaper's banner pledge to William Jennings

---

* The first Whitin advertisement in the *Textile Excelsior* — and apparently the company's first regular advertisement in the South — was placed in December, 1894. Probably Cramer's happiest advertising scheme was a set of handbooks which he compiled for the use of mill men. First published in one volume in 1898, *Useful Information for Cotton Manufacturers* was issued in a second edition in 1904 in an expanded two-volume form, the first volume being concerned with textile machinery and the second with miscellaneous mill equipment including power plants. In 1906 a third volume on "Dyeing and Special Finishing Machinery" was added, and in 1909 a fourth on air-conditioning.

Bryan and Free Silver. Cramer hastily explained that a cancellation of the advertisement would be a stroke of unhappy diplomacy, for news would soon spread among Whitin's Free Silver customers that the Whitin people were gold crucifixionists. Reluctantly Lasell acquiesced and the advertisement remained.

Cramer's contribution to the company's success cannot be easily overstressed. Entering at a critical point in the development of the industry, he was in large part responsible for the Whitin firm's gaining first place among its competitors in the ruthless race for Southern business. He had the necessary strength and energy required by a job that took him through a country where traveling and sleeping accommodations were poor and where malaria and typhoid fever were prevalent.* In a highly competitive game he enjoyed the contest. With a flare for histrionics, he took pride in fitting his selling approach to his customers' temperaments. If he could not get orders by reason of his thoroughgoing knowledge of textile machinery, he won them through the sheer force of his personality.

If Cramer had any major fault it was his failure to go far enough beyond North Carolina in his search for orders. Even today the Whitin company feels the effect of this neglect, for its sales are still not proportionally so strong in the other states of the South as in North Carolina. But if Cramer had to have a fault, this at least was a good one, for although North Carolina stood second in place to South Carolina in the South's early mill development, it surpassed its Southern twin early in the 1920's and in the 1930's went ahead of its Northern rival, Massachusetts, to become the leading cotton manufacturing state in the Union.

As the South prospered, Cramer added more men to his selling staff and received increasingly larger allowances, until by 1911 his gross annual salary from the Whitin company alone amounted to $30,900. In addition he was, by then, drawing income from various other sources and was counted among Charlotte's wealthy citizens.

---

* In May, 1898, Cramer complained of an attack of malaria, and again in August, 1904. In August, 1898, he was in bed for several weeks with typhoid fever. So that his family might avoid the unhealthful summers, he customarily sent them to vacation in Portland, Maine. In August, 1905, Whitin advised the erectors working at the Lane and Maginnis mills in New Orleans to use their discretion about remaining on the job during a yellow fever epidemic.

The salary plan proved a great success in fostering Cramer's early missionary work, but in later years, when the South's mill development began leveling off, it turned out to be something of a sedative to Cramer's once-spirited salesmanship.

In later years Cramer, like Tompkins, engaged in many outside activities. He became financially interested in the Ryder Wagon Company and, with his father, in the Cramer Furniture Company (chairs). He established the Cramer Air Conditioning Company to manufacture one of the standard air-conditioning units of the time and took on such a large line of supplementary mill equipment that he came to be regarded as one of the leading manufacturers' agents in the South. From these several sources he received what must have been a substantial income. Indeed, in the later years of his career he was often needled by Whitin for spending so much of his time in activities aside from his machinery interests. But the fortune and renown that came to him during his quarter-century as Whitin agent was in large measure deserved, for in any history of the Whitin Machine Works, Cramer must rank as one of the four or five top contributors to the company's success.*

4. TERMS OF SALE

Cramer's innate conservatism in financial matters was revealed in his careful selection of customers. In an era when the promise of high profits gave encouragement to weakly financed mill promotions, attention to credit risks was an important part of salesmanship, for the bad debt of one large customer could have seriously embarrassed Whitin, and even unduly slow collections could have put a heavy strain on the company's working-capital resources. It was natural, therefore, that Cramer should have wanted to concentrate

---

* Being a reserve officer, Cramer did duty in Washington during World War I. He retired from business in 1919, and the Whitin Machine Works bought out his Charlotte office and turned it over to his two assistants, Robert I. Dalton and William H. Porcher. These two men divided the Southern territory between them, Dalton taking Virginia, North Carolina, and Tennessee, and Porcher South Carolina, Georgia, Alabama, Mississippi, Louisiana, and Texas. Cramer was active in Republican politics and in the cotton textile industry of the South for twenty years after his retirement. He died 2 July 1940. Adulatory obituaries appeared in the Charlotte *Observer* (4 July 1940), the Gastonia *Gazette* (3 July 1940), and the Charlotte *News* (3 July 1940).

his selling effort in North Carolina where he was best acquainted and where he was most familiar with the credit rating of new mill enterprises.

As a market for cotton-textile machinery, North Carolina was by no means the best in the South in the 1890's; Georgia was about equally good, while South Carolina was a match for the other two states combined (see Appendix 31). But in respect to credit risks, North Carolina was probably the most desirable Southern market, for its mills typically were small ventures, commenced with equity capital and enlarged out of operating earnings.[32] The graph lines in Appendix 32 show vividly how strong Cramer's influence in North Carolina actually was; by concentrating more than half his sales in his home territory, Cramer was able to make many mill centers in the state virtually Whitin preserves.

Marston Whitin seems to have endorsed Cramer's policy of reducing credit risks by selling principally to the better-financed, medium-sized mills, although on occasion he seems to have regretted that there was no large mill in the South using Whitin machinery "right straight through."[33] At one time he even requested Cramer to withhold publication of a list of Whitin customers and the number of spinning frames they had bought, because, while the list established Whitin's ring frames as unquestionably the most popular in the South, it showed that few Whitin frames were to be found in the largest and best-known Southern mills.[34]

Even though the Whitin company deliberately chose to limit its market to the more conservative mills, it could not completely escape all credit risks in a situation as volatile as that which existed in the early years of the Southern mill development. It is true that in cases of bankruptcy the company usually managed to collect its debts, since as a creditor it held a prior claim on the bankrupt mills' assets. But such collections were frequently slow and troublesome. Often it was necessary to take preferred stock in reorganized mills and even, on occasion, to assume direct management of mills that had fallen into trouble.[35] But in general the Whitin Machine Works suffered surprisingly little from bad-debt losses.

Beginning about 1898, Marston Whitin made regular use of R. G. Dun & Company's credit reports as an aid in checking the financial reliability of customers. For a time in 1901 he also tried Bradstreet's reports. But after comparing the two he wrote to Cramer, "We are a little surprised that Bradstreet is thought more of in the South than Dun. Last year we took Bradstreet's Agency in order to compare it with Dun's, which we had had for years before. Our opinion, from the year's observation, was that Dun's reports were more promptly rendered and more satisfactory as to details." [36]

Yet in the South even mills with the best credit ratings found prompt payments sometimes difficult to make. In busy times, just when they needed more machinery, many mills had their available resources tied up in inventories. Additional funds were difficult, or at least expensive, to obtain in an economy that was short of investment capital. Not uncommonly they found themselves forced to pay for a large portion of their machinery in promissory notes. In such cases Whitin insisted that the notes be signed by all the directors of the enterprise.

There *were* occasions when Whitin wanted to take a *particular* order; perhaps he needed to fill a temporary gap in the productive capacity of a shop department; perhaps he felt that the mill involved had a promising future and would make a good long-term customer; or perhaps he simply wished to exclude other competitors from a particular area. Under such circumstances he sometimes ignored an unfavorable credit report from Cramer or Dun's agency and accepted an order — but only on condition that title to the machinery remain in his hands until the order had been completely paid for. In a highly competitive market, however, conditional sales were difficult to negotiate. Some mill owners would take almost any make of machinery rather than have their equipment bound by such an agreement. Moreover, Cramer was not always an enthusiastic sponsor of the idea. Most Southern states treated conditional sales as chattel mortgages and required that they be registered in a local courthouse. In many instances Cramer was not anxious to have the terms of his contracts thus made available to public scrutiny. Moreover, under such an agreement promissory notes could not be accepted at the time of sale, for such notes legally constituted "payment in full" and would have caused title to the machinery to revert to the mill.[37] As a result, the conditional sale was used as a protective instrument far less often than one might have expected.

One of the reasons why it was important to have some check on a customer's credit was that collections in the South were hedged about with difficulties. Laws in many of the states were admittedly designed to protect the debtor from his creditor. From 1896 to 1906 Whitin found it expedient to hire, on a retainer fee, the services of "Judge" Armistead Burwell of the Charlotte firm of Burwell, Walker & Cansler, simply to have available the advice of someone familiar with local technicalities.*

TABLE 8

Analysis of Terms of Sale for the Year 1909

Terms	Sales to New England (Per cent)	Sales to the South (Per cent)	Sales to Other States (Per cent)	Total Sales (Per cent)
Cash—30 days.................	47.6	19.5	51.6	37.3
—60 days.................	18.3	1.0	2.6	10.6
—120 days................	13.7	.3	7.5	8.2
—6 months...............	3.1	10.5	....	5.6
Half cash—balance in 1 year....	1.5	26.4	14.7	11.9
—balance in stock....	1.5	5.9	....	3.0
Third cash—balance in 1 year...	1.6	....	....	.9
—balance in 2 years..	1.6	2.5	....	1.8
Quarter cash—balance in 1 year.	2.1	....	....	1.2
—balance in 2 years	.9	18.8	....	7.5
—balance in 3 years	2.9	.8	3.7	2.2
Title retained.................	.5	6.1	....	2.5
Terms not recorded...........	4.7	8.2	19.9	7.3
Totals.......................	100.0	100.0	100.0	100.0
Per cent of total sales..........	54.4	37.4	8.2	100.0

Source: Machinery book No. 1, and Letterbooks 79–85.

* Why Burwell left the Whitin employ in 1906 and immediately became counsel for the Draper Company is not recorded. It is known, however, that a short time before his resignation, a stenographer in the Whitin company, when asked to send Burwell copies of all correspondence dealing with a particular mill failure, had inadvertently included a letter from Cramer to Whitin in which a recent course of action taken by Burwell was severely criticized. Following Burwell's departure, Whitin, in typical industrialist fashion, decided to do without legal counsel (which he said was "pretty expensive"), although from time to time he did hire lawyers for advice on particular problems.

Gradually Whitin became accustomed to the fact that his Southern business could not be carried along on the same credit terms as his business in the North. (The figures in Table 8 show how different was the treatment expected by, and extended to, the customers in the two regions.)[38] In the North the standard selling terms were "cash, 30 days," while in the South the most common terms were "half cash, the balance payable within a year." Whereas in the North over 80 per cent of all bills were collected within six months after presentation, in the South only about 30 per cent were collected within that period and about 20 per cent were allowed to ride for two years or more.

It is natural that the Whitin company, in view of the high costs incidental to selling machinery in the South on such long terms, should have been willing to grant more liberal prices to their Northern customers. Beginning about 1901 and continuing until the time of World War I, Whitin machinery was sold in New England f.o.b. the railroad station nearest the customer's mill and was erected without charge.[39] By this means Whitin (and his competitors as well, for it became a standard practice in the industry) could favor Northern customers without deviating from published price lists. The differential created by such a concession varied under differing conditions. Erection costs usually added about one per cent to the bills sent by the company to its Southern customers. Shipping to the South added another 5 per cent or more to the machinery's cost.[40] In addition, many Northern mills enjoyed the advantage of receiving cash discounts of 2, 3, or even 5 per cent on bills paid within ten days of delivery. Moreover, when giving notes in part payment for machinery, Northerners had to pay only 5 instead of 6 per cent interest. Consequently, Northern mill owners usually had a decided advantage over their Southern competitors in the prices they paid for machinery.

5. COMMON STOCKS FOR COTTON MACHINERY

Southern mill promoters commonly had to bear yet another expense — that of raising capital. In the North, mills usually could depend either on their own ample resources or on their well-established financial connections for any expansion capital they needed.

Southern mills seldom had either of these sources to depend on. D. A. Tompkins once stated that Southern mill men could count on obtaining from local investors no more than half the capital they needed; for the remainder, they usually had to look to the North.[41] Unfortunately, the normal channels through which Northern capital flowed were all but closed to them, for most Northern investors had no way of judging the soundness of — and hence had no faith in — the hundreds of small Southern mills that were seeking new capital funds. Even in the South there is said to have been no regular market for mill securities until about 1890.[42] Hence, when the promoters of the earliest mills found themselves unable to tap established reservoirs of capital, they turned for financial assistance to those individuals in the North who had reason to be interested in their success — the machine-builders who hoped to sell them machinery and the dry-goods commission houses who hoped to sell their goods.

Often the dry-goods firms were financially the better of the two connections. True, a commission house usually dealt with no more than perhaps six or eight mills, but in all of them it stood ready to carry a substantial investment, first as a means of assuring itself of a dependable source of supply and, secondly, as a lever to control the type, quality, and price of goods manufactured by the mills. Since a mill customarily sold its entire output through one commission house, the association between the two was usually mutually beneficial and hence long-continuing.

The typical association between mill and machine shop was of a somewhat different nature. Instead of doing business with a small scattering of mills, the machine-builder dealt with dozens, if not hundreds, of them — too many for him to hold blocks of stock in very many. Moreover, the machine-builder's primary interest in a mill extended only through the period when the mill's machinery was under construction. Thereafter, except for service calls and repair work, the builder had no further business with a mill until it decided either to replace its existing machinery or to enlarge its capacity. In both cases the builder might find it to his advantage to be a stockholder in the mill, but usually the mere fact that his machinery was already in the mill was enough to establish his priority to any new business that was to be had. Consequently, a machine-builder, in contrast with a textile commission house, had little to gain by retaining any stock that he might take in a mill as a means of encouraging either its initial promotion or its later expansion. Under such circumstances companies in the textile machinery industry typically followed one of two courses.[43] Some agreed to take stock in the mills of a few key (and usually well-established) customers partly as friendly gestures and partly as thoughtful investments. Others, to satisfy the demands of their customers, took stock in part payment for nearly every lot of machinery they sold, only to resell the stock as soon as the market was favorable.*

In general the Whitin Machine Works belonged to the group which took stocks infrequently — and then only as investments. It might be argued that the reason why the company took securities so seldom was that it had few connections with Boston investment circles (in contrast, for instance, to the Pettee Machine Works) and hence had little opportunity to unload the stocks it was offered. Moreover, the more conservative policy was clearly better suited to the temperament of George Marston Whitin, who was a subscriber to the tenet that a manfacturer should always stick to the business he knows best.

Unfortunately the Whitin records contain an incomplete account of the mill stocks taken by the company in settlement of its machinery bills. Apparently the company kept no regular statement of its stock holdings; at least, none has been preserved. Perhaps the bundle of certificates locked away in some vault drawer was considered record enough. From references to stock negotiations contained in Marston Whitin's correspondence, it seems clear that comparatively little stock was taken before 1895 and that between 1895 and 1905 (during which years the company took about 75 per cent of all the stock it ever took) not more than 5 per cent of its total sales were paid for in that manner. When one considers that the other principal producer in the industry, the Lowell Machine

---

* One of the companies in the industry fell outside both these categories; until 1905 the Lowell Machine Shop scrupulously avoided taking any mill stocks whatsoever.

Shop, took absolutely no stock during that period, one is led to believe that the machinery manufacturers as a group were not heavy contributors of capital to Southern mill developments. Nevertheless, one should not lose sight of the fact that in many specific instances machinery builders did supply up to 20 per cent of the capital going into individual mill ventures.*

One of the reasons that the acceptance of stock was not more widely engaged in by machinery companies during the initial years of the Southern development was that such inter-corporate stock transactions were not then believed to be permissible under common law. In the case of the Piedmont Manufacturing Company already referred to, Lasell had been obliged to write, "As a company we are not able to hold stock." [44] Since the Whitin firm was believed to be legally unable to hold stock, John C. Whitin had stepped forward with the offer to buy the stock personally. What followed thereupon was merely a bookkeeping transaction, but it met the requirements of the law. Lasell merely credited the Piedmont account with the value of the stock purchase and debited Whitin's dividend account accordingly. In other words, John C. Whitin was agreeing to accept a part of his dividends in the form of Piedmont stock instead of in cash.

Following the Piedmont precedent, Whitin stockholders on several occasions agreed to assist their company by subscribing privately to the common stocks of customers. However, since none of the Whitin stockholders was wealthy enough to be able to forego his cash dividends on many successive occasions, such cases were understandably few. Inasmuch as the owners of competing companies must have been similarly situated, the acceptance of stock did not become an issue within the industry until about 1893, when there seems to have occurred a revision of attitude toward the meaning of existing statutes. All stock taken in payment for machinery after

---

* At the request of William F. Draper, Whitin drew up a careful estimate of the complete cost of erecting a mill. This estimate appears in Appendix 18. From the figures given, it is apparent that the cost of machinery amounted to about 40 per cent of the total cost of the fixed assets in a typical mill venture. When machinery builders sometimes accepted common stocks in payment for half their machinery bill, they were in effect subscribing to only about a fifth of the total capitalization of the mill.

that date was made out directly to the Whitin Machine Works. Yet no Massachusetts statute or judicial interpretation was passed in or around 1893 making legal what company officials had once considered to be against the law. In New Jersey such a law was passed in 1888, and in many other states similar laws were enacted soon thereafter. But in Massachusetts no law specifically permitting corporate stockholding was ever passed. Instead, a reappraisal of existing statutes seems to have convinced lawyers and their clients that the investment in common stocks by corporations was in fact perfectly legal. Since the right of Massachusetts companies to hold stocks in companies outside Massachusetts was never actually challenged in court, the privilege came to be generally recognized even though it was without specific legal sanction.*

For a short time after 1893, George Marston Whitin fell in with the suddenly popular practice of letting Southern customers pay part of their machinery bills in common stocks. Soon, however, he realized that competitive practices were leading him to tie up too much of his working capital in unnegotiable securities, and so he began a campaign within the industry to have stock acceptance outlawed by general agreement. For a time his efforts were successful, as will be related in the following chapter, but after 1900 the competitive struggle for the booming Southern market grew so keen that it became impossible for him to exert effective restraint of any kind on the industry's selling methods. For a while the Whitin company, perhaps because it catered to the conservatively

---

* The only judicial interpretation affecting corporate stockholding in Massachusetts at that time was an opinion rendered in 1895 by the Attorney General of the Commonwealth whereby a corporation organized for the express purpose of buying and selling stocks in other corporations was considered legal under an act passed in 1874. There was no amendment to Massachusetts statutes during the 1890's such as the 1888 New Jersey law, and in fact even today there is no specific grant of power to companies incorporated under Massachusetts laws to hold stock in other companies. Nor was there any change in the Whitin Machine Works charter which might have given the company any special powers. I am indebted to Professor E. Merrick Dodd of the Harvard Law School for help in tracing through the legal aspects of the Whitin company's holding of mill stocks. See also the Commonwealth of Massachusetts *Report of the Committee on Corporation Laws*, January, 1903, chap. 4, pp. 202–204, which, although it discusses laws passed by other states making it legal for companies to hold stock in other companies, is silent regarding any such law in Massachusetts.

financed mills of North Carolina, was able to maintain, and even to increase, its Southern sales without being forced to accept large blocks of securities.*

Even the few stocks that the Whitin company did accept put a strain on its liquid resources, for its inventories and receivables were just then expanding under the pressure of business activity. To conserve cash, Whitin, whenever possible, distributed some of the more reliable mill stocks in place of cash dividends. Since the company had few stockholders, it was possible to make the distribution on an informal basis. At stockholders' meetings the owners merely discussed which stocks should be distributed without making any attempt to arrive at a decision regarding fair market values. If a security was sound — and Marston Whitin would not allow the distribution of any stock he considered unsound — it was arbitrarily valued at par. No attempt was made to prorate stocks among the Whitin company's owners. An owner simply expressed his willingness to accept the securities of a particular mill. The next owner

---

* When stock was accepted in part payment for machinery, the machinery was usually billed at list price and the stock was accepted at par value. However, Whitin was frank to admit that he was willing to give a 10% discount rather than take an order involving stock. In actual practice it was possible for Cramer to cut his prices on "cash" sales even further than 10% without reducing the company's profit margin below what it would have been on a "stock" sale. Under even the most favorable circumstances the stock of a new mill, had Whitin wanted to dispose of it, could not be expected to command any market whatsoever until the mill had been in operation for at least a year. Since dividends were seldom paid during the first year, and since new stocks seldom could command a price of more than 90 on a par of 100 even when a market for them did develop, Cramer could usually cut his prices on no-stock sales by about 15% without affecting the company's profit margin. When, to the differential in costs between doing business with a New England mill on a cash basis and dealing with a Southern mill on a long-term credit, was added the differential of dealing in stock certificates, the price to mills which financed their purchases out of stocks seemed to many observers to be extortionate. As a result, the machinery companies were widely criticized for taking undue advantage of their Southern customers. There were also irresponsible charges that Northern mill men put pressure on machine-builders to charge their Southern customers higher prices, but there is no evidence to support such accusations. One other technical aspect of stock acceptance should be recorded. In Massachusetts, stock issues were required to be paid for in cash. In North and South Carolina, however, corporation laws permitted the giving of property (i.e., machinery) in exchange for stock. Thus, in those states it was possible to negotiate a stock sale simply by making a book entry, whereas in Massachusetts stocks had to be paid for in cash, after which the mill returned the cash in part payment for its machinery.

might prefer the securities of another mill, and so forth. Human judgment and mere luck played an inescapable part in such chance allocations, for some securities later increased in value while others declined. However, an owner could always sell his mill securities immediately, if he so chose, at a figure that was usually close to or above par. If he held the securities as an investment, the risk was entirely his.

Despite the practice of distributing mill stocks as dividends, the company continued to be embarrassed by a shortage of cash funds. A letter written 24 April 1901 to the manager of the Worcester branch of R. G. Dun & Company reflects Whitin's concern over how others might react to his balance sheet's odd appearance:

If you have looked over our statement to the State you will see that our [current] debts are about $1,200,000 but that our assets, cash accounts, and bills receivable amount to $1,550,000, our stock in process to some $300,000, leaving a balance in our favor of quick assets over liabilities of some $600,000, and the plant free which in this statement amounts to $525,000, and we think this a conservative estimate of the value of the plant. We have been doing a much larger business during the last year than for some years past, which is the occasion for our having been obliged to borrow money. Considerable of our business is done on a basis of half cash, one-quarter six and one-quarter twelve months, which, owing to the large volume of business, takes a large amount of money.

During 1902 the situation grew worse. Warring within the industry, even in the face of considerable business activity, drove prices to the lowest point they had ever been and forced machine-builders through competitive necessity to accept mill securities with practically every order. By the end of 1904 the Whitin company was holding at least $825,000 of mill stocks, figured at par value. Meanwhile it was having to borrow $625,000 from banks in Providence and the surrounding area to finance its working capital.[45] In a sense Whitin was using its own well-established credit standing to help its customers, whose line of credit was limited, by accepting their corporate securities in place of cash.

As prosperity continued, however, Whitin decided, sometime in 1905, that stock acceptance was no longer necessary to keep his shop busy. Orders from Northern mills were coming in with gratifying frequency. In fact, many in the North believed that Southern mill development had reached the peak of its rapid climb and that thenceforth something like a state of equilibrium would exist between the two regions.[46] After 1902, the Whitin company's sales to Southern mills gently but steadily declined, while its sales to mills in the North constantly mounted until they reached the highest peak on record in the years 1909 and 1910.

The most prosperous mill area in the North was the city of New Bedford, where many new combed cotton mills were being erected. Marston Whitin was especially anxious to sell equipment in that area, for he was eager to promote the new combing machine he had just put on the market (a later section will be devoted to the Whitin High-speed Comber). For that reason he decided to reverse his policy of four years' standing and in 1909 again began accepting mill stocks in part payment for machinery. Since prosperous conditions were already putting heavy demands on his working capital and since he was already borrowing heavily at the banks, he was faced with the necessity of unloading some of the Southern mill securities his company still had on hand if he was to take on any more.[47] To avoid offending his Southern customers, however, he disposed of their securities with judicious care. Usually he felt morally obliged to give the issuing mill first refusal before putting a block of stock on the market; in fact, in some instances he had agreed, at the time he took the stock, that he would give the mill owners an opportunity to buy back their stock if he ever decided to sell. In any event he was always careful to act only with the full knowledge of the mill owners concerned. Generally he sold to brokers or bankers in the South, seldom to Northern investors.

*   *   *

In 1917, the first year in which the company formally appraised its security assets, the market value of its mill-stock holdings was set at $893,694. In the years immediately following World War I, the account grew slightly larger as the company continued to accept what were generally regarded as blue-chip securities in New Bedford's growing mills. But after 1923 its investment portfolio steadily contracted — not so much through liquidations as through the general decline in mill-stock values in the 1920's. Fortunately, at this period the company did not need the funds it held in its portfolio and so was able to retain its stocks until World War II when most of them more than recovered their values. During the war period an average of roughly $100,000 worth of securities was sold each year, until by 1946 the Whitin company's mill-stock account had been virtually closed out.

Because the Whitin company made no effort to record its early transactions in mill securities, it has never been certain whether or not its willingness to accept stocks proved profitable in the long run, but the general belief is that it did. Up to the 1920's, stock acceptance was advantageous to all parties concerned. It helped the company to sell machinery; it provided a high-return investment to those of the company's stockholders who chose to retain their dividend-distributed mill stocks; and it gave fairly marketable securities to those stockholders who chose to liquidate their mill-stock dividends. In the 1920's, however, practically all mill stocks declined in value, and many of those distributed as blue chips a few years earlier turned worthless in the hands of their owners. Some stockholders, notably in the Taft and Marston Whitin families, lost small fortunes in New Bedford securities. The one redeeming feature was that those stockholders who retained their Southern mill securities long enough were able to offset some, if not all, of their losses when security values in general returned to a higher level.

CHAPTER XII

WHITIN AND THE INDUSTRY, 1880–1900

ONE cannot help being surprised at how infrequently before the 1890's Whitin executives made any reference to their competitors. Apparently the company was so close to its customers that it had no reason to fear losing orders to other machinery builders. "Once a Whitin customer, always a Whitin customer" seems to have been taken as something like a foregone conclusion.

In general there were only two circumstances under which the Whitin firm corresponded with its competitors: (1) when it wished to order a type of machine it did not make and (2) when it wished to discuss with others in the industry the question of tariff protection against imports of textile machinery from England. Neither occasion occurred very frequently. Except for the Drapers, who were politically ambitious, no one either in the Whitin company or in the rest of the industry did much to advance the "Home Market" cause beyond contributing financially to the support of a lobbyist in Washington. It is true that the tariff question did succeed in bringing the industry together in a trade association, but except for two brief periods later in history (in 1895–1903 and 1933–35) the association was not very active.

What really brought the units of the industry into a sudden and bitter awareness that they could not do business without taking each other's actions into account was the rise of cotton manufacturing in the South. In a relatively short space of time the traditionally tranquil textile machinery industry was thrown into near-pandemonium by the realization that an almost completely new market for machinery products was opening in the South. With their Northern customers experiencing one of the worst depressions in history (1893–95, 1897–98), every New England textile-machinery manufacturer turned his attention to getting orders from mills in North and South Carolina, Georgia, and Alabama.

Everywhere in American industry, at that time, cutthroat competition was prevalent, but in the textile machinery industry it had a special reason for existing: manufacturers were meeting each other for the first time in an all-out struggle for a new market where no one had the customary advantage of tightly cemented customer contacts and friendships.

One might have expected such a period of stiff competition to produce radical changes in product design, but, with the exception of the revolving top-flat card, it did not. Excessive competition proved disruptive rather than constructive and revealed itself in underhanded competitive practices rather than in product improvements. There were many efforts on the part of competitors to reach mutually agreeable standards of competitive ethics, but most such efforts were unsuccessful.

What distinguished the textile machinery industry from many other industries in the 1890's and early 1900's was its reluctance to amalgamate its forces in one huge merger. Rather late, as mergers went, the three leading shops in the Boston area combined to form the present-day Saco-Lowell Shops. But firms in the Providence area, still family-owned and family-managed, declined to follow the trend. If for no other reason than from a sense of pride, they maintained their personal independence by keeping their companies free of entangling alliances.

I. FORMATION OF A TRADE ASSOCIATION

The first evidence of coöperation between the Whitin Machine Works and the rest of the industry occurred in 1872 when Josiah Lasell, acting apparently on behalf of all cotton-machinery builders, paid a man named William F. Goulding $1,174.01 for lobbying services in Washington.[1] Members of the industry seem to have become concerned over the fact that Southern legislators in the Capital were trying to have English machinery admitted to this country duty-free and seem to have felt that they needed a paid representative in Washington to state their case.[2] There is no evidence as to whether or not the industry formed a trade association at that early date, although the establishment of such organizations was common in the years immediately following the Civil War. The first mention of The American Cotton Machinery Builders Association to be found in the Whitin records is a letter signed in 1878 by Josiah Lasell as treasurer of the organization.[3]

The industry had good reason to be concerned over the import of machinery from British machine-builders in the early 1870's because, in the hope of getting quick delivery, new mills such as those in Fall River were turning to England despite the high duties they had to pay on British equipment. The postwar duty level was 35 per cent ad valorem on "manufactures of iron" and 45 per cent on "manufactures of steel," whereas the duty immediately before the war had been 24 per cent on both categories (see Appendix 8). However, most British textile machinery escaped being taxed at 45 per cent since the few steel parts could easily be removed and shipped separately. Hence, for all practical purposes the duty was 35 per cent.[4]

The 35 per cent level seems to have been high enough to have excluded all British textile equipment where promptness of delivery was not a factor. But American builders wanted to be doubly sure of their position and therefore sought to have the duty increased to 45 per cent on all manufactures of metal. "At the present price of gold," Lasell wrote to his Congressman, George F. Hoar,[5] "foreign machinery is coming into a very close competition with our own, and should gold go to par, the business would be a losing one unless there should be a very large decline in the cost of labor — and all this under the present tariff."

The industry's gentle agitation for a tariff revision did not, however, achieve results until the general revision of 1883 at which time, principally through the activities of William F. Draper, the industry succeeded in getting a 45 per cent duty on all textile-machinery imports. "I think we have reason to congratulate ourselves and our associates in business on the results of our labors," Draper wrote to Lasell. "The most important thing in our business that I know of now is to endeavor to have the customs laws properly administered by the Port of Boston."[6] Getting a favorable tariff law was only half the battle won. There remained the fact that customs officers took great liberties in interpreting the law, especially if they had strong political feelings on the matter.*

After 1883 the Association seems to have lapsed into inactivity. Even Lasell's death in 1886 was not enough to bring the members together to appoint a new treasurer.† In 1888 George Marston Whitin wrote briefly to William H. Bent, treasurer of the Mason Machine Works and secretary of the Association, stating, "It seems to me as though we should make some organized effort to protect ourselves against the British competition that I find is affecting our business so seriously." However, no action resulted. In 1890 William Draper stirred up some interest by calling a meeting on pending tariff matters, but the only tangible result was a resolution authorizing Draper and Bent to act as official spokesmen for the industry. The meeting is historically noteworthy only because it reveals which of the companies in the industry were considered to be most coöperative:[7]

---

* "It seems to me that we should make an effort to protect ourselves from English competition by having some one whose duty is to follow up each importation," wrote Marston Whitin to the treasurer of the Mason Machine Works in 1891, "as I understand nothing is now being done to see a fair valuation and it seems reasonable to me that there is undervaluation." In the following year Chester Lasell wrote to Stockton Bates, "the importation of machinery in the finished state as unfinished material in order to escape the duty should be prevented if possible." In 1895 J. M. Lasell added his protest by writing to both Senators from Massachusetts, "Mr. Dodge [the U. S. Appraiser for the Port of Boston] appears to us to have developed proclivities looking toward freer trade since the Cleveland administration went into power. As far as we can judge there have been some flagrant cases of undervaluation of manufactures of metal and steel, under which schedule our product comes. We want to see a man as appraiser who will execute the laws conscientiously and afford us what protection the present law gives."

† George Marston Whitin was appointed to the vacant treasurership about 1892. At irregular intervals the Association assessed its members at the rate of 1/10 of one per cent of their capital stock. Assessments were apparently used only to pay for lobbying activities; at least, there is no evidence that they served as fines or were used as a means of pooling profits as they sometimes were in other industries at that period. One such assessment was made in September, 1900, the amounts being as follows: Whitin Machine Works $1,000, Lowell Machine Shop $1,000, Draper Company $1,000, Crompton & Knowles Loom Works $1,000, Saco & Pettee Machine Shops $1,000, Mason Machine Works $600, Fales & Jenks Machine Company $500, Woonsocket Machine & Press Company $250, Kitson Machine Shop $250, Providence Machine Company $250, Fall River Machine Company $100. In January, 1904, a similar assessment was made except that meanwhile the Fall River Machine Company had dropped out of the Association.

Crompton Loom Works (looms)
Davis & Furber Machine Company (wool machinery)
Fall River Machine Company (partial line, particularly looms)
Franklin Foundry & Machine Company (spinning frames)
Lewiston Machine Company (looms)
Lowell Machine Shop (full line)
Mason Machine Works (nearly full line)
Pettee Machine Works (cards)
Providence Machine Company (roving frames)
Saco Water Power Machine Shop (roving and spinning frames)
Whitin Machine Works (nearly full line)

Notably not invited were:

Atherton Machine Company (partial line, particularly pickers)
S. Colvin & Company (looms)
Gilbert Loom Company (looms)
Kilburn, Lincoln & Company (looms)
Kitson Machine Shop (pickers)
Knowles Loom Works (looms)
George W. Stafford Manufacturing Company (looms)

Presumably the uninvited were companies that had shown little disposition to coöperate with the Association on former occasions. Later
on, when the industry tried to establish minimum prices for its
products, the producers of pickers and looms caused great consterna-
tion by remaining outside the agreements.

The Association continued semi-somnolent until 1894, when the
Wilson-Gorman Tariff Act caught it napping. Two years earlier a
Democratic President, Grover Cleveland, had been elected on a
tariff-reform platform, but except for William Draper, no one in the
industry seems to have thought the danger of a tariff reduction
very threatening. By the provisions of the 1894 act, the duty on all
textile machinery was reduced from 45 to 35 per cent ad valorem.*

---

* It appears that the Wilson-Gorman tariff reduction affected principally the importation of cards. In a letter written 25 January 1894, Marston Whitin explained
why the proposed reduction would probably not affect spinning frames and looms.
"Spinning . . . cannot be imported on account of spindle patents here. The owners
of the patents insist that the spindles are placed in American-made frames. As to
looms, I do not think it [the tariff] will alter prices at all as the English loom is
not popular here."

Under other circumstances the industry might have received news of the tariff reduction with a degree of equanimity, but, in the depression of 1894, the threat of increased competition from British imports seemed like a dash of gall in the industry's cup of distress. Since the fall of 1893, business had been paralyzed by a sudden contraction of the economy that had caught the textile machinery industry with almost no backlog of orders. Within five months the Whitin company had been forced to lay off 440 workers — about 40 per cent of its employment at peak operation. Furthermore a new, and potentially strong, competitor was entering the industry — the Howard & Bullough American Machine Company, Ltd. — the first textile-machinery firm of any significance organized in America since the boom period following the Civil War, when several medium-sized firms had been started.

The new company was a subsidiary of Britain's renowned textile-machinery builders, Howard & Bullough, and was expected to serve its British owners as a means of getting inside the American tariff wall. Its charter was British-granted, its capital was British-furnished, and its products were to be British-designed. The motivating force behind the new company was the dynamic personality of a persuasive salesman named Charles E. Riley, an Englishman who for about ten years had been Howard & Bullough's American agent.[8] It was Riley who sold Howard & Bullough the idea of a plant in America and who became treasurer of the new organization.

As a site for the new plant, Riley picked South Attleboro, Massachusetts, just across the state border from Pawtucket, Rhode Island, and not very far from the shop of the Fales & Jenks Machine Company.* The new plant's initial 90,000-square-foot capacity made the Howard & Bullough American company only about a fifth the size of either the Whitin Machine Works or the Lowell Machine Shop, America's two largest textile-machinery builders, but the interna-

---

* In the 7 April 1894 issue of Wade's *Fibre and Fabric* there appeared a notice that "the Howard-Bullough American Machine Co., who have been looking over the ground at Lowell, Providence, Fall River, and Pawtucket for a site to locate an $80,-000 plant in which to build the latest improved cotton machinery, have been offered 25 acres of ground and exemption from taxation for ten years, equal to about $60,-000, to locate about five or six miles from the center of Attleboro, Massachusetts. This offer has not as yet been accepted." The 2 June issue of the same publication carried an announcement of the acceptance of the offer and told of the work that was being done on the new factory building.

tional reputation and strong financial backing of its British parent firm made it a dangerous competitive rival. Moreover, the new company immediately began operations with a full line of all the machinery needed to equip a spinning mill (i.e., everything but weaving machinery). The only other company in America so well equipped to outfit new mills was the Lowell Machine Shop. Furthermore, many American mill owners had come to prefer English-type machinery and were glad to see a British firm establish a branch in this country. Especially was this preference common among mill owners in New Bedford where, in the 1880's, there had been a mill-building boom comparable to the boom in Fall River in the 1870's. All things considered, the announcement that the Howard & Bullough American Machine Company was being organized was probably the most unnerving bit of news the textile machinery industry had heard in a generation. Coupled with the depression, the tariff reduction, and the instability of business conditions in the South, it made the industry's future look bleak and grim.

2. PRICE AGREEMENTS

The first consequence of the unhappy state into which the industry was plunged in 1894 was an intensified effort to cultivate the Southern market, one phase of which, as has already been mentioned, was the appointment of D. A. Tompkins as Whitin agent. A second consequence was the outbreak of uninhibited price-cutting.

In previous depressions, machinery builders had pretty much let their costs govern their prices. Knowing that most of their regular customers would not buy equipment in bad times no matter what the price, they were unwilling to make any reductions below a certain point. Frequently during the 1870's Lasell had complained that he was taking orders at prices which returned him no profit, but he never mentioned taking an order at a loss. Regular customers could be counted on to buy machinery when prosperity returned. Meanwhile the company had simply tightened its belt and waited out the famine; on no occasion had it ever before gone looking for business in new quarters.

The business of the 1890's was different. Though the North was depressed, there was business to be had in the South if the conditions of sale could be made liberal enough. There were always a few underfinanced mill owners who were willing to buy machinery provided that they could get low enough prices, liberal enough credit, and acceptance of enough stock in lieu of cash. No machinery builder wanted that kind of business; on the other hand, no builder really dared to pass it up. The maker who first got his machinery installed in a new mill had a good chance of getting a customer who would stick with him permanently. Some builders were even willing to take a loss on their initial orders if they thought the order would lead to a lasting relationship.

To cope with this demoralizing state of affairs, eight members of the American Cotton Machinery Builders Association, all of them producers of ring spinning frames, met to discuss the feasibility of maintaining minimum prices on their spinning-frame products. Since the Draper company was by that time in complete command of the spindle business, it is not illogical to suppose that the meeting was called by one of the Drapers. The names of only five of the eight participating firms are definitely known — George Draper & Sons, the Fales & Jenks Machine Company, the Lowell Machine Shop, the Mason Machine Works, and the Whitin Machine Works — although two others are known to have joined in the final agreement, the Davis & Furber Machine Company and the Franklin Foundry & Machine Company. How long their discussion lasted is not recorded. There is some evidence that the plan was being considered as early as May, 1894,[9] but the sudden jump in Whitin's spindle prices from $2.87½ to $3.00 in June, 1895 (at which point it remained until late in 1899) seems to indicate that the agreement went into effect in the latter month.

Unlike so many of the pricing agreements effected by other industries during the 1890's, the spinning-frame agreement was a success. Most agreements sought to peg their minimum prices unrealistically high, and in fact the spinning frame industry made somewhat the same mistake, for the Whitin Machine Works had not previously sold its frames at a price as high as $3.00 for over four years (see Appendix 25). However, business in the spinning-frame field was so completely dominated by the Draper company that none of the frame-builders seems to have dared to violate the agreement. In April, 1897, Marston Whitin was able to write, "Spinning has been under agreement for 2 years now with no cutting noticeable."[10]

The stable level of prices in the spinning frame business during the cutthroat period of the 1890's should be noted and then heavily underscored. Spinning-frame sales constituted the largest single part of the Whitin machinery business. Probably no other manufacturer, except perhaps the Fales & Jenks Machine Company, devoted such a large percentage of its capacity to ring-frame production as Whitin did. With such a large portion of its business safely out of reach of destructive price-cutting, the Whitin company was in a strong fighting position to combat price-cutting in other fields.

Perversely enough, the worst competition for orders broke out not where business was hardest to get but where it was easiest — in the carding branch of the industry. In 1887, carding technology had been revolutionized by the introduction from England of the revolving top-flat card. (The top flats on this type of card, instead of being removed individually for cleaning, as in the Wellman-type card, were joined side-to-side in an endless revolving chain and were cleaned as they slowly traveled, upside down, across the top of the card on their way back to their original operating position.) The new card almost immediately made the old stationary top-flat card obsolete.* Suddenly card sales became as critical a part of the textile machinery business as spindle sales had been a decade or so earlier.

The original promoter of the revolving top-flat card in America was the Pettee Machine Works, one of the three leading producers of textile machinery in the Boston area. The Pettee company had fallen on bad times in the 1880's but had been resuscitated by the aggressive business tactics of its new managers, Frank J. Hale and Rodman P. Snelling. Under Hale and Snelling the Pettee firm became practically a specialist in card production and by 1894 was far in the lead of American cotton card manufacturers.

By 1889 Marston Whitin realized that the Whitin Machine Works would have to put a card of the new type on the market if it was

---

* It also made railway heads obsolete. In 1895 the Whitin Machine Works put on the market a new model of drawing frame, known as the "Wamsutta," to take the place of its old railway-head frame.

not to lose its carding business altogether. After looking about for a man who was experienced in designing revolving top-flat cards, Whitin encountered John Wild, who was an employee of Evan Arthur Leigh, the American agent for the Platt Brothers, of England. At Whitin's behest, Wild came to Whitinsville to work on a new card design, but it took over four years to develop a machine that was efficient and at the same time free of the danger of infringing on existing designs.[11]

The Whitin company put its first revolving top-flat card on the market in January, 1894. No sooner had it done so than the bottom fell out of the card business. Whitin's first cards sold for $750. Six months later its cards were selling for $650. By March, 1895, the company was asking $550 and was settling for $525 or less. Meanwhile the Howard & Bullough American Machine Company had begun production on its excellently designed card, and other British concerns, all of which had switched to revolving top-flat cards several years earlier than the Americans had, were beginning to take advantage of the lowered tariff to sell their cards to American mills.

Unfortunately the carding branch of the industry had no Draper firm to dominate it and keep it in line. The leaders in card production were the Pettee Machine Works and the Howard & Bullough American Machine Company.* Both were essentially new firms, Pettee having been recently reorganized. Both had strong financial ties, the one in Boston, the other in England. Both were headed by men who had the reputation of being the industry's top salesmen — Frank Hale at Pettee and C. E. Riley at Howard & Bullough American. The leadership of the two firms, far from being measured and temperate like Draper's, was aggressive, dynamic, and withal disruptive.

By May, 1896, conditions in the card business had become so deplorable that the card-building members of the American Cotton Machinery Builders Association gathered in Boston to arrive at some agreement such as that which had proved so successful in the spinning-frame branch of the business. Rather curiously, one of the

---

* In 1897 Marston Whitin estimated that Pettee was producing about 1,500 cards a year. The Whitin Machine Works did not reach that rate of production until the early part of World War I.

leading card producers, the Howard & Bullough American Machine Company, was omitted from the conference. Apparently it was not welcomed as a member of an association that was primarily devoted to keeping British competition out of the country. At the meeting, Marston Whitin insisted that the group consider not only minimum prices but also the question of accepting stock. Both Hale and Riley had been quick to perceive the potentialities of stock acceptance as a competitive weapon and, with their strong financial connections, both had been willing and able to make extensive use of stock deals to further their sales. Marston felt, and quite rightly, that no price agreement would be workable unless controls were also placed on the taking of common stocks.[12]

As a result of the card-builders' conference, the industry agreed to adhere to what was in effect a voluntary code of competitive ethics. In essence the code contained seven major points:[13]

1. Certain minimum prices were to be observed in the sale of all cards and associated machines, such as drawing frames, railway heads, and grinders. (For instance, the price of a standard revolving top-flat card was to be not less than $600.)[14]

2. No stock was to be taken in payment for machinery.

3. No manufacturer was to offer credit terms more liberal than half cash, a quarter in notes payable in six months, and the remainder in notes payable in twelve. Interest was to be computed at the rate of 6 per cent and was to be figured from the average date of shipment.

4. Each bid was to be itemized, and every manufacturer was to stand ready to take any part of an order at the prices he had bid.

5. No commissions were to be paid except to regularly announced agents. (By this provision it was hoped to halt the practice of bribing textile-mill superintendents with commissions for swinging orders from one manufacturer to another.)

6. Erectors' services were to be paid for at the rate of $6.00 per day plus traveling expenses. (Mills had formerly paid $2.00 per day plus room and board as well as traveling expenses. This clause in the agreement was soon changed, however, and the old arrangement was reverted to, except that the $2.00 charge was increased to $4.00.)

7. The agreement was to go into effect as of 1 June 1896, but members

of the trade were to be allowed 30 days in which to close outstanding options. To prevent any firm from exploiting its knowledge of the planned increase in prices, a list of all outstanding options was to be submitted to the Association. Mills not reported on this list were to be sold no machinery at less than the new minimum prices.

The provision requiring members to submit a list of the mills with which they were currently negotiating sales contracts nearly resulted in a breakdown of the agreement before it had had a chance to get started. Apparently the Association did not intend that option lists be made public; however, a few days after the conference, names on the lists began to leak out. Cramer hastily wired Whitin, complaining that others knew the mills he was negotiating with and demanding that he be sent a list of the mills that others were dealing with. Soon everyone in the industry knew which promoter groups in the South were in the market for machinery. Prices went lower than ever. For three frantic weeks Cramer traveled constantly, trying to get his share, or better, of the business that was known to be obtainable. Finally on the July first deadline, the hectic race ended as abruptly as it had started, and the industry settled down to observe the ethical code it had imposed on itself. Worn out, Cramer left for a vacation in Portland, Maine.

For a while business remained at a standstill. Many textile-mill owners rebelled at the announcement of higher prices and waited to see whether the agreement was strong enough to last. Only a few of the older and more conservative owners, such as H. P. Hammett's son-in-law, Colonel James L. Orr, of Piedmont mills, and Colonel J. A. Brock, of Anderson, were hopeful that the agreement would be a success, for they deplored the state of affairs that had allowed new competitors to begin operations with low-cost machinery.

It was not long before Marston Whitin began seeing evidence of how advantageous an agreement he had signed. Freed of competition on a price or stock-acceptance basis, the Whitin firm could at last benefit fully from the superlative ability of its Southern representative and from the high reputation of its products. "I sincerely hope," Cramer wrote in triumph, "that you will be able to maintain the card combination, because the way things are now we have a big advantage." Two months later he reported, "We have probably gotten more business recently in this territory than the rest of our competitors put together." [15]

For nearly a year the builders of cards stuck conscientiously to the letter of their agreement. Business in 1896 was unexpectedly brisk — a brief revival amidst a lengthy depression, something like the revival of 1937 — and so for a short time competitive pressures let up. But by April, 1897, orders were again difficult to secure and Cramer was complaining that mills he had felt confident were going to buy Whitin machinery were suddenly placing their orders elsewhere.

Investigation satisfied Cramer that the agreement was being violated, though proof was hard to obtain. Apparently both the Pettee Machine Works and the Howard & Bullough American Machine Company were giving their customers undercover concessions. However, both companies were cautious to conceal their activities, since, as Whitin remarked, both were anxious not to have the agreement break down. "Riley . . . is not going to kick over the traces," Whitin wrote to Cramer, "for he is the fellow who wants the agreement kept worse than anyone, unless it comes to Pettee." [16]

Violators of the agreement were fairly safe from discovery as long as they kept their sales contracts in proper order and as long as their customers were careful to keep any extra-contractual concessions confidential. But always there was some customer who would let slip a boast about how he had managed to get his cards at a shaded price. For instance, Cramer reported having heard that the Pettee Machine Works on one occasion required a customer to sign the six- and twelve-month notes called for by the agreement and then, in confidence, assured the customer that he could renew his notes as often as he liked. In another case he heard that the Pettee company had given a mill owner a sizable credit memorandum in advance so that, although the mill's machinery was billed at list price, the owner was required to pay only a portion of the full amount in settling his account. Sometimes card-builders installed machinery on a trial basis and then never sent bills for it. At other times they gave high turn-in values for old machinery, an easy loophole that the industry strangely overlooked in drawing up its agreement.

Anyone with a will to evade the agreement had no difficulty in finding a way.

Probably the most common means of side-stepping the agreement was to sell pickers — which were not covered by any price regulation — at a heavy loss. Customers did not care what they paid for individual machines so long as their total bill was low. Realizing this fact, both the Pettee Machine Works and the Howard & Bullough American Machine Company practically gave away their pickers. Howard & Bullough was especially well situated to take advantage of this handy competitive device, since its pickers were among its best-known machines. But the Pettee Machine Works, which made no pickers, had to negotiate an undercover arrangement with the A. T. Atherton Machine Company, a small, specialized manufacturing firm, in order to get control of a supply of picking machinery.* Finally, on 1 July 1898, the other card-builders forced Pettee and Howard & Bullough into an agreement to maintain minimum prices on their pickers as well as on their cards.

The loom-makers were the only group that never reached an agreement. (A minimum price on roving was effected at least by 1899.)[17] The reason seems obvious. In the loom business there were more small, specialized producers than in any other branch of the industry. True, looms for fancy goods were built only by the Crompton Loom Works and the Knowles Loom Works, both of Worcester, but looms for plain goods were built by at least nine manufacturers.[18] Moreover, in contrast to the card, which was fairly standardized, looms varied widely in design and price. Several manufacturers built light looms that sold for as little as $35, while at the other extreme were the automatic looms sold by the Drapers for $150 each. The Whitin loom was a heavily built, heavy-duty machine that sold for about $55. All manufacturers of plain-goods looms competed directly with each other; yet because of the range of their products, it is probable that the country's loom-builders could never have settled on a scale of prices that would have been satisfactory to all concerned. For-

* The form of control exercised by Pettee over Atherton is not known to me. The Atherton company remained a separate entity, but apparently the Pettee Machine Works owned most, if not all, of its stock. Cramer reported to Whitin on 18 May 1897 that A. T. Atherton was traveling in the South as a salesman for the company of which he had once been the owner.

tunately, however, price-cutting in the loom business had comparatively little effect on the card branch of the industry, since the companies that built both cards and looms — the Lowell Machine Shop, the Mason Machine Works, and the Whitin Machine Works — were the three companies that were most diligently trying to keep peace in the industry.

Apparently Marston Whitin's attitude toward price agreements was completely pragmatic. Since it was to his benefit to do so, Whitin did everything in his power to see that the agreements were observed, and since his word carried considerable weight in the Association, he was the one generally looked to as the preserver of harmony in the industry. Insofar as he could, he held Cramer responsible for carrying out all the terms of all agreements, if for no other reason than to avoid the embarrassment of being challenged in Association meetings for things Cramer had done. But he was too shrewd a judge of human character to make the mistake of quenching Cramer's enthusiasm for selling by putting too many restrictions on him. When Cramer could give evidence that others were offering terms below the agreed minima, Whitin granted him authority to undercut the agreement. Of course, whether or not a competitor was in truth shading prices was often a matter of pure surmise and frequently led to mutual recriminations. Whitin seems to have been perfectly aware that such was the case and he insisted that Cramer be sure of his facts before launching an attack on a competitor. On only one occasion, at a slightly later date, when Cramer had given an embarrassingly low quotation to J. W. Cannon, one of the toughest bargainers in the South, did Whitin take Cramer to task for exceeding his authority. But even on that occasion Whitin's tone was more reproving than reprimanding: "We will have to arrange some way in which you can lie gracefully to your people [i.e., your customers] so as not to make a discount to them on account of this trade with Cannon. This would not seem to be hard to do as Cannon is close[-mouthed] and your morals are poor." [19]

As a result of the flexible way in which Whitin handled Cramer, the Whitin Machine Works seems to have suffered very little from the subsurface price-cutting that went on continually. The firm that did suffer was the Lowell Machine Shop. Apparently it honored every word of the agreement — a naïve and unrealistic approach to the situation, revealing an unfamiliarity with true market conditions. Because it refused to grant secret concessions to its customers, the Lowell shop lost order after order to its competitors' salesmen — the men whom Cramer jokingly called the "rough boys." According to H. C. Perham, the treasurer of the Kitson Machine Shop, the Lowell company had been unable to sell a "d—— thing" since going into the agreement.[20] Cramer insisted, however, that the trouble at Lowell went deeper than the agreement. "The fact of the thing simply is," he wrote, "that this is another case of the same old trouble that has afflicted the Lowell shop for some time past, and that is, while they are very nice people, the management of the concern is in the hands of old and cranky people who do not always exercise the best business judgment or tact in dealing with a customer." [21]

Finally in March, 1898, General Robert H. Stevenson, the treasurer of the Lowell Machine Shop, became so exercized over the apparent duplicity of his competitors in their contract negotiations that he made a personal tour of the South. Cramer was quick to report the presence of Lowell's chief executive officer in North Carolina and to pass on to Whitin the rumor that Stevenson was threatening to leave the Association because he was finding repeated evidence of flagrant price-cutting. What piqued Stevenson more than any other single violation of the code was the fact that a competitor's salesman was trying to lure away the Sterling Mills, one of his very best customers in the South.

News of Stevenson's wrath spread rapidly, and within a week the generalissimos of the industry — Hale and Snelling of the Pettee Machine Works, one of the Drapers from the Draper Company,* and C. E. Riley of the Howard & Bullough American Machine Company — had converged on the South to be on hand, should a price war break out. Only William H. Bent of the Mason Machine Works and George Marston Whitin remained quietly at home. But Whitin made it clear to Cramer that Stevenson, if he should repudiate the agreement, was to be taught a lesson concerning what real competition was like; Cramer was to get the Sterling order no matter how low a price he had to bid.

Stevenson, however, delayed taking any action until he had re-

* George Draper & Sons had incorporated as the Draper Company in 1896.

turned home to talk things over with Whitin. At a private meeting in Boston he informed Marston that he intended to withdraw from the code group. Reporting the meeting to Cramer, Whitin wrote, "The Lowell people are satisfied from their trip South that there have been serious violations of the agreement. They think that this matter has been confined to Pettee and Riley although I am not sure that they do not think that you differ from Caesar's wife." [22]

Apparently Whitin commiserated with Stevenson on the deplorable state of the market and suggested that he delay official action until enough members of the industry had returned from the South to permit him to call an Association meeting. What took place at that fateful meeting will probably never be known. At the time the meeting was taking place, Cramer paid a visit to Whitinsville. Consequently there is no correspondence on the subject in the Whitin-Cramer files. But the outcome is clear. Not only did Whitin manage to hold Stevenson in the Association, but he extracted from the other members a pledge to refer all alleged violations, such as those reported by General Stevenson, to Eben Draper as industry arbitrator. If there had been any doubt before, none remained that George Marston Whitin was the most powerful single individual in the industry. Indeed Whitin's reputation for holding the whip hand in the Association caused Cramer to fear for a time that Southern customers might begin looking upon the Whitin Machine Works as the initiator and defender of high prices. [23]

The agreement to refer disputes to an arbitrator was reached on 23 March 1898. By May, business had begun to pick up, and by the end of the year prosperity had returned. For a time all companies in the industry were so busy filling orders that maintenance of minimum prices ceased to be an issue. Business in 1899 was so good, in fact, that by the end of the year Cramer had seriously oversold the Whitin company's capacity to deliver.

As the turn-of-the-century boom began to subside, however, prices started a downward movement again. This time, when a meeting of card-builders was called, the Lowell Machine Shop, convinced that its competitors were without honest intentions, flatly refused to attend. With one of the industry's major producers thus in a position to snipe at those who remained in the agreement, minimum prices

became difficult, if not impossible, to maintain. On several occasions between 1901 and 1903 the industry attempted new agreements,
but without success. Minimum prices became merely standard
figures on which all manufacturers gave regular discounts.

If any price agreements were attempted after 1903, they must have
been negotiated by telephone or in personal conversation, for Marston Whitin's correspondence contains no further reference to Association price meetings. The political climate by 1903 had caused
most manufacturers to become cautious in their collaboration with
competitors, for price agreements were being declared within the
purview of anti-trust legislation in both state and federal courts.*
The rising public sentiment against price-fixing was unmistakable
and was probably the cause of the textile machinery industry's dis-
continuance of any further attempts to set minimum prices.

Thus threatened on one side by unbridled competition and on the
other by action against pricing agreements, many American industries enthusiastically embraced the merger movement. In the steel
industry, the electrical and automobile industries, the shipping industry, the farm machinery industry and many others, large numbers of companies combined to form a few powerful and dominant
concerns. Not so in the textile machinery industry. Even at the
height of the movement only two mergers of any note occurred
among New England's cotton-machinery builders, and they were
fairly small. In the spring of 1897, the Crompton Loom Works and
the Knowles Loom Works combined to form the only company
specializing in the production of fancy-goods looms, and later in
that same year, the Saco Water Power Machine Shop, makers of
roving and spinning frames, joined with the Pettee Machine Works,

---

* In Texas, for instance, the state anti-trust statute went so far as to forbid "any
contract or agreement not to sell, dispose of, or transport any article below a common figure" (quoted in S. C. T. Dodd, *Trusts,* p. 100). So unequivocal was the
wording of the act that Whitin decided, as he expressed it, "not to send anything
down to Texas unless we have a written agreement there to waive their law or
[unless] something is done to protect our interests" (letter of George Marston Whitin
to H. C. Perham, 13 April 1901). Most similar laws were more loosely drawn, however, as in the case of the Georgia statute about which Whitin wrote, "I do not see
how it can affect us in any way as we have no combination," by which he seems
to have meant that the industry had no *formal* combination (letter of George Marston
Whitin to Stuart W. Cramer, 3 March 1897).

makers of cards and drawing frames, to form the Saco & Pettee
Machine Shops, a company with a fairly well-rounded product line.
A full-scale merger did take place in the card-clothing section of the
textile machinery industry, however. The American Card Clothing
Company was formed in 1890 as an amalgamation of the leading
card-clothing makers of the country, most of whom were located
around Worcester.[24] The rest of the industry staved off the pressure
to consolidate by resorting to a compromise alternative — coöperative selling.

As early as 1894 the industry learned that there were advantages
in being able to offer Southern mill promoters all the equipment
necessary to outfit a new mill. As has been pointed out, most
Southern mill men, having little experience at their jobs, preferred
to rely on a single manufacturer for their mill equipment even if
that manufacturer did not make all the machinery needed for a complete installation. Furthermore, most mill men were looking for the
best price and the best credit terms they could get, plus the chance
to pay for the largest possible part of their machinery with stock. By
purchasing *all* their equipment through one machinery company,
or through one Southern agent, they felt they had the best chance
of getting favorable terms. Agents, too, were anxious to carry a full
line of equipment if they could, for they often found it less difficult to sell a customer a complete installation than to interest him
in a particular make of pickers or cards. Thus, from all sides — from
the manufacturers, from the mill owners, and from the machinery
salesmen — came pressure to integrate horizontally. To meet this
pressure, and yet stop short of outright merger, the industry resorted to the formation of a number of informal marketing groups.

3. INFORMAL MARKETING GROUPS

On the surface a marketing group in the textile machinery industry was merely a number of manufacturers selling through a
single manufacturers' agent. But actually it was far more than that,
for in practice each group had an informal organization. In each
group one company dominated the rest. Domination was never admitted by the dominating company, or for that matter by anyone
else, but it existed nevertheless. The dominant company led the

group by setting sales policies — policies that the others had to follow if they wished to maintain their place in the group. Actually
the membership of various groups changed from time to time, as is
shown in Appendix 17, but the stronger combinations remained
fairly stable.

Quite logically, the coöperative form of marketing took its origin
in the South where leading manufacturers' agents organized marketing groups in order to be able to bid on full mill orders. But the device soon spread to the North and even to the foreign market. For
instance, in 1899, the Whitin Machine Works and the other members
of the marketing group it dominated decided to coöperate in offering
their products to the Mexican market. In so doing, this marketing
group made the same contractual arrangements with its Mexican
agent, J. M. Anderson, that it had entered into a few years earlier
with its agent in the South.

The first of the marketing groups in the South seems to have
been the one formed in or about 1894 by the Charlotte Machine
Company, a firm which, although possessing a small repair shop, was
primarily a manufacturers' agency. Among the New England companies for which the Charlotte company served as agent were the
Pettee Machine Works (cards and drawing frames), the Providence
Machine Company (roving equipment), the Fales & Jenks Machine
Company (spinning frames), the Cohoes Iron Foundry & Machine
Company (slashers), the Easton & Burnham Machine Company
(winders and spoolers), the Knowles Loom Works (looms), and the
Curtis & Marble Machine Company (finishing machinery). Of
course, not all agencies represented so many companies; in some
cases a marketing group consisted of only three or four large firms.

A few firms refused to join any of the newly formed marketing
groups, preferring to sell their products through their own employee-
salesmen. The Lowell Machine Shop was one of them. Its line of
products was so complete that it did not need to coöperate with other
firms. The Howard & Bullough American Machine Company was
in somewhat the same position, for it made all the machinery necessary to outfit a spinning mill. A third company, the Mason Machine Works, also refused to join any of the marketing groups, but
in its case there seems to have been no logical reason for its disdain-

ful independence. The Mason company had the same serious deficiencies in its product line that the Whitin company had, for it produced neither picking nor roving machinery.* Moreover, it was in need of just the kind of competitive reinforcement that coöperation with other units in the industry might have given it, for in the 1890's the Mason company was rapidly losing its relative position in the industry.† Without knowing all the facts, one is tempted to guess that Mason's failure to join a marketing group in the 1890's was an important factor contributing to its decline.

The Whitin Machine Works first engaged in coöperative marketing during the year 1895 at the time when D. A. Tompkins was its Southern agent. Tompkins, it will be recalled, was under contract to sell Whitin machinery on a commission basis. At the same time, he was selling Kitson pickers under a similar arrangement.‡ It appears that he also tried to get the agency for the roving line made by the Woonsocket Machine & Press Company, but for some reason was not successful.

When the Whitin Machine Works broke with Tompkins in 1896, the Kitson Machine Shop followed suit almost as though it were a Whitin subsidiary. When Cramer became Whitin's representative, he became Kitson's representative as well. When Marston Whitin agreed to give Cramer a salary instead of a commission on sales, the Kitson Machine Shop agreed to share part of the cost. When Whitin agreed to bear such extra expenses as the cost of advertisements and of making trips outside the Southern territory, Kitson agreed to bear its share. Because the two companies differed so widely in size, the Whitin Machine Works bore 90 per cent of such

---

* Mason produced mules, which Whitin did not, but by the 1890's the possession of a mule line was of little advantage since ring spinning was rapidly replacing mule spinning even for the finer counts of yarn.

† Until the 1870's or 1880's, the Mason Machine Works had been a leading company in the industry, second only perhaps to the Lowell Machine Shop. By 1900, however, it was not more than fourth in size and perhaps was only fifth.

‡ It is important to note that the Kitson Machine Shop, which for many years had been selling its pickers to the Lowell Machine Shop so that the Lowell shop did not have to make a picker line of its own, continued to do so even after arranging to have its own sales representative in the South and even despite the fact that its sales representative combined with his sale of Kitson pickers the sale of Whitin machinery.

expenses, leaving Kitson to bear the other 10 per cent. Later, this ratio was also used when the two companies had to agree on what portion of a block of stock each should assume when the stock was taken in part payment for a combined order of machinery.

Like Tompkins before him, Cramer was anxious to round out his marketing group by bringing in the Woonsocket Machine & Press Company with its line of roving equipment. It seems clear that Marston Whitin would have preferred having his company linked with the Providence Machine Company, whose roving equipment he considered superior to Woonsocket's, but the Providence firm already belonged to the Charlotte Machine Company's marketing group and so was not available. Therefore, Whitin consented to Cramer's efforts to bring the Woonsocket Machine & Press Company into the Whitin-Kitson group, and in fact assisted Cramer by personally discussing the matter with Woonsocket's owners. Finally, in 1897, after extensive negotiations, Cramer was able to convince Malcolm Campbell, the treasurer of Woonsocket, that the trend toward integrated marketing groups was so strong that specialists who continued to act independently would soon be frozen out of the Southern market.[25] In addition to the salary paid Cramer by Whitin and Kitson, Campbell agreed to pay $2,400 a year. He also agreed to bear 20 per cent of Cramer's incidental expenses. Thereafter the three companies in Cramer's marketing group coöperated in everything on a 10–20–70 basis.*

Although the Woonsocket Machine & Press Company undoubtedly profited by its arrangement with Cramer, Malcolm Campbell was anything but pleased with the deal he had made. It was not not long before he realized that he had virtually turned his entire Southern business over to Marston Whitin and Whitin's irrepressible Southern representative, Stuart Cramer. If for some reason Whitin

* The Woonsocket Machine & Press Company traced its corporate ancestry back to the Woonsocket Foundry, a firm established in 1838. (See *Biographical History of the Manufacturers and Business Men of Rhode Island*, pp. 284–288.) Its textile machinery history dated back only to 1884, however, at which time it adopted the name, the Woonsocket Machine & Press Company. In 1888, the Woonsocket company increased its machinery line by purchasing the patents, patterns, and machinery of the City Machine Company, a Providence firm that had been manufacturing roving frames since 1868. Unlike most of the firms in the Providence area, the Woonsocket company was not a family concern but was owned by a group of local bankers.

did not care to bid on a certain order, there was never much chance that Cramer could get the roving part of the order for the Woonsocket Machine & Press Company. If Whitin was willing to cut prices to the bone, the Woonsocket company either had to share in the discount or else run the risk of incurring the displeasure of the other companies in the group. If Whitin agreed to accept stock from a customer, the Woonsocket company was obliged to take 20 per cent of the block. Yet much as he chafed under these conditions, Malcolm Campbell kept his company in the group. From that fact alone, one surmises that he either feared returning to independent selling or else that he found the ride on Whitin's coattails more profitable than he was willing to admit.

* * *

As a temporary expediency, coöperative marketing was a highly successful arrangement. Yet, by its very nature it was unstable, since nothing prevented a member from withdrawing affiliation and threatening the very existence of the group. The merger of the Saco Water Power Machine Shop and the Pettee Machine Works is a case in point. Before 1897 the Saco company numbered among the independent marketers — and as such enjoyed only limited success in the South. The Pettee company, on the other hand, was highly successful as the dominant firm in the Charlotte Machine Company's marketing group. It was natural, therefore, that the Pettee company would want to bring its new affiliate into the Charlotte group. But its decision to do so created somewhat the same effect on the group that a man would create by bringing his mistress home to live. The other companies packed up and left to form their own marketing organizations (see Appendix 17).

Under such volatile circumstances, coöperative marketing could never have provided the industry with a permanent solution to its competitive problems. Eventually a more stable relationship had to be realized. What is remarkable under the circumstances is how long some of the marketing groups lingered on. The informal Boston group was not replaced by a formal merger until the year 1912, while in the Providence area, one of the groups — the one dominated by the Fales & Jenks Machine Company — remained in active existence until 1930. The destiny of the Whitin group is not so easily summarized. Its affiliation (through Cramer) with the Kitson Machine Company was disrupted when the Kitson company discontinued marketing its machinery in the South through Cramer and instead joined the Boston merger of 1912. Whitin's association with the Woonsocket Machine & Press Company, never a very happy one, was terminated when the Whitin company decided to buy out the roving business of Woonsocket's competitor, the Providence Machine Company. Because of the important bearing they have on Whitin's history, both events will be dealt with at greater length in the following chapter.

CHAPTER XIII

WHITIN EXPANDS AND INTEGRATES, 1900–1913

THE depression of 1897–98 was one of the important turning points in Whitin history, a turning point much as 1873 had been and as 1923 would be later on, except that those years marked the change from a sellers' to a buyers' market, whereas 1897–98 marked the reverse. Previously, for a period of about fifteen years, business had been slow, or at best moderate; sales in only one year (1896) had measured up to the record levels set during the boom years of the early 1870's and 1880's. Profits, as measured in dividends, had also been moderate or low; distributions to stockholders had averaged only 8 per cent on net worth.[1] During the fifteen-year period before 1897 manufacturing capacity had expanded only a fair amount; the company's floor space had grown by about 25 per cent. Competition, once a negligible factor, had become a dominant consideration in nearly all business decisions. Competitive ethics had reached an all-time low; firms in the industry found that they had to be constantly alert to what others were up to and usually had to retaliate in kind or risk losing out in the struggle. During those fifteen years the giant of the industry, the Lowell Machine Shop, refusing to engage in the unseemly free-for-all for business, had gradually lost its tremendous lead over its competitors and in the closing years of the period had seen two other companies forge ahead of it — the Whitin Machine Works and the Saco & Pettee Machine Shops.

With recovery in 1899, a new secular trend began.* Business was so good that even the sharp depression of 1907–08 was not enough to prevent the first decade of the new century from ranking as the

---

* It is important to note, however, that Whitin's spinning-machinery prices, as shown in Appendix 25, deviate from the general trend of prices after 1898 and continue downward until 1915 before turning up again.

most prosperous in Whitin history. In every one of those years, depression years included, Whitin's sales surpassed even the record years of the preceding century. Dividends averaged 13 per cent on net worth — and at the very time when the company was doubling its plant and was paying for most of the increased investment out of earnings. Competition from England was less than it had been for many years, for English machine-builders were as busy as the Americans, meeting the demands of the greatest mill-building era in Great Britain's history.[2]

Yet, oddly enough, these seemingly favorable times were not propitious for America's smaller textile machinery builders. Apparently, as the larger builders achieved national reputations, customers deserted or shunned the smaller manufacturers in favor of those whose names were better known. Before the end of the decade, many of this country's oldest machinery concerns — especially concerns in the loom-building trade, where competition with the Drapers' automatic loom was causing great distress — had closed their plants forever. In some cases weak companies saved themselves by merging with stronger ones. Others sold out or went into liquidation, until by the end of 1912 the number of firms in the preparatory branch of the industry had declined to six, whereas once there had been three times that many.

In the contest for first place in the industry the Whitin Machine Works won most of the initial rounds. With a hard-hitting and smoothly coördinated team, Whitin sought to strengthen its competitive position by filling the gaps in its product line and by attracting the disgruntled customers of the Lowell Machine Shop. On both counts the company was so successful that in the end it lost out to others, since the very threat of Whitin's mounting strength drove the Lowell Machine Shop and the Saco & Pettee Machine Shops to merge into a firm of over-shadowing size.

The first part of this chapter deals with the manner in which the Whitin company built up its independent strength as a producer of all types of preparatory machinery. The remainder of the chapter tells how this new strength affected the industry and how the industry's reactions in turn affected the future of the Whitin company.

I. NEW PLANT AND NEW VILLAGE

When one reconstructs the events of 1899-1900 from the records of the Whitin company, one is struck by the amount of building activity engendered in Whitinsville by the revival of business at the turn of the century. After fifteen years of dull or depressed business conditions, one might have expected Marston Whitin to take a cautious attitude toward any business revival, no matter how promising. A typical reaction was that of Malcolm Campbell, of the Woonsocket Machine & Press Company. Fearing that the boom of 1899 would immediately be followed by another depression as the boom of 1896 had been, Campbell flatly refused to expand his productive capacity even though Cramer threatened, and finally found himself forced to place his customers' heavy roving orders with Woonsocket's rival, the Providence Machine Company. Perhaps Marston Whitin's willingness to meet the sudden rise in demand by increasing his productive capacity is attributable to his desire to push his company into the leading position in the industry. His rationalized explanation was that, because of the long-continued poor business, mill men had to begin to buy machinery if they were to provide the cotton goods needed by the public. Future events were to bear out Whitin's analysis of the situation, but one wonders if, at the time, many others in the industry were not convinced that success had converted Marston Whitin, the arch-conservative, into Marston Whitin, the foolhardy.

Late in 1899, after Cramer had seriously oversold the Whitin company's capacity to deliver, Marston Whitin made plans to build Shop No. 4, a structure large enough to increase the company's productive area by 95,000 square feet — as much as the entire capacity of the recently built Howard & Bullough American shop at South Attleboro. While the shop was under construction, Marston stepped up production in the other parts of his plant by instituting a night shift and adding 50 per cent more workers to his payroll, making a total of 1,800 employees.

Whitin realized that his expanded plant could not be manned by the work force then available in Whitinsville and that additional company houses would have to be erected. Therefore, during

1900–01, he added no less than four hundred dwellings to the three hundred already owned by the company.* The construction of additional housing turned out to be a major task, for it meant the development of almost a complete new village. In fact, the project was known from the first as the "New Village" — and is still known by that name, even though it is now approximately a half-century old.

The first difficulty encountered was the choice of location. The employee houses built by John C. Whitin had been erected across the road from the plant and in such a way that they were bounded on the second and third sides by family estates and on the fourth side by Arcade Pond. Consequently, in building the New Village, the company had to go a considerable distance westward, beyond Arcade Pond, to find an expanse of land broad enough to accommodate four hundred dwellings.†

Locating so many dwellings so far west of the village proper in turn created a need for a new water-supply system, since the old system was badly placed and completely inadequate to meet the new demands. Consequently, beginning in 1901, the company undertook an ambitious program of reservoir construction involving the damming of three large ponds along Cook Allen Brook, a tributary of the Mumford River. These reservoirs were built specifically to store

---

* By 1907 the company was again hard pressed for housing. On 25 February 1907, Marston Whitin wrote, "It is getting very hard to find additional labor and I do not believe that we shall be able to increase our working force very much, if at all, from now until next fall." However, the depression of that year forestalled any further house construction until after World War I.

† Unlike its other housing projects, most of which were made up of two-family units, the company's New Village development was laid out for dwellings of the so-called parallel type. Under one roof were combined sometimes four but usually six individual, two-story units, located one beside another in a long, straight row. The dwellings were simply and inexpensively constructed so that rents could be kept low enough to attract immigrant day laborers. The feeling of urban congestion, so typical of large-scale industrial housing, was avoided by leaving generous spaces between buildings. The attractive natural roll of the open landscape was made good use of by the construction of curving roads and by the planting of shade trees. Two new boarding houses were included to accommodate the unmarried among the company's workmen, and a small store was added to meet the essential needs of local larders. (The origin of the small store is particularly interesting since it was set up at Marston Whitin's direction to give a source of income to the widow of Daniel Connolly, the man killed in the steam-pipe accident described in a preceding chapter. The company built a full-scale grocery store in the New Village in 1927.)

water for the New Village, but from the time they were finished they served as the water supply system for the entire community. (Appendix 13 sets forth in some detail the history of Whitinsville's water supply and of the part played by the Whitin Machine Works in its development.)

Building the New Village and a new reservoir system was only a partial manifestation of Whitinsville's pulsating activity at the turn of the century. Of perhaps greater significance, though not so immediately apparent, was the way in which the company's product line was undergoing gradual but radical change. At the beginning of the century, the company produced an incomplete line of machinery ranging from cards to looms. By the end of the century's first dozen years, the company's line, while not so broad in range as formerly, was fully complete within its limits so that the company no longer had to depend on the aid of an outside marketing group in selling its machinery.

2. THE WHITIN HIGH-SPEED COMBER

The first step taken by the company in rounding out its product line was the development and perfection of combing machinery, a type of equipment designed to help mills produce fine cotton yarns. Previously, most American cotton manufacturers had either restricted themselves to the production of coarse yarns or else had used double carding to achieve whatever refinements in yarn quality they desired. For two generations the combing of cotton had been almost exclusively a European practice. Consequently the few Americans who had used combers had necessarily gone to the British, the French, or the Germans to procure their equipment.[3] Beginning around 1875 a scattering of American mill men had given British-built combers a trial in their mills, but American operatives, being unaccustomed to the delicate adjustments of foreign-built combers, had found difficulty in keeping the machines in operating condition. For a time the Providence Machine Company tried to interest domestic mill owners in an American-built comber copied from British models. But in general, mill owners in this country continued to prefer the higher productivity, if somewhat lower quality, of double carding.

The circumstance that forced American cotton manufacturers to buckle down and learn how to make use of the comber was the competitive struggle between mills in the North and South. Once Southern mills had shown that they could produce coarse yarns more cheaply than Northern mills could, the mills of the North were forced to shift to fine yarn production in self-preservation. Even then, the comber's real success came only after mill men had learned that the comber enabled them to get more production as well as better quality out of a given grade of raw cotton.

Most of the combers bought by Northern mills during the 1890's were imported from England, although a few were bought from the Glabasch & Mumford firm of Germany and from the Société Alsacienne de Constructions Mécaniques of France. The first American shops to meet the new demand for combers were the Mason Machine Works and the Whitin Machine Works. At first the Mason company made its own combers. Then for a while it built Glabasch & Mumford combers on license.[4] The Whitin company began experimenting with its new machine at the Paul Whitin Manufacturing Company, where it gave most of its new products trial runs before putting them on the market.* Then, in 1899, it announced its new comber to the trade.[5] The three machines that comprised the Whitin combing set — the sliver lap, the ribbon lap, and the comber itself [6] — were copied almost directly from British machines of Heilmann type (so named because they incorporated the principles of the original cotton comber, invented by Josué Heilmann). In fact Marston Whitin insisted, as if it was a point of strength, that there was no real difference between his company's machines and the Heilmann combers built by the British.

The success of this first Whitin comber was immediate but short-lived. By 1902 several European manufacturers had brought out new comber models designed to operate at a speed roughly twice that of the Heilmann machine. Most successful of the European-built products was the Nasmith comber, designed by John W.

* Ownership of the Paul Whitin Manufacturing Company was inherited equally by George Marston Whitin and his older brother Henry ("Harry"). It is said that Marston gave his brother a small part of his stock in the mill so that Harry could have undisputed control. Marston's near-half share is still owned by those in the machine-shop family who are his heirs.

Nasmith of Manchester, England, produced by John Hetherington & Sons of the same city, and imported to this country by Stephen C. Lowe of New Bedford.

As Whitin saw his newly established comber business disappearing into the hands of his British competitors he set a staff of men to work developing a comber that would contain improvements beyond those incorporated in the Nasmith machine. Heading the developmental staff was Elwin H. Rooney, comber specialist for the company and former overseer of combers in a mill in New Bedford. Assisting him were Oscar L. Owen, head of the drafting room, and Harry A. Haselden, chief electrician, as well as three other men who seem to have been hired specifically to help develop the new product.[7]

For approximately twelve months during 1904–05 these six men worked at their assignment. Eventually all six men applied for one or more patents, which in due course they assigned to the Whitin Machine Works. The machine which they finally produced was a triumph in the American art of rationalized simplification. Although in principle not greatly different from the original Heilmann machine, the Whitin High-speed Comber was in fact a totally new mechanism. The old Heilmann comber had been so intricate in design that a minimum of ten hours had been required to set its nippers properly.[8] The Nasmith machine was somewhat easier to set but still had carried over many of its predecessor's complexities. As Whitin exclaimed, "Take the Nasmith machine with its toggle joints and bell-angle connections — it is impossible for it to run without wearing on the joints."[9] The Whitin comber corrected these defects, simplified the design, reduced the number of parts, made each component sturdier, and in general made the comber capable of withstanding the harder wear commonly inflicted on machinery in American mills.

The first Whitin High-speed Comber was shipped in October, 1905. For a time Marston Whitin was distressed to find that mill owners did not grasp the significance of the simpler design. But by the fall of 1909 he was cheered to see the machine beginning to take hold among Northern cotton hosiery mills. "There is no other machine that we sell," he wrote, "that I have so much confidence in recommending . . . as being superior to those of our competitors as I have this machine."[10]

Once the Whitin comber had gained the recognition it deserved, it drove European combers almost completely out of the market. By May, 1910, Marston Whitin stated the belief that nine-tenths of all the combers being sold in the United States were Whitin products.[11] Although he later revised his estimate to read "3/4 to 4/5" he still had good cause for rejoicing.[12] Not only did the Whitin comber account for 24 per cent of the company's dollar sales in 1910, but it added immeasurably to the company's prestige. (It also led to the company's acceptance of large blocks of common stocks in New Bedford mills, many of which mills later went bankrupt, bringing heavy losses to their stockholders.)

Meanwhile the Whitin company, encouraged by its success in the domestic market, had the temerity to challenge the Nasmith people on their home field. After a series of negotiations, Whitin granted the Howard & Bullough parent firm a license to build Whitin combers in England, making arrangements to collect all royalties through Howard & Bullough's American affiliate. After several years' trial, however, the English project was abandoned. So typically American was the Whitin High-speed Comber that its acceptance abroad was inversely proportional to its success at home.

After 1910 the Whitin comber gradually declined in importance relative to the company's other products. But in the American market it has continued to maintain its place of dominance down to the present. For years it was without competition from other domestic producers. Even foreign competition gradually disappeared, until in 1914 the British and French manufacturers had to abandon the production of combers altogether because of the war. Cut off from his supplier, Stephen C. Lowe decided to close his Hetherington agency and thereupon accepted a temporary job with the Whitin Machine Works as a Whitin comber salesman.[13]

Following World War I, an Englishman named Harry Tunstall established a small plant in Worcester to build a comber like the one made by Dobson & Barlow, the British firm where he had worked before the war. Apparently Tunstall was encouraged in this venture by the Boston machinery importing firm of Atkinson, Haserick & Company, for Atkinson, Haserick, which had been acting as American selling agent for the Dobson & Barlow firm, thereafter sold Tunstall's combers. Tunstall's success was, however, only moderate, and it was not until after the Saco-Lowell Shops had bought Tunstall's firm in 1933 and had set up a comber department of their own that a machine capable of competing with the Whitin High-speed Comber was put on the American market.

3. PURCHASE OF THE PROVIDENCE MACHINE COMPANY

While the Whitin Machine Works was endeavoring to create market acceptance for its comber, it was further integrating its product line by acquiring control of the Providence Machine Company, one of the country's leading producers of roving equipment. It will be recalled that throughout the Whitin company's previous history, except for John C. Whitin's brief and abortive attempt to develop a fly frame immediately following the Civil War, the firm had steadfastly, if reluctantly, refrained from competing in the roving field. To remedy this defect in its product line, the company had chosen to ally itself with a marketing group in which the Woonsocket Machine & Press Company was the roving-frame producer. The results of this unnatural alliance were, however, never satisfactory to either party concerned; the Woonsocket company constantly resented Whitin's leadership, and the Whitin company forever complained of Woonsocket's reluctance to follow.

It is easy enough, therefore, to understand why the Whitin Machine Works was anxious to develop a roving line of its own. It is also easy to understand why the Whitin company wished to buy a going concern, especially in view of the difficulties it was currently having with its new comber. But why did Marston Whitin buy the Providence Machine Company instead of the Woonsocket Machine & Press Company, especially after he had spent the previous ten years advising his customers to buy Woonsocket machinery in preference to any other make? Had he offered to buy the Woonsocket Machine & Press Company only to have his offer rejected? Or did he still carry the conviction that the machinery made by the Providence Machine Company was superior to Woonsocket's? If so, was he the one who approached the owners of the Providence company, or did a spokesman from Providence, acting either directly or through an intermediary, approach Whitin? In either case what prompted the Providence owners to sell? And what were the terms of sale? Only one thing is clear among all these uncertainties: the negotiations must have been carried on in person or by telephone, for not one word of them found its way into the Whitin company's letterbooks.

The Providence shop, it should be noted, was one of that august group of machine shops founded by pupils of Samuel Slater — shops such as the Fales & Jenks Machine Company, the Bridesburg Manufacturing Company, and the Cohoes Iron Foundry & Machine Company. One of the Providence company's original owners was Thomas J. Hill, the machine-shop superintendent of Slater's Providence Steam Cotton Mills.[14] In 1834 Slater separated his shop from his mill and established the Providence Machine Company with Thomas J. Hill as part owner. On Slater's death in 1846, his heirs sold Hill the remaining interest in the shop. Although Hill ran the company as a proprietorship until his death in 1894, he relied increasingly after 1885 on his grandson, William C. Peirce, to manage the firm.

William Peirce was only forty-five at the time he agreed to sell his family's firm to the Whitin Machine Works. It would seem that his willingness to surrender his active interest at such an early age must have been an indication that he had been managing the company in something less than a wholehearted manner. In addition it would seem that the company's failure to convert to the use of United States standard sizes — most progressive shops had adopted the new standards at least a decade earlier — must have been an indication of technological stagnation. If these were the circumstances, then, it may well have been that Peirce was anxious to retire and was consequently willing to sell the company even at a sacrifice price. On the other hand, however, the fact that the company was operating at capacity, plus the fact that Marston Whitin later brought many of the company's machine tools to Whitinsville, would seem to stand in the way of any conclusion that the company had become very far run-down under Peirce's management.

The exact date of the Providence purchase is not known, though it must have taken place in the early fall of 1909.[15] The first word of the sale to leak out to the public was a rumor printed in a Providence newspaper early in October, 1909.[16] Fearing that the news article would cause a general exodus of workers at a time when the

Providence shop was booked far in advance with orders, Marston Whitin authorized Peirce to confirm the rumor to his men and to announce to them that, although the shop in Providence would eventually be shut down and the machinery moved to Whitinsville, the Whitin Machine Works would offer jobs to any Providence men who wished to change locations.[17] (Actually about fifty men did decide to join the Whitin company, among them the superintendent of the Providence shop, Walter S. Brown, who became Whitin's roving specialist.)

For several reasons the transfer of men and machinery was not made at once. Because of booming conditions in the industry there was such great pressure on the Providence shop to meet its delivery schedules that Whitin was reluctant to sacrifice any of the roving shop's productive time until after the demand had subsided. Furthermore, the machine shop being constructed in Whitinsville to house the Providence company's equipment (Shop No. 5) was not yet ready for occupancy. Therefore the transposition of men and machines to their new location was not begun until December, 1909, and was not finally completed until October of the following year.

A word in passing about Shop No. 5. Although in part it eventually housed the machinery brought up from Providence, it was not originally intended for that purpose. As early as the spring of 1907 Marston Whitin had seen the need for further plant enlargement. The company's growth had reached a point where a major revision in plant layout was necessary if there was to be any further expansion of capacity. Lying across the only logical path of growth was the foundry, parts of which dated from as early as 1847. Focusing his sights far into the future, Whitin decided to build a new and much larger foundry west of the old one, at the same time filling in part of the water-power pond to make new ground. He then tore down the old foundry and built in its place a new machine shop. Work on this immense project carried over the 1907–08 depression and helped to give employment to machine-shop workers who would otherwise have had nothing to do. The Providence purchase thus came at an opportune time, since the plans for an expanded plant were already sufficient to accommodate the additional machinery.[18]

News of the Providence purchase seems to have taken the Woonsocket Machine & Press Company by surprise. With Cramer handling the Providence line of roving, Woonsocket had no outlet through which to sell its roving machinery in the South. How the Woonsocket managers solved their difficulty would ordinarily lie beyond the scope of this history were it not for the unexpected assistance given them by an internal rupture in the Whitin Machine Works management.

Back in 1896, shortly after Cramer had become Whitin representative in the South, the Whitin company had sent a young card erector, John H. Mayes, to Charlotte as chief erector for the Southern territory. Mayes proved so able that shortly after 1900 he was made assistant to Cramer and was given independent authority to negotiate sales. Prospering at his work, he decided in 1906 to establish a small cotton mill near Charlotte as a side investment. Apparently he was joined in the venture by other members of his family. The firm became known as the Mayes Manufacturing Company, and the village that grew up around it as Mayesworth.

Unhappily, in gathering together his work force, Mayes committed the unforgivable sin of hiring a Whitin erector to supervise the carding department of his new mill. This inept move exercised Marston Whitin so much that he wrote to Cramer recommending that Mayes be discharged. Apparently, Cramer interceded for his assistant; at least, it is clear that he neglected to follow Whitin's recommendation. During the next few years, however, something seems to have caused Cramer's friendship for Mayes to wear thin, for on 10 January 1910, without advance warning, Cramer wired Whitin that he had been forced to dismiss his energetic assistant.* There is some shadowy evidence that the younger executives at Whitinsville were sorry to see such a capable salesman leave their company, but Marston Whitin unhesitatingly supported his representative's action.[19]

As might have been expected, Mayes immediately set about establishing an agency rivaling Cramer's. His first and most natural

---

* Mayes' dismissal made way for the promotion of Robert I. Dalton and William H. Porcher, as assistants to Cramer. These two men are still in charge of Whitin's Southern sales.

contact was the Woonsocket Machine & Press Company whose roving frames he had for many years sold as Cramer's assistant. It was only a month or two before Mayes' dismissal that Woonsocket had officially severed connections with Cramer because of Whitin's deal with the Providence Machine Company. Within three months Mayes was advertising Woonsocket products over his name.[20] Gradually he secured other agencies for the Southern territory — the agency for Nasmith combers and for many of the firms that had formerly been associated in the Providence Machine Company's marketing group (see Appendix 17).

This new group, centering in Mayes, eventually came to be known as "the combine" and managed to survive the others of its kind by almost two decades. At length, however, it, too, disbanded in the face of competition from better-integrated concerns. In 1930 the two major companies in the group, the Fales & Jenks Machine Company and the Woonsocket Machine & Press Company, sold their assets to the Whitin Machine Works and went out of business. But that is a story for a later chapter.[21]

Having digressed for a moment, let us quickly summarize what had been happening in Whitinsville in the few years just preceding the Mayes episode of 1910. The Whitin Machine Works had gradually rounded out its line of preparatory machinery, first, by its ingenious development of a heavy-duty, high-speed comber and, secondly, by its purchase of the Providence Machine Company. It had at the same time been confident enough of its future to expand its plant capacity (as measured in floor space) by about 75 per cent.

During that same period, however, the Whitin company lost ground where once it had been a leader — in the loom business. *Losing ground* is a relative term and sometimes cannot be measured even statistically. When a company sells 7,875 looms in a given year (1896), thereby setting a record for itself, and then breaks that record by selling 8,455 (in 1909), one hesitates to declare that it has lost much ground in the interim. Nevertheless during those twelve intervening years the Drapers had put on the market their automatic loom, a device so efficient that it eventually drove the Whitin company out of the loom field. Therefore, once again it is necessary to to take a look at what was going on in Hopedale to understand what was happening in Whitinsville.

4. COMPETITION FROM THE DRAPERS' AUTOMATIC LOOM

In 1888 the Drapers, realizing the ephemeral nature of their patent-based control of the spindle business turned their attention toward the development of an automatic loom.[22] The trouble with existing looms was that they ceased to operate as soon as their shuttles ran out of filling. Since a shuttle was capable of carrying at best a small load of yarn, shutdowns were frequent, averaging about twelve an hour. The Drapers felt that by automatically replacing a spent shuttle, shutdowns could be virtually eliminated and a great reduction made in labor costs, which were higher per pound of cotton in the weaving shed than in any other mill department.

As a starting point the Drapers used the experiments which James H. Northrop, one of their former employees, had been conducting in his farmyard henhouse. By July, 1889, Northrop's shuttle-changing device was deemed workable and was forthwith installed for trial purposes in the Seaconnet Mills at Fall River. Unfortunately the device proved clumsy under actual operating conditions. As a result, Northrop started off on a new theory. To change the entire shuttle was impractical, he decided; to change the bobbin within the shuttle was the only feasible solution.

Convinced by then that an automatic loom was coming within reach, the Drapers poured every effort and resource into further experimentation. One man was assigned to investigate every previous development of a similar nature either here or abroad. Others were set to the task of inventing a warp stop motion. In the course of investigation, some sixty patents were either taken out or applied for by thirteen of the men engaged in the research. The size of the project, together with its ultimate success, was to earn it a rank among the triumphs of directed research by American business firms.

Not until 1894 was the so-called Northrop loom ready to begin regular operation, and even then the Drapers decided that first they should try it out in a mill of their own where they could study its performance at close hand. For this purpose they organized the Queen City Cotton Company, in Burlington, Vermont.[23] At the Queen mill the Northrop loom proved to be everything it was expected to be. Because a single operative could handle twice as many looms when the bobbins changed automatically, labor costs in the weave shed were cut in half. Since weave-shed labor ordinarily constituted half the labor in a mill, the potential saving was enormous.

Even before they were ready to begin producing their new loom in commercial quantities, the Drapers were inundated with orders. To meet the heavy demand they decided to license other producers as they had done in the case of the Sawyer and Rabbeth spindles. The Mason Machine Works, the Lewiston Machine Shop, and Kilburn, Lincoln & Company agreed to coöperate. But the Whitin Machine Works and the Lowell Machine Shop objected to certain contract clauses in which the Drapers required them to pay a royalty equivalent to the full price of a plain loom and to sign over whatever improvements they might add to the Northrop looms they manufactured. Whitin's formal reply to the Draper proposition was couched in measured words: "In regard to the license that you sent us some little time ago, we do not feel satisfied to sign it in just the form it is until we have looked the matter up a little further." [24]

After the first rush of orders, however, the Drapers were surprised to find that the high cost of the Northrop machine (about three times the cost of a common loom) and the rumored difficulty of keeping it in good operating condition were preventing its wide acceptance. Furthermore, equipping a new mill with Draper looms increased the cost of organizing a new mill by about 13 per cent, as is shown in Appendix 18.

In January, 1899, the Drapers ran in the *Textile World* an advertisement which reflected their exasperation at the failure of mill men to recognize the merit of their product:

Eighty mills have now ordered Northrop Looms. With a record of 25,000 sold the skeptics should be thoroughly silenced. We are not only selling a machine requiring but one half or less of the usual attention, but one which produces a better, as well as a cheaper product.

We believe we have called this fact to the attention of the manufacturing public before, but constant reiteration is sometimes necessary with that class of human nature which persistently overlooks its own self-interest.

Cramer was equally surprised at the market's reaction to the new mechanism. "The Drapers are pushing the loom for all it is worth," he wrote, "and it certainly does take in the South, and it seems to be doing well, yet it is not being bought in the North. Again several of the Northern shops have been licensed to build the loom, but they don't build it and they don't try to sell it." [25] Awakened to the fact that the Northrop loom would require aggressive promotion and that other manufacturers were unwilling to push it properly, the Drapers decided in 1899 to build what was in reality their first great manufacturing plant, a plant sufficiently large to meet the entire national demand for automatic looms.

Of all American loom manufacturers, the Whitin Machine Works probably stood to lose most in competition with the automatic Northrop device, for the Whitin product was the highest-priced non-automatic loom on the market.[26] Whitin's loom appealed principally to mill men who were not unwilling to make a large initial capital investment if it promised to yield them lower operating costs — the very men who could be expected to find the Northrop loom attractive. Curiously enough, Marston Whitin met the Drapers' threatened expansion almost with indifference. He seems to have believed that the automatic loom would soon find its natural limits and that the non-automatic loom would continue to command the residual bulk of the market. Therefore, when the Drapers began an expansion program[27] which would make them the rivals of the largest producers of cotton textile machinery in the country,* the people at Whitinsville, far from treating them as foes, gave them many helpful bits of information of the kind known only to those with long practical experience — information on foundry techniques, layouts for erection floors, materials and methods, wage levels, box-car loading arrangements, and so forth. Perhaps one should add that in the end the Whitin company was amply repaid for its magnanimity; the new foundry built by the Drapers incorporated so many features stemming from the best-known practices here and abroad that it

---

* During the first years of the new century, four firms came to dominate the cotton-textile machinery industry: the Whitin Machine Works and the Saco-Lowell Shops in preparatory machinery, and the Draper Company and the Crompton & Knowles Loom Works in weaving machinery. The Crompton & Knowles Loom Works is seldom mentioned on these pages only because, being a producer of looms for woolens and fancy cottons, it seldom came into direct competition with the Whitin Machine Works.

later served in part as a model for the foundry built in Whitinsville in 1908.

Indifference to the Northrop invention was not so complete among Whitin executives, however, that it prevented them from toying with the idea of developing a similar machine to complement their line of common looms. As early as 1898 they were telling customers that they were slowly perfecting an automatic loom of their own.[28] Ironically, just at that time the idea of an American-built comber seized Marston Whitin's imagination and caused him to divert his experimental staff's attention toward its development. From time to time independent inventors — for instance, J. C. Bryan, of South Carolina, and L. E. Bromeisler, of New York City — approached the Whitin Machine Works with various devices designed to enable a common, plain-goods loom to operate automatically, but in each case the Whitin company decided that the invention either would not survive the strain of mill operation or else that it would not stand clear of Northrop's broadly drawn patent claims.[29]

In 1898 the Whitin Machine Works considered entering competition with the Crompton & Knowles Loom Works by developing a line of drop-box (non-automatic) looms — that is, looms capable of weaving fancy goods with various colors of filling.[30] Crompton & Knowles, however, was already at work on ways of making their fancy-goods looms automatic. By 1905, only a short time after Whitin had produced its first 2x1 and 4x1 drop-box machines, the Crompton & Knowles firm was able to announce its new automatic machine. By so doing it stepped into as commanding a position in the fancy-goods loom business as the Drapers occupied in the plain-goods loom field.

By 1909 the Drapers had gone still further in perfecting the Northrop loom and had again offered the Whitin Machine Works a licensing arrangement similar to that suggested in 1896. The offer could have been extended at no less propitious time. Before Whitin, who was ill when the Draper proposal arrived, was well enough to give it his consideration, his company was "simply overwhelmed with loom orders." [31] Under such circumstances it is less difficult to understand how Marston Whitin was able to convince himself of the unshakable strength of the plain loom than it is to explain how the non-automatic loom, in the face of the Northrop loom's increased indefectibility, was able to stage such a remarkable comeback.

Had it not been for the unexpected reanimation of Whitin's non-automatic loom business in 1909, Marston's reply to the Drapers might well have been written in different words — although it is possible that his basic objection to the proposal's terms might still have prevented him from accepting it. As it was, he took pen in hand, as the Draper-imposed 31 December deadline drew near, and wrote the following:[32]

I wish we were situated so that we could take up the building of the looms for you, but at present we are not in condition to do it. Unexpectedly, this last year we have sold a great many plain looms, and we have had to double our output in this department. We are crowded to the limit in this branch, and this work is going to keep up for a number of months. We are also trying to move up the Providence Machine Works so as to get to building Roving in our shop, here, and I do not see how we are going to be in a position to do anything with a new loom for some time to come. Then too the other complications about our building an automatic loom are still in force so I am afraid that we shall have to decline this opportunity of doing this line of work.

Unhappily the 1909–10 hum of activity in Whitin's loom department proved to be the swan song of the Whitin non-automatic machine. In 1911 loom sales dropped 61 per cent and thereafter continued falling steadily until by 1917 they were accounting for less than one-tenth of one per cent of the company's total sales (see Appendix 27).

Here there arises a question of fact in connection with Marston Whitin's attitude toward his loom market. Did the threat of competition from Draper's automatic loom have any bearing on his decision to buy the Providence shop? If in truth he had realized that the loom market was irretrievably slipping from his grasp, might he not have reasoned that the best way to retrench his position in the industry was by strengthening his preparatory line? Yet, though such may have been his original reasoning, his ultimate motives in buying the Providence shop must have been somewhat different, for by the summer of 1909 (that is, before the Providence purchase had been made) orders for non-automatic looms were arriving with every mail. If Whitin looked upon those orders as an unreliable indication of the true demand for his looms (as indeed they proved to be), he gave no sign of it in his letters. Rather his willingness to carry through an expansion of his loom department, as noted above, seems to indicate that he greeted the boom as a justification of his oft-expressed faith in the unassailable position of the non-automatic machine. Thus one concludes that the Providence purchase must have been made on its own merits and not primarily, or perhaps even secondarily, in response to any pressure that Whitin may have felt from the competition of Northrop's loom.

A final word about the disposition of the Whitin loom business. For a while after 1910, Whitin's experimental staff made a renewed effort to work out various ideas for an automatic loom that would not encroach upon the Northrup principle. Several patents resulted, one or two of which were of considerable value. By 1917, however, it had become evident that a device mechanically superior to Northrop's was virtually impossible.[33] For a time, during the busy days early in World War I, the Whitin company leased its loom patterns to the Mason Machine Works.[34] Then, in 1918, it decided to abandon the loom business entirely by selling its collection of loom patents to the Drapers.

Since the Drapers were well on their way toward a monopoly in the plain-goods loom field, their purchase of a rival firm's loom patents might easily have opened them to a charge of conspiring with Whitin to restrain trade. It was thought best, therefore, to make the sale a personal rather than an intercorporate transaction. On 25 June 1918 the directors of the Whitin Machine Works voted "that there be distributed from the surplus of the Company as a dividend to stockholders of record at the close of business this day" seven letters patent of the United States, one of Canada, two of Great Britain, and two of France, plus eleven applications for letters patent of the United States. The patents were to be distributed in lieu of a $225,000 dividend that had previously been declared by the directors but that had not yet been paid.

What followed was of course a personal matter between the

Whitin stockholders and the Draper Corporation. Consequently it did not become a part of the Whitin records. It was no secret in the industry, however, that the Whitin stockholders in turn passed their patents to the Draper firm. How much they received in return is not known, but almost certainly it was enough to compensate them for the cash dividend they had foregone.[35] It was also no secret that at the same time the Drapers discontinued manufacturing twisters, the only other of their products that competed directly with the Whitin line. In neither case, it might be added, did the two companies sacrifice very much. Their actions were rather admissions that each had ceased to be very strong in the other's field. Thereafter the two firms concentrated their efforts on non-competing products, the Whitin Machine Works specializing in preparatory equipment and the Draper Corporation in looms.

5. WHITIN MAKES PICKERS AGAIN

The final move in the checker game by which the Whitin Machine Works became an integrated producer of cotton-textile machinery was the purchase of the Atherton Picking Machinery Company. The purchase itself was anticlimactic, however, compared with the long series of dramatic events that brought it about. The purchase did not take place until 1913, but the first directly traceable event leading up to it had occurred a dozen years earlier.

It will be recalled that 1901 was the year when the Lowell Machine Shop, convinced of the perfidy of its competitors, refused to enter a new pricing agreement with them. It will also be recalled that the refusal was a show of weakness, not of strength. Already Cramer had written what looked like a forecast of Lowell's doom: "[The Lowell people] have been driven out of North Carolina and then South Carolina and are partly driven out of Georgia, and they know they have got to make a final stand in Mississippi." [36] Realizing the desperateness of its situation, the Lowell Machine Shop embarked on a price war, even though conditions in the industry were generally prosperous and despite the fact that a sellers' market prevailed.

By 1904 Lowell's competitive price-cutting had driven spindle prices to their lowest point in history and had aroused among machinery men a grave concern over the contagion that was being spread by this sick giant in their midst. On 24 October 1904 Cramer wrote Whitin a long and acrid letter describing Lowell's most recent reckless price-cuts. In general, Cramer thought that Lowell was weakening itself and its competitors by transacting business wholly on a price basis instead of trying to win and hold customers on the strength of its products and the reliability of its services. At the conclusion of his letter Cramer sized up his view of the sordid situation:

I merely mention all this that you may understand what the Lowell people are doing, notwithstanding what they say they are doing. I see no way of getting better prices until that shop is out of the way, and it strikes me that somebody will have to get it out of the way before you will ever get prices up again. The business is getting so terribly disorganized, at least in this part of the country, that I do not see how we can get decent prices again for a long time.

It is improbable that Cramer's idea about getting the Lowell shop "out of the way" was original with him. More likely, he was aware that the industry was already considering some method of forcing Lowell to refrain from selling at prices below its costs. Knowing that Marston Whitin was in a position either to promote or to prevent such a scheme, Cramer was possibly taking this means to sway his employer toward support of the measure.

How Whitin felt about Cramer's proposal that someone get control of the Lowell shop has not been recorded. Either he was passive to the idea or else he was careful not to set forth his views in writing. Eventually, when the industry decided to join in buying control of Lowell, Whitin participated financially, but beyond that he was apparently not involved. The instigator of the joint-purchase was, in fact, not one of the textile-machinery men but rather a distinguished Boston lawyer and financier, named Robert F. Herrick.* Apparently Herrick had seen in the situation at Lowell an oppor-

* Herrick was not unknown to Marston Whitin, for he had sponsored the Loray Mills promotion in which the members of the Whitin family had invested $100,-000 only to be forced to follow up their investment with eventual control when Loray fell into financial difficulties. At the time of the Lowell purchase, however, Loray had not yet failed. Whitin and Herrick remained lifelong business friends despite the fact that their personal interests sometimes clashed.

tunity to acquire a splendid piece of property at a reasonable price. Apparently also he was aware that the members of the textile machinery industry were so vexed at Lowell's irresponsible price-cutting that they would be willing to back him financially.

Therefore, in March, 1905, Herrick announced his willingness to buy the outstanding shares of Lowell Machine Shop stock at a price sufficiently above the market to ensure his gaining control. Backing his offer were — so the trade journals of the day reported[37] — the financial resources of the Saco & Pettee Machine Shops, the Whitin Machine Works, the Draper Company, the Mason Machine Works, the Howard & Bullough American Machine Company, the Fales & Jenks Machine Company, and the Woonsocket Machine & Press Company. About a fifth of the total amount needed to purchase the outstanding Lowell stock was subscribed to by the Whitin Machine Works.

On its surface the purchase of the Lowell shop by a group that included most of its competitors had all the appearances of an act in restraint of trade. And perhaps it might have been found so to be if the matter had been adjudicated in the hostile courts of the time (where the decision in the Northern Securities case had recently pointed toward making such acts illegal even if they placed only *potential* restraints on trade).[38] Yet in its final results the Lowell purchase violated the Sherman Act neither in fact nor in spirit, for the purchasing companies were given no voice in the Lowell shop's management. It is true that under Herrick's direction Lowell's prices were stabilized, but perhaps no more so than would have been the case under any prudent new management. Meanwhile, Herrick infused the company with such renewed vitality that within two years Lowell was a stronger competitor than it had been for ten years past. Indeed, by 1907 Whitin was chastising Cramer for letting Lowell salesmen outsell him in the South.[39] Perhaps it is evidence of Whitin's desire to wash his hands of the whole Lowell deal that in the year following Herrick's purchase he wrote the Whitin Machine Works' investment in Lowell stock completely off his books, as though it had been an unavoidable expense undertaken in behalf of industry tranquillity and best forgotten.

Meanwhile, and almost coincident with his acquisition of control over Lowell, Herrick bought control of the Kitson Machine Company and made it a wholly owned subsidiary of the Lowell Machine Shop. He also bought the A. T. Atherton Machine Company, of Pawtucket, the only other picking-machinery producer in the country and the firm that previously had been controlled by the Saco & Pettee Machine Shops. Herrick immediately closed the Atherton plant (whereupon Abel T. Atherton turned around and established the Atherton Picking Machinery Company, the firm which Whitin bought in 1913), but he kept the Kitson plant in operation as an integral part of the Lowell shop's operations. At the same time he moved H. C. Perham from the treasurership of the Kitson company to the treasurership of Lowell.

These complicated corporate maneuvers may seem singularly remote from the Whitin story, but it must be remembered that the Kitson Machine Company had for ten years been a member of Whitin's marketing group and was in fact still the only source of picking machinery available to Whitin's customers. Therefore it was necessary for the Whitin Machine Works to effect some sort of working arrangement with the new Lowell management regarding picker sales. The final decision allowed Cramer to remain as the Lowell Machine Shop's picking-machinery agent in the South, despite the fact that Lowell continued to sell all its other machinery direct. This awkward and anomalous arrangement continued in effect until 1912, when the situation was suddenly changed by the merger of the Lowell Machine Shops with the Saco & Pettee Machine Shops.

It is not known to what extent Marston Whitin was able to anticipate the merger of the second and third largest companies in the industry (the Saco & Pettee Machine Shops had in fact outsold Whitin in five of the preceding sixteen years); it *is* known, however, that almost exactly a year before the merger occurred, Whitin had agreed to sell to Robert F. Herrick the block of Lowell stock held by the Whitin Machine Works.* Whether Herrick in November, 1911, was already planning the merger, or whether he was simply

---

* Whitin sold the stock to Herrick at its original cost. Thus the only direct financial gain enjoyed by the Whitin Machine Works from its investment in Lowell Machine Shop stock was the 6 per cent return which it received in the form of dividends.

relieving the Whitin Machine Works of a stock interest that might prove embarrassing, should the matter ever be brought up in court, is also something that is not known. Because of Marston Whitin's close friendship with Herrick and because that friendship continued even after the Saco-Lowell merger, one is tempted to assume that Herrick willingly kept Whitin informed of his plans and that Whitin made no strenuous effort to prevent Herrick from carrying them through. Whitin never commented on the merger in any of his letters except to explain to his customers that, despite the fact that the combination of the Lowell-Kitson and the Saco-Pettee plants under one management had produced the largest textile machinery *organization* in the country, the Whitin Machine Works could still boast the largest single *plant*.

The formation of the Saco-Lowell Shops became effective in November, 1912. A few days after the announcement of the merger had appeared in the press, Marston Whitin received a letter from Charles T. Atherton, the son and heir of Abel Atherton. Apparently Charles, having acceded to the difficult task of managing the Atherton Picking Machinery Company, had been looking about for a buyer and upon seeing the notice of the Saco-Lowell merger had guessed that the Whitin Machine Works would now be in the market for a picking-machinery plant. The fact that Marston Whitin promptly rejected the offer would seem to indicate that he had some reason to believe in his ability to continue on a working basis with the Kitson branch of the merged organization.

"As regards the matter in question," he wrote to Atherton, "we do not think we would be interested in making a proposition to buy out the business. We have a great many other irons in the fire at the present time and expect our energies to be pretty well concentrated along regular lines for the next year or two." [40]

In the succeeding months, however, something occurred to shake Whitin's confidence in the possibility of continuing his relationship with Kitson, for by November, 1913, he had reversed his stand and was offering to buy the patterns and patents of the Atherton concern. Apparently the Saco-Lowell Shops had decided to discontinue selling pickers through Cramer, thus forcing Whitin to develop his own picker line or do without.

Although Whitin paid only $10,892 for the Atherton assets, he got no bargain.* Before the Atherton picking machine could be made to compete with the Kitson product it had to be completely redesigned. Because of the attendant delay, Whitin-Atherton pickers did not finally reach the market until 1915. Even then they met with considerable consumer resistance. Even in Cramer's office the imbedded notion that there were no pickers quite like Kitson's worked to prevent wide acceptance of the Whitin-Atherton product. Essentially it was the design of the machine that was still at fault. The company's agent freely confessed, "There is nothing new about our picker. It is the old Atherton type, incorporating the best features of the [English] Dobson & Barlow machine."

At length, in April, 1924, the Whitin Machine Works brought to Whitinsville an Englishman, Edward Mills, for the sole purpose of developing a new Whitin picker.[41] Mills' qualifications for the job were excellent, for he had been manager of the picking department in the Taylor & Lang shops in Taylor Bridge, England, where the far-famed Buckley opener had been developed. Just as it had done thirty years earlier in the case of the revolving flat card, the Whitin firm was turning in time of trouble to English know-how for assistance.

Edward Mills remained in Whitinsville for about ten years. During his stay the quality of Whitin's pickers gradually improved until at last they were able to compete with Kitson machines. Finally, late in the 1920's, and for the first time in its history, the Whitin Machine Works could lay claim to being a producer of a strong and fully integrated line of cotton preparatory machinery.

* As part of the sales agreement, Charles T. Atherton attempted to persuade Whitin to hire him as foreman of the new Whitin picker department. Whitin saw fit, however, to hire Atherton's superintendent, J. J. McGowan, and his son, Frank, instead. The elder McGowan became a Whitin picker salesman while his son became department foreman.

CHAPTER XIV

MARSTON WHITIN RETIRES, 1913-1915

THE tremendous expansion of business in the decade following 1899 caused the Whitin Machine Works to become too large an organization to be managed by one man unassisted. Formerly, except perhaps for a half-dozen clerks to keep the accounts in good order and to compute the weekly payrolls, Marston Whitin had carried the executive load of the company almost completely without the help of a staff organization. With the exception of the two Lasell brothers, the company officials had all belonged to the line of command. Whitin himself had performed all the duties of a general sales manager. He personally had purchased all the major supply items. He alone had kept the company's financial records. And almost single-handedly he had conducted the company's correspondence. Except in the lower reaches of management — at the foreman level — he had permitted no decentralization of control.

Following 1900, however, Whitin had been forced to divest himself of his diverse responsibilities. In so doing he did not disturb his line organization; he merely delegated to others what once he had done unaided. To his secretary, George B. Hamblin, he turned over a major share of the purchasing work and a good deal of the routine correspondence. As the office force grew in size he also made Hamblin office manager. In addition he referred to Hamblin the petty legal and personnel problems that so often rose out of the shop's participation in town affairs, until eventually Hamblin became in fact if not in name the company's public relations representative.

At about the same time, Whitin began assigning to others the task of contacting customers. By 1900 he was finding it impossible to keep in intimate touch with the purchasers, or potential purchasers, of his machinery, so large had grown the number of cotton mills in the country. Meanwhile the aggressive selling efforts of his competitors had taught him that business could be had only by energetic solicitation and by offering services beyond those offered by others. As a result he began the assembling of what was to be the first real salesforce in the history of the company.

In general the new salesmen were specialists in one product only. Because of their specialized knowledge, Marston hoped that mill men would look to them for technical advice — advice on how a machine should be set up, how operated, and in case of later malfunctioning how put again in working order. Some of the specialists hired by Whitin have already been mentioned in other connections. J. J. McGowan was the company's specialist in picking, John H. Mayes in cards, Walter S. Brown in roving, and Elwin H. Rooney in combers.[1]

These specialists became the company's field agents. They scouted prospects, followed leads, rendered service to customers in an advisory capacity, and acted as trouble-shooters when operating failures occurred. In their work they were responsible only to Marston Whitin, who continued as the firm's master salesman and contact man. In a way they were a sign of the times. The upsurge of Southern mill incorporations was beginning to spend itself. The Whitin company was finding that its products were going less into the outfitting of new mills and more into the replacement of existing machinery or the expansion of existing capacity. By 1913 the day of the full-mill order was all but past. To the new era, the specialist-salesman was what the mill engineer had been to the old. Having none of the mill engineer's broad knowledge of a variety of machines the specialist-salesman nonetheless knew far more about what mill men had come to be interested in — the performance of individual machines.

I. ENTER THE FOURTH GENERATION

To assist in the work of managing the company, Marston Whitin also started the practice of bringing in several of his young relatives to train them for executive posts. The first young relative admitted to the firm during Marston's time was Lawrence Murray Keeler, the younger brother of Mrs. Chester W. Lasell. Following graduation from Phillips Andover Academy in 1893, Lawrence entered upon the customary tour of apprenticeship duty in Whitinsville, working first on the floors of the shop and then with an erection crew in the field. For a time thereafter he engaged in a miscellany of jobs, including the supervision of the company's exhibit at the 1895 Exposition in Atlanta, Georgia. Then, about 1903, he became salesman for the Northern area outside New England, a territory that extended from Baltimore to Montreal and from New York to Indianapolis.

It would appear that Keeler became a salesman more by circumstance than by inclination, but he enjoyed entertaining and became widely known in the industry at a time when personal contacts were often the basis on which sales were made. He was by nature restless and so took pleasure in being much on the road. If his gruff frankness made him less persuasive at his job than he might have been and if his aloof demeanor sometimes prejudiced men against him, both traits were usually excused by those who knew the New England temperament and who were acquainted with the fact that he was related to the company's owner-family.

In 1905 Keeler became even more a part of the family by marrying his brother-in-law's niece, Elizabeth Whitin, the eldest of Marston Whitin's four daughters. In the following year he became company agent with responsibility for sales in the entire Northern territory, including New England. (The Southern territory continued under Cramer's supervision.) As company agent Keeler took up residence in Boston, then the center of the textile machinery trade. But Keeler's wife, in rebellion against being left so often at home by a husband who was forced to travel a great deal, pressed for a transfer of their headquarters to a location nearer her family. As a result, in 1913 the Keelers moved their place of residence to Whitinsville, high on the hill above the village, overlooking the Mumford Valley.

The Keelers' return to Whitinsville terminated the only period when the Whitin company maintained a selling headquarters in Boston.* This fact is in marked contrast to the practice of the Saco-

---

* Since Lawrence Keeler is the only member of the younger generation of executives no longer living, it would perhaps be well at this point to follow through to the end of his career. It was his often-announced plan to retire in 1930 — at the age of sixty. As that time drew near, however, business became so inactive that he decided to retire somewhat earlier. He occupied his leisure by traveling, entertaining, and painting a little. On 28 March 1935, while vacationing in Florida, his retirement was cut short by a sudden and fatal heart attack. His age at death was sixty-four.

Lowell Shops which, from the beginning down to the present, never maintained their selling or administrative offices anywhere but in Boston, even though their manufacturing plants were always located somewhere else.

In the fall of 1909 Marston Whitin's second daughter, Elsa, married a young Worcester man, Sydney Russell Mason. Mason had attended Harvard College, but he had been forced by the sudden death of his father to leave school and to begin work in his family's Mason Brush Works, in Worcester. After his marriage to Elsa, however, he left the management of the brush shop to a brother and changed his abode to Whitinsville. Mason was a slight man in stature, but in his dogged capacity for work he revealed a tyrannical command over details. Marston realized that a man like Mason would be valuable to the company in the repair department to which, with vexatious frequency, customers were wont to apply for parts that had been out of current manufacture for twenty or thirty years. Just at that time the replacement-parts market was growing rapidly and the servicing of old Whitin machines was becoming an increasingly important item in the company's sales account. Formerly the sale of parts had amounted to less than 10 per cent of the company's business and so the superintendent's office had been able to handle such orders with ease. Between 1910 and 1913, however, the dollar sales of parts had increased by 56 per cent and the proportion of parts to total sales had mounted to 18 per cent. Therefore, in 1913, Marston Whitin decided to relieve the superintendent's office of its responsibility for parts orders and instead established a completely independent department to handle the work. Mason was one of the first employed in the new department and within three years had become its head, a position he is still occupying after more than thirty years of service.

Whitin's third daughter,* Katharine, married a man who, like Lawrence Keeler, was already related to the family. Her husband, E. Kent Swift, was Marston Whitin's first cousin — which is to say, he was the nephew of Marston's mother. Although Kent Swift thus

---

* Whitin's fourth daughter, Lois, was the youngest in the family by almost ten years. In 1920 she married a United States Army officer, William C. Crane, and for many years lived in Japan where her husband was stationed. Consequently neither she nor her husband figures prominently in the subsequent history of the company.

belonged to Marston Whitin's generation, he was in fact young enough to have been Marston's son. Swift's ancestors had lived originally in Falmouth, Massachusetts, where their shipbuilding interests had led them eventually into lumbering. As the lumbering business had moved westward, the Swifts had moved with it; consequently Kent Swift's birthplace and home had been Wisconsin. He had become intimately acquainted with his Whitinsville relatives during his years of study at Williams College in Massachusetts. In fact, it was during a visit to Whitinsville shortly after his graduation and before his scheduled matriculation in summer school at the Massachusetts Institute of Technology, where he intended to work on a mining degree, that he had been induced by Marston Whitin to change his plans and remain in Whitinsville as an employee of the shop. Not least among the inducements that caused Swift to accept the offer was the opportunity to live in the Whitin household, where he had found life on vacation to be congenial and stimulating. Therefore, after taking the summer off, Swift returned to Whitinsville in September to serve his apprenticeship in the shop.[2]

Having no son of his own, Marston developed a strong attachment for his young cousin. He was pleased to see what self-assurance Swift displayed in going about his work as a beginner, and he keenly watched the development of the young man's executive qualities. In 1906, at the 15 January meeting of the board of directors, Marston recommended that Swift be appointed assistant treasurer of the company, a post left vacant two years earlier by the retirement of J. M. Lasell. Swift was only twenty-eight at the time. But one of the characteristics of the Whitins was their willingness to thrust heavy responsibilities on young men. As assistant treasurer, Swift became second in command to Whitin, with full authority over the shop whenever Whitin was out of town.

At first Swift's responsibilities were not heavy, for with Whitin absent only a few days at a time important decisions could usually be delayed until his return. But in the spring of 1909 Whitin suffered an attack of appendicitis and on 10 April was hospitalized for an operation. During Whitin's absence, Swift assumed command and for two months or more remained in charge while Whitin took a leisurely trip to Europe in search of rest and recovery.

During that brief period the office was suddenly deluged with orders in the unexpected manner that had come to be typical of an incipient boom in the textile machinery industry. In addition Swift was confronted with a series of problems arising out of the demolition of the old foundry and the beginning of work on Shop No. 5, the renewal of the Drapers' effort to negotiate a licensing agreement for the manufacture of automatic looms, and further litigation with a man named Lewis T. Houghton over an alleged patent infringement involving the Whitin firm.* Through these treacherous management shoals the young man piloted the company so expertly that in the general consensus his succession to the treasurership was a matter of course.

A year and a half later, Kent Swift and Katharine Whitin were

---

* In 1904 Lewis T. Houghton, of Worcester, obtained a patent on a threadboard made of metal. Formerly all threadboards had been wooden. (Their function was to hold in place the thread guides on a spinning frame that conducted the yarn from rolls to rings.) Shortly after the issuance of Houghton's patent, the Whitin Machine Works offered its customers a similar metallic device. Houghton immediately sought and obtained a reissue of his patent so that his claims might be made broad enough to cover Whitin's product. In 1906 he brought suit against Whitin in the Massachusetts District Court, charging infringement. On the grounds that a substitution of materials (metal for wood) did not constitute a patentable idea, the court stated that Houghton's patent was without force and that consequently the Whitin Machine Works was not guilty of an infringement. In 1907 Houghton appealed to the Circuit Court and obtained a reversal based on the opinion that his substitution of materials had vastly improved the operation of the whole mechanism. The case was remanded to the lower court where the judge issued an interlocutory decree pending ascertainment, by an accounting Master, of Whitin's threadboard profits. Other manufacturers meanwhile signed licensing agreements with Houghton, but the Whitin company sought to escape paying royalties by developing a non-infringing device. In this attempt it was in part successful, thanks to the efforts of its assistant superintendent, W. O. Aldrich. Immediately the company started to convert to the new "Whitin C" model all the frames it had sold with the old type of infringing threadboards. In 1908, therefore, Houghton dismissed his original suit against Whitin in order to bring a second suit that would cover Whitin's new device as well as the old. As a result of the new suit in May, 1909, the District Court judge enjoined the Whitin company from making any further threadboards of metal. Thereafter Whitin had to send out all its new frames with wooden boards to serve until such time as it could legally replace them with metal ones. The case dragged into the summer of 1910. By then, Houghton had begun to doubt whether he was going to succeed in getting a decision against Whitin. On 1 August 1910, therefore, he signed with Whitin an agreement that was not unlike the agreement once signed by Whitin and Draper in regard to the Gravity spindle. In return for a nominal and preferential royalty, Houghton allowed the Whitin firm to equip frames with its own Whitin C model.

married. As a wedding present, and in evidence of his great joy over the match between his daughter and his foster son, Marston Whitin built for the couple a magnificent Georgian home far up on Northbridge Hill opposite the Keeler home. Like most of the construction work carried on in the self-sufficient village, the mansion at "Galesmeet," though planned by outside architects, was built by the shop's employees. Its high location makes it visible for miles around. To the villagers it has become a sight to be shown every out-of-town visitor, an object of pride second only to their pride in the shop.

By 1913, Marston Whitin was turning over to young Swift many of the management details of the business. Increasingly Whitin enjoyed spending his time in the company's experimental room, toying with ideas on how to improve his favorite machine, the Whitin High-speed Comber. Then, with unexpected suddenness, one day in April, 1915, he suffered a stroke. His age was fifty-eight.

In their uncertainty over how serious Whitin's illness would prove to be, the company's officials carefully explained in the letters they answered for Whitin that their treasurer was unable to write, being "a little indisposed" or "somewhat under the weather." [3] Their dark concern for him dissolved, however, as soon as it became evident that Whitin's typical Yankee fortitude was not going to let his illness keep him away from his desk for more than a month.[4]

Once recovered, Whitin again went regularly to his office as he had in the past. But though his perception was still keen, his strength was no longer capable of sustaining him through the gruelling requirements of a day's work. Thereafter, his command of the company was more nominal than real. Increasingly his interest was in the experimental room. His son-in-law, Swift, received a free hand in running the company's affairs, subject only to an occasional consultation with Whitin or an infrequent review of policy matters.

A second stroke seized Whitin in January of the following year (1916) while he and his wife were in New York attending the funeral of Mrs. Whitin's long-time friend, the actress, Ada Rehan. For many days his condition was so serious that it was thought unsafe to move him from the hotel where he had been staying. When he was finally well enough to travel, he was accompanied by his wife and daughters to Florida in a quest of sunshine and strength.

Never again was Whitin able to take active part in company affairs, though at times his strength and mental acuteness welled up together until his restless nature forced him to go to his office for an hour or two of work. On such occasions he found everything in readiness for his arrival. With his nurse in attendance, he went to his regular desk, lifted a freshly sharpened pencil that had been placed just as he liked it, read the morning mail, made notes, issued orders, and perhaps looked over current operating figures. For a few hours he recaptured the pleasure of doing what in life he enjoyed doing most.

Not until 1920 did he cease to hold the title of company treasurer. His health then had become so uncertain that the chance of his surviving the year seemed slight. For some time he had been confined to a wheelchair, and finally was seldom out of bed. At the annual stockholders' meeting, held 26 January 1920, E. Kent Swift was elected to succeed him.

Five days later, during the sub-zero temperature of a winter's night, Marston Whitin's home — the residence built for Josiah Lasell upon his removal from Holyoke to Whitinsville — was completely destroyed by fire. In sympathetic loyalty to the leader whom all respected, the villagers braved the midnight cold to man the village fire equipment only to find the pressure low and the hand pumps frozen. Volunteers carried Whitin to safety and removed all portable furnishings from the house, then stood by in wretched helplessness to watch the building burn.

Finally, on 8 December 1920, death came to the invalid body of George Marston Whitin. As in the case of his great-uncle, John C. Whitin, his passing was noted by few of his customers. In the shortness of human memory, the Whitin Machine Works had already come to be identified with the name of E. Kent Swift.

2. REVIEW AND SUMMARY

In the village of Whitinsville, however, Marston Whitin was still remembered — and revered. Even now, among the company's veteran employees, many hold their first allegiance to his memory. To them Marston Whitin was the Masterbuilder, the man responsible for the fact that the Whitin firm has continued to be a success de-

spite the difficulties of past years. During his active career he over-
saw the construction of 40 per cent of the company's present plant
and approximately 45 per cent of its present houses. Under him the
company-owned Blue Eagle Inn[5] was built to accommodate customers who wished to stay overnight and to house pensioners who
had no family to care for them. With support from Marston and
from other members of his family, a magnificent sandstone Congregational Church was erected — in typical Whitin fashion, with
an eye so far to the future that it was then, as it still is, somewhat
larger than required — an edifice so handsomely designed and so
painstakingly constructed that it is still unmarred by time, though
it is in fact now over a half-century old. Much of what Whitinsville
is today, it became during Marston Whitin's time.

No one now questions the wisdom of Whitin's building program.
It is considered one of the sources of the company's great strength
today. Yet it is equally a source of weakness. Three of the company's
most perplexing current problems stem directly from the policy of
expansion which Whitin followed between 1900 and 1910. The firm
is now faced with a plant that is poorly located in relation to its
Southern market; it is possessed of housing that has come to be a
source of expense as well as a cause of friction; and it is burdened
with an investment in municipal activities that it would like to escape but knows not how.

Could a wiser man have foreseen these problems? Foreseeing
them, could he have acted to prevent them? In Marston Whitin's
time the greatest challenge to the cotton-textile machinery trade was
the development of the Southern market, a market removed from
New England by nearly a thousand miles and one that was concentrated in a fairly small area around a Charlotte-Atlanta axis. If
Whitin had decided to build a branch plant in that area in 1907
instead of deciding to expand his facilities in Whitinsville, his company might today be in a better position to serve its customers and
at the same time might be less troubled by local village difficulties.

Unfortunately we know all too little about what would have been
the risks involved in such a move. We do know, however, that a
few machine-builders did undertake to build machinery in the South
in the early years of this century, only to falter and fail. The Mason

Machine Works once had a small shop in Charlotte where it built new machinery and repaired old.[6] So also had the Charlotte Machine Company, that erstwhile affiliate of the Saco & Pettee Machine Shops. But if the way those two concerns handled their sales organizations is any indication of the way they managed their shops, their respective failures do not necessarily indicate that manufacturing in the South was impracticable — although Marston Whitin may have been influenced by them to think that it was.

Perhaps the need for a Southern branch was not so clear-cut then as it now appears to have been. True, by 1907, approximately half of Whitin's machinery production was going to the South. Yet in those days the primary need of Southern mill owners was not for the low prices and prompt service that a near-by producer could have provided, but for capital — or that substitute for capital, credit. As we have already seen, the Northern machine-builders met the Southern demand for credit with real vigor. That they did not meet the demand for lower prices and better service by setting up branches in the South is perhaps only an indication that those considerations were often of subordinate importance in the minds of their customers. Prompt repair service to customers — a matter that later became a stiff competitive necessity — was at that time comparatively unimportant because of the relative newness of machinery in the South. As for prices, the cost of shipping machinery from New England to North Carolina amounted to only about 5 per cent of the total figure. In view of the risks involved, probably no machine-builder was willing to venture establishing a Southern plant merely in the hope of benefiting from a 5 per cent saving in shipping costs.

Chief among the risks that discouraged machine-builders from moving South in the early 1900's was the scarcity of skilled labor in that part of the country. Cotton mill owners had been able successfully to overcome that handicap by importing overseers from the North and by standardizing work loads so that unskilled laborers could be used to handle the bulk of the work, and conceivably the Whitin Machine Works might have done likewise. Indeed the Whitin company must already have been using some such technique in Whitinsville, else it could not have adjusted itself to the large numbers of unskilled foreign laborers it imported around the turn of the century. Perhaps, in fact, the reason that Marston did not build a Southern branch was because he wanted to take advantage of the skilled and smoothly coördinated labor force he already had in Whitinsville where, by increasing the supervisory load of his foremen and by spreading more thinly the work of his skilled men over a large number of unskilled employees, he was able to achieve high productivity at a low labor cost.

Were it not that the question of developing a large branch plant in the South is still a very real issue in Whitinsville, this discussion of the problem's pros and cons would be purely academic, for there is no evidence to support the belief that Marston ever gave the matter any consideration whatsoever. Surely if he had thought about the subject for any length of time, he would have mentioned it in his letters to Stuart W. Cramer. Why, then, if in retrospect it would appear that Whitin would have been well advised to have carried out his expansion plans in the South rather than in Whitinsville, did he pay the matter so little attention?

For one thing, it must be remembered that from his earliest years as treasurer, Marston had been a disciple of management by personal contact. The strength of his organization was a strength imparted to it by his personal familiarity with all its parts. An organization such as would have been essential to branch management would have been alien to his personality. It is doubtful, for instance, whether he would have continued to operate the Providence plant of the Providence Machine Company even if it had been economical to do so, simply because of his aversion to carrying on any business that was not under his personal supervision. Unlike his friend and neighbor, William F. Draper, who followed the course of dabbling in a multiplicity of activities — banking, mill operation, diplomacy, state and national politics, and Society — Whitin believed in concentration of effort. To him, expanding operations by building a branch in some other locality was something not to be thought of.

Similarly, to have abandoned his Whitinsville location, even in part, was beyond consideration. In a mind that was otherwise coldly rational, the shop and village occupied a spot governed by emotion. Marston believed in Whitinsville. He believed in its people — in the company's responsibility to them and theirs to it. He believed in the way of life made possible by a rural industrial feudality where day laborers could be ensured of a healthful environment by the company that hired them. He believed especially that it was his task to build where his predecessors had left off. To do so he felt that he must have a centralized firm. He believed also that the interests of that firm should be paramount to all things, even to the interests of the family. The family was to be compensated for its subordinate rôle by its continued close control over the company's ownership. This belief he successfully instilled into his daughters. It is no mere coincidence that three of them made Whitinsville their home and throughout their lives maintained an intimate interest in shop affairs. Indeed, as has been stated above, two of them married men already employed by the shop, while the third induced her husband to relinquish his interest in his own family's concern in order to aid in developing the Whitin Machine Works.

To the business historian a strong, stable firm is a pleasant fact to contemplate. Among old American firms the Whitin company is remarkable for its exceptionally long-continued strength and stability. The historian sees too often the hardships visited upon stockholders, employees, community, customers, and suppliers — roughly in that order — by a firm that is weak and victimized by mismanagement. But at the other extreme the business historian is apt to consider corporate strength such an unequivocal blessing that he fails to see the cost at which it is attained.

It is apparent that the Whitin stockholders were asked to sacrifice a great deal in dividends to make their company as strong as Marston Whitin thought it should be. Within not too many years the wisdom of that policy was to reveal itself. Yet, like anyone who has delayed taking his profits until an era of high taxes is upon him, the Whitin family have in the end been losers. The present generation will not suffer from Marston's policy, for its income and inheritance will be taxed no matter what the source. It is the members of the older generation who lost by leaving their money in the company with the hope that the younger generation would benefit thereby. They lost, that is, unless the pleasure they took from reinforcing the company and the community was greater than any pleasure they might have received from spending their larger dividends.

The employees and community were in a sense forced to put the interests of the company in a paramount position. The village surrendered its political and financial autonomy to the shop. The workers, in return for benefits received, acquiesced in hard times to the company's decisions regarding partial employment and job transfers.

The company's customers, too, could expect no favors that threw back to the shop any part of the cost of its products. Whitin operated his business on two basic principles. The first of these was: never sell machinery at a loss. The second principle was correlative to the first: maximize your profits.

Although he was well aware that others in the industry were willing to sacrifice profits on a first sale in the hope of offsetting their loss on later business, he was never an advocate of the practice. Whitin firmly believed that customers obtained on such a basis were insubstantial friends and hence were less reliable than those who bought for reasons other than price alone. Because of his insistence on prices that would cover costs, Whitin was sometimes condemned by cotton-mill owners; many considered his friendliness with competitors a sinister attempt to get the machine-builders to uphold each other at the expense of their customers. Some among the cotton-mill men would have preferred to see competition force prices below manufacturing costs, even if in the process certain manufacturers were driven from business. So far as Marston Whitin was responsible for preserving the price agreements of the 1890's, he probably was responsible for preserving stability in prices. But to just that same extent he was also responsible — by his strengthening of the weaker units in the industry — for holding off a merger movement in the textile machinery business until a considerably later date.

Operating in a producers' goods industry among remarkably loyal customers, Whitin seems to have been keenly aware that he was competing not only with other builders, but at times even with himself. A customer who was convinced against his better judgment to buy machinery in depressed times, often would agree to do so only at low prices; the same customer a few months later might otherwise have been willing and happy to buy the machinery at a price that would yield the manufacturer of the machinery a much higher profit margin. Moreover, orders taken at or near the end of a depression were especially risky, for in a surge of prosperity profits could easily be squeezed away between the millstones of fixed prices and ascending costs. Therefore, it was not uncommon to find Whitin warning his salesforce to discontinue all selling efforts until the promises of returning prosperity were either fulfilled or repudiated. Such a policy called for accurate diagnoses of the country's economic ills, a skill which in Whitin seems to have been innate rather than developed; one often suspects him of having been essentially right in his estimate of current business situations, but for the wrong reasons. Yet, because he had the boldness to maintain his prices while others were slashing theirs in their competitive anxiety, he was viewed by many as a cautious and hidebound conservative. A conservative he was. Over that there would be no caviling. But there are two distinct types of conservatives: the cautious, uninspired, preserver of the *status quo,* and the bold, hard-minded, dynamic realist. Whitin was definitely of the second type. He was never rash or speculative. Yet he was often willing to take what other men would have considered great risks. So confident was he in his analysis of the situation that he thought of such risks rather as near-certainties.

One aspect of Whitin's conservatism was his attitude toward his company's products. Being acutely conscious of costs, he was ever on the lookout for improved methods of production, better jigs and fixtures, automatic machines, finer materials. But in product design he was slow-moving. With the single and rather remarkable exception of the comber, he was an imitator rather than an innovator. The best gauge of his company's rôle in invention was its experimental room which, despite its name, was used more often to run tests for customers than to develop new types of machinery. So far behind did the company lag in the development of the revolving flat card that by the time it had a model on the market, the Pettee Machine Works had sold nearly seven thousand machines, as many as Whitin was to sell in the next ten years.

In the development of electrically driven machinery, Marston Whitin also revealed his passive attitude toward technological change. In 1907 the General Electric Company attempted, but without success, to induce him to promote the sale of spinning frames equipped with electric motors. Whitin believed, with some justification, that he was looked to by his customers for advice backed by actual experience. He was unwilling, therefore, to urge the advantages of electrification until electric motors had proved themselves in use.[7] However, since the typical mill superintendent was antipathetic to change, Whitin's attitude probably did not detract so much from this effectiveness as might be supposed.

What, then, was the source of the Whitin company's strength under Marston Whitin's management? If the company was not an innovator, was it a low-cost producer? Probably no other question confronting the business historian is more difficult to answer. Not only is the historian seldom able to get comparative statistics for other companies in an industry, but frequently he cannot even get a true idea of costs in the company he is studying. So it is in writing the history of the Whitin Machine Works. The Whitin company's cost system was, to say the least, inadequate, and no really satisfactory data are available for any of the other concerns in the industry. The only published figures on the industry's costs in the period before the 1920's are contained in a report made in 1916 by the United States Bureau of Foreign and Domestic Commerce,[8] but like most government reports on business, the figures in the Bureau's study are cloaked in anonymity. That particular difficulty may be resolved by checking the report against original company records, so that it is possible to establish with reasonable accuracy the names of the six companies investigated and to compile the study's key findings in the comparative form shown in Table 9. But beyond that point any use of the government's figures becomes treacherous. An analysis of them is attempted here only because it is impossible to ignore entirely the only industry figures available on the subject, especially when those figures are government-compiled.

In analyzing the figures in the study (as given in Table 9) one must keep in mind that the various data on which the figures are based are far from comparable. First, the methods of bookkeeping then in use by the several companies differed radically. And, since each company's operating statistics were accepted by the Bureau with few revisions, variations in the basic data were automatically reflected in the report. Secondly, since three of the six companies manufactured nearly complete lines of machinery, their operating statistics were bound to be not wholly comparable with the statistics of the other three companies which, by the time of the report, were specializing in the production of at most one or two machines. Therefore, if the report is of any use at all, it is useful only within very wide margins. For instance, it is immediately apparent that the Kitson Machine Shop enjoyed first place in nearly every category of analysis and that the Lowell Machine Shop was equally often in last place; consequently the evidence would seem to bear out the general conclusion that Kitson was a more profitable company than Lowell and that Lowell, at least during the early part of the century, was being poorly, or at any rate unsatisfactorily, managed. For the other four shops, however, the figures are sufficiently similar to make any distinction among them uncertain. Perhaps the most that can be said is that the Howard & Bullough American Machine Company's record seems to have been somewhat better than Whitin's.

The place where the Whitin Machine Works seemed to have a poor record was in its cost of labor as a proportion of total costs. In that one respect, its cost ratio was higher than the cost ratio of any competitor. Yet it is wholly possible that Whitin's high labor ratio was merely the result of especially careful workmanship and that because of the quality of its products the Whitin company was able to protect its profit margins by getting higher prices for its machinery (as it is known often to have done). In fact, had such not been the case, the company would not have been able to keep its profit-to-sales ratio on a par with its competitors'.

The only clear result of the Bureau's survey, so far as the Whitin Machine Works is concerned, is the lack of any evidence that the company was a more efficient producer than its competitors. There does seem to be evidence, however, to bear out the theory, already suggested in the company's correspondence, that although the Whitin firm did have high unit costs, its products were of commensurately high value and were therefore able to command a price and a market.

Since the cost of machinery comprises a small fraction of the total

TABLE 9

A Comparison of the Operating Efficiency of Six Major American Producers of Cotton-textile Machinery, 1906–1914

Plant No.	Probable Identity of Plant[a]	Profit as Percentage of Sales			Labor Cost as Percentage of Total Costs		
		1909	1913[b]	Average 1906–14	1909	1913	Average 1906–14
1	Pettee shop	29.09	.37	22.33	35.32	38.85	37.10
2	Biddeford shop	30.61	7.17	21.84	40.37	44.62	42.51
3	Lowell shop	13.30	17.42	5.35	48.53	53.66	44.17
4	Kitson shop	39.07	34.68	35.16	26.47	37.35	27.15
5	H & B American Machine Company	29.37	19.13	26.11	39.40	33.89	37.97
6	Whitin Machine Works	30.14	6.71	22.28	45.38	50.90	47.52

[a] By the time of the study the first four shops identified had been merged and had become divisions of the Saco-Lowell Shops.
[b] The year 1909 was chosen as being representative of boom conditions; 1913 was chosen as a representative depression year.

Source: *The Cotton Spinning Machinery Industry: Report on the Cost of Production of Cotton-Spinning Machinery in the United States,* U. S. Dept. of Commerce, Bureau of Foreign and Domestic Commerce, Misc. series, no. 37 (Washington, 1916), p. 11.

cost of producing cotton goods, the unit price of textile machines is an important item to the mill owner only when funds for capital investment are scarce, as they were in the early years of the South's industrial development, or when confidence in the future is shaken, as it was in the textile industry during the 1920's and 1930's. Under either of these circumstances unit prices may become the determining factor in the sale of textile machinery. But during other periods, a mill owner is more likely to consider factors that help to keep maintenance costs at a minimum, such as the durability of machinery and the ease of its repair. Initial price then becomes secondary. Quality is paramount — quality in a sense of the durability rather than the precision of the product in operation.

Knowing the needs of the textile industry, Whitin laid stress on the endurance of his company's products. At the same time, he underwrote his products with good service in an effort to keep Whitin machinery always in useful condition no matter how old. The accent he put on product performance enabled Whitin to secure as customers the more stable units in the cotton textile industry — those companies which looked toward long-term profits rather than short-term gains. Such customers were sufficiently willing to pay a premium for Whitin machinery to make it possible for Marston to price his products on what approached a cost-plus basis. Although competition, coupled with natural inclination, made Marston a cost-conscious producer, it did not necessarily force him to become the most efficient producer in the industry. It merely established the upper reaches beyond which he could not push the premium that he asked for his machines. Others were better salesmen than he; others were more willing to promote radically new designs; and still others were more lenient with their terms of sale. But in product performance and in quality of service no other company appears to have outdone, and probably few could equal, the Whitin Machine Works during the years when it was operated under George Marston Whitin's management.

In summary then, Marston Whitin was an industrial capitalist of the very essence. As such his opposite number in the industry was the venturesome, imaginative, financial capitalist, Robert F. Herrick, of the Lowell Machine Shop. In the business man's meaning of the word, Herrick was not even a business man. But his financial mind gave him a special knack for business that was not to be found among industrialists of Whitin's type. The two men exemplified divergent methods in business administration. The one knew nothing of the technical aspect of the textile machinery business. His control was remote, his emphasis was financial, his weakness was his unfamiliarity with detail, his strength was his breadth of view. The other knew the business from long personal experience. His control was immediate, his emphasis was production, his strength was his command of facts, his weakness was his limited imagination. With all the deftness of a financial capitalist, Herrick had reached out to exercise control over the old Lowell Machine Shop without personally exerting the command of ownership. Then, having built a weak company into a strong one, he had arranged a merger that was to produce a new unit in the industry, the Saco-Lowell Shops, larger than all others, not by virtue of strength through growth but by reason of amalgamation. The Whitin Machine Works, meanwhile, after a long, steady, single-purposed climb, had become, by the turn of the century, the largest textile machinery company in America, only to see its old opponent, the Lowell Machine Shop, suddenly forge ahead as part of this new merger. To the people of Whitinsville, in whom pride in company was so pronounced, the merger of the Saco-Lowell Shops could have given nothing but umbrage. To them the fable of the tortoise and the hare must have seemed a travesty on reality.

PART III

THE PERIOD OF E. KENT SWIFT

CHAPTER XV

THE WAR PERIOD AND ITS AFTERMATH,
1915–1922

E. KENT SMITH came of age as a business man in a dangerously prosperous era. Between the completion of his college education in 1900 and the celebration of his forty-second birthday in 1920, American firms encountered almost no obstacles in their growth. Prosperity bred a whole generation that knew nothing of managing its affairs in a contracting economy. When the 1929 crash occurred, there were few business men less than fifty years of age who had ever experienced a protracted depression. Any executive who had sufficient business ability to bring his company through the credit contractions of 1907–08, 1913–14, and 1921–22 found that during the rest of his career he had little difficulty in keeping his organization strong, healthy, profitable, and expanding.

What lay ahead was therefore a new experience for most Americans. It was a particularly critical experience for men in the textile machinery industry inasmuch as the hard times that followed began so early and lasted so long. We have come to think of the great post-World War I depression as beginning in 1929; for American textile machinery it started in 1923. Consequently the latter half of Swift's business career was to be spent managing a company in a chronically depressed industry. What seems remarkable in view of the prosperous environment in which Swift had grown up is that he met later reverses so well. Over at Saco-Lowell, young Robert F. Herrick, Jr., succeeding his financier father, became so enchanted by what had appeared to him to be a series of ever-recurring booms that he embarked on a tremendous plant-expansion program just before the long depression began and thereby steered his company breathtakingly close to business disaster. Had Swift been equally susceptible to the contagion of prosperity, he might have been tempted to follow Herrick's bold and seemingly progressive lead. As a disciple of Marston Whitin's philosophy of conservatism, however, he looked with natural skepticism on Herrick's optimistic schemes. In so doing he saved his company from overextending itself at a crucial point in its history.

There is no reason to suppose that Swift perceived with clairvoyance the early approach of a protracted depression. Even now, making use of whatever advantage hindsight may bring, one has difficulty in singling out any adumbration of what lay ahead. The cotton textile industry, and with it its servitors, the textile-machinery builders, had rushed forward pell-mell, ever expanding, from 1899 onward. During the first decade of the new century the total number of mills in the country had increased by no fewer than two hundred and thirty-five — as against only sixty-eight in the decade preceding. Since outfitting new mills was the very essence of the textile-machinery business, activity in those early years of the century had been unprecedentedly high.

Only two brief depressions — in 1907–08 and 1913–14 — marred an otherwise unblemished record. The first was sharp but brief. The second was more protracted and might possibly have developed serious proportions but for events in Europe.* Meanwhile one boom followed another in quick succession, the first in 1899–1901, the second in 1906–07, the third in 1909–10, the fourth in 1916–17, and finally a fifth in 1920–21, five of the biggest booms in the textile machinery industry's history. Table 10 gives comparative statistics for three of the peak periods as they affected the Whitin Machine Works. For Whitin it would be difficult to single out which of the peaks was highest, and for the industry as a whole it is equally difficult. There is some evidence, insubstantial to be sure, that the two years 1909 and 1910 were the busiest in the textile machinery industry's history. If so, it seems possible that the cotton textile industry had entered upon a long, gradual, but almost imperceptible decline even earlier than has been generally believed. It is possible

* Whitinsville inhabitants remember the 1913–14 depression as a period of general gloom around the Whitin Machine Works. For the first time in a generation, sons of company employees could not count on having a place made for them in the company when they came of working age.

that the prolonged depression which began in that industry in 1923 might have begun in 1913–14 instead, had not World War I intervened.

Bearing that possibility in mind, one should perhaps look upon the prosperity of the years 1915–22, the years covered by this chapter, as being the abnormal and hectically prosperous years of a war-disrupted economy rather than as the brilliant culmination of the industry's youthful growth and vigor.

TABLE 10

SOME COMPARATIVE FIGURES FOR THE WHITIN MACHINE WORKS IN THREE BOOM PERIODS, 1909–1910, 1916–1917, AND 1920–1921

Years	Spinning Frames Sold (in terms of spindles)	Cards Sold	Peak Number of Employees	Average Number of Hours Worked per Week	Peak Number of Man Hours Worked in Any One Week
1909–10	1,021,700	2,510	2,944	57	171,000
1916–17	917,002	2,700	2,958	55	209,000
1920–21	858,120	2,058	3,234	50	168,000

Source: Sales ledgers, payroll records, and letter books.

I. SWIFT IN COMMAND

Throughout the war and the long depression that followed in the 1920's, Swift served the company as its gyroscopic compass and stabilizer. To him is due much of the credit for navigating the Whitin Machine Works through the turbulent seas in which so many of its competitors foundered. When most other companies in the industry were at best being squeezed through reorganization and at worst being completely liquidated, the Whitin Machine Works showed profits, paid dividends, and kept its working force intact.

To achieve this remarkable performance Swift had to possess a will of iron. Yet he would doubtless have failed at his task had his metallic coldness in business affairs not been countered by the warmth of his genial personality. Because of his deep interest in human beings he took pleasure and pride in carrying to completion the Whitins' dream of a workers' village, a village with a close-knit community of interest and a social stability such as had once been known in the feudal manors of medieval times. Because of his personal magnetism he acquired a host of friends among mill men and so became, as had his predecessors, the company's leading sales-man. Because of his irrepressible and unflagging optimism even in the days when business conditions seemed remediless, he engendered in his associates a feeling that in the end all would be well.

Upon his entrance into leadership of the organization, Swift brought with him many personal characteristics not found in Marston Whitin and the other members of the Whitin family. For instance, Swift was of more than average height, and as a young man was an active athlete and a local tennis champion. (He still is an adept and enthusiastic golfer.) Being an inveterate smoker, he was seldom without a cigar.* In the office he showed a genial manner and the corners of his mouth, instead of turning down, lifted in a spontaneous smile. Being a friendly person, he entered thoroughly into enjoyment of the hospitality extended to him on his annual trips to the South.

Yet, much as his personality and appearance differed from his father-in-law's, E. Kent Swift was much like Marston Whitin in his management of the business. Indeed nearly every feature of Swift's method of administration may be traced directly to the influence of his predecessor in office, a fact that seems less surprising when one remembers that his education for business was gained during nearly fifteen years under Whitin's personal tutelage. Like Marston Whitin, Swift had no formal training in mechanical engineering. Still his searching mind and retentive memory enabled him to acquire a remarkably comprehensive if not a commanding knowledge of the machinery his company made and sold. In highly technical matters he relied on his staff of experts, but his familiarity with the needs of mill men and the performance of Whitin machinery was sufficient to make him a competent judge of the advice his experts gave him.

---

* During World War II the office personnel bought every box of JA cigars they could find, turning them over to the company's purchasing department so that "the boss" could be kept supplied with his favorite brand.

E. Kent Swift, Treasurer, 1920–1947, Chairman of the Board, 1946–

George Marston Whitin Gymnasium

No aspect of the business escaped Swift's personal attention — the experimental room, the patent office, the shop's working conditions, the repair of village streets, the level of the tariff, or the latest Supreme Court decision. But the core of his activities was his concern with the financial condition of the company. No capital expenditure — whether for new machine tools or for company trucks — was made without his approval. Reports on production costs, on bank balances, on foreign credits, and on sales contracts received his careful scrutiny. But one would err in concluding that Swift ran the Whitin Machine Works through the remote control of daily or weekly reports. Only a small portion of what came in and went out of his office took the form of paper and ink; personal interviews obviated impersonal reports.

The committee system of management was something he never adopted. Swift met his junior executives individually — not with any prearranged schedule but usually as they passed the open door of his office. At no time did he succumb to the temptation, to which every busy executive is subject, of protecting himself from intruders by throwing across the entrance to his office a moat-like secretary's reception room. Appointments were never necessary. Conversations once started were often interrupted to settle minor office or shop difficulties as they arose. Disorganizing as such a policy was, it gave to Swift's administration an air of informality that, in a small New England community where democratic ideals were cherished, was an important ingredient in his success.

In like manner Swift carried his informal friendliness into the shop. On his frequent tours through the various component buildings he never failed to nod to or pass the time of day with the workmen he encountered, all of whom knew him by sight, though it was impossible for him to know all of them. Like his office procedure, his trips through the plant were conducted informally and at irregular intervals. Perhaps, on returning from lunch, he would leave his car at the foundry entrance and would make his way to the front office on foot through the intervening shops. As he passed along between rows of machinery he would stop to ask about the performance of a new machine tool or to inspect a new type of jig. He alone, of all the shop's production men, had a general view of the plant's entire operations. No one else in the company could conduct a visitor on such a comprehensive tour of the shop as he. Unlike Marston Whitin, Swift was not a driver. It has been said that, whenever Marston walked through the shop, production increased by 10 per cent. Not so with Swift. He believed that people worked best when they enjoyed what they did. No stenographer was ever embarrassed to be found gossiping with a friend; no worker ever feared for his job for having been seen away from his machine.

Yet the outstretched hand of genial amity had a grip of bone and sinew. Like all his forerunners, Swift held unchallenged sway over both the shop and the village. His word was law — not because he was feared by the villagers, but rather because no one ever thought to question his authority. Under him directors' meetings were only slightly less perfunctory than under his father-in-law, for although others may have held sufficient proxies to vote his measures down, they never undertook to do so. The company functioned as a team — about that there seems no doubt — but the undisputed team captain was always E. Kent Swift.*

---

* Swift's wide connections in New England and the South brought him many invitations to serve on boards of directors. Following is a list of the important directorships and executive positions held by Swift at one time or another. The list may not be complete, for no accurate record of Swift's diversified business interests has ever been kept. It reads like a list of directorships held by the president of a prominent bank. It includes 39 directorships, 6 presidencies, and 8 miscellaneous other titles. Positions marked by an asterisk are those still held by Swift in 1949 after his semi-retirement.

American Textile Machinery Corporation, Boston, Massachusetts (director); Arlington Mills, Lawrence, Massachusetts (director); Ashworth Brothers, Inc., Fall River, Massachusetts (director*); Associated Industries of Massachusetts, Boston (director); Bigelow-Sanford Carpet Company, New York City (director*); Boston Manufacturers Mutual Fire Insurance Company, Boston (director*); Brogon Mills, Anderson, South Carolina (director); Calhoun Mills, Calhoun Falls, South Carolina (director); Crown Manufacturing Company, Pawtucket, Rhode Island (president and director); D. O. Pease Manufacturing Company, Palmer, Massachusetts (director); Dunean Mills, Greenville, South Carolina (director); Fayscott Corporation, Dexter, Maine (director* and chairman of the board*); Home Bleach & Dye Works, Pawtucket (president and director); Home Market Club, Boston (director and member of the executive committee); Kilburn Mill, New Bedford, Massachusetts (director); Lawton Mills Corporation, Plainfield, Connecticut (director); Linwood Street Railway, Whitinsville, Massachusetts (director); Loray Mills, Gastonia, North Carolina (director); Manomet Mills, New Bedford (director); Massachusetts Mutual Life Insurance Company, Springfield, Massachusetts (director*); Mutual Boiler Insurance Company, Boston (director*); Nashawena Mills, New Bedford (director); National Association of

2. WORLD WAR I

Among his other traits, Swift had a habit of looking at business from a long-range point of view. Years of selling capital goods had apparently accustomed him to thinking in terms of general movements in price levels and prosperity. As a result his customers often sought his opinion on current business conditions before deciding to place an order for machinery.

In February, 1917, less than three months before America's declaration of hostilities against the Central Powers, one such customer wrote Swift asking what he thought of the outlook for the year ahead. In his reply Swift dealt with several of the variables likely to affect the future of the cotton industry, but he made no mention of the chance that America might be drawn into the European struggle.[1]

To a generation that had known almost nothing of war, the possibility of a world-wide conflict was difficult to conceive. Even during the Spanish-American War, Marston Whitin's only recorded worry concerning the effect of hostilities on his business was the fear that Stuart Cramer, a naval reservist, might be called to active duty. In a fray that threatened to involve all the world's most powerful nations, few business men had any idea what to expect.

As it happened, the experience of the Whitin Machine Works in World War I proved to be not unlike its experience in the Civil War. With the nation's armed forces ordering quantities of wearing apparel, bedding, tents, bandages, and the many other military items

---

Cotton Manufacturers, Boston (director); National Association of Textile Machinery Manufacturers, Boston (president and director); New England Council, Boston (director); Nonquitt Mills, New Bedford (director); Nyanza Mills, Woonsocket, Rhode Island (director); Paul Whitin Manufacturing Company, Northbridge, Massachusetts (director,* president, and chairman of the board*); Pepperell Manufacturing Company, Boston (director*); Respro Incorporated, Cranston, Rhode Island (director*) Scott Lumber Company, Burney, California (president* and director*); Seaboard Foundry, Providence, Rhode Island (director* and chairman of the board*); Second National Bank, Boston (director*); Sharp Manufacturing Company, New Bedford (director); Trion Manufacturing Company, Trion, Georgia (director); United Lace & Braid Manufacturing Company, Providence (director); Whitinsville National Bank, Whitinsville (director*); Whitinsville Savings Bank, Whitinsville (vice-president* and trustee*); Whitin Machine Works, Whitinsville (director,* treasurer, president, and chairman of the board*); Worcester Bank & Trust Company, Worcester (director).

made of cotton, textile mills began looking to their machinery suppliers to stock them with repair parts and to keep them equipped with whatever new machinery they required for a changeover to production for war. Unlike the Civil War, however, the war of 1917–18 did not cut off mills from their supply of raw cotton. But for other reasons it caused a depression in the textile machinery trade just as the Civil War had done. To prevent mills from using scarce materials for expanding their plants during the war, the government placed stringent restrictions on all mill building.

Yet despite those restrictions, business in Whitinsville might have boomed had there not been a shortage of men and materials. By government direction, the country's man power and raw materials resources were allowed to flow where the need was greatest. War plants were given priorities on scarce materials and were permitted to assemble the labor forces they needed through the liberal provisions of their cost-plus contracts and through the high wages they could afford to pay their men. The textile machinery business, being an important but not an essential cog in the wheel of war, experienced repeated difficulties in getting raw materials and in general found it impossible to bid against war plants for the services of workers. Thus, while many metal-working firms in the country were experiencing a war-inflated prosperity, the Whitin Machine Works found that the war brought it a period of gradual recession.

When war became imminent the first thought among manufacturers was the protection of their plants from saboteurs. In Whitinsville a great stir occurred when word got round that some of the Turks in the community were sheltering a German underground agent.[2] Rather than risk an explosion or fire, Swift called the Pinkerton agency in Providence and requested the services of a private detective. Ironically enough, since it was important that the detective be able to speak Turkish, an Armenian was sent to investigate the matter. After conducting a series of interviews with one Hassen Mustapha and his sworn enemy, Tefic Saduch, the detective concluded, to everyone's embarrassment, that the origin of the rumor lay merely in the false criminations of two feuding Turks who had been calling each other German sympathizers.

Following the declaration of hostilities, an executive of the company dictated a letter to an acquaintance in Denver in which he described the impact of the war on Whitinsville — rather implying that the West was somehow not involved:[3]

We are having quite stirring times here in the East, at present. Quite a bit of interest in garden planting, and, of course, in preparedness in every form. Practically every house in our village flies an American flag, and every job in the shop has had its flag-raising.

At the time our participation in the war began, the company was booked with orders for nine months ahead. As new orders came pouring in from mill owners urgently in need of new machinery to expedite the war contracts they had just signed, Swift faced the dilemma of making proper allocations of the company's output of machines. He felt it his patriotic duty to send machinery where it was most needed, and he hesitated to be guided by those customers who were most vociferous in their demands. Therefore, in June, 1917, he sent out what was to be the first of a series of form letters, requesting customers to report the amount and type of war work they had contracted for.[4] Fortunately Swift found mill men very coöperative. By using the information he obtained from them, he was able to temporize with an informal priority system of his own until the War Industries Board was able to put into effect its standard priority ratings.

The information that Swift received from his customers served in turn as a basis for his own claim to raw materials priorities, especially to priorities on pig iron and coal, both of which were made extremely scarce by the sudden war demand. In fact, during January and February, 1918, the shop was closed for five successive Mondays as part of the general campaign to conserve fuel.[5] In May, 1918, Swift reported to the Priorities Committee of the War Industries Board that, in addition to iron and coal, his company was in urgent need of tin plate, steel (band, roller, spindle, cold-rolled, and cold-drawn), and lumber (yellow poplar and North Carolina pine). Believing the manufacture of textile machinery to be important to the war effort, the Priorities Committee granted Whitin generous ratings, enabling the company to go through the rest of the war without any further serious delays resulting from materials shortages.[6]

Some delays, though relatively minor ones, did occur, however, as a result of the critical railroad situation. Almost from the beginning of the war the railroads were unable to cope with the sudden demand placed on them. At the end of three months the government was commandeering so many freight cars for its own use that rail lines could not send the Whitin company the cars it needed to make prompt deliveries.[7] In addition, a curtailment of rail operations cut off from Whitinsville its key southbound mail train and delayed by more than twelve hours the bulk of the company's daily output of 500-odd pieces of mail.[8] A similar efficiency measure inaugurated by the government after 26 December 1917, when it took over the railroads, was the abolition of all regional offices operated by the various railroad lines. As in the case of its canceled mail service, the company lodged a vigorous, but futile, protest, for much of the success it had had in getting scarce materials was the result of experienced expediting work done by friendly railroad agents.[9]

Even when train service was not reduced by a shortage of rolling stock or a change in scheduled runs, it was likely to be disrupted by unpredictable rail embargoes. During the first four months of 1918 the Whitin shop was almost completely cut off from its Southern customers by a rigid ban on north-south shipments.[10] From time to time the ban was lifted, but while it was on, finished machinery piled up in the shop and plagued the management for storage space. At one time the company toyed with the idea of shipping machinery to the South by water as in the days before 1880, but the cost of boxing for coastwise shipment (by then increased to 10 per cent of list value), together with the constant hope that the embargo would soon be lifted, seems to have prevented anything from coming of the idea.[11]

As the war continued, total shop productivity dropped steadily. The cause of the decline was not, however, so much the shortage of materials or the difficulties of rail shipments as it was the acute scarcity of labor. Fortunately for the company in the early months of the war few of its employees left to take jobs in other industries or to join the armed forces. Between April and July of 1917 only "30 or 40 men" enlisted in the National Guard.[12] But meanwhile the draft drawing of 5 June 1917 was making many of its employees subject to call. In the following April the company really began to feel the effects of the draft. Throughout the remaining seven months of the war, men left the shop at the rate of over a hundred a month. Total employment fell 20 per cent despite Swift's effort to place women in the jobs that men had left.

A few women had worked in the plant before, although Marston Whitin had always felt that a machine shop was no place for the weaker sex. As early as 1900 the company had hired four or five girls to do the delicate needle-setting work in the new comber department, and by 1910 there were twenty-five women in that department. But with a few such minor exceptions the firm had carefully avoided the personnel problems involved in employing female help. If a Whitinsville woman wished to work, she usually applied for a job in one of the near-by cotton mills owned by the other branches of the Whitin family. Consequently the company was not equipped to handle a large number of women trainees (the limiting factor being rest rooms). By the end of World War I, the company had hired not more than fifty women to replace the seven or eight hundred men who had left its employ.*

As a result of the labor shortage, 1918 was a year of semi-depression for the Whitin company. At the beginning of the war the shop had been operating at a level of about 160,000 man hours per week; by the war's end the level was down to about 110,000 man hours (Appendix 23). Dividends, too, reflected the adverse circumstances brought on by the war. Whereas many of the metal-working companies that had converted to war work earned and paid unprecedented sums to their stockholders during the war, the Whitin Machine Works cut its annual dividend payments to $300,000 from a 1916 high of $600,000.

Still, the company's private wartime recession had its own compensations. The War Industries Board's restrictions on mill building during the war caused a temporary stunting of the country's normal growth in mill capacity. Thus, once the war had ended and the

---

* Many of its women employees stayed with the company throughout the postwar boom. However, as they began to drop out, they were not replaced, so that by 1923 few of them remained.

building restrictions had been rescinded, the textile machinery industry found itself enjoying a ready-made demand for its products.

The war also had the beneficial result of inducing the company to give further attention to the new management techniques just then becoming popular. In fact, the cautious movement in the direction of scientific management, which the company had started several years earlier, was stimulated by the abnormal conditions of World War I.

3. SCIENTIFIC MANAGEMENT

The scientific approach to management evolved so gradually that one finds difficulty in determining when it began. The most convenient date, and the one most often referred to, is the 1903 publication of an article on "Shop Management" by Frederick W. Taylor in the *Transactions of the American Society of Mechanical Engineers,* although Taylor himself had been an advocate of rationalized production methods since the 1880's.[13] In respect to the influence of scientific management on American business administration, however, the year 1910 is probably a more realistic starting date. In November of that year the able Jewish lawyer, Louis D. Brandeis, later to be a Supreme Court Justice, announced to the Interstate Commerce Commission with his usual dramatic and convincing eloquence that the railroads of the country, far from needing the boost in rates which they were demanding, should be forced to cut their rates and to increase their efficiency by adopting the scientific methods that the Santa Fe Railroad had just instituted with so much success. His charge was widely reported in the newspapers and was directly responsible for the extensive interest in the subject expressed by business men during the following year and for several years thereafter.

Taylor had hoped to develop his ideas into a broad philosophical discipline that would include every aspect of management, but the many followers who flocked to his standard after 1911 were content to concentrate on narrower aspects of the subject, especially on those aspects concerned with job analysis where the most dramatic and remunerative results could be obtained. Enterprising individuals — sometimes with ability, sometimes without — were soon organizing firms and were hiring out their services to manufacturing concerns at high fees. One such firm was a New York partnership named Suffern & Son.

E. Kent Swift chanced to encounter the younger Suffern on a return voyage from Europe. Becoming interested in the work the Sufferns were doing, Swift proposed to his father-in-law that the Whitin Machine Works give "efficiency engineering" a trial. Marston Whitin was not easily convinced and perhaps would not have assented to the proposal had not the Drapers initiated a similar project at about the same time.[14] Therefore, in the spring of 1912, Whitin agreed to give efficiency engineering a test by letting the Suffern firm start work in one department of the shop on a trial basis. Although no assurances were given, it was generally assumed that if the Sufferns were successful they would be retained for further work in other departments. Before hiring the Sufferns, however, Marston Whitin insisted that they agree not to accept as a client on any subsequent occasion any competing textile-machinery firm that might benefit by learning the techniques employed at Whitinsville.[15]

The department selected was the "flyer job," where roving flyers were made for use on Providence roving machinery. Since the department was a fairly new one and since its work was fairly standardized, it was chosen as the most logical place to commence installing the new efficiency system. Beginning in the summer of 1912, three Suffern men, Messrs. Marble, Armstrong, and Knoeppel, spent a portion of several months in the Whitinsville plant making time and motion studies, setting up piece rates, and improvising new manufacturing procedures.

From the first, Marston Whitin was impatient with the idea that men having no knowledge of the manufacture of textile machinery could presume to instruct the company in production methods. He was equally irritated by the fees that the Sufferns charged (approximately $450 per man per month). A letter written by Swift at Whitin's behest conveys something of this irritation: "Mr. Marble is doing what we have done on other jobs here in the shop with our own men . . . analyzing mechanical features of the work done on flyers and jigging up in an intelligent way . . . [so that] we feel that we are being charged entirely out of proportion for the work that is being done."[16] A few months later, and in somewhat the same tone, Swift again complained to the New York office of the Suffern firm: "[Our] product has not shown improvement over our regular output, and the men have been holding back on account of efficiency work being in progress."[17] Consequently when the Sufferns had completed their work in the flyer department (December, 1912), their further services were not requested.[18]

Later on, when prospective Suffern clients wrote to the Whitin Machine Works for information as to the quality of work done by the Suffern firm, Swift addressed himself to Ernest F. Suffern in part as follows:[19]

Our experience with efficiency work . . . could not be termed conclusive at all as regards its ultimate success. What experience we have had has been more or less satisfactory, but we are testing the thing out now on a practical basis, and we do not feel in a position to generally endorse the proposition to every one, although the letters we have written are what you would wish to have come from us. The point I am trying to bring out is we do not want you to place us as one of the monuments in this field of work, as we do not feel that we hold such a position, and we do not wish to go on record so frequently in this respect.

Yet, although Suffern's work was looked upon as no more than a qualified success, it was nonetheless retained by the Whitin Machine Works and was extended to other departments in the shop by employees in the Whitin organization who had been trained to make time studies by Suffern's own men. In fact, for a time in 1914, C. E. Knoeppel, by then the head of a consulting firm of his own, was brought back to Whitinsville to carry on the work started by the Suffern firm. Under Knoeppel a completely new shop organization was worked out and plans were laid to convert the shop's departmental setup from a product organization (in which all the operations on a particular product were performed in one area) to a functional organization (in which each department specialized in the performance of a particular operation). Because of ill health, Knoeppel did not remain to complete his job, but under Stuart F. Brown, one of the company's employees, a production department was organized to carry on the work which Knoeppel had laid out.

Meanwhile, the war had brought to the front office a revolutionary change in its accounting procedures. As has already been related, the Whitin Machine Works for years kept only single-entry accounts. Its balance sheets were skeletal and far from realistic, while its income statements were hardly worthy of the name. Yet in a sense the company had never had need for better records-keeping. Since no one outside the Whitin and Taft families was financially interested in the company, it mattered little what the statement of assets or earnings was from year to year. Not since 1909 had there been a transfer of stock or a change in the number of stockholders.

In past years the government had brought some slight pressure to bear against the company to reform its accounting methods, but never intensively enough to produce results. A statute passed in 1897 required all Massachusetts corporations to have their books audited annually,[20] but the Whitin Machine Works had simply hired as auditor the town clerk, a man who happened also to be company paymaster.* Beginning in 1913 the federal income-tax law had specified that all companies follow a prescribed form in reporting their profits, but the form had been loosely drawn and so it had been easy enough for the company to meet all the requirements with its existing method of records-keeping.[21] Moreover, the corporate income tax at that time amounted to only 1 per cent on profits (for Whitin the tax was thus less than $10,000 a year) and hence was not large enough to make it worth the company's while to install a completely new accounting system in order to be able to be certain of figuring its tax accurately.

The wartime excess profits tax of 3 October 1917, however, proved to be a completely different matter. It has been said that the business of public accountancy gained its first firm footing in this country as a result of the enactment of that tax. Superimposed on the existing tax structure, the excess profits act levied a graduated tax on all profits exceeding 9 per cent of average net worth in the three prewar years (1911, 1912, and 1913).[22] The Whitin stockholders suddenly realized that they were faced with a tax liability of something like $200,000 for operations during the year 1917. (Taxes for the five

---

* To prevent companies from hiring their own employees as auditors, the statute was later amended to read, "but no bookkeeper, treasurer or other officer of the corporation shall be appointed as . . . auditors."

years 1919–1923 averaged 17½ per cent of net profits.) Under such circumstances errors in computing income could easily pile up large tax liabilities. More important still, the provisions of the tax worked to the disadvantage of any firm like Whitin that had consistently undervalued its assets, for undervaluations meant low net worth, and low net worth meant low exemption from the excess profits tax.

Consequently, on advice of counsel, the company hired a Boston firm of public accountants, Scovell, Wellington & Company, to determine a more nearly accurate value of its tangible assets and at the same time to inaugurate a double-entry system of accounts. To work out a solution to Whitin's problems, Scovell, Wellington sent to Whitinsville a member of its staff named Edward S. Alden. Alden possessed a shrewd and nimble mind for figures and a pertinacity that carried him through a difficult job in the short space of a few months. By March, 1918, he had (1) reconstructed the company's asset accounts, (2) arrived at balance sheets and income statements for the years 1909–17, and (3) reorganized the company's accounting system on a double-entry basis.

Of the three accomplishments the reconstruction of the company's asset accounts was by far the most arduous.[23] As a beginning point, Alden picked the year 1896 (21 years earlier) on the theory that any machinery bought before that date should already have been written off the books by 1917. In assigning values to the land, water rights, and buildings owned by the company at that early date, however, he encountered serious difficulties, for few records of original costs existed. To resolve this particular problem he took the value that had been placed on the company's property in 1896 by the local tax assessors ($525,000) and arbitrarily divided it among the three types of fixed assets in question. Admitting that the figure was "ultra-conservative" — perhaps no more than half the liquidating value — he stated that he could determine no other reliable basis on which to proceed. By going through all the cashbooks page by page he was then able to add each year the amount spent on capital improvements and to deduct a proper depreciation figure from the accumulated total. In so doing he made no attempt to assign any values to the company's large collection of patterns, drawings, foundry flasks, and small tools, all of which were essential to

the company's operation and had been expensive to acquire but none
of which would have brought much at a forced sale. Nor did he
attempt to revise the company's method of taking inventory by
weight instead of by count. He did try, however, though not always
with success, to establish the original cost and current market value
of the cotton-mill stocks held by the company.

To be certain that Alden had arrived at defensible figures, the
company engaged the Associated Factory Mutual Fire Insurance
Companies (with which it carried its fire insurance) to make a
separate appraisal of its plant and equipment. To no one's surprise
the fire insurance values turned out to be considerably higher than
Alden's computed values. Separate appraisals of the company's elec-
tric-railway and water-supply system were also made by a qualified
outsider, Charles T. Main, a Boston engineering consultant, who
likewise arrived at figures considerably higher than Alden's. To
avoid any criticism for having inflated its asset values, the company
decided to adhere to Alden's lower figures. Consequently on 1 January 1917 it entered on its books a value of $2,761,831.17 for land,
plant, and equipment, where the day before the reading had been
$1,008,769.85 as computed by Marston Whitin's outdated method
of valuation.*

Swift was so pleased with the work which Alden had done that
he asked Scovell, Wellington to release their Whitinsville representative so that he might stay on as an employee of the Whitin Machine
Works. Contrary to what might have been expected, Scovell, Wellington took kindly to the suggestion perhaps because they were not
averse to having one of their men working for a company that promised to become a good client.

Unfortunately for the company, Alden did not remain merely an
accountant for very long. In the ensuing years the company could
have used someone well trained and alert to the rapid strides then
being made in cost accounting and control techniques. But at just
that time the financial aspects of the business became crucial (as
will be related in the following chapter), and Alden's attention was
absorbed in the handling of Whitin's finances somewhat to the

---

* Other asset revisions caused the final asset figure to be adjusted upward by a
total of $2,439,169.81.

detriment of the company's accounting. Having made a long stride forward, Whitin again fell behind in its accounting techniques, until it once more brought itself up to date in 1938. However, one notable advantage accrued from the company's static accounting practice. Year after year (from 1918 through 1937) Whitin's income statements and balance sheets as drawn up by Scovell, Wellington & Company were exactly alike. There is consequently a comparability among them that is rare among annual statements of American companies in that period when auditing firms were forever recommending changes in methods of valuation and hence were constantly destroying the comparability of their data.

4. FOREIGN SALES

For a short time following World War I there was a temporary lull in the textile-machinery business, which resulted partly from a drop in the cotton-commodities market. Mill owners, uncertain of what readjustment the peace would bring, refrained from binding themselves with any future commitments in the form of orders for machinery. Before three months had passed, however, business was humming again. The War Industries Board was quick to remove its restrictions on mill building, and mill owners soon found the demand for textile goods sufficient to warrant their making large additions to and improvements on their productive facilities.

Yet sizable as was the pent-up demand for textile machinery in America, it was as nothing compared with the swollen demand registered by the rest of the world. Since 1914 the mills of the world had been shut off from their principal suppliers of cotton-mill equipment, the machine shops in England. Not only had mills been prevented from expanding their capacity during the war years, but in some cases they had even been forced to cease operations because of lack of repair parts.

It is literally true that without England the world cotton industry could not have developed as it had done. The only area on the globe not dependent on that country for at least a part of its textile machinery was the United States. Mills in Mexico and South America, in France and Italy, in Russia and Egypt, in India, China, and Japan, looked to the machine-builders of Great Britain for their new equipment and for repairs on their old. The largest of the British firms, Platt Brothers, of Oldham (near Manchester), had a productive capacity in 1914 that was probably greater than the entire American textile machinery industry combined.* In some parts of the world, Platt machinery was virtually the standard equipment for all cotton mills.

Unlike the American machinery industry, which had become so customer-conscious in its competition for the Southern market that it had grown used to granting individual mill men all manner of special concessions in matters of design, the British industry had traditionally insisted on standardized products. Their argument had always been that under no other arrangement could they keep their far-flung customers supplied with repair parts. A significant result of their policy were the low prices at which they were able to sell such standardized machinery.

After the outbreak of hostilities in 1914, British producers had become engaged in war work and had inadvertently bequeathed their machinery market to the enterprising business men of countries that had remained neutral. Among the first to seize this opportunity were three New Yorkers, George A. Gaston, W. H. Williams, and J. A. Wigmore. These men banded together in October, 1914, to form a trading company under the name of Gaston, Williams & Wigmore. With their New York company as a parent firm, they established subsidiaries in the leading cities of South America, the Mediterranean region, and the Orient. By 1916 they owned a fleet of ten steamships and were making nearly five million dollars a year in net profits.[24] In January, 1916, this firm approached the Whitin Machine Works with the proposition that it be allowed to sell Whitin machinery in the world market.

Before 1916 the Whitin company had never sold actively abroad. True, almost from its beginning the company had had a few customers in Canada and Mexico,† but in no single previous year had

---

* Hartmann & Company (or more correctly, the Sächsische Maschinenfabrik vorm. Richard Hartmann), of Dresden and Chemnitz, Germany, was equally large, but its line included many products other than textile machinery (see *Handbuch der deutschen Aktien-Gesellschaften,* 1928, vol. i, p. 471).

† In 1899 Marston Whitin had endeavored to increase his company's Mexican sales by appointing J. M. Anderson, an American resident in Mexico City, as Whitin representative. This appointment was based on a salary agreement which was entered into by the other members of the Whitin marketing group, the Kitson Machine Shop,

foreign sales accounted for as much as one per cent of the shop's output. Therefore, when Gaston, Williams & Wigmore first approached the Whitin Machine Works with their proposition, Swift was frankly skeptical of their ability to secure the market they were after. Still, the terms of their offer were so liberal and the chance of financial loss seemed so slight that Swift could see no reason for not accepting.

According to their proposal, the Gaston partners would buy Whitin machinery for export, especially to China and Japan, but also to Russia and India. They would acquire title to the machinery and would pay for it in cash, f.o.b. the Whitins station. They would then forward the machinery to their customers abroad, charging enough to cover the cost of the machinery, the charges for freight, and whatever commission they wished to collect (understood to be about 10 per cent). Swift warned the Gaston partners:[25]

In the past the American manufacturers of textile machinery have not been able to compete in foreign fields with the English builders. England has some very large and well established machinery plants — Platt Brothers alone employing 12,000 men — and, with their shipping and financial arrangements, have been able, with their low cost of manufacturing, to monopolize the world's textile business outside of this country.

But Swift conceded that, with England's shops converted to war work, there was no reason why American firms should not step in to meet the demand.

Therefore, in March, 1916, Swift appointed Gaston, Williams & Wigmore as Whitin agents in the Orient. Six months later he dispatched to Shanghai an employee of the company's experimental department, Edward G. Whittaker, with a battery of Whitin ma-

and the Woonsocket Machine & Press Company. Results had proved to be disappointing for several reasons. As Marston Whitin later explained to his son-in-law, Lawrence Keeler: "Anderson I think is able and has done all he could, but the trouble has been that whenever he got near to closing a job, the English people have been unwilling to let it go and have reduced the price below where anyone was willing to sell" (letter from George Marston Whitin to L. M. Keeler, 21 January 1905). Therefore, at the end of a trial year, Anderson had been put on a commission basis, and the Whitin Machine Works had resigned itself to getting only occasional orders from below the Rio Grande.

chines to be erected in Gaston's China offices for demonstration purposes.[26] Whittaker was just getting established in Shanghai when America declared war on Germany. With production at the Whitin plant limited by priorities and a labor shortage, there was nothing for Whittaker to do but to last out the war, meanwhile becoming acquainted with the region and establishing as many contacts as possible.*

Whittaker's wartime activities began to pay dividends, however, as soon as the war ended. In fact the orders from Chinese and Japanese mills were to prove an embarrassment to the company, coming as they did on top of more domestic orders than the firm could handle. For as long as it could, the company delayed fulfilling its Oriental commitments, knowing that the only sound policy was to satisfy its domestic customers first. However, in order to placate the Gaston partners, it did allocate a production of 5,000 spindles a month to the Far Eastern market.

In January, 1921, nearly all world markets suddenly collapsed following a disastrous fall in commodity prices. Within the space of a few weeks Whitin's attitude toward its foreign customers abruptly shifted. At home the downdraft in cotton prices brought a blast of order cancellations from the company's customers. However, because of the postwar boom in automobile manufacturing there had developed in New England a speculative interest in tire-cord mills. In those days cotton manufacturers believed that suitable tire cord could be made only from carded and combed, long-staple cotton (it is now made from shorter cotton and is simply carded). Since Whitin was the principal domestic producer of combers, the bulk of the tire-cord market fell Whitin's way. Had it not been for a colossal order from the tire-cord mill being built by Bedford's Manomet Mills,† together with its backlog of orders from the Orient, Whitin

* One such contact resulted in Whittaker's marriage to an American missionary. The executives in Whitinsville were relieved to learn that she was a woman from America, for they had been worried that their bachelor representative might succumb to the "unsettling" influences of the Far East.

† Among the several tire-cord mills completely equipped by Whitin following the war, the Manomet Mills in New Bedford were by far the largest. No other mill in the country, save only the Amoskeag Manufacturing Company, had a capacity so large. Before Whitin had completed delivery of the Manomet machinery, the depression of 1921 had revealed what a serious overcapacity the tire cord industry had developed.

would have been forced, by midsummer 1921, to close down perhaps as much as 40 per cent of its plant operations.

Others in the industry were not so fortunate. As Swift remarked in July, 1921, "Pettee [meaning the Pettee branch of the Saco-Lowell Shops] and ourselves are practically the only ones doing well in the textile field and running full. Howard & Bullough have let a lot of men go and Woonsocket and Fales & Jenks are running on short time. Mason is still shut up." [27] Even Whitin and Saco-Lowell were not without their troubles. Saco-Lowell's foreign agents, the firm of Andersen & Meyer, were having to cancel further operations because of financial embarrassment,[28] while Gaston, Williams & Wigmore were tottering on the verge of bankruptcy.

Swift had begun to suspect that all was not well in New York as early as December of the preceding year (1920). From Shanghai he had learned that the Gaston firm was having difficulty meeting its obligations. "Whitin," said Whittaker in warning from Shanghai, "is in the hands of a company respected by none and with no friends available." [29] Then, in quick succession, Gaston's Shanghai agent, a man named Boulon, quit the partnership, offered his services to Whitin as an independent agent, was threatened with suit by Gaston, Williams & Wigmore for misappropriation of funds, and himself in turn threatened to sue the Gaston firm for back pay. The *affaire Boulon* was followed by a complete shake-up in personnel in Gaston's New York office.

When the Gaston firm's annual statement appeared, showing a heavy loss for the year 1920, Swift became thoroughly alarmed. The Whitin company had over a million dollars of orders on its books for which Gaston, Williams & Wigmore were financially responsible. Employing the services of Minturn de Suzzara Verdi, a New York lawyer and Chester Lasell's son-in-law, Swift approached the Gaston partners with an offer to assume the financial liability of the textile-machinery orders they held from mills in the Far East. Swift was afraid that, if the Gaston firm went into receivership, the

---

Nevertheless the Manomet owners continued with their plans. As another New Bedford mill (Wamsutta) had done in the depression of 1861, Manomet with its million-dollar order of machinery, almost single-handed, carried Whitin through the crash of 1921. With its inauspicious beginning, Manomet's tire-cord mill was never a success. The mill was sold to the Firestone Rubber Company in 1922.

receivers might cancel all contracts that threatened to cause the Gaston firm further loss, since the Gaston company had already received and dissipated the down payments on many orders. Swift was willing to take over the orders, including liability for the down payments, because he felt that his profit margins were sufficient to cover the financial risk involved and because he was anxious to keep his shop active.

Consequently, on 8 February 1921, Swift reached an agreement with Gaston, Williams & Wigmore the terms of which he described in part as follows:[30]

We took over all of the contracts which they held for textile machinery of Whitin make. At the same time . . . we severed all connections with [them]. . . . While we took over the contracts we did not take over the obligations which Gaston had under these contracts, but all we did was to agree that if the contract . . . went through we would assume in each case the bargain money [down payment] . . . and see that the mill received due credit for it in the execution of the contract. We also listed up all the contracts and agreed that we would keep careful record of them and if the execution of each and all contracts . . . went through we would then split 50/50 with them in what profits might remain. . . . What we are doing in New York is to use our own forwarding agent independent and separate from Gaston. . . . We have taken one of Gaston's former men, Frank Whitworth. He has an office near Gaston's so that he has full access to their old records.

It is probably an indication of the shakiness of the Gaston firm that such a sweeping arrangement was possible. Exactly one week later the stockholders of the firm, made apprehensive by rumors of insolvency, appointed James G. Blaine, Jr., chairman of a Stockholders' Protective Committee. On 16 March 1921 George A. Gaston resigned as president of the firm. The following day Gaston, Williams & Wigmore went into receivership.[31]

Thanks to the happy fact that Whitin executives had foreseen the possibility of Gaston's financial difficulties, the Whitin Machine Works was unaffected by the bankruptcy. If anything, it was in a stronger position than before, since the agreement of 8 February had put it into direct contact with its customers. Originally Gaston,

Williams & Wigmore had tried to keep Whitin completely in the
dark as to where its machinery was being sent, the implication
being that the Gaston partners were anxious to prevent Whitin from
becoming familiar enough with the Far Eastern market to be able
to deal with it directly. If such was the reason for Gaston's secretive-
ness, its fears were not without grounds, for the men at Whitinsville
had always been diffident about dealing through intermediaries and

TABLE 11

Japanese and Chinese Mills to Which More Than $200,000 of Whitin
Machinery Was Shipped during 1921–1922

(Listed in order of size of total shipments)

Name[a]	Location
Dai Nippon Boshoku	Tokyo, Japan
Ashikaga Boseki	Ashikaga, Japan
Dah Sung	Nantung-chow, China
Chuka Boshoku	Nagoya, Japan
Kikui	Nagoya, Japan
Dah Kong	Shanghai, China
Hattori Shoten	Nagoya, Japan
Fuji Gas Spinning Co.	Nagoya, Japan
Naniwa	Osaka, Japan
Awa Boshoku	near Kyoto, Japan
Toyoda Spinning & Weaving Co.	Shanghai, China

[a] All firms except Dah Sung, Chuka Boshoku, and Awa Boshoku, owned by Mitsui & Co., Ltd.

Source: Machinery Sales Books and Machinery Order Indexes.

it is clear that they would have preferred to by-pass the Gaston firm
had they been able to do so.

It was impossible, however, for the Gaston firm to hide from
Whitin everything concerning its customers in the Orient, for it had
to rely on Whitin men to erect Whitin machinery. In 1920 Swift
had sent a mill engineer, Frederick R. Pratt, to China as an assistant
to Whittaker and at the same time had sent an erector, Philip J.
Reilly, to Japan. There was no concealing from those men, and
hence from Swift, the identity of the mills into which Whitin machines were being sent. From their numerous reports one gathers
that most of the company's products before 8 February 1921 were

going into Chinese mills. After that date, however, it is clear from the Whitin records that the preponderance of machinery was being sent to Japan (see Table 11). Moreover, even the equipment being shipped to China was destined principally for mills owned by the Japanese, especially by the firm of Mitsui & Company, Ltd.

At the time of the Gaston failure, Lawrence M. Keeler was in Japan where he was being introduced to Japanese mill men by Whittaker. Since Keeler, as agent of the Whitin company, had charge of foreign sales,[32] he was sizing up the possibility of Whitin's selling to the Orient directly instead of through an intermediary. Keeler had been planning to make the trip for over a year but had been forced to postpone his plans because of the serious illness of Marston Whitin, his father-in-law. By the time that Marston's death had freed him to make further arrangements for the trip, his sister-in-law, Lois Whitin, had married an army officer, William C. Crane, who was stationed in Tokyo. Consequently Keeler took with him both his wife and his sister, Mrs. Chester Lasell, combining a business trip with a family reunion.*

While the Keelers were still abroad, Swift decided to take a trip to England, ostensibly to attend the World's Cotton Conference in Manchester and Liverpool, but also to check on how long it would be before the British could be expected to recommence the export of machinery. A part of what he found, he set forth in a letter as follows:[33]

Last Fall the [British] machine shops were operating at about 40% of their pre-war capacity. At the time I was there they were getting 60% and in some cases 70% of their pre-war capacity. . . . Platt Bros. were

---

* The Keelers must have felt that catastrophe had been biding its time till they were away from home, for in the short period of their absence (1) the commodities market broke and precipitated a national depression, (2) Gaston, Williams & Wigmore went into bankruptcy unexpectedly, leaving the Whitin Machine Works to shift for itself in the Far East, and (3) the Keelers' home in Whitinsville burned completely to the ground. Fortunately a plucky nurse was able to save the lives of the three Keeler children, but the enjoyment of the trip was marred by the succession of calamitous news forwarded to the travelers. Nevertheless the travelers returned with such glowing reports of their trip that the following year Mr. and Mrs. Mason and Mrs. George Marston Whitin made the same tour, and the year after that Mr. and Mrs. E. Kent Swift went also.

doing as poorly in productive capacity as any of the shops as well as Dobson & Barlow and Hetherington. Brooks & Doxey have recently changed their management. . . . Howard & Bullough were doing rather poorly as regards their management and the impression over in England was that they were going behind.

At the time I was there they were being threatened with a big engineering strike. [Two months earlier Swift had written that Platt Bros. were closed because of a coal strike.] The men had been offered a reduction of 20% from their present wages and were voting as to whether they would strike or not. . . . For a year at least it does not look as if very material deliveries can be expected from English machine shops.

As regards deliveries the English machinists claim to be sold about two years ahead. Their prices today are about equivalent to our $6.50 base. For instance a 40″ card would be sold in England for $1425.00 at the present rate of exchange . . . and our price . . . is $1450.00. They are a little lower on roving as a general rule than we are. . . . Of course English export prices are very apt to be governed by conditions found in the export field and may be higher in one country and lower in another.

Swift's interest in the British situation was prompted not only by his desire to know how much competition to anticipate in the Orient in the future (orders inherited from Gaston, Williams & Wigmore were sufficient to last only about a year and would have to be added to soon if the Whitin Machine Works expected to cultivate that market further),[34] but also because of a desire to size up the market on the continent of Europe. For decades France, Spain, and Italy had been important British customers, but it seemed likely that for a while at least they might be induced to buy American cotton machinery. Both Whitin and Saco-Lowell desired to tap the Continental market, but they realized that there was no hope to do so in competition with each other. Unlike the Far Eastern market, where both companies hoped there was sufficient promise of continuing business to make it worth their while to travel alone, the Continental market gave promise of being available only during the immediate period when England was too busy to meet its demands. Therefore, the American Textile Machinery Corporation was formed in November, 1919, as a Massachusetts company with main offices in Boston and branch offices on the Rue de la Paix in Paris. Both Saco-

Lowell and Whitin were behind the firm, both companies shared in the orders it secured, and executives from both companies made up its personnel, J. Fred Havey, head of Saco-Lowell's foreign sales department being also president of the export firm.

The firm was not, however, a success. European mill owners were unwilling to buy machinery that differed from the equipment they already had in their mills and that might give them service trouble in later years. Consequently, serious as Swift found the plight of the English shops to be, he felt that it was not serious enough to encourage the Americans to keep their Paris office open when it was getting no business. In 1922, therefore, the work of the American Textile Machinery Corporation was discontinued.

Meanwhile in the Orient the Japanese had decided to manufacture their own textile machinery rather than rely thenceforth on either the American or the British. By duplicating the Platt line of equipment, the Japanese machine shops were able to put on the market such acceptable and inexpensive machines that within a short time they had not only driven out all foreign competition but had actually succeeded in challenging the British in other parts of the world. Whitin therefore was excluded from any further selling in either China or Japan. Upon completion of its last Gaston order in June, 1922, the company's Far Eastern business came to an abrupt and, for most purposes, a final end.

5. THE SIGNIFICANCE OF THE POSTWAR BOOM

The profits of the years 1919 through 1922 were, to use the understatement of business jargon, most gratifying. The company's net return on sales for those four years were 26, 15, 25, and 41 per cent, respectively. In that short period its surplus account almost doubled. Many factors conjoined to produce such a record. First was the inflated condition of the nation's currency: the company's products were selling for double the price they had sold for before the war, and profit margins were correspondingly wide. Second was the intensive and efficient utilization of the company's productive facilities made possible by the high level of postwar operations. Third was the company's exactment of 5 per cent indemnities whenever mill owners, worried by the depression of 1921, sought to cancel their contracts for new machinery. Fourth was the advantage gained by the company from contracts it had signed in a period of high prices and filled in a period of low costs.

By 1922 the firm's surplus had reached $13,432,859, about twenty-two times the par value of its capital stock. The owners of the business agreed at their 8 December 1922 meeting that the surplus account had grown unreasonably large in relation to the company's capital structure and that some adjustment should be made. For that reason the stock account was increased to $9,000,000 (by transferring $8,400,000 from surplus), and 14 new shares of $100 par value were added for each of the 6,000 shares of $100 par already outstanding. The move was merely an accounting transaction, but it brought the book value of each share down from the awkwardly large figure of $2,272 to a more convenient figure of $151.

Only a minor portion of the firm's profits for the 1919–22 period — about 22 per cent — was paid out in dividends. The rest was retained in the organization — largely in the form of current assets, but partly in the form of additions to the company's plant and village properties. In 1918 the company had bought from the Paul Whitin Manufacturing Company a section of town known as Plummer's Woods.[35] On this property in 1921–22 it erected approximately one hundred new employee dwellings, the best-constructed and most attractive in Whitinsville.* The following year it also built fifty additional two-family houses in the New Village. These hundred and fifty dwellings were to represent the company's last large-scale housing effort.[36] On a few occasions thereafter it constructed single houses, and whenever possible, sold such dwellings to private owners.

A new plant, the company's sixth machine shop, was commenced in 1920 at a time when Whitin was embarrassed by an inability to fill orders from the Far East. A tremendous rock ledge stood in the way of construction and delayed final completion of the plant until March, 1923, by which time the need for it had passed. It is now quite impossible to know whether or not the company would have

---

* Philip B. Walker, an engineer who left the Boston Elevated Railway Company to accept the job of supervising the Plummer's Woods project remained in Whitinsville to direct the company's entire maintenance program.

been better off without the new and redundant half-million-dollar shop. Errors in business timing, like doctors' mistakes, have a way of burying themselves. But there came a time in the 1940's when the additional space was sorely needed. Probably if the company had delayed putting up the building till then, the added cost of construction would have more than offset all the money the company could have earned by investing its half-million dollars in some other way.

The end of the postwar boom marked something of a turning point in the company's history. Previously the backbone of the textile-machinery business had been the complete outfitting of new mills. The replacement of worn-out machinery had never constituted more than a small portion of the industry's sales. The rate of obsolescence had been slow and machines had traditionally been kept in serviceable operating condition for thirty or forty years. From its beginning, the growth of the cotton textile industry had continued at a slightly accelerating rate until about 1910. As one region matured, another always seemed ready to step forward; Lowell took its bow in the 1820's, eastern Connecticut in the 1850's, Fall River in the 1870's, New Bedford in the 1880's, and the Piedmont region of the South in the 1890's and 1900's.

By the First World War, however, the hope for new areas of exploitation had been all but abandoned when suddenly, with the outbreak of war in Europe, American machine-builders fell heir to the entire Far Eastern market. Many machinery men immediately saw visions of limitless opportunities in the Orient where the potential market for textile machinery had hardly been touched. These visions quickly evanesced, however, when the enterprising Japanese entered the field and drove British and Americans out of the oriental trade.

Within the space of the next few years, the entire American textile machinery industry experienced a basic change in its market. From the building of new capacity, its principal function changed to the servicing of capacity already in existence. No longer could it sell complete mill installations. Its new market consisted of replacements, changeovers, repairs, and services. Since its new task was lighter than its old had been, a depression in the industry became inevitable. The fact that the country's cotton mill industry became depressed at exactly the same time only helped to spread the infection.

CHAPTER XVI

THE GREAT TEXTILE DEPRESSION, 1923–1933

THE 1920's are generally thought to have been years of high prosperity. And so they were for large portions of the American economy. But in some of our oldest and most basic industries — in agriculture, in textiles, and in railroads, to name only a few of the most important — the 'twenties were years of financial distress.

The very fact that most of the suffering industries were old is in itself of vast importance. With advancing years, aged industries seem to lose their earlier resiliency. Their margins of profit tend to contract. Their rates of growth slow down. Their ability to attract young and aggressive executive talent declines, for they cannot extend the promise of advancement and reward that newer and more rapidly growing industries can offer.

As a result, the older industries are the first to feel the chill winds of business adversity. The chilliest of such winds are often the recurrent downdrafts of commodity prices like those which were felt throughout the 1920's. In a period of declining prices, businesses can be active and sales can grow — as indeed happened even in the depressed industries of the 'twenties — but, with prices falling, margins of profit become harder to maintain and business failures become more difficult to avoid.

Among the victims of depression in the 1920's were the cotton textile industry and its confrere, the textile machinery industry. Both were among the oldest manufacturing industries in the United States, having derived from the very beginning of the American Industrial Revolution. And both were among the hardest hit by the depression. No doubt the decline of the one brought on the decline of the other, but the mere fact that the manufacturers of textile machinery were so ill-prepared to meet and weather a depression among their customers, when the job of meeting depressions lay at the very heart of such a boom-and-bust producers' goods industry, is evidence enough that the textile-machinery manufacturers of America had lost their former flexibility.

It is instructive to consider that not all companies in the textile machinery industry were similarly affected by the depression. Here is a good example of how easily we can overstress the importance of external forces. All too often we forget that most forces are man-made and therefore can be man-countered. All the units in the textile machinery industry were about the same age and were subject to about the same dependence on the prosperity of customer mills. Yet some companies in the industry failed while others remained strong — and largely for reasons that can be traced not to external forces but to the behavior of individual men.

The depression performance of the Whitin Machine Works is an example of what a company can do to alleviate, if not to remove, the ill effects of adverse economic conditions. For the Whitin company, the 'twenties were the years of its greatest glory. By 1929 virtually every other company in the industry, winded and exhausted by past rash and ill-directed exertions, had dropped by the competitive way-side, while the Whitin company, with its near-century-long policy of persistent and tortoise-like conservatism, had moved ahead at a steady, if unspectacular, pace. This is not to say that the depression did not take a toll of the Whitin company, for it did. Yet, considered in relation to the rest of the industry, the Whitin Machine Works succeeded in adding constantly to its stature through fifteen years of one of the hardest and most prolonged depressions ever visited upon an American manufacturing firm.

Much has been written about the cotton textile industry's many years of unprofitable operations during the 1920's and 1930's and many a theory has been advanced as to why that particular industry suffered so much and for so long.[1] It seems preferable to concentrate here on only those particular aspects of the depression that most directly affected the builders of textile machinery. This chapter deals with the decade of market decline from 1923 to 1933, but it is important to note that the depression did not finally release its strangle hold on the textile machinery industry until 1939. The New Deal and the National Recovery Act brought some promise of revival, but not until 1937 did the Whitin company enjoy a really profitable year, and even then its prosperity was short-lived, inasmuch as 1938 was nearly as bad a year as the worst in the depression. It was not until the world was again at war that the company really extricated itself from the depression's grip.

1. OVERCAPACITY IN THE COTTON TEXTILE INDUSTRY

The great textile depression in America first gave indisputable evidence of its existence in 1923. For two years before that, the industry had been in a depressed state, but so also had the rest of American business, 1921 and 1922 having been years of postwar readjustment. In 1923 the general economy bounced back vigorously. To some extent the cotton manufacturing industry in the South did likewise, but in the North many small textile mills found the going too difficult to allow them to remain in business. Then, in the following year, when even the Southern mills returned to a state of depression, it became generally evident that all was not well in cotton textiles.

With a few fluctuations, business throughout 1925, 1926 and 1927 remained in the doldrums, the firms in the North suffering most. Mills lost money. Mills failed. Mills reorganized. Mills in New England moved to North Carolina seeking lower costs of operation. Most important for the textile machinery industry, mills virtually stopped buying new machinery. By 1929 both the cotton textile industry and its suppliers, the builders of machinery, had already experienced a depression of major proportions. The nationwide depression of the 1930's only aggravated a condition that had already become seriously unhealthy. What had brought about this deplorable state of affairs? Frequently the old term *overcapacity* was referred to; for the textile machinery industry, this word had a special meaning.

Before World War I the cotton textile industry of the United States ran almost exclusively on a one-shift basis. When additional output was desired, additional capacity was built. The war abruptly changed that pattern of operations by suddenly placing on the industry a demand for goods that a single-shift operation could not handle. Being prevented by government fiat from expanding their physical plants, mill owners met the increase in demand by operating their plants day and night. This meant employing women as well as men for night-shift work, since typically about a third of the jobs in a cotton mill were performed by female labor. After the war a brief readjustment took place during which one-shift operations were resumed. Then, as soon as mill owners realized the true nature of the heavy postwar demand, they returned to a two-shift basis.

One cannot emphasize strongly enough how important was the precedent set by those several years of two-shift operations. Like the wearing of slacks by women in World War II, night work in the cotton textile industry became socially acceptable during and after World War I. To the builders of textile machinery the change was of peculiar significance, for it enormously increased the potential capacity of the country's cotton mills without requiring the construction of a single additional card or spindle.

As the price of cotton goods fell off, along with the general decline in commodity prices following 1920, mill men saw their profit margins being squeezed to the vanishing point. If the industry had not been an atomized dispersion of small independent plants, manufacturers might have organized to control their output and hence might have achieved some stability in their prices. As it was, however, they acted independently, each trying to increase his profits by operating his plant at capacity. To keep their plants fully occupied, textile mill men were willing to accept excessively low prices. Even when prices fell beneath their break-even points, mill men endeavored to produce as much as they could just to cover some of their overhead expenses. Consequently they retained the second shift, even though it had ceased to be necessary or even desirable.

Two-shift operations became especially common in the South where state legislatures left manufacturers free to run their establishments pretty much as they chose. In the North, however, the laws of several states purposely made a second shift uneconomical. In Massachusetts, for instance, cotton manufacturers were prevented by state regulation from employing women after six o'clock at night.[2] Of course nothing in the law prevented mill owners from manning their second shifts entirely with male help, and in some instances they did just that. But the wages they had to pay male operatives were so much higher than those they paid women that most Northern manufacturers preferred to limit night-shift work to a few bottleneck departments.

Hand in hand with New England's stringent labor laws went its comparatively high wage rates. Hourly wages in the North were nearly half again as high as those in the South. Some of the differential was attributable to the greater skill of the average Northern mill operative. And the extra non-wage compensations given Southern workers, such as low-cost living accommodations and educational facilities, tended to make the real cost of labor in the South somewhat higher than the stated hourly wage rates would indicate. All modifying factors considered, however, labor costs in the Piedmont area must still have been considerably lower than those in New England.

The decline in profit margins following 1920 laid bare the fundamental difference that existed between Northern and Southern operating costs. Annual statements printed in red ink soon indicated which were the marginal producers. After 1920 some New England mills were never able to earn a profit. So sour did the market for Northern mill stock become that, by 1928, investors were often willing to sell their securities for less than the liquidating value of the assets their securities represented; investors preferred to take their losses in order to invest in the innumerable other common stocks that at just that moment seemed so promising. Some Northern mills closed forever, selling their machinery wherever they could as secondhand equipment. Others took what funds they had and moved to the South, sometimes translocating their machines, sometimes buying new. Only a few of the strongest Northern textile mills managed to remain where they were, and in so doing they usually either concentrated on the production of fine goods or else added Southern mills to their holdings so that they could distribute their production between the two localities as operating economies dictated.

The liquidation of manufacturing establishments in New England was a drastic remedy for the cotton textile industry's overcapacity. Though all too familiar to textile men, the baleful contours of Chart IX dramatically illustrate to the layman the physical shrinkage that the industry experienced beginning in 1923 and continuing down to date. In 1923 there were 36,260,000 active cotton spindles in the United States; by 1947 there were only 22,779,000 — a 38 per cent decline. At the end of World War II there were fewer operating spindles in this country than there had been at any time since 1904.

CHART IX

NUMBER OF SPINDLES IN PLACE AND ACTIVE
IN AMERICAN COTTON MILLS, 1910–1948

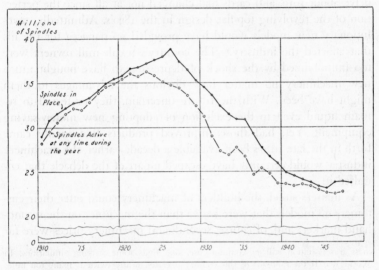

Source: Figures published annually by the Association of Cotton Textile Merchants of New York.

In 1920 there were 432 firms in the cotton textile industry; in 1940 there were only 300. Yet all the while the production of cotton goods was increasing, partly because of the fuller utilization of existing spindles and partly because of improvements in machine efficiency. By 1940, 25 per cent fewer spindles were producing 50 per cent more cloth with the help of 10 per cent fewer workers than in 1920.*

* The experience of the textile industry in the decade following World War I raises a fundamental question. Is the manufacture of cotton textiles an example of what other industries face as they age? In the railroad industry, the oldest mode of

It seems now that the depression in the cotton textile industry aggravated the depression in the machinery industry more than was necessary. If the machine-builders had been prepared to put on the market machines of radical enough design to make existing equipment obsolete, they might have induced their customers to buy their products as money-saving devices. But they had made no preparations for such an undertaking. From 1915 to 1922 they had been too busy turning out old models to give attention to any new ones. Spinning frames had changed little since the introduction of the tape drive about 1910, and cards had changed not at all since the perfection of the revolving top-flat design in the 1890's. Admittedly, revolutionary new models would have provided no panacea for the ills that afflicted the industry.* The country's textile-mill owners were too immobilized by the shock of depression to have bought much new machinery no matter how obvious the advantages to them might have been. With the future uncertain, they preferred to remain liquid even to the exclusion of adopting new money-saving equipment. Yet, had those improved products that finally came forth in the late 1920's been available a decade earlier, the machinery industry would certainly have escaped a part of the debacle that engulfed it.

As matters stood, the builders of machinery could offer their customers no models that were better than the machines on the secondhand market; and, of course, secondhand machinery prices were far

---

mass transportation still in common use, one finds some striking similarities. In World War II the railroads of this country operated nearly twice as many ton miles of freight as they did in World War I and with 25 per cent less rolling stock. In the year 1907 freight-car construction reached its peak, and 1919 was the year when the number of cars in existence began to decrease. The experience of industries such as these has helped to sponsor the theory that our economy has reached maturity. If the theory has validity we may well expect others among our older industries to begin describing a similar downward graph sometime in the near future; perhaps the next depression will be the acid test which, as in the case of litmus paper, will separate the red from the blue.

* The textile machinery industry was only experiencing what the rest of American industry would encounter a decade later, though in a less dramatic way. During the 1930's, industry in the United States made very little net addition to its capital investment. Of the sixty billion dollars of gross capital formation in plant and equipment between 1931 and 1940, ninety per cent was for replacement. The increased productivity during that decade came not from *more* machinery but from *better* machinery.

below the level of prices for new equipment. So serious became the competition between Whitin's new machines and the ones which it had manufactured and sold years before, that on at least one occasion the company gave serious consideration to entering the second-hand market and buying up its own old machines for renovation and resale.[3]

2. REPAIR SALES BECOME A MAINSTAY

For the machinery manufacturers there was one hope of salvation in their trip through the purgatory of the 'twenties and 'thirties: machine parts eventually wore out and had to be replaced. Furthermore, competition in the repair market was subject to certain natural limitations. Once a mill installed Whitin machinery, it usually looked to the Whitin company for service on that equipment. Sometimes, in fact, it could get the replacements it needed from no other source. But more often it chose to do business with Whitin simply because it realized the advantages of dealing directly with the original manufacturer and of utilizing the services which the manufacturer's salesforce had to offer.

Repair parts were the only items in Whitin's list of products that did not suffer from the textile depression of the 'twenties.[4] By 1928 and 1929 repairs constituted more than a quarter of the company's sales volume.* By the early 1930's repairs were accounting for as much as 40 per cent of all sales. More important still, the sale of repair parts contributed to the company's operating profits far more than their relative proportions would indicate. The company followed no set policy regarding individual profit margins on its repair parts, but the executives of the firm generally agreed that repairs could and should bear a higher markup than the company's regular machinery line. It would be only a guess, but possibly a good one, that repairs contributed more than half the money needed to cover

---

* Spinning-frame and twister parts (including rings and spindles) accounted for two-thirds of the company's repair sales. Comber, roving, card, and loom parts could be counted on for about a hundred thousand dollars' worth of business each year. One of the best gauges of the stability of the repair market was the fact that the general level of repair prices held up throughout the depression. In contrast, spinning-frame prices declined from a high of $7.00 per spindle in 1920 to $4.25 in 1925 before becoming steady (see Appendix 25).

the company's overhead expenses during most of the industry's depression years. In large part the firm was living on the achievements of the past.

There were at least three reasons that repair sales held up as well as they did during the depression. First, most mill men, being desirous of keeping their finances as liquid as possible during such uncertain times, chose to repair their old and worn machinery instead of buying new. Secondly, when machines were operated almost continuously, as they often were in the South, they wore out with even greater rapidity than might have been expected because of the extra hours they were worked. It would seem that machines, like human beings, require occasional periods of rest to render optimum service. Thirdly, producers of textile fabrics frequently shifted from one product to another in an effort to reach a market that would yield them a better profit; changes in their product lines meant the purchase of new machine parts.* They, therefore, applied to the machinery manufacturers for the rings and spindles necessary to alter their output from one type of yarn to another. It happens that rings and spindles are the two devices in the preparatory process that wear out most rapidly. Consequently, when the normal replacement market for such items was supplemented by the market created by changes in styles, Whitin's ring and spindle business prospered. Between 1923 and 1929 those two items alone accounted for 38 per cent of the company's total repair sales.

Yet Whitin's repair business was not without its tribulations. Carrying an inventory of all the parts which the company had manufactured over the past thirty years was obviously impossible. One firm, the Universal Winding Company, manufacturers of a line of textile machinery that did not compete directly with Whitin's, solved its inventory problems by manufacturing *only* for stock, each new machine being assembled from parts already on hand.[5] But Universal's line of machinery was small and its products were almost completely standard. As compared with Universal, the Whitin company's line of equipment not only was much larger but was made up

---

* Before the 1920's American cotton mills typically specialized in one type or class of goods only. In fact, the textile industry's difficulties during the 1920's were to some extent traceable to this rigidity in its production habits. The more agile managers in the industry, however, soon saw opportunities in the production of new types and styles of cloth.

of far more complex machines. It is true that Whitin's cards and combers usually followed a set design, but its spinning-frame parts were only about 60 per cent standard. The chassis of its spinning frames were all much the same, but the superstructures were governed by the type of fabrics which its mill customers wished to produce. Moreover, there were always innumerable petty reasons why a mill wanted its frames a little different from other frames. For one thing, every mill superintendent had his own idea how a spinning frame should be made, and any manufacturer who failed to heed customers' suggestions was running the risk of having frames develop a dozen real-imaginery performance failures as soon as they were installed. Then, too, mill men usually placed heavy emphasis on having the machinery in their mills as uniform as possible. Therefore, if Whitin succeeded in selling equipment to a mill that was already equipped with another machine-builder's products, the Whitin company often found it had to modify the designs of its new machines to make them similar to those of its competitor's old ones.

The most troublesome repair orders came from owners of machines that were as much as thirty and even forty years old. To accommodate such business, the company felt obliged to preserve more than 125,000 patterns in its lofts. Even then it received an occasional order for which it had to make a complete new set of patterns and jigs. If such orders came from mills that had bought Whitin machinery secondhand, the company usually felt no obligation to fill them, but if a request came from a regular Whitin customer, the customer was generally accommodated even though at an out-of-pocket loss to the company. An article which appeared in the July, 1939, issue of the *Whitin Review* (a house organ distributed by the company to the trade at irregular intervals beginning in April, 1933) gave a half-humorous, half-serious illustration of the difficulties such an order involved:

. . . . We build one hundred and fifty machines that might be called standard, which require nearly fifty thousand different parts. There are one hundred and twenty-five thousand patterns in our lofts from which castings can be obtained quickly. Millions of stock parts are ready for immediate shipment on order.

An order for six "special" gears comes in, marked RUSH. They are needed for machines that we built for a mill back in 1907 — thirty-one years ago. These gears are like nothing we have recently made, and we have no pattern from which to make the blanks. We really ought to write the customer, and say, "No soap." However:

We put in two days making a new pattern, get castings three days later. New tools are needed to cut the teeth — three more days gone. All our gear cutting machines are on production work, but one of these must be stopped while a special set-up is made for this little order. For the complete operation, it happens that three special set-ups are required. Special attention is given to the order on every job. Special handling is necessary at the hardening furnace. Finally, the job is done; but four weeks have elapsed since the order was received.

Anyway, we have given the mill service, and we hope for the best. It has cost us some money and we take a stiff loss on the order, which includes:

Special pattern for gear blank	$20.00
Special tools for cutting	8.00
Special set-ups for machines	12.00

and the added cost of individual attention, follow up, overhead, and what-have-you. The bill for the gears is sent along in due course, at our regular charge for standard gears: amount, $22.26.

A little later, in the mill office: "Hey! here's a bill from Whitin for those six gears. We asked them to hustle the order and they took four weeks on it. By the way, we don't need 'em now, put them in stock. And write Whitin their service is rotten, and the price is awful. Tell them at that price we could buy a whole new frame. . . ."

Orders for parts that were in current production were fitted in with the regular production schedule and were billed at cost (the company had no regular price list for repairs), but orders for parts that were neither current nor among the obsolete patterns had to be run in special job lots (one of the reasons why the prices charged for them were so high). Usually the company counted on its customers to stock their own supply of such parts and to order in economical lots, well in advance of their requirements. The company's only attempt to stock its own inventory of repair parts was the informal system carried on by its individual foremen. Often small rush orders could be filled simply by having foremen go to the stock bins where they kept over-runs of previous orders. The company's policy in handling repair orders was thus informal, direct, and individual.

For many years that policy was a success. But during the early 1930's a number of enterprising business men in the South saw the opportunity of getting into the repair parts business by offering Southern mills better service than the faraway Northern machinery builders could give. Before then the South had been by far Whitin's best market for repair parts. New England, a veritable hive of small-scale, metal-working shops, had always gone far toward supplying locally the repair requirements of its mills; but in the South metal-working was a fairly uncommon trade, and so Southern mills had traditionally looked to the North for their replacement supplies.

As early as 1923 the Whitin board of directors had discussed the advisability of erecting a branch plant in Charlotte to care for the Southern repair parts business, but the depression and the seeming necessity for conserving liquid funds had given the project its quietus. By 1932, however, so many small shops were nibbling at Whitin's lucrative repair business in the South that the board decided to go through with its original plans. Taking over a part of the office building which Cramer had erected in Charlotte and which the Whitin company had bought from Cramer at the time of his retirement, the Whitin management equipped the space with used machine tools sent from the plant in Whitinsville. A nuclear work force was sent from Whitinsville to Charlotte in the belief that suitably trained men could not be recruited in the South.[6] Operation of the Southern shop, which was begun in August, 1932, was placed nominally under Robert I. Dalton, the man in charge of the company's North Carolina-Virginia-Tennessee sales territory, but since Dalton was not a trained production man, the shop's superintendent was permitted considerable autonomy and became accustomed to looking for directions of a policy nature from Sydney R. Mason, head of repairs in Whitinsville.[7] During the first ten years of its existence, the shop employed an average of only about fifty men. It was small in relation to its parent concern, but in comparison with the other independent repair shops in the vicinity of Charlotte it was a sizable establishment. Without involving a heavy financial investment, it managed to rescue the Whitin company's threatened share in the repair business of the South.

The Charlotte shop also dramatized the change that had occurred in the cotton textile industry in the preceding ten years. By 1932 probably as much as two-thirds of Whitin's market potential for cotton machinery lay south of Mason and Dixon's line. Furthermore, by 1932, Whitin had become the only cotton-machinery builder in the country financially able to extend its productive facilities at the very bottom of the cyclical downswing.

3. THE TEXTILE MACHINERY INDUSTRY RETRENCHES

In 1923 there were still nine major plants producing cotton preparatory machinery in America. Four of the nine were the members of the Saco-Lowell combination (the Lowell and Kitson shops in Lowell, the Pettee shop in Newton Upper Falls, and the Saco shop in Biddeford). The remaining five were the shops of the Whitin Machine Works, of the H & B American Machine Company, of the Mason Machine Works, of the Fales & Jenks Machine Company, and of the Woonsocket Machine & Press Company. By 1933, after ten years of industry depression, only three of the nine remained in operation.

The first to shut down was the Mason Machine Works. Like most other units in the industry, Mason was a family-owned and family-managed concern. Right up till the time of the firm's demise it was operated by descendants of its founder, William Mason. As late as 1924, Frederick Mason, the founder's only son, was president of the company. During World War I, active management of the firm had been vested in Arthur R. Sharp, a son-in-law of one of William Mason's two daughters. Sharp was a flamboyant business man — the owner or promoter of several New England mills, among them the Sharp Manufacturing Company, one of several fine-goods mills established in New Bedford in 1910 with the financial assistance of the Whitin Machine Works. Under Sharp, the Mason Machine Works in 1917-18 turned heavily to government war work, making gun-barrel drilling, reaming, and rifling machinery, as well as 2,500-horsepower marine engines, four-inch gun mounts, gasoline air compressors, and other military appurtenances. The settlement of government contracts in 1919 made it apparent that the company had lost heavily on its war work and in the process had sacrificed most of its liquid capital. As treasurer of the company, Sharp gave way to Thomas A. Cox, formerly the company's Southern agent, but Cox, though earnest, was incapable of meeting so hopeless a financial situation. After considerable debate, the family decided to liquidate the enterprise rather than risk further losses. During 1922 and 1923 the Mason company took only what few scattered orders it could get on favorable terms. In January, 1924,[8] it shipped the last complete machines it was ever to build.*

Saco-Lowell was the next to experience difficulties. During the postwar boom its sales had been phenomenal ($21 million *vs.* Whitin's $11 million for 1920), and young Robert F. Herrick, Jr., had become convinced that the firm had reached a new high plateau in its growth. In 1920 the company began construction work on two new shops at Biddeford and an ambitious new foundry at Newton, and in 1923 (by which time the depression in textiles was in wide evidence) it also began work on two additional shops at Lowell, one of which was to specialize in the manufacture of worsted machinery. Herrick expected American machine shops to step into the world position occupied for so long by shops in England and was willing to back his optimism by investing large portions of his company's postwar earnings in a heavy expansion program. His plan was to make each type of machine in a separate plant. The depression had not been under way long, however, when his over-ambitious project showed its vulnerability. The new worsted-machinery shop at Lowell was never, in fact, put in operation. During 1923, 1924, and 1925 the Saco-Lowell company lost an average of a half-million dollars a year *before* depreciation.

The resultant steady drain on working capital forced the once-

---

* Textile machinery companies die hard. With so many of its machines still operating in cotton mills, there was strong incentive for the Mason company to continue in the repair parts business. In 1925 Whitin and Draper put out feelers to see if the owners of Mason might be interested in selling the company's drawings and patterns, but they met with no encouragement. Section by section the family sold off the various shop and foundry buildings, the largest sale being made to a lumber and building-supply firm named L. Grossman & Sons. But not till the late 'thirties did the owners finally dispose of the company's repair parts business. Though the Mason firm no longer exists, there are still Mason machines in operation, the newest being at least a quarter-century old. A small Taunton firm named Textile Parts, Inc., still uses the old Mason drawings and patterns to service whatever Mason machinery is still running.

proud Saco-Lowell company into reorganization.* David F. Edwards, a sometime professor at the Harvard Business School and executive of the General Motors Corporation, was brought in to rebuild the firm. One of his first major decisions was to close the Lowell and Kitson shops (1928), bringing to an end the careers of two among America's most illustrious old manufacturing plants. In their day both had been by far the largest producers in their respective fields. Before long (1932) Edwards had also decided to abandon the Pettee shop at Newton Upper Falls. Thereafter all manufacturing activities of the Saco-Lowell company were conducted at the Saco shop in Biddeford.

Although Saco-Lowell's experience in the 1920's was almost as far removed from Whitin's as failure is from success, the casual observer might not have noticed the difference. Until 1932 Saco-Lowell consistently led Whitin in sales and, even after that time, continued in close second place. In 1931 and 1932 it experienced operating profits while Whitin was suffering operating losses. But Saco-Lowell's fixed non-operating expenses had become so heavy that in most years its net showing was much worse than Whitin's. In the years 1924–29, when Whitin was making net profits of about a half-million dollars a year, Saco-Lowell, even with its larger sales volume, was running a deficit of about the same amount. The tremendous productive capacity built up by Herrick would have been a great boon in times

* There are many, both in Whitinsville and in Boston, who firmly believe the story that Saco-Lowell was so prostrate in 1926 that the Whitin Machine Works could have driven it to the wall and that Whitin would have done so had not a controlling interest in Saco-Lowell been held by E. Kent Swift. The fact that the rumor of such control could inspire credence (such control would have been in direct violation of the Clayton Act) is the best possible evidence of the awe in which Swift was held by many. As a matter of fact, Swift did avail himself of an opportunity to buy a small block of Saco-Lowell's stock when it was selling for a low price, but it constituted less than a 2% interest in the company. He never at any time had any voice in Saco-Lowell's management and he never became more than a casual acquaintance of Saco-Lowell's president, David F. Edwards.

As for the allegation that Saco-Lowell was prostrate enough to be driven out of business, that was true only in a corporate sense. A business enterprise is more than just a legal entity, opinion to the contrary notwithstanding. It is a corps of workers, an executive force, and a group of satisfied customers. Saco-Lowell found itself compelled to make changes in its financial structure and in its executive force, but its labor force and its customer relationships remained strong. Many mill men in the country continued to regard Saco-Lowell's pickers and cards as superior to Whitin's and continued to buy them even when Saco-Lowell was going through reorganization.

of peak demand, but in a period of depression it meant an inescapable assessment on the company's resources. Even Edwards' drastic decision to concentrate the company's manufacturing facilities at Biddeford introduced heavy non-operational expenses that the company could ill afford to bear.

At about the time when Edwards was concluding that the demand for cotton machinery was not sufficient to warrant keeping the Pettee plant open, two other machine shops went out of business — the Woonsocket Machine & Press Company and the Fales & Jenks Machine Company. It will be recalled that in 1910 those two firms had made John H. Mayes, a former Whitin employee, their joint Southern agent. Over the years between 1910 and 1929 the corporate tie between the two firms had grown increasingly strong — so that by the latter date they possessed identical boards of directors. What changes occurred in the ownership of the two companies I do not know, but it would appear that the center of control lay in the Fales & Jenks concern and that members of the Fales family were the ones who held sway. It is said in the trade that the principal weakness in each of the two companies was the failure to train suitable replacements for the old management as it departed through death or retirement.

About mid–1930 J. Richmond Fales approached the Whitin Machine Works with an offer to sell both the Fales & Jenks Machine Company and the Woonsocket Machine & Press Company. At that particular point in its history Whitin was none too anxious to increase its manufacturing facilities, for its own plant in Whitinsville was currently being operated at less than 50 per cent of capacity. Moreover, there was always the possibility that the government would look with disfavor upon any further consolidation in an industry that already had very few companies. Certain aspects of the offer were tempting, however. The opportunity to make sure that these two companies would not revive later on to become troublesome competitors must have been a powerful if unexpressed factor in the final decision. Moreover, the Fales & Jenks twister was highly respected by the trade and promised to be a valuable addition to the Whitin line. Something favorable could also be said of Woonsocket's line, for certain features of its roving machinery were distinctly superior to Whitin's, and, in addition, Woonsocket, over the years, had added to its line both cards and picking machinery.[9] Some slight advantage was also to be gained from transferring to Whitinsville some of the newer machine tools and the more skilled employees of the two companies.

But no matter what the advantages, they were minimized by the depressed conditions that prevailed in the industry. Hence, the Whitin company was not an eager buyer. At the same time, J. Richmond Fales must have realized that he was in no position to force a favorable bargain; he was anxious to sell and Whitin was his only possible customer. No outsider would have been likely to dare an entry into so demoralized an industry and no other firm in the industry had the financial strength to consider making the purchase. Fales must, therefore, have resigned himself to accepting a very low price.

After submitting the proposed transaction to the United States Attorney General's office to give the federal government an opportunity to object to the purchase if it saw fit to do so, the Whitin company agreed to buy the physical assets of the two companies. It obtained thereby only real estate, buildings, machine tools, and inventories; it received none of the two concerns' cash, none of their accounts receivable, and neither of their corporate franchises. It did, however, obtain the right to use the names of the two firms in its advertising and on the pages of its catalogues. The agreed price for the Fales & Jenks Machine Company was $600,000; the price for Woonsocket was $350,000; and a $50,000 fee was paid to J. Richmond Fales as negotiator. Hence the total cost to the Whitin Machine Works was a flat million dollars, a fraction of the book value of the two concerns.

The transaction was consummated 16 December 1930.[10] A year later the Whitin Machine Works made claim, in a pictorial volume commemorating the company's hundredth year in existence, that the purchase of Fales & Jenks and Woonsocket had reëstablished the firm as the largest builder of textile machinery in America.*

After the liquidation of Fales & Jenks and Woonsocket there remained only three shops in the preparatory textile machinery indus-

---

* The company has published pictorial volumes on three occasions. The first volume, called *A Trip through the Whitin Machine Works* (1925), contained pictures of the shop, its executives, their homes, and various views of the village. The

try — the Biddeford plant of Saco-Lowell, the Whitin plant, and the plant of the H & B American Machine Company at South Attleboro. "H & B" was the smallest of the three, being only about a quarter the size of either of its competitors. Although it owed its start to the English firm of Howard & Bullough and was 60 per cent owned by that firm, its control had always rested in the hands of Americans — first in the person of Howard & Bullough's American representative, Charles E. Riley, and later in the hands of Mrs. Riley's nephew, Edward L. Martin.[11] In 1911 Riley had succeeded in convincing the British that the Howard & Bullough American Machine Company, Ltd., should relinquish its English charter on the grounds that its British connections prejudiced American mill owners against the company, and that it should change its name to the H & B American Machine Company, with a charter in Maine.

In the years following World War I, the H & B company shared with others in the industry the profitable business to be had in the Far East. Unlike the Saco-Lowell Shops, it retained its profits by keeping them in the form of current assets. With about five million dollars in liquid funds the company was a choice piece of property.

Around 1922 Riley and Martin decided to try to buy from the British a controlling stock interest in the company. Since H & B had just passed through several years of high prosperity, the two men felt that the British would consider it an opportune time to sell. Both Riley and Martin made trips to England and in the end succeeded in buying half the British-held 60 per cent interest in the firm. With control indisputably in their grasp, H & B's management began to invest the company's excess funds in common stocks. Throughout the 'twenties they received a return on their investments that was more than enough to offset their manufacturing losses.

But 1929 turned the tide for them. Some of H & B's securities lost nearly all value. Among their heaviest investments was a block of International Match Company stock. Like so many investors follow-

---

second, called *Looking into the Second Hundred Years* (1931), was published in honor of the hundredth anniversary of the company's "founding." The third, *In This Quiet Valley* (1945), was a pictorial record of the shop's contribution to victory in World War II; it contained a hundred pages of informal shop photographs showing approximately 350 of the company's employees.

ing the crash, the H & B American company salvaged only a fraction of what they had put into the market. By 1932 they had lost nearly half their working capital. At the very time their need for extra resources was greatest, they saw their enviable financial position vanish. Had the company's ownership been less closely held (in 1932 it had only 22 stockholders)[12] or had a less dynamic man than Edward L. Martin been in charge,* H & B would doubtless have entered liquidation. Instead, it kept going. But its stock-market losses of 1929–32, followed by the operational losses of subsequent years, left the company permanently debilitated.

4. WHITIN WEATHERS THE DEPRESSION

Alone among the textile-machinery manufacturers, the Whitin Machine Works was able to maintain its financial equilibrium. Charting a careful course, it avoided the rocks and shoals that decommissioned its competitors. Unlike the Mason Machine Works, it did not venture outside the pilot marks set by its experience in the textile machinery business. While Mason turned to the production of marine engines and gun machinery during World War I † and lost heavily on the venture, Whitin chose to stick with textile machinery, as it had done in the Civil War, even if by so doing it became forced to operate at less than capacity. By its cautiousness it avoided the losses that eventually forced Mason out of the machine-building business.

Like the H & B American company, Whitin was able to retain a substantial portion of the profits it had made following the First World War. But unlike H & B, Whitin did not part with those profits in the stock-market crash. Between 1919 and 1923 its total income (before depreciation expense but after taxes)[13] amounted to $11,492,864. Of this amount the company distributed $2,880,000 in dividends and expended $4,722,655 on new plant, equipment, and housing. The rest, nearly four million dollars, it added to its work-

---

* Riley had fallen ill with pernicious anemia; he died in 1935.

† There was a precedent at the Mason Machine Works for this departure from its main line of endeavor. Almost from its founding the Mason company had made products other than textile machinery. For years it had been a well-known producer of locomotives. And until shortly before the outbreak of World War I it had also made a line of printing machinery.

ing capital. Ordinarily in a company like Whitin a current ratio of 10 to 1 would have been an ample margin of safety, but by 1925 the firm had achieved so strong a liquid position that its current ratio was 118 to 1.

At first, most of Whitin's increased working capital took the form of receivables. Because of depressed conditions in the cotton mill industry, debts owed the company by its customers were difficult to collect, and receivables were slow to liquidate. The company's average day's sales in 1925 were 125, or roughly four months; by 1925 they had risen to 226, or more than seven months. As mills completed paying for their machinery, however, Whitin found itself with a remarkable surplus of cash. By 1927 the company had nearly five million dollars that it no longer needed in the business and that it was free to invest in interest-bearing and dividend-paying securities.

In contrast to H & B American, the Whitin company chose the way of caution. Renouncing the profits that were to be made in the stock market of the latter 'twenties, Swift decided to concentrate on municipal and utility bonds. More than that, he bought only bonds that were nearing maturity, so that his turnover was high and his risks low. Such a policy required constant attention. Alden, the company's comptroller, spent much of his time studying security issues and rebuffing the constant efforts of such investment firms as Lee, Higginson & Company to interest him in the flotations they had underwritten. So ably was the fund administered that, even in the 1929 crash, losses were negligible.

Although it can be said that Swift's chief reason for choosing to invest his funds so conservatively was because he felt a sense of trusteeship for the money his family had left in the firm, it is nevertheless true that in the prosperous 'twenties many others who felt their trusteeship no less keenly were convinced that common stocks were a safe and sane investment. The fact that Swift did not go along with that sentiment marked him as a man of remarkable financial acumen. Others have been lauded as investment geniuses for less reason.*

* Beginning in 1930, the company's cash fund slowly but steadily dwindled. In 1931 and 1932 out-of-pocket losses were over a third of a million dollars. Moreover,

The result was a happy one for the company. In fact, the business life of Whitinsville in the 1920's remained so tranquil that it may be described as becalmed rather than as distressed. From 1925 through 1929, the company's total sales volume varied by less than 8 per cent from one extreme to the other. Operations were delicately balanced at a break-even point. Only a matter of accounting definition stood between a final determination as to whether the company was experiencing an operating profit or loss.* Since, in addition to its operating profits the company had a respectable income from the investment of its idle funds, its annual statements remained in the black for all but three years of the depression — in 1930, 1931, and 1935. Through the entire depression, the company missed not one quarterly dividend payment, though necessarily the rate was trimmed in several years.[14]

5. WHITINSVILLE IN DEPRESSION

The inhabitants of Whitinsville later looked back with nostalgia to the halcyon years in the 1920's — years when there was neither pulsating prosperity nor yet dispirited depression. The decade 1900–10 may have been the community's most prosperous era, but most villagers would agree that 1923–29 was its most felicitous. The firm's stability in the midst of the textile machinery industry's general decay gave the people of the community an immense pride in their company and a comfortable sense of security.

Swift was far more liberal in his interpretation of the company's rôle in the village than his predecessors had been. The earlier managers of the shop had felt that the company should proceed no

---

dividends exceeded income in every year from 1927 through 1935. Since Swift seems to have looked on the company's invested funds as money left in the firm by family stockholders, he believed that it was only right that family members should be allowed to withdraw those funds in the form of dividends even though the company's operations were not profitable enough to permit the payment of dividends based on earnings. The revival of business after 1935 gradually drew all remaining surplus cash funds back into use in the company's working capital.

* The company's audited statements show housing expenses as operating costs but do not show rental as operating income. As a result the company's statements show a small operating loss for most years between 1925 and 1935. If, however, rentals are included as an offset against housing expenses (as they are in Table 12), the operating losses are transmuted into small profits in all years except 1929–1932 and 1935.

further into village affairs than was necessary to attract and house an adequate supply of labor. In contrast, Swift believed that the company had much to gain by entering also the civic and social life of the community and by making Whitinsville an inexpensive place to live and a pleasant place to work.

Swift's policy was born not wholly of altruism. Until the 1920's the Whitin Machine Works seems to have been a relatively high-cost producer. It is difficult to prove that statement — in fact, it is even difficult to define its real meaning — but stated negatively it seems

TABLE 12

TWO DECADES OF DEPRESSION OPERATING FIGURES, 1920–1940

(In thousands of dollars)

Year	Machinery Sales[a]	Repair Sales	Total Sales	Operating Income[b]	Other Income (Net)[c]	Net Income before Taxes
1920	$8,860	$1,850	$10,710	$1,374	$237	$1,611
1921	9,421	1,457	10,878	2,708	18	2,726
1922	7,911	1,153	9,064	3,125	590	3,715
1923	7,927	1,332	9,259	2,103	390	2,493
1924	4,900	937	5,837	359	485	844
1925	3,821	1,202	5,023	26	686	712
1926	4,045	1,268	5,313	77	538	615
1927	4,089	1,272	5,361	272	200	472
1928	3,918	1,144	5,062	60	432	492
1929	3,926	1,356	5,282	−39	421	382
1930	2,202	1,228	3,430	−270	442	172
1931	2,007	1,104	3,111	−746	300	−446
1932	1,058	1,028	2,086	−578	194	−384
1933	2,159	1,540	3,699	47	176	223
1934	3,051	1,645	4,696	51	207	258
1935	3,291	1,060	4,351	−448	213	−235
1936	5,208	1,415	6,623	328	163	491
1937	8,854	1,845	10,699	1,236	255	1,491
1938	2,916	1,920	4,836	141	−87	54
1939	5,302	2,651	7,953	820	−32	788
1940	6,822	3,029	9,851	1,303	−39	1,264

[a] For sales figures from 1885–1915, see Appendix 29. Sales in 1916 were $5,510,000; in 1917, $6,500,000; in 1918, $6,332,000; and in 1919, $7,918,000.

[b] Includes profits arising out of the company's investment in housing.

[c] This column represents the difference between non-operating income and non-operating expenses. It is composed principally of interest and dividends received from the investment of idle funds.

Source: Audited annual statements.

at least to have been true that the Whitin Machine Works was never thought of in the industry as a leader in the reduction of costs. Of course, high-cost production need be no millstone so long as one's products can command their price. But a depression, especially a long one, is no time to have one's costs of production out of line. Swift saw the village as an opportunity to keep his labor costs and taxes at a minimum. By allowing the company to undertake functions that it could perform more economically than its employees could, he felt that the cost of living in Whitinsville could be kept relatively low. By projecting the company into civic affairs, he could visualize reflected benefits in low taxes on the company's properties. By providing, through the company, social welfare and security, he could envisage a stable, loyal, and at the same time efficient force of employees.

Swift's policy was not unrealistic in conception; it certainly was not unrealistic in results. Being the sort of business man who expects each undertaking to earn its own way, Swift was not the type to sponsor a project for sentimental reasons. During the 1920's he invested a few well-placed hundred thousand dollars in community betterment and in return obtained peaceful, friendly labor relations despite low-scale wages.[15] At Biddeford in 1923–24 the foundry employees of the Saco-Lowell Shops went out on a sixteen-month strike that began and ended in acrimony, while in Whitinsville labor rest prevailed with average wages that were 5 per cent or more lower than those in the Saco-Lowell plants.* Some men did leave the village in search of better-paying jobs as was to be expected, but so many of them eventually returned that one is never surprised in Whitinsville to be told by a man about the period when he too was a prodigal son of the village.

Such tranquil labor relations were the result of a complex of factors that would warrant a special study of their own, for no one man, no one policy, no accident of time or place, could be used in simple

* See Appendix 24, and for comparative figures consult George S. Gibb's history of Saco-Lowell. Biddeford's wage rates were much lower than those at Lowell and Newton. After 1932, by which time all Saco-Lowell's production facilities were concentrated in Biddeford, the wage differential between Saco-Lowell and Whitin disappeared. It revived again, however, after World War II, when Saco-Lowell adopted the policy of appeasing labor in order to avoid a costly strike at a time of peak demand.

explanation of so harmonious a management-labor relationship as that existing in Whitinsville during the 1920's and 1930's, when elsewhere there was so much unrest. Yet one would probably come near the heart of the matter if one said that Swift succeeded in making the people of Whitinsville feel politically free and at the same time economically secure. Such a feeling was difficult to achieve and probably was an ephemeral condition attainable only for a short period of time, for political freedom and economic controls (of the type seemingly necessary for economic security) have in the past always ended at cross-purposes, the one giving way to the other. And so it happened eventually at Whitinsville. But for two decades Swift conducted an experiment in a type of industrial feudalism that might well have aroused the admiration of some sociologists and the condemnation of others.

Swift realized from the first the danger of seeming to combine political with economic controls. Family tradition had established a practiced though unpreached policy that no top executive of the company should hold an elective public office. Other family members might, and often did, enter local politics, but the company executives kept their individual distances from the political arena.

Shortly before World War I there occurred a chain of incidents that, while trivial in themselves, are illustrative of how scrupulously Swift avoided the appearance of bringing any pressure to bear on the town's governing selectmen.[16] As has been said before, Whitinsville's location, somewhat off the main highway between Worcester and Providence, made it a difficult place to find. Realizing the situation, Swift petitioned the Northbridge Board of Selectmen in 1915 to have a suitable road sign placed on the main highway near the Linwood crossing. No action resulted, however. Again in 1916 he wrote a letter. Again no action. Once more in 1917 he reiterated his patient but persistent plea. This time he suggested that the Whitin Machine Works be allowed to bear the full cost of erecting the sign which he proposed. One cannot be sure that the selectmen had all along been waiting for him to make such an offer, but by their action they laid themselves open to a suspicion that such was the case, for on the third attempt Swift was granted the permission to erect the sign he wanted — provided that it was done at the company's expense.

There was good reason for Swift's not wishing to serve as selectman, for as chairman of the town's finance committee, he occupied a far more vital post and a post that was appointive, not elective.* As committee chairman, Swift brought to the town's finances the same shrewd management that he had brought to the company's affairs. Comparison of Massachusetts town statistics is an exceedingly treacherous undertaking, but even allowing for a wide margin of error, one must conclude that Northbridge has been among the most efficiently operated political units in the state.[17] While the tax rate in Northbridge has been fairly high, the assessed values have been unusually low. Roads are maintained in fair condition and schools are sufficiently superior to those of neighboring towns to attract an embarrassingly large number of transfer students.[18] The town's major tax burden is of course borne not by the inhabitants but by the company, which not only pays about half the total taxes collected by Northbridge but in addition contributes a great many utility services in lieu of taxes (e.g., the water system and the fire department). Even then the company pays unusually low taxes. During World War II, when the company valued its Whitinsville property for fire insurance purposes at about $20,000,000, its assessed valuation for tax purposes was only about $3,000,000, roughly half of that sum being for plant and half for company houses.

One reason the town could be economically run was that many an activity which might normally have been town-sponsored was supported by trust funds established by family members. The town hall was endowed by the Whitin family and was owned and operated not by the town but by a group of self-perpetuating, probate-approved trustees, most of whom were traditionally company officials.[19] The town's library was similarly endowed,[20] and the town's principal cemetery was operated by the Pine Grove Cemetery Association, an organization established by the original four Whitin brothers.[21] The employees of the company saw nothing unusual in having the cemetery association's main offices housed in the basement of the Whitin firm's administration building.

Before Swift's time gifts to the town had always been made in the name of individuals in the Whitin family, seldom by the company

* The finance committee was established in 1916, at which time Swift was made chairman; he has been chairman ever since.

itself. On occasion, when the company owned land that was needed for a public purpose, it donated the property if the cause seemed to be a worthy one — as when it gave the triangular plot of land between Church Street and Linwood Avenue for a public park (1890),[22] or when it gave the corner property across from the park for a bank building (1906),[23] or when it gave a house and lot in the Plummer's Woods section for a village hospital (1913)[24] — but such gifts were few. The firm's officers had always felt that their principal function was to run a sound and efficient company and that by so doing they were contributing to the community the greatest social good possible.

Swift agreed in principle with the policies of his forebears but he felt that under some circumstances their policies could be made more liberal. Being essentially a pragmatist, however, he followed no predetermined scheme in advancing the company's participation in civic affairs. Usually, in fact, he held back until it was apparent that matters were not proceeding well under private direction; then he stepped in either to take charge or to lend a helping hand, depending on which mode of action the situation seemed to require.[25] In 1919, following the death of John C. Whitin's widow, the company took ownership of historic Castle Hill Farm[26] and, under Swift's personal direction, converted it from a hobby showplace to a paying business.* In 1921 the company assumed financial responsibility for the town's baseball team,[27] an organization which a decade earlier had hired some of the finest semi-professional ball players in New England but which in subsequent years had fallen on bad times largely through lack of financial support.†

In all his dealings with the community, Swift was especially anxious to promote anything that might make life in Whitinsville more pleasant or that might reduce the cost of living for Whitin's workmen. One way that the company enabled its employees to live better on the wages they received was through the Whitinsville Home Garden Club, an organization that is still in active existence.[28] The Club

* One of the markets that Swift developed for the farm was in the company's shop where milk-vending machines were installed for the refreshment and nourishment of laborers and where competing Coca-Cola machines were excluded by fiat.

† Under company sponsorship the team dropped its professionalism, but even as an amateur organization it developed such a strong backing in public enthusiasm that it remained an established Whitinsville institution.

was initially formed in the summer of 1917 as a result of the food shortage during World War I. But so popular did the Club prove to be that it was continued even after the war had ended — in fact, as depressed times and slack work in the 1930's made gardening an increasingly rewarding occupation, the Club's membership grew in size. At times as many as a third of the families living in company houses joined for the season. Dues of a dollar were collected to provide a fund out of which cash prizes could be paid for the best gardens of the year. The real expense of the project was, of course, borne by the company. Members were each assigned a 50′ x 100′ plot of land which the company plowed and harrowed in the spring and for which the company provided ample fertilizer. The company also piped water to the several garden plots and then at the end of the season hauled away the refuse that remained — all without charge to Club members. The cost of raising a vegetable garden was thus only a dollar a year in membership fees, plus the price of seeds, which could be ordered through the company's purchasing department.

The Home Garden Club was but one example of the benevolently responsible attitude that the company assumed toward its employees — more especially toward those employees who lived in company dwellings, although by the late 'twenties very few employees were not company-housed. The company's icehouse furnished ice to employees at cost. The purchasing department provided furnace coal at wholesale prices. The company piped its houses with free water from its reservoirs. A maintenance crew kept the company's houses in constant repair and redecorated each dwelling on an average of once every seven years. Maintenance men even mowed the lawns surrounding company houses. A worker had to do little around his house to keep it livable. To ensure adequate fire protection the company sponsored the village volunteer fire department, bought the fire trucks, provided garage space for them, and honored the volunteer firemen at annual dinners. Because it did not wish to rely on the town, and because it wanted to keep its taxes down, the company built and maintained the streets that led through its various housing projects. It also plowed them in the wintertime — and at the same time plowed the sidewalks. Such extra services did not go unnoticed by the employees; conscious of the uniqueness of their community, they delighted in regaling their out-of-town friends with tales of the extraordinary services they received in the ordinary course of a day's existence.[29]

Operating such a community was not without its tribulations. Probably the most troublesome aspect was the assignment of dwellings.[30] By the late 1920's the company was maintaining almost a thousand family units. Of these about fifty were houses for executives and were assigned by Mr. Swift personally. The assignment of the rest was handled by a three-man shop committee which met once a week to consider applications and complaints.[31] From 1920 onward, there were seldom less than a hundred applications on file, so that the committee was never without work to do. Applications were acknowledged in part according to the date they were submitted, but the crucial test of priority was the valuableness of the applicant to the shop.[32] Even after a tentative priority list had been agreed upon, many other problems remained to be solved. The size of a worker's family or of his level of income sometimes held up the assignment of a house until a suitable vacancy occurred. Furthermore, the committee soon learned that Yankees and Irish did not make good neighbors and that the French got along with neither of the other two groups. It was best also, the committee found, to keep the Armenians segregated, not because of any racial prejudice but because their incessant brewing of lamb stew created odors offensive to most non-Armenians.

Of course, trouble really began only after assignments had been made. Whenever a vacancy occurred, there were always a dozen or more renters who thought they should be permitted to move. Renters by choice might have put up with their neighbors' idiosyncrasies, but renters by assignment found it easier to blame the company than themselves for the troubles they had with their neighbors. Even satisfied families presented their own problems, for after they had inhabited a dwelling for twenty years or more, such families felt a proprietary interest in it and hated to give it up when circumstances required that they should. Especially was this attitude common among workmen whose families had grown up and moved away. They no longer had need for large dwellings, and the company was anxious to have them make room for those who did; but the head of a family usually liked to have a home large enough to accommodate the families of his visiting children and so stoutly resisted the company's efforts to relocate him.

Yet, despite the many personnel problems inherent in the situation, the housing committee seems to have handled matters with tact and consideration, for the workers were remarkably loyal to the company and, in contrast to the attitude generally thought of as typical under paternalistic régimes, they were surprisingly appreciative of what the company was doing for them. They did not hesitate to criticize the company's policies among themselves but to outsiders they presented a united supporting front.

The crowning achievements in Swift's effort to promote the community life of Whitinsville were the construction of a gymnasium and the laying out of a golf course. In earlier years George Marston Whitin had expressed the thought that what the community most needed was a recreational center. The high school's auditorium was nothing more than a drill hall and was completely inadequate for organized sports. Had Marston remained in good health, he would doubtless have converted his idea into reality. As it was, his daughters, shortly after his death, decided to erect such a community center in his honor. The project called for a single building housing a gymnasium, a bowling alley (later dispensed with), various game rooms, and a swimming pool. Land for the building was parceled off from the grounds of the John C. Whitin estate, directly across the road from the shop, and was donated by John C.'s three surviving grandchildren — Mrs. George Marston Whitin, Chester W. Lasell, and J. M. Lasell. The gymnasium proper was financed by Marston Whitin's four daughters, Mrs. Keeler, Mrs. Mason, Mrs. Swift, and Mrs. Crane. Money for the swimming pool was contributed by the company. Construction work on the project was turned over in its entirety to one of New England's best-known contracting firms, the Aberthaw Construction Company; so far as I know, it was the only instance in the company's history when a major construction job was carried on completely outside the framework of the company's organization. In all, the cost of the project[33] amounted to something over $140,000.*

* As had been done in the case of several other family-sponsored projects, an association (the Whitinsville Community Association) was formed to conduct the ad-

Soon after completion of the townspeople's gymnasium, the company began construction work (1924–25) on a nine-hole golf course that was meant principally, though not exclusively, for its executives. Swift had long been aware of the need for a center where the company's officials could meet socially. Being an ardent golfer, he was also aware of the distance one had to travel from Whitinsville to find a course with good fairways and greens. Unfortunately, however, Whitinsville's rough topography almost precluded any thought of a local course. The only suitable site lay south of the river on property owned by the Whitinsville Cotton Mills. Swift once approached Arthur F. Whitin, the mill's lone surviving owner, with an offer to buy the property, but Arthur, being an ardent Congregationalist, refused to do anything that might so easily be interpreted as collaborating with the devil to keep men from church on Sunday morning.

In 1923, however, the Whitinsville Cotton Mills, along with so many other small New England mills, was forced to close its doors because of the generally depressed condition of the cotton textile industry. Desiring to liquidate his property, Arthur Whitin offered the mill building to Swift as a warehouse for the machine works. With the mill went the mill's employee houses plus the property south of the river. No doubt Swift would have bought the building even had the question of the property not been involved, but probably the inclusion of that strip of land did much to sweeten the deal, for it at last gave Swift the opportunity he had been seeking to construct a golf course for the community.[34] A club house, planned by outside architects, but erected by company maintenance men, was designed to provide not only locker and shower facilities, but a place for dances and card parties and a dining room for executives.*

---

ministrative affairs of the recreation center. To make the organization at least in part self-supporting, nominal membership dues were charged. Direct management of the Association was left in the hands of a board elected by dues-paying members; nevertheless, the Association's bylaws were so contrived that a self-perpetuating board of family trustees could exercise veto power if it felt the need to do so.

* Again a separate association was set up to acquire ownership of the new property. The association in turn leased the club house and golf course back to the company for a fee that, when added to membership dues, was expected to enable the club to cover its operating costs. Whenever it did not, the amount of the leasing fee was simply increased.

By such means did Swift enhance the values of living in a community that was somewhat removed from any metropolitan center. As a result of his efforts Whitinsvillagers took most of their entertainment locally. Even the families of top executives left the village only infrequently to shop in Worcester or to see a play in Providence or to attend the Boston Symphony. Harvard football games, especially the end-of-the-season contest with Yale, attracted many villagers to Boston in the fall, although usually they showed greater enthusiasm for the Red Sox whenever that club played an especially good season of baseball. But except for such occasional outside diversions, Whitinsville's social life centered in the village. Departmental parties, birthday and engagement celebrations, and a plethora of clubs kept the people of the community always occupied with banquets and committee work.

Typically at such social functions, shop affairs were the dominant topic of conversation. For executives the intimate social life of the village made possible the accomplishment of an extraordinary amount of after-hours business, but for the women it was a battlefield of rivalry. No tea, no bridge game, no supper, no dance was, in the minds of the women, without importance to their husbands' careers. Always jockeying for position, always hoping for the promotion that so seldom came, the wives of employees engaged in a constant, spirited, social struggle that kept the village constantly alive with activity.

The contest was saved from bitterness principally because the contestants had no fear of losing. The company took pains to make every man confident that his job was secure. If, in extremity, an employee had to be replaced by a younger, more aggressive man, another job was created for him; he was not fired. More commonly a man was left at his post for life, a younger man simply being made his assistant. When Albert H. Whipple died in 1924, he had been with the company for fifty-three years, of which his last twenty-seven had been spent as superintendent. William O. Aldrich, who had become Whipple's assistant in 1907, served under the older man for seventeen years and was not finally promoted to the superintendency until after Whipple's death.

The company had no general retirement plan,* preferring to handle each case on its merits. If a man chose to retire and if he had no other place to live, he was often given a room at the Blue Eagle Inn, there to eat and sleep and reminisce. But most men preferred to continue working, in which case they were given jobs commensurate with their strength.[35]

This problem of guaranteed security is one of the major challenges confronting American business today. An attempt to solve the retirement aspects of the problem is currently being made by many companies through foresighted pension schemes. But no company — at least, none whose labor costs are as substantial a portion of its total costs as Whitin's are — can be financially foresighted enough to tide its workers over long downward dips in the demand for its products. Many seasonal industries have gone far in ironing out their labor fluctuations, but as yet no one has adequately resolved the dilemma that faces a company when its market falls off in a long depression. Spreading the work helps for a while, but very soon unit costs begin to increase — and at the very time when it is most important to keep them low. Layoffs eventually become inevitable, causing distress to the workers and disruption to the company's trained labor force. It has been generally assumed that the industries most likely to succeed in an effort to achieve employment stability are those in the consumers'-goods field that make a product for which there is a fairly steady demand. Manufacturers of producers' goods, it has been assumed, are the ones least likely to find an easy solution to the problem of guaranteed employment.[36]

Yet, notwithstanding the difficulties inherent in its position as a manufacturer of producers' goods, the Whitin Machine Works endeavored to maintain employment in its village throughout the de-

* On 1 September 1943 the company put into effect a Pension Trust Plan with the Second National Bank of Boston as the repository of its pension funds. The stated purpose of the pension was to supplement Social Security benefits for those earning over $3,000, the maximum figure recognized by the Social Security Act. An elaborate formula (past service in excess of 5 years multiplied by .0075, multiplied by monthly salary in excess of the Social Security maximum of $250, plus number of years left till retirement at 65, multiplied by .01, multiplied by monthly salary in excess of $250) gave employees a monthly pension income that amounted to about a fifth of their current earned income. All payments toward the pension fund were made by the company.

pression. During its entire history the company had followed the basic depression policy that John C. Whitin had established whereby the heads of machine-shop families living in Whitinsville would be certain of employment. In the early 1920's the Whitin company had been able to cut back its pay lists gradually by not replacing workmen as they left its employ, until by 1926 it had stabilized its crew at about two thousand men. From 1926 until 1930 its work force undulated gently and regularly between 1,800 and 2,000 employees, the high being in winter months and the low in summertime. Not that the company's business had any normal seasonal pattern; employees just wanted to take time off in the summer, and with business slack, the company was glad enough to have them do so.

In 1930, however, a curtailment of operations became unavoidable. In an effort to spread employment, the company cut its workday to seven hours and its workweek to three days. On two occasions it also cut wages. But to reduce the burden of its shorter hours and smaller wages as much as possible, it also reduced its rentals on company houses by 25 per cent.[37] Rentals were already low — $14 a month for an eight-room house with all modern conveniences, and $8.50 a month for a five-room house; after the reductions such rentals were only $10.50 and $6.38 respectively. Swift estimated that villagers could rent in Whitinsville for about half the going rate in the surrounding rural countryside.[38] The company also gave its employees the privilege of paying whatever amount toward their rent they felt they could afford, the understanding being that, when better times returned, back rent would be deducted from the payroll in small installments. If workers wished to heat their homes with wood, the company permitted them free access to its reservoir preserves where they could chop all the wood they needed.

There are people in Whitinsville today who will tell you that the villagers never knew what the depression was really like. In a sense they are right; at least, no one in Whitinsville experienced the economic distress that was common in the rest of the Blackstone Valley area. And of course it is to the company's advantage that the villagers now *remember* themselves to have been well off, whatever the real situation may have been.

But in actual fact the economic contraction in Whitinsville during the years 1930–33 was severe. The worst of the depression came in the summer of 1932. In May and June the company had so little work that it was forced to lay off all men who had some other means of subsistence or who had no dependents. Still, it allowed no head of a family to miss a week's pay, even when there was not enough work to keep him busy. The bottom of the cycle occurred in July — not only for Whitin but for the rest of the textile machinery industry and for the cotton mill industry as well.[39] For the first time since 1898 Whitin's employment fell below 1,100. For a period of about three months it looked as though the plant might have to close down altogether. But by October, optimism had returned and men were being called back to work. By the following March — the month popularly regarded as the nadir of the depression — Whitin's recovery had become so rapid that its order books were fuller than they had been at any time in the preceding two years.

The National Recovery Administration's code for the cotton textile industry (the first of the codes to be put into operation, with approval granted 9 July 1933) further stimulated business activity. At first the machinery builders were concerned over what effect the code would have on machinery orders, since one of the code's clauses virtually forbade mills from buying new machines for any purpose other than the replacement of worn-out or obsolete equipment.[40] However, the general recovery in the cotton mill industry's demand for machinery was strong enough to offset the disadvantages of any single code provision, and the limiting clause was soon forgotten.

In October, 1933, the textile-machinery builders secured approval of a code for their own industry. The industry had had no active organization since the tariff and price-agreement days in the early 1900's, and even in those days the organization had been limited to the principal builders of preparatory and weaving machinery. In 1933, however, at the government's behest, the industry established in Boston the National Association of Textile Machinery Manufacturers and invited all manufacturers of finishing equipment and general machinery supplies — more than three hundred in number — to join. Still, as in former days, control of the Association remained in the hands of the large manufacturers. Whitin, Saco-Lowell, Draper, and Crompton & Knowles employed more than half the workers in the entire textile machinery industry, even including all the finishing equipment and machinery supply firms; hence (since the Association's dues were based on numbers of employees) these four concerns contributed the bulk of the Association's financial support and direction.[41] Swift, who was basically opposed to government interference in business and who had not signed the President's Blue Eagle agreement, was happy enough to see the presidency of the new association go to the politically more liberal Edwards of Saco-Lowell. Swift did, however, accept the chairmanship of the Cotton Preparatory & Yarn Division of the Association and later, some time after the NRA had been declared unconstitutional,* became the Association's president.[42]

The textile-machinery code did little toward solving the industry's basic problems. Companies in the industry were unaccustomed to dealing together and were uncertain of each other's good faith. Consequently the code's provisions were loosely drawn and with obvious reluctance. Such stipulations as the limiting of the workweek to forty hours were almost without meaning; except for brief intervals, the Whitin Machine Works had been working less than forty hours a week for nearly three years. The real job facing the industry — the development of new cost-saving products and the aggressive sale of such machines to reluctant customers — was incapable of solution by joint action. That job had to be left to the initiative of each individual concern.

Whitin, however, was solving its particular problems in noteworthy fashion. In fact, the new machines which it was developing were chiefly responsible for its ability to hold together its work force in the depths of the depression. In 1932, 40 per cent[43] of the firm's income from machinery sales came from types of equipment it had not built in pre-depression years. The exigencies of the times had forced the company to abandon its century-old practice of turning out machinery primarily for cotton mills and had introduced the company to a whole new field of textile fibers. It was to be perhaps the most far-reaching policy change in the company's entire history, a decision whose final results are yet to be known.

* Immediately after the Supreme Court decision on the Schechter case (27 May 1935), the textile-machinery code authority (which had been under the executive direction of one W. S. Pepperell) was disbanded, but the textile-machinery manufacturers' association continued in existence and is still active, though its membership now includes only about sixty-five firms.

CHAPTER XVII

NEW PRODUCT DEVELOPMENTS, 1927–1940

For Whitin the Great Textile Depression was at once a calamity and a blessing. It has often been observed that depressions goad business concerns to their best efforts. The depression of the 1920's certainly goaded Whitin. Except in the early development of the picker and in the later adaptation of the comber, the Whitin Machine Works had never been an industry leader in product design. Its forte had been reliability, not innovation. Beginning in 1927, however, Whitin embarked on an extensive program of experimentation. For the first time in its history the company was to concentrate its main efforts on development and research.

Before 1927 there had been a persistent hope that the textile industry's depression would soon be over and that the good old days would shortly return. Indeed, part of Saco-Lowell's willingness to continue its program of expansion even after the passing of the postwar boom was attributable to the broad general optimism that underlay the immediate distress of a declining market. When at last it became obvious that only drastic measures would remedy a situation that was continuing to grow worse with each succeeding year, Saco-Lowell submitted to a reorganization, while Whitin, being better financed, began looking for new products to occupy its idle capacity. Whitin was especially sensitive to the need for stabilizing its production, for it had a village to support and a group of local employees to consider. Saco-Lowell, on the other hand, could and did reduce its operations by closing whole plants and by laying off complete segments of its labor force.

Whitin's reservoir of idle funds proved at this point to be of vital importance, for it gave the company the confidence needed for venturing into new realms where profits were not likely to be immediately forthcoming. For the next several years the company spent much of its energy and financial strength on the development of new products — always judiciously and nearly always effectively. For the first time in its history, it ventured beyond narrow specialization in cotton-textile machinery and became a producer of preparatory equipment covering a wide range of uses. Almost every conceivable type of fiber was considered — wool, worsted, silk, rayon, asbestos, ramie, even pig's bristles and twisted paper.[1] The company followed no set policy in its developmental work, but generally concentrated its efforts either on machines that were like the cotton machines it was accustomed to making or on processes that it could adapt to the cotton system of manufacture.[2] For instance, when the decision was made to add wool machinery to the line, the company avoided making such equipment as washers and driers, with which it had had no previous experience, and concentrated instead on carding machinery, which was very much like the cotton-waste equipment it had been making. And when Whitin decided to make a wool spinning frame, it did not try to perfect the wool spinning mule which it had never made, but instead redesigned the traditional cotton ring spinning process so that the frame could be used on wool fibers. As a result most of Whitin's developmental work was adaptive, not inventive. The company succeeded in putting on the market a number of vastly improved machines, but nothing startlingly new was added to the technique of textile manufacturing.

Though it may seem paradoxical, the principal problems experienced by the company in the expansion of its product line occurred not in the experimental room, nor yet in the plant, but in the field. Reaching a new market, contacting new mill men, and above all selling new machines absorbed the main attention of Swift and his lieutenants from 1927 until the outbreak of World War II. The company made various attempts to speed up the marketing of new products by short-cutting normal channels, but with indifferent success. On two occasions it bought firms that were already producing non-cotton machinery, in order to obtain their sales contacts. And, on a third occasion, Whitin established a joint sales agency with another producer. But in general the best way to sell its new products was through its own salesforce, augmented by a few men who were employed specifically for their experience in selling particular types of machines.

It is perhaps significant that the company's main developmental period was concentrated in the years 1927–32. For Whitin at least, too much depression was apparently as ineffective a goad to risk-taking as too little depression had been in the years 1923–26. For, as the company felt the constricting effects of the national depression on sales in 1932–33, it curtailed all expenses that were not absolutely essential to continued operations. Then, when better times returned, it found itself fully occupied with perfecting the new machines it had developed and so did not attempt any further expansion of its line. After 1932 the company's experimental room concentrated on redesigning parts for the machines already in production and running tests to show what sort of work could be accomplished on Whitin products.

This chapter deals only with the advances made by the Whitin company in the design of non-cotton machinery; consequently it passes over one of the century's most important innovations in cotton-machinery technology — the development of long-draft spinning and roving. So that it will not be altogether disregarded, the long-draft story has been set forth in Appendix 15. With it has been included a recital of the basic facts involved in the Reynolds patent suit, a suit which grew directly out of Whitin's developmental work on long-drafting and which became one of the important legal controversies in Whitin's history.

I. WOOL CARDS AND SPINNING FRAMES

Whitin's first important departure from its cotton line was in the field of wool machinery. The story of how the company got into that field is a devious tale beginning in the early years of the twentieth century.[3] The principal character in the story was a man from Hampden, Massachusetts, named Durrell O. Pease, an inventor-promoter who was everything an inventor-promoter should be — versatile, erratic, independent, energetic, and excitable, an abominable penman as is shown by his letters, and an equally poor man of business as is shown by his career. Yet Pease deserves to rank among the great in the history of American wool manufacture, for it was his idea that ultimately resulted in the abandonment of the old-fashioned mule and the adoption of the more proficient ring method of spinning wool. For a half-century before Pease's time virtually all woolen yarn, both abroad and in this country, had been spun by mule, just as before the 1880's all cotton filling had been mule-spun. The idea of ring spinning had often been proposed for use with wool, but never before had its adherents achieved practical success. Indeed, even Pease's frame did not completely measure up to the performance of the slow but precise mule; yet it was the immediate forerunner of a wool frame that did. The frame that was eventually successful was a Whitin development based on the original Pease idea.

About 1929 a catalogue published by the firm of Johnson & Bassett, Inc., of Worcester, Massachusetts, manufacturers of wool mules (and hence opponents of spinning by the ring method), set forth a brief but substantially accurate account of Pease's misadventures in his attempt to market his ring spinning idea to the machine-builders of America. The account reads in part as follows:

The [wool ring spinning] machine was first conceived by the late D. O. Pease in the year 1888. He worked on the machine for several years and finally in the year 1895 he had a finished machine ready to demonstrate in Hampden, Massachusetts (near Springfield) where he lived. The machine was first offered to us [i.e., to Johnson & Bassett] in 1895 (nearly thirty-five years ago). We went up and saw it and spent several weeks up there examining the machine from all angles. We finally turned it down on the ground that it did not spin, but merely twisted. From that time on the machine has had a varied and checkered career.

M. A. Furbush & Son Machine Company, of Philadelphia, Pa., at that time large builders of carding machinery [and now a part of Proctor & Schwartz, Inc.] took over the manufacture of the Pease frame and spent some considerable time and money on the machine, but finally turned it down in disgust, and turned it back to Mr. Pease. Mr. Pease then took the machine to the Woonsocket Machine & Press Company, Woonsocket, R. I., and they spent more time and more money on it, but they too gave up the machine in despair and turned it back to Pease. Mr. Pease then took it to Platt Bros. & Co., Ltd., Oldham, England,* who

---

* This statement seems to have been not strictly true. Apparently Pease succeeded in interesting the British Wool Research Association in his idea, and was able to get that organization to place a sizable order for his frames with the Platt concern. It was the BWRA that took out the British patents on Pease's frame. A later statement that Platt Brothers turned the machine back to Pease in 1910 seems also to be

are the largest builders of textile machinery in the world. They spent a great deal of money on it. Mr. Pease went over and stayed with them for four years [1906–10]. They built a large number of these machines, some 200 to 300, but at the end of four years they turned the machine back to Mr. Pease. He brought it back to this country and formed another connection [with the Whitin Machine Works] for the manufacture of this machine. More money was spent on it and a very handsome looking machine turned out, but the principle remains the same. It never did spin, it does not spin now, and it never will spin.*

This quoted account omits the devious way in which Whitin came to adopt the Pease idea. It must be assumed that Marston Whitin was cool to the suggestion that his company manufacture wool spinning machinery, for he was undoubtedly among those whom Pease had been unable to interest in his frame in the years before 1906. What eventually aroused Whitin's interest in Pease's frame was not its wool-working possibilities but the fact that the British had used the Pease frame in processing cotton hard waste.† At that time the

---

in error; Pease simply returned to this country and took out American patents on his invention, while Platt Brothers continued producing his frame in England.

* In all fairness to John & Bassett it should be admitted that the Pease frame, because it did very little drafting, was in fact more a twister than a spinning frame. What made possible the Pease frame's low drafting ratio was the high proficiency of the tape condenser developed by European machine-builders in the early years of the twentieth century. (In the traditional method of wool manufacture, there is no roving operation; the tape condenser performs a similar function.) Indeed, had it not been for the perfection of the tape condenser, Pease's frame would never have been a success.

When Pease returned from Europe he brought with him the ideas about tape condensing that he had learned in England. So superior were the new condensers to those being used in America at that time that they were almost guaranteed a ready market. The Whitin company decided to take advantage of the situation and so became the first company in America to make wool tape condensers, all previous tape condensers having been made abroad. Thus, it is not wholly correct to say that Whitin remained a cotton-machinery specialist until 1927; the company added several non-cotton machines to its line before that date, but none was of very great importance in relation to its cotton business.

† Hard waste is the twisted by-product of the regular cotton-manufacturing process and is used in the production of mop yarns, insulating materials, and such other items as inexpensive draperies and low-grade blankets. Before it can be reprocessed the twist in it must be eliminated; hence the machinery required to do the work must be heavy and harsh in its treatment of the fibers — more like wool machinery than like cotton. (Soft waste is the by-product of the earlier cotton-manufacturing processes before twist has been applied; usually soft waste is either fed back into the manufacturing cycle or else is reprocessed on worsted-type machines.)

British were the world's leading producers of cotton hard-waste machinery; no United States manufacturer had ever been able to compete with them even for the American market. Whitin was understandably anxious to break the British monopoly in hard-waste machinery and so was willing to give Pease's frame a trial. Therefore, in February, 1909, he ordered a sample Pease hard-waste frame from the British firm of Platt Brothers & Company.[4]

To prevent others from knowing his intentions, Whitin sent Pease (who was still in England) money for the frame in advance and instructed him to buy the machine from Platt Brothers on his own account and to ship it to Boston in care of himself. Whitin further informed Pease that if the frame proved satisfactory, the Whitin Machine Works would be willing to pay for the exclusive rights to build it for hard-waste mills in America at a royalty not to exceed one dollar per spindle. The following summer he sent young Swift to England to view the Pease hard-waste machine in operation and to discuss its merits with mill men who had used it.[5] Upon Swift's favorable report, Whitin decided to offer Pease a job with the company as a salesman, erector, and general consultant on cotton hard-waste equipment.

Thus began several years of collaboration between Pease and the Whitin firm, but the object of that collaboration was principally cotton-waste machinery, not wool. For a time Whitin's hard-waste line was very successful. The outbreak of World War I cut off the cotton-waste mills of America from their British suppliers and forced them to turn Whitin's way for help. With Pease's assistance, the Whitin company added to its cotton-waste line a hard-waste card and eventually became the largest builder of cotton-waste equipment in America.[6]

In the meantime the Pease wool frame, while not forgotten, was pushed well into the background. As a Whitin salesman, Pease continued trying to interest mills in his invention* and from time to time succeeded in obtaining small requests for wool frames which Whitin built on special order. But at no time before 1927 did

---

* Pease was interested in selling his frames for wool purposes not because of any sales commission but because of the royalty he would get. Whitin salesmen were always (and still are) paid on a salary basis because so much of their time is necessarily spent on non-selling missionary work.

the company's production of wool equipment exceed 2 per cent of its total machinery output.[7] Discouraged by the continuing poor reception accorded his wool ring frame, Pease eventually turned his attention to new fields. Oddly enough, in so doing he encountered a man who was to do more to make his frame a success than he himself had been able to do in a lifetime of promotional effort.

Backed financially by E. Kent Swift and A. F. Jealous, a junior executive in the American Woolen Company, Pease went to Worcester in 1921 to establish the D. O. Pease Manufacturing Company. The new firm was set up to manufacture fabrics made of asbestos yarn with a core of cotton to give it strength and to reduce its cost. By 1923 Pease was already producing asbestos materials in a plant he had built in Palmer, Massachusetts (between Worcester and Springfield), though he had still not found a manager for his enterprise. A chance trip to Cleveland to remedy certain troublesome defects in some Whitin-made Pease frames operating in the Cleveland Worsted Mills solved his problem by bringing him into contact with J. Hugh Bolton, a junior executive in the mills and a son of one of the senior officials. Pease so beguiled Bolton with tales of his asbestos company's prospects that he talked Bolton into investing money in the enterprise and persuaded him to give up his job in Cleveland in favor of an executive post at Palmer.

Bolton had not been in Palmer long, however, when he became aware of the hopeless situation he had stepped into. Pease's production plans had been based on an estimated market potential for his products that was little short of fanciful. Furthermore, his working capital had become so depleted that his company had no other choice than to raise additional funds or close its doors. After conferring with the stockholders, who felt that putting in more capital would be throwing good money after bad, Bolton decided to liquidate the company. Meanwhile, he and the other stockholders had found it necessary to oust Pease from the firm, for the founder of the concern adamantly refused to go along with what he considered a conspiracy among the stockholders to wreck his business.*

---

* Pease retired to his farm in Hampden, where he lived out his few closing years on the proceeds of his license royalties. On his death the executors of his estate negotiated a lump-sum settlement covering the remaining years of the Whitin-Pease contract.

The skill with which Bolton negotiated the Pease company's liquidation[8] so impressed Swift that, in October, 1925, he offered the young man, who had sacrificed his contacts with the wool and worsted trade and had lost most of his savings in the Palmer fiasco, a position in the Whitin Machine Works' cotton-waste department. When R. T. Comer, the head of that department, suddenly died about nine months later, Bolton was promoted to take his place.

Being a wool man, Bolton quickly swung the department's center of gravity from cotton-waste to wool products. In so doing he had the full support of Swift, who at just that time was beginning to think of ways to increase the shop's production and who was of the opinion that the wool machinery industry offered sales opportunities that had never been exploited.

The wool machinery industry, it should be noted, was much smaller than its cotton-machinery counterpart, the demand for wool machinery in America being only about one-eighth the demand for cotton-mill equipment.[9] In certain respects wool machinery differed radically from cotton machinery, for wool, being an animal not a vegetable fiber, needed washing and chemical treatment instead of simply the mechanical opening and cleaning treatment given cotton fibers. Nevertheless, three-quarters of the expense of equipping wool mills with machinery went towards the purchase of machines that were not very different from standard cotton-waste equipment: i.e., cards, spinning frames, and looms.*

As the first machine needing improvement and promotion, Bolton picked the wool card. Using as his starting point the cotton-waste card which the Whitin company had developed in World War I, he first borrowed and perfected certain features of the wool card made by the country's leading producer of wool-mill machinery, the Davis & Furber Machine Company.[10] Then, learning that another

---

* Wool cards were made principally by the Davis & Furber Machine Company, of North Andover, Massachusetts, although a few cards were produced by Proctor & Schwartz, Inc., of Philadelphia, and by a fairly new firm in Worcester named the Cashiko Machine Company. Spinning frames (i.e., mules) were produced by Davis & Furber and by Johnson & Bassett, Inc., of Worcester. Looms for wool were made almost exclusively by the Crompton & Knowles Loom Works, of Worcester. Since Whitin had abandoned its loom line, it made no attempt to enter competition in that field.

wool-card manufacturer, the Cashiko Machine Company,* was having financial difficulties, he scouted the possibilities of Whitin's acquiring its ownership. As a result, on 21 December 1927 the Whitin company bought Cashiko outright, paying $150,000 for its entire capital stock, and hiring two of its owners, Kovar and Shimek, as wool-card salesmen.[11]

Getting a company that was already in the wool machinery business was worth the expense, for more difficult even than the development of a competitively successful machine was the establishment of contact with an almost totally new market. Unlike the country's cotton mills, its wool mills were still located predominantly in New England — not merely New England, but northern New England (Maine, New Hampshire, and Massachusetts) — although North Carolina and Georgia were beginning to develop as wool-manufacturing centers. Wool mills were typically small and venerable enterprises and were habituated, as a result of long personal contact, to dealing with specific wool-machinery firms. For a cotton-machinery firm to have succeeded in penetrating the wool-mill industry without the assistance of men trained in the wool-machinery business would have been exceedingly difficult. The two groups literally talked different languages. Similar processes were not uncommonly called one name by cotton men and another by men in the wool business. Missionary work was bound to be an important part of Whitin's developmental program, and Cashiko's contacts were consequently as valuable as its card.[12]

When Whitin began pushing its wool-card sales with earnestness in 1928, it received assistance from two unexpected sources. First of all, 1928 was a year of unusual prosperity in the wool industry; hence sales were easily made. Secondly, many wool mill men, without abandoning their loyalty to their regular wool-machinery sup-

---

* The title *Cashiko* (pronounced CASHiko) was derived from the names of the three partner-owners, Alexander *Ca*vedon, treasurer, Joseph *Shi*mek, assistant treasurer and manager, and John H. *Ko*var, president. Shimek and Kovar had come to America in 1912 to erect tape condensers for the Austrian firm of G. Josephys Erben, one of the Continent's largest producers of wool carding and spinning machinery. Seeing the opportunity of selling cards and tape condensers in America, the two men had enlisted the financial help of Cavedon and had started a small shop of their own in Worcester in 1918. During their busiest years (1922–24) they had employed about 160 workers.

pliers, were willing to encourage a strong new producer in the field, for they felt that greater competition in the wool-machinery business would yield better machinery at lower prices. Because of those two factors, the new Whitin card almost outdid the company's fondest hopes in sales. Billings for 1928 amounted to $482,179. Only the company's cotton spinning frames and cotton cards brought it larger receipts.* Thereafter the Davis & Furber company had to share the wool-card market about equally with its new competitor.

It seems probable that the wool card's immediate acceptance did more than anything else to persuade the Whitin company that there was a future in non-cotton machinery lines. Whitin suddenly discovered how little competition there was in the wool-machinery business and by what easy means the wool market could be invaded. Whitin technicians also found that non-cotton manufacturing techniques had progressed less far than cotton techniques and that, by the simple method of adopting cotton know-how to non-cotton lines, substantial improvements could be made. Finally, and more important psychologically than the other two reasons combined, Whitin's executives were impressed by the fact that the cyclical behavior of different fibers did not necessarily coincide. The year 1928, so prosperous for wool mills, was the worst year the cotton industry had experienced in a decade and a half. To the executives of the Whitin Machine Works it seemed possible that diversification of product line might prove a cure for the company's depression ills.

Therefore, gratified by the success of the wool card, Swift and Bolton turned their attention back to the still not wholly satisfactory Pease wool spinning frame. They soon learned, however, that selling wool men anything so radical as a ring frame was far more difficult than selling them a mere improvement on the standard card. Especially was it difficult because, although by 1928 the wool frame was producing yarn as uniform and strong as that made by mules, it was not producing it at an appreciably lower cost. Wool yarn was so bulky that it quickly filled the small 2½-inch or 3-inch space inside the spinning ring, forcing frequent, and hence expensive, bobbin changes. Using larger rings, so that larger bobbin packages could

---

* Some idea of the instantaneous success of the Whitin wool card may be gained from the fact that the first year's record sales were not surpassed until 1941.

be spun, had always been deemed impractical since, in any event, loom shuttles were incapable of taking packages of filling yarn larger than 1⅝ inches in diameter.

There was no such natural restriction on the size of warp yarn packages, however; in fact, the larger the warp package, the less handling was required in transferring the yarn from bobbin to beam. If handling costs could be sufficiently reduced, Bolton argued, wool mills could afford to buy special frames for spinning warp yarns, thus reserving their mules for filling production only. Therefore, about 1929, the Whitin wool department began work on increasing ring sizes on frames that were intended specifically for warp yarn production.

At that time no one knew how large a ring size was feasible. As ring diameters grew larger, the ballooning strain on yarn fibers necessarily increased until at some point breakage was bound to occur. For a while the problem of keeping a large ring from burning up its traveler at high speeds stood in the way of progress, until the self-lubricating vertical ring was developed.

From the first, Bolton was fearful of putting on the market a machine that was too radical or one that had not been sufficiently tested under mill conditions. Therefore he installed in the American Woolen Company's Assabet Mills, in Maynard, Massachusetts,* a ring frame on which he tried out ring sizes up to five inches in diameter. After nearly two years of experimentation he felt that the kinks had been satisfactorily worked out of the frame and that it was ready for the trade.

Because of the severe depression existing in 1931, the new frame did not immediately show its strength in sales. But its potential threat to the mule-building industry was soon recognized by the Davis & Furber company, which quickly assigned a former Whitin employee named Henry A. Owen to the task of developing a similar ring frame to supplement the regular Davis & Furber line of wool

---

* Starting in Assabet was hitting at the heart of Davis & Furber's business, for Assabet was the largest of the American Woolen Company's mills, and American Woolen had always been a staunch Davis & Furber customer. Assisting Bolton in his experiments at Assabet were Harry Moss, later Bolton's successor as head of Whitin's wool department, and William Ferguson, an erector who spent almost his full time at Assabet watching the performance of the experimental frame.

mules. When better times returned, however, Whitin's long experience with ring spinning stood the company in good stead, and from the beginning Whitin led Davis & Furber in changing the country's standard method of wool warp yarn production from the mule to the ring spinning process.

Meanwhile some small progress was also being made in converting the production of wool *filling* yarn to the ring principle. It was discovered that, in some cases, the savings in labor made possible by large-package ring spinning were sufficient to warrant rewinding the yarn from a large-package bobbin back on a shuttle-size package by means of the Universal Winding Company's non-automatic No. 90 winder. Still, the mule continued to be generally purchased for filling yarn purposes until just before the outbreak of World War II, when the Whitin company became the exclusive American agent for the Swiss automatic Schweiter winder.[13] So rapidly and inexpensively did the Swiss machine perform the rewinding operation that it made large-package ring spinning much more economical than the old mule system of spinning and almost put an end to further wool mule sales in this country.*

After 1933 the Whitin company made no important alterations in its wool spinning equipment.[14] Yet it sold approximately three times as many wool spinning machines as its only competitor, the once dominant Davis & Furber Machine Company. Thus, in the space of a few years Whitin had changed, so far as its interests in wool machinery were concerned, from being merely a job-order shop, to being the largest builder of wool preparatory equipment in the country.† In part that achievement was traceable to its having been the first company ever to make practical the ring spinning of wool. It is ironical that the Whitin Machine Works, whose name has always been associated with cotton machinery, should have made what is probably its one unchallengeable claim to a "first," not in the cotton but in the wool field.

---

* Wool ring spinning has far to go before it completely replaces mule spinning, however. In March, 1948, the Whitin company estimated that there were still 1,110,000 wool mule spindles in place, as against 450,000 of the ring type.

† Whitin's sales of wool machinery are still limited principally to cards and ring frames. It builds a few wool twisters, but the demand for twisted wool is so limited (in contrast to the demand for twisted worsteds, which is extensive) that its sale of such machines is negligible.

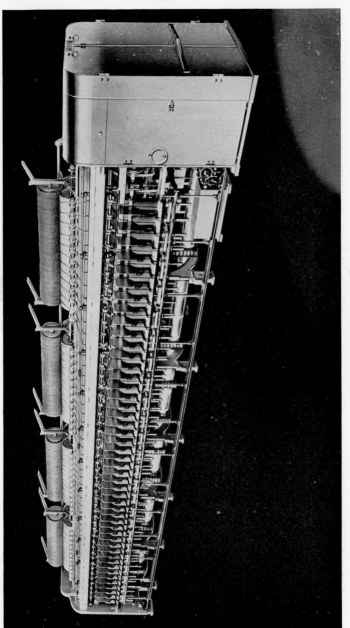

Wool Ring Spinning Frame

B-W Worsted Ring Spinning Frame

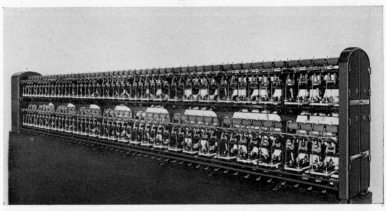

Silk and Rayon Upstroke Twister

2. FILAMENT RAYON SPINNING FRAMES AND TWISTERS

The Whitin company's striking and rather easy success in the wool machinery business opened its eyes to profit possibilities in other fields. As early as 1925 Swift had given some thought to making machinery for the processing of what was then known as "artificial silk," but he had not yet made a definite move in that direction when, in 1929, the Industrial Rayon Corporation, of Cleveland, approached the Whitin company with a request for a special order of rayon twisters.[15] In former years Whitin might have turned down such a request on the grounds that it was not prepared to enter a new and unfamiliar business, but with its successful experience in wool behind it and with the need to keep its village people employed by whatever means were at hand, the company agreed to accept the order and to follow Industrial Rayon's specifications.

The full import of that order can be appreciated only if one knows the general state of the rayon machinery industry in the late 1920's. The manufacture of rayon on a commercial basis began in the early 1890's when a Frenchman, Count Hilaire de Chardonnet, succeeded in deriving silk from mulberry leaves by artificial means. Shortly thereafter the viscose process, still one of the two basic methods of obtaining rayon, was discovered in France as a by-product of what was then a widespread search for a suitable electric light filament. Following World War I, the second of the two basic types, acetate rayon, was discovered by the British as a by-product of their experiments in photographic film solutions and airplane wing coatings.

During the early years of rayon's development, and indeed until very recently, Europeans led the world in rayon technology. So far advanced over Americans were they, that most of today's large producers of rayon in the United States owe their start to foreign capital and ability.[16] It was consequently natural for the rayon machinery industry at first to center abroad. The initial producer of rayon in this country, The American Viscose Company (incorporated in Pennsylvania in 1910) was a British-owned concern and is believed to have been equipped in large part by machinery imported from England.[17]

During its initial years the rayon industry was so secretive about its chemical processes that it was inevitably secretive about everything else, including its machinery. American rayon producers, if they did not buy their machines from affiliated concerns abroad, either built their own equipment or else farmed out orders for parts and assembled them into machines inside their own plants. They especially shunned any contact with established textile machinery companies for fear that information about their secret machinery designs would leak out to other customers of such concerns.

Producers of rayon were able to avoid relying on machinery builders principally because their early demands for machinery were small. The industry did not really begin to mushroom until after 1920, when the last of the basic patents held by American Viscose expired. Moreover, the production of rayon, by its very nature, requires precious little machinery. Rayon technology completely eliminates the first four basic steps in the manufacture of cotton (opening, carding, drawing, and roving) by producing directly from a chemical solution a number of filaments which are immediately spun into yarn. After the spinning operation, which may be called step one, the only machinery operations left to be performed in the plant of a rayon producer are (2), the imparting of a slight additional twist to bind the spun filaments together and (3), the winding of twisted filaments on packages suitable for shipping.* Since

---

* Rayon producers usually ship their goods directly to concerns called "throwsters." These concerns are generally small outfits that are paid on a commission basis by weaving and knitting mills to put added twist into the slightly twisted rayon yarns turned out by the large bulk rayon producers. Many throwsters were formerly silk concerns which had switched to rayon twisting because the silk industry had begun to decline. Moreover, the machinery used by throwsters had been built by companies that had once been silk-machinery manufacturers — the Atwood Machine Company, of Stonington, Connecticut (now owned by the Universal Winding Company), the Fletcher Works, Inc., of Philadelphia, and the U. S. Textile Machine Company, of Scranton, Pennsylvania.

In the throwster-machinery business, sales were made strictly on a price basis, a type of competition the Whitin company had never cared to engage in. However, Whitin did become involved, almost inadvertently, in the throwster-machinery business for a while (1938–41) by obtaining control of the U. S. Textile Machine Company. For years this Scranton concern had been a customer of Whitin, for it had bought many of its twister spindles from the Whitin company. In 1938, however, the business outlook seemed so bleak that U. S. Textile Machine's owner-managers approached Whitin with an offer to sell their controlling interest. After reviewing the situation, the executives at Whitinsville reported that they thought the company not worth saving and that liquidation was the best solution. Unwilling to part with both their investment *and* their jobs, the Scranton owners demurred. Finally it was

Whitin at that time made no equipment in the winding field, the only products that it could sell to rayon producers were spinning machines and twisters. The Industrial Rayon Corporation's order gave Whitin a nice opening to the rayon *twister* market.

Realizing how expensive it was to continue the manufacture of its own twisters, Industrial Rayon had originally turned to the silk machinery industry for the necessary machines. To its disappointment it had found silk-type twister frames too light and too poorly constructed (they were usually just bolted together) for the heavy-duty and precise work of rayon manufacture. The Industrial Rayon Corporation turned, therefore, to the Whitin firm whose cotton twisters, though considerably different from silk machines, were nearer what the Industrial Rayon engineers wanted in the way of construction. Whitin's production men agreed that they could build the uptwisters Industrial Rayon had in mind (though Whitin's previous cotton experience had always been with downtwisters) and in May, 1929, accepted an order for 72 of them. So pleased was the Cleveland company with the first machines produced by Whitin that it forthwith ordered 78 more of the same design.

Whitin was still in the process of filling its Industrial Rayon order for *twisters,* when the rayon *spinning*-machinery market also opened in a sudden and unexpected manner. It seems that a number of the

---

agreed that Whitin should buy a 50 per cent interest (later increased slightly to a controlling interest) for $20,000.

Henry R. Bailey, a promising young Whitin executive who had come to Whitinsville at the suggestion of his Harvard College roommate, Lawrence M. Keeler, Jr., was made assistant treasurer of the Scranton firm and was appointed to its board of directors. Serving as liaison man between Whitinsville and Scranton, Bailey supervised the revision of the U. S. Textile Machine Company's cost accounting, plant layout, and production techniques. By such means, and by loans of working capital, the Whitin company put its Scranton subsidiary back on its feet. The flow of benefits was not just one way, however. Whitin's sale of parts to U. S. Textile Machine brought it a handsome return on its relatively small investment.

The arrangement might have continued to be mutually beneficial had not World War II intervened. As U. S. Textile Machine turned to war work, its management problems mounted while its purchases of Whitin parts declined. Therefore, in 1941, the Whitin company decided to dispose of its controlling interest and agreed to sell its stock to the Scranton company's managers at the same price it had paid for it; it did, however, bring up from Scranton one of U. S. Textile Machine's junior executives, Eugene M. Kennedy, whom it eventually made assistant to its manager of foreign sales, J. J. Foley.

early rayon plants in America had been designed by a German mill engineer named Baron Oscar von Kohorn. Kohorn was more than an ordinary mill engineer; he was also owner of one of the Continent's leading rayon-machinery manufacturing concerns, the firm of Oscar Kohorn & Company.[18] Through New York representatives, he contracted with American promoters not only to design American rayon plants but to build their machinery as well. Unfortunately the 40 per cent American tariff on textile machinery was a grievous handicap to Kohorn's activities and a threat to his continued success. Therefore, in 1929, he decided to ally himself with some American manufacturer who would agree to build machinery for him on order.

In September of that year American representatives of the Baron made informal advances to the Whitin Machine Works, followed a month later by a formal proposition by the gruff and blustering Baron himself, who came to this country to make all the arrangements in person. The New York *Journal of Commerce,* reporting on the Baron's arrival in this country, speculated in print on the purpose of his trip:[19]

Further rayon plant expansion in the United States was forecast yesterday when it was learned that Baron Kohorn, the head of Oscar Kohorn & Co., leading European manufacturers of rayon machinery, would arrive in this country October 8 on the Olympic. Kohorn machinery is already in use in a number of the large American rayon plants, and the announcement that Baron Kohorn is now on his way to this country to pay the visit schedule[d] for last summer is regarded as an indication that his advice has been sought concerning the equipping of new plants.

It will be recalled that these well known textile engineers only recently secured a large contract with the Soviet Government. By this Russian transaction the Chemnitz concern has considerably extended its field of activity. So far the Kohorn firm has erected plants in England, Japan and other countries abroad producing more than 200,000 kilos (approximately 400,000 pounds) of rayon daily.

Chemnitz is now regarded as the center of the comparatively new rayon machinery industry, not only for Germany but also for other countries. . . .

Swift was attracted to Kohorn principally because the Baron could give Whitin the entree to the rayon spinning-machinery market it was looking for, since as a mill engineer he was in a position to specify the type of spinning machines to be used in his clients' mills. Swift therefore entered an agreement with Kohorn to build German-style rayon machinery for sale in the American market. A separate New York selling firm, the Whitin-Kohorn Company, owned fifty-fifty by the Whitin Machine Works and Oscar Kohorn & Company, was established to handle the sales end of the agreement. Swift consented to have Whitin bill its machinery to the sales firm at cost. Announcement of the agreement was made early in November, 1929. Kohorn engineers were immediately dispatched to Whitinsville, and by June of the following year they were turning out drawings of machines designed to spin rayon by both the pot and the spool methods.[20]

The agreement was drawn to last ten years, but as it turned out it lasted less than two. The planets were simply not in the right position. Only a week before Kohorn had set sail for America, the world had been astounded by news of the spectacular Clarence Hatry failure in London. By the time Kohorn had arrived in America, a steady decline in United States Steel stock quotations had given Wall Street investors the jitters. The ink had hardly dried on the Whitin-Kohorn agreement when the New York stock market crashed. The world-wide credit contraction that followed seems to have seriously disarranged Kohorn's business affairs, though he kept his difficulties carefully hidden from his associates. Consequently, the announcement in May, 1931, that Oscar Kohorn & Company had suspended payment on its liabilities (unlike the similar news of the Gaston, Williams & Wigmore failure) caught Swift completely by surprise.[21] Fortunately, the Whitin-Kohorn enterprise had not yet succeeded in getting many orders for spinning frames; as a result, Kohorn's difficulties had little effect on Whitin. Swift simply closed the Whitin-Kohorn New York office and had the firm dissolved.*

Even discounting the fact that the depression caught the Whitin-Kohorn Company at a weak point, it is doubtful whether the company's venture into rayon spinning would ever have been a success. The designs of rayon spinning machinery were among the most jealously guarded secrets in the rayon industry, for it was in the

---

* Oscar Kohorn & Company reorganized and soon again became recognized as a powerful force in the rayon industry, not so much in the United States as in other parts of the world.

spinning machine that the key conversion of chemicals into filaments took place. Whitin had proceeded on the assumption that it could evolve a chassis (together with the necessary spinning attachments) which would eventually become standard equipment, leaving the rayon producers room to bolt on their special chemical baths and other attachments after the chassis had been delivered. The scheme might have been feasible had not rayon development engineers insisted on continuing to make alterations that affected not only the chemical part of the machine but the mechanical part as well. Such changes reduced Whitin's work practically to a job-shop status, for which type of business the company was not then properly organized. Consequently, after the dissolution of the Whitin-Kohorn firm, Whitin all but completely abandoned the rayon spinning field; thereafter, rayon producers had their spinning frames built by small job shops on special order or by the H. W. Butterworth & Sons Company, of Philadelphia, one of the few machinery firms that has specialized in that type of work.

Whitin's failure in rayon spinning was fortunately more than offset by its success in rayon twisting. The Industrial Rayon order had immediately established the firm as an important builder of uptwisters for *viscose* rayon and had led to a series of orders from other viscose plants. Meanwhile the company had been given an opportunity to build downtwisters for use in the production of *acetate* rayon. In 1929, the Du Pont Rayon Company had built its first acetate rayon plant in Waynesboro, Virginia, and had equipped it with standard throwster-type uptwisters. Its uptwisters proved to be so unsatisfactory under operating conditions, however, that, after they had been in use only a few months, the Waynesboro officials started the search for a better machine with which to replace them. Learning of the work Whitin had done for viscose producers, a group of Du Pont engineers visited Whitinsville to discuss the possibility of creating a new type of twister that would be especially designed for use on acetate filaments. Whitin's experimental men agreed to coöperate and began work on adapting the conventional cotton ring downtwister for use with rayon filaments. At the same time, Du Pont's alert and extremely able engineers contributed ideas of their own on how the new machine should be designed. The final result was a combination of ideas from the two groups, but it was a source of no small satisfaction to the Whitin developmental men that their long experience with twisting machinery made it possible for them to save the theoretical Du Pont engineers from committing many grievous errors in construction designs.

The Du Pont's Waynesboro order came at a propitious moment in Whitin's history: it was one of the few orders that helped carry the company over the months of the depression's nadir in 1932. It also helped Whitin on its way to becoming the leading — indeed almost the exclusive — supplier of twisting machinery to the nation's large rayon producers, both in the viscose and in the acetate fields. By 1937, rayon twisters were Whitin's largest selling non-cotton product and were accounting for about a sixth of the company's dollar sales volume.

So pleased was the Du Pont company with the performance of its Whitin-designed machinery that it returned to Whitin in 1937 with another design problem — the job of constructing special machinery to handle its new Fiber 66, later called nylon. Du Pont was at that time setting up an experimental installation at its rayon plant in Buffalo and was anxious to begin work on developing special, high-speed machinery for use with the new fiber. Working in collaboration, as before, Du Pont and Whitin men began with the standard cotton-twister chassis as the starting point of their design. Their first machine twisted yarn at the rate of 250 feet per minute, about five times as fast as the standard cotton twister. However, Du Pont's top engineers rejected it, arguing that nylon was enough tougher than any previously known fiber to warrant a considerably greater increase in the speed of operation. Further experimentation proved the Du Pont men right. Whitin abandoned the conventional cotton chassis and began again from the ground up until at length its twister had achieved a speed of 1,600 feet per minute (later to be increased to 2,000 feet per minute). When the Du Pont company set up its first nylon producing plant, at Seaford, Delaware, all the twisters installed were built by Whitin.* When Du Pont was ready to build a second nylon plant at Martinsville, Virginia, that too was Whitin-

---

* These twisters were named draw twisters because they were designed to draw or stretch the filaments as well as twist them; they had to be so constructed that they allowed not more than 1 per cent variation in yarn diameter, since variations greater than 1 per cent produced noticeable changes in shade when dyed. It was the maintaining of this high standard that had made increases in speed so difficult.

equipped. So also was the third plant at Chattanooga, Tennessee. Consequently, every inch of nylon yarn produced in this country, at least up to the date of this book's publication, has been drawn and twisted on Whitin machinery.

Now that the Whitin Machine Works has established itself as the leading supplier of twisters to synthetic fiber producers, it has good reason to be concerned over how long its new market will last. During its early years, when it was tooling up, the synthetic fiber industry needed a large number of machines. But it is inconceivable that the rate of growth enjoyed by the industry in the last decade can be continued indefinitely. At some point the industry will have to begin leveling off, at which time the demand for twisters will decline markedly. Moreover, so incredibly fast do the new twisters operate and so enormously productive are they, that even if synthetic fibers were to replace natural fibers completely, the number of twisters needed by the industry would not be tremendously large. Hence, unlike the wool-machinery field where thousands of wool mules still remain to be converted to ring spinning frames, rayon-twister sales may be fast approaching a point beyond which the only likely direction is downward. In that case Whitin will no longer be able to count on a business that it has gained with little selling effort and has held against little competition.

*　　*　　*

It should be made clear at this point that synthetic fibers can be used in two different ways. Historically the first, and for many years the only, method of using them was in filament form. Viscose or acetate solution was extruded through many fine spinerets to form gelled filaments, which were then slightly twisted about each other to give them the strength and appearance of natural silk yarn. Later the filaments were given a variety of additional twists and were woven or knitted into fabrics or stockings. All machines discussed in the above section were designed to handle such "filament" yarns.

In the late 1920's, however, producers of rayon in Europe, where rayon technology still held world leadership, commenced using rayon as a substitute not only for silk but also for cotton (and later even for wool). By cutting filaments to prescribed lengths and sometimes by putting an artificial crimp in them, the Europeans succeeded in producing a second type of rayon fiber known as "staple" rayon. Staple rayon can be used either alone or in mixture with cotton or other fibers. Most important of all, it can be processed on regular textile machinery.

The use of staple rayon did not become common in America until the mid-1930's, but by 1939 the demand for it was nearly as great as the demand for the filament type. Unfortunately the effect of the staple rayon development on Whitin's sales cannot be accurately measured. Since staple rayon machinery is almost, if not completely, identical with other textile machinery, the company often finds that its cotton-machinery products are converted for use on rayon staple after they have been installed. Insofar as the introduction of staple rayon has helped generally to revive the textile industry, the company has probably benefited through increased machinery sales. But staple rayon machinery should not, from a developmental standpoint, be classed among the company's important new product lines.

3. WINNING THE WORSTED MACHINERY MARKET FROM FOREIGN COMPETITORS

While Whitin was pushing its way into the wool and rayon machinery fields, it was not neglecting to explore the market for worsted machinery. Previously the only large American producer of worsted machinery was the machine shop at Lowell, which from 1898 to 1926 had built worsted machinery of the Bradford type.* All

---

* It should be noted that worsted spinning machinery is of two general types. The one type is used with long, combed fibers in the manufacture of hard, men's-type worsteds. Since machines of this type are manufactured principally in the Bradford region of England, they are commonly referred to as Bradford frames. The other is used with shorter fibers and is employed chiefly in the production of women's wear. Frames of this type are made principally in Alsace and are referred to variously as French or Continental machines depending on one's views regarding the proper nationality of the Alsace region. Most Bradford-type mills in America have traditionally been located in Massachusetts and Rhode Island; French-type mills have also tended to concentrate in those two states, although large numbers of them may also be found in New Jersey and Pennsylvania.

For many years Atkinson, Haserick & Company, of Boston, have handled all importation of worsted machinery to this country from Europe's two leading builders, the *Société Alsacienne de Constructions Mécaniques,* makers of French worsted equipment, and Textile Machinery, Ltd., a British cartel formed at the end of World War II by such Bradford equipment builders as Prince, Smith & Sons, Platt Brothers & Company, and Hall-Stells, Ltd. See Stone's *History of Massachusetts Industries* for a brief history of the Atkinson, Haserick firm.

other worsted machinery used in American mills had been imported from abroad. However, because of financial difficulties in the mid–1920's, the Saco-Lowell Shops had dropped their worsted-machinery line, leaving the American market again completely in the hands of European machine-builders.

It is easy enough to understand how European machine-builders first got their fingerholds on the American worsted business, but it is difficult to explain how they managed to hold on for so long. Worsted manufacture was late in coming to America. Both the wool and the cotton industries were well established in this country and most of the important American wool and cotton machinery manufacturers were already in business when this country's first worsted mills were built in Lawrence, Massachusetts, in the 1850's. For years the American worsted trade was so small that it did not require enough machinery to make worth while the organization of shops specializing in that type of equipment. Consequently early American worsted mill owners characteristically bought their machinery abroad.

By 1898, however, the manufacture of worsted goods had become such a sizable industry in this country that the Lowell Machine Shop decided the time had arrived to pick off the luscious worsted-machinery plum. Business was in the doldrums at the time, and Lowell was looking for a new line of products just as Whitin began looking about for new products in the depression of the 'twenties. The worsted machines that Lowell put out were almost exact duplicates of Bradford worsted machinery, but Lowell's costs were so high that even a 45 per cent tariff could not keep out competitive products from abroad. Nevertheless, Lowell continued its manufacture of worsted equipment over the next twenty-five years — and with fair success.

Meanwhile, Whitin, too, had ventured into the worsted business, but only in a very small way. The company still has a picture of a worsted spinning frame that it is supposed to have built in 1887. And in 1890 it developed a worsted loom which, unfortunately, did not sell.[22] In 1910, when it bought the Providence Machine Company, it obtained the patterns and drawings of a worsted cone roving frame that the Providence company had been manufacturing,[23] and to satisfy a limited but continuing demand from Providence's former customers, Whitin kept the Providence frame in production. But, although the Whitin firm thus became the leading American builder of worsted roving equipment, the home market was small, and there was little incentive for the company to spend money on improving its worsted roving products. Consequently, the worsted roving frame has undergone very little change in recent decades and has never been a significant item in Whitin's product line.*

Following World War I the builders of machinery in America thought they saw their opportunity to capture the domestic worsted-machinery market for themselves. European manufacturing costs had risen so much more rapidly than American costs following the war that serious competition from abroad seemed unlikely. In 1923 Lowell decided to build a complete new plant for the manufacture of Bradford-type worsted machinery, and in 1924 Whitin, too, decided to embark on a concerted worsted-machinery program — though on a more cautious scale than Saco-Lowell's. Through friends in England, Swift induced two British worsted specialists to accept jobs with the Whitin Machine Works. One of them was Ellis Hartley, chief draftsman of Hall-Stells, Ltd., a leading British manufacturer of worsted equipment; the other was Cornelius Lane, erector for the same company.[24] Hartley and Lane were technicians, not inventors, and so produced for Whitin a worsted spinning-frame design that slavishly imitated the British product even to the extent of duplicating the European cap type of spinning arrangement.

The sojourn of the two men in Whitinsville can hardly be said to have been a commercial success. Whitin's worsted cap-spinning

---

* The place where Whitin has made its greatest success in the worsted roving field has been in the conversion of about three-quarters of the country's old-style flyer roving frames (the type made at Lowell) to the ring method of roving. Whitin has never made worsted cards, for that market is as limited as the market for worsted roving. In 1945 the Whitin company estimated that there were only about 2,000 worsted cards in the country against 5,500 wool cards and 80,000 cotton cards. Technological change in worsted cards has been so slight that 50-year-old machines with new card clothing are still able to compete with new machines. America's principal worsted card-builders are Proctor & Schwartz, Inc., and the Davis & Furber Machine Company. Later on, Whitin added worsted twisters to its line, but since worsted twisters are virtually the same as cotton twisters, they are not discussed in this section.

frames proved to be not sufficiently distinguishable from competitive British products to arouse any appreciable interest among mill men, especially since in most cases the Whitin frames were as high-priced as the British machines which they attempted to supplant.

Finally, in 1929, the Whitin company hit upon the idea of adopting ring spinning techniques to worsted manufacture by making use of what is known as a stationary ring rail.[25] The new idea proved a success for two principal reasons: stationary ring-rail spinning permitted larger package bobbins to be spun and at the same time produced a more even yarn with fewer breaks. It is true that ring spinning did not appreciably reduce worsted spinning costs, but it did reduce costs in subsequent operations, since larger packages and better yarn permitted speedier handling in the warping and weaving stages. Worsted mills found, therefore, that ring spinning could net them sufficient savings within two or three years to pay for converting their frames from the old cap system. Most of Whitin's work in the worsted field between 1930 and 1937 consequently centered in the conversion of existing British-made cap frames to the ring method of spinning, although the company did make a few complete machines which incorporated the ring spinning system from the start.

In 1937 the company decided to try the same idea on French-type frames, and to its surprise experienced considerable success. Table 13 gives an estimated breakdown of the various types of worsted spinning frames in this country in 1948 and shows the extent of Whitin's influence on the design of American worsted machinery. As the table reveals, the Bradford system has been strongly challenged by Whitin but still accounts for about two-fifths of the worsted spinning machinery now in place. The French system, though as yet less strongly challenged, accounts for only about a fifth of the nation's worsted spindles. The other two-fifths have, in one way or another, felt the influence of Whitin's developmental work. The figures in this table are, however, merely a static representation of the *existing* situation at a particular moment of time. If we had figures showing a breakdown of the types of worsted machinery currently being *installed* in this country, we should probably find that the Whitin company has become a far greater factor in the American worsted-machinery business than has generally been known and that the British and French producers have lost their control of the market.

The Whitin worsted-machinery development that has shown the most recent promise has been the so-called American System of worsted manufacture, although its real potentialities, since it was developed during and following World War II, have not yet been tested in a truly competitive market. During the war, worsted mills

TABLE 13

AN ESTIMATE OF WORSTED SPINNING MACHINERY IN PLACE IN THE
UNITED STATES IN MARCH, 1948

Type of Machinery	Number of Spindles	Type of Spinning	Where or by Whom Built
Bradford (British)	905,000	Cap	Mostly imported from England
	480,000	Cap frames converted to ring	Built by British and the Lowell Machine Shop; converted by Whitin (1930–48)
	110,000	Ring	Built by Whitin (1930–48)
Continental (French)	487,000	Mule	Mostly imported from France
	100,000[a]	American System	Mostly built by Whitin (1943–48)
	83,000	Ring	Built by Whitin (1938–48)

[a] The Whitin company estimates that another 25,000 cotton spindles have been converted to worsted uses by mill maintenance men.

Source: United States Department of Commerce figures brought up to date by Whitin Machine Works estimates.

in America found that getting new machinery either from abroad or from domestic manufacturers was virtually impossible. One of the first to recognize the possibilities of using cotton machinery in the production of worsted yarns was Harold J. Walter, president of the Uxbridge Worsted Company, a firm with headquarters only a few miles from Whitinsville. Robert J. McConnell, Whitin's vice-president in charge of cotton and spun-rayon development and sales, soon saw the possibilities of Walter's experiment and led the Whitin campaign to sell worsted men on the new system.[26]

Unknowingly the Whitin company had been preparing for this new development for several years, since it had gradually been increasing the roll distances of its cotton frames until the frames were capable of handling rayon staple fiber lengths up to three inches. These lengths were within the range of worsted fibers and so were usable, with slight rebuilding, for the production of worsted yarns. Under Whitin sponsorship the American System of worsted manufacture met with rapid acceptance in the field. Though as yet applicable only to a narrow range of worsted yarns, it has attracted many followers, some of whom have extemporized with their own version of the system by having cotton frames converted to worsted use by men in their own maintenance departments.

4. DIVERSIFICATION *vs.* SPECIALIZATION

As this chapter has already shown, the depression forced Whitin to make a radical shift in its product policy. Presumably that shift could have headed in either of two directions. The company was in a position to choose whether to make far-reaching changes in its cotton-machinery line, thus exciting an increased demand for its traditional products, or to diversify its product line, thus reaching out for a broader market in non-cotton lines. Actually it tried a little of both, but its greater attention focused on diversification.

Meanwhile, Saco-Lowell was making the opposite decision. Being financially embarrassed, the Saco-Lowell Shops could not risk putting money into a broad developmental program. It chose, instead, to abandon such non-cotton lines as it had and to concentrate almost exclusively on the production and sale of cotton preparatory machinery. By this action Saco-Lowell retreated to the narrowest and most specialized line of equipment it had dealt with in its entire history. Thus, having followed completely different courses for a century, the two companies crossed each other's paths in mid-passage, each proceeding in the direction in which once the other had traveled. Whitin's method of meeting the decline in domestic cotton-machinery sales was to expand into non-cotton machinery lines; Saco-Lowell's method was to drop its non-cotton lines. Girding its loins, Saco-Lowell went out after cotton-machinery business especially in the foreign market, where it had always had a fairly strong foothold and where Whitin had never been a very important competitor. As yet it is impossible to determine which of the two courses of action was the more efficacious. Certainly both companies have encountered difficulties in putting their policies into effect,* but at the time they were adopted, and under the conditions then existing, both policies seemed eminently desirable. Perhaps in the end both will prove to have been best suited to the individual company concerned.

From the narration of events in the earlier part of this chapter, it must seem clear that diversification at Whitinsville was not a planned program but rather one that came about in *ad hoc* fashion. Yet, in retrospect, one can distinguish a certain logic in its development. Undoubtedly diversification helped the company to preserve its labor force during the depression. One point not clear, however, is whether the company would have been as well off if it had stuck strictly to cotton machinery, for, remarkably enough, Saco-Lowell, without diversifying, weathered the worst years of the depression as well as Whitin did. Diversification tended to level out the company's short-run business cycle, for, as experience had shown, the cycles of different textiles did not always coincide (although the company made no study to determine just to what extent the industry's various cycles had diverged in the past). In an industry that appeared to have become chronically depressed, diversification and flexibility seemed a logical safeguard against extreme fluctuations.

At Biddeford the Saco-Lowell officials marveled at the casual way Whitin turned its attention from cotton machinery, the bread-and-butter of its old-time business, to wool, worsted, and rayon equipment, the cake-and-frosting of the machinery trade. Nevertheless, Whitin was convinced that its gamble would pay off in the long run

---

* One of the difficulties yet lying ahead of the Whitin company in a major way is the complex problem of supplying repair parts for such a diversity of products. As Whitin complicates its product line, it doubly complicates its repair business, for more parts would mean not only higher costs but slower deliveries. Already specialized repair shops in the South are eating into the company's lucrative repair business by offering better service at lower prices. Meadows & Company has become a formidable competitor in the changeover business, and the Dixie Flyer & Bobbin Company has built up its spindle trade till it is able to better Whitin's job-order repair system by using mass-production techniques. Thus the company may be jeopardizing one anti-depressive (repairs) by emphasizing another (diversification).

since it felt that, in diversifying, it was spreading the risk inherent in a highly volatile business. Admittedly, though, in diversifying its product, the company was building up an enormous and unwieldy overhead that it might have difficulty controlling in depressed times. In 1900, white collar workers comprised only 1½ per cent of Whitin's payroll; by 1940, 18 per cent of the company's employees did their work behind desks.*

However, diversification performed one great favor for the village of Whitinsville: it once again made the village a logical place for the location of the Whitin Machine Works. By 1939 only 22 per cent of the nation's cotton machinery (in terms of spindles) was to be found in New England mills; two-thirds of it was located in the four Southern states of North Carolina, South Carolina, Georgia, and Alabama. The logic of the situation had begun to demand that the Whitin plant be moved southward. Once Whitin had branched into the manufacture of wool and worsted machinery, however, the desirability of moving south diminished, since most customers for that line were located in the New England area.†

One of the adverse results of the Whitin company's diversification program was the management problem it created. Soon the models of machinery produced by the Whitin firm had become so numerous that the old production-control methods were rendered obsolete. It will be recalled that following 1913 the company had installed a new production department which had undertaken the job of converting the plant from a product-line organization to a functional organization, set up to take greater advantage of mass-production techniques. The plant's reorganization on a functional basis was slow to reach completion but was wholly accomplished by 1927, at which time the policy of product diversification was introduced. Ten years later the company's line of products had grown so large that the advantages of mass production could be realized only by the most careful planning. Yet the company had made no fundamental change in its plant organization. Its lethargy was principally owing to the fact

---

* In 1947, when Whitin sold substantially more machinery than Saco-Lowell, it nevertheless made a smaller profit, principally because the cost of getting out such a large volume of non-standard machinery was so great.

† Contrariwise, the Saco-Lowell Shops, having concentrated on cotton machinery, have continued under heavy pressure to relocate in the South.

that activity during those years had been at such a low level that it would have been difficult in any event to have distinguished unavoidable inefficiencies from avoidable ones.

The first step toward remedying the situation was taken in 1937. For two years the company had reported unsatisfactory profits. In 1935, when Saco-Lowell was enjoying a small profit, Whitin suffered a near-quarter-million-dollar loss. In 1936, the company's most active year since 1923, Whitin's profits were 7.4 per cent of sales, whereas Saco-Lowell's were 10.2 per cent. Troubled by the company's poor showing, Swift had asked William Hoch, his chief assistant in plant matters, to study the situation and suggest a solution. It happened that only a little over a year earlier Hoch had hired the accounting firm of Ernst & Ernst to study the operations of Whitin's village maintenance crew with an eye to setting up some type of incentive wage structure. Since the representatives of Ernst & Ernst were still in Whitinsville when the matter of Whitin's poor showing came up for discussion, Hoch consulted them and agreed to let their division chief, William W. Tuttle, study the situation and submit a report. Tuttle found that the company had no adequate knowledge of its manufacturing costs, that it compiled no monthly statements of profits or loss, and that it needed a modern system of standard costs as a check on its production department's effectiveness.[27]

Accepting Tuttle's findings, Swift permitted Max F. Thompson, an Ernst & Ernst cost accountant and budget specialist, to install the necessary cost and budgetary controls. After nearly six months of work (July–December, 1937), Thompson was ready to convert the company's plant accounts to a standard cost basis. Instead of instituting his system department by department, he used the shock method of installing it all at once. Probably his decision was a wise one, for it is doubtful whether any such radical change had ever taken place in the memory of men in the shop, and it was well that he went about getting it over with in a hurry. To win coöperation from the company's foremen, Thompson held advance meetings to explain what he was attempting to do, but his success in getting acceptance of his new ideas was at best limited. Opposition was widespread and many among the company's old-timers felt it their duty to preserve the firm from the enmeshments of so much red tape. For a long period some departments continued to keep the old system of records alongside the new, just in case the new should break down. Thompson's missionary zeal only added fuel to the flames. A remarkably able man, he was impatient with the irrational attitude taken toward his system and sometimes drove his reforms through to realization even over the opposition of the older executives.[28] Swift recognized Thompson's great abilities, however, and persuaded Ernst & Ernst to release him for a permanent job with the Whitin Machine Works. Meanwhile, Whitin discontinued the use of Scovell, Wellington & Company as its auditing firm and transferred its auditing business to the Ernst & Ernst firm, where it could also secure the advantages of management advice. Since that time the company has profited greatly from the consulting services of Ernst & Ernst's William W. Tuttle.

Tuttle's chief contribution was to bring to the company's inbred management an outsider's point of view. But he could do no more than offer competent suggestions. The executives of the firm still had to make all the important decisions, and the problem of managing a complex and diversified line of products still remained inescapably the responsibility of the company's top officials.

Beyond the management problems involved, the company's diversification of products carried risks of a special nature, for the non-cotton machinery market for which the company was striving was severely limited in size. It has been estimated by men in the industry that 75 per cent of the dollar volume of preparatory textile machinery produced in this country is machinery of the cotton type. Wool and worsted machinery accounts for about half of the remainder and rayon machinery for the rest.[29] Thus, Whitin, in diversifying, was concentrating its development and executive energies on a small portion of the total machinery market, while Saco-Lowell was bending its chief efforts toward the area where the market was largest.* Under such conditions there were possibilities of unfavorable developments: Would Saco-Lowell's concentration on cotton machines eventually enable it to outdistance Whitin's tech-

---

* By the later 1930's, Saco-Lowell was again running neck-and-neck with Whitin in total sales. Both companies were selling about equal amounts of cotton machinery in the domestic market, while Saco-Lowell was meeting Whitin's non-cotton-machinery sales with an equal volume of cotton-machinery sales to customers located abroad.

nological developments in the cotton-machinery field? Would the Whitin shop, fighting many battles on many fronts, be able to meet its great cotton-machinery opponent on equal grounds? At the same time, would the Whitin company's non-cotton-machinery market continue as flourishing as in the past?

Many felt that the Whitin company was skimming off the cream of the wool, worsted, and rayon markets, and that difficult times lay ahead in that branch of its business. Much of Whitin's success in its non-cotton lines had derived from its ingenious application of the more advanced principles of cotton manufacturing to the less well-developed manufacturing processes previously used on other fibers. By World War II, the task of up-dating the manufacturing processes of other lines was somewhere between half and three-quarters finished. Once the job was completed, would the company be able to find ways of replacing the adaptive work it had been doing? Certainly the task would not be easy and would require a heavy expenditure of time and money at the experimental level. Could the Whitin Machine Works, or for that matter any other firm in the industry, meet the demand for product innovation in a manner forceful enough to prevent the industry from slipping back into another chronic depression? If the Whitin company had greater need for product development than any other company in the industry, it was only because Whitin had so many more products to worry about. Everyone in the industry realized that the textile-machinery business would have to look to its experimental rooms if it was to create the obsolescence so necessary to future sales.

But if product innovation seemed the hope of the future, why had it not been the industry's salvation in the past? There was nothing new in the charge that the industry needed to spend more time on developing new products. For eighty years critics had been saying that textile-machinery designs were behind the times. One still occasionally hears statements to the effect that cotton-manufacturing techniques are the same now as in the days of Arkwright and Slater. And to the uninitiated there seems to be considerable truth in what is said, for only a person of technical sophistication can detect the basic differences between the sketches of cards used by Slater and of those in use today. Yet the difference is enormous, and in that difference lies part of the explanation why the textile machinery industry has never appeared to be an innovator and why innovation in that particular industry has been, and probably will continue to be, so difficult to achieve.

5. THE PROBLEMS OF INNOVATION

Men in the industry give several reasons why textile machinery firms have not been able to promote radically new ideas in textile-machinery design. In every instance they emphasize the nature and limitations of the market for their products.

In the first place stands the close relationship that has always existed between machinery builders and their customers. In most other business situations, buyers shop around for their goods before making their purchases and in so doing assume sole responsibility for whatever purchases they make. In the textile industry, however, very little shopping takes place — partly because there are few producers to choose from and partly because mills have found it to their advantage to deal with one producer only. Consequently mill men depend heavily on the advice of their machinery builders when they decide to install new equipment.

Under such conditions the responsibility for selection of product rests squarely on the producer's shoulders. When seven members of Great Britain's cotton goods industry made an official tour of the United States in 1944 in an effort to learn how British productivity per man hour could be increased, they were greatly surprised to see how close was the coöperation between the textile mills and the machinery builders of this country and how conscientiously the one group followed the recommendations and advice of the other. As a result of this close tie, American machinery builders have had to be certain that their products would stand the test of rigorous mill conditions before being ready to recommend them to the trade. When mills buy equipment, they expect it to last under harsh treatment for thirty years or more.* Consequently, a new type of machine cannot be said to have been fully tested until it has been in operation for a number of years. To mill owners, initial costs are not so important as maintenance expense, and quick is the exchange of in-

---

* Tax regulations take recognition of this fact by requiring that mill owners depreciate their spinning and weaving machinery over a period of twenty-five years.

formation in the industry if a new machine begins to develop "bugs" after it has been in service awhile. No textile machine carries a formal guarantee that it will meet the continuous heavy treatment given it on the floor of a mill, but, because of the resulting injury to its reputation, no textile-machinery firm can afford to have a machine render unsatisfactory service. Consequently, machine-builders have learned from experience to be cautious in their choice of machines to put on the market. It is not surprising, therefore, to find them holding to machines that have proved their merits after long years of service.

Then, too, developing and testing a new machine before putting it on the market is often so costly, when such a careful job must be done, that the potential sale of the new product may not warrant the expense involved. Many machines in the textile line are in such limited demand that there is no point in spending money on their improvement. The worsted roving frame, already mentioned, is a case in point. A research program large enough to assure the development of a successful new machine might easily cost the Whitin company more than the entire net profits from such a machine for a generation to come. A concerted effort to produce a completely new machine to replace one of Whitin's best-selling machines would undoubtedly require a minimum expenditure of a million dollars. With no assurance that such an expenditure would pay for itself in new sales, the company has hesitated to risk its financial substance in such a way.*

---

* Some critics of the textile machinery industry have argued that the reason for the industry's lack of interest in developing its own new machines is that it has too comfortably relied on its lucrative repair-parts business. The following quotation from the May, 1944, issue (p. 220) of *Fortune* magazine sums up the general attitude of condemnation: "The textile-machinery industry has largely confined itself to existing types, spare parts, and accessories. For millowners would have to install a whole set of radically new machines if they installed one, which they cannot afford. If there were new machinery and wealthier millowners installed it, the machinery manufacturers' poorer customers would not be able to compete. The fear of their demise and losing their lucrative spare-parts business keeps the machinery manufacturer sitting in his chair." It is undoubtedly true that the existence of a dependable repair-parts market has softened the urgent necessity for machine-builders to get out and drive for new machinery business, but it is naïve to imagine that a manufacturer would be willing to sacrifice an opportunity to sell a complete new machine to any customer, wealthy or not, just to preserve his market for parts of old machinery.

Consequently, the Whitin company, like most companies in the industry, has felt that much of the work of original invention must fall to others. It has held that the principal function of a textile-machinery concern is the building of textile machinery. It has seen to it that its products have always been made according to the best-known and proved designs, but its accent has always been on the word *proved*. In short, it has pursued a policy of watchful waiting. Its theory has been that the greatest number of practical new ideas are those constantly bubbling up from the cotton mills themselves. Acting on that theory it has made the manager of each of its sales departments the manager also of its corresponding development programs, so that the flow of information from a customer's mill floor to the company's experimental room has been direct and unimpeded.

Looking to its largest and most progressive customers for design improvement has made the industry appear to be trailing behind the country's leading mills in product development, but it has given the industry a source of developmental ideas far more prolific than anything that could have been fostered from within. The larger mills in this country are many times the size of the largest machine shops and have greater financial resources to spend on developmental work. Furthermore, mills are in a favorable position to detect deficiencies in existing machines and are able to run practical operational tests on new equipment of their own design. Unfortunately, developmental work in mills is largely adaptive and so the textile-machinery firms, by depending on mills for their new ideas, have allowed their product designs to move forward by slow stages and not by any revolutionary leaps.*

---

* In addition to the cotton mills of America, a traditional cradle of textile-machinery innovation has been the machine shops of Europe. For generations the British textile machinery industry was the world's source of new cotton-manufacturing techniques. But since World War I, Britain has lost that leadership and the American industry has had to look elsewhere for new ideas. At present Switzerland produces machinery that is in some ways, especially in the precision with which it is made, superior to that produced in America, and, in at least one case, that country has been the source of new Whitin products (the Schweiter winder). But the Swiss tend to build single-purpose machines which are inflexible and difficult to keep in operation. In addition, their equipment is over-designed; consequently, for American uses, it is too expensive to manufacture and too expensive to maintain. Whitin, for instance, was forced to redesign its Schweiter winder completely to permit eco-

Because Americans are fond of change and are admirers of the new as against the old, they have tended to give credit to the industry or to the firm that has been an innovator and to neglect the one that has achieved progress through evolutionary means. Actually, although never leading the parade, the textile machinery industry has consistently held rank and thus has achieved greater advances in technology than it has been given credit for. The best way to measure progress in a materialistic world is to calibrate it against man-hour productivity. It is generally conceded that America has attained its present high standard of living by achieving a cumulative rate of advance in its man-hour output amounting to an average of about 2 per cent per year, a rate unequaled by any other country in the world. Efforts to determine to what extent the cotton textile industry has kept up with the national advance have revealed that it has in fact very nearly equaled the national average. A detailed study of the situation was made in 1936. The study compared mill conditions in 1910 with those in 1936 and came to the conclusion that the rate of advance in the intervening twenty-six years was approximately 1.5 per cent a year.[30] Since, in 1936, the introduction of long-draft spinning and roving had not as yet had much effect on the figures, it is not unlikely that the rate of advance since that date has been somewhat higher.

For a bit of contrast, one should read the 1944 *Report of the* [British] *Cotton Textile Mission to the United States of America,* already referred to a few pages back. In their report the British stated that they were not a little surprised to find that nearly all American looms were automatic, whereas very few English looms were; that long-draft had been applied to more than half of America's spinning frames, while in England its adoption had been not more than spotty; and that labor efficiency had steadily increased here because of the use of faster operating and more nearly automatic machinery, while in England, man-hour output had hardly increased at all since 1910.[31]

---

nomical manufacture and to minimize service complaints. In short, the foreign shops, once a prolific source of technological information, are still a summer visiting place for American textile-machinery executives but are not likely to be so dependable a source of usable ideas as they were in the past.

To some extent the charges of backwardness that have been voiced against the American textile machinery industry recurrently since the Civil War have been one of the contributing factors in developing an attitude of complacency toward radical change within the industry. Having heard for so many years the carping judgments of those who have not understood the difficult problems it has been faced with, the industry has grown indifferent to all criticism and has tended to shrug off adverse comment with an air of tired resignation to the inevitable. In so doing, it has shut its mind to its real shortcomings. Probably the spectacular technological achievements of other industries would not under any conditions have been possible in the textile machinery industry, but certainly the industry could have been more alive to its opportunities than it has been.

Possibly the American textile machinery industry has been too conservative for its own good: it might have accomplished somewhat more than it has if it had been a little more willing to accept the risks of developing new products. But any industry that is functioning in a declining market, as the textile machinery industry has done for the past quarter-century, is loath to risk investing its capital in the long-range future. A new industry on the upgrade can afford to put its hopes on the future. An old industry, knowing that the question is not so much whether it can get more business as whether it can hold what it has, must keep its eyes focused close to the present.

Perhaps it is asking too much that the conservatism laid down in Whitinsville in deposits of four generations — a conservatism that has made the company the strong corporate unit it is today — should be drastically modified. Possibly the correct solution is for the Whitin company to divorce long-time developmental work from actual manufacturing and to continue largely as a manufacturer in the area of achievement where it has proved itself so proficient, meanwhile leaving the more fundamental developmental work to other institutions. At the Massachusetts Institute of Technology, a Slater-endowed laboratory has spent several years running exhaustive tests on textile fibers in an effort to discover mathematical formulae that will accurately describe fiber properties. Proceeding from a purely theoretical base, the Institute's research men hope to learn enough about fiber behavior to be able eventually to recommend a completely new approach to textile manufacturing, an approach that may conceivably have the features of line production and electronic control. The end is still far off, but perhaps research such as this will prove the solution to some of the textile machinery industry's most pressing problems. As yet, however, the machinery manufacturers are not involved in the M.I.T. experiments, either financially or psychologically, and certainly, before the program could leave the laboratory and enter the world of practicality, a vast deal of money and enthusiasm would have to be spent on it. For the present, therefore, it remains to be seen whether the manufacturers themselves, through their own developmental departments, are going to be able to meet the challenges of the future.

CHAPTER XVIII

THE IMPACT OF WORLD WAR II, 1941–1945

For Whitin, as for most American companies, World War II began somewhat before the bombing of Pearl Harbor. War in Europe made itself felt in American industry during 1940–41 both directly, through the placement of war orders with American firms, and indirectly, through the general speed-up in the world's economy. For Whitin the war brought an end to a fifteen-year depression, though it did not completely succeed in restoring the firm to capacity operation. Business became good, but not booming. Business would have been worse, had not a number of textile mills in Cuba, Brazil, Argentina, and other Latin American countries turned to the Whitin Machine Works for the equipment they needed but could not get from England on account of the war.

Because of its idle capacity, the Whitin company was in a receptive mood when, in April, 1941, it was approached with a suggestion that it bid on an order for auxiliary steam engines to be built for British cargo ships. Ordinarily the company would have considered steam engines too far out of its field, but, with war threatening, some of the company's younger officials felt that they should be gaining some experience in war work. Therefore, the contract was sought and won.

The contract was placed through the New York shipbuilding firm of Gibbs & Cox, American purchasing agent for Great Britain, and thence through the B. F. Sturtevant Company, of Hyde Park, Massachusetts. The Sturtevant company was an old family-owned concern,[1] located near Boston, and was one of three American producers of auxiliary steam engines for the United States Maritime Commission. Its chief product was blowers, however, and the small capacity that it could make available for the production of steam engines was already overtaxed by orders from the American government. For that reason, Sturtevant was willing to subcontract to Whitin its entire British order for 312 Liberty-type engines.[2] Since Whitin received the privilege of using Sturtevant's drawings and specifications, the arrangement was a mutually satisfactory one.

Within a few months Whitin had completed the order and had sent the engines on their way. At the time, the matter seemed routine enough; but once war had been declared, its significance became evident, for in the chaos that followed Pearl Harbor, Whitin knew at least one wartime product that it was capable of making efficiently.

The first real evidence that war was drawing close was a meeting of textile-machinery officials called by representatives of the Office of Production Management (later called the War Production Board) in Boston on 25 November 1941. At that meeting New England's textile-machinery companies were advised to begin considering what work they could do in case of war, since it was evident that materials allocations would soon be necessary and that materials for textile-machinery production would be placed low on the list. In response to this advice the industry agreed to submit to the government a list of the textile machinery for which it currently held orders; in addition, it agreed to take further orders only on a conditional basis. Before the plan could be put into effect, however, war broke out.

I. REPERCUSSIONS OF PEARL HARBOR

Immediately all attention focused on Washington. The country's business men knew so little about what was expected of them that they deluged the capital city with their representatives. Everyone went to seek instructions, clarifications, privileges, and exemptions. Several Whitin men traveled to Washington in those early weeks of the war, but one among them was especially important, for it was his trip to the capital which precipitated the first of those successive and far-reaching organizational shifts that produced such a change in the Whitin company during and after the war. That man was William H. Hoch, for many years Swift's chief assistant and his closest Whitinsville friend.

"Bill" Hoch was reared in Worcester as part of the social group to which the younger members of the Whitin family belonged.[3] Like Swift, he took his schooling at Williams College, though his class was seven or eight years later. It is said that soon after graduation Hoch applied for a job at the Whitin Machine Works, but was turned down by George Marston Whitin because business conditions at the time (the depression of 1907–08) did not warrant hiring a college-trained man.

On reapplying in 1909, however, Hoch was hired and was put to work in the shop. In 1913, when Suffern & Son recommended that the company establish a production department to coördinate the shop's activities, Hoch was the man put in charge. In 1917 when the United States entered World War I, Hoch was moved to enlist in the Army and was assigned first to Plattsburg and then, as an officer, to the Boston headquarters of the Quartermaster Corps.

After the war Hoch returned to Whitinsville, and Swift soon made him a member of the closely knit trio that was to serve for many years as the company's unofficial executive committee. Previously the trio had consisted of Marston Whitin, Kent Swift, and George B. Hamblin, but Marston's retirement and death had prepared the way for a new person. At first Hoch held the title of works manager, while Hamblin remained purchasing agent. But in 1923 Hamblin was moved to the works manager post, and Hoch was promoted to the vacant assistant treasurership.[4] At the same time he was made a member of the board of directors, the first non-family employee so honored since the days of the Tafts.

As assistant treasurer, Hoch filled a real niche in the company. Not only did he see that Swift's orders were executed, but whenever Swift was out of town he acted in Swift's stead as executive head of the company. Most important of all, he served as a communications medium between Swift and the rest of the shop. Men soon learned that Hoch spoke for the "boss" and that his words carried weight. They also learned that Hoch was a good listening device for Swift and that matters they might otherwise have hesitated to discuss with the chief executive they could easily discuss with Hoch, for he was an understanding person and, better still, he knew how to convey information to Swift at the proper time and under the proper circumstances. Especially was Hoch valuable in ironing out petty differences or misunderstandings and in tempering the occasional vindictiveness that Swift was wont to show when angered.

Everyone liked and trusted Hoch, even though some envied the position of authority he occupied.

Hoch's station in the community was unique. He was a bachelor, and so, like a minister with no wife, was looked on as belonging to everyone. For many years after his appointment as assistant treasurer he continued to live unpretentiously at the Blue Eagle Inn along with the company's other bachelor employees and its elderly pensioners.*

Hoch was especially friendly with the Lasell branches of the family and, as a member of the board of directors, was permitted to vote their stock. Since between them the two Lasell branches still owned a silent but controlling interest in the company, Hoch's proxy votes were enough to control the board. On at least one occasion, in an expansive mood, Hoch was indiscreet enough to state that in his hands lay control over E. Kent Swift and the company. Literally speaking what he said was true, but only in the narrowest possible sense. If he had ever used his vote to oppose Swift in a board meeting, he would never have been allowed to do so again. His strength was not his own but was the strength of his position, and his position depended wholly on the backing of E. Kent Swift.

Such was the personality and background of the man Swift sent to Washington in the early days of the war. While there, Hoch encountered Robert Stevens, an old friend and a member of a prominent family of wool-mill owners. Stevens was an officer in the Army's Quartermaster Corps and was anxious to see the armed services get all the good men they could. Being a man of enthusiasms, he pommeled Hoch with arguments concerning the national crisis and the government's need for able administrators to help carry on the war. Swayed by Stevens' earnestness, Hoch called Swift by long-distance telephone to announce his decision to remain in Washington in government wartime service.

Swift was thunderstruck. His company was facing the most criti-

* During nearly three years Hoch was absent from Whitinsville because of illness. In December, 1928, the symptoms of muscle spasm in his neck became so pronounced that he resigned his duties and left for Bermuda in search of relief. After seeking the advice of several doctors he underwent an operation which proved successful and permitted him to return to his duties in Whitinsville in 1931; from then on, he made Worcester his home.

cal test in its history. Within the following months it would have to change to completely new fields of endeavor, with what consequences no one could predict. At the age of sixty-three, Swift felt entitled to the full support and coöperation of all the men under him. To him, Hoch's action seemed an inexcusable defection. During their heated telephone conversation Swift informed Hoch that his departure from the company would be considered a resignation and not a leave of absence. In anger, Hoch replied that his decision remained unaltered. The conversation ended with each man irreconcilable to the other's position.

How such word gets about one never knows, but in no time the village was aware that the two men had had a falling-out. Thereafter Hoch's name was mentioned in Whitinsville only in the undertones usually reserved for the dear departed dead.*

For years Hoch's affiliation with the company had stood between Swift and the need for appointing a successor: not because Hoch was heir-presumptive to the treasurership — he was too near Swift's age for that — but because in the event of the unexpected, Hoch could have been relied on to fill in till a younger man — preferably one of the family — could be trained for the job.

Swift had been prevented from training a young man earlier by the family's failure to provide him with a suitable business heir. Previously there had been among the younger generation of Whitins at least one son-in-law of such energetic purposefulness that the family had never been forced to go outside its ranks for managerial talent. For a number of reasons the situation had changed by 1941, and for the first time in one hundred and ten years the owner-manager relationship in the company seemed threatened with extinction. Among Swift's children were three girls, all of whom had received fine educations and all of whom had chosen professional men as husbands — a lawyer, a doctor, and a professor. Thus the traditional line of Whitin management descent from son-in-law to son-in-law to son-in-law was, in any event, bound to be broken.

---

* At the end of the war, Hoch went to Japan to serve on the staff of General Douglas MacArthur. Later he returned to Washington as a civil servant. On occasion he still visits friends in Whitinsville but never in any official capacity and never for more than a few days at a time.

Swift's only son, E. Kent Swift, Jr., was not yet eighteen at the time.

On his wife's side of the family, Swift had only four nephews, the three sons of the Lawrence M. Keelers and William C. Crane, Jr. Young Crane, being the son of a United States Army officer had lived in many parts of the world and consequently had never developed an interest in the Whitin company. Lawrence M. Keeler, Jr., had attended the Harvard Business School and had just begun to show executive promise when a cerebral hemorrhage left him incapacitated for several years at a critical time in his career. A second Keeler boy, Marston, was likewise not well enough to assume any rigorous duties in the company. Murray Keeler, the eldest of the three, was thirty-three at the time and was a restless, independent sort, who had left preparatory school to enter the business without completing his education. Preferring the freedom of bachelorhood and the conveniences of life at home, he had not married. Similarly in business he had preferred the salesman's freedom to the confining responsibilities of the executive.

Nor in the Lasell branch was there prospective executive timber. Chester's two daughters, like Swift's, had married professional men — a lawyer and a doctor. Among J. M. Lasell's seven children there had been three girls, of whom two had never married and the third had married a Philadelphia business man. Of the four boys, three had been associated with the Whitin shop at one time or another, but only for short periods; the fourth had become an artist.

When it came to hiring members of the family, Swift had followed the policy laid down by Marston Whitin that every member should be given a fair chance to prove his mettle; however, promotion should always be made only on merit. Two of J. M. Lasell's sons, Chester and Josiah II, either because Swift did not encourage them to stay or because they found other opportunities more attractive, severed their respective connections with the company after only a few years of service.* The third, John Whitin Lasell, might possibly have become Swift's successor if the treasurership had been

* Josiah Lasell II became a salesman for the company around 1919 and a member of the board of directors in 1921. In 1924 he severed all connections with the company to take up residence abroad. Chester served on the board from 1937 to 1948, when he resigned because duties on Wall Street kept him from attending meetings.

a publicly elective post instead of a self-perpetuating one, for he was extremely popular with the townspeople of Whitinsville.

Handsome, gregarious, a convivial drinker, well-married, and the father of four attractive children, John had all the social and political assets a man needed. In the village he was as idolized by the people as the other members of his family were held in awe. First as town selectman, then as state representative, and later as Air Commissioner for Massachusetts, he climbed steadily in the political world, never suffering defeat. As his political life encroached further and further on his business activities, however, he gradually relinquished his duties in the Whitin company. Perhaps, in fact, it was his ineptness as a business man that made him turn to politics, for in his only major company assignment — the advertising managership — he had expended funds so fruitlessly that Swift had been forced to replace him with the less spectacular but more discreet William H. Greenwood. Some of John's spark was precisely what the company needed,[5] but he lacked the balance and judgment so necessary to a top executive.*

Thus, having no one to turn to as his successor among the family's younger generation, Swift's only choice lay between going outside the company for an executive vice-president or looking for someone within the organization. I think it is true that the first alternative was never given serious consideration. Even had it been considered, the securing of a good man just then, early in the war, would have been an exceedingly difficult task, since never before in history had such a high premium been placed on managerial ability. Moreover, it was typical of the textile machinery industry to believe that a good executive could be developed only within the industry. Always in the past the chief executives of textile-machinery companies had been also their firms' chief salesmen. It was not enough that they be simply able administrators; they had also to be thoroughly conversant with the products and personalities of the trade. A notable exception was David F. Edwards, a former professor and automobile

* Having been a pilot in World War I, John Lasell felt morally impelled to volunteer his services to the Air Force in World War II. While he was serving as an Observer in the Burma Theater, his plane disappeared without a trace (1 December 1943) and later all aboard were declared missing. Meanwhile, his wife resolutely carried on by serving as the company's wartime director of women employees.

executive, but even in his case it is instructive to note that his selection as head of the Saco-Lowell Shops was made not by textile-machinery men but by the banks in charge of Saco-Lowell's reorganization.

This question of management succession ranks high among the critical problems in business administration and, if anything, receives less emphasis than it deserves, for a business organization can never be strong if its top management corps is weak. All other factors are necessarily subordinate. Indeed, sometimes it is difficult to explain the success of a business on any other grounds than the ability of its chief executives. Consequently the choice of a new management team is always critical, for if a company is to enjoy a continuity of management unbroken by the disruption that results when one management era comes abruptly to an end and a completely new one takes over, plans must be laid far ahead. It seems safe to say that the Whitin company's notable success over four generations of family ownership was owing in large part to the continuity of its management — coupled always, of course, with a willingness on the part of each succeeding generation to depart from the model set by the old when changing times made such a departure necessary.

The task of picking a new executive vice-president from within a corporation instead of from without is made easier by the chance to observe a man at close range and under varying conditions of strain. It is complicated, however, by the difficulty of predicting how any particular man will react to increased authority. In some, responsibility brings out latent qualities of leadership greater even than expected; in others, promotion brings nervous disorders and anxiety at one extreme, and inflated egos at the other.

In 1941 the Whitin company had three vice-presidents from among whom it was logical to assume the company's executive vice-president would be selected. First, there was Frederick E. Banfield, Jr., the man who had come to Whitinsville from Biddeford in 1935 to replace George B. Hamblin as works manager. As an executive he was soft-spoken, amiable, scholarly, and technically expert, not a driver, not an administrator, and not trained in sales or finance. Secondly, there was Ralph E. Lincoln, the man who had succeeded

George B. Hamblin as purchasing agent when Hamblin moved up to the works manager's post in 1923. If any one person in Whitinsville could be picked as a personification of the spirit of the Whitin Machine Works, it was Lincoln. Of all the company's executive officers only Swift had been with the firm longer. Lincoln had joined the office force in 1901, while he was still in knee-breeches, at a time when the only office equipment was paper, pen, and ink, and when the company's accounts were computed inside a few nimble heads.* When Lincoln succeeded to Hamblin's place as purchasing agent, he took over a job that had become work enough for two men and for the rest of his career he continued to carry a load that steadily mounted in size. Coming to the office always on Saturday, sometimes on Sunday, seldom taking a vacation, going for years at a time without missing a day of work, delegating little authority, and doing as much as he could do personally, he retained more in his memory concerning what went on in the office and plant than could possibly be set down in a five-volume history of the company. Lincoln was a lone-working genius who gradually came to be recognized as the key man in the front office. His preference was for the old days, but he kept up with the new: he ordered flat-top desks for executives who wanted them, but his personal choice was the roll-top type. He kept the affairs of the company always at his finger tips and in so doing created for himself a place that was vital to the firm's operations. To have disturbed his position in the office would have been disastrous if for no other reason than that no man could have taken his place.

* Lincoln was always quick to point out that modern youths are mathematically illiterate. And so they *are* when compared with his standards. Men in the Whitin office still enjoy seeing him add long columns of figures in his head. No other man in the company has ever gathered about himself such a profusion of tales and fables. Those who know him only slightly are awed by his infallibility; those who work under him are unswervingly loyal. An employee in the company's drafting room tells a story that, even if apocryphal, catches the spirit of the man. Given the job of redrawing the floor layout plan of the main office, the drafting-room employee purposely came to work early one morning to avoid encountering Lincoln. But before he had finished his work Lincoln arrived, early as usual. When Lincoln learned what was going on he barked out, "Why didn't you ask me? The dimensions are . . . ," and he gave some figures. The draftsman nevertheless continued his job in silence. He was not at all surprised, however, to discover, when he had finished, that the figures Lincoln had remembered were right.

The third of the vice-presidents was J. Hugh Bolton, the man who had come to Whitinsville from the D. O. Pease Manufacturing Company and the one who had been instrumental in diversifying the company's product line. Bolton's temperament was quite different from the temperaments of the other two. Whereas Lincoln drove himself but not others and Banfield drove neither, Bolton drove both. Moreover, he was considerably younger than the other two, being only forty-five at the time. Though his choice for the executive vice-presidency seems now to have been the right and obvious one, to many at the time it seemed far from such. Bolton had been in Whitinsville for sixteen years and was known by nearly everyone in town. Yet he was still regarded as something of a newcomer. Certainly no one during those years had ever thought of him as a successor to Swift. There were two main reasons why such an idea was unthinkable. First of all, Bolton was a wool and rayon man. He was virtually unknown to the cotton industry. Already, by 1941, only half Whitin's sales were being made to cotton mills, and many skeptics imagined that the company's cotton-to-wool machinery ratio might decline still further, and dangerously so, under Bolton's administration. Secondly, Bolton was a salesman, in fact one of the best in the industry. Now, it was all very well for the executive head of the company to know sales — indeed, it was a prerequisite of the job — but he must also know administration and production. Fortunately Bolton's wide experience in developmental work meant that he had gained intimate familiarity with a large portion of the company's products, but it is true that, as a salesman, he had had little occasion to do administrative work. However, Swift was a person who had great faith in men and he believed Bolton could handle the job. Therefore in March, 1942, he recommended that Bolton be made first vice-president and a member of the board of directors.*

During the rest of the war Bolton served virtually as Swift's *alter ego*. Swift stuck close to Whitinsville watching carefully the shop's problems and progress, while Bolton ranged up and down the East Coast, trouble-shooting, making the necessary contacts, and representing the company in Washington. Fully half his time during the

---

* At the same time, the other two vice-presidents were also made members of the board.

war was spent away from the plant. But meanwhile the people in Whitinsville were becoming adjusted to the idea that a non-family executive would one day be vested with an authority that came to him simply by reason of appointment and not because of the stock he held in the company or because he was related by blood or marriage to the Whitin family.

2. THE SHIFT TO WAR WORK

When Bolton was promoted to be second in command, he was already in the midst of negotiating a series of war contracts for the company. Immediately after the declaration of war the company had received notice to cancel all its unfilled machinery orders and to complete only those approved by the War Production Board. It was obvious, therefore, that the company could expect to remain in the textile-machinery business for only a few more months. Beyond that time its work on textile machinery would have to be limited to the manufacture of enough repair parts to keep the equipment in the nation's mills operating.

It was at once evident to both Swift and Bolton that their best opportunity in war work lay in the production of auxiliary steam engines for Liberty ships such as the ones built for the British before the war. Each ship required a minimum of five such engines: three to generate electricity, one to drive the ship's main water-circulating pump, and one to drive its air-circulation blower. The existing capacity for building such engines in this country was severely limited. The three American firms that had built auxiliary engines in the past were small establishments.* To meet the huge demand brought on by the war, the Maritime Commission would either have to enlist the help of other manufacturers or else build its own additional plant capacity. What made other manufacturers difficult to find was the fact that Liberty engines required many cast-iron parts and consequently had to be made by a company with a large iron foundry. Very few companies with foundries as large as Whitin's still existed in America. The textile machinery industry was the only industry

---

* Besides the B. F. Sturtevant Company, there were the Troy Engine & Machine Company of Troy, Pennsylvania, and the Ames Iron Works of Oswego, New York, each of them an approximately half-million-dollar concern.

J. Hugh Bolton, President, 1946–

left in the country that was still using castings on a large scale. The other two industries that had formerly made wide use of foundry products — the farm equipment and the machine tool industry — had, by 1942, largely converted to the use of weldings and forgings. Thus Swift and Bolton felt that Whitin was peculiarly suited to meet the Maritime Commission's needs.*

However, he soon discovered that the ways of the Commission were not easily changed. Having had satisfactory dealings with its three regular suppliers of auxiliary steam engines, the Commission was not anxious to establish connections with a fourth. The fact that Whitin had shown its ability to produce similar engines for the British carried little weight, especially since in making the British engines Whitin had relied entirely on the Sturtevant company's drawings and specifications. Having no steam-engine model of its own, Whitin could hope to get a contract from the Commission only by borrowing Sturtevant's design, which Sturtevant was unwilling to have it do, or by designing a wholly new engine, which would cause more delay than the Commission was willing to sanction.

With dogged persistence, however, Bolton approached the problem from a new angle. Through his friends in the American Wool Association he learned of a Washington lobbyist named Morris Rosner who was influential in Maritime circles. Rosner was one of those behind-the-scenes men who was so reviled during the war and yet who did so much to cut across the administrative red tape of governmental bureaucracy. Certainly without his assistance the Whitin company would have had great difficulty in unseating the champions of *status quo* in the Maritime Commission. And the Commission itself would have paid far more for its engines and would have obtained them much later than it did.[6]

Meanwhile Bolton also busied himself by approaching friends in the General Electric Company to get their assistance on a design for an engine that would meet the Maritime Commission's critical ap-

---

* To increase its foundry efficiency during the war, Whitin (along with all the other major New England textile-machinery builders) engaged the National Engineering Company, of Chicago, to install a continuous molding system which greatly increased the output of the foundry and remarkably improved its working conditions. It would be interesting to speculate on how long those installations will delay the industry's eventual abandonment of casting on a large scale.

proval. As it developed, the principal difficulty in arriving at a new model was the limitation put on deviations from accepted steam-engine construction. Not only was the Commission loath to accept anything that had not been tested thoroughly, but since the ships on which the engines were to be installed were already being built, no really fundamental change in the engine's general dimensions was possible.

Once Bolton had obtained approval of the proposed designs, the Whitin company rapidly prepared itself to make steam engines on a mass-production basis.* To expedite matters it also provided for

* An unfortunate incident grew out of the company's contract with the Maritime Commission. Early in 1943 the SS *Henry Bacon,* a Liberty ship operated by the South Atlantic Steamship Line under government contract, developed trouble, on its maiden voyage, with the governor on its Whitin-built electric generator engines. While anchored off Balboa at the western end of the Panama Canal (18 January 1943), Chief Engineer Charles O. Stokes and First Assistant Engineer George E. Marsters attempted to remedy the difficulty. In so doing they inadvertently switched the entire electrical load onto one engine, allowing the other to run free. Thereupon the lights in the ship went out and the free engine speeded up to many times its normal rate of operation. Endeavoring, in the dark, to turn off the runaway engine, Stokes closed the exhaust valve (instead of the throttle valve as he should have) and thus jammed the engine. Under the terrific strain of coming to an immediate stop the engine's flywheel flew into bits, injuring Stokes seriously and Marsters to a less extent.

Stokes brought suit against the steamship line (and hence against the federal government for which the line was operating) and won a partial victory, the court declaring that 70 per cent of the accident was due to the unseaworthiness of the engine and 30 per cent was due to his own negligence. On appeal, however, the lower court's decision was reversed to the extent that the whole fault was laid to the unseaworthiness of the engine. The government paid Stokes $44,600.98 in damages plus $6,500 in expenses; shortly thereafter it settled with Marsters out of court for $10,000. In September, 1945, the government in turn sued Whitin to recover the damages it had been forced to pay the two men plus the $55,080.14 cost of repairing the ship — a total of $116,181.12. The government argued that a piece of flywheel had been found with a casting flaw in it; the company countered that such flaws are both inescapable and undetectable in casting work and that even a flawless wheel would have shattered under the circumstances.

Since Whitin was protected against liability suits by the Travelers Insurance Company, it was defended in court by that company (the suit was brought in the District Court of Massachusetts). However, it also assigned its own law firm, Herrick, Smith, Donald, Farley & Ketchum to advise on the case, for it felt that its reputation was involved, especially since the matter concerned the production of what was alleged to be defective war equipment, an extremely serious charge.

When the District Court judge decided in favor of the federal government, the insurance company appealed the case and won a reversal of the lower court's decision, thus securing for the Whitin company a complete release from blame. Meanwhile, however, extensive newspaper and radio comment had brought to the public's

assembling the engines with the units they were to drive. Engines that were to be attached to circulating pumps were sent to the Worthington Pump Company for final assembly, but engines that were meant to drive either generators or blowers were assembled in Whitinsville. On subcontract from Whitin, the General Electric Company reconditioned an old plant specifically to build 20-kilowatt Liberty ship generators. The American Blower Company likewise built blowers on subcontract from Whitin and shipped them to Whitinsville to be assembled with a steam-drive unit. (Toward the end of the war, steam engines were replaced by turbines which the company also built; see accompanying illustration.)

One of the reasons why Whitin was able to act on its war work so promptly was that it experienced no shortage of working funds. Although theoretically a war plant could obtain "progress payments" from the government on partly finished war work, such payments were difficult to arrange for and aggravatingly slow to collect. But as the Whitin Machine Works liquidated its textile-machinery orders, it accumulated large cash reserves on which to draw. Consequently it was able to go through the entire war without having to secure advances from the government and without borrowing from the banks.

During the war the company produced a total of about eleven thousand auxiliary Liberty-ship steam engines — somewhere between 80 and 90 per cent of the country's total requirements. On 7 November 1942, in recognition of the quality of its products and the promptness of its deliveries, the Maritime Commission awarded Whitin the coveted Maritime "M," * the second such award made in New Eng-

_____

attention the government's suit against Whitin. Not without justification the company felt that the government, in seeking to settle a hundred-thousand-dollar claim, had done many times that amount of damage to the company's reputation and on insufficient grounds. (Information in this footnote was obtained from a brief prepared by Herrick, Smith, Donald, Farley & Ketchum for *U. S.* v. *Whitin Machine Works*.)

* As a matter of detail, the Whitin "M" was specifically awarded for proficiency in the production of bleeder plugs, small threaded plugs that allow fuel-oil tanks to be drained and cleaned. Early in the war there was an acute shortage of bleeder plugs. No ship could sail without them. By greatly simplifying the method of manufacturing such plugs, Whitin broke the shortage and earned the gratitude of the Maritime Commission.

During the war the company also received the Victory Fleet Flag, awarded to any plant that furnished materials to the Victory Fleet; the "A" award for proficiency in its Air Raid Precaution drill; and the Defense Bond Award for subscribing 10

land.[7] An elaborate presentation ceremony was attended by Massachusetts' Governor Leverett Saltonstall and by various state, federal, and Maritime Commission dignitaries and was broadcast to the region by radio.

If the company's work on steam engines may be said to have been an accomplishment in speed and production, its second major wartime job was a feat in care and precision. To keep the B-24 bomber program running smoothly the government needed literally hundreds of thousands of magnetos, for each bomber required an initial installation of eight, plus enough for servicing purposes. The government's principal contractor, the American Bosch Corporation,[8] of Springfield, Massachusetts, was unable to meet the demand without assistance and so began looking about the surrounding territory for plants that could serve as subcontractors. The Bosch company found that Whitin had two very important production assets: (1) ample plant facilities, since it was not making use of its large machinery-erection floors and (2) an abundant local supply of female labor.[9] What it lacked were the proper machine tools and the necessary skilled labor. Bosch felt confident, however, that the tools could be obtained through the Defense Plant Corporation and that the necessary skills could be acquired through training.[10]

Therefore, in April, 1942, Whitin signed a contract with the American Bosch Corporation to build magnetos for Pratt & Whitney engines on a subcontract basis.[11] The Whitin company at once sent a corps of men and women to Springfield for training and began to clear its spinning-erection floors for a line-production setup. By November it was ready to start turning out magnetos.

Since nothing in Whitin's experience had prepared it for the job, the remarkable achievement in the manufacture of magnetos is the more unaccountable. Some magneto parts had to be held to within two-*tenths* of a thousandth of an inch, while tolerances on textile-machinery parts seldom fell below one- to two-thousandths of an inch. Furthermore, most of Whitin's magneto work force was green,

---

per cent of its payroll to government savings bonds. (See illustration showing the flags being flown from the Administration Building.) As the illustration shows, a service flag was also flown from the bell tower. On the flag was sewed the number of employees who were serving in the armed forces and, in gold, the number who had been killed. Whenever news of an employee's death was received the company's American flag was flown at half-mast.

and most of its administrative force was inexperienced in the type of line production that required such carefully balanced adjustment to achieve high-speed, efficient operation.

One intangible factor seems worth mentioning — and being an intangible is perhaps worth more weight than at first seems warranted; that is, the *esprit de corps* of the Whitin workers, most of whom had relatives in the service and felt that they were lending a hand toward fighting the war. The bomber program, even as small a part of it as the production of magnetos, had its glamorous aspects, especially in a small town where patriotism ran higher than was likely to be the case among more cynical workers in larger cities. Moreover, the magneto project was run as a wholly separate unit — a shop within a shop. The resulting close-knit camaraderie among the magneto employees may well have been an important factor in producing their high-level performance. In addition, the establishment of the magneto job as a department completely separate from the rest of the shop and one that did not have to tie in with the plant's other operations may help to explain Whitin's success in meeting its heavy magneto production quotas.*

During the war Whitin produced approximately seventy-three thousand complete magnetos with additional spare parts sufficient to assemble thirty-five thousand more. Not only did it meet all its own quotas, but it occasionally assisted the American Bosch Corporation and the Veeder-Root Company (another Bosch subcontractor) in meeting theirs. Every magneto produced by Whitin had to be inspected first in Whitinsville and then again in Springfield before it could be accepted. As a result Whitin's magneto workers became accustomed to working well inside the allowed tolerances in order to be always on the side of certainty. It would be impossible to state with any accuracy the proportions of the wartime B-24 magnetos built in Whitinsville, but certainly it was not less than 25 per cent.

Steam engines and magnetos do not by any means exhaust the list

---

* Perhaps, also, it explains why so little of the precision work learned on the magneto job carried over to the postwar work on textile machinery. The company argues that it can tighten its tolerances, but that the benefits of closer tolerances on equipment like textile machinery are not worth the added costs involved. What the magneto job taught the company were inspection techniques and methods of achieving quality control, both of which carried over into the firm's postwar work.

of the company's war products. The accompanying illustration shows a few of the many others.* But in dollar volume, steam engines, turbines, and magnetos accounted for about three-quarters of the war work done by the company in the years 1942–44. (Whitin's total sales for those years break down as follows: war work 61.4 per cent, textile machinery 21.6 per cent, parts for textile machinery 17.0 per cent.) †

3. RECONVERSION

Because the major portion of Whitin's war work was devoted to helping build the fighting arm of the military services rather than to keeping the forces overseas supplied, its rôle in the war ended somewhat earlier than the war itself. By January, 1945, its final steam-engine order from the Maritime Commission had been completed and its magneto work for American Bosch had nearly run out. Meanwhile, so much strain had been put on the textile industry during the years of heavy war production that considerable pressure had built up to get the textile-machinery manufacturers back into regular production on mill equipment.

The pressure was especially strong in the twister line since the demand for tire-cord yarn had increased enormously during the war, especially the demand for heavy-ply yarn to be used on truck and bomber tires. Therefore, the War Production Board had called representatives of the industry together in a series of conferences, during June, 1944, to discuss the best means of meeting the crisis. It was generally agreed that each company should engage in the production of the twister model best suited to its productive facilities. The Attorney General's office was consulted to make certain that there

---

* The company also kept about a hundred workers busy on orders for torpedo parts manufactured for the Newport (Rhode Island) Torpedo Station.

† As in the previous war the company's profits were kept low by the federal Excess Profits Tax — and for much the same reasons. The base years 1935–39, on which the tax was figured, were years of very low earnings for Whitin, and since the company still followed a policy of keeping assets extraordinarily undervalued, very little benefit was received from the alternative privilege of computing its excess profits on the basis of capitalization. Through the constant reduction of prices to the government, earnings were kept within limits, and consequently, when renegotiations were entered into, a refund had to be made to the government for only one year (1943), and then for only a little more than a million dollars.

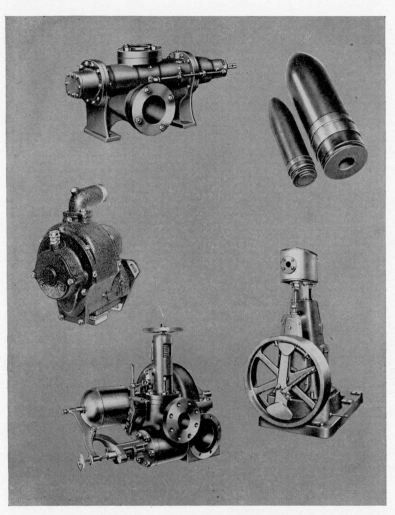

OIL PUMP   PROJECTILES
MAGNETO
TURBINE   STEAM ENGINE

WORLD WAR II PRODUCTS

BELL TOWER AND VICTORY FLAGS, 1945

would be no objection to such industry-wide coöperation; then, with the Justice Department's formal approval, the industry embarked on a joint effort to meet the nation's twister requirements. All sales were made directly to the Defense Plant Corporation, which was charged with responsibility for seeing that mills obtained the twisters they needed to meet their war production quotas.

Such a frontal attack on the twister shortage was of benefit to the industry as well as to the government, for it helped to fill the gap that threatened to occur as war work began falling off, and while peace work remained still impossible because of materials shortages.

In those intervening months between war and peace, Whitin's management took occasion for thorough self-analysis. The job that lay ahead promised to be enormous; already customers were asking to be put on the list for postwar machinery. Capacity operations appeared to be foreseeable for at least three years. Every line promised to be in heavy demand. Whitin's executives knew that their organization was not equipped to handle such a load. Except for the installation of a standard cost system in 1938, techniques of administration had undergone little change since the mid-1920's, when it was still possible for the company to have a relatively simple plant organization and when much of the necessary coördination of activities was carried on personally and by word of mouth. Comparatively few types of machines were being made in those earlier years, and many of them were standard. Of course, a certain amount of job work existed and had existed since as far back as the 1870's, for American manufacturers had always encouraged mill men to write their own machinery specifications. But with experienced foremen at the helm such deviations from true course had not been troublesome.

By the 1940's, however, conditions had radically changed. The old foremen who had successfully added to their accumulated knowledge each new deviation from standard as it came along had been succeeded by younger men who were overwhelmed when faced with such a multiplicity of manufacturing details. Furthermore, the company's diversification program had nearly tripled the number of products it was offering its customers and had added to the problems of production control by geometric progression. During the 1930's

low-capacity operations had enabled the company to get along satisfactorily with its old organization despite an increasingly complicated product line, but the prospect of a postwar production boom
made drastic changes in plant organization imperative.

Once again problems led to progress. In 1938, when Saco-Lowell
was showing a better earnings ratio than Whitin, Whitin had taken
the lead by installing a standard cost system. In 1945, when Whitin's
production difficulties looked infinitely more complex than Saco-
Lowell's, Whitin again led by instituting a far-reaching administrative reorganization. Already, because of the war, one significant step
forward had been taken — the adoption of a job-evaluation and job-
classification system. Previously men had been hired and promoted
on a strictly individual basis. Consequently, wage rates on similar
types of work had become far from comparable. What helped to
bring on the decision to begin a program of job evaluation and
classification was the desire to get increases in wages for shop employees. During the war, wages had become virtually frozen; the
only way management could give an employee a raise was to promote him. Since such promotions had to be carefully defined, job
classifications became almost inevitable. At the time, of course, such
classifications were applied to only those jobs currently involved in
war work; when peace returned, the system, which had been installed by men from Ernst & Ernst, was easily extended to the rest
of the shop.

Two large jobs required immediate attention at the end of the war.
First, the entire plant layout needed reappraisal. Departments that
had been efficiently located a quarter-century earlier had often remained where they were simply because there had seemed no pressing need to move them. Castings sometimes traveled for miles
through the shop, much of the distance unnecessarily. No one in the
company had the experience or the detachment which the plant layout job required. For that reason, in the fall of 1944, Whitin hired a
firm of New York management consultants, Wallace Clark & Company,[12] to study the problem and make recommendations.

The second problem concerned the company's production department, which necessarily had to be made the brain center of the organization if Whitin was to conduct successfully its huge postwar

job-order business. Even before the war, W. W. Tuttle, of Ernst & Ernst, had urged upon Swift the necessity of revamping the production department. At that time the production department was still scheduling all production on the basis of the time each operation was known to require. No attempt was made to approach the problem from the standpoint of the productive capacity in each department, and some departments were basing their work schedules on the same form of building orders used back in the 1880's. When the shop was not busy, the system worked well enough, but at peak capacity one schedule inevitably competed with another for the available men and machines in a department until near-chaos developed. Consequently, the plant reorganization that had seemed unnecessary to the Whitin management before the war became inescapable as soon as the war was over and capacity operations were in prospect.

The company could have picked no more difficult period to make such a complex adjustment in its management routine. In a period of slack activity the adjustment would have been difficult enough. But in 1945 Whitin was facing the largest backlog of orders in its history and was beginning textile-machinery production again from scratch. When a plant the size of Whitin's suddenly resumes production on dozens of different kinds of machines, it must do everything at once. It must try to produce each part in sufficient quantities to be economical. Yet it must not tie up a machine with the production of parts that will not be used for six months, when parts that could be used within six hours are waiting to be made. It must not keep nearly completed spinning frames standing on the erection floor with only a few final parts missing, yet it must not obtain those parts at the cost of disturbing the flow of work in the rest of the shop.

Nevertheless, with the odds against them, the men of the Ernst & Ernst organization, under the immediate direction of W. W. Tuttle, undertook the job of reorganizing the production department in the summer of 1945.[13] Immediately conflicts developed. Tuttle wished to have Whitin set up a highly centralized production-control system with everything focused on a central ledger control. Swift and Bolton insisted that the system be decentralized to as great an extent as possible, and held to that view throughout. Tuttle also advised that an experienced production-control man be hired to supervise the installation and to make it operate. But the company insisted that a Whitin employee be trained to handle the job.

Outside conditions helped to complicate the task of getting Whitin's production back on a smooth-flowing schedule. Everywhere, in the fall of 1945 and the spring of 1946, plants were struggling to reconvert. Materials were short and deliveries were spotty. Strikes frequently forced the customers of a struck plant to close down for lack of parts, and the shortage of such raw products as pig iron drove firms like Whitin to go into the world market to buy materials for which they had to pay two and three times as much as they had ever paid before.

By the summer of 1946, conditions in the Whitin shop had reached a critical state. Production had been running along at a high rate, but poor coördination had resulted in the building-up of a dangerously large inventory of unfinished parts. Machines were being shipped minus critical parts, and the production department's expediters were running themselves into exhaustion in their vain effort to locate the reasons for the shortages which were appearing on every order.

Observing the difficulties that the Whitin management was having, the Wallace Clark consultants, who had been hired to work on plant layout, offered to lend their services and promised to straighten out the production department's entanglements within a year's time.[14] By agreeing that greater decentralization was desirable, they won the sympathetic ear of the Whitin management and so received authority to take over the reorganization of the production department from the Ernst & Ernst group. (Ernst & Ernst, however, was still retained as the company's auditors.)

Almost the first thing that the Wallace Clark men did was to convince Swift and Bolton that a trained production-control man was needed to head up the reorganized department. On their recommendation the company hired Fletcher O. Rizer, formerly production-control manager in the Dallas plant of the North American Aviation Corporation. Rizer was a typical son of the Southwest — aggressive, energetic, self-confident, and impervious to criticism. To the quiet village of Whitinsville he seemed like a football player at a D.A.R. tea. Indeed, he often referred to himself as the new quarter-back on the company's management team. But Rizer was exactly the sort of man the job required, for the new production-control system cut across so many established ways of doing things that it had to be jammed through in order to be effective.

One of the things that surprised Rizer on his arrival in Whitins-ville was the coöperative spirit evinced by the plant's foremen. Despite the nerve-wracking pressure they had been forced to work under, they still obligingly gave way to the urgencies of every new rush order that came their way. Soon Rizer realized, however, that their very obligingness lay near the root of the shop's difficulties. Having been trained in a tradition of coördinating their efforts with their fellow-foremen through personal and informal contact, the Whitin foremen were not accustomed to laying out their work in advance and then saying "No" to requests that disturbed their production routine. As a result, work was sometimes laid aside to meet an immediate emergency only to create a much greater emergency further along in the production cycle.

In consultation with Wallace Clark's management experts, Rizer set about remedying the situation. With the idea of determining how much work a department was capable of handling, he had studies made of the machine capacities in each department. Then, instead of scheduling each job individually without reference to department bottlenecks, he laid out production schedules based on the known capacity of each department. To keep track of how well the work was flowing through the shop, he assigned a corps of checkers to assist the foremen in planning their work and to report any deficiencies in the system's operation. These checkers, young and unskilled — often girls just out of high school — became official representatives of the front office to the people in the plant. In laying out a department's work they followed a fairly simple and mechanical procedure, but the logic of what they did was usually so inexorable that, even though they gave every foreman the privilege of approving or disapproving their plan of production for the day, in most cases they really seemed to have taken over the brain work of the department where they worked — and so, down went the foreman's standing one rung lower on the ladder of prestige.

For two and a half years, the Wallace Clark men worked with Rizer on smoothing out the complicated problems of planning the huge volume of job work in which the Whitin Machine Works was engaged during the postwar boom. The best evidence of their success in stepping up the shop's productivity is the fact that twice during that short period the production department was forced to abandon the graphs it had been using because the chart lines had run off the top of the page.

The postwar readjustment in Whitin's management brought many new names to the company's organization chart.* Probably the change that had the greatest meaning for the future was the replacement of Banfield, as works manager, by thirty-eight-year-old Erik O. Pierson. Before the war Pierson had been one of the company's cotton-machinery salesmen and before that an employee of a mill-engineering firm with experience in many parts of the world.[15] When Whitin's selling function fell into limbo during the war, Pierson took charge of the complicated and critical task of handling the shop's relations with the government on matters of priorities and allocations. So impressed was Bolton with Pierson's wartime performance that in September, 1947, he decided to give him an opportunity to prove himself in production, though Pierson had had no previous experience in that line.

* Besides those mentioned here and elsewhere in the text there were Leonard White, former salesman for the Jones & Laughlin Steel Corporation, hired to handle the company's steel purchases, and Robert Waters, former liaison man between the Whitin company and the American Bosch Corporation, hired to handle sales of Schweiter winders.

If the Whitin company could be said to have an executive hiring policy, it was to find a job to fit an able man rather than to find an able man to fit a job. To my knowledge the company has never in its history conducted an organized search for executive talent. Yet on occasions too numerous to mention it has found jobs for able men who chanced to come within its purview. Such men usually were appointed to staff positions (line executives continued to be selected from within the company). That such men were willing to give up other jobs to work in Whitinsville speaks eloquently for the attractiveness of life in the village.

The company has almost never hired graduates just out of engineering or business schools, for it has always placed more emphasis on experience than on formal education. Following World War II it did inaugurate a program of advanced apprenticeship training in which young engineers were given an opportunity to learn the problems of textile-machinery manufacture. But whether in the long run the program would be successful in training a younger generation of executives depends in part on the level of salaries the company will be willing to pay and in part on the prospects of promotion it will be able to offer young men in the future.

Pierson's promotion was made especially significant by the fact that less than a year earlier, in December, 1946, there had been a change in the other key production post, the superintendency. At Christmastime, the man who had been shop superintendent throughout the war, Harry Mitchell, a Scotsman noted for the burr on his tongue and the brusqueness of his manner, was stricken with a fatal heart attack. Bolton's choice of a man to succeed Mitchell was as much a surprise to the successor as to the rest of the company, for John H. Cunningham was only thirty-one years of age when he was informed of his promotion. Like Pierson he had never had experience in factory management. Both men were, however, graduate engineers, Pierson having attended Rensselaer Polytechnic Institute and Cunningham having attended Harvard's Division of Engineering Sciences. During the war Cunningham had risen in rank to become a Lieutenant Commander in the submarine service and had served as Sound Material Officer aboard the U.S.S. *Growler* (during which tour of duty he earned the Bronze Star Award) and as Executive Officer of the U.S.S. *Sailfish* (the former *Squalus*). Returning to Whitinsville after the war, Cunningham had been made staff assistant to Bolton, which position he held at the time of his promotion. Sensing the man's innate leadership ability and again overriding a serious lack of training in manufacturing, Bolton had appointed Cunningham to the vacant superintendency in January, 1947. Throughout the tense and hectic days of postwar capacity operations, Cunningham went about his work with cool good humor. Extremely popular with men and management alike, he was a good antidote to the nervous tension of the times. Under the circumstances he could hardly have been expected to be a master of his job, but at least he never let the job master him.

Pierson's and Cunningham's promotions were significant parts of a larger transition. The company that had once been run by its family-owner group was gradually being turned over, under Swift's watchful eye, to a corps of hired managers. The transition had begun, perhaps unwittingly, when Bolton, Banfield, and Lincoln were made vice-presidents in 1939. It did not really gather momentum, however, until Bolton began to take over many of Swift's executive duties in 1946. As administrative head of the company, Bolton astounded both supporters and detractors with his unsuspected executive ability. Under him the all-comprehending personal management practiced by Swift gave way to a decentralized, committee system of management. Whereas formerly allegiances in the plant had run vertically, Bolton encouraged horizontal teamwork and communications. The transition was not accomplished without friction. That it was accomplished at all was owing in part to the still pervasive influence of Swift who, even in the semi-retirement he affected, remained the company's most dynamic personality.

4. SHIFTS IN OWNERSHIP

Swift's partial retirement from active management and his delegation of authority to non-family executives was but part of the trend away from family ownership and control. Beyond the family's failure to provide a member from its ranks as Swift's successor, two other forces were weakening its influence in company affairs.[16]

For one thing, the family was growing larger. John C. Whitin had been survived by only one child. That child in turn had been survived by only three. But those three had had thirteen children and had had twenty-four grandchildren. Consequently the family-ownership group was becoming diffused, and many heirs were inheriting a financial interest in a company they had no personal interest in.

In addition, inheritance taxes had begun to take their toll. By the 1940's a large concern owned solely by one family had become an anachronism. Except where members of the Whitin family had been able to set aside large reserves in non-company investments, their estates necessarily had to sell part of their Whitin stock to realize enough cash to pay the taxes on inheritance.

In general, the George Marston Whitin branch of the family (40 per cent interest) had fared better than the two Lasell branches (30 per cent interest each) — and for three very good reasons. In the first place, the members of the Marston Whitin family had lived somewhat less pretentiously than the Lasells and had tended to invest their income in a productive rather than a consumptive way.*

---

* The George Marston Whitins would have done still better had they not lost heavily on the New England mill stocks they held. In general, the Lasells sold their mill stocks while they were still bringing high prices and then enjoyed spending the proceeds therefrom.

Moreover, they had earned larger total incomes than their Lasell cousins. Three of Marston Whitin's sons-in-law had become top executives in the company, whereas none of the Lasell sons had; and, although the combined salaries of the three men did not average higher than $110,000 a year (a moderate sum for a company Whitin's size), such salaries enabled their recipients to live comfortably while putting the major portion of their dividend incomes into other investments. Finally, through a combination of foresightedness and good fortune, Mr. and Mrs. George Marston Whitin had been able to pass on their holdings to their heirs with a minimum of tax liability. Marston Whitin had died in 1920, long before inheritance taxes had become confiscatory, and had left his 10 per cent block of stock in trust for his descendants. Mrs. Marston Whitin did not die until 1940, but as early as 1917 she had begun distributing her stock to her daughters, to her sons-in-law, and in trust to her grandchildren, so that by the time of her death little remained to be taxed.

The Lasells were not so fortunate. Chester Lasell died in 1935 when the tax was not yet heavy, but in his estate he left notes payable to the company for $140,000, secured in part by company stock.* Not wishing to settle the debt in cash, Chester's estate offered to pay the company in Whitin Machine Works securities. At the time, the company would probably have preferred cash, although in theory a stock settlement was attractive enough. Because of the extreme depression and the poor showing of the industry for so many years past, and because there was virtually no public market for the company's stock, the Lasell family was reconciled to accepting a very low price. The figure finally agreed upon, about sixty-five dollars a share, was roughly equivalent to the per-share value of the company's net current assets. Yet, on a yield basis, the price was a fair one, for the company was currently paying dividends equal to four dollars a share. From the standpoint of the company, the reacquisition of its own stock was the equivalent of investing its funds at 6 per cent, with the chance of a considerable increase in earnings-value.

The problems of Chester's heirs were further complicated by the

---

* The bulk of Chester's indebtedness to the company dated back to 1924, at which time he had drawn on the firm's men and materials to reconstruct a magnificent colonial farmhouse a few miles north of Whitinsville.

fact that Chester had left half his stock to his wife and half to his other heirs. By the terms of his will, his wife thus became (after J. M. Lasell's death) the company's largest single stockholder, with about a 13 per cent interest. But some day Mrs. Chester Lasell's heirs (Mrs. Lasell died 26 April 1950 while this book was in press) would have to pay another tax on *her* stock — in contrast to the single tax paid on stock inherited directly from Chester.

J. M. Lasell, before his death in 1939, had foreseen the difficulties that would one day face Chester's heirs and therefore had left *all* his stock to his seven children (most of it in trust with the Boston Safe Deposit & Trust Company). By 1939, inheritance taxes had become so heavy that J. M.'s estate, in order to meet its obligations, had no other recourse than to sell some of the company stock that he had owned. Again the company agreed to act as purchaser. This time a low price was beneficial to both parties, since the valuation of Lasell's estate for tax purposes would in large part hinge on the price at which his Whitin stock was sold to the company. But business had improved considerably since 1935 and the company knew, from the state's demurrer to the 1935 price it had set on Chester's stock, that a higher value would have to be set. Therefore, in 1940, the company bought 4,500 shares of its own stock from the J. M. Lasell estate for $75 a share.

By that time there were 6,854 shares of Whitin stock lying fallow in the company's treasury (about 7 per cent of the company's total issued stock), and Swift was beginning to consider what should be done with it. I am not sure that I know all his reasons for eventually deciding to put the stock back into private hands, but the fact that he chose to sell it to company executives is an indication that even before Pearl Harbor he was giving thought to the day when non-family executives might assume major responsibilities for the firm's affairs.

Three problems were involved in selling stock to executives. First, the transaction could not be so large that it might be considered a public offering, for in that case the stock would have to be listed with the Securities & Exchange Commission, and the company was not anxious to divulge all the information that such a listing required; nor was it anxious to go to the necessary expense (approximately

$200,000). Secondly, the price had to be carefully established. Too low a price would have brought charges that the company was giving its employees hidden earnings. Finally, the stock had to meet the provisions of Massachusetts' Blue Sky laws, a formality that had never before been necessary. Whitin's lawyers finally agreed that a sale to sixteen executives would probably not be interpreted as a public offering and that $75 per share (the price established by the purchase of stock from the J. M. Lasell estate) would probably be considered fair. Because of the company's unassailable financial reputation, the approval of the state's Public Utilities Commission was obtained without difficulty.

In 1941, therefore, 1,200 shares of treasury stock were offered to the company's top sixteen executives in blocks of from 25 to 150 shares apiece. Payments were to be made 10 per cent in cash and the balance in regular installments over a six-year period with interest at 4 per cent. To the executives the investment was an attractive one, for dividends in the first year alone were almost enough to cover the down payment. The company reserved the right to buy back the stock at the paid-in price, if an employee defaulted on his payments or if he died or left the company before completing his purchase. But once a man had finished paying for his stock it became irretrievably his.*

Meanwhile the Lasell branches of the family were beginning to bring pressure to have the company's stock split into shares of smaller denomination so that a market for the stock could be fostered. Some of the heirs of Chester Lasell found themselves in the uncomfortable position of having the bulk of their personal fortunes tied up in Whitin stock, for which there was virtually no market. At the same time, the trustees of J. M. Lasell's estate were giving thought to the advisability of diversifying the trust's holdings. Since the war's prosperity had enhanced the value of Whitin stocks, both Lasell groups felt that the time was opportune to sell. Wishing to accommodate the family and learning that stock divisions were easily and

---

* Again, in 1944, the company offered treasury stock to its executives under similar provisions, except that this time 3,221 shares were offered to thirty-five executives in blocks twice as large as formerly and for $80 a share. The remaining undistributed shares still repose in the company's treasury. A third sale to executives does not seem likely without a formal listing with the Securities & Exchange Commission.

inexpensively negotiated, the board of directors authorized a stock split of four shares to one on 12 February 1945, thus increasing the outstanding shares from 90,000 with a par value of $100 per share to 360,000 with a par value of $25 per share. At the same time, they made the Second National Bank of Boston the company's transfer agent, allowing an agency outside the company to perform that function for the first time in history.

There is something magical about stock splits. Nearly always the split shares assume a greater total value than the unsplit shares have had. The increased value of Whitin's shares was startling. Only a few months before the split occurred, Whitin's stock was considered worth $75 per share. A year later the heirs of Chester Lasell and the administrators of J. M. Lasell's trust were making small private offerings of Whitin's $25 shares at as high as $43.50 per share.* A small over-the-counter interest in the stock developed in the Boston area and boosted the price at one time to over $50 — the equivalent of $200 before the split or about two and one-half times the price paid by the company's executives a few years earlier. The company was especially pleased to see that some of the purchasers of its stock were such venerable New England institutions as the Lowell Institute, the Massachusetts General Hospital, and the Boston Museum of Fine Arts, proof that the company's common stock was looked upon as having many of the qualities of a preferred security.

In the space of six years nearly 10 per cent of the company's stock thus passed into the hands of the public, and the number of stockholders increased from less than a hundred to nearly four hundred. Though still not having proceeded far, the trend toward dispersion of ownership was marked and irreversible. Holdings in the Chester Lasell branch of the family had fallen to about 25 per cent and in the J. M. Lasell branch to about 20 per cent, and both promised to fall

---

* Chester Lasell's heirs sold through the Providence brokerage house of G. H. Walker & Company. The J. M. Lasell trustees sold through the Boston office of Kidder, Peabody & Company and through the Worcester brokerage firm of Kinsley & Adams.

At the end of 1948, the company's stock was selling for only about $43 per share; the company's net current assets at that time were alone worth $39 per share. The stock was so conservatively valued that the Fitch Bond Record rated it only one step below such blue chip securities as the stocks of the General Electric, General Mills, and General Motors companies.

still further once the company had listed its stock publicly, an action it could not much longer defer.

Only the George Marston Whitin branch had held its own (in fact, it had gained about 2 per cent through the executive purchase plan). But even there the establishment of trusts promised to reduce the likelihood that in the future any one member of the family would be able to govern the company's affairs simply through the leverage of stock ownership. Nevertheless, the future balance of power lay within the Marston Whitin branch. Financially, it was prepared to meet all inheritance taxes for at least one more generation without being forced to liquidate any of its Whitin stock. Socially, it was still a closely knit group that gave promise of working in concert for the short-term future at least.

Soon the chief executive of the company would, for the first time, be the servant and not the master of the board of directors. No chief executive in the company's corporate history had ever held stock control in his own hands, yet his authority had never been questioned by those who served on the board. With someone outside the family occupying the presidency, however, the board of directors, as representatives of the family, would take on new authority. In large part the future of the company would depend on the tranquillity of the board's relations with the man in the president's office.

CHAPTER XIX

UNIONIZATION AND LABOR TROUBLE, 1943–1948

For one hundred and twelve years the Whitin company maintained a proud record of freedom from labor trouble. During those years it had never been confronted with the problem of unionization; no union movement had even gained a start. Whitin workers had never gone out on mass strike; they had never engaged in violence of any kind. Their demands for shorter hours and higher pay had percolated up through the shop's foremen to top management and had always been met in one way or another without serious disturbance to labor-management tranquillity. The company had followed a consistent policy of frank paternalism toward its employees and had always taken care to give its workers the impression that their best interests would be served in the long run by acquiescence to management's over-all plan for their welfare. In return for the interest shown in them, the workers evinced remarkable loyalty to their employers. When they spoke of the company's owners as the "Royal Family" as was their custom, they did so not in the sneering manner one might have expected, but with a tone of respect such as the British use in referring to their Windsor family. The Whitins may not always have been democratically popular among the villagers, but there was never a time when they were not held in high esteem.

During the 1930's, while militant unionism was advancing the cause of organized labor in other parts of the country, Whitinsville managed to escape completely the storms of industrial disharmony and strife. In so doing, however, it gradually separated itself from what was going on in other industrial centers, until by World War II its wage and hour policies were considerably out of line with those of other companies in other industries.

This disparity of conditions was made possible by Whitinsville's singular insularity. For two decades — roughly from 1920 to 1940 — the people of Whitinsville lived a detached and almost static existence, removed to a remarkable degree from the influences of life in the surrounding countryside. Between 1920 and 1940, the number of inhabitants in the village remained almost stationary.* Labor turnover in the shop became so slow that promotions seldom occurred except in case of deaths. Almost no one moved into the village. What movement occurred was outward. The more impatient among the town's young men took jobs elsewhere. Only two of the local lads of that period rose to executive positions in the company — George McRoberts, who became advertising manager, and Harry Moss, who became vice-president in charge of wool-machinery development and sales.

Gradually the average age level of employees mounted. Almost no one chose to retire, and in those days of financial stringency very few young men were hired. The number of "old-timers" in the shop came to be an object of pride in Whitinsville. In 1921 the company began the practice of awarding service pins to men who had been in its employ for long periods of time, and in the space of 27 years it gave out no less than one hundred and nine diamond-studded emblems to men who had actively served the company for a period of fifty years,† a record that could never have been achieved had retirements been compulsory.

Work went on in Whitinsville during the nineteen-twenties and 'thirties at a quiet, steady tempo, and management took pride in not having a "drive" shop. Nearly everyone went home for lunch, taking an hour off and sometimes more. Hours of work were flexible, and lateness to work was thought no more of than voluntary overtime duty at night or on Sundays.

To outsiders the serenity and security of life in Whitinsville

---

* The census of 1920 reported 10,174 inhabitants in Northbridge; the census of 1940 reported 10,242, a net change of only 68 persons.

† Information furnished by W. Hanna of the Boston office of Whitehead and Hoag, manufacturers of advertising novelties and commemorative pins. The Whitin company presents jeweled pins to all employees who have completed 5, 10, 15, 20, 25, 30, 40, and 50 years of service. As is fitting, the 50-year pins are the most elaborately designed. They are made of 10-carat gold and set with ten 1½-point diamonds. In 1948 these pins were costing the company more than eighty dollars apiece.

seemed old-fashioned — an evidence that the company was growing inefficient. Yet, in a way, the Whitinsville experiment was more modern than the latest book on sociology and more advanced than the newest theory on industrial relations, for the people of Whitinsville had come to have a sense of security that few industrial workers are ever able to attain. In addition, they had come to feel a proprietary interest in their company, an interest far stronger than any that could have been fostered in them merely by a stock-sharing plan designed to make them part-owners of the firm. The shop was more than a factory to them; it was almost a social club. One's fellow-employees were not men one saw only during work hours; they were friends with whom one spent evenings and holidays. No one seemed to mind the fact that wages in Worcester were considerably higher than those in Whitinsville. One could always point to the offsetting low rents, the garden facilities, the public services, and the genial atmosphere to be found in Whitinsville.

How long the Whitin Machine Works could have continued to support a policy that held the community almost stationary in size and that tended on the one hand to discourage young men from joining the company, while on the other hand it advanced the average age of company employees until there was danger that corporate arteriosclerosis would set in, is now a moot question. The Second World War suddenly changed the entire situation by forcing the Whitin company to do what it had never done before: to expand by venturing into the unknown territory that lay outside the textile-machinery field. That the company succeeded in meeting its challenge is much to be applauded; that, in succeeding, it sacrificed much that it had previously stood for will, to many, seem regrettable. It seems clear, however, that what occurred was in any case inevitable and that eventually Whitin's insularity had to give way if the firm was to remain a vitally strong institution.

I. THE END OF WHITINSVILLE'S INSULARITY

Nowhere was the impact of the war on the village so dramatically evident as in the change which it brought to the company's employee-housing plan. For years the Whitin firm had operated its houses at or near the break-even point, all the while keeping its buildings in excellent condition and its rents very low. During the early 1930's, however, when conservation of liquid capital became the keystone of Whitin's financial policy, the firm postponed village improvements and allowed a large backlog of deferred maintenance requirements to accumulate, until it could no longer delay making repairs and improvements on its buildings if it was to preserve the quality of its housing accommodations.

By 1937 business had begun to revive, and Swift finally felt justified in again diverting funds to village maintenance. But meanwhile costs had started rising, and operating losses on the company's houses seemed almost inescapable. In an attempt to avert those losses the company called upon Ernst & Ernst, as has already been related, to develop a scheme of pay incentives that would make maintenance work more efficient. But the steady rise in wages was too great to be offset by incentive schemes alone. What the company needed was a parallel rise in rental income. Yet Swift hesitated to upset the local stability he had struggled so hard to achieve. Though he recognized his inability to control the outside forces that were causing an increase in village maintenance costs, he nevertheless did his best to keep rents at a low level. His only concession to the inevitable was to charge slightly higher rents to employees who requested the installation of modern furnace or bath facilities* and to raise rents by 10 per cent upon the first occasion of a change in tenants. But the turnover of employees was so slow that many dwellings continued for years with the same occupants renting at the same rates. In the years 1938 to 1940 the company was losing an average of $152,000 annually on its housing operations.

Then came the OPA. With the establishment of rent ceilings, the income from company houses became frozen at levels that had been in effect since about 1933. Yet maintenance costs continued to rise with uncontrollable velocity until the rental income from company houses was not enough even to pay local taxes. By 1944 the Whitin Machine Works was standing a loss on housing of $286,000 a year,

---

* Here Swift's liberal policy backfired. By allowing individuals the privilege of choosing between low rents and improved housing, he in effect encouraged workers to be satisfied with existing standards. Consequently until recently, there were houses in Whitinsville with outdoor toilets — and probably some would be there still had not the company changed its policy and made modern plumbing compulsory.

of which only $56,000 was depreciation expense. The social experiment that had seemed so promising a decade earlier had, for the time at least, become an onerous financial burden.

Meanwhile the war had conspired to shatter the stability of Whitin's labor force.[1] The demand for employees soon exceeded anything the company had known before, and at the very time when most of the village's young men were leaving town for service in the armed forces. Yet, thanks to the automobile, Whitin no longer had to depend solely on the village for its supply of workers. Practically the entire Blackstone Valley could be drawn upon. Consequently nearly half the people employed by the firm during and immediately following the war came to work from outside Whitinsville (see Appendix 19).

It is not to be wondered at that these outside workers brought with them an attitude toward the company that was wholly unlike the attitude held by the villagers. Many of the new employees had previously worked in union shops and had been active in union affairs, whereas the only familiarity the Whitin workers had with the union movement was their memory of a bitter and unsuccessful struggle at neighboring Rockdale in 1934–35.*

Many of the new employees also failed to understand the complacent attitude of Whitin's workers toward the company's wage and hour policies. From years of experience in the violently fluctuating textile-machinery business, the Whitin company had learned to absorb the shock of business reverses by cutting or increasing hours rather than by hiring or discharging men. The villagers were consequently not unfamiliar with long workweeks as well as with short ones, and when the company stepped up its operations to 54 hours a week during the war, the local reaction was not so much one of surprise as of satisfaction over the opportunity to earn more overtime

---

* In 1934, workers in the mill of the Paul Whitin Manufacturing Company (a large interest in which was owned by the heirs of George Marston Whitin) had gone on strike in sympathy with the whole New England movement to force higher wages for textile-mill workers. The strike was long and finally drove the mill to sell the houses it owned in Rockdale. Eventually the strike was terminated, but only after the union had been broken and the strikers had agreed to return to work on company terms. The Rockdale strike was not quickly forgotten in Whitinsville and was considered by many as an example of the evils of unionism.

pay. But workers from outside saw little merit in so long a week when most of their friends were working 48 hours. They also thought it strange that the company did not institute a second shift (only a few men worked a twelve-hour night shift, from 6:00 P.M. to 6:00 A.M., in departments where round-the-clock operations were unavoidable). Furthermore outside workers resented the company's practice of giving paid vacations only to salaried workers.

The company soon sensed the tension caused by the introduction of workers who were accustomed to such different working conditions, and as rapidly as possible it brought its wage and hour policies into line with those in the surrounding territory, although at every step it was delayed by the necessity of getting approval from the War Labor Board. But one fundamental source of malcontent it could do nothing about. Two employees working side by side might receive precisely the same wages in money; yet if one lived within the village and the other lived outside, a marked difference in their real wages was inevitable. The village worker had no commuting expense, since he customarily walked to work and walked home again for lunch. Moreover, he lived in a house the rental cost of which was inconsequential. The non-village worker had the expense of riding to work, eating in the shop cafeteria,* and paying perhaps three or four times as much for his rent.

Being unable to adjust its rents because of the OPA, the company sat by helplessly watching the fuse burn closer to an explosive situa-

---

* The cafeteria, a handsome brick structure built in 1943 next to the George Marston Whitin Gymnasium at a cost of nearly $50,000, was erected specifically to accommodate Whitin's out-of-town employees. With typical independence, the company declined to allow industrial caterers to manage the cafeteria, even though experienced managers of eating establishments might have helped to keep down the deficit at which the cafeteria was operated. The company felt, however, that quality of service was of the essence and so chose to do its own managing of the cafeteria as a means of keeping quality control in its own hands. Also typical of the company's abiding concern for its villagers was Swift's decision not to split the lunch hour into shifts. A lunch period designed to run from 11:30 to 1:30 with different departments taking lunch at different times would have made possible service to more people and would have thereby cut down the cafeteria's operating deficit. But in many a village home, where more than one family member worked in the shop, the lunch hour would have been disrupted if its working members had come home in shifts. Consequently Swift insisted that the 12:00 to 1:00 period be retained for everyone.

tion. That the rental question did not become a point at issue when the explosion finally occurred is only an indication of how delicate the rent subject had become. During the war several groups of union leaders attempted to organize the Whitin shop, but not once in their organizing campaigns did they allude to the discrepancy that existed between the real incomes of local and outside workers. To have done so would have been to alienate village sympathy with their cause. Yet, for all its hush-hush nature, the fundamental conflict of interest existed, and villagers who were lulled into a false sense of security by the unions' careful avoidance of the rental topic, were simply not conscious of what the full meaning of unionization was. The low rental policy of the company and the high wage policy of the unions were essentially antithetical and could not be expected to exist side by side for long.

The challenge brought by union leaders to the management of the company was a bitter blow to pride and precedent. Whitin's history had contained almost no taint of labor difficulty. In 1896 a journalist, setting out to explore a number of American companies that had shown outstandingly successful labor relations, had chosen Whitin as one of his examples.[2] On several occasions the company stated that it never discouraged men in its employ from joining unions and never consciously favored employees who were not union men. As George B. Hamblin once wrote, "We employ union and non-union men indiscriminately, that is, we do not ask whether or not a man belongs to a union, as this being a close corporation and located in favorable territory, we do not have any contentions whatever with any form of organized labor."[3] Nor had the company ever joined anti-union organizations. "We have been receiving a great many letters from the National Founders Association, of Detroit, asking us to join," wrote Marston Whitin in 1911, "but so far we have not paid any attention to them. It seemed to me that it was foolish for us to join any Association so long as our relations with our men are pleasant, and they, on their part, have not taken any part in labor organization."[4] Partly, of course, the Whitin company's remoteness from industrial centers accounted for its freedom from union agitation, but even in its day-to-day relations with its employees, harmony prevailed. Swift once described the village as being "a quiet place, somewhat apart from the centers . . . a pleasant community and a force of men working together with the utmost loyalty and coöperation."[5]

In its entire history the shop had experienced only two labor disturbances of any significance, and even they had not had serious consequences. The first, involving the animosity between Turks and Armenians (in 1895), was described in an earlier chapter. The second, a walk-out of about fifty men in the foundry's cast iron room (17 September 1915), resulted from a foreman's refusal to grant the men an increase in wages. Three days later all fifty of them were back at work — and at the same pay.

2. THE DRIVE TO ORGANIZE WHITIN

With such a record behind them, the owners of the Whitin Machine Works greeted with open incredulity the labor agitation that started fomenting during the war. No less than four international unions tried to organize Whitin between 1943 and 1945. Three of them were affiliated with the American Federation of Labor; the fourth was a member of the Congress of Industrial Organizations. To be exact their titles were:

International Molders' and Foundry Workers' Union of North America (AFL)
Pattern Makers' League of North America (AFL)
International Association of Machinists (AFL)
United Steelworkers of America (CIO)

For simplicity's sake they will be called merely the Foundrymen's, the Patternmakers', the Machinists', and the Steelworkers' unions, respectively.

The first group to open an organizing drive in Whitinsville was the Foundrymen's union. How they knew of the vulnerability of Whitin's labor relations at that particular moment in history I have not been able to learn, but the mere fact that Whitin had one of the largest unorganized foundries in the country was reason enough for them to have kept in close touch with the situation there.

It was not illogical for Whitin's first labor trouble to break out in the foundry, for foundries have traditionally been cursed with poor working conditions. A certain amount of heat, dust, and weight-lifting are inevitable. Rather ironically, though, when the organizing drive began, Whitin was in the process of remedying many of the most unpleasant aspects of its foundry conditions through the installation of an automatic sand-distributing system and a continuous molding system.

A brief leaflet campaign ensued, following which the Foundry-men's union requested an election to establish its right to bargain collectively for the company's founders and molders. To this request the company rather sanguinely consented, for Swift felt confident that a test of strength would reveal the loyalty of his workers; 23 September 1943 was set as the date for the election.

On the afternoon preceding the election Swift called a temporary halt to work in the foundry. Then, over a public address system that had been installed to carry recorded music to workers during periods of relaxation, he read a personally prepared speech. In those days, court interpretations of the Wagner Act were very strict regarding personal addresses to workmen by business executives, and any executive who chose to take his case before his men did so at the risk of being charged subsequently with attempting to coerce his employees. Consequently, Swift very carefully read his speech and judiciously limited what he had to say to personal reflections. Yet, cautiously worded as it was, the speech was later credited by many in the company with having contributed to the union's defeat. For that reason, it is worth quoting in part:

I am an old timer here in the shop. I came to work in 1900, and since 1913, I have been responsible for the operations of this company — some thirty years. I naturally am proud of its position today in the trade, in the quality of machinery it manufactures, and in the character of men who are working for it. But what means as much, if not more, to me is the happiness and contentment of those connected with this company. We have tried to make this a friendly shop. It is not a drive shop. We have tried to make Whitinsville a place where a man with a family would want to settle down and become a good citizen, and I think we have made such a community. Through these years, the relations between men and management have been friendly. I do not mean to say that from time to time irritations or local troubles or local misfits have not occurred, but given time we have remedied any situation which caused discontent. In other words, we have tried not to have any condition in this plant which would make a man feel that he was not being fairly treated. This is our condition today.

I naturally view with hesitation any change in the relationships which we have had heretofore. If you have complaints, and I understand there are a few, I think you can rely upon your management to remedy them. If, on the other hand, you feel that you have got to go to an outside organization to represent you in your relations with this company, you are entirely within your rights. . . . Business, as I look upon it, is a partnership. You have got to have capital to put into the plant; you have got to have management to direct its efforts; you have got to have workmen to produce the goods. It is a delicate machine which has got to work in harmony and without friction.

The vote was 174 opposing the union, 156 favoring. Although the margin was narrow, it appears to have been considered decisive by both union and management and was sufficient to discourage the Foundrymen from further organizing attempts for nearly a year and one-half.

Not until 21 February 1945 did the union resume its campaign to organize the men in the Whitin foundry. On that day it distributed leaflets containing a list of advantages to be gained by Whitin workers if they selected the Foundrymen's union as their bargaining agent. Ordinarily such election promises are extreme and sometimes even completely fanciful, but in this case the union's promises were reasonable enough: guaranteed vacations, an "honest" hourly wage, no pay cuts, time and a half for work beyond eight hours in any one day or forty hours in any one week, time and a half for any work on the sixth consecutive day of work, and double time on Sunday.

On 3 May 1945 the company again consented to a foundry election. This time the number of foundry voters totaled only 285, in contrast to the 330 who had voted a year and a half earlier during the wartime peak in employment. Either most of those who had left the company in the interim had been anti-union men (which seems unlikely) or else a number of men who had previously voted against the union now voted in favor of it, for, although the number favor-

ing the union was 153, almost the same as before, the number opposing dropped from 174 to 132. Therefore, for the first time in its
history, the Whitin company found itself faced with the necessity
of bargaining collectively with a trade union.

Three weeks later, on 24 May 1945, a second AFL union achieved
recognition. In the patternmakers' department, adjacent to the
foundry, the small and conservative Patternmakers' union succeeded
in obtaining 17 of the department's 24 eligible votes. These two elec-
tions, involving as they did only about three hundred of the shop's
three and a half thousand employees, were only preliminaries, however, to the major bout, the struggle for jurisdiction over workers in
the company's machine shop where 70 per cent of the Whitin labor
force was employed.

The campaign to organize the machine shop began about a week
after the opening of the second phase of the campaign to organize
the foundry, that is to say, around the first of March, 1945. Headquarters for the campaign was the Worcester office of the United
Steelworkers of America (CIO). Sensing that the World War was
drawing to a close, the Steelworkers' Worcester branch had begun
laying plans to bring within their jurisdiction the two largest plants
in the southern section of Worcester County, the Whitin Machine
Works and the Draper Corporation. Believing that, of the two, the
Whitin management was the less hostile to labor, the Worcester
group chose Whitinsville as the scene of its first great postwar
drive.[6] With all the vigor and enthusiasm of an organization that
had been held in check by wartime conditions, the CIO launched its
first attack.

"On the basis of numerous requests by workers at the Whitin
Machine Works over the past year," its initial leaflet read, "the
United Steelworkers of America announces that it is undertaking
a campaign to bring [to Whitinsville] the benefits of unionism."
Unlike the Foundrymen's promises, the Steelworkers' pledges were
both numerous and comprehensive: high minimum wages, night-
shift premiums, vacations with pay, seniority on layoff and promotion, equal pay for equal work, no differential in wage rates between
men and women doing similar work, a method for adjustment of
grievances, protection against unfair discharges, safety and health

protection, satisfactory overtime pay, reporting pay (a guarantee of work, or pay, for each day an employee reports for work), daily guarantee for piece workers, and a guarantee against postwar wage cuts.

Nearly a month elapsed before the AFL took up the challenge flung down by the Steelworkers' CIO union. With two AFL unions already recognized in Whitinsville, the International Association of Machinists (AFL) felt that it had prior claim to the votes of Whitin's machine-shop workers.[7] But the Machinists' plan of attack was as imperfectly executed as it was slow to get under way. Whereas CIO organizers conducted a leaflet campaign that was direct and personal, often referring to company executives by name, the AFL organizers held themselves completely aloof from internal shop affairs. Indeed, they seem never even to have been sure of the company's correct name, for they often referred to it as the Whitin Manufacturing Company, or the Whitin Machine Shop, or the Whitin Machine Company, and only occasionally, as if by accident, as the Whitin Machine Works.

Typical of the AFL leaflets was one that boasted of the maturity and experience of their organization. To this, the CIO quickly replied — with wit, if not with logic:[8]

Some organization passing leaflets at the gate last Friday morning boasted about the fact that they have been organized for 50 years. This is supposed to constitute a reason for you to join their organization. The Steelworkers have been organized for 10 years. We are not proud of the fact it took us 10 years to bring the benefits of a union to the employees of Whitin Machine Works. However, we would be ashamed to admit it took us 50 years to find Whitinsville.

Still another CIO leaflet gave evidence of the disdainful attitude of the Steelworkers' union toward its AFL rival:[9]

As you all know, the Machinists of the A. F. of L. did not come to Whitinsville until after the Steelworkers started to organize. They have held few meetings, perhaps because no one attended them, and they have not conducted a vigorous or progressive campaign. They have passed few leaflets, and only partly covered the plant when they did pass one. They have almost no members in the shop as was proven yesterday when they could not get even one employee of the Whitin Machine Works to attend the conference in the Company Office, while the Steelworkers had a full committee of twelve (12), and they have absolutely no chance of winning the election.

In contrast to the AFL campaign, the CIO conducted its drive with vigor and intelligence, giving evidence of careful planning and close attention to detail. Leaflets were distributed to workers regularly either on Tuesday or Wednesday of each week. No two consecutive leaflets used the same style of presentation. Some carried cartoons which, although containing little information, were eye-catchers. Others were more explanatory in nature, setting forth behind-the-scenes reasons for current happenings. And since everyone was curious to know what really *was* going on behind the scenes, everyone read them, including the men in the company's front office.

Generally CIO leaflets also contained an announcement of a meeting to be held later in the week, usually in the local I.O.O.F. hall. At several of these meetings special speakers were presented, often organizers attached to the union's Worcester office, though sometimes they were officials of various local unions in the Worcester area.

The CIO's membership drive, like its leaflet campaign, was conducted with a vigor that the AFL's drive did not match. Stapled to each CIO leaflet was an addressed, prepaid post card on which a worker might apply for membership in the Steelworkers' union simply by giving his name and address; an impulse made a worker a member. In contrast the AFL's application blanks were printed at the bottom of its leaflets, and were so designed that a worker had to take several preliminary steps before he could apply for membership. First he had to tear the application blank from the leaflet and then fill it out in detail. Next he had to mail it to the union in his own envelope and with his own stamp. And finally he had to pay a $5.00 initiation fee in advance. The CIO's initiation fee was only $3.00 and could be paid at the worker's convenience.

By 16 April, the CIO had received enough membership cards to enable Martin J. Walsh, the Steelworkers' New England director, to write Swift stating: "A majority of your employees have designated the United Steelworkers of America, C.I.O., as their bargaining agent. We desire a conference at your early convenience for the purpose of negotiating an agreement covering wages, hours, and other conditions of employment." [10]

Swift agreed to meet with Walsh on 27 April 1945 in the company's offices, but at the meeting he declined to accept the Steelworkers as bargaining agent for the machine shop's employees until the union had verified its membership claims in a duly conducted election. Walsh therefore petitioned the National Labor Relations Board's regional office in Boston for an election among "all employees of the Company at its Whitinsville, Massachusetts, plant except for executives, foremen, office and clerical employees, guards, pattern makers, foundry employees, and all supervisory employees with authority to hire, promote, discharge, discipline, or otherwise effect changes in the status of employees or effectively recommend such action." [11] In reply to Walsh's petition, the Labor Board's regional director appointed field examiner William I. Shooer to investigate the case.

Meanwhile on 27 April (the day the CIO first met with the company to present its claim as bargaining agent for the machine shop) a few Whitin employees attempted to organize a local union in opposition to those from outside. The leaders of the movement seem to have been men who were opposed to unionization in any form, but who felt that the best way to fight fire was with fire. They appear to have had no real desire to act as bargaining agents for their fellow-employees and they seem to have had almost no ability to create or organize. One of their first acts was to look to the company's executives for support and ideas, but the executives reluctantly replied that, although sympathetic, they could have no part in such a movement. After only a few, poorly attended meetings, the group disbanded.

On 18 May the NLRB examiner held a public hearing in Memorial Hall, Whitinsville, to determine whether the CIO was eligible to petition for, and the company was willing to agree to, an election. Again the company declined to grant a consent vote, thereby forcing the matter to the NLRB in Washington.

During the six weeks that it took the NLRB to reach its decision, the CIO stepped up its leaflet campaign in frequency and punch to keep interest at a high pitch. Finally, on 29 June, the Steelworkers triumphantly announced that the Labor Board had ordered an election.

On 5 July representatives of the company and of both the CIO and the AFL unions met to determine on what date the election should be held and in what manner the voting should be conducted. The company agreed to make up pay lists (together with job classifications)* of all men eligible to vote and consented to let representatives of both unions inspect the lists to ascertain their accuracy.[12] On 23 July the representatives examined this list and questioned the admissibility of thirteen names on the grounds that those particular people were engaged in part-time or marginal supervisory work and so could not belong to the bargaining union. The company agreed to remove eight of the thirteen challenged names, leaving a total of 2,350 workers who were eligible to vote at the forthcoming election.

The election was held 25 July 1946 and turned out to be a resounding victory for the CIO. Of the 2,003 votes cast and declared valid, 1,311 favored the CIO, only 91 favored the AFL; 601 voters wanted no union at all.

3. BARGAINING COLLECTIVELY FOR THE FIRST TIME

Now came the task of drawing up contracts with the three unions that had been declared official bargaining agents for the company's employees.† The first contract to be negotiated was with the Pattern Makers' League of North America. To initiate matters the League mailed Whitin a copy of its standard contract form. To the company's surprise the contract was extremely conservative in its wording and demanded little that Whitin was not already giving its pattern-shop employees. An amicable correspondence ensued, and

---

* By an unfortunate slip, these pay lists, bearing as they did full information about job classifications, were the ones posted at the time of the election. Naturally the publication of every man's job rating stirred up a hornet's nest of resentment against the company and doubtless swayed many wavering votes to the union's side.

† The local Steelworkers' union (no. 3654) was formally organized 14 August 1945 and was chartered by the Pittsburgh headquarters of the United Steelworkers of America on 25 August 1945.

after a leisurely interval, was followed by a pleasant visit to Whitinsville by the union's top officials. At length, on 10 April 1946, both
parties signed a contract that differed only in minor particulars from
the standard contract originally proposed.

The contract with the Foundrymen's union took less time to negotiate than the Patternmakers' contract but it generated considerably
more heat. Mainly because of a personality clash between union representatives and the shop's superintendent, negotiations broke down
on 21 September 1945 and a brief week-end strike ensued, the specific
area of disagreement being over seniority provisions. But the temper
flare-up seems to have helped clear the air, for immediately thereafter agreements were reached on all disputed points and a contract
was signed 1 October 1945.

When the CIO representatives learned how moderate the terms
of the Foundrymen's contract were, they snorted their disdain and
boasted openly that the company would get no such easy contract
from them. (Their boast was not in vain; Appendix 22 compares
the provisions of the pattern department, the foundry, and the machine-shop contracts and shows how much more exacting were the
clauses won by the CIO.)

The representative designated by the CIO to negotiate the Whitin
contract was Kenneth Glynn, a former Worcester machinist whose
enthusiasm for labor's cause and whose ability as a leader had attracted the attention of CIO executives. The Whitin contract was
his first major assignment, and he gave it all the care and attention
due a first-born child. A quiet man, soft-spoken and imperturbable,
he was nonetheless self-assured, well-informed, and quick-witted.
Those who attended the negotiation meetings conceded that no
man on the company's side was a match for his carefully planned
maneuvers, his surprise attacks, and his rapidly shifting basis of
argument.

Glynn began his negotiations by presenting the company with a
model contract much as the Patternmakers had done earlier, but the
demands of this contract were considerably more importunate. (An
analysis of the proposed contract is contained in Appendix 21 with
an indication of the points the union lost and won.) The first meeting between union and company took place 21 September 1945, fol-

lowed by several more over a period of two months. Tentative agreements were reached on nearly all points, but only tentatively, for neither side was willing to commit itself definitely until the all-important matter of wages had been settled. The war had just ended, and no one could be certain what economic changes the postwar period would bring. The crux of the matter was the price ceiling imposed on textile machinery by the Office of Price Administration. Until it was known what policy the OPA would follow regarding postwar price levels, the company was unwilling to consider any change in its wage pattern whatsoever, for it knew that even without any pay increases it would find difficulty in operating at a profit if existing price ceilings were continued.*

Because the question of machinery prices impinged so directly on Whitin's contract negotiations, a brief review of what had previously taken place in Whitin's relations with the OPA is necessary. The price level established by the OPA dated back to a time even before the declaration of war. In the summer and fall of 1941, business in the textile machinery industry had been very good, and many in the industry had felt that it was time to increase machinery prices from the level where they had remained since 1937. Swift was one of those who did not share this view, for he felt there would be an added stimulus to sales if prices were maintained. Under the pressure of rising costs, however, Swift finally gave way and allowed the level of Whitin's prices to rise about 8 per cent, effective 1 December 1941. Meanwhile the OPA was laying plans to place controls on the nation's price level. On 18 May 1942 it announced its decision to freeze prices, but in so doing it chose 1 October 1941, seven and a half months earlier, as the effective date for its price "roll-back." Consequently the 8 per cent price increase put into effect by the textile machinery industry in December, 1941, was rescinded, and the dwindling machinery business conducted by the Whitin company during 1942 brought in little or no profit.

---

* On 31 October 1945 President Truman had announced that general pay increases throughout industry should be a matter of collective bargaining and should be absorbed by corporate profits without change in price ceilings. Whitin, along with nearly every other company in the nation, maintained that other costs had risen so high that there was no profit margin from which to squeeze pay increases without raising prices.

Throughout the war Whitin managed to make a small profit on its sales of repair parts, since the profit margin on that branch of its business had always been generous and was enough to keep the company above the high-watermark of costs even under price control. But with its return to the production of complete machines, the Whitin Machine Works realized that existing price levels were far too low for profitable operations. Along with the rest of the industry, Whitin pointed out this fact to the War Production Board at the time the government was asking for a speed-up in the production of twisters, and at that time the WPB agreed to endorse the industry's applications to the OPA for relief.

Whitin filed its first request for price relief on 9 November 1944.[13] The request covered only cotton machinery and was based on cost figures for the months June, July, and August, 1944. The company was frank to admit that its war profits were enough to carry it through 1944, but it stated that at least a 25 per cent increase in cotton-machinery prices would be necessary if it was to show a profit in 1945. Since both Saco-Lowell and H & B American were similarly situated, they too submitted requests for relief.

The OPA admitted that under existing circumstances such requests were perhaps valid and so sent investigators to the three companies to examine their books. After a careful study of comparative costs at the three plants, the examiners recommended that Saco-Lowell be allowed to advance its prices an average of 21.57 per cent, H & B American 18.75 per cent, and Whitin 11.50 per cent. Theoretically, the OPA's findings were a great compliment to the Whitin company. Any concern that could profitably undersell its competitors, as the OPA claimed Whitin could do, would ordinarily have been in an extremely favorable competitive position. But in a booming postwar market when questions of delivery were far more important to customers than questions of price, Whitin felt that it was being penalized for the efficiency the OPA examiners reported they had found. It appeared that, by a deft shift, the OPA was becoming an agency for regulating profits instead of prices.

Swift was not one to let such an inequity go unchallenged. In a strongly worded memorandum to the OPA, dated 1 May 1945, he expressed his protest:

If relief to industry is to be based on the profit earned in the base years without regard to the production of the individual concern or the trade customs in the art, all incentive for economical production is eliminated and it puts in the power of your Board the ability and the power to wreck individual concerns and destroys competition in the industry.

As stated previously we build other machinery besides cotton mill machinery which is our principal line. This consists mainly of woolen machinery, rayon, and a small amount of worsted [on which the company had been given no price relief]. We are advised that our principal competitor in woolen machinery (Davis & Furber Machine Company of Andover, Massachusetts) has been granted a 7% increase on all of their production — machinery, repair parts, changeovers, etc. This woolen machinery which we are building today on today's costs is showing us a loss. This relief granted to our competitor will enable him to build this machinery on a basis much more favorable than what we are receiving with the same general effect as stated above.

Our operations for the first three months of 1945 cover a total of $3,527,819.59 of sales. In this business we have a small loss and the loss would have been a great deal more if the profit which we received from the remaining war work which went over into this quarter had not been included. . . . In other words we have petitioned for relief and have not received it.

Despite this protest, the OPA took no action, leaving the company's price level only about 3 per cent higher than it had been at the outbreak of war. Meanwhile costs had risen disproportionately. Thus, at the very time Whitin was negotiating its contract with the CIO, its operations were precariously balanced at a break-even point. Any increase in wages would have thrown the company into deficit. In an attempt to avoid the deadlock that the wage issue threatened, the company suggested to the union that they sign a six months' contract without a wage clause in the hope that a further OPA increase could be obtained within that breathing spell. The union insisted, however, that it was morally obligated to obtain a wage increase for its members. Therefore, on 21 November 1945, Local 3654 of the Steelworkers' union filed notice of the intention to strike.

During the month's interval required by law before the actual strike vote could be held,[14] the company, in line with its paternalistic principles, took occasion to make several adjustments in wages and hours rather than allow the union to gain prestige by negotiating the benefits. First it reduced the workweek from 54 hours to 45. Then it announced a flat wage increase (effective 31 December 1945) of 7 cents an hour to all straight hourly employees and 5 cents an hour to all piece-rate workers (the equivalent of 7 cents an hour to hourly workers). In addition it announced ½-cent increases wherever inequities occurred.*

Instead of placating the workers, as the company hoped it would, the unilateral announcement of wage-and-hour adjustments fanned the workers' resentment and led, on 21 December 1945, to an overwhelming vote in favor of a strike.† The strike ballots carried no indication when the strike would be called; the Worcester organizers thus had the privilege of setting the date to coincide with the great nationwide strike planned by their International union.

4. THE STRIKE

In compliance with orders from Pittsburgh, the strike commenced on Monday morning, 14 January 1946, a bitterly cold, though snowless, day. Simultaneously workers began picketing major steel plants all over the country. By month's-end the nation was in the midst of the worst strike wave in its history.[15] The Whitinsville plant had ceased to be a manufacturer of textile machinery and had become merely one of many producers of lost-man-hour statistics.

At first the workers in Whitinsville greeted the strike as if it was an exciting adventure. Most of them were sated with the monotony of long wartime hours and were ready for a vacation. Volunteer

---

* The company realized that these increases would probably cause it to operate at a loss, but it hoped to obtain approval of them from the Wage Stabilization Board, which approval would in turn force the OPA to reconsider its decision regarding Whitin's price ceilings. At about the same time, the company applied for permission to raise its rents under a provision that allowed for relief where losses exceeded losses in the base years 1938–40.

† However, the company felt, and with some justification, that the vote was not a true reflection of sentiment, since the ballot form was somewhat misleading. The form used was the one required by the War Labor Disputes Act (the war was not yet "officially" over); consequently Whitin's employees were asked to vote on the question: "Do you wish to permit an interruption of war production in wartime as a result of this dispute?" Since the war had (unofficially but nevertheless actually) ended four months earlier, the question made little sense.

duty on the picket line was merely part of the game. No one expected the strike to last very long. There was no real feeling of animosity, no strife, no violence of any kind. In fact, the only significant event in the first seven weeks of shutdown was a brief flare-up of tempers that would hardly be worth recording except for the insight it gives into the relations between the company and the officials of the local and international unions.

As the incident gives evidence, the central personality in the strike was the Worcester representative of the CIO, Kenneth Glynn. His seems to have been the guiding mind back of all union strategy. Indeed one is tempted to believe that he was even behind the democratic proceedings in the union hall, so regularly did the voting proceed in his favor. For instance, Glynn realized that it was highly desirable for him to have the local union appear completely indigenous; consequently it was to his advantage when all three top offices in the Local were filled by villagers. Similarly, it was to his advantage to have as the first president of the Local a man who would not object to taking orders from Worcester. Richard Malmgren was such a man — soft-spoken, tractable, and a worshiper at Glynn's feet. The firebrand and real potential leader in the local organization was the vice-president, John Andonian, an Armenian with traits exactly opposite to Malmgren's. It seems almost more than coincidence that soon after the end of the strike, when Glynn needed someone in Whitinsville to carry on the organization he had launched, Malmgren decided that the burden of the presidency was more than he wanted to handle and so resigned in Andonian's favor.*

The day the strike began there was considerable confusion regarding which workers should be allowed to pass the picket line. It was generally understood that all foundrymen and patternmakers, since they belonged to AFL unions, would be allowed entrance to the plant along with all clerical and executive employees, who belonged to no union at all. But the CIO was anxious to bring the

---

* When Andonian became president he quit his job at the machine works and devoted full time to his union duties, with the Local paying his salary. The third official of the Local was James H. Jones, a pleasantly daft individual who was by nature more an artist than a machinist and who had drunk deeply of intoxicating Marxisms.

foundry to a halt if it could, though Glynn realized that it might be desirable to allow a partial inventory of castings to be built up against the possibility that the machine shop might resume operations on short notice. However, Glynn happened not to be on hand when the critical issue arose.

Among those included in the CIO bargaining unit were the yard crane operators who unloaded and loaded the company's pig iron, coal supplies, and scrap metal. By law, these men had to be licensed operators. The foundry was dependent on them for its coke, scrap, and pig iron, and the village was dependent on them for its heating coal. Being CIO members, these men were among those who went out on strike.

When Mitchell, the irascible plant superintendent, learned that the union had refused to let its crane operators load supplies for the foundry and village, he very nearly had a coronary thrombosis. Adrenaline immediately began flowing on both sides of the argument, and only after Glynn had been summoned posthaste from Worcester was a reasonable compromise effected. Glynn realized that it was important to keep the villagers supplied with coal and so he authorized the coal operator to return to work. But the other crane operators remained on strike, and at the end of two weeks the foundry had to be closed for lack of supplies.

For seven weeks neither side moved toward a settlement of their dispute over wages. Each believed that victory could be won through attrition. Glynn was anxious to achieve as much as possible for the union on this, his first major assignment, while Swift saw the union's defeat as the only means of erasing the blot on his company's otherwise unsullied labor record. To Swift the rebellion of his workers against a company that had done so much for them was enough to shatter all that he had stood for in his thirty years as head of the community. It came to be commonly believed in the village that Swift considered the strike a personal rebuff, and many of the inhabitants who might otherwise have supported the strike opposed it because they hated to see injury done to a man who had worked so hard for the town.[16]

On Friday, 1 March 1946, the anti-union workers in the village announced that on the following Monday they intended to exercise their right to return to work. But when Monday morning arrived only a few die-hards showed up and those few were confronted by so many union pickets that they made no attempt to carry through their boast. What made the otherwise ignominious end of the back-to-work movement seem dramatic, however, was what happened at the company's annual meeting in the main office building a few hours later that same day. To the surprise of most of those present, and with unconcealed emotion, Swift tendered his resignation as president of the company and recommended that Bolton be elected to take his place.

Actually the resignation caused no fundamental change in the company's management hierarchy, for Swift remained as treasurer and ascended to the chairmanship of the board.* Yet the significance of Swift's move escaped no one's attention; by his action he turned over to Bolton the direct responsibility for managing the company and — what was of more urgent importance — the immediate responsibility for settling the strike.

Bolton let two weeks elapse before making his first official overture to the union. Even then he might have taken no action had he not unexpectedly received word from the OPA, on March 20, that Whitin had been granted a further price increase amounting to 16.8 per cent. (The upward adjustment was to be made on whatever machines and in whatever manner the company considered warranted, so long as the final average of all increases did not exceed the specified figure.)[17] The OPA announcement removed the company's basic argument that it could not grant a raise to labor without suffering an operating loss. In reality it marked the turning point of the strike, though relations between company and union had by then deteriorated to such an extent that final settlement of differences required several additional weeks of negotiations.

As soon as Bolton had learned of the new OPA ruling, he sent word to the union that the company was willing to make a compromise wage offer. Meeting with the union on 21 March, Bolton proposed an eight-cent hourly increase which, when added to the seven

---

* Previously the president of the company had always served *ex officio* as board chairman. Until 12 May 1942 the chief executive officer had been the treasurer, but on that date the bylaws had been changed to make the president the chief official in conformity with the standard practice of younger firms.

cents granted immediately before the strike, meant a total raise of fifteen cents an hour. (The terms of Bolton's proposal are set forth in detail in Appendix 20.) Only two weeks earlier, however, President Truman had given official support to a recommendation that the United States Steel strike be settled on the basis of an eighteen-and-one-half-cent hourly increase; hence Glynn felt obliged to decline Bolton's offer, though he countered with a suggestion that negotiations be resumed on the non-wage clauses of the contract, in regard to which no definite agreement had ever been reached. To this Bolton assented, and a meeting was scheduled for the following Tuesday, 26 March.

The heat that was generated in the negotiations at that next meeting — after all, this was the contestants' first effort, since the beginning of the strike, to make any serious headway toward reconciling their differences of opinion — is a good indication of how taut nerves had become. The conference did not get past the formal preamble of the contract. Glynn insisted that, according to the Steelworkers' constitution, the contract had to be an instrument between the company and the International union.* Bolton replied that he would negotiate only with Local 3654 and not with the International. Seeing that he was getting nowhere, Glynn led his union negotiators out of the meeting. On the following day, Bolton resolutely ordered all machinery in the shop slushed with heavy grease in preparation for a long strike. Yet, as later events revealed, all that really stood in the way of final settlement was a calm approach to the dispute.

In an effort to introduce such calmness from the outside, Glynn asked Federal Conciliator Henry W. Tucker to see what he could do to establish the nature of the area of disagreement between the two parties. Tucker must have brought to his task a consummate skill in handling men, for at his first meeting he brought the contestants together on all but seven of the points in dispute — and two days later he reduced the number of disputed points to two. In essence the final agreement was an offer by the company of a twelve-cent raise (a total of nineteen cents in all) and a withdrawal of the

* The Steelworkers' constitution stated: "The International Union shall be a party to all collective bargaining agreements, and all such agreements must be signed by the International Officers." Quoted from Florence Peterson's *Handbook of Labor Unions*, p. 357.

union's demands for maintenance of membership (again see Appendix 20 for details).

On 15 April 1946, exactly thirteen weeks after the strike's beginning, company and union officials sat down to sign a contract. Only a week earlier, on 8 April 1946, newspapers had carried an announcement that the OPA had released all textile-machinery prices from ceiling controls. All parties felt that they had won their major points: the union had its contract; the workers had their raise; and the company had the reassurance that it could pass these higher costs on to its customers.

5. THE STRIKE IN RETROSPECT

It would be easy to conclude from the narrative as it appears above that the villain in the Whitinsville strike was really the Office of Price Administration. And indeed there is a certain logic in that view. Yet it is probable that the strike would have occurred even had price ceilings not plagued the company. It must be remembered that, at the end of 1945, all branches of the Steelworkers' union were spoiling for an opportunity to test their strength in a coördinated national strike. Under such conditions almost any company would have become a pawn in the chess game of power politics. Equally basic was the company's unwillingness to give serious consideration to organized labor's postwar demands for a twenty-five-cent increase in hourly wages. No increase of like proportions had ever before been granted by American industry; and, considering how much such a raise threatened to distort manufacturing costs (see Appendix 24 for a graphic representation of how much the eventual raise actually did distort Whitin's costs), probably no company in the country would have been willing to grant such an increase, had not the President of the United States officially backed labor's demands.

Yet it is equally a mistake to think of the strike as being wholly the result of a dispute over wages. Unionism came to Whitinsville not only over the issue of wages but also over the question of working conditions in the shop — and in particular the shop's handling of workers' grievances. Before the war the company had never really needed a formal system of communicating grievances between the shop and the front office since its informal system functioned with fair smoothness. But for many reasons the informal system broke

down during the war. Newcomers to Whitinsville were unacquainted with each other or with old-timers in the shop; instead of
being able to settle their grievances on a personal and friendly basis,
they had to deal with people they did not know and in a way they
were unaccustomed to. Foremen had complete authority in their
own departments, and under wartime pressures probably often exercised that authority with unintentional tyranny. A worker could,
of course, appeal his case to the superintendent, but in most instances the superintendent felt obliged, in the interests of good morale, to support the decisions of his foremen. The company had no
real personnel director, only a keeper of the personnel records.* Consequently, the war period saw the company's relations with its
employees degenerate sharply in the short space of a few years. Preoccupied with the tough technical problems of the war, Whitin's
management neglected what seemed to be the less pressing problems
of personnel administration. In so doing it issued an engraved invitation to unionization and created a condition without which it is
unlikely that the actions of Truman or the OPA or Glynn could
have induced the Whitin workers to strike.

Once started, the strike continued as long as it did largely because
there was no pressing financial need on either side to bring it to an
early end. The company's position was such that it was almost as
well off closed as operating. Critical materials were in such short
supply, and widespread strikes had cut off the sources of so many
of the company's raw and semi-finished goods, that the Whitin firm
would almost certainly have operated at a loss during those three
months even if it had kept going.† Furthermore, the knowledge that
the government stood ready to indemnify it for reconversion losses

* Two and a half weeks after the strike vote had been taken, the company's first
true director of industrial relations reported for work. He was Frank N. Stone, an
able lawyer who, during the war, had gained experience in personnel work at Veeder-
Root, Inc., Whitin's fellow subcontractor on the American Bosch magneto job. Stone
brought intelligence, industriousness, and skilled administration to a job that had
previously been seriously neglected, but he also brought a lawyer's propensity to stick
by everything contained in the fine print.

† The Davis & Furber Machine Company, Whitin's principal competitor in the
wool field, was on strike at the same time; consequently the company felt some
relief in knowing that it was at least not losing place competitively in the wool-
machinery market. The Saco-Lowell Shops, however, managed to go through the
entire postwar period without a strike, but only by making broad concessions to
union demands.

by allowing credits against its former excess-profits taxes, helped to reassure the firm that it could afford to wait out a long dispute.[18]

The workers were similarly provisioned for a lengthy siege. During the war they had accumulated an unprecedented backlog of savings on which they were able to draw during the period when pay envelopes were not forthcoming. As a result, severe hardship was almost unknown among strikers' families. During the entire three months of the strike, the Village Welfare Society received only twenty-two requests for relief. Foundrymen, inadvertently laid off because of the strike, were liberally provided for by the AFL "pay-off" benefit plan. And six hundred of the company's clerical and executive workers remained at work on full salary throughout nearly the entire shutdown. Only the twenty-six hundred men employed in the machine shop were without continuing financial support. Of those, the thirteen hundred or so who lived in Whitinsville cashed, at the two local banks, government bonds averaging $13.50 per person per week, enough to meet at least the minimum food requirements of their individual families.[19] In addition, the CIO distributed baskets of food to its members in exchange for a day of picketing, and the company gave employees who lived in its houses the privilege of deferring payments on their coal and rent bills till after the strike was over, and even then it gave them several months to settle their debts. Because of these favorable circumstances, the union, despite its youth, was able to face up to the company without fear that its members would feel the squeeze of personal hardship and withdraw their support from the union cause.

For weeks following the strike, villagers argued over the outcome. Neither side felt that it had gained a clear victory. Management had given way on point after point where once it had held unchallenged sway. Only on the question of maintenance of membership had it won a major issue.* Workers were disgruntled by the terms of the settlement since, even though their hourly rates had been advanced, their take-home pay had actually been reduced below what it had

---

* In later months Swift came to believe that the union and the strike had not been without their merits. At the Draper Corporation the fear of unionization had forced management to grant even larger-than-current increases, and at Saco-Lowell the fear of a shutdown had caused executives to submit to union demands that made the Biddeford shop increasingly a high-cost producer.

been when the strike began. Because Glynn was forced, for reasons of prestige, to get at least an eighteen-and-one-half-cent raise for his men, he had agreed to compromise on a forty-hour week, and by so doing had cut his men off from all overtime allowances.* Gradually it became apparent that the real victor in the dispute was the United Steelworkers of America. True, the strike had been expensive, and the local union had not been provisioned with a strong financial reserve. But an increase in membership dues from $1.00 to $1.50 a month soon remedied that situation. The real test of success came as the local union membership began to rise. The reduction of the workweek to forty hours forced the company to inaugurate a second shift, bringing the union hundreds of additional members. By October, 1948, when the company was operating at peak capacity, its Whitinsville plant was employing 5,615 men, 2,639 of whom belonged to the local CIO.

Yet, viewed in perspective, the strike seems to recede somewhat in significance. Had it not been for an unusual conjunction of circumstances, the strike might never have occurred. Only about half the company's workers ever became self-announced members of the union. Far more fundamental than the strike was the fact that unionism had at last arrived in Whitinsville. Into the rigid social structure of the village the union had inserted a wedge that was to separate the company's owners from its employees more than ever before. Perhaps a social psychologist would say that the separating process had been under way for several years, for with Swift's choice of Bolton as his successor, it must have been clear to most people that the family's close bond with the village was being weakened. Of course, no one can know in any precise way how Swift's approaching retirement was regarded in the village, but it is evident that by 1946 the company's employees had begun to lose whatever confidence they may have had in the ability of the family to see them through adversity — whether it be the adversity of a depression or of an inflationary spiral.

It would seem that in our industrial civilization employees must

* It may be that Glynn expected the company to continue operating a forty-five-hour week anyway because of the heavy demand for production, but on that point he was wrong, for the company instead instituted a second shift.

be a dependent group — whether on a company, on a union, or on a government. In the last analysis the Whitin company's employees had always been dependent on the Whitin family. They had looked to the family for stability of employment in depressions and they had relied on the family to manage the company in a way that would keep it a vital and profitable concern. In both cases their confidence had been well placed. But now conditions had changed. The family's position had been weakened by lack of youthful leadership and by the hostility of the government to inherited wealth. Whether in the future the other executives of the firm might take over the family's feeling of responsibility toward the village, no one could predict.*

In place of the uncertainty of a new and untried management, the union offered a kind of security that was different — and in many respects more attractive — from that offered by the family. The family had always followed the policy of sheering off the peaks of prosperity and shoring up the bottoms of depression. The union's policy was to enjoy the peaks while they lasted and to rely on the government to prevent the depressions. What made the union's cause especially appealing was this latter prospect. If depressions were to be outlawed, then there was no point in the company's insistence on austerity-in-boom as a preventive of austerity-in-bust. Furthermore, most workers had come to look on the national government as a powerful force in the interest of their general welfare, and so they felt safer in placing faith in an institution that stood in the government's favor, as the union did, rather than continuing to rely on an

---

* For the near future one thing was certain: rents had to be raised, and raised sharply, for the company could not afford to continue underwriting the deficit it was running on its housing project. Yet every time rents were raised, a blow was struck at employee relations — and at the very employees who, historically, had been most loyal to the company, the employees living in company dwellings. On 1 November 1948, the company announced just such an increase in rentals; on 2 November 1948, the day Harry S. Truman was elected President of the United States, traditionally Republican Whitinsville went strongly Democratic.

Various solutions of the rent problem have been suggested. It has been thought that a separate corporation might be established to own and manage the houses. It has also been thought that the company's dwellings might be sold to some outsider, if an outsider could be interested in the venture. Or perhaps, despite their multiple construction, they might be sold unit by unit to employees. In any case the company would not be able to escape its responsibility very soon. Whatever the solution a delicate readjustment of company-employee relations would be necessary.

institution, such as the Whitin dynasty, that was the object of government attack.

How far metaphysical interpretations of history may be valid, one can never know, but it seems to be true that the workers of Whitinsville abandoned their allegiance to the Whitin family very soon after it had become apparent that the family was ceasing to be a bulwark of strength, and in so doing they shifted their allegiance to a group that was currently waxing in strength and basking in the sun of a laboristic government. The change was not to be wondered at or even lamented. Such shifts of allegiance have marked every era of our history. New leadership replaces the old, and the men who are followers change their loyalties accordingly.

By 1946 the owners of the Whitin Machine Works were no longer in full control of their company any more than they had been in real control of their personal fortunes since around 1935. In all the important matters of personnel relations they had come to a place where they had to look to Worcester; and in all important matters of accounting and finance they necessarily had to look to Washington. Family-owned and family-controlled concerns were rapidly becoming an institution of the past. Whitin had survived as a family-owned company longer than most. But now its stock was being scattered and its management was being turned over to professional executives. The process was only just beginning, but there was little chance that it would be reversed. Whitinsville was losing much of what had once made it unique. It was feeling the leveling force of the national trend that was socializing the American democracy.

CHAPTER XX

EPILOGUE

ANY story of a live business, brought down to the present, runs the risk of having its final chapter appear as a climax. Unlike the final pages of a novel, the end of an historical study cannot be neatly turned into a satisfactory denouement. In the Whitin study, recent events have made it impossible to end the narrative on any other note than on labor strife or high prosperity. Yet neither theme reaches very far back into the past or gives any certainty of continuing very far into the future. Being forced by circumstances to choose between the two, I selected the strike and its immediate aftermath as my ending point, not because I considered the strike a climax or turning point in the company's history — although the time may come when it will be looked upon as such — but simply because it saved me from having to bring the story down too near to the date of publication. Perhaps some future historian, viewing the tangled threads of Whitin's labor story as here set forth, will single out, from the threads that lead nowhere, the ones that lead on into the future.

Viewed in retrospect, the pattern of an historical fabric is always more readily distinguishable than when viewed from a contemporary vantage point. The pattern of Whitin's historical fabric has seemed especially clear because of the remarkable evenness of its texture. Whitin's threads reach far back and come down to the present in unbroken order. Few companies in America today have a background so homogeneous. The past is very close to the present in Whitinsville, and the policies of today are often policies which the company has followed for three or four generations. The fact that those policies have endured for so long is no guarantee that they will not be changed in the future, but it is an indication that the changes, when they come, will be so without precedent that they will be achieved only after a period of difficult transition.

An attempt to appraise the company without a thorough knowledge of its history would be as impossible as an effort to understand a person's psychological behavior without a knowledge of his background and experience. For instance, no one today could explain the location of the Whitin Machine Works in Whitinsville without knowing that the company orginated from a partnership of four brothers whose loyalty to each other and to their community was engendered in them by a spirited and able mother. Nor could the existence of a company village in Whitinsville be explained without the knowledge that, during most of its history, the company has lived in an area of labor scarcity, a fact which, during the depressed days of the nineteen-twenties and 'thirties, was almost completely forgotten by the people of the village — all that stuck in their minds was the distressing abundance of labor produced by the depression in the region's cotton mills. Correlatively, it was the shortage of labor that produced Whitinsville's population of foreign extraction, and in turn it was the community's foreign-born inhabitants who determined the kind of houses that the company built. It was also the shortage of labor that, at a later date, created a situation favorable to the company's unionization.

It would be impossible for anyone to know the motivating forces behind Whitin's present management without knowing that the company has been family-owned since its inception and that the family has fashioned the personality of the company in its own image, but that now, for the first time, the company's active top-level management is not composed of family members. There is always something tristful about the break in a long and honored tradition, and at first it seems regrettable that a closely held company should lose its family leadership. But a family that has provided four generations of top executives has more than fulfilled its social obligations. The task of producing superior executive material is too heavy a responsibility for any one family to continue bearing indefinitely. It would have been sheer accident if, in its fifth generation, the Whitin kindred had produced a member ready to take over at the proper time and of such ability that his qualifications outweighed those of any other candidates for the job from outside the family's ranks. One of the great strengths of a democratic society is the opportunity it gives to a firm like Whitin to select its officials from a wide range of executive timber.

With non-family men in top managerial positions, the company's board of directors, as it has always been constituted, becomes an anomaly. Historically, the Whitin board has never exercised a veto power over the company's management; in the future it may wish to begin to do so. In early years there was no need for the board to exercise any such power since the company's directors were in fact its executives as well; and in recent years the board's function has tended to be largely advisory, since the men elected as directors have been put on the board not so much to represent the family as to give competent advice to the family-managers. Now, however, with a management that is no longer in family hands and one that, given a reasonable degree of continuity, will some day be working for a group of trustees and younger stockholders who have had no voice in its selection, a purely advisory board of directors will hardly be suitable to changed conditions. If, however, it should happen that the future stockholders of the company, in electing directors to represent their interest, should create a board that is hostile toward, or at least critical of, the incumbent management, then the Whitin company will have lost one of its great points of strength, for it has been the company's monolithic one-man management that has always in the past given the firm its unity of drive and purpose.

Closely held stock ownership over a period of four generations has quite naturally produced a company of individual pattern. Consequently, it would hardly be remarkable if a dispersion of that ownership were to cause fundamental changes in the company's personality. Two of the credos by which the company has always guided its destiny may well be challenged. One is the belief that the company, as an institution, should always be put ahead of the interests of any individuals in it, whether they be executives, employees, or stockholders. The second is the conviction that the company should act as its own bank and that it should rely as little as possible on commercial banks and not at all on investment bankers. Both policies have been made possible by the autocratic form of one-man rule that has guided the company's destiny in the past. Under a more democratic form of management, with more persons having a voice in corporate affairs, both policies may give way to the selfish interests of individuals. In the past these two policies have caused the company to add to its financial strength in periods of prosperity by leaving earnings in the firm. Even in the boom period following World War II, the stockholders plowed back the major portion of their profits. With the labor union growing stronger, however, and demanding its share of the company's profits, with a management no longer tied to the firm by family interests, and with a stockholder group that is rapidly expanding and at the same time becoming more interested in dividends than in earnings, not to mention a government that officially frowns on withheld profits, the conservative financial policies of the past will become increasingly difficult to maintain.

Already there is a noticeable change of attitude on the part of the stockholders toward their company. The old sense of pride is still there, but it has been shaken because of the strike of the company's employees against their would-be benefactors. There is a conscious decision that, in the future, the paternalism of the past should be gradually abandoned. The company's owners, being disillusioned by the fact that men can be completely lacking in gratitude for what is given to them without their asking for it, have decided that henceforth the village will have to pay its own way. Meanwhile, there are to be no further additions to the family's investment in Whitinsville. Three of E. Kent Swift's fondest plans for the future have been abandoned. One was the extension of the company's multiple housing units in the village east of Plummer's Corner. Another was the construction of a group of moderately priced, single-family dwellings on the hillside south of the river — not for rent but for sale to returning veterans. The third was the erection of a new machine shop on the south bank of the river, adjacent to Shop No. 3. The first and second projects never got beyond the planning stage. The third got as far as blueprints and almost to the point of being contracted for and then was suddenly abandoned. Only a fourth postwar project has become reality — the construction of a new and much larger Southern shop near Charlotte, North Carolina.[1]

Because of the decision not to expand productive capacity in Whitinsville, the company has gone through the postwar boom with a plant much smaller than would have been ideal. In the long run, however, the decision not to expand promises to be a wise one, for it has forced the company into a program of subcontracting that has immensely increased output without at the same time causing an unnecessary addition to fixed overhead.[2]

When a group of laborers go so far toward alienating the sympathy of their employers that those employers decide against continuing to underwrite the prosperity and stability of the local community, one cannot help wondering what the long-run implications of their actions may be. Security is everywhere being demanded by laboring groups in America, yet the group in Whitinsville has turned its back on security — at least of the type it has had in the past. To many, the welfare state is the next goal in mankind's achievement; yet in Whitinsville, where there has been a limited form of the welfare state for many years, the people are not content with it. What is the explanation of this apparent contradiction? For a while it seemed as though villages like Whitinsville might furnish an answer to the insistent problem of how to provide security for industrial workers. According to the Whitinsville answer, the national economy would some day be decentralized into garden cities operated on the Whitin plan. In those garden cities living conditions would be healthful and there each worker would have a plot of ground on which to rely for his sustenance during difficult times. Depressions would be combated by spread-the-work programs, and every family would be guaranteed at the very least an existence wage. In other words, scarcity would be shared by everyone on an equal basis, and in return everyone would have security. In addition, there would be all manner of social benefits — little luxuries that would not be unduly expensive but that would help make life enjoyable — free snow-shoveling services, free lawn-mowing, free garden facilities and athletic programs.

Why should any experiment as promising as the one in Whitinsville chance to come under a cloud? Is it because in any period of prosperity the very reason for its existence as a low-cost way of life is temporarily removed? Is it because, in a period of rapidly rising maintenance costs and slowly rising rents, the company begins to feel uneasily apprehensive about the financial burden it must carry?

Or is it because the vision of a national welfare state has made men impatient with experiments on any smaller scale? A social program conducted at a national level substitutes the federal government for the local business firm as the guarantor of stability. It does more than that: the best that the individual firm can promise is to help men *survive* depressions; the government promises, or will strive, to *prevent* depressions altogether.

If, then, in the final analysis, it should come to pass that the social experiment in Whitinsville is to be set down as merely a divertissement in history's over-all program and not as an overture to the future, it seems possible that the people in Whitinsville who are responsible for directing the company's affairs may look for the first time with a dispassionate eye on the question of whether there is really any rational reason for the company to be located where it is. In John C. Whitin's time, Whitinsville was favored over Holyoke because it was the location of the family homestead. In Marston Whitin's time, it was preferred to Providence for reasons equally personal. In the present generation the question of whether Whitinsville is a better location than Charlotte has never been fairly faced. Perhaps some day it will be, and a final decision will be reached.

In the midst of uncertainty, one fact seems clear — at least for the present. Despite the blow to its pride, the family does not yet intend to relinquish its interest in the firm. For at least another generation there is a likelihood that the heirs of George Marston Whitin will hold control. On two occasions since the recent war, New York financial interests have approached the family with offers to buy controlling interest in the firm, but in both cases they have been politely but firmly turned down. It is always possible that the family will some day follow a common trend and decide to sell, but for the present it has made its decision to stay.

In looking back over the past, one becomes conscious that every generation has to face some one critical problem. In John C. Whitin's time, it was production. As long as the company could turn out high-grade machinery at reasonable cost, it could count on having its products create their own sales promotion. In Marston Whitin's time, the emphasis shifted to sales, for it made little difference, during the period of Southern mill development, what quality a company built into its machinery or what price it placed on its products if the company's salesman was not on hand to make the original sale to a mill promoter and to bind that mill man to the shop as a loyal and continuing customer. In Kent Swift's time, both sales and production became subordinate to finance, and the questions of liquidity and break-even points became the paramount issues of the day. What the critical issue of the present régime will be cannot yet be determined, but possibly it will be product development. If so, the Whitin Machine Works will have to alter sharply a number of the venerable policies set forth in previous chapters or see itself slip behind.

One of the policies indirectly related to product development is the one followed by the company in connection with its selection and training of executives. A product-development program can be no better than the men who are chosen to conduct it; therefore, the manner in which those men are trained for their jobs is of first importance. Traditionally, executives in Whitinsville have been developed, not hired. They have been selected either from persons at hand in Whitinsville or from the family's roster of friends and acquaintances. The system was a natural outgrowth of the fact that the family relied on its sons and sons-in-law to fill its principal executive posts and so developed the habit of making the best possible use of the executive material it had available. Men were chosen at an early age and were quickly given heavy responsibilities on the theory that a man's best qualities are developed under fire. The system worked well. It gave full recognition to the latent abilities in an individual and it caused men of ordinary parts to do jobs well over their heads. The success of the policy was so noteworthy, in fact, that the company still adheres to it. The only important exception in recent years occurred when the company hired, as the head of its reorganized production department, a man from the outside with whom the executives were unacquainted and who had had no previous connection with the textile industry. Yet, suitable as this policy has been, it is questionable whether it will be appropriate for the future. The complexities of modern industrial organizations put high premiums on specialized educations. Ability is still a prerequisite, but today ability must be honed by theoretical knowledge if its cutting edge is to work with maximum efficiency.

If the key problem in the present generation of the textile machinery industry turns out to be product development, the cause will be the continued threat of a contracting market for textile-mill equipment. It is still too early to know whether a chronic depression will settle down again over the industry as it did after the First World War, but many of the ingredients exist. The physical production of cotton textiles has not increased since 1941 despite a 12 or 13 per cent rise in population and a notable increase in national income. Wool production has shown only a very slight rise. Rayon and other artificial fibers have accounted for practically all the expansion in textile output and, as has already been said, filament rayon production requires precious little textile machinery. Consequently most of the increased use of textile machinery in the past few years has been in the manufacture of staple rayon goods.

It does little good to reflect that one-half of the country's cotton spinning equipment is over thirty years old; the Whitin company knows that age and obsolescence have not always been telling arguments when it came to selling capital goods. For twenty years before World War II, E. Kent Swift kept insisting that the nation's textile industry was replacing its machinery less rapidly than it should. It must have brought him a wry smile when so many of his customers finally acknowledged his point by placing their orders at postwar peak prices and when deliveries were hardest to get. Thanks to the boom in textile goods, mill owners at last felt able, after the war, to buy the equipment they had delayed buying for so long. In the last analysis, the prosperity of the textile machinery industry has always been, and will probably continue to be, closely linked with the prosperity of the textile industry it serves.

In the depression of the 'twenties and 'thirties, the textile machinery industry chose two paths out of the slough. The one, leading into the wool, worsted, and rayon fields, was followed by the Whitin Machine Works. The other, leading abroad, was followed by the Saco-Lowell Shops. In case of another depression, and if those same two paths again seem to lead outward, each company may well try to follow the other's course. In such an event, Whitin would have to abandon still another policy of long standing, for the company has never, with certain important exceptions, actively pursued business abroad. For a short time it had an agent in Mexico and following

World War I, under very favorable conditions, it sold machinery to
the Orient. But, knowing that selling in the export market required
special skills it did not possess, the company generally refrained from
promoting its machinery in foreign countries. During the latter
1930's and again following World War II, Whitin did a spirited
business in South America, particularly in Brazil, but more as
a result of international conditions than because of sales promotion. During the postwar boom, when orders from Cuba, Brazil,
Mexico, Peru, Bolivia, Argentina, and Chile were especially heavy,
the company would have liked to ship as much as 50 per cent of its
output to that part of the world, knowing full well that once the
British were back in competition, orders from Latin America would
again be difficult to get. But, knowing also that domestic customers
would resent any show of favoritism to foreign mills, the company
discreetly limited its shipments abroad to 20 per cent of production.

Over against the possibility that the textile machinery industry
will return to semi-depressed conditions stands the basic fact that
the industry provides the mechanical wherewithal for the production of one of the elemental goods in a civilized economy — textile
fabrics. The level of demand may fluctuate, but there is no fear that
the demand will disappear. Perhaps that is one of the reasons why
institutional investors have faith in Whitin securities.

The present management is well aware of the problems that it
faces; being aware, it has won half the battle. So long as the company has an alert management it has nothing to fear, for, financially
and competitively, it is as strong now as at any time in its history.
The Whitin Machine Works has a rare tradition behind it. Success
will result from living up to that tradition, not in looking back on
it with nostalgia.

To the historian, viewing several generations of accomplishment,
the chief conclusions lie in the fact that one enterprising family has
given employment to men from the neighboring valleys and from
overcrowded parts of Europe, has turned out an excellent product,
has contributed to the reduction of costs of production and hence to
the advance of the nation's standard of living, and in the process has
attained the stability and security for itself and for its employees
that the modern world so highly esteems.

APPENDICES

APPENDIX 1

CHANGES IN OWNERSHIP IN THE NORTHBRIDGE COTTON MANUFACTURING COMPANY

(Numbers indicate fractional share of ownership)

Date	Deed[a]	Northbridge Group				Leicester Group			Rhode Island Group										Total	Comments
		Paul Whitin	James Fletcher	Samuel Fletcher	Abram Wilson	Pliny Earle & Bros.	Timothy Earle	Silas Earle	Charles Sabin	John Sabin	Henry Sabin	Jonathan Adams	Joel Lackey	William Howard	Amasa Southwick	Thos. & Wm. Buffum	Samuel Shove	P. Whitin & Sons		
24 May 1810	177/396	6	4	2	1	8	2		4			3		2					32	@ $ 500 [b]
29 Dec. 1810	180/266	6	4	2	1	8	2		4			3							30	@ 1,000
4 Apr. 1811	180/267	6	3	2	1	8	2		4			4							30	@ 1,100
14 Jan. 1812	183/207	6	2	2	1	8	2	1	4			4							30	@ 1,100
14 Jan. 1812	184/421	6	2	1	1	9	2	1	4			4							30	°
28 Feb. 1812	183/443	6	2	1	1	7	2	3	4			4							30	@ 1,000
22 Dec. 1812	186/308	7	2	1	1	7	2	3	4			4							30	@ 1,000
8 Jan. 1813	186/309	6	2	1	1	7	2	6	4			4							30	@ 1,000
29 Jan. 1814	192/31	6	2	1	1	7	2	6	4	1		1							30	@ 1,800
8 Feb. 1814	192/110	6	2	1	1	7	2	6	4	1		1	1						30	@ 1,800
24 June 1824	239/200					4	2	6	4	1	5	1	1						30	@ 1,800 [d]
25 Mar. 1825	249/30					4	2				3				3	18			30	@ 555
16 Nov. 1825	249/29					4	2				1				3	20			30	@ 333
28 Nov. 1825	249/27					4	2								3	21			30	@ 333
6 May 1826	257/202					4									3	23			30	@ 333
1 Oct. 1830	280/579					4									3		23		30	°
10 June 1831	282/92					4									3			23	30	@ 670
15 Oct. 1832	289/347														3			27	30	@ 500
26 Dec. 1832	290/450																	30	30	@ 500 [f]

[a] These deeds are registered at the Worcester County Court House, Worcester, Mass. The first of the two numbers indicates the book in which the deed may be found, the second the page number.   [b] William Howard forfeited his option to buy two shares.   [c] Silas Earle withdrew from partnership with his brothers.   [d] As collateral for a debt of $4,617.22, Pliny Earle transferred to Amasa Southwick a 3/30 share in the enterprise. Meanwhile, Henry Sabin had become administrator of the estates of Charles and John Sabin.   [e] The terms of sales are not given.   [f] Actually, the 3/30 purchased by P. Whitin & Sons from Amasa Southwick cost $3,000, for Pliny Earle still claimed ownership, although the debt for which the share was security apparently remained unpaid; therefore, to settle the claim P. Whitin & Sons had to pay both parties for the share involved.

APPENDIX 2

LIST OF COMPANY OFFICIALS
1870–1948

Presidents

John C. Whitin	1870–1882
Josiah Lasell	1882–1886
Chester W. Lasell	1887–1932
E. Kent Swift	1933–1946
J. Hugh Bolton	1946–

Treasurers

Josiah Lasell	1870–1886
George Marston Whitin	1886–1920
E. Kent Swift	1920–1947
Edward S. Alden	1947–

Assistant Treasurers

J. M. Lasell	1891–1905
E. Kent Swift	1906–1920
William H. Hoch	1923–1942[a]

Vice-Presidents

George B. Hamblin	1929–1939
Frederick E. Banfield, Jr.	1939–
J. Hugh Bolton	1939–1946
Ralph E. Lincoln	1939–
Robert J. McConnell	1943–
Harry Moss	1947–

Agents

Gustavus E. Taft	1881–1888
Cyrus A. Taft	1888–1902
Lawrence M. Keeler	1906–1929

Works Managers

William H. Hoch	1919–1923
George B. Hamblin	1923–1935
Frederick E. Banfield, Jr.	1935–1947
Erik O. Pierson	1947–

Superintendents

William H. Kendall	1847–1864
Gustavus E. Taft	1864–1881
Harvey Ellis	1881–1891
William L. Taft	1891–1897
Albert H. Whipple	1897–1924
William O. Aldrich	1924–1930
Ernest T. Clary	1930–1943
Harry Mitchell	1943–1946
John H. Cunningham	1946–

[a] Except for the years 1928–1931.

APPENDIX 3

LIST OF DIRECTORS OF THE WHITIN MACHINE WORKS, 1870–1948

(Only those years are shown when there were changes in the directorate; e.g., John C. Whitin was a director from 1870 to 1882, etc.)

1870	1873	1882	1887	1888	1908	1910	1917	1921	1923	1925	1928	1929	1932	1933	1936	1937	1940	1942	1943	1944	1947	1948
JCW	JCW																					
JL	JL	JL																				
GET	GET	GET	GET																			
CPW	CPW	CPW	CPW																			
'MW																						
		GMW	GMW	GMW	GMW	GMW	GMW															
			CWL	CWL	CWL	CWL	CWL	CWL	CWL	CWL	CWL	CWL	CWL									
			JML	JML	JML	JML	JML	JML	JML	JML	JML	JML	JML	JML	JML	JML						
			WLT	WLT	WLT																	
			CAT	CAT																		
							EKS	EKS	EKS	EKS	EKS	EKS	EKS	EKS	EKS	EKS	EKS	EKS	EKS	EKS	EKS	EKS
							SRM	SRM	SRM	SRM	SRM	SRM	SRM	SRM	SRM	SRM	SRM	SRM	SRM	SRM	SRM	SRM
							LMK	LMK	LMK	LMK	LMK	LMK	LMK	LMK								
								JLII	JLII													
									MV	MV	MV	MV	MV	MV								
									WHH	WHH	WHH	WHH	WHH	WHH	WHH	WHH	WHH					
															WHH	WHH	WHH					
										JWL	JWL	JWL	JWL	JWL	JWL	JWL	JWL	JWL				
															AW	AW	AW	AW	AW	AW	AW	AW
																CHL	CHL	CHL	CHL	CHL	CHL	
																		FEB	FEB	FEB	FEB	FEB
																		JHB	JHB	JHB	JHB	JHB
																		REL	REL	REL	REL	REL
																			NFA	NFA		
																				ESA	ESA	ESA
																					PK	PK
																						MWK

Key to code: John C. Whitin, Josiah Lasell, Gustavus E. Taft, Charles P. Whitin, John Maltby Whitin, George Marston Whitin, Chester W. Lasell, J. M. Lasell, William L. Taft, Cyrus A. Taft, E. Kent Swift, Sydney R. Mason, Lawrence M. Keeler, Josiah Lasell II, Minturn deSurzara Verdi, William H. Hoch, John W. Lasell, Chester H. Lasell, Frederick E. Banfield, J. Hugh Bolton, Ralph E. Lincoln, Nathaniel F. Ayer, Edward S. Alden, Phillips Ketchum, Murray W. Keeler.

APPENDIX 4

DISTRIBUTION OF OWNERSHIP OF WHITIN MACHINE WORKS STOCK, 1870–1910

Name	1870	1873	1876	1882	1883	1887	1888	1889	1892	1893	1896	1897	1910
J. C. Whitin d. 22 Apr. 1882	5980	5985		5									
J. M. Whitin d. 22 Oct. 1871	5												
C. P. Whitin	5	5	3895	3890									
G. Taft d. 29 Aug. 1887	5	5	5	5	5	5	5*	5*	5*	5*	5*	5*	
J. Lasell d. 24 June 1888			600	600	600	590	590	215*					
Mrs. J. Lasell d. 15 Mar. 1886	5	5	1500	1500	3450	3440*	950*	950*	950*				
G. M. Whitin† d. 12 Mar. 1895					1940	1940	2440	2440	2440	3390			
Mrs. G. M. Whitin					5	5	5	5	5	5	5	505	600
C. W. Lasell						5	500	500	500	500	1630	1630	1800
J. M. Lasell						5	500	500	500	500	1630	1630	1800
Mrs. Backus d. 9 Mar. 1892							500	500	500	500*	500*		
O. Backus							500	500	500	500	1630	1630	1800
C. A. Taft d. 6 Feb. 1908						5	5	130	202	202	202	202	
W. L. Taft d. 29 Dec. 1909						5	5	130	202	202	202	202	
E. M. Taft								125	196	196	196	196	
Totals	6000	6000	6000	6000	6000	6000	6000	6000	6000	6000	6000	6000	6000

* Estate.

† Death dates have been given only when death accounted for changes in stock ownership.

Source: Statements of Condition filed in the Secretary's Office, Massachusetts State House. Statements made as of the third Monday in January. No change in ownership during years not shown.

APPENDIX 5

NET WORTH AND DECLARED DIVIDENDS, 1876–1948

Year	Stated Net Worth	Estimated Net Worth[a]	Declared Dividends[b]	Dividends as a % of Est. Net Worth
1876........$	735,190	$ 749,000	$ 60,000	8.0
1877........	800,192	830,000	36,000	4.3
1878........	852,495	900,000	60,000	6.7
1879........	877,551	944,000	36,000	3.8
1880........	921,140	1,007,000	60,000	6.0
1881........	903,314	1,009,000	300,000	29.7
1882........	950,438	1,077,000	300,000	27.9
1883........	1,012,217	1,162,000	300,000	25.8
1884........	1,084,945	1,159,000	....	..
1885........	1,002,555	1,200,000	....	..
1886........	1,019,729	1,242,000	36,000	2.9
1887........	1,033,666	1,281,000	60,000	4.7
1888........	1,052,351	1,326,000	60,000	4.5
1889........	1,052,123	1,358,000	60,000	4.4
1890........	1,062,967	1,398,000	90,000	6.4
1891........	940,483	1,401,000	240,000	17.1
1892........	901,955	1,287,000	90,000	7.0
1893........	939,245	1,351,000	48,000	3.5
1894........	1,003,244	1,441,000	48,000	3.3
1895........	1,031,824	1,500,000	72,000	4.8
1896........	1,062,685	1,534,000	60,000	3.9
1897........	1,070,113	1,573,000	600,000	38.1
1898........	1,137,288	1,673,000	120,000	7.2
1899........	1,164,479	1,734,000	450,000	26.0
1900........	1,132,413	1,737,000	450,000	25.9
1901........	1,163,784	1,803,000	300,000	16.6
1902........	1,495,838	2,178,000	240,000	11.0
1903........	1,528,197	2,255,000	360,000	16.0
1904[c]......	1,646,200	2,466,000	420,000	17.0
1905........	1,755,495	2,627,000	300,000	11.4
1906........	1,707,396	2,630,000	600,000	22.8
1907........	1,802,197	2,786,000	120,000	4.3
1908........	2,215,374	3,257,000	120,000	3.7
1909........	2,182,413	3,288,000	120,000	3.6
1910........	2,772,082	3,956,000	600,000	15.2
1911........	3,308,765	4,581,000	420,000	9.2
1912........	3,381,337	4,748,000	120,000	2.5
1913........	3,232,463	4,691,000	180,000	3.8
1914........	3,228,667	4,780,000	180,000	3.8
1915........	3,098,240	4,743,000	330,000	7.0
1916........	4,408,478	6,174,000	600,000	9.7
1917........	7,034,175	....	300,000	4.3
1918........	7,738,010	....	300,000[d]	3.9

NET WORTH AND DECLARED DIVIDENDS, 1876–1948 (continued)

Year	Stated Net Worth	Estimated Net Worth[a]	Declared Dividends[b]	Dividends as a % of Est. Net Worth
1919	9,009,464	....	450,000	5.0
1920	9,681,012	....	300,000	3.1
1921	12,137,963	....	450,000	3.7
1922	14,722,767	....	600,000	4.1
1923	15,649,198	....	1,080,000	6.9
1924	15,593,469	....	720,000	4.6
1925	15,897,432	....	540,000	3.4
1926	15,922,812	....	540,000	3.4
1927	15,983,074	....	585,000	3.7
1928	15,802,708	....	585,000	3.7
1929	15,602,551	....	540,000	3.5
1930	15,364,678	....	450,000	2.9
1931	14,419,777	....	360,000	2.5
1932	13,639,504	....	292,500	2.1
1933	13,369,589	....	270,000[e]	2.0
1934	13,249,654	....	360,000[f]	2.7
1935	12,864,644	....	360,000	2.8
1936	12,958,333	....	360,000	2.8
1937	13,481,557	....	562,500	4.2
1938	13,302,022	....	292,500	2.2
1939	13,465,762	....	562,500	4.2
1940	13,835,657	....	630,000	4.5
1941	14,207,693	....	630,000	4.4
1942	14,557,548	....	630,000	4.3
1943	14,931,499	....	630,000	4.2
1944	15,491,959	....	630,000	4.1
1945	16,563,400	....	648,000	3.9
1946	17,177,535	....	648,000	3.8
1947	19,321,680	....	648,000	3.4
1948	....	....	....	..

[a] For the method used in computing Estimated Net Worth for the years 1876–1916, see footnote 1, chap. xiii; after 1916, stated net worth and estimated net worth are identical.

[b] Declared dividends not listed in table: 1872—$110,000 (of which $60,000 was declared as of 1871); 1873—$90,000; 1874—$300,000; and 1875—$110,000.

[c] Before 1904 balance sheets were dated as of the annual stockholders' meeting held the third Monday in January. Beginning in 1904 balance sheets were dated 31 December.

[d] Dividends amounting to $300,000 were declared, but only $75,000 were paid out in cash. In lieu of the remainder the company distributed its loom patents to its stockholders.

[e] Dividends amounting to $472,500 were declared in 1933, of which only $270,000 was to be paid in that year, the remainder to be paid in 1934.

[f] Dividends amounting to $360,000 were declared in 1934, of which only $157,500 was to be paid in that year, the remainder to be paid in 1935. In 1935 an additional $157,500 in dividends was declared and paid.

Source: Statements of Condition rendered annually to the Commonwealth of Massachusetts; Minutes of the Board of Directors' Meetings.

APPENDIX 6

SELECTED LIST OF AMERICAN TEXTILE-MACHINERY MANUFACTURERS

(A list of the competitors that have been significant in the history of the Whitin Machine Works)

Company Name	Location	Founder	Mill Origin	Machinery First Sold	Company Specialty	Liquidated or Combined	Present Name
COMPANIES MAKING PREPARATORY MACHINERY							
Whitin Machine Works	Whitinsville, Mass.	John C. Whitin	P. Whitin & Sons	1833	nearly full line	....	Whitin Machine Works
Providence Machine Co.	Providence, R. I.	Thomas J. Hill	Providence Steam Mills	1827	roving	1909	Whitin Machine Works
Atherton Picking Machinery Co.	Pawtucket, R. I.	A. T. Atherton	....	c. 1906	pickers	1913	Whitin Machine Works
Cashiko Machine Co.	Worcester, Mass.	Cavedon, Shimek & Kovar	....	1918	wool cards	1929	Whitin Machine Works
Fales & Jenks Mach. Co.	Pawtucket, R. I.	David Fales Alvin Jenks	....	1830	spinning & twisting	1931	Whitin Machine Works
Woonsocket Mach. & Press Co.	Woonsocket, R. I.	....	....	1868	roving	1931	Whitin Machine Works
Saco Water Power Co.	Biddeford, Me.	....	Saco Manufacturing Co.	1844	roving & spinning	1897	Saco-Lowell Shops
Pettee Mach. Works	Newton Upper Falls, Mass.	Otis Pettee	Elliot Mfg. Co.	1832	cards	1897	Saco-Lowell Shops
Lowell Mach. Shop	Lowell, Mass.	Paul Moody	Merrimack Mfg. Co.	1815	full line	1912	Saco-Lowell Shops
Kitson Mach. Shop	Lowell, Mass.	Richard Kitson	....	1849	pickers	1905	Saco-Lowell Shops
Howard & Bullough Am. Mach. Co.	Pawtucket, R. I.	C. E. Riley	....	1894	nearly full line	....	H & B American Machine Co.

Company Name	Location	Founder	Mill Origin	Machinery First Sold	Company Specialty	Liquidated or Combined	Present Name
COMPANIES MAKING WEAVING MACHINERY							
Geo. Draper & Sons	Hopedale, Mass.	Ira Draper	….	1816	plain cloth looms	….	Draper Corporation
Crompton Loom Works........	Worcester, Mass.	William Crompton	….	1837	fancy cloth looms	1897	Crompton & Knowles Loom Works
Knowles Loom Works........	Worcester, Mass.	Lucius Knowles	….	1862	fancy cloth looms	1897	Crompton & Knowles Loom Works
COMPANIES MAKING WOOLEN MACHINERY							
Davis & Furber Mach. Co.......	No. Andover, Mass.	Jona. Sawyer Russell Phelps	Abraham Marland Mills	1832	woolen machinery	….	Davis & Furber Mach. Co.
COMPANIES NO LONGER IN EXISTENCE							
Mason Mach. Works........	Taunton, Mass.	William Mason	….	1843	cards, drawing, spinning	1924	….
Hawes, Marvel & Davol........	Fall River, Mass.	Wm. C. Davol	Pocasset Mill	1842	mules	c. 1905	….
Jas. Brown Machine Shop........	Pawtucket, R. I.	Jas. S. Brown	….	1824	mules	1906	….
Kilburn, Lincoln & Davol Co.......	Fall River, Mass.	J. J. Kilburn J. T. Lincoln	Quequechan Mill	1845	plain cloth looms	1927	….

This appendix is meant only as an aid to the reader in comprehending the relationship of those units in the textile machinery industry that are mentioned in the text. It omits many companies and includes many others that are of lesser importance. It includes all the units which have gone to make up the present Whitin Machine Works but necessarily omits some of those that have gone into the Saco-Lowell Shops. Many of the names and dates have been arbitrarily selected as must always be the case if the complexities of corporate structures are to be summarized.

APPENDIX 7

MANUFACTURERS OF TEXTILE MACHINERY AND SUCH OF THEIR PRODUCTS AS WERE IN OPERATION IN 1874

Names of Companies	Location	Openers	Pickers	Cards	Drawing frames	Roving frames	Throstle frames	Ring frames	Mules	Spoolers	Warpers	Dressers	Slashers	Looms
American Builders														
Amoskeag Manufacturing Co.	Manchester, N. H.	x		x				x[a]		x	x			x
Bridesburg Manufacturing Co.	Philadelphia, Penna.							[b]						
City Machine Co.	Woonsocket, R. I.					x								
Fales, Jenks & Sons	Pawtucket, R. I.							[c]						
Franklin Foundry & Machine Co.	Providence, R. I.									x				
George Crompton	Worcester, Mass.													x
Geo. Draper & Sons	Hopedale, Mass.									x				
James S. Brown & Sons	Pawtucket, R. I.					x								
J. E. Van Winkle & Co.	Paterson, N. J.	x												
Kilburn, Lincoln & Co.	Fall River, Mass.													x
Kitson Machine Shop	Lowell, Mass.	x	x											
Lanphear Machine Co.	Phenix, R. I.							x						
Lewiston Machine Shop	Lewiston, Me.									x	x			x
Lowell Machine Shop	Lowell, Mass.			x	x			x[d]		x				x
Marvel, Davol & Co.	Fall River, Mass.	x								x				x
Mason Machine Works	Taunton, Mass.	x	x	x				x[e]		x	x	x		x
Pettee Machine Works	Newton Upper Falls, Mass.	x	x											
Providence Machine Co.	Providence, R. I.					x								
Saco Water Power Machine Shop	Biddeford, Me.	x	x	x				x[f]		x	x			x
Whitehead & Atherton Machine Co.	Lowell, Mass.	x	x											
Whitin Machine Works	Whitinsville, Mass.	x	x	x				x[f]		x	x			x
British Builders														
Curtis, Parr & Madeley	Manchester, England					x			x					
Howard & Bullough	Accrington, England	x	x	x									x	
Platt Bros. & Co.	Oldham, England	x							x					
Walker & Hacking	Stalybridge, England					x								
Wm. Higgins & Sons	Manchester, England					x	x							

Types of spindles:
  [a] Perry (dead).   [c] Rabbeth.   [e] Birkenhead.
  [b] Excelsior.   [d] Richardson and Pearl.   [f] Sawyer.

Source: Samuel Webber, "Tests of Power Required for Cotton and Other Machinery," N.E.C.M.A. *Transactions*, no. 16, 1874. The list is by no means complete; it simply contains the names of machine-builders whose products Webber tested.

APPENDIX 8

TARIFF ACTS AFFECTING THE LEVEL OF DUTIES ON IMPORTED TEXTILE MACHINERY

Year of Enactment	Wording of Pertinent Clause in Each Tariff Act	Level of Tariff (per cent)
1792	". . . all manufactures of iron, steel . . ."	10
1794	". . . above the duties now payable . . . five per cent. ad valorem . . . on all manufactures of iron, steel . . ."	15
1804	". . . for carrying on warlike operations against the regency of Tripoli . . . a duty of two and an half per centum ad valorem in addition to the duties now imposed by law . . ."	17½
1812	". . . an additional duty of one hundred per centum upon the permanent duties now imposed by law."	32½
1816	". . . all articles manufactured from . . . iron, steel . . ."	20
1824	". . . all manufactures, not otherwise specified, made of brass, iron, steel . . ."	25
1832	". . . all manufactures, not otherwise specified, made of brass, iron, steel . . ."	25
1833	". . . in all cases where duties . . . exceed twenty per centum . . ."	
	31 Dec. 1833	24½
	31 Dec. 1835	24
	31 Dec. 1837	23½
	31 Dec. 1839	23
	31 Dec. 1841	21½
	30 June 1842	20

Year of Enactment	Wording of Pertinent Clause in Each Tariff Act	Level of Tariff (per cent)
1842	". . . all other manufactures, not otherwise specified, made of brass, iron, steel . . ."	30
1857	[all articles in Schedule C of the Tariff Act of 30 July 1846 (which had continued the duties on manufactures of iron and steel at 30%) to be reduced to 24%]	24
1861	". . . all manufactures of iron not otherwise provided for . . ."	30
	". . . all manufactures of steel . . . not otherwise provided for . . ."	30
1862	". . . all manufactures of iron, not otherwise provided for, [an addition of] five per centum ad valorem."	35
	". . . all manufactures of steel . . . not otherwise provided for, [an addition of] five per centum ad valorem."	35
1864	". . . all manufactures of iron, not otherwise provided for . . ."	35
	". . . all manufactures of steel . . . not otherwise provided for . . ."	45
1883	"Manufactures . . . not specifically enumerated . . . composed . . . of iron, steel . . ."	45
1894	"Manufactured articles . . . not specifically provided for . . . composed . . . of any metal . . ."	35
1897	"Articles or wares not specifically provided for . . . composed . . . of iron, steel . . ."	45
1909	"Articles or wares not specifically provided for . . . composed of iron, steel . . ."	45
1913	"Articles or wares not specifically provided for . . . composed wholly or in chief value of iron, steel . . ."	20
1922	"Articles or wares not specifically provided	

Year of Enactment	Wording of Pertinent Clause in Each Tariff Act	Level of Tariff (per cent)
	for . . . if composed wholly or in chief value of iron, steel . . ."	40
1938	"[The Tariff Act of 1930 sustained the 40% level on textile machinery but was modified by a reciprocal trade agreement with the United Kingdom, effective 1 Jan. 1939, in which the rate was made 20% on all] textile machinery, finished or unfinished, not specifically provided for, for textile manufacturing or processing prior to the making of fabrics [thus the duty on looms remained at 40%]"	
1947	"The Governments of the Commonwealth of Australia, the Kingdom of Belgium, the United States of Brazil, Burma, Canada, Ceylon, the Republic of Chile, the Republic of China, the Republic of Cuba, the Czechoslovak Republic, the French Republic, India, Lebanon, the Grand Duchy of Luxemburg, the Kingdom of the Netherlands, New Zealand, the Kingdom of Norway, Pakistan, Southern Rhodesia, Syria, the Union of South Africa, the United Kingdom of Great Britain and Northern Ireland, and the United States of America . . . by entering into reciprocal and mutually advantageous arrangements . . . have through their Representatives agreed as follows . . . textile machinery . . . for textile manufacturing or processing prior to the making of fabrics [again looms were excluded] . . ."	10

APPENDIX 9

PATENTS CONTROLLED BY THE WHITIN MACHINE WORKS, 1832–1910

Compiled by George West, head of the patent department at the Whitin Machine Works.

Date	Patent No.	Inventor	Invention
July 20, 1832	....	J. C. Whitin	Picker
Nov. 4, 1856	16,028	Joel Smith	Regulating the Twist in Throstle Frames
Feb. 8, 1859	22,899	Joel Smith	Regulating the Twist in Throstle Frames
July 7, 1863	39,187	J. C. Whitin	Card Stripper
Jan. 19, 1864	41,268	J. H. Aldrich	Flyer
June 7, 1864	43,059	J. C. Whitin	Bolster for Flyer-Frame Spindle
Aug. 30, 1864	43,961	Aldrich & Pattee	Flyer
Oct. 27, 1868	83,436	J. H. Aldrich[a]	Flyer
Nov. 16, 1869	96,935	G. W. Prentice	Weight-Releasing Device for Spinning Rolls
Apr. 25, 1871	114,064	G. E. Taft[b]	Sliver Traverse Mechanism for Drawing Frames
Apr. 9, 1872	125,501	G. E. Taft	Card Stripper
Jan. 21, 1873	135,189	C. F. Wilson	Spindle-Step
Jan. 21, 1873	135,190	C. F. Wilson	Spindle-Bolster
July 8, 1873	140,740	G. E. Taft[b]	Card Stripper
Feb. 24, 1874	148,015	C. F. Wilson	Spindle-Bolster
June 29, 1875	164,948	G. E. Taft	Picker-Beater
May 8, 1877	190,525	G. E. Taft	Bobbin Adaptor (Paper Cop)
July 24, 1877	193,571	G. E. Taft	Cotton Card
Dec. 2, 1879	222,329	G. E. Taft[b]	Bobbin Building (Speed Change)
Mar. 2, 1880	225,181	G. E. Taft[b]	Spinning Spindle
Oct. 19, 1880	233,576	G. E. Taft[b]	Cotton Card
July 18, 1882	261,275	G. E. Taft[b]	Spindle-Bearing
Sept. 11, 1883	284,775	Taft & Woodmancy	Spindle-Bearing
May 19, 1885	318,405	G. M. Whitin[b]	Spindle-Drive
Jan. 5, 1886	333,898	G. E. Taft[b]	Thread-Board Lifter
Mar. 16, 1886	338,238	H. F. Woodmancy	Spindle-Bolster
Sept. 10, 1889	410,864	G. E. Taft	Card Cylinder
Oct. 15, 1889	412,996	Taft & Woodmancy	Spindle-Bolster
Mar. 4, 1890	422,849	C. A. Taft[b]	Support for Flats, Cotton Card
July 7, 1891	455,525	H. F. Woodmancy	Spindle-Bolster
May 31, 1892	475,994	H. F. Woodmancy	Spindle-Bolster
June 7, 1892	476,587	H. F. Woodmancy	Spindle-Bolster
Aug. 16, 1892	480,984	H. F. Woodmancy	Bolster Case
Aug. 16, 1892	480,985	H. F. Woodmancy	Spindle–Doffer Guard
Nov. 8, 1892	485,997	C. A. Taft[b]	Stop Motion for Drawing Frames
Mar. 20, 1894	RE 11,407 (480,985)	H. F. Woodmancy[b]	Spindle-Doffer Guard
May 1, 1894	519,295	C. A. Taft[b]	Stop Motion for Drawing Frames
May 28, 1895	540,198	C. A. Taft[b]	Separator for Spinning Frames
Feb. 13, 1900	643,343	H. F. Woodmancy	Ball-Bearing Spindle
June 7, 1904	761,934	W. O. Aldrich[b]	Thread Board
Dec. 1, 1908	905,386	C. A. Taft[b]	Thread Board
Apr. 10, 1910	953,732	W. O. Aldrich[b]	Thread Board

[a] Assigned to John C. Whitin and Aldrich.
[b] Assigned to Whitin Machine Works.

APPENDIX 10

A BRIEF HISTORY OF THE WHITIN FAMILY'S
COTTON-MILL HOLDINGS SUBSEQUENT TO
THE DISSOLUTION OF P. WHITIN & SONS

To facilitate the distribution of P. Whitin & Sons' assets among the company's shareholders, Betsey Whitin, on 31 December 1863, transferred to her four sons her one-eighth interest in the firm in exchange for the nominal sum of $29,000. (Worcester County deed book 683, p. 413.) The reason for the low valuation on Betsey's share is made clear, in part at least, by the terms of her will. (Registry of Probate, Worcester County, Probate series A, no. 64567.) She apparently wanted her estate to provide two trust funds of $18,000 each, one for her son, Nathaniel, and one for a daughter, Margaret. Since all her property, except for those two legacies, was to go to her four other sons in equal parts upon her death, she had no reason to require a high price for her share in the enterprise. (Where not otherwise noted, information about the subsequent history of the family was obtained in the course of conversations with Paul Whitin IV and Richard C. Whitin of the Paul Whitin Manufacturing Company, with Earl J. Liberty, formerly connected with the Whitinsville, Linwood, and Saundersville mills, and with Robert E. Hamilton, secretary of James Whitin, Inc.)

Paul Whitin, Jr., the oldest of the brothers, received the newest of the mills, the Rockdale and Riverdale properties which had been bought in 1856 and had been largely rebuilt and renovated in the following years. The size of these mills in 1864 is not known, but shortly after 1870, the year in which they were incorporated as the Paul Whitin Manufacturing Company, they were said to have a combined capacity of more than 16,000 spindles. (Spindle capacities have been obtained from Dockham's Directories and from Davison's Blue Books.) The Riverdale mill, however, did not remain in operation long. On 8 February 1889 a fire gutted the building and irreparably damaged the machinery. For several years the building was left a blackened shell until finally it was sold to the Riverdale Woolen Company in 1894. (The Riverdale Woolen Co., manufacturers of shoddies, remained in operation for about fifteen years after which the property was sold to the Kupfer Bros. Co., makers of coated paper products, in whose possession the property still remains.) Insurance collected on the Riverdale building was used for the first of a series of expansions of the Rockdale mill which, by 1908, had enlarged the mill's capacity to 72,000 spindles.

After 1886 the managements of the Rockdale mill and of the Whitin Machine Works functioned in active coöperation because of the close family tie established by the marriage of George Marston Whitin, grandson of Paul Whitin, Jr., to Catharine Whitin Lasell, granddaughter of John C. Whitin. From then until recently the treasurer of the machine shop always served also as president of the Rockdale mill. When the machine shop began developing new types of equipment, the Rockdale mill was used as a proving ground; consequently, the product line of the mill, which until the turn of the century had been limited to shirtings and print cloths, was gradually extended by the introduction of new machinery until it included not only such fancy cotton goods as cambrics, lawns, sateens, and twills, but some rayon fabrics as well. The Rockdale mill became one of the first to use rayon produced by The American Viscose Company after it was founded in 1910. By the beginning of the First World War, employment in the mill had reached nearly a thousand, a level at which it has remained fairly steady ever since. Because of a continuous succession of able managers who were willing to experiment with new materials and fabrics, the company has managed to weather the storms in which so many Northern cotton mills have foundered. For five generations the eldest son of each generation has carried on this tradition of family management. It seems that only one other family in the cotton textile industry can duplicate this record — the descendants of Samuel Slater.

It will be recalled that the youngest of the four Whitin brothers, James F. Whitin, held only a one-eighth interest in the partnership. For his share he received only one mill, the 10,000-spindle unit known as the Uxbridge Cotton Mills; in addition, however, he was given title to the water rights at Linwood, near his Uxbridge properties. These rights, although potentially valuable, were at the time undeveloped. Almost immediately, James persuaded his older brother, Charles, to lend him financial aid in utilizing the Linwood privilege, and by 1867 the two brothers had erected a mill of 15,000 spindles. From the beginning the Linwood mill overshadowed James' other mill at North Uxbridge, which was destined never to become an important producing unit. No major expansion was undertaken at the smaller mill until 1900, and even then the capacity was increased only to 17,000 spindles.

The active management of the Uxbridge Cotton Mills continued in the hands of James F. Whitin until well past the prime of his life, for the son on whom he had counted as a successor died in his early thirties, leaving James with only two minor grandsons as heirs to the Uxbridge mill. On James' death the management of the mills was entrusted temporarily to a nephew, Edward Whitin, who ran the mill until the two grandsons were old enough to assume their responsibilities. Eventually James Earle Whitin, the younger of the two grandsons, bought out the interest of Frederick, his older brother, and took over full management of the mill. Following the First World War, James realized that a small carded-cotton mill equipped with old machinery could no longer compete with Southern mills, so he closed the Uxbridge mill (1 July 1923) and devoted his full time to the Worcester carpet interests of Matthew J. Whittall whose daughter he had married. (James Earle Whitin married Edgeworth Paget Whittall and his sister, Betsey Whitin, married Edgeworth's brother, Matthew Percival Whittall.) Meanwhile, he had sold his interest in the Linwood mill to the Charles P. Whitin branch of the family.

In recognition of his quarter-interest Charles P. Whitin had received the firm's remaining mill properties: the stone mill in Whitinsville, the old brick mill which had ceased operations when the stone mill had been built, and the mill at East Douglas. Charles immediately set about adjusting the operation of his properties to meet the new conditions. Floor space of the stone mill was doubled by the addition of a wing in the rear and by the erection of a small picker building. The Douglas mill was then closed, and much of its machinery was transferred to the new wing of the stone mill, giving that mill a production capacity of about 12,000 spindles. Meanwhile, Charles had joined his brother James in the erection of the new mill at Linwood. By 1866 Charles was ready to consolidate his interests and to form with his two oldest sons a partnership to be called the Whitinsville Cotton Mills. In 1881 Charles and his sons, in an effort to prevent the financial ruin of Esek Saunders (whose daughter had married James F. Whitin), added to their mill holdings by purchasing from Esek the Saunders Cotton Mill located in Saundersville just north of Whitinsville.

On the death of Charles in 1887, his mills came under the able management of Edward, his oldest son. Edward continued the operation of the Whitinsville and Saundersville mills as units of about 14,000 spindles employing up to 200 workers each, but at Linwood during the 1890's, he undertook a major expansion program, increasing the mill's capacity from 15,000 to 28,000 spindles. By 1900, roughly a quarter of the mill workers under Whitin family management were working in the Linwood mill, while three-eighths were at Rockdale, and another three-eighths were divided about equally between Whitinsville, Uxbridge, and Saundersville.

The mills which had belonged to Charles P. Whitin were not, however, destined to enjoy the success of the Rockdale mill. Whereas Rockdale had diversified its product line after 1900, the Whitinsville, Linwood, and Saundersville mills continued to concentrate on the manufacture of plain cotton goods, which were already meeting stiff competition from mills in the South. Moreover, the continuous line of able executives which the Paul Whitin, Jr., and the John C. Whitin branches of the family had produced was paralleled in the Charles P. Whitin branch for only one generation, after which the family line died out. On Edward's death in 1913, ownership of the mills fell to his only surviving brother, Arthur F. Whitin, whose interests were absorbed by the problems of his own enterprise, the Whitinsville Spinning Ring Company (see p. 170). Actual management of the mills was therefore left first to the individual mill superintendents and later to Earl J. Liberty, who became assistant treasurer of the mills.

Finally, during the great New England textile depression which followed the First World War, the mill at Whitinsville was closed (October, 1923) and was sold to the Whitin Machine Works to be used for storage space. In 1926 the Saundersville mill, where unfavorable economic conditions had been aggravated by the peculation of one of its employees, was likewise closed. In 1928 Arthur F. Whitin died leaving no direct descendants. His mill at Linwood was continued for a time under the management (and after 1936 under the ownership) of Earl J. Liberty, but in July of 1940, it, too, was closed. After the machinery had been sold, the property and water power were disposed of (1945) to the United States Reconstruction Finance Corporation. After the war, the RFC sold the property to the Guild Pinecrest Mills and, in 1949, the Guild Pinecrest Mills sold it to the Whitin Machine Works.

Thus, in the two decades which followed the First World War, nearly a thousand workers in the Whitinsville vicinity found themselves in a community threatened with permanent unemployment as mill after mill closed, never again to open. The only diversification of industry in the nearby villages along the Mumford and Blackstone rivers was the machine shop, if indeed a business so closely affiliated with the cotton industry could be considered diversification. But gradually, as business conditions improved, the Whitin Machine Works and, to a lesser extent, the Paul Whitin Manufacturing Company at Rockdale were able to absorb into their employment the men and women who had formerly been employed in Whitin family cotton mills. To those workers the existence of a strong industrial organization in their community proved providential. And to the machine shop, located as it was at a distance from a large labor supply, the existence of a labor pool within easy commuting distance facilitated the problem of expansion with which the company came to be faced.

APPENDIX 11

WHITIN-DRAPER SPINDLE AGREEMENT OF
21 NOVEMBER 1885

ARTICLES OF AGREEMENT made and entered into this the
Twenty First day of November, A.D. 1885, by and between the
SAWYER SPINDLE COMPANY, a corporation duly established
under the laws of the State of Massachusetts party of the first part:
and the WHITIN MACHINE WORKS, a corporation duly established under the laws of the State of Massachusetts, party of the
second part:
WITNESSETH
THAT WHEREAS the parties of the first part are owners of Letters Patent No. 141441 granted to Barton H. Jencks August 5th.
1873 for improvement in Spindle Bolsters for Spinning Machines.
Letters Patent No. 215142 granted to Thomas Mayor, May 6th. 1879
for improvement in Spindles for Spinning Machines: and Letters
Patent No. 227129 granted to Francis J. Rabbeth, May 4th. 1880, for
improvement in Spinning Spindles and bearings: and also own and
control a number of other Letters Patent for improvements in Spindles and Bolsters for Spindles for Spinning and Twisting Machines,
and have applications pending for patents: and
WHEREAS the said parties of the First part have a large and varied
experience in the Manufacture and introduction of improvements
by Letters Patent and by litigation in the Courts a specialty: and
WHEREAS the parties of the second part are engaged in the manufacture of Cotton Machinery and are the owners of Letters Patent
No. 261275 granted to Gustavus E. Taft July 18th. 1882 for improvements in Spindles and Bearings therefor and Letters Patent No.
284775 granted to Gustavus E. Taft and Henry F. Woodmancy,
September 11th. 1883 for improvement in Bearings for Spinning
Frame Spindles, and are also the owners for the United States of
other improvements made by the same Gustavus E. Taft and

Henry F. Woodmancy, the applications for patents for which are now pending in the Patent Office: and

WHEREAS the parties of the Second part have manufactured and sold spindles containing the improvements shown and described in the Letters Patent owned by them, and in applications for Letters Patent referred to, and

WHEREAS it is the interest of both parties to this agreement to harmonize and unite their respective patents and to avoid litigation and controversy:—

NOW THEREFORE they have agreed as follows:

I

That they will submit their respective patents to three arbitrators one to be chosen by each of the parties respectively and the third to be chosen by those two: who shall hear the respective parties by one counsel each and upon such testimony taken within sixty days after the appointment of the arbitrators, each party having half of this time, as may be legally competent to aid in the determination of the question which is to be submitted to them for decision, which arises upon the following agreements between the parties and the facts herein submitted.

FIRST: In order to effect a consolidation of the interests, and to put the patents under one control, the parties of the second part agree to convey to the parties of the first part, their above enumerated patents and applications for patents which they have pending in the Office: to be held by the parties of the first part for the purpose of carrying out the objects of this agreement.

SECOND: The parties of the Second part shall have the exclusive right to manufacture use and vend, upon terms to be decided by the arbitrators, spindles such as are now known as the "WHITIN SPINDLE" made in accordance with the said patents, and with the applications for patents above referred to, for all other purposes except for use in old spinning frames and twisters: and the parties of the first part shall have a like exclusive right, without compensation to the parties of the second part, of applying spindles to old Spinning machinery, except that the parties of the Second part, shall have the right to apply such inventions to old machinery specified in a list made for that purpose, hereto annexed and marked A.

II

For the purpose of determining the pecuniary value of the consideration moving the respective parties to this agreement, the arbitrators as aforesaid shall decide what payment shall be made by either party to the other: and as a basis for determining this question it is agreed that the established license fee of the parties of the first part for the use of their patents, is thirty-eight (38) cents a spindle, which is to be taken by the arbitrators as the value of the inventions in said patents contained. And they shall thereupon estimate the value of the inventions exhibited in the Whitin Spindle, and covered by the patents and applications for patents conveyed by the parties of the second part to the parties of the first part, by comparing their value, with the value of the inventions owned by the parties of the first part and contained in their patents and applications, fixed as aforesaid. The value of the inventions covered by the patents conveyed by the parties of the second part shall be offset against the value of the inventions covered by the patents of the parties of the first part, which is fixed at thirty-eight (38) cents a spindle, for the purpose of ascertaining how much, if anything, shall be paid by the parties of the second part to the parties of the first part, for the spindles manufactured by them under this exclusive license.

III

In estimating the pecuniary value to the respective parties the arbitrators shall take into account the advantages which the respective parties may be found to possess for promoting and pushing their respective inventions and patents: and the benefits which the respective parties may derive from a consolidation of the patents, thereby avoiding conflicts in the Courts, and competition in business: and all other considerations which they may consider to be valuable as a consequence of the agreements between the parties herein referred to.

IV

It shall be the duty of the SAWYER SPINDLE COMPANY to bring suits against infringers, whenever any infringement of the

patents conveyed by this agreement shall occur, upon the request
of the parties of the second part: but if upon such request the said
SAWYER SPINDLE COMPANY should think that no suit ought
to be brought, then the question shall be referred to some disinter-
ested counsel, and his decision shall control. The expense of such
suits shall be borne by the respective parties in the proportion to
the number of spindles of the types referred to made by each of
them, their licensees, or agents, between the date of this contract
and the date of the decision of such suits. It is understood that
either party may bring suits on such patents, and have the right
to use such names and patents as may be necessary in law for the
purpose, without the consent of the other, by paying the expenses
of such suit, and in that case such party shall recover the profits
or damages for its own use.

V

It is agreed between the parties that the royalty upon all spindles
made by either of the parties under this agreement shall be considered at least thirty-eight (38) cents in addition to the manufacturers' profit so that neither party shall undersell the other so far
as the price is affected by the patent fee.

VI

It is also agreed that if at any time the parties of the first part
shall reduce the royalty below thirty-eight (38) cents charged by
them to any licensees for manufacturing spindles: then the royalty
to be paid, if any, under this agreement shall be reduced in like
proportion.

In witness whereof the party of the first part has caused these presents to be sealed with its common seal and signed by J. H. Sawyer,
its president, and Edward Sawyer, its treasurer, and the party of
the second part has caused these presents to be sealed with its common seal and signed by J. Lasell, its treasurer, the day and year
first above written.

SCHEDULE "A" comprising list of Cotton Mills in which the
Whitin Machine Works are at liberty to apply the Whitin Gravity
Spindle, so called, to old frames.

Whitinsville Cotton Mills
Uxbridge Cotton Mills
Linwood Mills
Rockdale Co.
Manchaug Co.

APPENDIX 12

HOW THE WHITIN COMPANY'S ELECTRIC LOCOMOTIVE MAY HAVE BEEN THE FIRST BUILT IN AMERICA, AND OTHER RELATED TOPICS

Beginning with the third or fourth picker built by John C. Whitin, the machine shop in Whitinsville experienced the disadvantage of being located off a main railroad line. For more than a half-century the company suffered the inconvenience of having to haul all its machinery a mile and a half down Linwood Avenue (then called Railroad Avenue) to the freight and passenger station at Whitins and then haul back its supplies and raw materials. To perform this drayage, it had to keep a score or more of horses on hand at all times, and even the oxen that were used for work in the shop yard sometimes had to be borrowed for duty on this route.

Perhaps it was merely a coincidence, but in the spring of 1889, the shop barn burned to the ground killing all the company's horses. Whether the barn disaster induced Marston Whitin to take a step he had long been contemplating, we do not know, but only a few months thereafter, Marston began searching about for some other means of hauling freight between the shop and the station.

In the course of his inquiries, he was led to discuss the matter with a representative of the Thomson-Houston Electric Company, of Lynn, Massachusetts, then one of the country's leading builders of electric motors and later one of the two principal firms merged to form the General Electric Company. That Whitin was led even to consider electric power seems the more remarkable when one recalls how new were electric traction engines in 1890. Less than two years had passed since the first successful installation of a complete streetcar system had been made in Richmond, Virginia. As yet no one had attempted to use electricity to haul anything so heavy as a commercial freight car.

The Whitin company's experience with electricity was anything but extensive. The company had been using an "isolated" arc lighting system in the shop only since 1888. (The installation had been made by the Waterhouse Electric & Manufacturing Company, of Hartford, Connecticut, at a cost of $7,735.02. See Cash Book, 19 December 1888.) Previously the company had used gas for lighting. ("We use gas made from rosin," wrote Josiah Lasell on 1 November 1871. "We have found it very satisfactory affording a very strong and clear light, and in ordinary times . . . [at] as cheap a rate as any. Our works were put in by Providence Steam & Gas Pipe Co.") The Northbridge Board of Selectmen had granted the Westinghouse Electric & Manufacturing Company the right to string lines in Northbridge on 3 June 1889, but the recently organized Uxbridge & Northbridge Electric Company's power plant, with its generating plant in Uxbridge, did not extend its street-lighting service into Whitinsville until 1891.

The Whitin Machine Works did not convert its source of power to electricity until 1896, at which time it built its own power house and shifted from water power directly to electricity without ever having used steam except for emergency purposes. Even then the company did not abandon its old Boyden water turbines, and today it can still generate up to 12 per cent of its peak 6,500-horsepower load by the use of power from its dams. (In 1920 the company tied in its power facilities with the New England Power Company at which time it had to convert from the old-style 40-cycle current to the newer 60-cycle phase. Information obtained from L. R. Ball, shop power engineer, whose father was power engineer before him.)

It is true that in 1890 there was much discussion concerning the potentialities of electricity; in fact one of the earliest of America's electric streetcar lines was located in Woonsocket, Rhode Island, about fifteen miles south of Whitinsville, near enough, surely, to have made Whitin conscious of electricity's ability to render competent traction service. But so unlike Whitin's personality was it to venture blindly into the unknown that one is surprised to learn of his trip to Boston to negotiate an order for an electric freight locomotive of a type that had never been built before.

As nearly as can be determined, the order was placed with Thomson-Houston about June, 1890. Mr. Curtis H. Veeder, later a founder of Veeder-Root, Incorporated, was an employee of the Thomson-Houston Company at the time the Whitin locomotive order was received and remembered it as being the first such locomotive order received by the Thomson-Houston organization. (Ltr., J. H. Chaplin, president of Veeder-Root, to EKS, 23 July 1945.) Since Thomson-Houston was a pioneer in electric traction motors, the claim to priority is an important one. The specifications discussed by correspondence called for an engine capable of hauling sixty tons at a speed of seven miles per hour, but whether the final product conformed to those limitations is not known. The illustration shown earlier in the book indicates that the engine, as delivered, was not a powerful unit.

In November, 1890, a corporation, known as the Whitinsville Street Railway Company, was organized apparently as a subsidiary of the Whitin Machine Works. Meanwhile, tracks had been laid, electric lines had been strung, and the generator required to furnish electricity had been delivered. But not as yet the locomotive. Whitin wrote insisting that the engine be sent not later than 1 February 1891. "The matter has hung fire for so long," he wrote, "that we are getting suspicious, and when the machine gets here we shall of course give it the hardest test we can." (Ltr., GMW to Chas. H. Guild, 20 Dec. 1890.)

Time passed, and for one reason or another the men at Thomson-Houston repeatedly revised their estimate of when the locomotive would be ready. Undoubtedly they were extremely busy, for the electrical business was just then expanding more rapidly than new personnel could be trained. More than likely there were also unforeseen difficulties that held up construction. Finally the engine was delivered in May, 1892, nearly a year and a half late. (There is no mention of the locomotive's delivery in Whitin's correspondence, but on 11 May 1892 Marston wrote saying that it was being given thorough tests.)

During its wait for delivery the company had begun using horses to pull loaded freight cars over the readied tracks. Oddly enough this practice was continued even after the engine had arrived in Whitinsville. It seems clear that the delay in putting the locomotive into use was not due to any defect in the locomotive, since strenuous tests had proved it to be all that was claimed for it. Instead the Whitin Machine Works must have encountered some legal obstacle to its ownership of a "company" that was engaged in the transportation business. It is difficult otherwise to explain why, in the fall of 1893, the Whitinsville Street Railway Company was declared bankrupt. (Ltr., JML to Tax Commissioner, Boston, 1 May 1894.) At auction the Whitin Machine Works bought the bankrupt concern's existing assets and in January, 1894, under the liberal provisions of its state charter, began running the mile-and-a-half-long line as an integral part of its manufacturing business.

Because of the delay in getting started, the Whitin Machine Works probably lost the honor of having operated this country's first electric locomotive equipped to haul standard freight cars, but its claim to credit for having bought the first locomotive built for that purpose seems fairly safe from challenge. Donald M. Shaw, of Springfield, Massachusetts, has made the history of electric traction his hobby and has come to the conclusion that several electric freight locomotives were in use by 1894. According to John W. Hammond, in his *Men and Volts* (Phila., 1941), the Baltimore & Ohio Railroad adopted the first electric freight locomotives used by a major steam railroad line, in 1895. The rapid advance in the state of the electrical arts is shown by the fact that the Baltimore & Ohio's locomotives, only three years older than Whitin's unit, were able to haul 30 freight cars at 15 miles per hour.

From the standpoint of the Whitin company's history, the important point is not whether the company was the first in a new field but that it was showing a willingness to venture into unknown territory.

From 1894 to 1899, the railroad line between the shop and Whitins station was used only to haul freight. Then on 1 January 1899 passenger service was started by the Linwood Street Railway Company, a private corporation formed by George Marston Whitin and a number of the company's lesser officials. From 1899 until 1925 the Linwood Street Railway Company leased the right to use the company's railway tracks. On 26 January 1925, the directors of the Whitin Machine Works voted to buy the physical property of the Linwood company for $4,908 (the line was consistently losing money) and agreed to keep the line in operation as long as there seemed a need for it. By 1935 bus service had removed the need for a streetcar line, and on 28 February 1935, passenger service was discontinued. The tracks are still being used, however, for freight service, although electricity gave way to diesel power in 1943.

APPENDIX 13

WHITINSVILLE'S POWER AND DRINKING-WATER RESERVOIR SYSTEMS

Historically Whitinsville has had four water systems. The first was purely a power system and was built in the days of the village pump when a drinking-water system seemed unnecessary. A glance at the accompanying map will help distinguish this system from the components of the drinking-water system. The power reservoirs were built many years before the Civil War at a time when the Whitin Machine Works was just getting its start. The purpose of the reservoirs was, of course, to store enough water to provide a steady source of power throughout the dry months of the summer. These reservoirs were constructed coöperatively by the manufacturing establishments along the Mumford River and were thereafter jointly maintained. Nearly all record of how they came into existence has been lost, but through custom the associations that provided for their maintenance are still alive. Except the Manchaug Reservoir Association, which is handled by James Whitin, Inc., the Whitin Machine Works administers the business affairs of all the associations and bills the other companies for their proportionate share of the upkeep expense. The other companies in the various power reservoir associations are the Hayward-Schuster Woolen Mills, Inc., Whitin Brothers, James Whitin, Inc., and the Uxbridge Worsted Co.

The second village water system was the fire-fighting system built in 1867, at the time Shop No. 2 was built, and now known as Reservoir No. 1.

The third system was the original village drinking-water system with two reservoirs built in 1889 and 1891. The construction of these was under the supervision of A. C. Moore, a civil engineer from Southbridge and the man who later supervised the construction of the Cook Allen Brook reservoirs. (At about the same time Moore added to the power reservoir system by constructing the Carpenter Reservoir.)

Water from the reservoirs built in 1889 and 1891 was the first to be piped to houses in the village. It is important to note that pipes were laid to private homes as well as to company dwellings. Since the Whitin Machine Works by that time owned about two-thirds of the

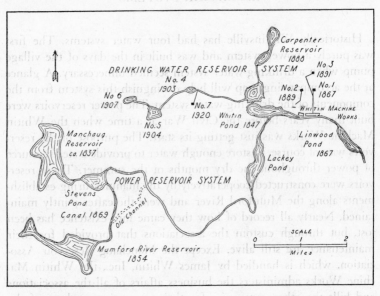

MAP SHOWING DRINKING WATER AND POWER RESERVOIR SYSTEMS
MAINTAINED BY THE WHITIN MACHINE WORKS

dwellings in Whitinsville, it was quite logical for it to extend its private water system to the rest of the village. Since there was plenty of precedent in New England for privately owned water companies, Marston Whitin probably gave little thought to the fact that his company was getting further and further into civic affairs. Even had he pondered the point, he would probably have dismissed it, for after all, what other choice was there? For the village to own and operate a separate water system would have been costly and wasteful. For it to own the whole system was unthinkable. With the company, through its plant and houses, the consumer of perhaps three-quarters of the water in the village, the possibility of rate manipulation by a politically elected body was too dangerous to risk.

The fourth system was the one mentioned in the text, the Cook Allen Brook reservoir system constructed west of the village. There are four reservoirs in this system, one built in 1901, one in 1904, and a third in 1907; the fourth was added in 1920 to bring the pressure level up to 110 pounds per square inch. Although much smaller than the others, the 1920 reservoir probably cost as much as the others combined. The other three were formed by building earthen dams across natural valleys. The fourth was built of concrete and was covered over so that purified water could be stored in it unharmed.

Originally the water, which was aerated by tumbling down Cook Allen Brook into the reservoirs, was considered pure enough to be piped directly into town. However, state regulations caused the company to adopt a filter method of purification. Since then all water has been allowed to flow into the lower ponds where some of it seeps down through the underlying beds of sand and gravel. It is then recovered by a series of wells drilled near the water's edge, is pumped to the 1920 covered reservoir and there is held till needed. The filter system in 1948 had reached its capacity. Meanwhile the gradual extension of Whitinsville eastward had created a need for a more balanced water system. Thus problems in distribution have arisen to make the Cook Allen Brook incapable of meeting current needs. But so far as volume of water is concerned, it seems unlikely that the Cook Allen Brook reservoirs will ever have to be extended. In 1948 the Whitin company's reservoir system was carried on its books at a value of about $650,000.

For further information on this subject see page 7 in the December, 1920, issue of the *Whitin Spindle*.

APPENDIX 14

THE WHITIN MACHINE WORKS' APPRENTICE
TRAINING PROGRAM

The Whitin company still maintains an apprenticeship course even though most companies of its size are now coming to rely more and more on trade schools to provide them with their skilled workmen. One reason why apprentice training has continued in Whitinsville has been the company's distance from the sort of industrial centers where trade schools have sprung up. Another reason has been the company's paternalistic desire to train the sons of Whitin workers for jobs in the Whitin plant.*

At one time (and to some extent still) an apprenticeship at Whitinsville was a coveted opportunity and was sought by the sons of some of John C. Whitin's best customers. Under Marston Whitin's régime, however, the apprentice program became principally a means of introducing first- and second-generation Europeans to the art of machine production.

Under both John C. and Marston Whitin the training of apprentices was the direct responsibility of the plant superintendent.† The superintendent, however, was usually too busy to give the boys much attention and so delegated all but the disciplinary part of his responsibility to foremen. Customarily the training period lasted for

---

* In Whitinsville there is a well-established tradition of family employment in the plant. The most notable present-day example is that of the Kelliher family. John Kelliher, now deceased, worked for the company for 46 years, much of that time as foreman on the polishing job. Four of his sons now work for the company, together with three daughters-in-law and three grandchildren.

† For information on the early years of the Whitin apprentice program see the *Whitin Spindle*, August, 1919, p. 11; August, 1920, p. 3; October, 1920, p. 7; and March–April, 1924, p. 3. Information on the later years was furnished me by John A. Kooistra, director of the apprentice school at Whitinsville. Some of the most oft-repeated anecdotes around Whitinsville concern the disciplinary measures taken by Gustavus E. Taft to curb the mischievous pranks of the apprentices under his charge.

three years, each apprentice serving time in three different departments, a year in each.

About World War I the company came to realize that its apprentices were learning only what the company's older employees knew, and hence nothing, or at least not enough, about the techniques of modern manufacturing methods — techniques such as blueprint-reading or micrometer measurements. To improve its apprentice program, the company proposed to organize a school with a full-time director and two part-time assistants. In such a school, trainees could be closely supervised and their courses could be tailored to their needs. Rotation of work in all departments was arranged for the first two years, with specialized instruction during the third year in any of several elective skills — machining, molding, pattern-making, plumbing, carpentry, and the like. At the same time formal classroom instruction in precision instrument reading, shop mathematics, mechanical drawing, and blueprint-reading developed in apprentices a flexibility that they could never have obtained by merely imitating what was being done at the bench.*

The man selected to head the new apprentice program was William T. Norton, the company's assistant paymaster. In 1918, Norton was sent to Cambridge, Massachusetts, to attend the Harvard Business School's newly established course in Employment Management and on his return was handed many of the responsibilities formerly assigned to the superintendent — among them the hiring of men and the training of apprentices.†

* Also in connection with the apprenticeship program a series of evening classes in basic English was offered to the shop's 100 employees who spoke no English and to the 200 others who spoke it only slightly.

† Among his other duties, Norton was given the job of organizing a plant magazine, the *Whitin Spindle*. Beginning as a monthly publication in August, 1919, the *Spindle* became a bi-monthly in March, 1924, and went out of existence after the May–June, 1926, issue. In February, 1948, it was revived on a monthly basis. The original *Spindle* was a magazine of about twenty pages, containing regular articles on various shop departments as well as short biographies of old-timers. Its center of interest was distinctly historical. The new *Spindle* is about the same size as the old, but is more generously illustrated and is filled principally with current news. The original magazine was meant to appeal to readers who had been with the company for many years; the new one has been purposely directed toward the large number of employees who come from outside Whitinsville and who know and care little about the company's history.

For the most part the apprentice program proved successful. True, the shop lost about a quarter of its trainees to other companies, but the men it retained, in addition to being familiar with all parts of the shop, were widely acquainted with workers in every department and therefore had a sense of "belonging" to the group. Indeed, the psychological results of the broadened training program were perhaps as valuable as the increased skills it promoted.

For a time during the depression, when the company was hiring no new men, and again during World War II, the apprentice school was discontinued, but on 18 October 1948 it was formally reinstated with approval from the Massachusetts Department of Labor Statistics and Industries, Division of Apprentice Training.

Since the war, the company has also been conducting an advance apprenticeship course, one of the members of which has been John H. Bolton, Jr., son of the president. The purpose of the advance course has been to give college-educated engineers the advantage of a practical education in the shop, but whether the company will be able to make room in its executive corps for the college men it has trained and whether it will pay them salaries that will be attractive enough to hold them in Whitinsville remains to be seen.

Recently the company has also encouraged the sons of South American mill men to spend a year or two in Whitinsville learning the tricks of the machinery trade. One is never surprised to sit down at one of the communal tables in the Blue Eagle Inn with a lad from Venezuela, Peru, or Brazil.

APPENDIX 15

THE DEVELOPMENT OF LONG-DRAFT COTTON SPINNING AND ROVING

It has been said that the development of long-draft cotton spinning was one of the only three important advances in the art of cotton manufacturing made in the last hundred years* — the other two being the high-speed spindle of the 1870's and the automatic loom of the 1890's.† If true, the statement has peculiar significance. Two of the three advances were of American origin, but the third and latest came from abroad. Both of those originating in America were Draper-sponsored; by corollary then, neither Saco-Lowell nor Whitin may be credited with any major inventive achievements for a period of at least the last century. From one of the two Draper-sponsored inventions, the spindle, Whitin gained certain indirect advantages, partly as a result of its being the nation's leading spinning-frame producer and partly in return for its contribution of the Gravity Spindle to the Draper patent pool. Because, however, it had no hand in the other Draper invention, the loom, Whitin lost a sizable portion of its machinery market. Whitin managed to gain considerable advantage from the third revolutionary invention, long-draft spinning, but in part at least by accident.

---

* (Southern) *Textile Bulletin,* 11 February 1937, p. 8.

† Some might add to the list the high-speed spooler and warper and the tying-in machine developed by the Barber-Colman Company, machine-tool manufacturers of Rockford, Illinois. Economically, however, the Barber-Colman advances were not so significant as the other three, since the cost-saving opportunities in the spooling and warping operations are not so great as those in spinning and weaving. It is significant, however, that a machine-tool builder was able to force its ways into the textile-machinery field with a product that was expensively and precisely made. Yet it is generally conceded that Barber-Colman could not have succeeded as it did, had it attempted to enter the preparatory machinery business, since there the improvement of one machine almost inevitably required the supporting improvements of other machines in the line.

The extent to which the American textile machinery industry may be blamed for its failure to produce more striking machinery improvements than it has, especially in the current century, is a question to be decided elsewhere; for the present it is enough to note that inventive leadership has been, and remains, elsewhere — either in the mills at home or in those abroad — and that on occasion the Whitin company, at least, has suffered by not contributing to that leadership.

Long-draft spinning was originally developed by Fernando Casablancas, a cotton-mill superintendent in Sabadell, Spain (near Barcelona).* Casablancas had been at work for some time on a method to improve spinning-frame drafting when, in 1913, he discovered that, by increasing the surface control of cotton fibers in the drafting operation, he not only could improve quality but could also enormously increase the amount of drafting possible. His discovery meant that a good deal of the drafting work done formerly on roving frames could instead be performed on the spinning frame itself, thus eliminating one of the three roving operations. It should be remembered that the drafting or attenuation of cotton slivers was traditionally accomplished in four or more steps, first on that type of roving frame known as a slubber, then on an intermediate roving frame, next on a fine roving frame, and last on a spinning frame just before the sliver was twisted into yarn. The possibility of eliminating one of the roving steps (the fine-frame operation) opened the way to substantial savings in labor-operating costs, against which the initial expense of installing Casablancas' fiber-control devices was relatively small.

Casablancas was not slow to realize the significance of his discovery and the profits to be gained from its exploitation. Organizing a company named Hilaturas-Casablancas, S. A., he began manufacturing long-draft attachments for sale to mills on the Continent. The manufacturing process was comparatively simple; a long-draft device consisted of little more than a set of small rolls and aprons. It is true that the changeover from conventional spinning to long-

* Except where otherwise noted, information in this section has been taken from the carefully compiled files of George West, patent expert of the Whitin Machine Works.

draft also required new gearing, but Casablancas left that part of the business, along with the actual job of making conversions in the mills, to the manufacturers of the original spinning frames. Letting the machine manufacturers in on a share of the changeover business, he hoped, would secure their good will and coöperation.

Everything seemed set for a drive to reëquip the cotton mills of Europe with long-draft spinning when World War I cast its trade barriers across the face of the Continent. For five years the spread of the long-draft principle was held up and the profits normally due Casablancas in recognition of his remarkable contribution to the art of spinning were delayed. After the war, however, Casablancas' device made rapid progress — and, as was to be expected, attracted many imitators, among them the French LeBlan-Roth system developed by Martin Roth and manufactured by LeBlan & Cie., of Lille.

The first in America to sense the importance of what was happening abroad seems to have been Charles F. Broughton, head of New Bedford's Wamsutta Mills. In 1922 Broughton ordered a set of Casablancas' attachments and gave them a trial run on his spinning floor. When he saw what a remarkable success they were, he got in touch with the Hilaturas-Casablancas firm and negotiated a deal (1923) that secured for him and the group he formed (the United States Casablancas Syndicate) * an exclusive selling agency for Casablancas' attachments in the United States.

Since Whitin, Saco-Lowell, and H & B American were anxious to get the service work involved in the installation of long-draft systems, they willingly coöperated with Broughton and the Casablancas Syndicate. But Swift believed caution to be the better part of business valor and waited to see how the system would work under actual mill conditions before giving it his personal endorsement. "My own impression about long-draft systems," he wrote on 21 January 1926, "is that sooner or later something will be done along this line, but our own position has been to keep in touch with the

* On 25 March 1926, the American Casablancas Corporation was organized in Delaware to take over the agency work of the Syndicate and to hold Casablancas' American patents. This corporation was dissolved in 1941. See Massachusetts State House, Secretary of the Commonwealth, Statements of Condition by Foreign Corporations.

different systems and cooperate with the various people as far as we can. The Casablancas looks good; on the other hand it has not been thoroughly tried out in this country and it has not been adopted by the English spinners." Still, Swift wanted his company to be ready to move quickly when the time seemed right and so put his development men to work in the summer of 1924 testing the various systems then being advanced and endeavoring to develop an original system that did not infringe on those already patented.*

Meanwhile the Saco-Lowell Shops, desperately seeking to regain their equilibrium after several years of heavy financial losses, had also begun looking for means of competing with the Casablancas Syndicate. After testing several rival devices they concluded that the French LeBlan-Roth system was the best to be had. In some ways in fact, it seemed to excel Casablancas, for it had fewer moving parts. It was less flexible than its Spanish counterpart, however, and was less readily adapted to fine work. After concluding a licensing arrangement with LeBlan & Cie. (1926) and after spending considerable time adapting the French system to American production requirements, the Saco-Lowell Shops announced to their customers (in the March, 1928, issue of their monthly *Bulletin,* a house organ similar to Whitin's *Review*) that they were prepared to make long-draft changeovers of the LeBlan-Roth type.

With the introduction of a fourth party the eternal triangle became two pairs. Previously Casablancas had had no reason to court the favor of either Saco-Lowell or Whitin. But once Saco-Lowell had expressed a preference for the French method of long-draft, Casablancas had to turn to the waiting and outstretched arms of Saco-Lowell's rival, the Whitin Machine Works. For with Saco-Lowell able to offer customers its own style of long-draft, Casablancas found its market limited almost exclusively to Whitin customers. Consequently, on 6 August 1929, the American Casablancas firm concluded an agreement with the Whitin Machine Works whereby Whitin was given sole right to manufacture Casablancas'

* One of the Whitin men assigned to the job was Henry A. Owen, the man whose several inexplicable developmental blunders proved so costly to the company that he was finally encouraged to resign. It was he who later headed Davis & Furber's wool ring spinning developmental program.

attachments in the United States. By December, 1929, Whitin was ready to make its first Whitin-Casablancas long-draft shipment.

Thus, almost by default Whitin had obtained exclusive American rights to what was basically the finest drafting system then known. Yet American mill owners, their perception possibly dimmed by the depression, did not begin to recognize the merits of long-drafting until after 1933 (by which time ironically enough, the basic Casablancas patents had nearly expired).* Beginning in that year, Whitin grossed about a half-million dollars annually on its spinning change-overs. Even that figure does not adequately indicate the important part long-draft played in the company's post-depression recuperation. A good share of Whitin's orders for new spinning frames came from mill owners who wanted long-draft spinning but preferred to buy completely new equipment rather than spend money to modernize their antiquated frames. Moreover, long-draft sales stimulated picking sales as well, for successful long-drafting was dependent on thorough opening and picking, an excellent example of how inter-related were the various preparatory operations.† Thirdly, the achievements in long-draft spinning led directly to the extension of the long-draft principle to the roving operation as well.

* The expiration date was 18 September 1934.

† One-process picking was essentially nothing more than the connection of three pickers in tandem. In fact it was possible to rebuild a mill's existing pickers into a one-process picker system if they were in good condition. The savings in horsepower and labor were claimed to be enough to repay the cost of the new device in four years. (*Whitin Review,* April, 1933, p. 2.) In 1924 a Canadian inventor named William Hardman, a resident of Hamilton, Ontario, perfected the picking operation by combining what had once been three separate operations into a single continuous one. His idea was not new, but his particular application seems to have been. He applied for an American patent and obtained it in August, 1926. Meanwhile, he gave his invention wide publicity. When it came to collecting royalties based on his patent, however, he found that his claims had been so inexpertly drawn that they gave him no protection against infringement. Meanwhile, all three American preparatory-machinery companies, sensing the advantages to be gained from one-process picking, had devised and patented their own applications of the principle. Whitin put its first one-process picker on the market in 1928, somewhat after the first appearance of Saco-Lowell's machine of that type (Saco-Lowell's Kitson picker division was still the country's leading producer of pickers). Because long-drafting required superior work in the picking room, one-process picking sold well. For some time Hardman's New York lawyers fulminated against the three American producers, charging infringement, but eventually dropped the matter without bringing suit.

One of the reasons Casablancas' long-draft device was superior to the LeBlan-Roth device was because it could be applied not only to spinning frames but to roving equipment as well and therefore could be used to produce yarns of exceptionally high count. The LeBlan-Roth system was so constructed that it could be used only on spinning and so was less flexible than its rival. Both systems eliminated one of the four traditional drafting operations, but Casablancas', by using long-draft on two of the three remaining drafting operations, was better suited to fine work than the LeBlan-Roth, which could be used at only one of the three stages (i.e., on the spinning frame).

However, Whitin's advantage over Saco-Lowell proved more theoretical than real, since the Biddeford concern, with the advantage of a head start, outsold Whitin in the long-draft field during all the critical years of the depression. Moreover, the paramount question soon came to be not whether Saco-Lowell could produce a competitive long-draft roving system but whether it could find a way to eliminate the remaining two roving operations altogether.

Following Casablancas' success in doing away with one of the roving operations, inventors all over the world became fired with enthusiasm to do away with all the other roving processes. Casablancas himself caught the fever and worked till he had produced what he considered a practical design for a device that could handle the entire drafting load at the spinning-frame stage. Sometime in the late 1920's he licensed his new multi-stage drafting idea to the firm of Richard Hartmann & Company, of Chemnitz, Germany, a concern which, a few years before (about 1925), had obtained the exclusive Casablancas rights for Germany just as Whitin was to do later for the United States.

From Casablancas' American representatives, Swift learned of the multi-stage drafting frames being built by Hartmann and in the fall of 1930 ordered one of them for experimental purposes. After giving the frame careful study, however, Swift's spinning specialists advised him that the Hartmann machine attempted too much drafting in one operation and for that reason turned out inferior work. Nevertheless they were impressed by the efficiency of the device and were of the opinion that a second of the three roving proc-

esses could be eliminated, if only multi-stage drafting could be perfected for use on roving. Proceeding on that theory, the men in
Whitin's experimental room worked for some time to convert the
multi-stage Hartmann device from use on a spinning frame to use
on a roving intermediate frame. Finally, in May, 1934, they announced to the trade their success in developing what they called
"Super-draft" * or one-process roving.

Meanwhile, Saco-Lowell had arrived at approximately the same
goal by a somewhat different route. Looking for a roving device to
compete with Casablancas' long draft, Saco-Lowell's vice-president,
Frederick E. Banfield, Jr., had come across a Southern mill man
named William G. Reynolds (superintendent of the Eastern Manufacturing Company, of Selma, North Carolina) who, like so many
others, had developed what he considered a spinning frame that
would completely eliminate all roving. Banfield was not impressed
with Reynolds' machine,† but he was impressed with the man's
ability. Consequently, when the developmental emphasis at Biddeford shifted from an attempt to equal Whitin's Casablancas roving

* The names "Long-draft," "Inter-draft," and "Super-draft" were adopted by
Whitin as registered trade names. I use them here only for convenience and not with
any intention of conveying the impression that they are generic terms. In a general
way "Long-draft" refers to drafts below 10, "Inter-draft" to drafts between 10 and
16, and "Super-draft" to drafts above that number. Saco-Lowell uses the term "Controlled draft" and H & B American uses the term "Hi-draft." Not only does multi-
stage roving eliminate all but one roving operation, but it increases the output of
the remaining roving frame so greatly that one roving spindle on the new system
could accomplish as much as four spindles on the old system had been able to accomplish only a few years earlier. Whitin's new device sold itself by being able to
effect sufficient savings to return its initial cost in from two to three years. About
three years were required to introduce the idea to the market, but thereafter, until
America entered the Second World War, sales averaged about four hundred thousand dollars a year, with Inter-draft accounting for nearly as much as the other two
types combined.

† Reynolds had submitted his frame to Whitin as well as to Saco-Lowell. Commenting on the frame in a letter to Reynolds written 26 April 1927, Swift stated
that the frame was not practical as it stood and that it would require too much
additional developmental work to make feasible any estimate of its worth. Swift has
ample reason to regret having written the letter, for it became a center of controversy later on. In the suit between Reynolds and Whitin, the judge considered the
letter evidence that Swift recognized Reynolds' idea as "revolutionary" and therefore
"original." Aside from the fact that the two words are not synonymous, the judge
seems to have ignored the fact that Reynolds' 1927 device was meant for use on a
spinning frame, while the device in question was meant for use with roving.

device to an effort to eliminate all but one of the roving operations, Banfield wrote to Reynolds and offered him Saco-Lowell's experimental facilities as a place where he might perfect his multi-stage drafting idea for use on roving instead of on spinning.

Reynolds started work at Biddeford in July, 1933. From the beginning, he found difficulty in achieving a suitable device to re-form fibers as they passed between the multi-drafting stages. When the sliver was attenuated so much and so rapidly as it had to be in multi-stage drafting, small loose fibers inevitably frayed out at the edges. A satisfactory yarn could be produced only if the disarranged stray fibers could be tucked back in and then pulled parallel again. Reynolds tried many ideas, but rejected them all until he hit upon a tongue-and-groove roll that formed the sliver in a U-shape and then crushed the edges toward the center. By the end of a year he had achieved what he had set out to do; on 23 July 1934 he submitted an application for a patent covering his tongue-and-groove device. Then, in November, he returned to North Carolina. In October, Saco-Lowell announced that it, too, could supply its customers with a multi-stage drafting device that reduced roving to a one-step operation.

The long-draft roving narrative would end at that point had not the re-forming devices of both Saco-Lowell and Whitin proved unsatisfactory in operation. Whitin's device was a rotary twister head, manufactured on license from the American Casablancas Corporation and designed to give the sliver a false twist. Technically it performed its job with complete satisfaction, but in actual practice it tended to jam with lint. If mill operatives had taken normal precautions in keeping the rotary head clean, there would have been no trouble. But piece-rate workers were likely to postpone the cleaning operation until lint filled the rotary head and prevented it from revolving. The machine shutdown that inevitably followed was not serious, but it did add materially to manufacturing costs, for the head had to be cleaned and re-threaded before the machine could be started again. During their first year or two on the market, both the Whitin and the Saco-Lowell multi-stage drafting devices provoked frequent complaints from disgruntled customers. At length the two companies realized that their devices would have to be simplified to meet the requirements of the market.

The events that followed thereon became the subject of such bitter controversy in later years that their true nature cannot now be ascertained. But some of the points in dispute are worth recording. In the early part of the summer of 1935, a threatened shake-up in Saco-Lowell management promised to relegate to the research department the Biddeford vice-president in charge of production, Frederick E. Banfield, Jr. Learning of the impending change, James Truslow, a Whitin salesman with contacts in all parts of the cotton industry, passed the word along to E. Kent Swift.* It happened that just at that time Swift was giving thought to a change in his own plant management and was looking for a new Works Manager. Since 1923 the Whitin shop's Works Manager had been George B. Hamblin, one-time confidential secretary to Marston Whitin and a key figure in the organization that Swift had inherited from his father-in-law.† No longer a young man, Hamblin had served the company for 42 years and was nearing the age of retirement.‡ Swift was especially interested in finding a man who was familiar with the machine-tool requirements of a textile-machinery shop, for in the lean years of the depression he had deliberately neglected replacing obsolete plant equipment in his overriding effort to keep his company strongly liquid and he needed a man with expert technical knowledge for the retooling job that lay ahead. Therefore, effective 1 July 1935, Swift hired Banfield and made him Works Manager of the Whitin firm.

Reynolds later charged that Banfield, who had been closely connected with the multi-stage drafting experiments at Biddeford, committed a breach of faith by taking with him to Whitinsville the Reynolds drafting know-how. Banfield, however, categorically

---

* The same James Truslow was instrumental in attracting to Whitinsville Robert J. McConnell. While making a long-draft installation at the Pequot Mills, in Salem, Massachusetts, Truslow learned that McConnell was dissatisfied with his job and informed Swift of the fact. Swift offered McConnell a job with the Whitin Machine Works and later made him vice-president in charge of cotton sales and development.

† Assistant Works Manager during those years was Ernest T. Clary, graduate of Harvard College, and from 1909 to 1921 an employee of Whitcomb-Blaisdell, manufacturers of machine tools in Worcester. Clary came to Whitinsville in 1921 and remained until his death in 1943.

‡ As was typical of men in Whitinsville he did not completely retire. From 1935 until his death in 1938 he continued to occupy a vice-presidency and remained in charge of the shop's village interests.

denied the allegation. His first months at Whitinsville, he said, had been such a nightmare of shop problems that he had given little attention to the work then being carried on in Whitin's experimental room by Carl Brandt and Otto Schlums, although he was aware that efforts were being made to simplify the re-forming device. Since Reynolds himself had discarded all his experiments previous to his tongue-and-groove device, Banfield felt that nothing he had learned as a result of his contact with Reynolds could possibly be of assistance to Brandt and Schlums. (Reynolds later denied that he had rejected his former work and insisted that the Saco-Lowell executives had been the ones who had decided to put their faith in the tongue-and-groove device instead of in some of the earlier de-vices he had proposed.)

In January, 1936, six months after Banfield's arrival, Brandt and Schlums made their first successful installation of what they con-sidered a completely original re-forming device. The new device did away with the rotary head so complained of by Whitin cus-tomers and substituted in its stead a curved surface that banked the strand of fibers and presented them on edge to the next set of drafting rolls. This device, being stationary, eliminated the faults of the twister head and proved completely satisfactory in operation. On 31 July 1936 Brandt and Schlums made a routine application for a patent.

Immediately upon learning of Whitin's success with a stationary device, the Saco-Lowell Shops began looking for a similar arrange-ment to offer their customers. The solution they hit upon was a trumpet design (patent applied for 23 February 1937) in no way similar to Whitin's device and far removed from Reynolds' tongue-and-groove rolls. What all three had in common was the folding-in of stray fibers, or at least so Reynolds claimed, although the ma-chinery manufacturers insisted that their devices did not fold.*

Reynolds first learned of Whitin's and Saco-Lowell's change in re-forming devices when he saw their roving machinery exhibited at the Southern Textile Exposition the following April (1937). To

---

* On 24 August 1937 the H & B American Machine Company also applied for a patent on a re-forming device known as a scroll condenser and containing some of the advantages of both the Whitin and the Saco-Lowell devices.

him it seemed apparent that Saco-Lowell had made its change in an effort to avoid paying him royalties on his invention and that Whitin had obtained its idea for the change from Banfield as a result of his shift in jobs. Therefore, on 18 August 1937, he petitioned the Patent Office in Washington (where as yet no final action had been taken on his application) to broaden the claims of his patent application so that they would cover the stationary devices developed by the textile-machinery concerns.

Realizing that Reynolds' broadened claims, if recognized by the Patent Office, would endanger their individual applications, both Whitin and Saco-Lowell strove vigorously to have the claims disallowed on the basis (1) that "prior art" had already established the general use of surfaces to re-form cotton strands and (2) that Reynolds was not entitled to a patent that covered all devices for folding stray fibers inward. The two companies were successful in winning most of their minor skirmishes in the Patent Office (they succeeded in having three of Reynolds' four new claims disallowed) but they failed to persuade the patent examiner that Reynolds was not entitled to his fourth claim regarding the folding of stray fibers. It was the examiner's view that a final decision in the matter was not within his jurisdiction but was a matter to be handled by a court of law. Therefore he permitted obviously conflicting patents to be granted — to Saco-Lowell on 23 January 1940, to Whitin on 4 February 1941, and to Reynolds on 15 April 1941. (H & B American's application had slipped through the patent office on 24 August 1937 before the office had taken note of Reynolds' petition for a broadened claim.)

Reynolds, together with his financial backer, Edgar A. Terrell, immediately brought suit against Saco-Lowell for infringement. Since Saco-Lowell was a licensee under the Reynolds patent and had sold machinery based thereon, it could not argue that the Reynolds patent was invalid. With its key argument thus denied it, the Saco-Lowell company lost the suit in 1943 and was forced to pay Reynolds $210,-265 in damages and back royalties.

Reynolds then turned to institute suit against Whitin (May, 1945). As in his case against Saco-Lowell, he brought action in a North Carolina District Court (at Greensboro). Fearing discrimination,

Whitin's lawyers* did everything in their power to have the venue of the trial shifted to a Northern court, but without success.† After many a trying and prolonged hearing, the case finally came before District Court Judge Johnson J. Hayes for decision in 1947.

Part of the suit involved the alleged breach of faith committed by Banfield when he moved to Whitinsville, but the North Carolina statute of limitations prevented any action on that aspect of the case. Nevertheless, the Judge assumed that Reynolds had committed the alleged tort and wrote his assumption into the opinion he delivered on the case (see quotations from the opinion at the end of this appendix).

The other part of the suit was highly technical and, to be understood, required a familiarity with both cotton-manufacturing technology and patent law. Judge Hayes was frank to admit that he was familiar with neither. "This is a very complicated case," he stated in his written opinion, "and the most skillfully contested patent case which has confronted the court. . . . It presents a striking example of a branch of federal court jurisdiction which should be set aside exclusively for determination by a court of competent patent experts instead of leaving it to judges who like myself are entirely devoid of mechanical skill and therefore unable to bring to the solution of the case the skill essential to the broader and better decision."

To the non-technical person, the case seems to have had two aspects:‡ (1) the strictly legal question of whether Whitin's device infringed on Reynolds' and (2) the socio-ethical question of whether

* At first Whitin's lawyers were the firm of Jeffrey, Kimball & Eggleston, a lineal partnership descendant (through Kimball, who handled the case) of the Wetmore & Jenner firm that had handled the company's two previous big suits (with Draper and Houghton). Unfortunately Kimball died in 1945, so the case was referred to the firm of Burgess, Ryan & Hicks. Hicks had been a former Kimball partner. Burgess handled the court work.

† Reynolds had previously offered to settle with Whitin out of court for $160,000 but Whitin's lawyers had advised Swift against the offer. They were of the opinion that a judge trained in patent matters would inevitably have to render Whitin a favorable decision. When their attempt to change the venue of the trial failed, they pinned their hope on an appeal to the Supreme Court.

‡ As an historian I cannot claim to be either a technically trained observer or an impartial judge of the points involved in the Reynolds case, for I am not expert in cotton-manufacturing technology and I have not seen the testimony presented by the plaintiffs at the trial. Nor have I talked or corresponded with either of the plaintiffs.

a man who has done pioneer work in a field should be entitled to a broad claim on the ultimate fruits of his endeavors. The original intent of our patent system was clearly to establish and maintain the rights in dispute under aspect (2) of the case; but in the actual operation of the patent system, it was soon discovered that broad claims could also violate the rights of others and that certain limitations, such as those inherent in aspect (1) of the Reynolds case, had to be adopted if such rights were to be protected. Having pronounced himself unqualified to deal with aspect (1), however, Judge Hayes proceeded to devote his entire attention to aspect (2). In so doing he chose as his orientation the position that he was acting as a protector of an individual set upon by an unscrupulous combination of Northern machinery manufacturers.

A few passages selected from Judge Hayes' opinion, though necessarily subject to the distortion always inherent in quotations out of text, will indicate something of the tone the Judge adopted:

Reynolds spent his life after he was seven years old in a cotton mill, working in all its departments up to the Superintendent and part owner. Through the hard way he struggled to overcome, what he and the industry in general recognized [to be], the cumbersome methods of roving in textile mills. . . . The correspondence between counsel for [Whitin] . . . and counsel for Saco-Lowell [over the fight to have Reynolds' amended application to the Patent Office disallowed] reveals an ugly episode of two powerful competitors combining their skill . . . to defeat [Reynolds' claim]. . . . If these manufacturers are competitors their joint conduct in an effort to defeat Reynolds' claim raises a serious question about that competition. . . . The improvement records of the device are written words made by [Whitin] employees . . . who were not adept in the use of technical words to conceal what they were doing. . . . The most favorable interpretation that can be placed on their [Whitin's] conduct in this connection, is that they were using ideas gained from Reynolds [through Banfield] in an attempt to manufacture a machine which would utilize the substance of his invention while technically avoiding infringement. We think that they succeeded in utilizing the substance of the invention but failed to avoid infringement.

Judge Hayes' decision was: "guilty of infringement," the plaintiffs, Reynolds and Terrell, to be entitled to "an accounting from

[Whitin's] profits from April 15, 1941, to the date of the accounting and to damages, and to . . . recover the cost of the action."

Whitin's lawyers appealed the case to the Circuit Court at Charlotte, but without getting a reversal of the District Court's decision. In making their final appeal to the United States Supreme Court they argued that Reynolds' patent was invalid and that the Patent Office had issued the patent with the explicit intention of allowing it to be tested in court. They argued further that the validity of Reynolds' patent had never been so tested, since Judge Hayes had admitted his inability to judge the case on its technical grounds. The Supreme Court, however, declined to review the matter. In the fall of 1948, the Whitin Machine Works settled its dispute with Reynolds by paying a sum considerably in excess of a quarter-million dollars (the company has seen fit to keep the exact amount of the settlement a private matter) and by agreeing thereafter to pay him regular royalties on all the long-draft roving devices it sold.

The Reynolds case became the third of four major cases in the Whitin company's history. Three of the four — the cases of Draper, Houghton, and Reynolds — the company fought and lost. The fourth case — the Maritime Commission suit — the company fought and won. In all four cases the issue was raised by the company's opponents. In the Draper and Reynolds suits, the company could have settled out of court for far less than it eventually had to pay. In the Draper and Maritime Commission cases, the company allowed itself to become involved only because it felt a moral compunction so to do.

At first glance it would appear that the company's ethical standards have been at odds with those of the courts. Yet if the company is remarkable for any one thing, it is remarkable for the strictness of its ethical code. On occasion it may have shown in its manner a certain New England self-righteousness, but it has never, so far as I have been able to discover, shown any of the high-handedness Judge Hayes thought he saw in its conduct before the Patent Office. If there is any one reason why the company has lost so many suits, it would appear to be because, in three out of the four cases, the judges have shown an inclination to favor the cause of the individual against the cause of the corporation, and certainly such a bias, if it has existed, is more to be desired than one operating in the reverse direction. However, one cannot help feeling that in the Reynolds case, if not in the others, the company came off rather worse than it deserved.

APPENDIX 16

ORDERS FROM SOUTHERN MILLS FOR MORE THAN $50,000 OF WHITIN MACHINERY

Year	Mill	Location	Size of Order
1888	Clifton Mfg. Co.	Clifton, S. Carolina	$148,693
1889	Piedmont Mfg. Co.	Piedmont, S. Carolina	174,684
	Troup Factory	La Grange, Georgia	62,952
1890	Galveston Cotton & Woolen Mills	Galveston, Texas	123,724
	Odell Mfg. Co.	Bynum, N. Carolina	96,514
1892	Henrietta Mills	Caroleen, N. Carolina	72,938
1893	Anderson Cotton Mills	Anderson, S. Carolina	74,961
1895	Henrietta Mills	Caroleen, N. Carolina	72,938
1896	Proximity Mfg. Co.	Greensboro, N. Carolina	69,111
	Southern Cotton Mill	Bessemer City, N. Carolina	59,197
	Erwin Cotton Mills	Durham, N. Carolina	125,303
	Henrietta Mills	Caroleen, N. Carolina	54,980
	Camden Cotton Mills	Camden, S. Carolina	62,336
	Gaffney Mfg. Co.	Gaffney, S. Carolina	76,900
1897	Spray Cotton Mills	Spray, N. Carolina	60,931
1898	Wiscasset Mills	Albemarle, N. Carolina	60,323
1899	Aragon Mills	Aragon, Georgia	52,892
	Proximity Mfg. Co.	Greensboro, N. Carolina	77,248
	Henrietta Mills	Caroleen, N. Carolina	79,249
1900	Henrietta Mills	Caroleen, N. Carolina	74,201
	Orr Cotton Mills	Anderson, S. Carolina	74,973
	Revolution Cotton Mills	Greensboro, N. Carolina	77,403
	Trion Mfg. Co.	Trion, Georgia	111,818

Year	Mill	Location	Size of Order
	Willingham Cotton Mills	Macon, Georgia	60,098
	Scott Dale Mills	Scottdale, Georgia	62,479
1901	Golden Bett Mfg. Co.	Durham, N. Carolina	96,773
	Gibson Mfg. Co.	Concord, N. Carolina	92,253
	Harriet Cotton Mills	Henderson, N. Carolina	58,913
	Loray Cotton Mills	Gastonia, N. Carolina	155,881
	Darlington Mfg. Co.	Darlington, S. Carolina	105,731
	Tucapan Mills	Tucapan, S. Carolina	61,993
1902	Chiquola Mfg. Co.	Honeapath, S. Carolina	51,270
	Williamston Mills	Williamston, S. Carolina	60,626
1903	Fulton Bag & Cotton Co.	Atlanta, Georgia	52,856
	Wiscasset Mills	Albemarle, N. Carolina	52,873
	Erwin Cotton Mills	Durham, N. Carolina	111,977
	Arcadia Mills	Spartanburg, S. Carolina	57,876
	Brogon Cotton Mills	Anderson, S. Carolina	157,753
	Orr Cotton Mills	Anderson, S. Carolina	132,192
	Woodside Cotton Mills	Greenville, S. Carolina	74,107
	Clifton Mfg. Co.	Clifton, S. Carolina	138,142
	Tucapan Mills	Tucapan, S. Carolina	131,781
1904	Highland Park Mfg. Co.	Charlotte, N. Carolina	76,320
	Loray Cotton Mills	Gastonia, N. Carolina	94,600
	Cox Mfg. Co.	Anderson, S. Carolina	86,090
	Chiquola Mfg. Co.	Honeapath, S. Carolina	68,044
	Williamston Mills	Williamston, S. Carolina	52,195
	Clifton Mfg. Co.	Clifton, S. Carolina	148,701
1905	Maginnis Cotton Mills	New Orleans, Louisiana	75,829
	Lane Mills	New Orleans, Louisiana	122,940
	Piedmont Mfg. Co.	Piedmont, S. Carolina	71,393
	Loray Cotton Mills	Gastonia, N. Carolina	78,420
	Cone, Moses H. & Caesar (Revolution Mills)	Greensboro, N. Carolina	62,720
	Cone, Moses H. & Caesar (White Oak Mills)	Greensboro, N. Carolina	145,326
	Highland Park Mfg. Co.	Charlotte, N. Carolina	64,232
	Gray Mfg. Co.	Gastonia, N. Carolina	58,691

Year	Mill	Location	Size of Order
1906	Cabarrus Cotton Mills	Concord, N. Carolina	64,689
	Pomona Mfg. Co.	Greensboro, N. Carolina	62,720
	Cone, Moses H. & Caesar (Revolution Mills)	Greensboro, N. Carolina	79,670
	Cone, Moses H. & Caesar (White Oak Mills)	Greensboro, N. Carolina	61,313

Source: Whitin Sales Ledgers.

APPENDIX 17

SOUTHERN MACHINERY AGENTS WHO BROUGHT NORTHERN MACHINERY BUILDERS TOGETHER IN INFORMAL MARKETING GROUPS

(Agency changes are indicated by the selection of three representative years)

1895

D. A. Tompkins Company, D. A. Tompkins, President, agent for
Pickers — Kitson Machine Shop
Cards & Drawing — Whitin Machine Works
Roving —
Spinning — Whitin Machine Works
Slashers —
Looms — Whitin Machine Works
Finishing Machinery —
Charlotte Machine Company, H. S. Chadwick, President & Treasurer, agent for
Pickers —
Cards & Drawing — Pettee Machine Works
Roving — Providence Machine Company
Spinning — Fales & Jenks Machine Company
Slashers — Cohoes Iron Foundry & Machine Company
Looms — Knowles Loom Works
Winders & Spoolers — Easton & Burnham Machine Company
Finishing Machinery — Curtis & Marble Machine Company
Specialized firms which joined one of the marketing groups within the following two years:
Pickers — A. T. Atherton Machine Company
Roving — Woonsocket Machine & Press Company
Roving & Spinning — Saco Water Power Machine Shop

Looms — Crompton Loom Works and Kilburn, Lincoln & Company (the Draper Company, soon to be the largest of American loom builders, always maintained its own representatives in the South)

Integrated companies which had nearly complete lines of machinery and which therefore maintained their own representatives in the South:

Lowell Machine Shop, represented by E. P. Dennis (complete line except for pickers)

Howard & Bullough American Machine Company, represented by E. Chappell (complete line except for weaving and finishing machinery)

Mason Machine Works, represented by Thomas A. Cox (complete line except for pickers, roving, and finishing machinery)

1897

Stuart W. Cramer, agent for

Pickers — Kitson Machine Shop

Cards & Drawing — Whitin Machine Works

Roving — Woonsocket Machine & Press Company

Spinning — Whitin Machine Works

Slashers — Cohoes Iron Foundry & Machine Company

Looms — Whitin Machine Works

Finishing Machinery — Curtis & Marble Machine Company

Charlotte Machine Company, H. S. Chadwick, President & Treasurer, agent for

Pickers — A. T. Atherton Machine Company

Cards & Drawing — Saco & Pettee Machine Shops

Roving — Saco & Pettee Machine Shops

Spinning — Saco & Pettee Machine Shops

Slashers —

Looms — Crompton & Knowles Loom Works

Finishing Machinery —

Sexton & Robbins, agents for

Pickers —

Cards & Drawing —

Roving — Providence Machine Company

Spinning — Fales & Jenks Machine Company

Winders & Spoolers — Easton & Burnham Machine Company

Looms — Kilburn, Lincoln & Company

Finishing Machinery —

Integrated companies which had nearly complete lines of machinery and which therefore maintained their own representatives in the South:

Lowell Machine Shop (same as in 1895)

Howard & Bullough American Machine Company (same as in 1895)

Mason Machine Works, represented by D. A. Tompkins, with the same line as in 1895

1913

John H. Mayes, agent for

Pickers — Potter & Johnston Machine Company

Cards — Potter & Johnston Machine Company

Drawing & Roving — Woonsocket Machine & Press Company

Spinning — Fales & Jenks Machine Company

Warpers — T. C. Entwistle Company

Winders & Spoolers — Easton & Burnham Machine Company

Looms —

Finishing Machinery —

Specialized firms which, by 1913, were again marketing their products independently:

Looms — Crompton & Knowles Loom Works and Kilburn, Lincoln & Company

Slashers — Cohoes Iron Foundry & Machine Company

Finishing Machinery — Curtis & Marble Machine Company

Integrated companies which had complete or nearly complete lines of *preparatory* machinery (by 1913 the Draper Company had achieved domination in the loom market) and which maintained their own representatives in the South:

Saco-Lowell Shops, represented by Rogers W. Davis

Whitin Machine Works, represented by Stuart W. Cramer

H & B American Machine Company, represented by E. Chappell

Mason Machine Works, represented by Edwin Howard (Mason's line still lacked pickers and roving)

Source: Correspondence between George Marston Whitin and Stuart W. Cramer, Dockham's Directories, Davison's Textile Blue Books, and American Textile Directories.

APPENDIX 18

AN ESTIMATE OF THE COST OF CONSTRUCTING A 42,660-SPINDLE MILL, BASED ON FIGURES PREPARED IN 1908 BY GEORGE MARSTON WHITIN FOR THE INFORMATION OF WILLIAM F. DRAPER[a]

Plant and Equipment	Mill Using Whitin Looms	% of Mach. Cost	% of Total Cost	Mill Using Draper Looms	% of Mach. Cost	% of Total Cost
10 lappers @ $925	$ 9,250.00	3	. . .	$ 9,250.00	2	. . .
62 revolving flat cards @ $660	40,920.00	13	. . .	40,920.00	10	. . .
120 drawing deliveries @ $60	7,200.00	3	. . .	7,200.00	2	. . .
8 slubbers @ $14.01 per spindle	. . . .	. . .	. . .	. . . .	. . .	. . .
16 intermediate frames @ $9.51 per spindle . .	. . . .	. . .	. . .	. . . .	. . .	. . .
40 finishing frames @ $6.40 per spindle	64,566.40	21	. . .	64,566.40	16	. . .
87 warp spinning frames @ $2.85 per spindle . .	. . . .	. . .	. . .	. . . .	. . .	. . .
81 filling spinning frames @ $2.75 per spindle . .	119,507.40	39	. . .	119,507.40	30	. . .
8 spoolers @ $3.00 per spindle	. . . .	. . .	. . .	. . . .	. . .	. . .
15 warpers @ $225	8,175.00	3	. . .	8,175.00	2	. . .
1000 looms @ $54 for Whitin looms and $150 for Draper looms	54,000.00	18	. . .	150,000.00	38	. . .
2 folders @ $250	. . . .	. . .	. . .	. . . .	. . .	. . .
1 press @ $300	800.00	0	. . .	800.00	0	. . .
Machinery totals	$304,418.80	100	40	$400,418.80	100	46
Buildings	290,000.00	. . .	38	290,000.00	. . .	34
Power plant	80,000.00	. . .	11	80,000.00	. . .	10
Land, tenements, etc . . .	82,750.00	. . .	11	82,750.00	. . .	10
Mill totals	$757,168.80	. . .	100	$853,168.80	. . .	100

Cost of machinery with Whitin looms—$7.14 per spindle
Cost of machinery with Draper looms—$9.38 per spindle
Cost of complete mill with Whitin looms—$17.74 per spindle
Cost of complete mill with Draper looms—$20.00 per spindle
Increase in cost of machinery when Draper loom is used—32%
Increase in cost of total mill when Draper loom is used—13%

[a] Values are based on average prices for the years 1903–08.

Source: Letter from George Marston Whitin to William F. Draper, 11 Dec. 1908.

APPENDIX 19

PLACE OF RESIDENCE AND COMMUTING DISTANCE OF WHITIN EMPLOYEES IN JANUARY, 1946

A. Place of Residence

Residence	CIO Unit		AFL Units		Non-union		Total[a]	
Company houses.......	915	35%	131	35%	203	48%	1,249	36%
Whitinsville[b] (excluding above)..............	421	16	76	20	71	17	568	17
Northbridge[c] (excluding both above).........	407	16	48	13	17	4	472	14
Elsewhere.............	862	33	120	32	131	31	1,113	33
Total................	2,605	100%	375	100%	422	100%	3,402	100%

B. Commuting Distance

Residence	No. of Employees	%	Cumulative %
Living in company houses.........	1,249	34.5	....
Living in Whitinsville (but excluding above)....................	568	15.7	50.2
Living within a radius of 5 miles[d] (but excluding above)..........	930	25.7	75.9
5–10 miles....................	569	15.7	91.6
10–15 miles....................	275	7.6	99.2
15–20 miles....................	12	.3	99.5
20–25 miles....................	17	.5	100.0
Totals.........................	3,620	100.0	

[a] Does not include erectors and southern shop employees.

[b] Of Whitinsville's 5,068 inhabitants (1940 census), 1,817 worked in the Whitin Machine Works (1946), or about one out of every three.

[c] Of Northbridge's 10,242 inhabitants (1940 census), 2,289 worked in the Whitin Machine Works (1946), or about one out of every five.

[d] Add about 50% to radius mileage to arrive at commuting mileage.

Source: Personal Record Cards, Company Employment Office.

APPENDIX 20

CHRONOLOGY OF THE STEELWORKERS' STRIKE AT THE WHITIN MACHINE WORKS, 1946

14 January	Strike commenced.
22 January	Board of Conciliation and Arbitration of the Commonwealth of Massachusetts Department of Labor and Industries called contesting parties to a conference at the State House, Boston. Nothing accomplished.
28 January	Foundry closed.
11 February	CIO candidates for Public Welfare Officer and Town Treasurer were decisively defeated in town election.
15 February	18½-cent wage raise was recommended by President Truman in settlement of U. S. Steel strike; became basis for settlement of strikes throughout the nation.
Early March	Citizens' Committee was formed. Purpose: to obtain and publicize views of both sides of controversy. Members:

Clergymen: Glenn D. Glazier, Methodist minister
            James A. Deery, Catholic priest
Business men: Francis E. Duggan, Oil agency owner
            Zaray A. Kizirbohosian, Shoe store owner
Selectmen: George L. Searles, Hardware man
            Curtis M. Carr, Banker

Though such action was without precedent, the two clergymen were permitted to sit in on negotiations.

4 March	Back-to-work movement. Union learned of it, was prepared with 200 pickets to prevent it. No disturbance.

Swift resigned as president of the company at a special stockholders' meeting.

20 March   Word was received from OPA that the company had been granted additional 16.8 per cent increase in prices.

21 March   Company proposed the following wage increases:
    (a) 8 cents per hour to hourly workers including office employees and job supervisors,
    (b) an equivalent rate to piece workers,
    (c) 10 cents an hour for assistant foremen,
    (d) 15 cents an hour for foremen, plus 10 cents an hour while the shop continued to work 45 hours a week.

Union rejected offer but proposed that negotiations be resumed on the rest of the contract, leaving wages till later.

26 March   Meeting got no further than preamble of contract. Union demanded that contract be signed with the international union, not the local. Union negotiators walked out of meeting.

27 March   Company officials decided to slush machinery to prepare for a long strike.

3 April   On invitation of Union Negotiator Glynn, Federal Conciliator Henry W. Tucker called the two parties together again and established area of disagreement.

Union demanded:	*Company replied:*
(a) 18½-cent pay increase	Choice of 8 cents for 45 hours per week or 11½ cents for 40
(b) Maintenance of membership and check-off of dues	Check-off voluntary but irrevocable
(c) Vacation eligibility based on work during 60 per cent of previous period	Based on 40 out of 52 weeks (about 77 per cent of previous period)

(d) Top seniority for un-   No
    ion officials

(e) Holiday pay for Labor   No
    Day

(f) Severance pay   No

(g) 75 cents minimum
    wage   70 cents

5 April   Agreement reached on all but two points:

            (a) Union accepted $11\frac{1}{2}$ cents for 40 hours, plus 2 cents for correcting inequities

            (b) No agreement on maintenance of membership

            (c) Compromise on 70 per cent for vacation eligibility

            (d) Company granted top seniority to union officials

            (e) Union withdrew Labor Day pay demand

            (f) Union withdrew severance pay demand

            (g) No agreement on minimum wage.

8 April   Newspapers carried article stating that price ceilings on textile machinery had been suspended. Company received official word two days later. The news had no apparent effect on settlement of strike.

10 April   Company offered non-striking patternmakers a choice of 8 cents-45 hours or $11\frac{1}{2}$ cents-40 hours. Patternmakers chose $11\frac{1}{2}$ cents. Similar offer made to foundrymen. They also chose 40-hour week. Father Deery said mass for speedy and amicable settlement of strike.

11 April   Union withdrew demand for maintenance of membership in exchange for additional $\frac{1}{2}$-cent raise and 73 cents minimum wages. Total hourly wage increase since end of war: 19 cents.

13 April   CIO members voted to accept contract agreement.

15 April   Contract signed; strike ended 13 weeks after it started.

APPENDIX 21

NEGOTIATIONS LEADING TO THE FIRST CONTRACT BETWEEN THE WHITIN MACHINE WORKS AND THE UNITED STEELWORKERS OF AMERICA, SIGNED 15 APRIL 1946

(x's indicate which party's point of view prevailed; in the case of compromise I have tried to indicate which party gave way least by use of the letters C for company and U for union; however, these evaluations are purely subjective and would probably be disputed by both sides.)

Section	Union demanded that:	Union	Company	Compromise	Final agreement
Preamble	Negotiations be between Whitin and the USA (CIO)	x			
1. Recognition	Bargaining unit consist of groups listed	x			
2. Maintenance of Membership	Members dropped from union must be fired			C	Voluntary, irrevocable check-off
3. Posting of Notices	Union notices be freely posted on bulletin boards in the shop			C	Only after Director of Personnel approves
4. Overtime	a. Double time be paid on Sunday		x		Only on 7th day's work
	b. Double time be paid on holiday		x		Only time-&-half
	c. Sunday holiday be observed on following Monday	x			
5. Seniority	a. Preferences not to be given those living nearest the plant			U	Permissible when all other factors equal
	b. Two separate zones of seniority be observed (based on type of job)			U	Six zones agreed on
	c. Layoffs, promotions, etc., be considered according to seniority provided man has ability to perform work required			C	Layoffs but not promotions
	d. Whenever vacancies cannot be filled within a department, notice shall be published, job bid on, and highest seniority given preference		x		Omitted
	e. Top seniority be granted union officials			U	Not more than 10 men; must have 3 years' seniority
6. Grievances	a. Grievance committee have 25 members			C	Not more than 6
	b. Procedure too complicated to summarize			U	Provision for appeal if Wks. Mgr. and Int. Rep. do not agree; otherwise accepted
	c. Committee paid when engaging in grievance work during work hours			C	Paid only half straight hourly rate
7. Leave of Absence	Two years be granted if man takes union job elsewhere		x		Omitted

APPENDIX 21 (continued)

Section	Union demanded that:	Union	Company	Compromise	Final agreement
8. Wages	a. All wage increases be retroactive to 25 July 1945, date of the NLRB election		x		Omitted
	b. Substantial pay increases be granted			U	(See Appendix 22)
	c. Minimum rate of $.70; later $.75			U	$.73
	d. $.10 per hr. premium be paid for shift work			C	$.05 for 2nd shift; $.10 for 3rd
9. Vacation	a. Work for 30% of past year be considered qualifying			C	70% of past year
	b. 1½ times base rate be paid for 2nd week of vacation		x		Omitted
10. Rents	Charges shall not be increased by company during period of contract		x		Omitted
11. Veterans	Veterans not be hired if company has to lay off employees to make room		x		Omitted
12. Safety	a. Safety shoes, etc., be provided by company		x		Provided at cost
	b. Safety committee be represented equally by union and company			C	Committee to include a union member
13. International Representative	International Representative have free access to shop			C	Must be accompanied by company representative
14. Insurance	Company sponsor elaborate insurance plan including life, disability, hospital, and medical insurance for employees		x		Omitted
15. Control	Control of manufacturing operations be left in management's hands				No difference of opinion on this point
16. Trial Employment	30 days be considered trial employment period			C	Three months
17. Severance Pay	In case company closes or moves part of its plant, severed employees be paid 4 weeks' pay if employed 1–3 years, 8 weeks' pay if more than 3 years		x		Omitted
18. Annual Wage	Annual wage be guaranteed		x		Omitted
19. Sick Leave	Workers get 7 days' sick leave if employed 1–3 years, 14 days if more than 3 years		x		Omitted
20. Local Conditions	Local conditions in the village remain as before				No difference of opinion on this point
21. Supervisors	Supervisors shall not perform productive or maintenance work	x			

APPENDIX 22

COMPARISON OF PROVISIONS OF THE FIRST CONTRACTS BETWEEN THE
WHITIN MACHINE WORKS AND THE THREE LABOR UNIONS THAT
REPRESENTED ITS EMPLOYEES

(x's indicate the existence of such a clause in the contract.)

Provisions	Machine Shop CIO	Foundry AFL	Pattern Loft AFL
1. Preamble, dated:	15 Apr. '46	1 Oct. '45	10 Apr. '46
a. agreement between company and international union			
b. agreement between company and local union	x	x	x
2. Definition of bargaining unit	x	x	x
3. Functions of management—management to have control of manufacturing operations	x	x	
4. Shop rules:			
a. to be given to union 48 hours before posting	x		
b. to become effective 48 hours after posting	x	x	
5. Seniority:			
a. to be considered in layoffs and rehiring if employee can perform work required	x		
b. to be considered in layoffs and rehiring only if abilities are equal		x	x
c. seniority is to apply:			
i. within zones; six zones or types of work to be established	x		
ii. in case of all transfers, voluntary or involuntary			x
iii. in former department if transfer was not voluntary		x	
d. company to submit layoff list one week in advance	x	x	
e. each employee (and the union) to be informed of date from which his seniority is to be figured	x	x	
f. seniority to cease when worker:			
i. quits	x	x	x
ii. is discharged for just cause	x	x	x
iii. is laid off and not recalled for 12 months	x	x	x
iv. fails to report for work within	48 hrs.	48 hrs.	3 days
g. seniority to become effective after employee has worked	3 mos.	3 mos.	1 yr.

APPENDIX 22 (continued)

Provisions	Machine Shop CIO	Foundry AFL	Pattern Loft AFL
h. local union officials to have top seniority, for purposes of layoffs and rehiring, during tenure of office	x		
i. company to give just consideration to length of service when making promotions	x		
j. no layoffs to be made until work falls below average of 24 hours per worker per week			x
6. Leaves of absence			
a. to be granted for sickness up to a year without loss of seniority	x		
b. may be granted for just cause without loss of seniority up to	60 days	reasonable time	
7. Veterans			
a. Selective Training and Service Act to be observed if discharged employee returns within	90 days	6 months	
b. company to make reasonable attempt to place employee who has been handicapped in service			x
8. Supervisors not to perform production work	x		
9. Maintenance of membership			
a. maintenance of membership but not check-off		x	
b. voluntary, irrevocable check-off, but not maintenance of membership	x		
10. Wages			
a. general increase[a]	12¢		7¢
b. minimum wage[b]	73¢		65¢
c. inequities to be adjusted, averaging 2¢ per worker	x		
d. no wage differential because of sex	x		
e. shift premiums (previously company had paid premiums of 5¢ an hour to women on cleanup shift —3PM–11PM— and 5 per cent for men on night shift —6PM–6AM, 5 days a week—	5 & 10¢		5¢
11. Overtime			
a. time-&-half for hours over 8 per day, 40 per week and holidays	x	x	x

APPENDIX 22 (continued)

Provisions	Machine Shop CIO	Foundry AFL	Pattern Loft AFL
b. Double time for seventh consecutive day	x		
c. Reporting pay for 4 hours, or promise of 4 hours' work	x	x	
d. holidays			
i. New Year's, Memorial Day, July 4th, Labor Day, Thanksgiving, Christmas	x	x	x
ii. to be counted as part of work week in computing overtime	x	x	x
iii. to be observed on Monday if occurring on Sunday	x	x	
12. Vacations			
a. 20 hours' pay for employees with 6 mos. to 1 year service; 1 week vacation with pay for 1 to 5 years' service; 2 weeks' vacation for 5 years or more service	x	x	x
b. vacation pay to be computed on basis of straight time hourly earnings for ___ previous pay periods (averaged)	5	10	10
c. if production demands, money may be paid in lieu of vacation	x	x	x
d. temporary shutdown any time between June 1st and Oct. 31st may be counted as vacation	x	x	x
e. to qualify, employee must have worked ___% of the time prior to vacation	70	60	60
f. if possible, employees to be given choice of vacation period	x	x	x
g. men inducted into armed services to be given vacation allowances if qualified	x	x	x
h. men returning from armed services to be given vacation allowances if otherwise qualified, even if they do not meet the provisions of section "e"	x		
13. Grievances			
a. Machine-shop procedure: employees to present grievances in writing to foreman; may be accompanied, if desired, by steward; first appeal to asst. supt. accompanied by member of Grievance Committee; second appeal to Director of Personnel with Grievance Committee as a body; third appeal to Works Manager with International Representative; final appeal to impartial judge, his de-			

APPENDIX 22 (continued)

Provisions	Machine Shop CIO	Foundry AFL	Pattern Loft AFL
cision to be binding; time limits imposed at each step	x		
b. Foundry procedure: employees to present grievances to foremen; first appeal (in writing) to superintendent; may be accompanied by Shop Committee; second appeal to Director of Personnel with International Representative; third appeal to impartial judge, but his decision not binding; time limits imposed at each step		x	
c. Pattern-loft procedure: employees may be represented by either Shop Committee or International Representative			x
d. grievances to be settled outside working hours if possible; if settled during working hours committeemen to be paid half straight time rates	x	x	
e. no union activities during working hours			x
14. Strikes and lockouts to be outlawed during term of contract	x	x	x
15. International Representative may enter shop if accompanied by company representative	x	x	
16. Union may post notices if Director of Personnel approves	x	x	
17. Union to have a representative on Safety and Health Committee	x		
18. Neither company nor union to discriminate between employees on basis of union membership		x	x
19. Company and union to set rules for apprentices			x
20. Duration of contract: one year, renewable for	1 year	1 year	6 mos.
Approximate number of words in each contract	5,400	2,700	2,000
Total membership of the international union[c]	725,625	67,177	11,000

[a] Although the foundry contract required no wage increase and the pattern-loft contract only 7¢, both groups were extended the same rights as those later written into the machine-shop contract.

[b] The pattern loft's minimum wage was raised to 73¢ at the same time that the machine shop's was.

[c] Florence Peterson, *Handbook of Labor Unions* (Washington, D. C., 1944). The International Association of Machinists (AFL) had 635,000 members in 1944.

Source: Printed copies of contracts.

APPENDIX 23

TOTAL MAN HOURS WORKED DURING THE FIRST WEEK OF EACH QUARTER BY WHITIN'S NON-ADMINISTRATIVE EMPLOYEES, 1865–1948

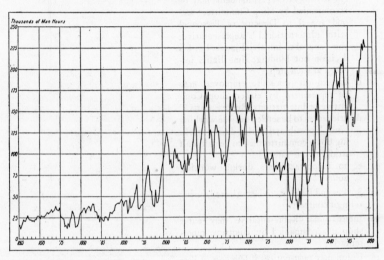

Source: Whitin Payroll Ledgers. Figures do not include man hours worked in the Southern Shop or at the company's Fayscott plant in Dexter, Maine. Method of computation: 1865–85, total payroll for first month in each quarter divided by 3/13, then the quotient divided by average hourly wage; 1886–1948, total payroll for first week in each quarter divided by average hourly wage.

APPENDIX 24

AVERAGE HOURLY RATES PAID WHITIN'S NON-ADMINISTRATIVE EMPLOYEES, AS OF JANUARY, IN THE YEARS 1860-1948

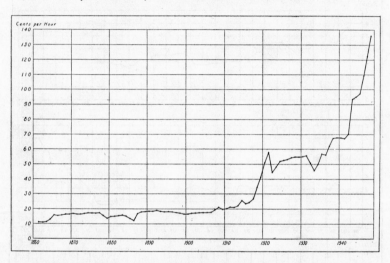

Source: Whitin Payroll Ledgers. Statistical method: 1862–86, total January payroll (less piecework extras) divided by total man hours worked during the month of January; 1887–99, same as above except computation has been arrived at on a weekly basis, the first full week in January being the week selected; 1900–14, figures compiled by the company by dividing total annual payroll by the total annual man hours worked; 1916–48, figures compiled by the company as above, but on a monthly instead of an annual basis, January being the month selected.

APPENDIX 25

WHITIN SPINNING-FRAME PRICES (IN DOLLARS PER SPINDLE), 1866–1948

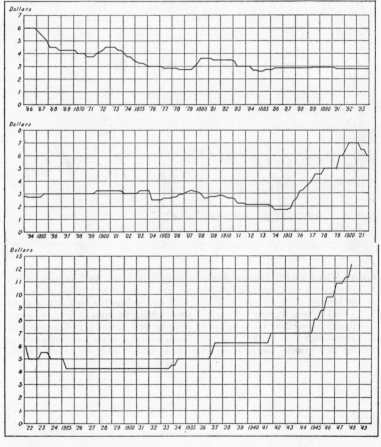

Source: Quotations found in Whitin Letterbooks and in official company price list books.

Explanation of Statistical Method Used in Compiling
Appendix 25

This chart violates several basic rules of chart making. Obviously it is meaningless to compare the price of a spinning frame made in 1860 with the price of one made in 1948. Furthermore "base prices" — the prices which are plotted on this chart — are widely affected by the number of extras which have been added to spinning frames in increasing numbers since they were first introduced in 1889. In addition there are many minor changes in comparability, all of which are set forth below. But the essential value of the chart is not altered by these unavoidable drawbacks. The chart is designed to show only the direction of price movements over any given period of time, not the dimensions of such a movement.

1862–79   Prices given are for frames with common spindles equipped with rings measuring 1⅛″ x 2½″, that is, rings with 1⅛″ diameter, spaced 2½″ apart. Until Oct., 1879, price quotations were made in steps of one-eighth of a dollar, just as stock market prices are quoted today.

1879–83   Few 1⅛″ x 2½″ frames were sold after 1879. The new standard became 1¾″ x 2¾″ and sold at 10 cents more than the old type.

1883–89   Gravity spindles, at 35 cents more than the old common spindles, became standard Whitin equipment after 1883.

1889–92   Beginning in Mar., 1889, threadboard lifters and in Apr., 1890, separators (each priced at 10 cents extra formerly) became standard equipment.

1892–95   Quoted prices remained fairly stable but actual "sale" prices sometimes fell as low as $2.45. Consequently the prices plotted for this period represent quoted prices rather than actual sale prices as heretofore.

1895–1904   Protected by the Draper pool of spindle patents, spinning frame prices remained fairly stable during this period of general price instability.

1904–15   Prices plotted for this period represent actual prices to customers rather than quoted prices.

1915–48   Prices plotted for this period are again quoted rather than sale prices. The standard spindle continues to be 2¾″ gauge for pricing purposes, although by 1948 few frames using so small a gauge were being sold by the company.

APPENDIX 26

SALES OF WHITIN SPINNING FRAMES
AND CARDS, 1850–1913

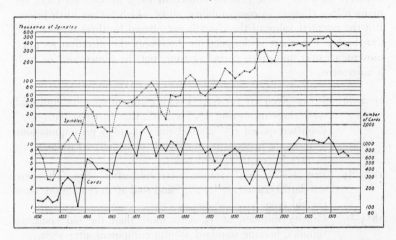

Source: Order Books, 1850–85; Day Book summaries, 1886–99; Machinery Book
summaries, 1900–1913. Statistical method: Since the company did not keep a
dollar record of sales until after 1900, the chart is drawn in terms of number of
machines sold. For the years up to and including 1886, the sales figures indicate
machinery ordered; for 1886 and afterwards, sales figures indicate machinery
delivered. To eliminate random variations and to compensate for the lag between orders and deliveries, running two-year averages have been charted. In
years before 1886 and after 1899, the average has been placed opposite the second of the two years averaged; in the years between 1886 and 1899, the average
has been placed opposite the first of the two years averaged. Hence the double
readings for 1886 (the two spindle readings are practically identical) and the gap
for 1900.

APPENDIX 27

SALES OF WHITIN LOOMS, 1850–1918

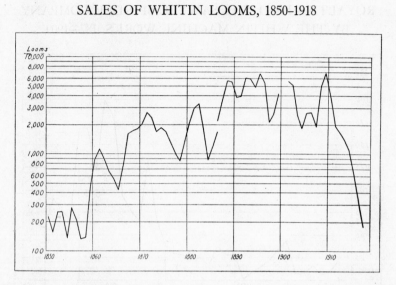

Source: Same as for Appendix 26.

APPENDIX 28

ROYALTIES PAID THE SAWYER SPINDLE COMPANY
BY THE WHITIN MACHINE WORKS, 1874–1909

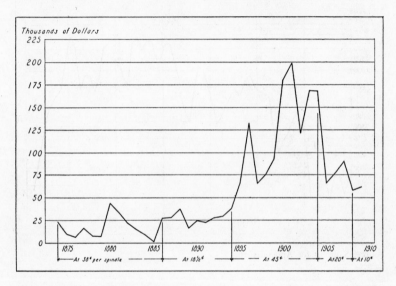

Source: Whitin Letterbooks.

APPENDIX 29

WHITIN'S TOTAL NEW-MACHINERY SALES AND THE PART OF ITS NEW-MACHINERY SALES THAT WENT TO THE SOUTH, 1885–1915

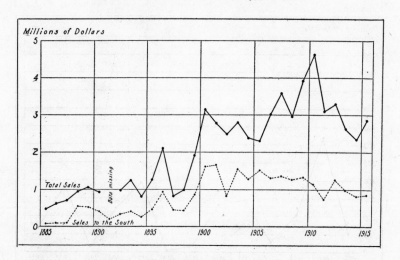

Source: Whitin's Sales Ledgers. Method used: Each account had to be totaled separately; then all accounts had to be totaled for each year

APPENDIX 30

SPINDLES INSTALLED BY ALL MANUFACTURERS IN NEW AND ENLARGED MILLS BOTH IN THE NORTH AND IN THE SOUTH, 1891–1903

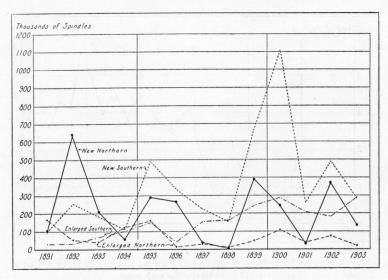

Source: *Textile Manufacturing World*. Figures for the years 1891–93 were furnished through the courtesy of the New York Public Library

APPENDIX 31

SPINDLES INSTALLED BY ALL TEXTILE-MACHINERY MANUFACTURERS IN THE FOUR LEADING COTTON-MANUFACTURING STATES OF THE SOUTH, 1891–1903

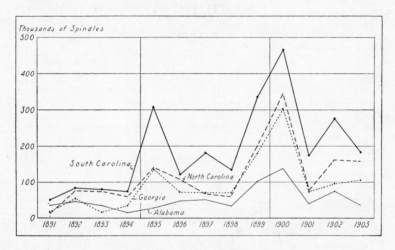

Source: Same as Appendix 30.

APPENDIX 32

WHITIN'S NEW-MACHINERY AND REPAIR SALES TO THE FOUR LEADING COTTON-MANUFACTURING STATES OF THE SOUTH, 1880–1915

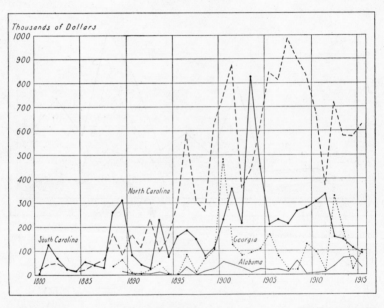

Source: Whitin's Sales Ledgers (a breakdown of the figures compiled for Appendix 29).

APPENDIX 33

A CENTURY OF PLANT EXPANSION
IN WHITINSVILLE, 1847–1948

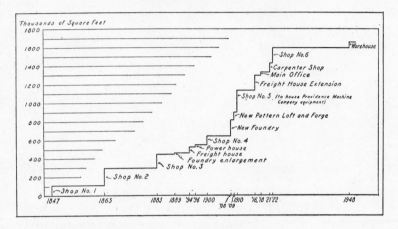

Source: Lay-out drawings on file in the Whitin maintenance office. Not shown: alterations that have added floor space to existing buildings; in 1949, the company's total floor space exclusive of its plants in Maine and North Carolina was
2,098,401 square feet.

NOTES AND REFERENCES

There is virtually no published information on the textile machinery industry. Apparently, being a producers' goods industry, it has held no romantic appeal for either writers or scholars. In 1916 H. H. B. Meyer, chief bibliographer of the Library of Congress, set about compiling a list of books and articles on the industry and in the end was able to find only eight pages of references. Even then, most of the books he found were on the design and operation of textile machines rather than on their manufacture. The Bureau of the Census, furthermore, did not give the industry separate attention until 1920. Consequently the materials for this book were, even more than is customarily true in business histories, drawn from company records. Such inside information is, of course, always subject to bias. The writer of a truly rounded business history should be able to see events not only through the eyes of the company he is writing about, but from the vantage point of the company's suppliers, its customers, and most of all its competitors. That this is the counsel of perfection would not be denied. But the historian who does not admit to himself and to his readers that his book is bound to be one-sided in spite of his conscientious efforts to make it otherwise is not being wholly candid.

Whitin's extant records date back only to 1849 and, in significant amounts, only to 1860. Consequently the information for the first two chapters of this book was drawn chiefly from outside sources. County histories contributed their share of the facts. But incomparably the most rewarding repository of information about the company's early history lies in the basement of the Worcester County Court House where copies of the County's old deeds are kept. At a time when corporate legal instruments were almost nonexistent, partners used the Registry of Deeds to record transfers of the "shares" they held in real and personal property. Consequently, deed records are one of the best surviving sources for business historians working in the period of the early nineteenth century. Northbridge town records were also helpful, especially vital statistics, which at least established the ages and family connections of men in the company, and tax valuation lists, which furnished otherwise unobtainable information on physical assets and values.

There is always a temptation for the historian to dwell over-long on the early phase of a company's history. And I confess to having succumbed myself. It is the one place where the historian can use his traditional research techniques to best advantage. And since the available information on the period is usually finite, he feels a challenge to exhaust every source, even at the risk of encountering diminishing returns. Yet there is no better way to waste precious time. Much of the sort of information that the historian spends weeks looking for in the early chapters of his book, he would cast aside as useless in a later chapter where he had plenty of information of far greater significance. The business historian is working in a new medium — the records of business concerns — and he can contribute most to human knowledge by exploiting that medium to his best ability. I do not mean that he should relax his standards of scholarship. I mean simply that, with limited time and energy at his disposal, he should be conscious of the need to distribute his work to the greatest advantage.

A word about the way company correspondence has been footnoted. Letters written by the company or by executives of the company have been indicated by appropriate initials. Key: WMW — Whitin Machine Works; JCW — John C. Whitin; JMW — John Maltby Whitin; JL — Josiah Lasell; GET — Gustavus E. Taft; GMW — George Marston Whitin; SWC — Stuart W. Cramer; GBH — George B. Hamblin; CWL — Chester W. Lasell; JML — J. M. Lasell; EKS — E. Kent Swift; LMK — Lawrence M. Keeler; JHB — J. Hugh Bolton.

In making my footnotes I have been not a little arbitrary. When using company sources, I have footnoted my materials only if the sources were not self-evident from the text or when a controversial point was involved. As a substitute for more elaborate documentation, I have written a short commentary on my sources at the beginning of each set of chapter footnotes. To some extent I have distinguished between documentary and informational footnotes by placing the former at the back of the book and the latter below the text. However, I have not always been consistent in this practice, and wherever an informational footnote simply elaborated a point already made or when for some reason an informational footnote seemed particularly dull, I have placed it at the back of the book.

Much of the information on which a study of this type is based is available only to the author of the book. Hence, more even than is true of most historians, business historians must measure up to the position of trust that their readers are forced to hold them in. Limitations of materials should be clearly set forth and handicaps under which the author has labored should be made clear from the first.

Sooner or later every business historian meets the skeptic who doubts whether the history of a business firm can ever be written with complete candor. Naturally the candor with which a history may be written differs from instance to instance and even in some cases from author to author when questions of taste are involved. But in any event the author owes it to his reader to set forth the circumstances under which his book has been written.

In general it may be said that most American companies have not yet reached the point where they are willing to let outsiders have full access to their materials without the exercise of a controlling judgment over what is written from those materials. Those companies that have reached that point are generally of two types. There are those firms who are proud of their past and who are conscious that no fair investigator could write anything seriously damaging to their reputations. The Whitin Machine Works belongs to this category of firms. There are also a few firms whose present-day managements, for one reason or another, feel no responsibility for the deeds or misdeeds of past managements and so feel free to have the past exposed to public scrutiny no matter what the consequences. In both cases it should be emphasized that companies feel free to waive censorship only when they have confidence that the authors of their histories have no preconceived theories for which they are merely seeking supporting ammunition. Free permission to publish the findings contained in the Harvard Studies in Business History could never have been obtained had the firms involved not had implicit faith in the fair-mindedness of Professor N. S. B. Gras. It behooves the business historian, therefore, to be as frank with his subject and his reader as he is when discussing his subject with his colleagues.

1. The best sources of information published on the life of Paul Whitin are: *History of Worcester County, Massachusetts* (Philadelphia, 1889), D. Hamilton Hurd, editor, vol. i, pp. 424–453; and William R. Bagnall, "Sketches of Manufacturing Establishments in New York City, and of Textile Establishments in the Eastern States" (unpublished), edited by Victor S. Clark (Washington, 1908), vol. ii, pp. 1464–1471. The former contains a long and informative article on the town of Northbridge written by John R. Thurston, who was, at the time of writing, pastor of the Whitinsville Congregational Church. The latter is a collection of historical materials made by William R. Bagnall just before his death in 1892. The Bagnall papers are especially valuable since the information on which their statements about Whitin are based was obtained from Arthur Fletcher Whitin, a grandson of Paul. Wherever in this chapter facts about the early history of the Whitin family enterprises have been presented without annotation, it may be assumed that they were derived from one of these two sources.

2. The Paul Whiting of Sutton was born 28 February 1761; thus he was six years older than the Paul Whiting of Northbridge. See William A. Benedict and Hiram A. Tracy, *History of Sutton, 1704–1876* (Worcester, 1878), p. 747.

3. Paul's great-great-grandfather appears to have been the Nathaniel Whiting who is credited with having owned the first grist mill on the Charles River. The mill was bought by Whiting around 1640 and for five generations remained in his family. It was finally sold about 1827. Thus, at Paul's birth, the mill must have been owned by a cousin of his father. See Erastus Worthington, *History of Dedham* (Boston, 1827), p. 37.

4. George L. Gibbs, "Reminiscences" (unpublished, written about 1884).

5. *Ibid.*

6. Before 1786 Northbridge had been the northern district of Uxbridge and even earlier, before 1727, had been a part of the town of Mendon.

7. Ezra Wood must be credited with the construction of the smithy, for no record of its existence can be found in the deed by which Wood bought the land where the smithy stood. It seems possible that Wood built the

smithy specifically for Whitin's use. At least Whitin appears to have been its first operator.

8. Copies of the deeds for these transactions are preserved in the Registry of Deeds, Worcester County Court House, Worcester, Massachusetts, in book 145, p. 436, and in book 207, p. 483.

9. The forge enterprise was given the firm name of Fletcher & Whitin. Although Whitin thus became Fletcher's legal partner, he continued to devote his entire energy to his own business.

10. See Victor S. Clark, *History of Manufactures in the United States* (Washington, 1916), vol. i, p. 477.

11. George S. White, *Memoir of Samuel Slater* (Philadelphia, 1836), p. 190.

12. *Ibid.*, p. 107.

13. Albert Gallatin, *Report on American Manufactures* (Boston, 1810). Although Gallatin's report is of questionable accuracy, it is the best available for that date.

14. A series of Worcester County deeds dated earlier than 13 Jan. 1798 give Northbridge as Jonathan Adams' residence.

15. William R. Bagnall, *The Textile Industries of the United States* (Cambridge, 1893), p. 445.

16. Worcester County deed book 177, p. 396, shows a deed, dated 24 May 1810, in which Fletcher transferred ownership in the mill site to his partners. By that date the mill building must have been completed and much of the machinery installed, for operations began 10 Aug. 1810. According to the deed, Fletcher received a credit of $2,800 for the $28/32$ part of his property which he turned over to his partners. The additional $4/32$ of the property, or $400, represented his own personal contribution to the firm. Thus, at least $3,200 of the $4,000-share he held in the enterprise consisted of the property he made available for the mill site.

17. Registry of Deeds, Warwick Court House, Apponaug, Rhode Island, deed book 15, p. 491.

18. In Worcester County deed book 183, p. 443, a deed dated 28 Feb. 1812 gives Sabin's residence as Northbridge.

19. Worcester County deed book 177, p. 396.

20. *Ibid.*, pp. 398–399.

21. White, *op. cit.*, pp. 96–97.

22. Worcester County deed book 180, p. 266. In 1813 Paul Whitin sold the partnership a dye house for $60. This may indicate that, for the first few years of the company's existence, the mill's yarn was dyed by Whitin on his own account.

23. Gibbs, *op. cit.*

24. Bagnall, *Text. Inds. of the U. S.*, p. 444.

25. Those authors who state that the mill had 1,500 spindles apparently refer to the capacity of the mill building. See James H. Lamb, *Lamb's Textile Industries of the United States* (Boston, 1916), vol. i, p. 295; and J. D. Van Slyck, *Representatives of New England: Manufacturers* (Boston, 1879), p.

498. Gallatin, *op. cit.*, chart C, reported a capacity of 800 spindles, but his report was made before the mill had been completed. As late as 1831, the mill had only 1,476 spindles.

26. Gallatin, *op. cit.*, chart C, indicates that the average number of active spindles per mill operating in the Providence area in 1809 was about 750. Mills in the process of erection in that year averaged a capacity of 1,700 spindles. Since the number of spindles employed is generally the limiting factor in mill production, capacity is usually referred to in terms of spindles.

27. It is interesting to note that, when the Northbridge mill was granted a state charter on 9 June 1814, it was limited in capitalization to $150,000, a figure which conforms to the investment recommended by Gallatin for a mill of 1,500-spindle capacity.

28. Worcester County deed book 213, p. 185.

29. Most writers have referred to this firm as Whitin & Fletcher, but it is clear from deeds of that time, and certainly it is more logical, that a final "s" was used.

30. Worcester County deed book 252, p. 359. Amos Armsby had sold his ⅛ interest to Arnold Walker for $1,500 on 11 May 1822 (deed book 229, p. 320). Two months later, on 27 July 1822, Walker had sold the share to James Fletcher, Sr., for the amount which he had paid for it (deed book 239, p. 558). On 18 Feb. 1823 Ezra Fletcher had sold his ⅛ interest to his father and two brothers jointly for $1,266.67 (deed book 252, p. 364); shortly thereafter he had moved to Providence, Rhode Island. When Paul Whitin bought out the firm, in 1826, the only deed recorded was the one showing the sale of the interests of Samuel and James Fletcher, Jr. (for the stated $2,000); but there can be no doubt that James, Sr., also sold to Whitin at this time. It is interesting to note the decline in values of the shares in the firm of Whitin & Fletchers. In 1822 a ⅛ share sold for $1,500, in 1823 for $1,266.67, and in 1826 for $750.

31. The firm was named Lee & Whitin and was located on Maiden Lane. Whitin had come to know Lee as a fellow-clerk in the Boston store of James Brewer.

32. Nathaniel is credited by George L. Gibbs with the invention of a pill-making machine and of a machine for spreading plasters. He is known to have received patents on a gas stopper and on a tin baking oven. See Edmund Burke, *Inventions and Designs Issued by the United States from 1790 to 1847* (Washington, 1847).

33. Although the new building had only two stories, it possessed a full basement and was 60 ft. long and 32 ft. wide. The costs of constructing the mill and of building new machinery for it soon depleted the Whitins' cash reserves. To obtain working capital they found it necessary to ask Daniel Waldo for a short-term loan of $2,600, payable in five months. See Worcester County deed book 252, p. 393.

34. Bagnall's unpublished papers, vol. ii, p. 1048.

35. Worcester County deed book 249, p. 30.

36. *Ibid.*, p. 29.

37. Worcester County deed book 252, p. 367, gives a full list of the notes.

38. J. Leander Bishop, *A History of American Manufactures from 1608 to 1860* (Philadelphia, 1868), vol. ii, p. 336.

39. Bagnall's unpublished papers, vol. ii, p. 965.

40. Worcester County deed book 282, p. 92. The deed of 1831, by which Shove sold the Whitins his interest in the Northbridge company, contains an inventory of machinery and equipment owned by the mill. Since such lists, for a period so early, are very rare, it seems worth while to reproduce this one in full.

1 picker	1 mule (144 spindles)
1 whipper	1 warper
1 lap machine	1 spooler
5 double cards	2 dressers
3 drawing frames	36 looms (power-driven looms were
2 belted speeders	introduced to mills in the Provi-
8 throstle frames (48 spindles each)	dence area during the early 1820's)
1 mule (216 spindles)	1 machine for cutting and connect-
1 mule (180 spindles)	ing top roller covers

For some reason the rest of the equipment was listed separately; perhaps the division was meant to indicate different physical locations.

18 cards	1 fluting engine
4 throstle frames (84 spindles each)	1 cutting engine
2 looms	preparation for grinding cards
1 mule (216 spindles)	4 stoves and pipes
1 woodturning lathe	1 press for baking cloth
1 engine for turning	2 desks in counting room

41. Worcester County deed book 280, p. 576.

42. *Ibid.*, 289, p. 347 and 290, p. 450. In later years a dispute arose over the final disposition of the notes which the Buffums had originally issued and which first Shove and then the Whitins had agreed to pay. On 4 Apr. 1843 the Whitins took steps to clear their title by paying to Robert Earle, administrator of Silas Earle's estate, the amount of $2,500 to cover the principal of the notes and all interest which had accrued thereon (Worcester County deed book 416, p. 47). On 24 Aug. 1846 a similar settlement was made with Henry Sabin in the amount of $600 (Worcester County deed book 416, p. 47). Although no record exists showing that similar adjustments were made with the Fletchers, it is possible that a private settlement was effected.

CHAPTER II

The only existing corporate records for the period 1831–59 are two small order books no larger than a schoolgirl's diaries. One dates from 1849 to 1853, the other from 1854 to 1859. Yet a surprising amount can be learned, even from such seeming trivia, once one has buckled down to the job of sifting out the available information.

These order books, kept in John C. Whitin's own handwriting, are a striking example of the informality of business records in those days. From their present good condition one would gather that they were books of final entry, not simply pocket notebooks. Yet, in addition to a chronological list of orders received, these books contain, on their front and back pages, jotted information such as formulae for solving simple problems in shop mathematics, lists of raw-materials suppliers, the names of lads who had applied for apprentice training, and even the ingredients for compounding Babbitt metal.

One important type of information is everywhere omitted, however: the price of machinery and the discounts given. Apparently Whitin wished to conceal those figures from his employees, for in place of price quotations he used such two- and three-letter codes as $RS, $LE, and $OMU. It was not until after I had become fairly familiar with the general range of prices in those days that I discovered the rather simple key to the code. Whitin was merely replacing figures with letters according to the following pattern: A = 1, E = 2, I = 3, O = 4, U = 5, L = 6, M = 7, N = 8, R = 9, S = 0. Thus the examples given above (which were for a railway head, a loom, and a lapper, respectively) stood for $90, $62, and $475. Since Whitin used these codes only infrequently and since the code prices averaged about 10% less than other known prices, it is possible that he used this means to remind himself of discounts granted to favored customers.

Beyond their usefulness to the study of the Whitin company's history, these order books are valuable for their mention of the names of contemporary business men. Up to the present date almost nothing has been known of the persons employed in the operating echelons of America's early cotton textile industry. Business directories for the pre-Civil War period are almost non-existent. The list of mill agents and treasurers contained in the Whitin order books goes part way toward filling the gap.

1. P. Whitin & Sons' repair shop was housed in a one-story, 18x43-ft. ell of the old brick mill. Bagnall's unpublished papers, vol. ii, p. 1470.

2. White, *Memoir of S. Slater,* p. 187 n.

3. Bagnall, *Text. Inds. of the U. S.,* p. 327.

4. See *Documents Relative to the Manufactures in the United States* (Washington, 1833), vol. i, p. 70, and Gallatin, *Report on Am. Manufs.,* p. 10.

5. Caroline F. Ware, *The Early New England Cotton Manufacture* (Cambridge, 1931), p. 23.

6. In England the picking and spreading steps were still separate as late as 1840. See James Montgomery, *Cotton Manufacture of the United States of America* (Glasgow, 1840), p. 28.

7. See Joseph W. Roe, *English and American Tool Builders* (New Haven, 1916), p. 63, for information regarding early use of gearing.

8. Montgomery, *op. cit.,* p. 30.

9. Northbridge town records show that Innis declared his intention to marry in December, 1825, at which time Whitin was eighteen years old. Recent publications of the Whitin company have made tacit admission of Innis' claim; e.g., "In 1831, John C. Whitin, with the help of one mechanic, made and patented an improved picking machine." *Information about Whitin* (Whitinsville, 1946), p. 5.

10. *Facts and Estimates Relative to the Business on the Route of the Contemplated Providence and Worcester Railroad* (Providence, 1844), p. 13.

11. Worcester County deed book 406, p. 363. Van Slyck, in his *Reps. of New Eng.: Mfrs.,* p. 500, states that the brick mill was converted into a machine shop in 1845. Thus the brick mill probably became the "lower" machine shop referred to by implication in the quoted deed.

12. Daniel W. Snell, *The Manager's Assistant* (Hartford, 1850), p. 14.

13. The *Whitin Spindle* of Aug., 1920 (p. 11), lists the following men as being 9 of the 11 employed by Whitin in 1839: Benjamin Innis, Arnold Whipple, Amos Whipple, Harkness Inman, Amos Arnold, William Nicholson, Edward Fuller, John Wilmarth, and Sylvester G. Keith. Note the Yankee surnames. Possibly S. F. Batchelor is one of the two missing names, for he is known to have been making Whitin's "spreaders" at that time.

14. John W. Barber, *Every Town in Massachusetts* (1839), p. 591.

15. Ltr., JL to Mountain Island Mills, 27 Mar. 1873.

16. Van Slyck, *op. cit.,* p. 327.

17. *Ibid.,* p. 208.

18. *Ibid.,* p. 265.

19. The stone mill, as it first stood, measured 48 x 162 ft. In 1864 a three-story ell (48 x 148 ft.) and a one-story picking house (48 x 50 ft.) were added. The building is still standing but is now used only as a storehouse.

20. In the following year a foundry (50 x 132 ft.) was built adjacent to the new brick machine shop.

21. Bishop, *Hist. of Am. Manufs.,* vol. iii, p. 321.

22. *New England Mercantile Union Business Directory* (New York, 1849), p. 223, and Bishop, *op. cit.,* vol. iii, p. 536.

23. *Business on the Contemplated Providence and Worcester Railroad,* p. 13.

24. William F. Draper, *Recollections of a Varied Career* (Boston, 1908), p. 5.

25. The purchase of the Rockdale Mill is recorded in Worcester County deed book 570, p. 26. The Worcester Bank, the mortgage holder, received $12,000 for the property.

26. For this date, I follow Bagnall's unpublished papers, edited by V. S. Clark (vol. ii, p. 1474), although I have found no corroborative evidence to support Bagnall's facts. There seems to be no record of the sale of the Riverdale property in the Worcester County Registry of Deeds. If it is there, it is improperly indexed. The Northbridge Valuation Lists for the years 1860–64 show that by those years the property belonged to P. Whitin & Sons, but it

also rather disturbingly refers to the property as "The Dunn Estate." To add another pinch of confusion, Rev. John R. Thurston states that during the Civil War the mill was operated by Harvey Waters as a scythe shop and that bayonets were made there.

27. Worcester County deed book 462, p. 233. The transaction, which was stated to have taken place on 9 Apr. 1847, was, for some reason, not registered until 24 Apr. 1850. Perhaps it was found desirable, when recording the deed, to predate the agreement by a few years in order to cut James in on some of the profits earned during the intervening period.

28. To reduce machinery sales to a common denominator for comparative purposes, it was necessary to make some assignment of dollar values however arbitrary. Figures used for the compilation of statistics in this chapter are given below. Except where otherwise noted they have been taken from a stray sheet of paper which somehow escaped destruction and on which are listed miscellaneous Whitin prices for 2 Aug. 1854. List prices, such as these, seem to have remained fairly stable for the period, but individual discounts often effected wide variations.

Willows (Montgomery, *Cotton Manuf. of the U. S.*, p. 115)					$100
Pickers (two beaters)	18"	24"	30"	36"	
Mumgrill	$300	$325	$375	$420	
Wood frame	—	375	425	475	
Iron frame	—	450	500	550	
(three beaters)					
Mumgrill	375	400	450	500	
Wood frame	—	475	500	550	
Iron frame	—	550	600	650	
Cards — 30"					130
36"					140
Small grinders (Order Books, *passim*.)					15
Top grinders (Order Books, *passim*.)					90
Breaker railway heads					110
Finisher railway heads					160
Drawing heads (Order Book no. 2, 20 Jan. 1849)					90
Iron drawing frames					200
Ring spinning frames (128 spindles, $4.00 each)					512
Spoolers — 3" bobbins					300
4" bobbins					325
Dressers					400
Warpers					100
Looms					70

29. Paul Whitin, Jr., was on the committee formed to "open the books of subscription to the stock of [a railroad company]." *Business on the Contemplated Prov. and Worc. R. R.*, p. 2.

CHAPTER III

From a research standpoint the Holyoke chapter constitutes a package unit. In reality it is a small business history in itself. Ordinarily it is never possible to determine exactly how profitable a company has been until after its liquidation, but in this case a final appraisal is made easy because the company lasted only four years. Furthermore, virtually all the company's records have been preserved. These records cover such a short period that the researcher can become familiar with them all, a rare achievement in the business history field where source materials are usually so voluminous that the only feasible research technique is a careful sampling process.

The key book of account among the Holyoke records is the cashbook. In it are entered all cash transactions, however trivial. Because the cashbooks are chronological in form and are nowhere summarized, they are tedious to work with, but they are very complete. If ever an historian were forced to choose which books of account to save, he would probably put cashbooks near the top of his list. Cashbooks are merely raw materials, however, and must be refined to be made useful. It would be possible of course to construct something like a modern set of accounts from them, but that would be an inordinately tiresome task. An alternative is to construct a Source and Application of Funds Statement (see for example Table 2), an invaluable device for discovering how a company has used its corporate funds. It is not surprising that historians have made little use of such statements, for business men themselves have used them for only a comparatively short time. But as tools of financial analysis they should be in every historian's work kit.

Auxiliary to the Holyoke cashbooks are four other types of account books which restate the information contained in the cashbooks, but in slightly different form. The payroll books are, of course, valuable because they contain the number and names of employees. But since few such records contain any reference to the positions held by employees, the information which they contain regarding rates of pay is seldom very useful.

The purchase journals tell the names of suppliers, which is helpful, but they too have their limitations, for they give scant information as to the materials bought; worse still, they have nothing concerning the really dynamic part of the purchasing function — the dickering between company and suppliers over the questions of price and quality. No adequate historical account of a company's purchasing experience has ever been written and it may be years before one will be, for the information vital to such an account is customarily not preserved.

The Holyoke sales journals present a chronological record of the company's shipments of machinery and are useful as a partial measure of business activity. But nearly everything useful in the sales journals is presented in more usable form in the company's ledgers, where sales information is accumulated under each customer's account. Oddly enough, though, the Holyoke ledger like so many other business ledgers, is less useful to the historian than to the accountant; although it is a book of final account and consequently contains much information in a conveniently summarized form, the very compactness of its data tends to obscure the individual details that are so often the heart of a business story.

Finally, Chapter III depends in part on the Holyoke shop's outgoing letter-books, but because letterbooks figure prominently as the source of information in two later chapters, a discussion of their usefulness will be postponed till then.

1. In her historical study, *Holyoke, Massachusetts: A Case History of the Industrial Revolution in America* (New Haven, 1939), Mrs. Constance M. Green repeats a rumor that John C. Whitin was forced to turn down a million dollars' worth of machinery in the early months of 1860. The amount is unquestionably overestimated, but the existence of such a rumor is worth noting.

2. Ltr., JCW to Henry Saltonstall, 3 Feb. 1863: "I have in connection with my brothers a considerable amount of unoccupied water power near my home."

3. For the early history of the machine shop at Holyoke, I have relied upon Green, *op. cit.,* chap. 2.

4. Otis Holmes' son seems also to have rented a small space in the shop. Ltr., JL to Otis Holmes, 27 Feb. 1862. Whitin later had to pay Wheeler & Pattee $2,000 to relinquish their lease. Ltr., JCW to W&P, 17 May 1860.

5. Vera Shlakman, *Economic History of a Factory Town: A Study of Chicopee, Massachusetts* (Northampton, 1936), pp. 39–42, and *New England Mercantile Union Business Directory.*

6. Holyoke *Transcript,* 11 Apr. 1863.

7. Bagnall's unpublished papers, edited by V. S. Clark, vol. 3, p. 1806.

8. Although Whitin made his final payment of principal on 28 Oct. 1862, or less than two weeks past the 2½-year anniversary of the sale, he was obliged to pay full interest charges for 3 years.

9. Louis H. Everts, *History of the Connecticut Valley in Massachusetts* (Philadelphia, 1879), vol. ii, p. 919, gives in detail the dimensions of the shop.

10. The dormer windows and the two-story extension shown in the picture were added by the Hadley Co. after Whitin had sold the property.

11. Green, *op. cit.,* p. 78; Nathan Appleton, *Introduction of the Power Loom and Origin of Lowell* (Lowell, 1858), p. 28; entries every June 30 and Dec. 31 in the Holyoke Machine Shop daybook.

12. There were 68 geared turning lathes, 48 plain turning lathes, 21 geared hand lathes, and 63 plain hand lathes.

13. Holyoke Order Book, p. 30, contains this statement: "Shattuck & Whitney want Four 600-spindle mules, if we make any — first we make."

14. Arthur T. Safford and Edward Pierce Hamilton, "The American Mixed-Flow Turbine and Its Setting," *Transactions of the American Society of Civil Engineers,* 1922, pp. 1237–1255. Probably the most important of the

builders of the Boyden turbine was the Lowell Machine Shop, one of Whitin's competitors.

15. The exact date when the lower rate became effective is not clear. The last indication of the $2.00 rate is a letter dated 10 June 1861; the first mention of $1.50 occurs on 29 Nov. 1861.

16. Jonathan Thayer Lincoln, "Material for a History of American Textile Machinery," *Journal of Economic and Business History,* vol. iv, no. 2 (Feb., 1932), p. 266. Lincoln points out that most textile-machinery companies, in the process of their evolution, passed through a stage of product diversification. The Whitin company was probably the only major producer in the field that did not follow this general pattern.

17. *Lamb's Text. Inds. of the U. S.,* pp. 302–303.

18. Bagnall's unpublished papers, vol. iii, p. 1806; Gibbs, "Reminiscences."

19. Income from the sale of castings amounted to very little, not more than a few hundred dollars a month; rentals from the company's houses amounted to nearly as much.

20. Ltr., JCW to JMW, 21 May 1860.

21. Customers located nearer to Whitinsville than to Holyoke were paid a refund by Whitin for any extra freight charges on machinery that had been made for them in the more distant shop.

22. For many months Whitin was so hard pressed for cash that he found it necessary to discount all notes payable at the local Hadley Falls Bank. Not until Feb., 1862, did he begin to allow his commercial paper to mature.

23. Materials traveled from Providence to New Haven by sloop and thence to Holyoke by rail. Ltr., JCW to French & Pierce, 7 May 1860. A spur connected the machine shop with the main line of the Conn. River R. R. *Report on the History and Present Condition of the Hadley Falls Company* (Boston, 1853), p. 13.

24. Shlakman, *op. cit.,* p. 153.

25. Van Slyck, *Reps. of New Eng.: Mfrs.,* pp. 177, 208, and 329.

26. Hayes, *Am. Text. Mach.,* p. 59.

27. To deliver these machines on time Whitin worked his men until 10 o'clock at night. Ltr., JCW to Jas. T. Ames, 6 Mar. 1862. The fact that overtime was paid for this work is shown by individual payroll entries for as much as 36 "days'" work during the month of Feb., 1862. (A standard day's work consisted of eleven hours.)

28. Ltr., JL to E. Whitney, 9 June 1863.

29. Holyoke *Mirror,* 4 Jan. 1862, reported that the Glasgow Co. was running full time and that the Hampden Mills were running extra time.

30. The relative size of these two orders is indicated by the fact that they, together with the earlier $65,000-order from Pacific Mills and a later order for $90,000 from the Hadley Co., accounted for more than a quarter of Whitin's entire business during the four years that he was in Holyoke.

31. Lamb, *op. cit.,* p. 299.

32. From timetables of the period it is possible to deduce that Whitin must

have left Whitins station at 8:51 A.M. and, after a half-hour delay in Worcester and an hour and a half delay in Springfield, must have arrived in Holyoke at 1:48 P.M., if the train was on time. See *Snow's Pathfinder Railway Guide for the New England States and Canada* (Boston, 1862), and ltr., JCW to Geo. M. Bartholomew, 11 Sept. 1862: "I shall be up here again I think Monday next at 2 o'clock. . . ." Today, travel between Whitinsville and Holyoke by public conveyance would be at least partly by bus and would require nearly as long as in Civil War days; but by automobile the trip would take only a little more than an hour and a half.

33. Though on vacation, Whitin did not neglect to take every opportunity to further his business interests. Ltr., JCW to C. H. Whitman Sons & Co., 27 Aug. 1861.

34. Henry Beetle Hough, *Wamsutta of New Bedford, 1846–1946* (New Bedford, 1946), pp. 35–36. No interruption of amicable relations between the two companies resulted from this episode.

35. Ltr., JCW to Andrew Robeson, treasurer of the Hadley Co., 9 June 1863. In this letter Whitin also gives indication of the irritableness which he may have developed with overwork and of the intolerance he held for sloth: "You will please remember such machinery as you will be satisfied with cannot be created by magic — but will take a *little time* — and a *few hard knocks* — which we are putting in while you are at Newport having 'a good time.' "

36. Ltr., JCW to J. S. Davis, agent of Lyman Mills, 21 Apr. 1863.

37. Holyoke *Transcript,* 2 and 16 May 1863.

38. *Ibid.,* 17 Oct. and 26 Dec. 1863. Only a handful of Holyoke Machine Shop employees (16) were transferred to Whitinsville. Among them were: Joshua T. Carter, a railway-head worker; David P. Chase, who became paymaster at Whitinsville; Henry B. Osgood, a draftsman; Harvey Ellis, who was to follow Taft as superintendent at Whitinsville; and John Aldrich and Patrick McSheehy, both experienced roving-frame builders on whom Whitin relied, in vain, to develop a successful roving line. To employ those who remained in Holyoke, Thos. H. Kelt, formerly Whitin's foundry foreman, undertook to establish a new foundry, though without success. Holyoke *Transcript,* 26 Sept., 7 Nov., and 12 Dec. 1863. However, Stewart Chase, agent of the Holyoke Water Power Co., succeeded in organizing a small shop, the Holyoke Machine Co., which absorbed most of the former Whitin workers and which later became well known as a producer of paper machinery. Holyoke *Transcript,* 5 and 19 Dec. 1863.

39. Ltr., JCW to J. S. Davis, 10 Mar. 1863.

40. Ltrs., JCW to J. T. Ames, 25 and 29 June 1863.

CHAPTER IV

Two distinctive sources were used in this chapter, both of them the personal contribution of townsmen who happen not to have been company employees. One of the men was George L. Gibbs, a local retailer whose marriage to

Charles P. Whitin's daughter, Helen, was one of the scandals of the day and whose status as a member of the family was tolerated by the Whitins but never stressed. In his "Reminiscences" (a copy of which is included with the Whitin records at Baker Library) he deals with the family and the village in personal and candid terms. The other man is Charles O. Bachelor, for many years the town clerk of Northbridge. With prodigious industry Bachelor compiled, principally from town records, a volume of facts and data on the town's history in the hope that they would some day be used in writing an official story of the community. This volume, written in Bachelor's own hand, is preserved in the Whitin company's vaults.

Nearly every company has its diarist or personally appointed historian. Data compiled by such men are often full of errors and need to be checked, but often the facts they have recorded about incidents and especially about personalities cannot be duplicated anywhere else.

Newspaper comment on company and village activities is all but nonexistent in the case of the Whitin Machine Works. Except for the Whitinsville *Compendium* (1870–73), Whitinsville's only local newspaper, the weekly *Times,* has been in existence only since 1929.

1. Mrs. Sydney R. Mason tells me that her great-aunt, Miss Anne Whitin, (who was born in 1839) could remember the first Irish workers coming to Whitinsville when she was seven. They were the town's first "foreigners."

2. See footnote 22, Chapter XVI.

3. Generalizations have been drawn from information found in Hurd, *Hist. of Worc. County;* Gibbs, "Reminiscences"; J. C. Whitin's payroll accounts; Northbridge Valuation Lists; the Eighth and the Ninth Census of the United States; and Charles O. Bachelor's "Materials for a History of Northbridge," compiled about 1876–78. Bachelor estimated that the population of Whitinsville in 1875 was about 2,100. In terms of the birthplace of heads of families, he estimated that 45% of the population was native-born, 40% was Irish, 7% English, 4% Scottish, 2% French Canadian, and 2% all others.

4. Conversation with A. J. Brown, head of the Whitin company pattern loft since 1914.

5. Ltrs., JCW to S. G. Allen, 7 Mar. 1868; JCW to Henry Coverdale, 26 May 1869; and JL to H. N. Gambrill, 1 May 1872.

6. Ltr., JCW to S. G. Allen, 7 Mar. 1868, gives the rates paid to apprentices and hence serves as a key to the names of apprentices appearing on the payroll for Mar., 1868.

7. Ltr., JCW to Orray Taft, 30 Oct. 1865.

8. Sarah S. Whittelsey, *Massachusetts Labor Legislation* (Philadelphia, 1900), pp. 12–13.

9. Henry Roland, "Six Examples of Successful Shop Management," *The Engineering Magazine,* Oct., 1896.

10. Ltr., JL to E. E. Manton, 2 Jan. 1874.

11. Northbridge Valuation List, May, 1864; map of Whitinsville *c.* 1871.

12. Ltr., JCW to D. Trainer & Sons, 18 Feb. 1867.

13. F. M. Peck and H. H. Earl, *Fall River and Its Industries* (New York, 1877), p. 132.

14. For an excellent analysis of the ambitious company town at Pullman, Ill., see *Report of Commissioners of the State Bureaus of Labor Statistics on the Industrial, Social and Economic Conditions of Pullman, Illinois, September, 1864.*

15. See article on "Company Housing" by Leifur Magnusson in the *Encyclopaedia of the Social Sciences.*

16. *Loc. cit.*

17. Jacob Strieder, *Jacob Fugger the Rich,* translated by Mildred L. Hartsough (New York, 1931), p. 175.

18. Morris Knowles, *Industrial Housing* (New York, 1920), p. 14.

19. *Shawsheen, the Model Community and the Home of the Officers and Staff of the American Woolen Mills* (Andover, 1924).

20. A study of employer housing made by the Bureau of Labor Statistics, in 1920, indicated that, as late as 1914, semi-detached frame cottages in New England cost from $800 to $1,000 per dwelling. Compare these figures with Whitin's costs a half-century earlier when he spent nearly $1,100 per unit on his houses. This same study indicated that the return on housing before depreciation for the years 1911–15 averaged only 8.3 per cent. See *Bulletin of the United States Bureau of Labor Statistics,* no. 263, Oct., 1920.

21. Ltr., JCW to S. J. Wetherell, 29 Jan. 1864.

22. Ltr., JCW to Geo. S. Ward, 24 Feb. 1864.

23. Ltr., JCW to L. Blackstone, 11 Mar. 1864. In ltr., JCW to H. Lippett & Co., 24 May 1867, Whitin also admitted that he was a higher-cost producer than Fales, Jenks & Sons.

24. Whitin was a regular subscriber to the Providence *Journal,* the Worcester *Spy,* and the Holyoke *Transcript.*

25. Ltr., JCW to A. Briggs, 13 July 1864.

26. Ltr., JCW to Geo. L. Ward, 28 Nov. 1864.

27. Ltrs. dated 1 Nov. and 3 Nov. 1864 respectively.

28. These were "seven-thirty" bonds. Whitin must have bought them a short time earlier, for they had been on the market only since Feb., 1865. See Henrietta M. Larson, *Jay Cooke, Private Banker* (Cambridge, 1936), pp. 165–175.

29. Ltr., JCW to Wm. Gregg, 24 Feb. 1866. According to Victor Clark (*Hist. of Manufs. in the U. S.,* vol. ii, p. 102), "during the [Civil] war and immediately afterwards, British machine makers could deliver equipment in America more promptly and at lower prices than could American shops."

30. The R.W.&O.R.R. was a prosperous line in upstate New York which formed the vital link connecting Boston with the Grand Trunk Railway and the far west. See Edward Hungerford, *The Story of the Rome, Watertown*

and Ogdensburgh Railroad (New York, 1922), and an article in the *American Railroad Journal,* 13 June 1863. The P.&W.R.R. stock was bought for from $127 to $130 a share; the R.W.&O.R.R. stock for from $112 to $121.

31. Ltr., JCW to M. Massy, vice-president of the R.W.&O.R.R., 24 Feb. 1869. "I thought I would like to make up my stock to 500 shares in your road if I could at the right price as a permanent investment."

32. Cf. Peck & Earl, *op. cit.,* p. 68.

CHAPTER V

A word about trade journals, their uses and their limitations. Since the textile machinery industry has never had a trade journal of its own, I have had to rely on publications of the cotton textile industry — on the *Transactions* of the New England Cotton Manufacturers' Association and, for later years, on such publications as the *Textile World* and *Fibre and Fabric.*

As business history sources, trade journals suffer from two major limitations. First, they deal principally with the technical problems of an industry. Consequently they contain very little that is useful to the historian who is interested in a company's business policies. (Of course there are wide variations in quality and content from trade journal to trade journal as well as from decade to decade, so that it is difficult to generalize in a way that will cover all cases.) Secondly, they are capable of absorbing a prodigious amount of research time without yielding a proportionate amount of information. Sometimes, of course, trade journals may be the only source of facts during a period when, for some reason or other, there may be a gap in a company's corporate records. But the Whitin records are so exhaustively (and exhaustingly) complete that I have felt my major job was to digest them and to record the information I found therein. Therefore, except for a fairly complete perusal of the N.E.C.M.A. *Transactions,* I have relied on trade publications only when I needed to check specific points, especially with regard to the activities of customers or competitors.

1. Gibbs, "Reminiscences."

2. For the period following the Civil War, these were handsome emoluments, especially since Lasell and Taft, though small stockholders, were in reality only hired managers of the firm. The presidency of one of the country's largest insurance companies, The Mutual Life Insurance Co. of N. Y., paid very little more — $20,000 in 1868, $30,000 in 1877. See Shepard Clough, *A Century of American Life Insurance* (New York, 1946), pp. 109 and 205.

3. Supreme Judicial Court Records, Worcester, Mass., vol. xx, p. 185.

4. Ltr., JL to A. D. Lockwood, 5 Sept. 1872; Gibbs, *op. cit.*

5. Because the firm was a proprietorship, Whitin was restricted in the extent to which he could discount promissory notes. Ltr., JCW to S. Williston, 5 Dec. 1866. "As it respects taking notes in pay[t] for the machinery I would be willing to accommodate you if I could, but I have not the means to do it.

I have been expending a very large amt. in building and [have] rec^d no return from it and shall not for a long time. I am alone in the machine business and cannot honour money as well as if I had other business connections."

6. Massachusetts State Library, Acts and Resolves Passed by the General Court of Massachusetts in the Years 1868 and 1869, chap. 140, p. 107. The form used in the Whitin charter was fairly standard. Notice how similar it was to the 1845 charter of the Lowell Machine Shop quoted in the Appendices of Gibb's forthcoming history of Saco-Lowell. Notice also that John C. Whitin seems to have had in his mind the possibility that he might some day want to consolidate his machinery business with cotton manufacturing as had been the case under P. Whitin & Sons.

7. In reply to my inquiries, Mr. H. Dwight Hall, vice-president of the Boston Manufacturers Mutual Fire Insurance Company with which the Whitin Machine Works has always carried its fire insurance, wrote me the following letter regarding the Whitin company's first policy:

I have searched our records to obtain the history of the insurance first placed by the Whitin Machine Works with the Boston Manufacturers Mutual Fire Insurance Company. After a considerable amount of research work I have located what apparently is the first policy, namely:

Policy No. 6498 for $66,500. issued to John C. Whitin as of December 29, 1869, attaching from January 1, 1870, and expiring January 1, 1871.

This policy insured against damage or loss by fire, divided to apply as follows:

$ 8,000.	On Machine Shop Building and Fixtures and Fixed Machinery.
30,000.	On movable machinery and all other movable property therein contained required in the manufacture of machinery therein.
15,000.	On new Machine Shop Building and Fixtures and Fixed Machinery therein.
13,500.	On machinery, tools and all other movable property therein used or required in the manufacture of machinery.

$66,500.

The rate was 1% and the premium $665. In addition there was a deposit note of $3,325. equal to five times the premium, the note being subject to pay all such sums as may be assessed by the President and Directors of the company, pursuant to the by-laws of the company, provided that they be not allowed to pay in the whole more than double the amount of said premium and deposit. Thus they assumed the liability to pay, if required by assessment, double the amount of the premium and double the amount of the note. In other words, they assumed assessment liability equal to twelve times the amount of the premium. It is interesting to note that for the year 1870, during which this policy was in force, the company paid an average dividend of return premium of 81.07%, which was on the high side of dividends for that period as the average for the 10-year period 1861–1870, inclusive, was 67.97% with an average cost of insurance of 27.95¢ per $100. per year, whereas the cost on this particular policy for the year 1870 was approximately 19¢ per $100.

This policy was transferred January 12, 1870, to Whitin Machine Works so it appears evident to me that this must be the first policy as, apparently, the plant was originally owned by John C. Whitin, personally, and after the corporation was organized in 1870 the Whitin Machine Works took over the property.

The first plan of the Mill which we have in our files is one issued in December, 1883. A later plan issued in January, 1892, shows the old frame Mill formerly designated Carpenter Shop, Saw and Grist Mill, with a footnote that it was 83 years old, which would indicate that it was erected in 1809 [the building here referred to was the mill of the old Northbridge Cotton Manufacturing Company]. It was on or near the site now occupied by the Power House. This plan also indicates that Machine Shop No. 1, now designated No. 14 on our plan, was 45 years old in 1892, indicating it was erected in 1847. The original survey of the Village Property is dated December, 1926, as formerly we did not insure the Village Property. . . .

8. Historical sketch of the company contained in the Minutes of the Stockholders' Meetings.

9. Massachusetts General Statutes (1860), chap. 68.

10. Conversation with Mr. James R. Ferry, who can remember seeing Whitin in his wheel chair.

11. The Stafford Mills and the King Philip Mills in Fall River, Mass., were among those which ordered portions of their machinery from England and were then forced to delay their scheduled date of opening for several months because of the inability of the English to meet delivery promises.

12. These mills were the Tallasee Mfg. Co., of Montgomery, Ala., the Georgia Factory, of Athens, Ga., and the Ettrick Mfg. Co., of Petersburg, Va.

13. Ledger no. 1, Whitin Machine Works.

14. Peck & Earl, *Fall River, passim.*

15. *Ibid.,* pp. 113–150, gives a brief history of each of the Fall River mills built before 1877 and, for some of them, gives the source of their machinery.

16. Ltr., JL to S. B. Bond, 6 Mar. 1872.

17. Mason was director of at least five mills, to some or all of which he supplied machinery. Peck & Earl, *op. cit.,* pp. 121, 123, 131, 141, and 145.

18. Kilburn was director of Border City Mills, King Philip Mills, and Weetamoe Mills; Lincoln was a director of Tecumseh Mills. Although Kilburn, Lincoln & Co. was a comparatively small firm, its specialization in looms allowed it to compete with the largest units in the industry. In the years 1871–73 the company was producing an average of 2,600 looms a year. See *Journal of Econ. and Bus. Hist.,* vol. iv, no. 2 (Feb., 1932), p. 277. During

1873, the Whitin Machine Works produced 2,500 looms. Ltr., JL to A. G. Ray, 9 Sept. 1874.

19. Ltrs., JCW to W. C. Chapin, 30 Nov. 1868, and JCW to J. G. Davis, 30 June 1869.

20. Because the cost of equipping a mill varies widely with the type of yarn or cloth to be produced, no accurate statement of average costs can be made. However, a rough division of the investment required by an 1870 mill that used ring frames for both warp and filling (and not including the power unit and transmission shafts) would approximate the following pattern:

Pickers, etc.	4%
Cards, etc.	13
Drawing equipment	5
Roving equipment	25
Spinning frames	35
Dressers, warpers, spoolers, etc.	6
Looms	12
Total machinery cost	100%

See New England Cotton Manufacturers' Association *Transactions,* no. 38, 1885, p. 85. A breakdown of the expense of equipping a modern mill would be roughly similar except that carding would be proportionately more expensive and roving would be proportionately less so.

21. No sale of Whitin ring frames to a Fall River mill was made until 1874. See ltr., JL to N. B. Borden, 12 Jan. 1874.

22. Ltr., JL to J. M. Campbell, 26 Mar. 1877.

23. Machinery shipped to the South was usually insured for its billed price, plus 10% to cover transportation costs.

24. Ltr., JCW to W. H. Thompson, 3 Mar. 1863.

25. Werner Sombart, *The Jews and Modern Capitalism* (London, 1913), pp. 119–127. Sombart believed that the Jews were the first to break down this professional attitude by their emphasis on the functions of selling and advertising.

26. Ltr., JL to Greenswood Co., 18 Mar. 1871; JL to A. A. Maginnis & Sons, 18 Mar. 1881; JL to G. H. Jones, 17 Dec. 1873.

27. Ltr., JCW to Hay, McDevitt & Co., 28 Dec. 1868.

28. Clark's letterheads indicate that he dealt also in secondhand wool and worsted machinery and in all sorts of secondhand parts, such as clothing, harnesses, reeds, shuttles, and top rolls. See ltr., Jeremiah Clark to GET, 17 May 1880.

29. Ltrs., JCW to Jas. T. Dumble, 25 May 1869; JL to J. Waterman, 17 Aug. 1882.

30. Ltr., JL to Warren Mfg. Co., 14 May 1881, " . . . we do not get for a large portion of repair castings what it costs to make them." From the extant records of the company it is impossible to learn what the costs of repair parts

were. Moreover, it is doubtful whether even Lasell, considering his inadequate accounting methods, really knew.

31. As was true, for instance, in 1874; the customer was the Chicopee Mfg. Co.

32. Whitin did not like to accept drafts on banks outside either Boston or N. Y. since they cost him ¼% to cash.

33. Ltrs., JL to Enterprise Mfg. Co., 6 May 1878; JL to Messrs. Inman, 5 Oct. 1878; and JL to W. B. Whiting, 13 Mar. 1879.

34. Whitin often complained that, when a new mill was not ready to receive finished machinery, it cost him three months' insurance, storage inconvenience, and a loss of interest on his money.

CHAPTER VI

Both Chapters V and VI are based on a page-by-page reading of the *outgoing* Whitin letterbooks for the years 1870–86. Consequently they contain many statements and generalizations that are based not on any particular letters but on a large number and not on any particular facts but on a "feel" such as one inevitably picks up after reading all the letters written by a firm over a considerable number of years. Such a "feel" is exceedingly difficult to annotate and being somewhat subjective is admittedly capable of misuse. Hence, where footnotes have not been possible, I have tried to convey to the reader the idea that evidence for certain statements is substantial but not conclusive by using such words as *seem* and *appear*.

There is always a tendency among historians, especially business historians, to rely heavily on correspondence for their basic information. Actually, although letters are perhaps the most usable of all corporate records, they are by no means the most useful, and their limitations should be recognized. The bulk of a company's outgoing letters are usually written to three types of addressees — to customers, to suppliers, and to employees (especially to salesmen but sometimes to executives who are away from the home office). Letters to the last-named can be extremely revealing, for they frequently discuss or set forth company policies. Letters to suppliers tend to be stereotyped discussions of quantity, quality, price, and delivery. Letters to customers may sometimes be the same, though generally they are more varied, for they are likely to discuss credit practices, new products, manufacturing difficulties delaying deliveries, and the like. Lying scattered among all these types of letters may be found a few diamonds in the rough — letters to business friends or competitors discussing economic conditions, general business policies, and individual personalities. However, if one is to learn about a company's costs, about its financial affairs, its shop practices, or employee relations, its executive compensation plans, or any of a myriad of other administrative problems, one must look beyond the concern's letterbooks for one's facts.

A note concerning *incoming* letters is also in order at this point, although I have made little use of that particular resource in writing this book. Whitin's incoming letters are not unlike its outgoing letters to suppliers — concerned principally with matters of quantity, quality, price, and delivery. Their chief use is as a source of critical comment on the company's products. In one respect, however, the Whitin company's incoming letters are as valuable as anything in the collection, for they span the years when the South was experiencing its industrial genesis. No historian of the South's early cotton-mill experience will want to miss using those letters even if he obtains from them nothing more than the invaluable information contained on the letterheads of stationery used by the owners of the South's nascent textile mills in writing to Whitin for machinery.

There is another set of Whitin records that I have made little use of but that should prove useful to many other business historians: the company's Statement Books. Any historian writing about an American textile mill will want to check these Statement Books for the information they contain on machinery installations made by the Whitin company in practically every textile mill in the country.

1. Ltr., JL to Farrar, Follett & Co., 13 Sept. 1871.

2. In 1877 a $275 combination card required 83 square feet of card clothing. At $1 a square foot, the cost of clothing thus added $83 to the price of a carding machine. In modern times clothing costs about $190, or only 6% of the $3,000 at which a carding machine now sells.

3. Gibb's forthcoming history of the Saco-Lowell Shops. As Gibb points out, between 1840 and 1860 the major developments in the industry were the widespread adoption of the self-acting mule, the ring frame for spinning, the railway system for drawing, and the intermediate frame for roving; yet all of these had been known either in this country or in England at a much earlier date.

4. The Union Card made use of Wellman's method of stripping top flats and also of Gambrill's method of stripping rollers. Its cylinder was 48 inches in diameter, whereas the cylinder of the ordinary card was only 36 inches.

5. Ltrs., JL to E. N. Steere, 9 Apr. 1873 and to G. M. Ives, 20 Sept. 1879.

6. N.E.C.M.A. *Transactions,* no. 12, 1872, p. 37.

7. Ltr., JCW to Oakley, Whites & Co., 16 Feb. 1869.

8. In 1862 Hardy was selling his grinder for $145; Whitin was selling his for $85.

9. The first slasher brought from England was a Howard & Bullough model imported by A. D. Lockwood. N.E.C.M.A. *Transactions,* no. 6, 1869, pp. 18-21.

10. A report presented in the N.E.C.M.A. *Transactions,* no. 64, 1898, pp. 199-200, estimated that the new slasher was about ten times as productive per dollar of labor cost as the old-style dresser.

11. Ltrs., JL to J. G. Barber, 18 Jan. 1870, and to Androscoggin Mills, 23 May 1871.

12. In the N.E.C.M.A. *Transactions,* no. 13, 1872, p. 8, both George Draper

and A. G. Cumnock opined that most inventions had come from the mechanic and overseer class in the mills.

13. Quotations from biographical sketches at the back of the Minutes of the Stockholders' Meetings of the Whitin Machine Works.

14. In 1884 the Whitin Machine Works was forced to pay John Lord $25 for every lapper the company had manufactured since 1877.

15. After 1879 no further addition to the carding line was made until 1894 when the company brought out its first revolving flat card.

16. This stripper made use of a Foss skip wheel and was commonly referred to as the "Foss Stripper," apparently because it threatened such direct competition with the Wellman stripper that Lasell was unwilling to have the Taft or Whitin name connected with it (Taft had consigned the patent to the Whitin Machine Works); in fact Lasell paid Wellman a royalty on all Foss strippers sold, just to avoid any possible litigation. The Foss-Taft improvement made possible the double stripping of those flats which stood nearest the feed rolls and which consequently performed the greatest stripping work. Taft tried to persuade Platt Bros., of Oldham, England, to introduce the new stripper in England, but apparently in vain.

17. The throstle was not, in principle, very different from the old Arkwright water frame. In fact Evan Leigh, in his *The Science of Modern Cotton Spinning* (Manchester, 1877), vol. i, p. 207, stated that the only reason the name water frame was dropped in England and the term throstle frame substituted in its place was because the advent of steam power had made the term archaic. He believed that the name throstle may have been adopted because the machine sang like a throstle, the Scottish name for a thrush.

18. Although bearing virtually the same names, the two Pollocks were no more closely related than, at the most, cousins. The father of C. E. was James Pollock, of Burrillville, R. I.; the father of C. H. was Samuel Pollock, of Blackstone, Mass.

19. See letterbook no. 9, p. 449.

20. Ltr., JL to Wm. Mason, 20 Feb. 1873.

21. Geo. Draper & Son also switched from Scotch to American pig iron at about the same time. N.E.C.M.A. *Transactions,* no. 20, 1876, p. 22.

22. A. D. Lockwood, one of the most prominent of the early mill engineers, had begun acting in that capacity at least as early as 1855 (see Van Slyck, *Reps. of New Eng.: Mfrs.,* p. 308); and C. T. James, at one time a superintendent of Slater's steam cotton mills, served as a consultant for many steam-powered mills built during the 1840's. *Textile World,* Dec., 1901, pp. 1083-1084, states that David Whitman (beginning around 1825) was probably the first mill engineer in this country.

23. The following mill engineers were recommended to customers by Lasell (the date indicates the first recommendation):

John Rhodes Brown	Montgomery, Ala.	(1871)
William A. Thompson	Boston, Mass.	(1871)
A. D. Lockwood	Providence, R. I.	(1872)

Daniel Keith	Columbus, Ga.	(1874)
D. M. Thompson	Providence, R. I.	(1878)
Shedd & Sawyer	Boston, Mass.	(1880)
John Hill	Columbus, Ga.	(1880)
Carlos Nudd	Providence, R. I.	(1880)

24. A gauge is determined by measuring the distance between spindle centers. Before 1879 the standard gauge was 2½ inches; after 1879, it became 2¾ inches.

25. Introduced in 1876, the narrow frame enjoyed for a time a remarkable popularity. In 1878 Lasell wrote that nearly all orders for ring spinning were for narrow frames. Their chief appeal was the small floor space they occupied, but apparently their narrowness reduced their stability. By 1883 the company had returned to the 36 and 39 inch widths which still remain the standard sizes. In later years George Marston Whitin commented on the narrow frame as follows (ltr. to SWC, 24 Oct. 1904): "We made a frame 28″ wide and the Saco shop made one 32″ wide. I think . . . we sold a great many of these narrow frames because people could get a large number onto the floor space, but we were never successful with the frame. After they had been running awhile people had trouble with the bands coming off."

CHAPTER VII

1. The account of Lasell's death is taken from an obituary sketch preserved by the company in its letterbook no. 22. The author of the account seems to have been Lasell's son, Josiah M. Lasell.

2. George Marston Whitin was elected treasurer of the company on 22 January 1886, two months before Josiah Lasell's death.

3. Taft's illness is described in an obituary sketch at the back of the Whitin Machine Works' Minutes of Stockholders' Meetings.

CHAPTER VIII

The primary source materials for Chapter VIII were a half-dozen Job Order books (1864–1911), George Marston Whitin's personal Treasurer's Book, and numerous conversations with veteran employees. The chapter is an attempt to get below the policy level of top management for a look at how shop operations were conducted in the 1880's and 1890's.

It is also an attempt to take a look at plant organization, especially at that part of plant organization that is sometimes called middle management. It deals with a group of men who are all too easily overlooked. For sake of simplicity we often say that a "company" has done this, or its "president" has done that, when in truth the former, as a legal concept, is incapable of any action whatsoever, while the latter, as a human being is capable of only a fraction of what is generally attributed to him. In permitting ourselves such free use of a figure of speech, we sometimes anesthetize our minds to reality. (Of course, what is true of subordinate officials is even more true of men at the bench; but being too numerous for individual recognition, they and their accomplishments seldom find a way into corporate records and so their deeds are lost completely to history.)

Because the source material on the Whitin supervisory group is so scant, I have not been able to deal with the subject at very great length. Since the job-work system has received such little attention from historians, I have concentrated on the subject as practiced in Whitinsville, even though most of the Whitin company's job-work records concern a period when job work was declining. When we have more information regarding job work, it may be that we shall conclude that the contract system of shop organization stood historically between the central workshop and the factory in the development of large-scale manufacturing.

In addition I have tried to present, in condensed form, an analysis of Marston Whitin's own personal accounting system — not because it is a model of accounting systems in that era, but because it is representative of the way so many industrialists of Marston Whitin's type ran their companies.

1. Except where otherwise noted, information in this section was obtained in conversation with four of the company's long-service employees — James R. Ferry, Albert J. Brown, C. T. Moffett, and Ernest Booth.

2. See George S. Gibb, *The Whitesmiths of Taunton: A History of Reed & Barton, 1824-1943* (Cambridge, 1943), pp. 70-71, and his forthcoming history of the Saco-Lowell Shops.

3. C. E. Pollock (spinning frames), B. L. M. Smith (rolls), Oscar Taft (bolsters), and Carlos Heath (gears).

4. In Jan., 1900, the first month for which Smith's department appeared separately on the payroll, he had 80 men, 22 of whom were being paid only 70 cents per day. The average pay for his department was $1.01 per day, whereas the average for the entire company in that year was $1.65.

5. Henry Roland, "Six Examples of Successful Shop Management," *The Engineering Magazine,* Oct., 1896, p. 76.

6. The following men were on job work at least as early as 1870 and continued until the date shown. Joshua T. Carter (card troughs) 1892, Robert Foster (planing) 1900, Joseph Hanna (rings) 1887, John Harrington (card parts) 1894, Henry F. Woodmancy (spindles) 1898, Carlos Heath (gears) 1900, Henry C. Peck (pickers) 1899, Charles E. Pollock (spinning frames) 1898, J. F. Schofield (card erection) 1890, B. L. M. Smith (rolls) 1906, David Smith (railway heads) 1898, Oscar F. Taft (bolsters) 1906, Orrin Wade (stands) 1887. Complete lists of job workers and foremen from 1894 to the present have been compiled and presented to the Whitinsville Free Library.

7. Leverett S. Lyon, *Education for Business* (Chicago, 1922), p. 270.

8. Ltr., WMW to W. C. Coker, 28 Aug. 1889. From Feb., 1873, to Jan.,

1883, the cashbooks contain no forwarding balances. No breakdown of dollar sales by types of machinery was made until 1901.

9. The first "statement of condition" was made in 1876. The balance sheets contained in these statements have not been reproduced in an appendix because they contain such limited information. They are available, for the asking, at the Massachusetts State House, in Boston.

10. In 1890, for instance, the inventory valuation was only $143,625.26, although the insurance carried on iron inventories alone amounted to $200,-000.

11. Physical asset inventories were taken only occasionally. Gustavus Taft once stated (see ltr. to O. B. Smith, 29 Jan. 1883) that the company depreciated its machine tools 5% the 3rd year, 6% the 4th, 7% the 5th, 8% the 6th, 9% the 7th, 10% the 8th and 10% on the remaining value for every year thereafter.

12. According to the ledger account (which may not have included all items of expense) Shop No. 3 cost roughly $92,000.

13. In 1900, when the plant and machinery account was being carried at $525,000, the insurance valuation (also no doubt conservative) was:

Buildings	$ 317,069
Machinery	289,750
Raw Materials (iron)	200,000
Work in Progress	201,140
Patterns	60,000
	$1,067,959

14. The company's depreciation of its boarding-house property is an example of Marston Whitin's approach to accounting. Boarders were charged $3.50 per week. Usually the charge was simply deducted from their pay. Whitin set up a depreciation reserve which he credited with 25 cents for each $3.50 deducted. Thus, his depreciation rate fluctuated with income. He seems to have considered the reserve as a loan to the company's working-capital funds, for he made a practice of crediting the account with a regular 4% interest payment. See ltr., GMW to Arthur Clark, 1 Nov. 1886.

15. During the years 1889–91, profits came from the following sources:

Manufacturing	50%
Spindle royalties	25
Interest on notes	15
Housing rentals	10
Total	100%

16. Gibb's forthcoming history of the Saco-Lowell Shops.

17. In the U. S. Bureau of Foreign and Domestic Commerce Misc. Series No. 37, five of the six companies studied enjoyed an average return of be-

tween 21.84% and 35.16% on sales. These figures do not include depreciation.

18. If extra charges for long-draft are omitted from modern spinning prices, the ratio between revolving flat-card prices and spinning-frame prices per spindle is still roughly 200 to 1.

19. In the company's printed price book of 1913, the roving constants are the same as those used today. It is not unlikely that these constants were in use as early as 1910 and that they came to the Whitin Machine Works with the purchase of the Providence Machine Co.

20. Until 1902, Marston Whitin also bought all lumber supplies personally. In that year, however, he turned over the responsibility for making iron and lumber purchases to his assistant, George B. Hamblin. Steel and other miscellaneous shop and foundry supplies were bought through the superintendent's office. Machine tools were bought on the advice of the master mechanic. (Conversation with R. E. Lincoln who began work in the company's front office in 1901.)

21. Ltr., GMW to C. L. Pierson & Co., 27 June 1898.

CHAPTER IX

Where possible I have striven to narrate the Whitin company's history in chronological form. For the years 1880–1900, however, the threads of the story become so entangled, with developments both in Whitinsville and in the South, that I have had to treat those two decades topically. Therefore, in Chapters VIII, IX, and X I have dealt with different aspects of the New England end of the business, and then beginning with Chapter XI I have concentrated for two chapters on what was happening in the South.

Most of the information contained in Chapter IX was obtained in conversation with villagers. Such information was obtainable from no other source. Inevitably, viewpoint and prejudice heavily govern the information gleaned in such a manner, so that I have felt constrained to distinguish, insofar as I could, between reportorial fact and unsubstantiated fancy.

In a village the size of Whitinsville, one is bound to encounter a considerable amount of rumor. The people in the valley never tire of discussing the people on the hill. Scandal is always a favorite topic of conversation, and certain branches of the Whitin family have contributed their share to the fund of gossip. But the members of the machinery branch of the family have been uncommonly circumspect in their behavior and have never allowed their personal life to do injustice to the reputation of their firm either in Whitinsville or elsewhere.

In treating of the family in this chapter, I have dealt only with the aspects of family life that have had an immediate bearing on the company's history. While it was still in manuscript form, I read the chapter to various family members to get a judgment on the accuracy of my statements. In a few cases I agreed to make certain changes and deletions which I considered unimportant to the machine-shop history. This chapter is the only one in the book that has been altered in any way by request of the company's owners.

In writing this chapter I adopted a piece of journalistic license that needs a word of explanation. To distinguish Josiah Manning Lasell from his father, Josiah Lasell, and from his son, Josiah Lasell II, I have referred to him simply as "J. M." Actually he was never known by his initials. His friends usually called him "Joe."

1. Conversation with C. T. Moffett who came to Whitinsville in 1894 from the Brown & Sharpe Mfg. Co., of Providence, to act as asst. foreman in the expanding foundry.

2. In 1948 the people living in Whitin Machine Works' houses belonged to the following nationalities:

Yankee and English	40%
Irish and Scotch-Irish	25
French and French-Canadian	15
Dutch	8
Armenian	7
All other	5
Total	100%

Averages based on 1948 Tenement Report compiled by James R. Ferry.

Averages have been rounded off on the assumption that intermarriages have made any list somewhat arbitrary.

3. Conversation with George Marston Whitin's daughter, Mrs. Sydney R. Mason.

4. See ltrs., GMW to Wm. Draper, 28 Apr. and 10 May 1886 and 5 Oct. 1893.

5. See ltrs., JL to Walcott & Campbell, 16 Jan. 1874, and to Henry A. Whipple, 5 Dec. 1874.

6. Conversation with Stephen M. Machoian, whose uncle sent him money to make the trip from Armenia to Marseilles, to New York, and then to Whitinsville.

7. Roland, "Six Examples of Successful Shop Management," p. 78.

8. James H. Tashijian, *The Armenians of the United States and Canada* (Boston, 1947), p. 20.

9. Conversation with Jacob Feddema, whose uncle's brother-in-law was John Bosma, the first Dutch settler in Whitinsville. Jacob arrived in Whitinsville with his mother and four brothers and sisters in 1888.

10. According to an entry of that date in a diary kept by the manager of Castle Hill Farm. The diary is among the Whitin Machine Works records.

11. Conversation with Anske Fortuin, whose father was minister of the Dutch Reformed Church in Whitinsville from 1906 to 1921.

12. Conversation with John Vanderbaan, who in 1895 was induced to

leave Utica, N. Y., for Whitinsville by news that a Dutch Reformed Church had been established there.

13. Even if the large company-owned herd on Castle Hill Farm (about 175 head) were included, the Dutch holdings would still account for 45 per cent of the town's dairy cows.

14. Conversation with James G. Mandalian, editor of the *Hairenik Weekly*. Also, Simon Vratzian, *Armenia and the Armenian Question* (Boston, 1943), pp. 80–82.

15. The dates have been supplied me by the following lodge secretaries (listed in the order in which their lodges appear in the text): John D. Leonard, Albert J. Brown, M. Lynn Richardson, A. Norman White, Mrs. Charlotte H. Clark, Mrs. Ethel Hix, John D. Leonard, and Miss Margaret Keeler.

16. See Worcester County deed book 412, pp. 453 and 593.

17. In his *Broken Fetters, the Light of Ages on Intoxication* (Boston, 1888), p. 303, Charles Morris writes, "The prohibitory movement of the present century within the United States began with the refusal to grant licenses in certain localities. The earliest case on record is that of the town of Harwich, Mass., where in 1829 the selectmen were instructed not to grant licenses."

18. Morris, *op. cit.*, p. 318.

19. In 1895, apparently after the adjoining town of Sutton had gone "wet," J. M. Lasell wrote a letter of protest to one E. E. Clark, superintendent of the Manchaug Mills and a leading figure in Sutton politics: "In behalf of the Whitin Machine Works I wish to enter a strong protest against granting any liquor licenses to parties to do business technically in the town of Sutton but practically in Northbridge. I have reference particularly to the locality known as 'Hockanum' in the west part of the town & to such a place as Horace Bachelor's hotel [now revived as the Green Lantern]. The influence of the former resort during those years when licenses have been granted there has been extremely demoralising to our workmen & the community. Two men have ended their careers practically on the premises from the result of alcoholism. If further proof is needed of the character of this locality, we think the constable of the town will be glad to testify. We think you will agree with us that it is hardly fair that Northbridge should be subject to the disadvantages of legislation enacted by Sutton with no share in the financial gain. Hoping that your board will see the justice of our remonstrance — "

George Hanna, an old-timer around Whitinsville who is familiar with virtually everything, real and rumored, that ever happened in town, tells me that one of the men killed was a certain David Casey, who fell off a stone embankment as he was walking home, and that soon thereafter Bachelor's license was not reissued. Town Hall records show that one David Casey "accidentally fell from a bank wall" and died 4 Sept. 1893.

20. Conversation with William L. Taft, the son of Edmund and the only remaining Taft in Whitinsville, 3 Aug. 1948.

21. One daughter, Ruth, married and moved to Providence. The other, Myra, married and moved to California.

22. Patent no. 112,655 on a spinning-ring improvement, dated 14 Mar. 1871, granted to C. E. Trowbridge; patent no. 126,120 on a tool for boring spinning rings, dated 23 Apr. 1872, granted to Arthur Whitin; patent no. 127,-121 on a tool for grooving spinning rings, dated 21 May 1872, granted to C. E. Trowbridge.

23. The Whitinsville Spinning Ring Co. also sold a large number of rings to the Saco-Lowell Shops until that company bought its own ring-making company in 1919. Conversation with Stuart F. Brown, 3 Aug. 1948. Stuart Brown is the son of Robert K. Brown who was for many years bookkeeper of the Whitin Machine Works.

24. The hospital is located in a renovated dwelling given to the village by the Whitin Machine Works in 1915. See Minutes of the Board of Directors' Meeting, 18 Jan. 1915.

25. The franchise enabling the Blackstone Valley Street Railway to extend its line into Rockdale was granted by the Northbridge Board of Selectmen on 3 Apr. 1893. Minutes of the Meetings of the Board of Selectmen.

26. The franchise allowing the Worcester & Blackstone Valley Street Railway to extend its line from Rockdale to Whitinsville, via Riverdale, was granted by the Northbridge Board of Selectmen on 6 Mar. 1899. Minutes of the Meetings of the Board of Selectmen. The company had opposed the route through Riverdale, preferring instead a route through Northbridge Center. Ltr., JML to Whittall & Thomas, 4 May 1898.

27. The information concerning the Chester Lasells was gathered in a series of interviews with Mrs. Chester Lasell. Information concerning Mr. and Mrs. George Marston Whitin was obtained in conversation with two of their daughters, Mrs. Lawrence M. Keeler, and Mrs. Sydney R. Mason, and with a son-in-law, E. Kent Swift.

28. At his death Chester willed his farm to his groom, John White, who operated it as a stable for racers.

29. Something of the spirit of Jessie Lasell's vivacity is captured by Elizabeth Foster in her book, *The Islanders* (Boston, 1946), in which she relates how her grandfather, a Philadelphia lawyer, established a summer place on an island in Rangeley Lake, Maine. Chester, J. M., and Marston jointly maintained a lodge near Rangeley and came to be close friends of Mrs. Foster and her grandparents, the Dicksons. See especially pp. 15, 74, 206, and 267.

30. Except where otherwise noted, information concerning Sarah Elizabeth Whitin was obtained in conversation with her grandniece, Mrs. J. M. Lasell.

31. *Biographical Directory of the American Congress: 1774–1927* (Washington, 1928), p. 1421.

CHAPTER X

Most of the information contained in this chapter was found in sources outside the Whitin company's records. Particularly valuable were the lengthy transcripts of evidence taken during three key patent suits, *Oliver Pearl et al.* v. *Appleton Co. et al.*, *Sawyer Spindle Co.* v. *Eureka Spindle Co.*, and *Whitin Machine Works* v. *Sawyer Spindle Co.* All three cases were long-drawn-out affairs. The testimony in the Pearl-Appleton suit covered 3,360 printed pages and in the Whitin-Sawyer suit, 1,040 pages. Like most testimony, the facts recorded in these transcripts are involved, conflicting, inaccurate, and incomplete.

Part of the difficulty arising out of the use of testimony for historical purposes is the technique used by the lawyer when he wishes to emphasize specific truths at the expense of general ones. Time after time, in the testimony of the Whitin-Sawyer suit, the voluble William F. Draper seems about to state the essence of the case as he saw it, when he is cut off by objections from the plaintiff's attorney. The value of testimony is consequently restricted in many cases to the specific facts brought forth.

Added material was found in correspondence between the Whitins and the Drapers; however, since the two parties were located near each other geographically, it seems clear that many vital issues were discussed in person and consequently were not committed to permanent record.

The Whitin company also has in its possession a manuscript written by the late Bertram Sweet, formerly head of the company's spindle department. In his manuscript Sweet has presented a detailed history of the technical evolution of the Gravity Spindle. Because I was more interested in the administrative problems raised by the spindle controversy than in the spindle's technical performance, I made very little use of Sweet's report. I mention it here merely to have its existence on record.

I owe a special debt of gratitude in the preparation of this chapter to George West, the Whitin company's patent expert. He spent many hours of his time helping me dig through the printed material on the spindle controversy. His office is a mine of technical information that I could not have found duplicated in any other place.

1. Commenting on the modern spindle, Robert E. Naumberg stated, in the November, 1924, issue of *Mechanical Engineering,* "Improvements have been made in the process of manufacture, the quality of steel has improved, the heat treatment is more scientific, the workmanship more accurate, but the mechanical principles are practically unchanged. In recent years the number of applications for spindle patents has greatly decreased."

2. *Whitin Machine Works* v. *Sawyer Spindle Co.* (Boston, 1893), p. 393.

3. Materials on the early history of the ring spindle have been taken from the printed testimony given in the case of *Oliver Pearl et al.* v. *Appleton Co. et al.* (Boston, 1880). See especially the "Synopsis of Brief."

4. *Pearl* v. *Appleton Co.,* testimony of Gustavus Taft, pp. 1184–1192.

5. N.E.C.M.A. *Transactions,* no. 50, 1891, p. 23.

6. See N.E.C.M.A. *Transactions,* no. 10, 1871, pp. 47–52, "Description of a Recent Improvement in Ring Spinning Machinery," by J. H. Sawyer.

7. Later a slightly heavier spindle was found to be more satisfactory. The Sawyer patent bore the number 113,575 and was issued [eleven] Apr. 1871, a week before the invention was made public.

8. Virtually all the mills in New England were soon making dynamometer tests on every type and model of textile machine then in existence. The dynamometer had been designed by James B. Francis, the brilliant engineer of the Locks and Canals Company at Lowell. To meet the demand for running dynamometer tests, several men made themselves specialists in the trade. Probably the best-known was Samuel Webber, a man who was to run many tests for the Whitin Machine Works. After a varied career as the agent of several different mills he took up power testing in 1871 and for the next ten years made a good living doing nothing else. See biographical sketch, *Textile World,* May, 1902, pp. 875–876.

9. The exact date of the Sawyer-Draper agreement I have been unable to learn. It certainly preceded 11 Mar. 1871, the date on which Draper wrote to Taft to arrange for frames into which the Sawyer spindles for the Lonsdale order could be put.

10. N.E.C.M.A. *Transactions,* no. 13, 1872, p. 7.

11. N.E.C.M.A. *Transactions,* no. 11, 1871, p. 14; ltr., JL to Collins Arnold, 14 July 1871.

12. Draper, *Recollections of a Varied Career,* pp. 178, 182.

13. This agreement has not been preserved among the Whitin records, but its terms were so thoroughly discussed in later letters that its general provisions are evident.

14. Ltr., JL to Geo. Draper & Son, 7 Dec. 1876.

15. Ltr., JL to J. L. Bacon, 29 July 1876.

16. Ltr., JL to M. Gambrill & Co., 20 Sept. 1879.

17. See testimony of Wm. F. Draper in *Sawyer Spindle Co.* v. *Eureka Spindle Co.* (Boston, 1887), pp. 169, 173.

18. Most of the following account has been taken from testimony given in the case of *Pearl* v. *Appleton Co.*

19. Ltr., Geo. Draper & Sons to JL, 7 Feb. 1879.

20. See U. S. Circuit Court decision 3F153.

21. According to Lasell, Fales, Jenks & Sons did occasionally produce Sawyer frames, though only on a limited basis. Ltr., JL to Nathaniel B. Borden, 13 Feb. 1874.

22. Ltr., JL to L. Blackstone, 8 June 1872.

23. Ltr., Geo. Draper & Son to JL, 1 July 1874.

24. Ltr., Geo. Draper & Son to JL, 7 Sept. 1874. Draper based his case on patent no. 127,159, issued 27 May 1872 and reissued 18 Aug. 1874.

25. *Whitin* v. *Sawyer,* p. 394.

26. *Ibid.,* p. 390.

27. *Ibid.,* p. 397.

28. Ltr., JL to Asa Flansburg, 18 Mar. 1880.

29. Woodmancy had learned the spindle business while working in Spindle-ville, a part of Hopedale. (The *Whitin Spindle,* Sept., 1919, p. 12.)

30. Ltr., JL to Geo. Draper & Sons, 28 Nov. 1882, dates the beginning of experimentation on the Gravity Spindle back to Nov., or Dec., 1879. Taft and Woodmancy received their patent on 11 Sept. 1883. They also secured patents in Great Britain, France, Germany, and Belgium, but the Gravity Spindle attracted very little attention abroad. Taft assigned his share in the American patent to the Whitin Machine Works, but Woodmancy gave the company only "shop rights," reserving other rights to himself.

31. *Whitin* v. *Sawyer,* pp. 46–47.

32. Massachusetts Supreme Judicial Court Case no. 450, on file at the Worcester County Courthouse, Worcester, Mass.

33. By mutual agreement, the third arbitrator required by the agreement was dispensed with.

34. Application had been filed 3 Oct. 1885; the patent was granted 15 Oct. 1889.

35. Ltr., Geo. Draper & Sons to JL, 18 Jan. 1890.

36. *Ibid.*

37. Ltr., GMW to Edward Wetmore, 9 Oct. 1890. At the request of the Drapers the case was transferred to the Massachusetts Supreme Judicial Court.

38. Ltr., GMW to Wm. F. Draper, 16 Dec. 1890.

39. See ltr., GMW to Wm. F. Draper, 9 Aug. 1892.

40. *Whitin* v. *Sawyer,* p. 499.

41. *Ibid.,* p. 470.

42. *Ibid.,* p. 36.

43. Draper, *op. cit.,* pp. 216–217.

CHAPTER XI

Chapter XI is as conspicuous for what it leaves out as for what it includes. The rise of cotton mills in the South is a subject that a chapter like this can only scratch. Even Broadus Mitchell's book by that title is no more than a prologue to the real story, a story that business and economic historians alike have generally overlooked. We can only hope that history students will not continue to leave this fertile field untilled.

The portion of the story that the history of a textile machinery firm should deal with at length is the part played by machine-builders in financing the Southern development through stock subscriptions. The manner in which the growth of the American economy has been financed is a subject of peren-nial interest both here and abroad, and stock-taking by builders of producers' goods has played a leading rôle. (For instance, the early financing of the elec-tric power industry in the United States was aided in this fashion.) But un-fortunately the Whitin Machine Works kept so few records of its stock transactions that a full exposition of its contribution to the South's development has not been possible.

By a thorough reading of Marston Whitin's letters I was able to compile a list of mills whose securities he either agreed to accept or at least considered accepting. But such a list, though helpful to the researcher, is apt to be misleading to the reader, since there is no certainty that it is not filled with errors. Furthermore, such a list concerns the intimate corporate affairs of every cotton mill on it. To reproduce the list, I felt I should obtain permission from all the mills shown. My chances of success in that venture being small, I decided to confine my remarks about the Whitin company's stock holdings to generalizations.

1. N.E.C.M.A. *Transactions,* no. 71, 1901, p. 297.

2. Thomas P. Martin, "The Advent of William Gregg and the Graniteville Co.," *The Journal of Southern History,* Aug. 1945, pp. 411, 415.

3. Broadus Mitchell, *William Gregg* (Chapel Hill, 1928), p. 131. See also Mitchell's sketch of H. P. Hammett in the *Dictionary of American Biography,* in which he states that Hammett's father-in-law, when erecting his first mill in the South (c. 1830), used secondhand English machinery.

4. Edwin T. Freedley, *Philadelphia and Its Manufactures* (Philadelphia, 1858), p. 427.

5. Ltr., C. T. Harden to WMW, 13 Aug. 1880.

6. Compare Freedley, *op. cit.* (1867 ed.), p. 351, with Dockham's *Directory,* 1888, p. 4.

7. In Sept., 1873, Hammett wrote to the Whitin company asking for prices on machinery to outfit a 3,584-spindle mill. The reply, written by Josiah Lasell, quoted a total figure of $41,693, plus charges for boxing. A week later Hammett wrote Lasell, placing the order at the figure quoted. On 12 Nov., however, Lasell received a request to cancel the order; the widespread financial panic which had followed the failure of the banking firm of Jay Cooke & Co. had caused Hammett to delay his plans indefinitely. In August of the following year, Hammett seems to have seen reason for greater confidence in the future, for he again wrote Lasell for prices. His second order, virtually the same as the first, was not finally placed, however, until May, 1875, because of the difficulty he encountered in raising capital. So far had the prices of machinery fallen since the first order that the second was placed for only $30,216. Delivery was scheduled for July, 1875, but because the mill structure was not completed in time, the machinery was not shipped until August. The bill (which including extras amounted to $31,-825.20) was dated 31 Aug. 1875. Not a cent of this bill seems to have been paid upon its presentation. After dunning Hammett for nearly a year, Lasell (at the bidding of John C. Whitin) agreed to accept five notes for $5,000 each payable monthly beginning Aug., 1876, plus a sixth note covering the remainder of the mill's indebtedness, payable in Jan., 1877. In Nov., 1876, Hammett wrote confidently that the mill was running well, but added that he

would have to default his fourth note, just as he had the preceding three. Lasell replied with a request for a balance sheet of the mill and a report of current production. In May, 1877, with his bill still completely unpaid, Hammett wrote that he was in the process of raising more capital and hoped soon to be able to settle his debt. On 3 July 1877, the Whitin company received a draft for $25,200 from Piedmont. Nearly all the remainder of the debt was settled by John C. Whitin's offer to take $16,000 worth of newly issued stock, $8,000 of which he paid for at once. (Cumulative interest and orders for additional parts had meanwhile increased the debt to $34,642.65.) Within six days after he had settled his debt with the Whitin company, Hammett was writing for a bid on another and still larger lot of machinery.

8. Ltr., JCW to H. G. Hall, 28 May 1869.

9. D. A. Tompkins credits Piedmont's success to its being the first mill to be equipped with the new type of machinery that had been developed in the early 1870's. See D. A. Tompkins, *Cotton Mill, Commercial Features* (Charlotte, 1899), p. 189.

10. See the biographical sketch of H. P. Hammett in *Dict. of Am. Biog.*

11. Gibb's forthcoming history of the Saco-Lowell Shops.

12. GMW's Treasurer's Book.

13. Broadus Mitchell, *The Rise of Cotton Mills in the South* (Baltimore, 1921), pp. 105–112.

14. Ltr., SWC to GMW, 21 Apr. 1896.

15. Ltr., JL to W. Seabury Simmons, 17 Nov. 1885.

16. Ltr., C. T. Harden to WMW, 13 Aug. 1880.

17. There is no reference in the letterbooks or in the ledger to indicate that Whitin had a display at Atlanta; in contrast there are several references to the exhibit of machinery at the New Orleans Exposition of 1884–85.

18. Ltr., JL to Dwight Mfg. Co., 8 Aug. 1882. The Whitins station on the Providence & Worcester Railroad was constructed in 1866 at a cost to the railroad company of $3,271.40. See 22nd Annual Report of the P.&W.R.R.

19. Ltr., JL to Canada Cotton Mfg. Co., 9 Dec. 1879. When the standard car was enlarged from 30′ to 34′ and the door width was increased from 4′ to 5′, the end-door car became obsolete.

20. Ltr., JL to W. G. & O. M. Anderson, 4 Dec. 1867.

21. George S. Gibb, the author of Saco-Lowell's forthcoming history, has checked the Lowell Machine Shop letters for some evidence bearing on this point but has failed to find anything either in confirmation or rebuttal.

22. Ltr., W. H. Greenwood to the Draper Co., 6 July 1917.

23. Wade's *Fibre and Fabric*, 26 Aug. 1893, p. 316, and *Textile World*, Apr., 1895, p. 39.

24. See the biographical sketch of D. A. Tompkins in *Dict. of Am. Biog.* In *Cotton Mill, Commercial Features*, p. 40, Tompkins states that he began business in Charlotte in 1884.

25. Much of the following two paragraphs is paraphrased from a long letter written by Cramer to the Whitin Machine Works, 31 Oct. 1895.

26. Tompkins, *Cotton Mill, Commercial Features*, p. 31.

27. The company bore $500 of the initial cost of setting up the office. For display purposes the office was provided with the machinery that had been recently exhibited at the International Cotton Exposition in Atlanta. (In 1901 an Atlanta office was also opened.)

28. Ltr., SWC to GMW, 18 May 1897.

29. The agreement with Cramer read as follows:

This agreement entered into this day, December 3d, 1895, between the Whitin Machine Works of Whitinsville, Massachusetts, and Stuart W. Cramer of Charlotte, N. C., is as follows:

The Whitin Machine Works appoint said Cramer as their Selling Agent in the South, and agree to pay him for his services, the sum of $900.00 per month, payable the first of each month preceding.

It is understood that said Cramer is to maintain a suitable office and display room in Charlotte, N. C., and to maintain a suitable force consisting of a competent assistant, and stenographer and typewriter. The above sum to be paid includes all travelling and other expenses excepting travelling expenses incurred in our interests outside of the State of Virginia, North and South Carolina and Georgia.

It is understood that all contracts are subject to the approval of the Whitin Machine Works.

It is understood that either party may terminate this agreement by giving to the other sixty (60) days notice, in writing.

It is agreed that this contract dates from December 3d, 1895.

Cramer chose as his assistant Paul Bigelow, another Tompkins employee. However, in Feb., 1897, Paul married and moved to New York, after which A. C. Haskell became Cramer's assistant.

30. Tompkins, *Cotton Mill, Commercial Features*, p. 31.

31. For biographical data on Cramer see *Lamb's Text. Inds. of the U. S.,* pp. 63–65.

32. Although admittedly incomplete and no doubt in many cases inaccurate, the capitalization figures in Dockham's Directories seem to bear out the general statement that mills in North Carolina were better financed than those in South Carolina. Dockham's *Directory* for 1897 indicates that North Carolina mills had an average capitalization of $15.73 per spindle while on a similar basis South Carolina's capitalization was only $14.37.

33. Ltr., SWC to GMW, 1 Feb. 1897.

34. Ltr., GMW to SWC, 18 Oct. 1904.

35. Three examples will be enough to indicate the sort of problems the Whitin company faced.

When the Loray Mills (to which the Whitin company had sold $155,881 worth of machinery and in which Whitin family members were heavy investors) failed in 1905, the Whitin Machine Works, along with the Draper

Company and the Loray Mills' selling agent, Woodward, Baldwin & Co., took over control and put in as manager a friend of Cramer's named Thomas E. Moore. In 1913, Cramer and Moore having come to an unexplained disagreement, Cramer became president of the mills. In 1919, at about the time of Cramer's retirement, the mills were sold to the Jenckes Spinning Co., of Pawtucket, R. I.

The circumstances surrounding the Whitin company's interest in the Mayes Mfg. Co. are not wholly clear. The Mayes mill was apparently a promotional effort sponsored by John H. Mayes, an employee of the Whitin Machine Works. The mill was located in Mayesworth, a village near Charlotte. In 1910 Mayes was fired by Cramer. Almost immediately his mill passed into Cramer's hands. It may have been, however, that Cramer was merely acting for the Whitin company. During the preceding two years Mayes had given the Whitin firm $55,000 in notes which may not have been paid off. (The mill's total capitalization was listed at $200,000.) In the next seven years the Whitin company put $228,600 worth of machinery into the mill, taking stock in payment, one of the few instances of stock taking by Whitin during that period. After his retirement, Cramer took full possession of the mill, changing its name to Cramerton Mills, Inc. (See also Chapter XIII, 21n.)

A third instance in which the Whitin firm became involved in the control of a mill was in connection with the failure of the Overland Cotton Mills of Denver, Colo., in 1903. With unfavorable freight rates on its raw cotton, the mill was already having financial difficulties when its owner, John Jerome, died. The Whitin Machine Works, holding $214,000 in mortgage bonds, foreclosed and bought the property at auction. Disposing of the machinery was a comparatively easy matter, but the property itself was not finally and completely sold until 1947.

36. Ltr., GMW to SWC, 10 Mar. 1902.

37. Ltr., GMW to SWC, 24 Aug., 1900. In Mass., however, the recording of conditional sales was not required by law. See ltr., EKS to Wm. C. Peirce, 1 Nov. 1909.

38. The year 1909 was chosen for the purpose of this table, first because there is no complete information regarding sales terms before 1907, and secondly because 1907 and 1908 were years of unusual credit stringency. Unfortunately not even 1909 is wholly representative since the company was taking virtually no stocks at that time.

39. Ltr., EKS to S. C. Lowe, 22 Jan. 1915.

40. On machinery sent to the South the shipping rate per hundredweight in 1904 was 50¢. In 1887 it had been 70¢, in 1889, 64¢, in 1890, 60¢. Thus, on a machine that was heavy for its value, such as a loom, which cost about 5½¢ per pound, shipping rates increased the cost by as much as 10%. On machines that were light for their value, such as a spinning frame, which cost about 11½¢ per pound, the added cost might be not more than 5%.

41. Tompkins, op. cit., p. 39.

42. Mitchell, Rise of Cotton Mills in the South, p. 271.

43. In U. S. Bur. of For. and Dom. Com. Misc. series No. 37, p. 9, the H & B American Machine Company is said to have still retained, in 1916, "virtually all such securities accepted." Whitin is said to have retained, "the majority accepted . . . and the remainder disbursed to stockholders on a basis which required no determination of value." The Saco-Lowell Shops were reported as having "sold or disposed of practically all security [sic] accepted."

44. Ltr., JL to O. H. Sampson, 9 Mar. 1877.

45. In only a few cases was a record kept of the names of banks from which these loans were obtained. They were the Providence Institution for Savings, the Rhode Island Hospital Trust Co., the Home Savings Bank of Boston, the Fitchburg Savings Bank of Fitchburg (Mass.), and the Whitinsville National Bank. The inflated state of the company's notes payable in 1910 was no doubt due to its purchase, in the preceding year, of the Providence Machine Co. The Whitin company stopped using Providence banks around World War I because they persisted in charging ¼% more interest than banks in Boston and New York.

46. M. T. Copeland, *The Cotton Manufacturing Industry of the U. S.* (Cambridge, 1912), pp. 51–53.

47. On 18 Jan. 1909, the company adopted a bylaw reading, "The Treasurer shall have full power and authority to sell at such price and upon such terms as he shall determine, any stocks or bonds in any corporation or company held or owned by this company. . . ."

CHAPTER XII

The greater part of the information included in Chapter XII was obtained from the correspondence files of George Marston Whitin and Stuart W. Cramer. What made these files so rich as a source of materials was the fact that they contained an almost daily exchange of letters between two of the company's top executives. Nowhere is one likely to find better comment on company policies and on current business events than in the correspondence between men who are so situated that they not only have an intimate view of what is happening but in addition have a vital part in what is taking place. Here one finds frank comments on customers and competitors, on other employees of the company, on business conditions in general, and on what the company's policies are or what they should be under particular circumstances. Inter-executive correspondence is rarely found among the records of manufacturing concerns, unless the concerns have manufacturing subsidiaries. It is therefore all the more to be valued when found.

1. Ltrs., JL to Wm. F. Goulding, 7 May and 18 June 1872.

2. Ltrs., JL to Hon. Geo. F. Hoar, 4 May 1870, and E. P. Taft to JL, 19 Feb. 1880.

3. Ltr., JL to Albert Briggs, 3 Apr. 1878.

4. Hayes, *Am. Text. Mach.,* p. 64.

5. Ltr., JL to Hon. Geo. F. Hoar, 26 May 1870.

6. Ltr., Wm. F. Draper to JL, 6 Mar. 1883.

7. Ltr., Robt. H. Richardson to GMW, 20 Jan. 1890.

8. The first Whitin letter written to Riley's agency, the firm of Howard, Bullough & Riley, is dated 2 July 1883. The agency's first directory advertisements also appeared in that year.

9. Gibb's forthcoming history of the Saco-Lowell Shops.

10. Ltr., GMW to SWC, 27 Apr. 1897.

11. When the Whitin Machine Works at length brought out a revolving flat card, it was forced to pay a $5 royalty to McConnell & Higginson, of England, for the use of a grinding device and a $1.50 royalty to the Saco & Pettee Machine Shops for the privilege of manufacturing the Thompson stripping rolls.

12. See ltr., GMW to Robt. H. Stevenson (Lowell Machine Shop), 1 May 1896, ". . . The result of the meeting seems to me to leave the matter in this shape; we can probably bring about the understanding [concerning no stock taking] we wish, provided we can get Mr. Snelling [Pettee Machine Works] to engage with us. Mr. McMullan [Saco Water Power Machine Shop] has, by his own admission, so much stock on hand that he cannot be much of a factor in any arrangement we make for some time. In regard to the Pettee Machine Works, I do not think we can do anything with them unless we are willing to meet them with a fixed price on cards, railway heads, and drawing. While we both have objections to entering into such an agreement, would it not be better policy for us to do so if we can get rid of this serious evil of stock taking? . . . From our talk Wednesday, there seems to be at present, quite a wide difference as to the selling price of revolving flat cards. Mr. Snelling stated it at $650.00 and my view was that $600.00 was a fair price. I really think that a large order from a good concern could be placed at much less than the lower price. I presume, in making a minimum price for selling Cards, that it would not be necessary to make a high price — in which case would we be any worse off on the card question than we are today? The only disadvantage that I can see would be that it would prevent us from making an especially low price where we were for some reason anxious to obtain the order."

13. The seven points as given here are a paraphrased version of information contained in a series of explanatory letters written by GMW to SWC during June, 1896. These points were also printed in what appears to have been the company's first published price books. The price books were then distributed to all salesmen with an admonition that the terms of the pricing agreement were not to be violated.

14. The other minimum prices agreed upon were:

Traverse grinders	$60
Long roll grinders	$35
Burnishing brushes	$20
Stripping brushes	$20

Drawing (6 deliveries per head) — $60 per delivery
         (5 deliveries per head) — $62 per delivery
         (4 deliveries per head) — $64 per delivery
Single railway heads $200

All American card builders entered this agreement, but the Mason Machine Works was allowed to sell a few of its new revolving flat cards at $575 until a market for them was established.

15. Ltrs., SWC to GMW, 9 Jan. 1897 and 27 Feb. 1897.
16. Ltr., GMW to SWC, 10 Dec. 1898.
17. Ltr., GMW to E. S. Draper, 9 Mar. 1899.
18. See Jonathan T. Lincoln's, "The Cotton Textile Machine Industry — American Loom Builders," *Harvard Business Review* (Oct., 1933), pp. 94–105.
19. Ltr., GMW to SWC, 3 Dec. 1904.
20. Ltr., H. C. Perham to SWC, 31 Mar. 1898.
21. Ltr., SWC to GMW, 5 Dec. 1896.
22. Ltr., GMW to SWC, 7 Mar. 1898.
23. *Ibid.,* 16 Feb. 1903.
24. The companies merged were: J. & J. Murdoch, Bisco & Denny, H. A. White Mfg. Co., W. & J. Whittemore, E. C. Waite & Co., T. K. Earle Mfg. Co., Sargent Card Clothing Co., Card clothing depts. of Jas. Smith & Co. and Davis & Furber Machine Co., Decher & Bonitz Co., Stedmen & Fuller Mfg. Co., E. P. Stetson, D. F. Robinson, and the Lowell Card Co. About 1901 the Ashworth brothers (Henry and R. C.), of Fall River, began marketing a superior clothing for revolving flat cards. These brothers soon attracted the support of American card builders who had been experiencing difficulties with the high price and slow deliveries of Sykes clothing, the leading and indeed dominant English brand of clothing. Therefore, around 1905, several American card builders including Whitin agreed to help finance the Ashworth brothers so that they could expand (at the same time taking over the American Card Clothing Co.) and could supply the American market with high-grade clothing. In return for their stock subscription, the machine-builders were apparently given special price concessions. George Marston Whitin claimed that Ashworth clothing was in every respect equal to that made by Sykes, but not for nearly a decade was he able to convince his customers of that fact. The Whitin company still retains its original interest in the Ashworth company.

25. The exact date of Cramer's agreement with Campbell is uncertain because the letter in which Cramer announced to Whitin his success in reaching an agreement with the Woonsocket people is dated only "Sunday."

CHAPTER XIII

For full understanding, this chapter should be read in conjunction with the parallel chapter in Gibb's forthcoming history of the Saco-Lowell Shops.

Necessarily much of the information contained herein is based on a knowledge of what was happening at Lowell, at Newton Upper Falls, at Biddeford, and more especially at the Boston headquarters of all those companies. Consequently, even though footnotes have not always been possible, because of the general nature of the material used and because Gibb's book was still in manuscript form when this book went to press, I have relied on his research extensively in the preparation of this chapter.

It should be remembered that my sources for the section on the Draper automatic loom, like the sources for my chapter on the Draper spindle pool, are necessarily secondary and therefore this chapter may be subject to revision if and when the Draper history is written from inside sources.

The other sources for this chapter are as miscellaneous as the subject matter of the chapter itself. One thing the chapter points to clearly: the need for a better understanding of the textile machinery industry as it existed in Europe. At present we know little more than the names of the firms operating abroad and, in a rough way, the products they manufactured. We know very little of their relative importance, of the source of their technological developments, or of the extent of their markets. Probably it would be safe to say that we shall never fully understand the influence of European machine-builders on the American economy until we have studied their histories from sources available only in Europe.

1. See Appendix 5 for an effort to arrive at something like reasonable figures for the company's net worth prior to 1917. In that year the accounting firm of Scovell, Wellington & Co. recommended that the Whitin firm write up its fixed assets by approximately $2,000,000 (from roughly $1,000,000 to $3,000,000). Even then the accountants admitted that the company's assets were considerably undervalued. If one considers the amount of the write-up to be a fair, if conservative, estimate of the amount of hidden profits the company had enjoyed over the years since the company's first recorded balance sheet (1876), one discovers that the company had accumulated its hidden profits at the average rate of 2% of net worth each year. The figures in Appendix 5 under Estimated Net Worth are based on a computation of what the company's net worth would have been had it shown a profit of 2% (of cumulative net worth) each year more than it did show. (I have arbitrarily included all contingency reserves in my computation of net worth.) The statistical validity of such a method of arriving at true net worth is, of course, slight. The best that can be said for the method is that it attempts to bring the company's figures a little closer to reality. That the resulting figures are still understatements of value is hardly to be doubted.

2. *Report of the Cotton Textile Mission to the United States of America, March–April, 1944* (London, 1944), p. 23.

3. For a history of the comber's development see *Lamb's Text. Inds. of the U. S.*, vol. i, pp. 77 ff.

4. *Ibid.*, p. 88.

5. N.E.C.M.A., *Transactions*, no. 72, 1902, pp. 227–238.

6. One of the first Whitin letters mentioning the new comber reads as follows: "The Whitin Combing Machinery comprises three machines: Sliver Lap Machine, Ribbon Lap Machine, and Combing Machine. The Sliver Lap Machine takes 12 to 16 card slivers, forms them into one lap; 6 of these laps are passed through the Ribbon Lap Machine forming a ribbon lap; 6 ribbon laps then enter the Carding Machine which draws them out 20 to 26 times, producing 15–20% waste."

7. Timothy O'Connell, of Holyoke, Levi Rawlinson, of Pawtucket, and Dallas B. Hathaway, of New Bedford. Apparently these men were mill hands brought to Whitinsville because of the practical experience they had had in the operation of combing machinery.

8. *Textile World*, Sept., 1903, p. 1413.

9. Ltr., GMW to SWC, 13 May 1910.

10. *Ibid.*, 4 Nov. 1909.

11. *Ibid.*, 13 May 1910.

12. *Ibid.*, 18 May 1910. In the Bur. of For. and Dom. Com. Misc. Series No. 37 (1916), it is stated that 1,163 combers were imported to the U. S. between Jan., 1909, and Dec., 1912. During that same period, the Whitin Machine Works sold 2,221 combers; thus its share of the market was probably nearer two-thirds.

13. Lowe joined the Whitin Machine Works in Sept., 1914, at a salary of $12,000. His salary was cut to $10,000 in 1915. He ceased working for the company in July, 1916.

14. For a brief history of the Providence Machine Co., see *Biographical History of the Manufacturers and Business Men of Rhode Island* (Providence, 1901), Joseph D. Hall, Jr., editor, pp. 17–18. According to the *Whitin Spindle*, Feb., 1921, pp. 14–15, the capacity of the Providence shop in 1909 was one roving frame per day.

15. A letter written 26 July 1909 to Peirce mentions an audit of the Providence accounts by certain Messrs. Hamblin and French. Although Hamblin and French may have been professional auditors, it is more likely that they were men from the Whitin office, especially since at that particular time Marston's private secretary and confidential assistant was one George B. Hamblin. It is not at all unlikely that Marston decided to send Hamblin to Providence to check the company's accounts before making a final decision as to price. Just what that final price was cannot now be determined. The figure recorded on the Whitin books was $175,000, but it seems likely that this amount was for plant and machinery only and did not include inventory. Three years later the Thomas J. Hill estate, from which Whitin bought the Providence shop, was still in possession of a Whitin company note for $200,000. The purchase agreement included "the entire number of shares of the capital stock of the Providence Machine Co., of Providence, R. I." See ltr., GMW to Wm. C. Peirce, 26 June 1912, and Minutes of the Directors' Meeting, 17 Jan. 1910.

16. Ltr., GMW to Wm. C. Peirce, 12 Oct. 1909. An account of the sale also appeared in the *Textile World Record* in Nov., 1909, p. 160.

17. After the move had been made the old plant in Providence stood empty for many years. Finally, about 1918, it was sold to the Gorham Mfg. Co., makers of silverware.

18. The first heat in the new foundry was taken off 3 Aug. 1908. Demolition of the old foundry was begun 30 Apr. 1909. Steel work on Shop No. 5 was completed 15 Dec. 1909. These dates are taken from a typewritten copy of a diary of memorable events reputedly kept by H. A. Owen, one of the Whitin shop foremen. Unless its wording has been altered in transcription, the diary indicates that the Providence purchase caused no alteration in the plans for Shop No. 5. The diary entry for 30 Apr. 1909 reads, "Start tearing down old foundry to build new shop 421' x 135'." Since the present dimensions of that shop are 421' x 135', the Providence purchase could not have resulted in any enlargement of existing plans unless another floor was added.

19. See ltr., EKS to J. H. Mayes, 15 Apr. 1910.

20. See *Textile World Record,* Mar., 1910, p. 25.

21. Immediately after Mayes was fired, Cramer took over management of the Mayes Mfg. Co. Mayes had bought most of his machinery from the Whitin Machine Works with long-term notes. Probably those notes had not yet been paid. In 1919, when Cramer retired, he became full owner of the company and changed its name to the Cramerton Mills. In 1946 the Cramerton Mills were sold to the Burlington Mills Corp.

22. For various accounts of the development of the Northrop Automatic Loom see *Textile World,* May, 1895, pp. 30–35, and Sept., 1900, pp. 431–434. See also N.E.C.M.A. *Transactions,* no. 59, 1895, pp. 88–104.

23. The Whitin Machine Works made the cards and spinning frames for the Queen City mills. The Whitin family also contributed to the project by taking approximately $20,000 in Queen City stock.

24. Ltr., GMW to Wm. F. Draper, 16 Apr. 1896.

25. Ltr., SWC to GMW, 13 Feb. 1897.

26. Ltr., GMW to SWC, 18 July 1898.

27. *Textile Texts* (Hopedale, 1901), p. vii.

28. Ltr., JML to V. P. Polevoy, 8 Nov. 1898.

29. Ltrs., GMW to SWC, 26 May 1902 and 7 Feb. 1907, and to L. E. Bromeisler, 7 Feb. 1907.

30. Whitin wrote to Cramer, 13 June 1898: "I do not think they [the Crompton Loom Works] have any occasion for getting excited on the loom business at present. It is true that we are getting up a Loom following closely the Crompton style of Box Loom, but we do not intend to take anything that is poor from their design, neither do we intend to infringe any of their patents. Anything that is good and free, we intend to help ourselves to as far as we like. Think we are going to get a mighty good Box Loom before we are through with it. The 2x1 Box Motion we have had running for a month or six weeks and it is doing first class. We are already [*sic*] to sell it, but as

to the 4x1 Box Motion, we are now working on the patterns and it will take some little time to fill an order, should say sixty to ninety days. . . . I have an idea that Crompton's prices are very stiff, at least they say they are getting $90.00 for a 2x1 box and I suppose that would mean over $100.00 for a 4x1 box."

31. Ltr., GMW to SWC, 23 June 1909.

32. Ltr., GMW to the Draper Co., 29 Dec. 1909.

33. The only company that succeeded in developing an automatic plain-goods loom on a basis different from Northrop's was the Stafford Company. In its loom the shuttle came to a stop before the bobbin was replaced. Hence it was a slower acting loom than Northrop's. See *Textile World,* May, 1905, p. 167.

34. Ltrs., LMK to *Textile World Journal,* and to the War Industries Board, 31 May 1918. At the same time the Saco-Lowell Shops also leased their Lowell loom patterns to Mason. Eventually the Whitin Machine Works sold its duck-loom patterns to Mason, but it recalled its other patterns and continued furnishing repair parts to customers until Dec., 1936, when it sold its patterns to the Draper Corp.

35. Since the Whitin company had charged all the developmental cost of its loom patents against current operations, the company's loom patents had no bookkeeping value, and hence no bookkeeping entry was involved in the distribution of patents as dividends. The company still does not capitalize such items as patents, small tools, and patterns.

36. Ltr., SWC to GMW, 20 Dec. 1899.

37. For a lengthy article on the Lowell purchase see the *Textile Manufacturers' Journal,* 17 June 1905.

38. Said the court in the Northern Securities case: "The mere existence of such a combination, and the power acquired by the holding company as its trustee, constitutes a menace to, and a restraint upon, that freedom of commerce which Congress intended to recognize and protect, and which the public is entitled to have protected." 24 S. Ct. 436 (1904).

39. Ltr., GMW to SWC, 16 Sept. 1907.

40. Ltr., GMW to Chas. T. Atherton, 29 Nov. 1912.

41. See the *Whitin Spindle,* Dec., 1924, p. 7.

CHAPTER XIV

Research in the Whitin company's letterbooks after 1895 becomes both easier and more difficult — easier because letters are typewritten after that date and more difficult because, with the advent of typewriting, letters became far more numerous. In some American companies typewriters were used as early as the 1880's, but, in general, typewriting was not adopted until the mid-1890's. The Whitin company's first typewritten letter was dated 3 April 1890, but typewritten letters do not become common in the Whitin letterbooks until after 1895. The company's first typist, or "typewriter" as he was then called, was George B. Hamblin, the man mentioned in the early part of this chapter as being Marston Whitin's right-hand assistant.

The reason for the delay of five years between the initial trial and the general adoption of typewriting in Whitinsville was the company's adherence to the practice of letter-pressing all outgoing correspondence instead of adopting carbon paper as a means of preserving copies of letters that had been typewritten. Letter-pressing involved the use of bound letter-press books containing approximately a thousand pages of fine, porous rice paper. It also required a special kind of typewriter ribbon that had to be developed especially for letter-press use. To preserve a letter-press copy of outgoing correspondence, a secretary had to place the original letter beneath the first blank page of a letter-press book. Next she had to place a damp linen cloth over the blank page and atop the cloth place a blotter. The book was then closed and pressed in a letter vice. The combination of pressure and dampness caused the blank sheet of rice paper to absorb an imprint of the letter from underneath. Since the page was very thin, the imprint came completely through the paper and could be read off directly. As the book was filled, the letters it contained were alphabetically indexed according to addressee on the book's front pages.

Soon after typewriters had come into common use, most companies did away with the practice of letter-pressing and relied wholly on carbon copies for file purposes. But the Whitin company continued pressing its letters even though it also made use of carbon copies. By this method the Whitin company has kept a permanently bound, chronological record of all the letters it has sent out since 1860. In a firm that deals with customers who still own machinery bought decades ago, the system is well worth the expense — and certainly it is a boon to the historian. The chief drawback is the miscellany of unimportant correspondence that inevitably creeps into such a record. In their anxiety to press everything that may be of later use, the company's stenographers seldom omit anything, even routine inter-office memoranda.

1. Two other key specialists were James A. Cooper on spinning, and A. K. Pratt on cards.

2. Although he was paid an apprentice's wages, Swift's pay records were kept with the office accounts. Like other office employees he was paid on a salary rather than on an hourly basis. Also, like the other employees, he drew money against his account whenever he needed it rather than at regularly stated intervals. The practice of drawing at will against salary accounts was continued at the Whitin Machine Works until 1918, after which employees were required to draw their full pay regularly.

3. Ltrs., EKS to Ed. E. Leonard, 22 Apr. 1915, and to J. E. Dunson, 4 May 1915.

4. Ltr., EKS to Robt. Schofield, 15 May 1915. "Mr. Whitin is getting along nicely; has been able to play a little golf, and is making a very quick recovery. It is pretty hard to keep him out of the shop now."

5. The name of the Blue Eagle Inn is in no way connected with the Blue

Eagle of the National Recovery Administration. The reason for giving the Inn that name has now been forgotten, but it was in existence at least a third of a century before the NRA.

6. Ltrs., SWC to GMW, 25 Apr. 1898, and GMW to SWC, 27 Jan. 1910.

7. Ltr., GMW to SWC, 24 July 1907. "The General Electric Company are trying to have us father the entire scheme of motor connections, they simply furnishing the motors. We simply refuse to do this as we have had no experience whatsoever along this electrical line." As a matter of fact, mill electrification was not new, for the Columbia Mills of Columbia, S. C., had been electrified in 1894, but the use of individual motor drives was new to the trade. Though there is undoubtedly something to be said for Marston's argument that he could not assume the risk of promoting General Electric's products, he seems to have gone far to the other extreme, for soon customers were complaining that, when they ordered spinning frames equipped with motor drives, the Whitin Machine Works charged more for mounting the motors than it would have cost them to mount the motors themselves.

8. See *The Cotton Spinning Machinery Industry: Report on the Cost of Production of Cotton-Spinning Machinery in the United States,* U. S. Dept. of Com., Bur. of For. and Dom. Com., Misc. Series No. 37 (Washington, 1916).

CHAPTER XV

The introduction to this chapter raises the question as to when the American textile machinery industry reached its peak. In England the peak seems to have occurred about 1910. Did the experience of the American industry follow the same pattern?

Unfortunately, the United States Census is of limited use in establishing levels of production, for the data contained in the Census are static rather than dynamic. The Census simply records the number of spinning frames and looms in existence during census years; it gives no indication of the number of machines produced between census reports. The entire machine capacity of the cotton textile industry could have been scrapped and replaced between census years without affecting the total figures in any way.

The most reliable source of information about production would of course be the account books of the individual machine-builders themselves, but unhappily too few of those have survived to permit any accurate judgment about the whole. The only really large collections of textile-machinery records known to exist are those of the Whitin Machine Works, the Saco-Lowell Shops, and the Draper Corporation. The first two collections are deposited in Baker Library, the third is still in the Draper Corporation's offices in Hopedale. A smaller collection, consisting of the Kilburn, Lincoln & Company records, is also housed in Baker Library and has been only partially studied. (See Jonathan Thayer Lincoln's "Material for a History of American Textile Machinery," in the *Journal of Economic and Business History,* February, 1932, pp. 259–280.) The Crompton & Knowles Loom Works has few of its old records. Some of the H & B American Machine Company's records are known to have been destroyed although, so far as I am aware, no complete inventory of its records has ever been made. Nearly all the records of the Providence Machine Company, the Fales & Jenks Machine Company, and the Woonsocket Machine & Press Company were destroyed when those companies were purchased by the Whitin Machine Works. Most of the Mason Machine Works' records were burned, although a few scattered items were saved by, and are in the possession of, individual employees. Thus the industry has failed to preserve the story of its own achievement.

After carefully weighting all the intangibles involved, however, one is apt to come forward with general conclusions of this nature. For the Whitin Machine Works, the greatest period of activity in its history occurred following World War II, due chiefly to the subcontracting work it carried on outside of Whitinsville. For the industry as a whole, the boom following World War I probably holds the record for intensity of demand. But when one considers that the World War I boom benefited in large part from the accumulation of orders during the war years and from abnormal sales abroad, one is inclined to let the balance swing to the boom of 1909–10 when (again considering the industry as a whole and not just one company in the industry) one realizes that the industry achieved a record level of production without having to rely on the artificial and accumulated stimulus of war and a foreign demand.

1. Ltr., EKS to P. S. Tuley, 28 Feb. 1917.

2. Ltrs., Geo. B. Hamblin to J. B. Hanrahan, 15 and 28 Aug. 1917.

3. Ltr., LMK to Lawrence Lewis, 18 Apr. 1917.

4. Of the 99 mills to which the first letter was sent, 28 (or 30%) were located in North Carolina.

5. Reported in the *Whitin Spindle,* Feb., 1920, p. 15.

6. The company's only other serious difficulty over priorities came from the Emergency Fleet Corp., which for a time had control of pig iron allocations.

7. Ltr., EKS to W. P. Hazelwood, 25 June 1917.

8. Ltr., EKS to John D. Leonard, 9 Aug. 1917.

9. Ltr., Geo. B. Hamblin to Hon. Henry Cabot Lodge, 24 Apr. 1918.

10. Ltr., J. F. McGuiness to the Campe Corp., 20 Apr. 1918.

11. Ltr., Geo. B. Hamblin to New Bedford Board of Commerce, 14 June 1918.

12. Ltr., EKS to E. G. Whittaker, 1 June 1917.

13. For an account of the early development of scientific management see Horace B. Drury, *Scientific Management* (2nd ed., N. Y., 1918), pp. 15–97.

14. Ltr., EKS to F. J. Dutcher, 1 Feb. 1913.

15. Ltr., EKS to Suffern & Son, 16 May 1912.

16. *Ibid.,* 16 July 1912.

17. *Ibid.*, 29 Oct. 1912.

18. Commenting on the work done by the Suffern firm, Swift wrote to Geo. B. Stevens, 15 Apr. 1913: "We adopted the bonus system which did not disturb the day wages of the men, but gave them a bonus on their work after it passed a certain point. . . . We have not had any trouble with our employees, although the efficiency system did have the effect of weeding out the poor ones, as men who could not maintain a fair efficiency dropped out to be replaced by others who could."

The Bur. of For. and Dom. Com. Misc. Series No. 37 (pp. 51–52) contained the following comment on the Suffern work in Whitinsville:

"One large plant undertook an efficiency experiment in 1912 which, although the firm did not apply the results to its other departments, was so interesting and conclusive that it is worthy of special mention here. A firm of efficiency engineers was called in, and under their direction an important part of a machine, in itself a complete manufacturing unit when finished, was selected as the basis to work upon.

"The results were obtained by means of a time study and bonus system, which brought about a reduction of 25 per cent in the labor cost while increasing the production nearly 50 per cent and increasing the earnings of workmen more than 26 per cent. A member of the efficiency firm described the bonus system as follows:

" 'Most of the gain came through having the work at hand for the men and through the men's own initiative under the spur of an increased wage.

" 'The standard was set with the idea that a good man working consistently for 9 hours out of 10 at his machine or bench could earn 20 per cent in addition to his regular wages, and the bonus began to be paid at 81 per cent of the standard. . . .

" 'The standard was obtained by observation of actual work done with the use of a stop watch. Where more than one man was doing the operation, studies of each individual were made. . . .

" 'Remarks: Workmen are satisfied and contented; only one man had quit because of dissatisfaction. No rates have been cut. Conditions were intensely complicated to begin with. Professional service discontinued after five months, and work turned over to client.' "

19. Ltr., EKS to Ernest F. Suffern, 23 Apr. 1913.

20. See *Acts and Resolves Passed by the General Court of Massachusetts in the Year 1897*, p. 486.

21. Paragraph G (c) of the income-tax law passed 3 Oct. 1913 reads in part: "All corporations . . . shall render a return . . . setting forth (first) the total amount of its paid-up capital stock outstanding, or if no capital stock, its capital employed in business, at the close of the year; (second) the total amount of its bonded indebtedness at the close of the year; (third) the gross amount of its income received during such year from all sources . . . ; (fourth) the total amount of all its ordinary and necessary expenses paid out of earnings in the maintenance and operation of the business and properties

of such corporation . . . within the year, stating separately all rentals or other payments required to be made as a condition to the continued use or possession of property . . . ; (fifth) the total amount of all losses actually sustained during the year and not compensated by insurance or otherwise, stating separately all amounts allowed for depreciation of property . . . ; (sixth) the amount of interest accrued and paid within the year on its bonded or other indebtedness not exceeding one-half of the sum of its interest bearing indebtedness and its paid-up capital stock, outstanding at the close of the year . . . ; (seventh) the amount paid by it within the year for taxes imposed under the authority of the United States . . . ; (eighth) the net income of such corporation . . . after making the deductions . . . authorized."

22. The War Revenue Act of 1917, Title II, Sec. 201, considered corporation income not excessive when it did not exceed the average rate of income on capital in the three prewar years, but that rate could not be less than 7% or more than 9% of capital — with some further modifications. Because of Whitin's low asset valuation, its average return on capital for the three prewar years was 14.9%. Hence its effective rate was the maximum 9%, which meant that it was subject to excess profits taxes on anything above approximately $300,000. Earnings above that figure were subject to taxation according to the following schedule:

20% on all profits over 9% but not more than 15% of capital
25% on all profits over 15% but not more than 20% of capital
35% on all profits over 20% but not more than 25% of capital
45% on all profits over 25% but not more than 33% of capital
60% on all profits over 33% of capital

23. A copy of the report rendered to the Whitin Machine Works by Scovell, Wellington & Co. may be found in the Minutes of the Board of Directors' Meeting held 29 Mar. 1918.

24. Moody's *Analysis of Investments, Public Utilities and Industrials* (N. Y., 1916), p. 1799.

25. Ltr., EKS to Gaston, Williams & Wigmore, 24 Jan. 1916.

26. Whittaker was allowed a drawing account of $250 a month. He had joined the Whitin company about 1909, coming from the Boston Duck Co. where he had served as a spinner. During most of his years in Whitinsville he had been connected with the experimental department so that he had a wide knowledge of textile machinery. He worked for the Whitin Machine Works in the Orient for seven years or more, after which he became, and for many years remained, the representative in the Orient for the Universal Winding Co.

27. Ltr., EKS to Frederick R. Pratt, 11 July 1921.

28. Ltr., EKS to W. H. Swift, vice-pres. of Gaston, Williams & Wigmore, 14 Jan. 1921.

29. Quoted in ltr., LMK to Gaston, Williams & Wigmore, 13 Dec. 1920.

30. Ltr., EKS to Frederick R. Pratt, 25 May 1921.

31. New York *Times,* 17 Mar. 1921, p. 23. Some of Gaston, Williams & Wigmore's business was salvaged by Elbrook & Company, of which George R. Coleman was vice-pres. The present-day Coleman & Company is thus a lineal descendant of Gaston, Williams & Wigmore. Mr. Yang, a one-time representative of the Gaston firm in China, is still an agent for the Whitin Machine Works in that country.

32. Keeler's "assistant in charge of foreign sales" was J. F. McGuiness.

33. Ltr., EKS to Frederick R. Pratt, 11 July 1921.

34. At the board of directors' meeting 10 Nov. 1921, the directors considered arranging for a new agency in China, but nothing ever came of the matter.

35. Directors' minutes, 27 Dec. 1918. The price paid was $10,000.

36. Whitin Machine Works' additions to the village were made roughly as follows:

76 family units — 1864 (acquired as a result of the dissolution of P. Whitin & Sons)		
200	" "	— 1865–69
32	" "	— 1888
425	" "	— 1900–01
150	" "	— 1919–21
82	" "	— 1923 (purchased from the Whitinsville Cotton Mills)

In addition the company has from time to time purchased private homes in the community. In the summer of 1948 the company owned 983 family units, or 72% of the 1,364 family dwellings in the village.

CHAPTER XVI

With Chapter XVI, I have begun to use three of the business historian's handiest tools — the profit statement, the balance sheet, and the minutes of directors' meetings. Before 1918, none of these three was complete enough to be of much value to anyone interested in Whitin's history. The company's earlier profit statements and balance sheets have been described in Chapter VIII. Its early directors' minutes were too perfunctory to be more than a lead to what was going on in the company. Since 1918, however, all three types of records have been very complete and consequently very helpful — although it would be folly to attempt, as has been done in some volumes, to base an entire history on those alone with no attention to other sources except published ones.

I have decided not to reproduce the Whitin company's balance sheets in an appendix, first, because the most important information obtainable from the balance sheets has been summarized in the text, and secondly, because copies of the balance sheets are available on request at the Massachusetts State House. The company's profit statements before 1918 are so meaningless that I have also omitted them. An abbreviated form of company profit statements for the years 1920–40 may be found in Table 12. This table contains the first profit information ever made public by the Whitin company.

Recently company officials have given serious thought to publishing the firm's profit statements annually, but they have felt that the unusually high level of sales during the war and postwar periods might give the public a misleading impression of the volume of business done by the company in more normal times. They have therefore postponed the decision to begin making their profit statements freely available until some later and perhaps more normal period. It is easy to recognize the reason for such a decision, but it is equally easy to regret the fact that the decision has been made. Often companies are far more fearful of the adverse results of public disclosures than they have any need to be.

Despite this hesitancy regarding sales figures, the company gave me access to all current sales records. At the same time, however, I was asked not to print any figures later than those for 1940. Since I found that the war and postwar sales were no more inflated than were the sales for most companies during that period (and hence that they did not in themselves constitute an unusual facet of the narrative), I conceded that the story could be told fully and clearly without the use of sales figures for the recent period. It was mutually agreed, however, that, for the reader's benefit, the reason for the omission should be set forth clearly at some appropriate place in the book.

1. From the point of view of business administration, an excellent summary of the causes of the textile industry's depression in the 1920's is to be found in C. E. Fraser and G. F. Doriot, *Analyzing Our Industries* (N. Y., 1932), pp. 114–137.

2. *Acts and Resolves Passed by the General Court of Massachusetts in the Year 1909,* p. 740. The law forbade the employment of women in textile mills between the hours of 6 P.M. and 6 A.M.

3. Directors' minutes, 15 May 1933.

4. Information on repair sales is based in large part on conversations with Sydney R. Mason and with Robert McKaig, manager and assistant manager, respectively, of the repair-sales department.

5. Conversation with Robert Leeson, president of the Universal Winding Co., 15 June 1946.

6. *Whitin Review,* Apr., 1933, p. 4, and Aug., 1937, p. 15.

7. Report on the management problems of the Southern Shop rendered to J. Hugh Bolton by Curtis Grieb, Oct., 1948.

8. J. S. Eaton, of Taunton, Mass., formerly purchasing agent for the Mason Machine Works, has shown me the Mason company's last order-specifications book, which he has in his possession. Mr. Eaton was the source of much of my information on the Mason company's demise.

9. *Whitin Review,* July, 1933, p. 6.

10. Ltrs. EKS to the Fales & Jenks Machine Co. and to the Woonsocket Machine & Press Co., 6 Nov. 1930, and Minutes of the Stockholders' Meeting,

26 Jan., 1931. After several adjustments the assets of these two companies were recorded on Whitin's books as follows:

	Pawtucket Property	Woonsocket Property
Land	$ 50,000	$ 25,000
Building	50,000	25,000
Machinery & equipment	428,071	350,000
Total	$528,071	$400,000

At first Swift hoped to keep the Fales & Jenks foundry operating on job orders from local Pawtucket concerns (see ltr. to Robert and Richmond Fales, 2 Jan. 1931), but that failing, he decided to have the plant buildings demolished as a means of avoiding the high taxes imposed by the City of Pawtucket. The Woonsocket buildings were left standing and over a period of years were sold off gradually to a number of small, independent manufacturers until by 1939 the company had disposed of its last piece of Woonsocket property.

11. I am indebted to Edward L. Martin and to his son Winslow Martin for much of my information on the H & B American Company. According to E. L. Martin, the British did not even place representatives on the American company's board of directors.

12. *Moody's Manual of Investments, Industrial Securities,* 1932. The H & B American company made its first appearance in Moody's in 1931; the Whitin company first appeared in 1924.

13. Depreciation expense amounted to $1,103,533.

14. Roughly two-thirds of the dividends paid out between 1924 and 1929 were covered by non-operating earnings. About half the remainder was covered by operating income, the rest being covered by earnings previously made.

15. In 1932 Swift estimated (in a letter to Jas. C. White, 18 Feb.) that labor rates in Whitinsville were 10% lower than those in the surrounding territory. If such was the case, the company's savings in labor costs were approximately $250,000 a year. The expense of maintaining the village was as follows:

Depreciation on housing investment at 2% (the company figures its housing investment worth $1,750,000 or approximately $1,750 a dwelling)	$ 35,000
Maintenance on housing	115,000
Gross housing expense	$150,000
Less: income from rentals	105,000
Net housing expense	$ 45,000

In another letter (26 Mar. 1934) Swift estimated that the net village cost was $24,000 a year plus insurance and administrative expenses. The reservoir system paid for itself, he said. An initial investment of $400,000 had been

written down (by 1932) to $240,000. On this investment the company was able to draw water for its own use and to deliver water for the free use of its tenants at a cost of about 10 cents per thousand gallons. Swift stated in his letter that the lowest commercial rate in Massachusetts at that time was 17.4 cents per thousand gallons. Thus, even when the expense of maintaining the hospital, church, gymnasium, club, and the like is included it is apparent that the company benefited greatly from the village it had sponsored.

16. Ltrs. EKS to the Northbridge Board of Selectmen, 29 Mar. 1917, 20 Apr. 1917, 14 June 1917.

17. Of the 40 most populous towns (townships) in Mass., Northbridge stands 31st in size. It has the lowest per capita valuation of the group and has the second lowest per capita tax. Only North Attleboro is lower.

18. The 1948 town school board was composed of Richard Whitin, treasurer of the Paul Whitin Mfg. Co.; Elizabeth Lasell, daughter of J. M. Lasell; George McRoberts, shop advertising manager; Henry Crawford, assistant shop personnel director; Dr. Bovier, Whitinsville medical doctor; and Dr. Cassidy, Whitinsville dentist.

19. The Northbridge town hall seems to have been built as a part of John C. Whitin's make-work program in the depression of the 1870's. The spot chosen for the hall was the geographical center of Whitinsville, where stood the old Paul Whitin homestead. It was thus but a few yards from the location of the original smithy out of which the Whitin Machine Works had grown. At the 4 Mar. 1872 meeting of the Northbridge Board of Selectmen, "John C. Whitin offered, for himself and brothers, to build said building at their own expense." The first meeting in the new hall was held 7 Nov. 1876. Until 1885 the hall was referred to in the Minutes of the Board of Selectmen's Meetings simply as the "Lower Town Hall, in Whitinsville," the "Upper Hall" being the one that had been previously used at Northbridge Center. Since 1885 the building has been known as Memorial Hall. To be certain that the hall would be properly maintained, the Whitin brothers, who believed in public democracy but who knew the failings of public finance, set up (in 1882) a self-perpetuating board of trustees consisting of Josiah Lasell, Gustavus E. Taft, Edward Whitin, William H. Whitin, and George Marston Whitin, and sold to those gentlemen the hall and property for $1.00. The two brothers also established a $10,000 trust fund for maintenance purposes, the fund to be administered by the trustees under the general direction of the Probate Court. Since many of the trustees then (as now) were members of the Whitin firm, it was natural that the company should take over the work of maintaining the building and of keeping account of the trust's financial affairs. The trustees in 1948 were: E. Kent Swift, chairman of the board, Whitin Machine Works; Oliver S. Chute, nephew of Swift and salesman for Whitin; Philip B. Walker, head of Whitin's maintenance department; Laurance M. Fuller, assistant to the treasurer of the Whitin company, and son of the man charged with maintaining the company's reservoirs;

and Laurence Hale, vice-president and agent of the Paul Whitin Mfg. Co.

20. When Sarah Fletcher, a sister of Betsey Whitin, died in 1844, she left a $100 legacy to establish a "social library" in the village. The library that was established as a result of her legacy was a private organization and was located in a room above the village store that stood in front of the stone mill. No doubt Josiah Lasell, having a literary bent, became one of the library's active patrons; a record of those who had paid their fifty-cent dues in 1869 appears in the Whitin Machine Works letterbooks in his handwriting (letterbook no. 1, p. 231). The library's books were moved to the "Lower Town Hall" in 1876 and in that year were made available to the public without charge at a time when public libraries were just coming into vogue. In return the town was to pay a yearly sum of "not less than Three Hundred Dollars." Since 1913 the library's books have been housed in their own library building, a Georgian structure of local, gray granite donated to the town by Arthur F. Whitin and his brother Edward. *Worcester County History,* p. 441; Directors' minutes, 16 Jan. 1882; *Whitin Spindle,* Jan.–Feb., 1926, p. 3.

21. Paul, John, Charles, and James Whitin, in 1878, established the Pine Grove Cemetery Association as a public benefaction. Previously Whitinsville had had no suitable burying ground; those able to afford it had had a "yard" of their own set off on some remote section of their property, and a privately operated "yard" was located where the high school now stands. (This was transferred, grave by grave, to the Pine Grove Cemetery when the present high school was built.) To remedy the situation, the Whitins formed a cemetery association under the public statutes of the Commonwealth of Massachusetts and endowed the organization with 27 acres of land and a superintendent's house (Worcester County deed books 1088, p. 287, and 1149, p. 360). Again the trustees became self-perpetuating under the jurisdiction of the Probate Court and again the actual management of the Association devolved upon the Whitin Machine Works. The trustees in 1948 were: E. Kent Swift, Sydney R. Mason, Philip B. Walker, and Laurance M. Fuller, all of whom were in the Whitin Machine Works (see n. 19 above for their positions in the company); Earl J. Liberty, administrator of the Arthur F. Whitin estate; Curtis M. Carr, cashier of the Whitinsville National Bank; Paul and Richard Whitin, owners of the Paul Whitin Mfg. Co.; and John B. Dunbar, Jr., furniture store proprietor.

22. The Whitin company bought the plot from the estate of Paul Whitin, Jr., and gave it to the town (Directors' minutes, 20 Jan. 1890). At first the plot was only landscaped, but in 1905 the Whitin company contributed $4,000 toward the cost of a Civil War monument to the town's 39 war dead (checkbook stub, 8 July 1905). In 1922 it gave $5,500 toward a World War I monument to be placed in the park in honor of the 19 men who had died in their country's service (Directors' minutes, 22 Jan. 1923). The town lost 51 men in World War II and has begun a public subscription in their honor, but town

sentiment seems opposed to using the money for a third monument. The
Pine Grove Cemetery Association maintains the park and charges the town
for its services. Since the Pine Grove Cemetery Association is managed from
the Whitin company's administration building, the park is in fact, if not in
law, another of the company's many adjunctive activities.

23. Stockholders' minutes, 26 Jan. 1931.

24. Directors' minutes, 18 Jan. 1915.

25. For example, during World War II the company took over the town's
ambulance service when the funeral director who had been operating it declared that it was a losing proposition and one that he could not continue to
operate.

26. The farm had probably never before made money. Mrs. Whitin had
often remarked that its only profitable venture had been the raising of pigs.
It was in fact so far indebted to the Whitin Machine Works for the advances
the shop had made to keep it in operation, that little real equity remained.
Therefore the company bought from Mrs. Whitin's heirs all the John C.
Whitin property (including the 375-acre Castle Hill Farm, but excluding
the Whitin mansion across from the shop) for $108,560 and the cancellation
of $68,171 in indebtedness.

27. At least as early as the beginning of the present century, Whitinsville
had a baseball team in the old Mill League. In those days the team was
sponsored by personal contributions, George Marston Whitin and J. M. Lasell
being among those whose support could always be counted on. In 1921, when
the company became the team's sponsor, it was reorganized on an amateur
basis and was entered in the Industrial Triangle League along with teams
from the Norton Co. and Walden-Worcester Wrench, Inc., both of Worcester,
the American Optical Co. and the Hamilton Woolen Co. of Southbridge, and
S. Slater & Sons, of Webster. (The name of the league derived from the
fact that the towns formed a roughly equilateral triangle with its apex at
Worcester.) However, the Whitin Machine Works remained in the Industrial
League for only a few years. In 1925 it transferred its club to the newly organized Blackstone Valley League, in which were teams from the neighboring
mill towns of Rockdale, Uxbridge, Douglas, Fisherville, and Millbury. Like
the teams in the old Mill League (and in contrast to those in the Industrial
League) the Blackstone clubs were organized on a semi-professional basis.
Many players were imported from out-of-town and were paid on a per-game
basis. The Blackstone League still exists but it has not been without its vicis-
situdes. In some years it has not functioned, and from time to time its status
has shifted from semi-professional to amateur and back again. But one cannot easily over-estimate its importance in the social life of the valley. Baseball
games have for years provided the area's favorite topic of summer conversation and its most popular summertime relaxation. They have also given to
the inhabitants of the region a sense of intimacy with the sports world, for
many of the rooky players on valley teams have gone on to make names for
themselves in the major leagues. Apparently the executives of the Whitin

Machine Works have seen in league baseball a valuable morale builder, for they have financed a fine baseball park equipped with bleachers capable of seating a thousand spectators and have spent a thousand or more dollars a year to make their team one of the best in the League. Meanwhile intra-shop sports have not been neglected, though they have been given less publicity than has league baseball. Since 1919 the shop has sponsored, on an inter-departmental basis, both bowling and hardball teams. The intra-shop hardball teams constitute what is known as the Sunset League. Oddly enough, softball has never played an important part in shop sports. The people of Whitinsville are quick to point out that theirs is chiefly a "hardball town." *Whitin Spindle, passim;* conversations with Henry Crawford of the shop Employment Department; and Harley E. Keeler's diaries, shown to me by Harley's son, Robert.

Another popular summer pastime was picnicking at Purgatory Chasm. To the people of Whitinsville, Purgatory was nothing to fear; it was a pleasant place, a rocky primordial gorge left apparently untouched by the erosive ice movements of the glacial ages. It had once belonged to John C. Whitin, having been acquired by him in what seems to have been the discharge of a mortgage debt. In 1873 Whitin transferred his ownership to the Whitin Machine Works. In 1920 the shop in turn deeded the property to the Commonwealth of Massachusetts (for a nominal $3,202.50). Since then Purgatory Chasm has been a state reservation and a favorite playground for Whitins-villagers.

28. Most of the information concerning the Home Garden Club was contributed by Dana Heald, for many years the Club's president. Through cooperation with the Worcester County Extension Service, the Club is able to obtain expert judges who stage a surprise inspection sometime about mid-July and who determine the winners of the Club's cash prizes. In 1948 dues were increased to $2 to make the cash prizes more attractive. Then, on the Saturday after Labor Day the Club sponsors a gala garden show in the George Marston Whitin Gymnasium. The company has several field plots available for gardening, one of which, as the frontispiece shows clearly, is on the hill just above the shop.

29. The complexity of the company's interest in its employees' welfare is best shown by the fact that the payroll department, in 1948, was making ten different types of deductions from weekly pay checks: Social Security, federal income taxes, Blue Cross (hospital insurance), Blue Shield (surgical insurance), rentals, garage repairs and gasoline, coal, ice, purchases through shop departments, and union dues.

30. The difficulties of managing the company village were related to me by the company's public works manager, Philip B. Walker.

31. The committee consists of the company's Public Works Director (Philip B. Walker), a representative of the Employment Department (Henry S. Crawford), and an old-timer in the village (James S. Ferry). In 1946 the assignment of workers to company houses was as follows:

Production men	564
Maintenance men	195
Desk workers and supervisory men	468
Pensioners, widows, etc.	56
	1,283

Since there were 989 tenements at that time, the average number of employees per housing unit was about 1⅓. Thus in one out of three families, the head of the house had a son, daughter, or wife also working for the company.

32. When the plant became unionized, one of the union's demands was that houses be allotted strictly according to seniority.

33. Directors' minutes, 26 Nov. 1923. Dedication of the gymnasium took place 7 July 1923. Dues are now (1948) $6.00 a year. The Association has also built three tennis courts near where the John C. Whitin mansion once stood (it was torn down in 1943 to avoid taxes). Floodlights to permit night playing were donated by E. Kent Swift. Copy of the Association's bylaws given to me by Sydney R. Mason, one of the Association's trustees.

34. The Whitin company paid $221,000 for the Whitinsville Cotton Mills property.

35. Conversation with a retired molder, named James McGinniss, related to me by N. S. B. Gras.

36. Joseph L. Snider, *The Guarantee of Work and Wages* (Boston, 1947).

37. The first wage cut was a blanket 10% on 12 Oct. 1931. The second was an individual downward adjustment on 1 Dec. 1931. Rentals were reduced in Mar., 1930, because of reductions in hours worked. They were restored in Aug., 1931, reduced again in June, 1932, and restored again in July, 1933.

38. Ltr., EKS to P. A. O'Connell, 26 Mar. 1934. This letter was written *after* the 25% rent cut had been restored.

39. See charts printed in *The Blue Eagle,* 9 Jan. 1935, p. 8, and 15 Mar. 1935, p. 8.

40. Industrial Code No. 1, clause VI, sect. 3, read, "prior to the installation of additional productive machinery by persons engaged or engaging in the cotton textile industry, except for the replacement of a similar number of existing looms or spindles or to bring the operation of existing productive machinery into balance, such persons shall secure certificates that such installation shall be consistent with effectuating the policy of the National Industrial Recovery Act during the emergency."

41. Out of the estimated 17,578 employees in the industry on 9 Nov. 1933, the following numbers were employed by the 10 largest firms:

Whitin Machine Works	2,799	H & B American Machine Co.	779
Saco-Lowell Shops	2,671	Proctor & Schwartz	524
Draper Corp.	2,643	Davis & Furber Machine Co.	456
Crompton & Knowles Loom Works	2,003	Fletcher Works, Inc.	407
Universal Winding Co.	949	Atwood Machine Co.	404

42. Swift served as president of the N.A.T.M.M. from 1937 to 1946.

43. This figure does not take into account the fact that nearly all the company's regular lines of cotton machinery had also undergone substantial model change. The company's 1932 total sales divided themselves roughly as follows: 50 per cent repairs, 30 per cent cotton machinery, 20 per cent non-machinery.

CHAPTER XVII

Chapters XVII and XVIII are based to a large extent on interviews, followed up by whatever checking was required by the nature of the information so obtained. Interviewing has not yet gained a recognized place in historical methodology, for it has been looked upon as an unreliable source of facts and data. Unreliable it is, but no more so than the written word on which historians have always placed so much faith. The limitations in interviewing lie more with the interviewer than with the person interviewed. Information obtained through interviews must be checked with more than usual care, but interviewing should not be shunned simply because it is a difficult technique to master. Surprisingly little of what goes on in corporate America ever gets into print. If the business historian were to shut himself off from the information existing nowhere save in men's minds, he would deprive himself of his most prolific source of facts.

1. Chapter XVII deals only with the more outstanding product developments. For instance, it omits the following four significant developments:

(1) At one time the company tried to promote the use of ramie fiber in the manufacture of cotton sheets. Around 1925 Swift went to Germany, where for $10,000 he bought the American rights to a patented mechanical method of treating ramie fibers. At the same time he bought a sample German machine and shipped it back to the United States. Under the management of a man named Elsner, Swift organized the Fibre Development Co., using the old Whitinsville Cotton Mills as headquarters. The fibers produced there were called "Eksonia" in E. K. Swift's honor. For a time the prospects seemed bright, for Eksonia could be produced at costs lower than the prevailing price of cotton. But when cotton prices fell, the Fibre Development Co. lost its reason for existence and had to be discontinued at a substantial loss to the Whitin Machine Works.

(2) The Whitin company also took a 20% interest in the Perlock Co., a firm controlled jointly by the Paul Whitin Mfg. Co. and the Cabot Mfg. Co. The Perlock Co. owned the rights to a process of breaking up rayon materials and reclaiming them for re-use. The company is still in existence, but Whitin sold its interest in 1936.

(3) In 1915, under the guidance of D. O. Pease, the company started making asbestos machinery, its first installation being made in the Johns-Manville

plant at Brooklyn, N. Y. By the late 1920's, Whitin had become the leading builder of asbestos machinery in America.

(4) When Germany entered World War II, America's dress-goods knitting mills were shut off from their principal suppliers of tricot-knitting machinery, German machinery shops. Whitin and others began building knitting equipment to meet the emergency, but what the postwar future of Whitin's war-born knitting machinery business will be is difficult to predict so soon.

2. Ltr., EKS to David F. Edwards, 26 Nov. 1928, "We are more and more impressed that cotton [type] machinery offers the cheapest method of producing yarns of any of the various systems, and there is going to be more of a trend toward utilizing it." Swift's prediction was amply borne out by subsequent events.

3. Where not otherwise noted, information for this section was obtained in conversation with J. Hugh Bolton, the developer of the company's wool-machinery line, and Harry Moss, currently the company's vice-president in charge of wool-machinery development and sales.

4. Ltr., GMW to Edmund K. Baker and Durrell O. Pease, 27 Feb. 1909.

5. Ltr., GMW to Wetmore & Jenner, 18 July 1910.

6. Ltr., EKS to Carolina Bagging Co., 14 Dec. 1928.

7. Ltrs., LMK to Messrs. Baere, Delcroix & Cie, 20 July 1917, and G. B. Hamblin to U. S. Shipping Board, 29 July 1918.

8. Bolton sold the Pease company's machinery to the medium-sized Union Asbestos & Rubber Co., of Chicago.

9. In Mar., 1948, there were only about 1,560,000 wool spindles in the U. S., as against 23,927,706 cotton spindles.

10. Whitin's wool cards and its cotton-waste cards are exactly the same, except that the rolls on waste cards are covered over to keep loose lint from flying around.

11. Whitin immediately wrote down its investment in Cashiko to $68,000 since a sizable part of what it had paid for was inventory. Whitin also hired one of the Cashiko company's salesmen, Julius Benedict. The other producer of wool cards, Proctor & Schwartz, was a merger of the Philadelphia Textile Machinery Co., makers of wool-drying equipment, and the Smith & Furbush Machine Co., makers of waste machinery. After World War II, Proctor & Schwartz dropped its line of wool cards but kept its worsted card line, with which Whitin did not compete.

12. Among Whitin's earliest wool customers were the Kent Mfg. Co., of Clifton Heights, Pa. (flannels), the Peerless Woolen Mills, of Rossville, Ga. (men's wear), the Chatham Mfg. Co., of Elkin, S. C. (blankets), F. C. Huyck & Sons, of Albany, N. Y. (felts), and the Cleveland Worsted Mills, of Cleveland Ohio (men's and ladies' wear).

13. Swift had seen the need for an automatic winder and had been watching for one to appear on the market when a Whitin salesman, James Truslow, reported from England that Schweiter, Ltd., of Horgen, Switzerland,

was displaying an automatic winder in Manchester. Without seeing the machine, Swift authorized Truslow to obtain its American agency for the Whitin company. When war broke out, interrupting delivery of the Swiss machines, the Schweiters sent Hans Theiler to Whitinsville to help the Whitin company get into production on the machine. The fall of France caught Theiler in America and forced him to stay in Whitinsville for the rest of the war, a visit which he seems to have enjoyed none the less for its having been involuntary.

14. In the summer of 1948, the wool department was working on a completely new model of the wool spinning frame.

15. Ltr., EKS to Wilbur Watson Assn., 28 Dec. 1925: "We are interested in artificial silk machinery, but our interest has not proceeded to a point where we are in a position to advise."

16. The influence of Europeans on America's rayon industry is shown by the fact that, of America's leading rayon producers, only two — Du Pont and Tennessee-Eastman — were founded by American promoters (E. I. Du Pont de Nemours and Eastman Kodak Co., respectively). All others were promoted from Europe: Industrial Rayon (Italy); American Viscose Corporation (England); Celanese Corporation of America (England); North American Rayon Corporation (Germany); American Bemberg Corporation (Germany); and Tubize Rayon Corporation (Belgium).

17. Where not otherwise noted, the information for this section was obtained in conversation with Robert A. Hargreaves, manager of Whitin's rayon department.

18. The firm now advertises itself as "the world's oldest and most experienced manufacturers of machinery and builders of plants for the manufacture of filament rayon, rayon staple, fiber and cellophane." (*Rayon Textile Monthly,* Jan., 1948, p. 9.)

19. Issue dated 3 Oct. 1929, p. 15, with a picture of the Baron. The article continues in part: "Practical experience gleaned from rayon plants in all parts of the world forms the basis for improvements in machinery which are constantly being made. Royalties of the Kohorn plants frequently run abroad as, for instance, in England, where the Hetherington machinery plant at Manchester serves for the purpose of erecting rayon machinery and building up the rayon machinery plants. Other enterprises at Chemnitz have also changed part of their program during the last few years, devoting greater attention to modern rayon machinery."

20. Drawings shown me by Cyril Taylor of the Whitin rayon department.

21. Ltr., EKS to the Oscar Kohorn Co., 14 May 1931.

22. *Whitin Spindle,* July, 1920, p. 13.

23. Providence Machine Co. machinery order book for July, 1900–Sept., 1910, in the Whitin Machine Works vaults.

24. The two men arrived in Whitinsville in the spring of 1924. See *Whitin Spindle,* Dec., 1924, p. 7.

25. *Whitin Review,* Apr., 1934, p. 1. The mills used as proving grounds

for the worsted ring spinning frame were the Glenark plant of the Uxbridge Worsted Co. (Woonsocket, R. I.), the Millbury Spinning Co. (Pascoag, R. I.), the Waskunut Mills (Farnumsville, Mass.), and the Rivulet Mill (No. Uxbridge, Mass.), all near Whitinsville.

26. According to McConnell, the term "American System" was first used by François Cleyn, of Huntington, Quebec, in an article that appeared in the Mar., 1946, issue of *Textile World*, p. 123.

27. Information in this section was obtained in conversation with Max F. Thompson, and from his files.

28. When the American Tobacco Co. began advertising its Lucky Strike cigarettes during World War II with the teaser initials LSMFT (Lucky Strike Means Fine Tobacco), Whitin employees said the letters stood for "look sharp, Max F. Thompson."

29. This is a rule-of-thumb estimate used by the industry. I know of no published figures that would either substantiate or disprove it.

30. Boris Stern, "Mechanical Changes in the Cotton-Textile Industry, 1910 to 1936," *Monthly Labor Review,* U. S. Department of Labor, Bureau of Labor Statistics, Aug., 1937. The material for the Stern report was collected by the Boston mill engineering firm of Barnes Textile Associates and was financed by the American Textile Machinery Manufacturers' Association.

31. *Report of the Cotton Textile Mission to the United States of America, March–April, 1944* (London, 1944), p. a–4.

CHAPTER XVIII

As a study of the administrative problems of a business concern, this book is particularly weak in Chapter XVIII since it treats so sketchily the challenging subject of Whitin's conversion from textile-machinery manufacture to war-materials production and back again. The reason for the sketchiness was lack of time. Better scheduling would have allotted less time for the middle chapters and more for the later ones. Under circumstances such as these, the historian comes to realize how much easier it is to be wise with the benefit of hindsight than to be foresighted without the benefit of wisdom.

Business historians of the recent past have one tool that helps to offset the discouraging volume of records being currently compiled by modern business firms, and I have used that tool wherever possible: present-day executives, themselves disturbed by the volume of data compiled for their use, have adopted the practice of asking for summarized reports on certain topics. Such reports contain a wealth of information in condensed form and serve the historian almost as predigested research materials. But the historian must keep to his awareness that such reports are, after all, compiled by fallible human beings.

1. Since that time the B. F. Sturtevant Company has been sold to the Westinghouse Electric Corporation.

2. All information concerning the Whitin company's work on auxiliary steam engines was gained in conversation with, or from the records of, J. Hugh Bolton, who was the executive most intimately connected with the company's steam-engine work.

3. Information in the following ten paragraphs was collected from various Whitinsville sources but was never corroborated by Mr. Hoch himself, although a copy of the paragraphs was sent to him for perusal.

4. Previously the assistant treasurer had been elected by the stockholders. In 1923 the company's bylaws were changed to allow the position to be filled by vote of the board of directors. The change was significant, for it meant that the person occupying that position was then regarded merely as an assistant to the treasurer and not as a successor-in-training.

5. Because its customers have always been few in number and because its contact with them has always been intimate, the Whitin company has never done much advertising. In 1917, George B. Hamblin wrote that the company had placed "no advertisements whatsoever within recent years." Often when the company did advertise it did so more from a desire to help support certain trade journals than from any thought of monetary return. Such an attitude necessarily precluded any likelihood that new and unorthodox promotional measures would be accepted.

6. In a series of articles published by columnist Westbrook Pegler during the summer and early fall of 1948, Rosner was so thoroughly denounced for his part in the motion picture industry's lobby that he was forced to abandon his profession, at least temporarily.

7. The first award made in New England was to the Wickwire Spencer Steel Co., of Palmer, Mass.

8. American Bosch was a government-controlled corporation, having been taken over at the beginning of the war by the Alien Property Custodian. In the years before World War I, Bosch had been a German-owned concern, known as the Bosch Magneto Co. In that war, too, it had been taken over by the government, but following the war the Americans who bought it from the government had seen fit to sell it back to German owners. Consequently, the government had felt obliged to re-appropriate it in World War II. Under the Alien Property Custodian, however, most of the former American-born management was kept on, and efficiency of operation was maintained at a very high level.

9. Whitin employed an average of 150 women in the years immediately preceding the war. The peak employment of women during the war occurred in Oct., 1943, when there were 935 on the payroll — nearly a quarter of the company's total work force (according to the company's annual reports to the Census of Manufacturers). The company started the war with 4,200 employees. The number declined gradually during the early months of the war until it reached a low of 3,600 in Aug., 1942. By Oct., 1943, the number had increased to 4,243, principally through the addition of women to the magneto job. The low point of employment during the reconversion period occurred in

Aug., 1945, when the number of workers fell to 3,085. Thus the total number of Whitin's workers fluctuated within a comparatively narrow range during the war, though the turnover was much higher than those figures would indicate. Over 1,500 men left the company to join the armed forces.

10. At the end of the war the Whitin company bought from the Defense Plant Corp. most of the machine tools used on the magneto job and converted them to use on textile-machinery production.

11. Information on Whitin's magneto program was obtained from Robert F. Waters, Whitin's liaison man at the American Bosch Corp. during the war.

12. For information about the previous work of Wallace Clark, especially in Europe, see Pearl Franklin Clark, *Challenge of the American Know-How* (New York, 1948).

13. Information concerning Ernst & Ernst's work was obtained principally from Max F. Thompson, but also from nearly every other executive in the company, for the effectiveness of Ernst & Ernst's work for the company was a hotly debated topic on which everyone had an opinion.

14. Information concerning the Wallace Clark & Co.'s recommendation was found in a report submitted to Bolton on 19 July 1946 by W. E. Camp, one of the Wallace Clark consultants.

15. For a brief biography of Pierson, see the *Whitin Review*, Mar., 1941, p. 18.

16. Information in this section was obtained from Directors' minutes, and from conversation with E. Kent Swift, Edward S. Alden, and various members of the family.

CHAPTER XIX

The time may come when Whitinsville's labor troubles during and after World War II will seem too unimportant to have been given as much space as a full chapter. Whitin's experience with organized labor is not unique, and its difficulty in learning to deal with a completely new labor situation is typical of the difficulties encountered by most companies under analogous circumstances. The reason I have given the subject such detailed treatment rests simply and frankly in the fact that I happened to be on hand during the strike period and had access to the leaders on both sides of the dispute. Since setting down current history seems to me to be one of the important parts of the business historian's task, I took the opportunity of recording, especially in appendices 19 through 22, a vast volume of data that would otherwise soon have been lost to memory. Future developments will determine whether the information here set forth will preserve its relevance.

1. Where not otherwise indicated information in this chapter was obtained from the personal files of Harry Mitchell, late superintendent of the plant, and from the detailed diary of shop events that he kept.

2. Henry Roland, "Six Examples of Successful Shop Management," *The Engineering Magazine,* Oct., 1896.

3. Ltr., WMW to National Civic Federation, 3 Oct. 1902.

4. Ltr., GMW to G. A. Draper, 23 May 1911.

5. Ltr., EKS to Wm. S. Howard, 23 June 1917.

6. Conversation with Kenneth Glynn, 15 Apr. 1946.

7. The first leaflet distributed by the Machinists' Union was handed out 6 Apr. 1945. It contained promises, in addition to those made earlier by the steelworkers, covering rest periods, holidays with pay, correction of unfair piece rates, a guarantee against sending work out of the shop, and arbitration of all disputes without strikes.

8. Quoted from a CIO leaflet distributed 6 June 1945, a copy of which is in the plant superintendent's files.

9. Quoted from a CIO leaflet distributed 24 July 1945, also in the plant superintendent's files.

10. Ltr., Martin J. Walsh to EKS, 16 Apr. 1945.

11. Ltr., Dr. A. Howard Myers (Regional Director of the NLRB) to WMW, 30 Apr. 1945, in which Walsh's petition is quoted.

12. In compliance with NLRB instructions, the company used as a voting list the names appearing on the payroll 22 June 1945.

13. Information on Whitin's relations with the OPA is based on records and letters contained in Mr. Swift's personal files.

14. Section 8 (a) (1) of the War Labor Disputes Act (Smith-Connally Act) of 1943 required unions to file with the Secretary of Labor, the National War Labor Board, and the National Labor Relations Board, a notice 30 days in advance of any strike. It is important to note that, although the announced wage-and-hour adjustments did not become effective until 31 Dec. 1945, their announcement was made 17 Dec., before the strike vote was taken.

15. *Wall Street Journal,* 12 Nov. 1946, p. 1.

16. I happened to be in Whitinsville just three days after the strike began. In conversing with various people in the village, I was impressed by the coincidental use of a certain phrase by a top executive of the company and by the president of the local union. Both men told me that they thought the strike would "break Mr. Swift's heart."

17. During the immediate postwar period companies customarily learned through the morning newspaper what the OPA expected them to do. Whitin did not receive official word that its prices had been relaxed until three days later. Official news arrived through the Washington Daily Reporter System, a publication of the Bureau of National Affairs that was sent out daily by airmail from Washington at a cost to its subscribers of $25 a week. Because of the volume of government regulations being issued daily, no large firm could afford not to subscribe.

18. When Congress repealed the excess profits tax, in Oct., 1945, it continued the carry-back provisions for the stated purpose of enabling corporations to meet heavy reconversion expenses with tax refunds. As it turned out,

some of the heaviest reconversion expenses were the costs of postwar strikes. Whitin estimated that its strike cost $858,000, but its earnings for the rest of the year more than made up for this loss. For Whitin's earnings figures since 1943, see *Moody's Industrials*.

19. During the three months of the strike, $229,000 worth of government bonds were cashed at the local banks. Of course some of these bonds may have belonged to people from outside the village, but for every non-resident who cashed a bond in Whitinsville there may have been a village resident who cashed his bonds elsewhere just to avoid public notice. It has been estimated that Whitin employees held, at the end of the war, about $300,000 in government bonds. (All through the war they had cashed two bonds at the bank for every three bonds that were deducted from their pay checks.) Consequently, it would seem that the company's employees had very nearly used up all their war savings by the time the strike ended.

CHAPTER XX

1. The new shop was opened on 1 November 1947. Property for the new shop was bought from Dalton & Hedges for $25,000. The old shop was sold to the City Industrial Bank for $30,000 and was leased back during the period when the new shop was being built. The new shop was estimated to cost $200,000. In 1948 the management of the new shop was placed in the hands of B. Curtis Grieb, formerly the manager of Air-Shields, Inc., manufacturers of aircraft radio shielding, in Hatboro, Pennsylvania. Grieb is a brother-in-law of Bolton, but under the circumstances it is apparent that the relationship was less a reason for his being given the job than an obstacle he had to overcome in getting it.

2. Rather inadvertently, the company's subcontracting program has resulted in its acquiring a subsidiary. Whitin's principal subcontractor during the postwar period was the firm of Fay & Scott, a small but reputable company manufacturing engine lathes in Dexter, Maine. Ownership of the company was vested in a family trust managed by Portland bankers. Business conditions before the war had not been favorable, but war work had put the firm on its feet and had permitted an extensive modernization of its equipment. Whitin signed its first contract with Fay & Scott on 3 Oct. 1945. At first the Dexter plant took over the production of Whitin cards, the most standard machine in Whitin's product line; then, later, it added drawing frames. By the summer of 1947, the bankers who were directing Fay & Scott's affairs were convinced that the time had come to sell the Dexter plant while the boom was still going strong. With some reluctance, but with a fear that the plant might otherwise go to the Saco-Lowell Shops, the Whitin company bought the Dexter plant and, on 16 July 1947, set up a wholly owned subsidiary, the Fayscott Corp., to hold the property. Fayscott was distantly located and was even farther from the Southern market than Whitins-

ville was, but the price was favorable (roughly the liquidating value of the inventory and equipment) and within two years the plant had paid for itself.

In addition to the arrangement with Fayscott, Whitin subcontracted as much of its work as it could. At one time it was buying nearly as many pounds of castings from subcontractors as it was making in its own foundry. It even went so far, in one case, as to finance and give management advice to a small Providence foundry called the Seaboard Foundry, Inc.

One other postwar expedient ought to be mentioned in this connection: the manner in which the company solved the problem arising out of the acute shortage of pig iron. Along with several other users of pig iron, Whitin was instrumental in getting the old Mystic Iron Works, of Boston, to reopen its furnaces. In July, 1948, however, Mystic's old furnaces broke down and were out of operation for about four months. During that period, Whitin was forced to buy pig iron in the world market and at times had to go as far as Mexico and the Netherlands for it.

INDEX